THE NEW SOCIOLOGY OF SCOTLAND

Sara Miller McCune founded SAGE Publishing in 1965 to support
the dissemination of usable knowledge and educate a global
community. SAGE publishes more than 1000 journals and over
800 new books each year, spanning a wide range of subject areas.
Our growing selection of library products includes archives, data,
case studies and video. SAGE remains majority owned by our
founder and after her lifetime will become owned by a charitable
trust that secures the company's continued independence.

Los Angeles | London | New Delhi | Singapore | Washington DC | Melbourne

THE NEW SOCIOLOGY OF SCOTLAND

DAVID McCRONE

Los Angeles | London | New Delhi
Singapore | Washington DC | Melbourne

Los Angeles | London | New Delhi
Singapore | Washington DC | Melbourne

SAGE Publications Ltd
1 Oliver's Yard
55 City Road
London EC1Y 1SP

SAGE Publications Inc.
2455 Teller Road
Thousand Oaks, California 91320

SAGE Publications India Pvt Ltd
B 1/I 1 Mohan Cooperative Industrial Area
Mathura Road
New Delhi 110 044

SAGE Publications Asia-Pacific Pte Ltd
3 Church Street
#10-04 Samsung Hub
Singapore 049483

Editor: Natalie Aguilera
Assistant editor: Delayna Spencer
Production editor: Katherine Haw
Copyeditor: Neville Hankins
Proofreader: Rebecca Storr
Indexer: Elizabeth Ball
Marketing manager: Sally Ransom
Cover design: Shaun Mercier
Typeset by: C&M Digitals (P) Ltd, Chennai, India
Printed in the UK

Library of Congress Control Number: 2016952262

British Library Cataloguing in Publication data

A catalogue record for this book is available from
the British Library

ISBN 978-1-4739-0388-3
ISBN 978-1-4739-0389-0 (pbk)

At SAGE we take sustainability seriously. Most of our products are printed in the UK using FSC papers and boards.
When we print overseas we ensure sustainable papers are used as measured by the PREPS grading system.
We undertake an annual audit to monitor our sustainability.

'This masterly book is the vital text for understanding contemporary Scotland. It is comprehensive in treatment, convincing in argument and a most accessible read.'

Professor Sir Tom Devine (University of Edinburgh)

'The book is utterly marvellous: wonderfully clear and amazingly comprehensive.'

Professor John Hall (McGill University)

'Effortlessly understands the myriad of social influences and historical complexities that make up modern day Scotland.'

Professor Chris Yuill (Robert Gordon University Aberdeen)

'David McCrone has written an expertly-judged and thought-provoking book. He situates Scotland within a sociological imagination that will prove vital for the orientation of a small nation through the turbulence of the twenty-first century. Its predecessor *Understanding Scotland* virtually invented the sociology of Scotland from scratch more than a quarter of a century ago. This time around, *The New Sociology of Scotland* has radically upped the stakes. It is packed with fundamental issues and illuminating examples, ranging from power, inequality, crime, culture, through to how we belong in different ways to local, national and global communities. As the world appears to become more uncertain and unpredictable, this will become the essential guide for all students of the political, economic and social processes transforming contemporary Scotland.'

Professor Alex (Abertay University)

'This is a monumental achievement. It is the definitive account of modern Scotland but its significance goes beyond this. David McCrone's theoretically sophisticated book will become a classic analysis of on how modernity plays out in specific places with their own histories, cultures and politics.'

Professor Michael Keating (University of Aberdeen)

'This is an ambitious and hugely timely book, broad in scope but with detailed and balanced argumentation throughout. *The New Sociology of Scotland* provides a new benchmark in our understanding of Scotland and its significance to a much broader social science. The book goes far beyond Scotland, providing a theoretically informed and empirically rich contribution to some of the most pressing contemporary sociological questions (identity, globalisation, belonging). McCrone's previous work placed our understanding of Scotland at the forefront of better understanding a broader world – this book raises that bar very significantly again.'

Professor Michael Rosie (University of Edinburgh)

'This marvellous book explores the complexity of Scotland through the many and varied ways in which the experience of Scotland is lived: through the expression of its history and politics, its religion and its sport, its sense of place and its rich popular culture. In the process it draws upon an exhaustive range of academic and literary sources. It is a beautifully written, magisterial study built on a lifetime of impeccable research and scholarship. As the successor to McCrone's own *Understanding Scotland*, this book will be the authoritative and indispensable reference for the next twenty five years. It is a model for how fine sociology should be done.'

Professor Anthony Cohen (University of Edinburgh)

'A most useful book for grasping the meaning of new social and political developments in Scotland. David McCrone is a long-standing academic with an authoritative reputation for dissecting the social fabric of Scottish contemporary society. This volume is a most timely contribution for understanding current debates and future scenarios for Scotland and its relationship with the UK and Europe.'

Luis Moreno (Spanish National Research Council (CSIC))

'McCrone's writing has provided much of the intellectual superstructure for the Scottish Society course I have taught for a quarter of a century. This new book adds further to that construction, given the challenging evidence-based debates and broader sociological canvas it offers up to the reader.'

Professor Douglas Robertson (University of Stirling)

'David McCrone's authoritative work on Scotland – and more broadly, nationalism – is deservedly well known. Deploying his formidable knowledge, and drawing at times on contributions by his colleagues, he has devised a monumental, clear and well organised textbook. This will be a key point of departure for those seeking to understand Scotland today. Moreover, in the fraught context of continuing debate about Scottish independence and in the wake of the far-reaching repercussions of proposed Brexit for the United Kingdom, this is both illuminating and necessary reading.'

Professor Philip Schlesinger (University of Glasgow)

CONTENTS

LIST OF FIGURES

LIST OF TABLES

ABOUT THE AUTHOR

David McCrone is Emeritus Professor of Sociology and co-founder of the University of Edinburgh's Institute of Governance. He is a Fellow of the Royal Society of Edinburgh and a Fellow of the British Academy. He has written extensively on the sociology and politics of Scotland and the comparative study of nationalism. He is author of: *Understanding National Identity* (2015) (with Frank Bechhofer); *Living in Scotland* (2004) (with Lindsay Paterson and Frank Bechhofer); *Understanding Scotland: The sociology of a nation* (2001); *The Sociology of Nationalism: Tomorrow's ancestors* (1998); and *Scotland – the Brand: The making of Scottish heritage* (1995) (with Richard Kiely and Angela Morris). His edited books include: *The Crisis of Social Democracy in Europe* (2013) (with Michael Keating); *National Days: Constructing and mobilising national identity* (2009) (with Gayle McPherson); and *Nationalism, National Identity and Constitutional Change* (2009) (with Frank Bechhofer).

Notes on contributors

Steve Bruce, who has written Chapter 14 on religion, is a graduate of the University of Stirling. He has been Professor of Sociology at the University of Aberdeen since 1991. He is a Fellow of the British Academy and a Fellow of the Royal Society of Edinburgh. He has published extensively on the sociology of religion in the modern world and on the links between religion and politics. His *Scottish Gods: Religion in Scotland 1900–2012* won the Saltire Society Best History Book for 2014. His other books include: *Politics and Religion in the United Kingdom* (2012); *Why Are Women More Religious Than Men?* (2012) (with M. Trzebiatowska); and *Sectarianism in Scotland* (2004) (with T. Glendinning, I. Paterson and M. Rosie).

Susan McVie, who has written Chapter 12 on social order, is Chair of Quantitative Criminology in the School of Law, Director of the Applied Quantitative Methods Network (AQMeN) and Co-Director of the Edinburgh Study of Youth Transitions and Crime (ESYTC) at the University of Edinburgh. Her research interests include: crime patterns and trends; youth crime and justice; criminal careers and developmental criminology; crime and place; violence and homicide; and gangs and knife crime. She sits on a number of government committees, including the Building Safer Communities Programme Board and the Independent Advisory Group on Stop and Search in Scotland. She is an editor for the *British Journal of Criminology, Youth Justice* and *Criminology and Criminal Justice*. She is a Fellow of the Royal Society of Edinburgh and was awarded an OBE for services to social science.

Lindsay Paterson, who has written Chapter 10 on education, is Professor of Educational Policy in the School of Social and Political Science, University of Edinburgh. His main academic interests are in education, civic engagement and political attitudes. He has published widely on the expansion and purposes of higher education, on social mobility, on the relationship between education and civic values, on the twentieth-century history of Scottish education, and on Scottish politics. He has provided policy advice to the Scottish Parliament's Education Committee and to the Scottish government. He is a Fellow of the British Academy and a Fellow of the Royal Society of Edinburgh.

PROLOGUE

The simple definition of sociology is that it is the science of society. If Scotland is a society, then it follows that we can have a sociology of Scotland. At that point it gets interesting, for what do we mean by 'society'? If we equate society with the state (or even something called the nation-state), then Scotland is neither, because it does not have a seat at the United Nations between Saudi Arabia and Senegal. But if Scotland is a society, what does that mean? Simply put, it means that its institutions and social structures are relatively self-contained and meaningful to those who live in the place. The key term in that sentence is 'relatively', for it is a matter of degrees of self-containment. Having a separate system of law, education and religion (when it mattered), institutionalised since 1999 in a parliament at Holyrood, has helped to create a frame of reference within which people think of themselves as 'Scots'.

This is not to imply that they can only be Scots, for many consider themselves British too, for the UK also has the capacity to translate institutional 'governance' into identities, just as being 'European' derives from similar structures. Being 'European' was not ruled out by the UK 'Brexit' vote on 23 June 2016. On the contrary, it reinforces that claim as an aspiration precisely because there was a 'Remain' vote in every single Scottish local authority. Thirty-eight per cent of people in Scotland may have voted for Brexit, but according to the electoral rules, a singular majority of Scots voted to remain in the EU, and thus a new piece of distinctive Scottish (and British) history was made: Scots are 'European'.

That may seem to stress the 'political' nature and impact of institutions, but sociology is more than that. The sociologist Zygmunt Bauman once said that sociology is first and foremost a way of thinking about the human world. Bauman considered the central questions of sociology to be:

> in what sense does it matter that in whatever they do or may do people are dependent on other people; in what sense does it matter that they live always (and cannot but live) in the company of, in communication with, in an exchange with, in competition with, in cooperation with other human beings? (1990: 8)

The sociological imagination

The sociological way of thinking is that we are in essence *social* creatures, even if we live on a desert island, or deny that we are social at all.[1] We are, of course, not determined by people around us; we are not puppets on strings, but sentient and frequently contumacious human beings. The tension between being individuals as well as social creatures is often summed up in sociology by the tension between how much of what we do and think derives from institutions and structures, and how much we construct our own and shared meanings of our actions.

Nevertheless, the essence of sociology is the social. Sociology is not defined by the particular slice of human life which it studies – like economics or politics, for example, which are concerned, respectively, with monetary distribution and exchange between people, or how to resolve conflicting differences on the other. Sociology is defined in terms of the fact that we are social creatures; in Bauman's words, 'To think sociologically means to understand a little more fully the people around us, their cravings and dreams, their worries and their misery' (1990: 16). That will encompass anything that human beings get up to. To be sure, there are other social sciences like social anthropology and psychology which also are defined by their perspective, and not the slice of human life they study. Thus, social anthropology focuses on 'culture', the meaning systems people generate in their lives, and psychology on the study of 'mind'. Sociology, on the other hand, is the study of the social, and in that sense, society.

But is it a 'science'? Not if we think that means uncovering the basic laws of human nature, like the laws of gravity in physics. Bauman again: 'Can you imagine a physicist using "we" of themselves and molecules? Or astronomers using "we" to generalize about themselves and the stars?' (1990: 10). The 'we' in sociology stands for both the people we study and ourselves who do the studying, because human beings are, by and large, aware that they are being studied, and patently molecules and stars do not (as far we can tell). 'Science', however, is more than 'natural sciences', as they are sometimes called. 'Science' refers to the systematic collection and analysis of all forms of knowledge, carried out to the best of our ability, and using all our ingenuity and experience. The German term *Wissenschaft*, the systematic pursuit of knowledge, is closer to what we mean than the Anglo-Saxon term 'science', which has come to equate to the natural or physical sciences.

Adopting a wider definition of 'science' does not mean that anything goes. The German sociologist Max Weber, who wrote his great work *Economy and Society* at the beginning of the twentieth century, 'especially abhorred the misuse of the rostrum for the indoctrination of students, who could neither answer nor argue. "The least tolerable of all prophecies is surely the professor's with its highly personal tinge"' (in Roth, 1978: LXI).

Readers of this book should not feel constrained in answering or arguing back, for writing a book on the *New Sociology of Scotland* is not a bully pulpit. It is one sociologist's way of telling the story of Scotland. That itself begs many questions: why this way, and not others?

Book outline

Consider the structure of the book. It is divided into four parts. The first, called 'Framing Scotland', has three key questions: Where did the idea of Scotland come from? What were the social forces which made Scotland in the twentieth century? And how should we understand Scotland in sociological terms? You may, if you prefer, read the third chapter first, but you might find it helpful to put some historical flesh on the sociological bones by reading the chapters in sequence. In that way you may get a better understanding of how Scotland evolved through time. To help you find your way through the history, you will find a timeline in the Appendix, which picks out some of the key events that we deal with later in the book.

The second and largest part of the book is called 'People and Power'. The aim of this part is to give you an account of the social structure of Scotland, its demography, patterns of economic ownership, how power is structured, making a living, how social class operates, and the ways education shapes people's life chances. The theme of 'power' is carried through the chapters on gender relations, social order and crime, 'race' and ethnicity, and the rise and fall of religion in Scotland. The rationale for this part is that, to understand Scotland or anywhere for that matter, we need to see how 'structures' shape the social contexts and the behaviours of people within them. They do not, of course, determine these, but set frameworks within which we operate. What is, or is not, acceptable behaviour is laid down by such structures, even though they are fluid and frequently implicit: we learn what not to do if and when we break the rules, hence the focus on power.

The third part of the book deals with 'Culture and Identity', with how 'place' – and that includes Scotland as a whole – is imagined. We will introduce the notion of Scotland as a 'landscape of the mind', a place of the imagination, much of which has been bequeathed to us by interpretations of 'history' and the past. In the interactions of 'structure' and 'culture' we can better understand who we are, what 'being Scottish' means, and how it has changed down through the years. In that context, we will examine the relationship between national identity and politics, an important topic in the light of political events, especially in the last fifty years.

The final part focuses on 'Representing Scotland', the idea that Scotland is sustained as much by those living furth of Scotland as within the country. Do we, for example, see ourselves as others see us? How is Scotland represented in sport and in the press, and does it make any difference to how we see ourselves? What, in any case, is the point of focusing on Scotland, which, in the words of one anonymous referee for this book, is one, small, damp and not particularly significant country in north-west Europe? Behind that view possibly lies an argument that we live in one, globalised, world in which what we consume and the social and economic forces which matter most are global ones. Perhaps, as Sigmund Freud once pointed out in another context, we are simply obsessed with the 'narcissism of small differences'. Having read the book, or at least dipped into it, you will be in a better position to see if you agree with that view, or whether you think that small, and large, countries matter.

How should you read the book? You may wish to read it through from the beginning, or dip into it according to taste. As far as possible, there will be cross-referencing to other chapters, without making it too turgid. You will find at the end of each chapter suggestions for further reading, as well as sets of questions you might like to think about. You should also come up with questions of your own, either based on material in the chapters, or where you think more might have been said. You might even think of different ways in which the Scottish question should have been addressed.

Now that you have some sense of how the book is organised, it may be useful to say what it is not. First of all, it is not a 'history' book, for sociology is not an adjunct to history, simply a way of telling the 'modern' story. Indubitably, history matters and underpins much of the way the book has been written. Neither is it a 'politics' book, in which the focus is on explaining political developments like the recovery and development of a Scottish parliament. If anything, changes in society and culture have driven 'politics', rather than the other way round, but in any case the key point is the complex interaction of social, political and cultural forces, rather than the primacy of any single one. If there is more to Scotland than history and politics, then that is society and culture, and that is our focus in this book.

There are, naturally, perfectly good alternative ways of providing a sociology of Scotland. The obvious model would be to provide a general introduction to sociology, covering many of the chapter themes in this book, but in a more general way, with the specificities about Scotland used simply as illustrations. This is the model adopted by George Ritzer and Neil Guppy, also published by Sage, entitled *Introduction to Sociology: Canadian version* (2014). We learn a lot about the key institutions and structures in modern societies, but less about how Canada as state and society has evolved. You could, for example, write a sociology of Canada, but that would be a very different one to that of Ritzer and Guppy.[2] Another model of a sociology of Scotland might focus on public policy: that is, how Scotland 'works' in policy terms with regard to education, housing, welfare, its economy, and so on, both in terms of how policy is made as well as its outcomes. We would learn much about how Scotland itself works as a society, but arguably that would be incidental to the policy focus.

Why Scotland?

So what makes Scotland sociologically interesting? When, in 1992, I wrote *Understanding Scotland*, it was subtitled *The sociology of a stateless nation*. The point was that we could consider Scotland to be an 'imagined community', which is how Benedict Anderson defined a nation with four key dimensions: *imagined*, because its members believe they have something in common; *limited*, most obviously by its boundaries; *sovereign*, in having rights of self-determination; and a *community*, involving deep and horizontal comradeship (Anderson, 1996: 6–7).

Describing Scotland as stateless was less than accurate, even before the devolved Scottish parliament was created in 1999, because Scotland already had institutions of governance (such as the Scottish Office). Hence, in the 2001 edition of *Understanding Scotland*, the term 'stateless' was omitted, although possibly 'understated' might have been a more accurate descriptor. Regardless, Scotland is sociologically interesting because it is not a state in conventional terms, and shares that characteristic with the likes of Catalonia, Euskadi (the Basque Country), Quebec, Wales and many others.

The supposition that the world comprises 'nation-states' in which cultural entities (nations) correspond with political units (states) is no longer feasible. Robin Cohen (2008), for example, has pointed out that there are far more self-defining nations than actual states, possibly ten times the number. Indeed, so-called nation-states have been the exception, not the rule. So Scotland becomes an exemplar of an interesting geo-political phenomenon, a territory with a high degree of institutional identity, an 'imagined community', but not possessing a full-blown state. That is one important way in which Scotland is sociologically interesting: it provides an exemplar of the fact that 'society' is not a synonym for 'state'.

Furthermore, Scotland plays an interesting part in the debate about 'globalisation', both in terms of its 'understated' character as well as assumptions about its loss of economic autonomy. If, indeed, we increasingly lived in a globalised world, what would be the point of a movement towards greater political independence? Would there even *be* a point? Might it not represent something of a delusion? On the other hand, maybe globalisation is not quite the overwhelming process it is cracked up to be, and places like Scotland help to provide the exception which proves the rule that all is not what it seems.

And why the title of the book: *The New Sociology of Scotland*? Why, in particular, the definite article? Is this not somewhat presumptuous – that this is the only, proper, way to write such a thing? The title is not meant to pre-empt other efforts at understanding Scotland. Rather, since *Understanding Scotland* was first published in 1992, and then republished in revised form in 2001 to take account of new sociology thinking and new events, it seems reasonable enough to write a much bigger book without calling it 'Understanding Scotland 3'. For better or worse, these earlier books set the scene such that this book represent the 'new sociology' of Scotland in the sense that it builds on the previous versions. These set the pace, and others were invited to follow.

And why a prologue, and an epilogue, rather than an introduction and conclusion? The Prologue/Epilogue are theatrical devices first dreamt up by ancient Greeks to provide context for a play. They provide a voice for telling the tale. There was no presumption that this was the only tale worth telling, and that it had one simple message. And so it is here. There is no beginning or ending of Scotland's account, hence no introduction and conclusion. Indeed, as we shall see in the Epilogue, this is an ongoing tale. The Prologue is a device to provide a background, an insight into the author's or playwright's mind, concerning what they were aiming at. It is also personal.

I was one of the first students to take a sociology degree in Scotland, the subject being established in the mid-1960s, first at Edinburgh, and a year later at Aberdeen. My intention was to take a degree in English literature and, as the Scottish curriculum allows, two other subjects. I had heard of psychology (rather more about sticklebacks and pigeons than people, for my taste), and I also wanted to do history. My advisor of studies was a professor of African history, who said that doing history was off the agenda (full up, I seem to recall). Asking what 'resembled history', I was ushered into a new-fangled subject, sociology, and never looked back. One might say that John Hargreaves, that Aberdeen professor of history, made me a sociologist.

I was, however, puzzled about sociology. It seemed to be much more about family life in east London, or gangs in Chicago, and had nothing to say about the society most of us students knew best: Scotland. In other words, sociology was *in* Scotland, but not *about* Scotland; this, despite the fact that one could lay a claim that Scotland helped to create sociology in the form of the Scottish Enlightenment, notably by Adam Ferguson. With hindsight, the kind of sociology on offer in the late 1960s derived from two sources. On the one hand, there was the assumption that one society was much like any other society, and that what the United States did today, the rest of us would be doing tomorrow. On the other hand, sociology had grown up in the post-war context of the British welfare state, so 'society' really was equated with the state. Scotland was no different. With hindsight, this was the high noon not only of welfare statism, but of British political centralism.

By the early 1970s, things began to change. The ongoing crisis of British economic decline, the demise, especially in Scotland, of traditional heavy industries, coincided with the discovery of oil in the North Sea. Most bets were off. The marginal Scottish National Party was carried along by the rising tide, and borne also by another cultural revival matching the one in the 1920s and 1930s, but without the baleful assumption that Scotland was 'over'. My generation encountered distrust of the state, opposed the Vietnam War (as best we could) and bought into the notion that Scotland was 'different' somehow. Most of us in those days did not consider ourselves 'Nationalists' (with a capital 'N'), but Winnie Ewing's by-election victory at Hamilton in 1967 put the cat among the political pigeons.

In the mid-1970s I began to teach an undergraduate course at Edinburgh called 'Scotland: Social Structure and Social Change', and there were few comparators other than James Kellas' course on Scottish Politics at Glasgow. James and I, like prophets in the wilderness, met to compare notes. What followed thereafter was history. Cultural and political revivals reinforced each other and helped to stimulate a research agenda to try to understand Scotland. I doubt whether, in 1974, we could have predicted Winnie Ewing, as 'mother' of the parliament in 1999, saying 'The Scottish Parliament, which adjourned on March 25th 1707, is hereby reconvened', nor SNP governments in that parliament since 2007, nor 95 per cent of Scottish MPs elected in 2015 for the Nationalists, nor indeed an independence referendum in 2014 which has turned out to be ongoing and unfinished business. Or, perhaps, now being sufficiently wise after the event, we would have taken it for granted.

Understanding Scotland is, above all, a collegiate activity. I am grateful to Steve Bruce, Susan McVie and Lindsay Paterson for writing, respectively, chapters on religion, social order and education. They have done this far better than I ever could. The reader might take it further and ask why I have not assembled a battery of experts, and turned it into an edited book. Undoubtedly, the depth of expertise would have been greater, but the point of the book is to have an authorial voice. This book is how I see Scotland and its sociology. It is not intended to pre-empt anyone else's understanding, still less to assert the primacy of my discipline. It is what I know about, and I follow the comment by C. Wright Mills that, like the cobbler who thought there was nothing quite like leather, I am a sociologist.

Acknowledgements

Books do not write themselves, nor do single authors. In any case, three of the chapters have been written by my colleagues whose expertise is much greater than mine: Steve Bruce on religion, Susan McVie on social order, and Lindsay Paterson on education. I am grateful to them for their generosity and commitment. I am indebted to friends and colleagues for their support and helpful comments: to the anonymous seventeen reviewers (you know who you are) to whom Sage sent the proposal; to the six reviewers who read some of the penultimate chapters. Where I thought you had a good idea, I borrowed it.

Celeste Bertaux has been my 'intelligent reader', reading through the text when she had many other, more important, things to do in her life. She has also used her superior technical skills to improve many of the diagrams. The editors at SAGE, notably Delayna Spencer and Natalie Aguilera, have kept me on the straight and narrow, and answered my queries with courtesy and patience. It was a previous editor, Chris Rojek, who asked me to write this book, and I am grateful to him for giving me the opportunity.

Behind it all there are colleagues, friends and former students who have had bits of the book inflicted on them over the years. Prominent among these are: Frank Bechhofer, Michael Anderson, Ross Bond, Jonathan Hearn, Jimmy Kennedy, Lindsay Paterson and Michael Rosie.

Academic work is a collegiate activity, despite efforts by governments and university administrations to treat it as akin to producing widgets in a factory. I am especially indebted to Frank Bechhofer with whom I laboured long in the vineyard, and together we discovered quite a lot about national identity. Indeed, we have bored for Scotland on many occasions. Michael Anderson supplied many of the population graphs, along with helpful suggestions, with his characteristic generosity.

I have been encouraged to illustrate the book with diagrams and photographs, which I have happily done, even though it has cost me real money out of my own pocket. I did try to persuade the Carnegie Trust for the Universities of Scotland to help with research assistance and costs, but despite their claim that they were about 'improving and extending the opportunities for scientific study and research in the universities of Scotland', they declined to do so.

I have, however, been gratified by the willingness of so many organisations and individuals to allow me to use their photos and images free of charge. These are: The Bank of Scotland (especially Doug MacBeath); The Clydesdale Bank; Grandfather Mountain Highland Games (and James Shaffer); The National Library of Scotland; National Records of Scotland (especially Jay Gillam); The Scottish Parliament (especially Andrew Cowan); The Scottish Government; The Scottish Trades Union Congress; The Royal Collection in Trust; D.C. Thomson of Dundee (famously, *The Beano* and *The Dandy* and *The Sunday Post*); Glasgow University Special Collections; Friends of Glasgow Necropolis; Scottish Mining Museum; Scotland Street School Museum; University of Edinburgh; Michael Anderson; Brian Ashcroft; Dauvit Broun; Steven Camley (my favourite cartoonist); Robert Crawford; David Hawkey; Bob Morris; Stephen Smith (of National Records of Scotland); Chris Ramsay (of Forvie Media); Bruce Whyte and Tomi Ajetunmobi (Glasgow University); and Women for Independence.

The following organisations have allowed me to use their images for a fee: The BBC; Bridgeman Images; *The Herald*; The British Library; National Gallery of Scotland; National Gallery London; National Museum of Scotland; The Fleming Gallery, London; Imperial War Museum; The Press Association (special thanks to Sam Harrison); and Adrian McMurchie whose line drawings of Glasgow I much enjoy.

Those who live with me, notably Jan, Islay and Catherine, know that I can bore for Scotland, and frequently do. I thank them for their love and forbearance. They know I cannot change the habits of my lifetime.

For me, the sociology of Scotland has been a life's work and a labour of love. In words probably wrongly credited to Martin Luther: here I stand; I can do no other.

Notes

1   Like Robinson Crusoe we will carry social expectations around with us, even when we are entirely alone; and believing that we are freestanding individuals is in essence a *social* ideology.
2   There is, for example, a strong tradition in Canadian sociology which derives from 'political economy', associated with the work of Harold Innes, S.D. Clark, John Porter and Wallace Clement. They might recognise in this book something closer to their own.

HOW TO USE THE COMPANION WEBSITE

Visit **https://study/sagepub.co.uk/sociologyscotland** to find a range of additional resources for both students and lecturers, to aid study and support teaching.

For students

- **Word maps** presenting key themes covered throughout the book
- **Student notes** to help with your understanding of each chapter
- **Weblinks** which direct you to relevant resources to broaden your understanding of chapter topics and expand your knowledge
- **Key points** from each chapter to help you with your learning and revision

For lecturers

- **Tutor notes** which include seminar ideas and essay questions outline examples to use in class or for assignment
- **PowerPoint slides** featuring figures and tables from the book, which can be downloaded and customized for use in your own presentation

FRAMING SCOTLAND

1

WHEN WAS SCOTLAND?[1]

This is a 'sociology' book, not a 'history' book, but arguably you cannot write one without the other. It is for historians to decide how much, or how little, sociology they wish to include, but beginning to tell the story of Scotland, as this chapter tries to do, cannot be done without history. In any case, we might ask: when does the 'past' end and the 'present' begin? We cannot understand one without the other. Arguably, the sociology of any society must involve telling its story, at least in terms of how its structures, social, political and economic, and its cultures were formed.

That, however, raises an important question: how much 'history' to include and how to tell it? Since publishing *Understanding Scotland*, first in 1992, and in revised form in 2001, there has been a huge increase in historical scholarship and output. Nevertheless, the task in this chapter is to sketch out a 'sociological history': to focus on the key events and processes which have shaped Scotland and formed it as a society. To that end, it is necessary to be selective. We will focus on three key points in history at which Scotland's identity has been especially problematic and salient: (a) in the thirteenth century, and particularly relating to the Wars of Independence; (b) at the time of the Union of Parliaments with England in 1707; and (c) at the end of the twentieth century when agitation for greater self-government culminated in the recovery of a (devolved) Scottish parliament. Each time-point has as its central question: what is Scotland? Or, in the words of the chapter title, when *was* Scotland? How can we be sure that Scotland is meaningful in sociological terms?

Chapter aims

- To examine where the 'idea' of Scotland came from: what are its origins? In other words, *when* was Scotland?

- To discover what impact the Union of 1707 had on Scotland, its institutions and identity.

- To see how viable the arguments are that Scotland was 'over', that with the loss of formal independence it ceased to be a proper 'society', and that its culture was weak and divided.

In the subsequent chapter we will examine how the immediate history of the twentieth century shaped Scotland.

When was Scotland?

The historian Dauvit Broun has commented: 'However old this fundamental sense of people [Scots] and country [Scotland] may be, it must have begun sometime' (2015: 164). So when did 'Scotland' as an idea begin? Broun observes: 'to insist that Scotland was not a meaningful concept, or that Scottish identity did not exist before the end of the 13th century, would surely be to allow our modern idea of Scotland to take precedence over the view of contemporaries' (1994: 38).

So what is he alluding to? What *we* think of as 'Scotland' is shaped by our own experiences of it as a small, advanced, capitalist society on the fringes of north-west Europe. Trying to 'imagine' how our ancestors thought of it is much harder for us to do. Furthermore, there is an argument that notions of modernity so shaped our understanding of 'nations' that we simply have to treat them as modern creations.

We cannot know, the argument goes, what meaning and significance they had in the pre-modern era. Such is the view associated with Ernest Gellner, that the 'nation' is a cultural construction of modernity, dating from about the end of the eighteenth century. Gellner belonged to the 'modernist' school of nationalism studies, and Anthony Smith to the 'pre-modernist' one. In an engaging debate as to whether 'nations have navels', that is whether they derive from previous history or are simply creatures of 'modernity', Gellner and Smith argued whether modern nations have any or much claim to historic ancestry (see Gellner, 1996; Smith, 1996). All of this is part of a lengthy debate in nationalism studies about how old (or, indeed, how young) nations really are, and they have implications for Scotland.

Can we be at all sure that there is a clear historical lineage from past to present? We might take the view that our notion of 'Scotland' is a modern one, reflecting contemporary political and constitutional concerns, which we then read back into 'history', by way of ideological justification. We can use such justification for political purposes, to say, for example, that Scotland is one of Europe's oldest nations, but can we be sure that our ancestors thought of it as a 'nation', and, if so, in what senses? Hence Broun's comment that we cannot assume that the 'Scotland' we have inherited is that of the Middle Ages; that *medieval* Scotland means the same as *modern* Scotland. Much more difficult, then, as Broun observes, to ascertain whether people in the thirteenth century had any notion of 'Scotland', and what it might have meant to them. The author L.P. Hartley opened his novel *The Go-Between* (2004 [1953]: 5) with the words: 'The past is a foreign country; they do things differently there.' His original manuscript continued: 'Or do they?', a question cut from the published copy. Perhaps we can reinstate Hartley's question for the purposes of this chapter.

'Not-England'

Why, you might ask, the *thirteenth* century? 'Scotland' might have existed as early as the first millennium, but it was the twelfth and thirteenth centuries, and above all the 'Wars of Independence' at the beginning of the fourteenth century, which arguably 'made' Scotland in a way we now recognise. This is territory belonging to medieval historians. Broun contends that: 'it was not until the period between 1260 and 1290 that the idea of country, people and kingdom coincided to form what we recognise as the beginning of modern Scotland' (2015: 165).

So what brought this about? Broun argues that this was the outcome of a long process which had its origins in England, rather than Scotland. This was the unintended consequence of legal and administrative reforms between 1154 and 1189 during the reign of the English king Henry II: 'the main spur towards beginning to regard the Scottish kingdom as a single country may have been an intensification of royal power not in Scotland, but in England' (2015: 167). In other words, Scotland developed a sense of itself as 'not-England', at the point where regal authority south of the border was flexing its muscles. Not to be incorporated into England required active dissociation. In any case, by the 1180s we have the earliest indications that local lords thought of the Scottish kingdom as a land with common laws and customs, an unintended consequence of comparable legal and administrative reforms in England during Henry's reign.

By the middle of the thirteenth century, we have evidence of legal mechanisms in Scotland about the reporting of local land inquests to the king. Furthermore, the amount of money in circulation grew dramatically between 1250 and 1280, which was reflected in the creation of coinage mints from Inverness to Dumfries, as well as establishing sheriff courts throughout the land, both indicating jurisdictional expansion by the Crown.

We might assume, then, that the Crown was mainly responsible for shaping and imposing national institutions on 'Scotland', much as the monarchy did in France (Beaune, 1985). Broun argues that 'Scotland' came to be a phenomenon of the mind, an 'idea that, at some point, came to be thought of by its inhabitants as one-and-the-same as the kingdom they lived in' (2015:164). Furthermore:

> When economic growth and the increasing importance of burghs is combined with the change in the procedure for inquests ... it may be envisaged that those with property and possessions came more and more to identify with royal authority as a key background element in the pattern of their lives. (2015: 170)

Where was Scotland?

'Scotland' was envisaged in the twelfth century as the territory between the River Forth in the south, the Spey in the north, and the mountains of Drumalban in the west. However,

> by the late 13th century, a new sense of kingdom, country and people emerged which, of necessity, was based on something other than the logic of geography. At the end of the 12th century the kingdom was seen by contemporaries as comprising several countries, with the Scots identified as the inhabitants north

of the Forth. … this had begun to change by *ca*1220 when 'Scotland' appears to have meant the kingdom as a whole. By the early 1280s at the latest, not only had kingdom and country become one, but all its inhabitants were now Scots. (Broun, 2013: 6)

So strong was the conception of Scotland north of the Forth that it was thought of as an island, crossed by the bridge at Stirling (see map in Figure 1.1), which became a key battleground during the extended Wars of Independence.

Note, as shown in Figure 1.1, how the River Forth was imagined to be a continuous sea loch between east and west, with a single river crossing at Stirling (top, centre). For good

FIGURE 1.1
Matthew Paris map, fourteenth century

Source: Copyright British Library Board

measure, there are two walls dividing *Scocia* and *Anglia*, one, southern, approximating to Hadrian's Wall, and another emerging at Berwick in the east, north of the River Tweed.

Those described as 'Scots' (*Albanaig*) north of the Forth were later described as 'highland Scots', reflecting territorial expansion and diversity in the later period. Broun points out that the monks at Melrose ('chroniclers'), who derived authority from the king,

> may have become Scots, but this does not require that they ceased to be English. It depended on context. This 'new' kingdom-centric Scottish identity was grounded in obedience to the king of Scots. It is conceivable, therefore, that people continued to regard themselves as 'English' in the sense that their mother tongue was English, and at the same time identified as Scots. (2015: 168)

From the thirteenth century those living south of the Forth began to see themselves as 'Scots' living in 'Scotland', even if, like the Melrose monks, they viewed the northerners as somewhat unsavoury. Broun concludes:

> Overall … we seem to have kingdom, country and people coalescing round the image north of the Forth as an island, an image rooted in an awareness of a genuine topographical barrier. By the late thirteenth century kingdom, country and people has coalesced anew around the dawning concept of sovereignty. The sense of ultimate secular authority shared by both had moved its centre of gravity from geography to jurisdiction. (2015: 186)

Thus did kingdom/country/people coalesce imperceptibly into a new 'Scotland' as an independent realm, a view shared by its people at large.

Who were the Scots?

What we have inherited is the characterisation of Scots as a 'mongrel people', no pure race, but an amalgam of peoples united by territory rather than ethnicity. Scotland has no ambitions to be pure bred: we are a mongrel people, at least in our conception of ourselves. Such a descriptor has appeal to politicians. Thus, Alex Salmond in a speech in 1995:

> We see diversity as a strength not a weakness of Scotland and our ambition is to see the cause of Scotland argued with English, French, Irish, Indian, Pakistani, Chinese and every other accent in the rich tapestry of what we should be proud to call, in the words of Willie McIlvanney, 'the mongrel nation' of Scotland. (Speech to the annual SNP conference, Perth, 1995; quoted in Reicher and Hopkins, 2001: 164)

The conventional historical wisdom (e.g. Mackie, 1964), now disputed (Broun, 2013: 280), is that there were five 'founding peoples': the *Picts* in the north and east; the *Scots* around

Dalriada in the west; the *Britons* in the south and west; the *Norse* in the northern and west-ern isles; and the *Angles* in the south-east. Medievalists like Broun (2013: 276) are critical of this view, pointing out that it fits a narrative showing that they were inexorably united, by conquests or by dynastic unions, in order to conform to a conventional storyline.

Nevertheless, it helps to convey what the historian Christopher Smout memorably called a 'sense of place', rather than a 'sense of tribe'. This is no claim to be morally superior to any other people; it was simply *realpolitik*. Thus:

> If coherent government was to survive in the medieval and early modern past, it had, in a country that comprised gaelic-speaking Highlanders and Scots-speaking Lowlanders, already linguistically and ethnically diverse, to appeal beyond kin and ethnicity – to loyalty to the person of the monarch, then to the integrity of the territory over which the monarch ruled. The crit-ical fact allowed the Scots ultimately to absorb all kinds of immigrants with relatively little fuss, including, most importantly, the Irish in the 19th century. (Smout, 1994:107)

This fitted in with how other historians made sense of the history of these islands. In many ways, Scotland was less homogeneous culturally and linguistically than its Celtic neigh-bours. The historian Sandy Grant observed:

> during the Middle Ages the Welsh and the Irish surely had at least as strong a concept of racial or national solidarity as the Scots, and much more linguistic solidarity. Yet, between the eleventh and the thirteenth centuries, the whole of Wales and very substantial parts of Ireland were conquered by the English; subsequently both countries experienced many anti-English rebellions, but nei-ther was ever liberated from foreign rule. The contrast with what happened to Scotland is obvious, and demonstrates that success or failure in maintain-ing independence cannot simply be explained in terms of racial consciousness, nationalist myths, common language and the like. (1994: 75)

Grant's point is that territorial interests, reinforced by state authority in the shape of the Crown, held Scotland together despite its regional and ethnic diversity; or perhaps because of it, in the sense that national integrity had to be worked at actively to offset ethnic diversity on the ground.

Stating the nation

It is in this context that we can appreciate what the iconic Declaration of Arbroath of 1320 signifies. This was a political document from the barons of Scotland to Pope John XXII, which begins with a rewriting of the history of the people, which no modern historian could ever countenance. The Scots, the declaration averred, 'journeyed from Greater Scythia by way of the Tyrrhenian Sea and the Pillars of Hercules, and dwelt for a long course of time in Spain among the most savage tribes, but nowhere could they be subdued by any race, however barbarous'.

Having reached their promised land, the 'Scots' single-mindedly pursued their goal: 'The Britons they first drove out, the Picts they utterly destroyed, and though very often assailed by the Norwegians, the Danes and the English, they took possession of that home with many victories and untold efforts.' So much for being a mongrel people, for live and let live: the fourteenth century was not the time to make such an essentially modern and liberal claim.

We can only assume that conveying that strong national lineage was *de rigueur* in convincing the pope to recognise their claim; the Scots were a people distinct (from the English) and, crucially, they were winners. Broun's view is that the Declaration of Arbroath was a device to portray Scotland as exclusively Scottish in its formative years. He comments: 'the fact that the Picts were now seen as a historical nuisance is striking testimony to how the idea of kingdom, country and people had crystallised in the heat of war into a seamless unity without any consideration of geographical reality' (2013: 276).

The most famous part of the Declaration of Arbroath is well-known:[2]

> for, as long as but one hundred of us remain alive, never will we on any conditions be brought under English rule. It is in truth not for glory, nor riches, nor honours that we are fighting, but for freedom – for that alone, which no honest man gives up but with life itself.

Few readers, however, take note of what precedes these famous few lines. If 'our most tireless Prince, King and Lord, the Lord Robert [i.e. Bruce]',

> should give up what he has begun, and agree to make us or our kingdom subject to the King of England or the English, we should exert ourselves at once to drive him out as our enemy and subverter of his own rights and ours, and make some other man who was well able to defend us our King.

Little sign there of deferring to an absolute monarchy and the later divine right of kings. The message is clear: if Bruce (or any other king or queen, for that matter) did not defend Scotland's independence from England, then he would be usurped, and someone better suited would be put in his place. What this implies is that the Crown is conceived of as the state, and not the *person* of the monarch. Bruce could govern as long as he defended Scotland's interests, but if not, not (see Figure 1.2). Such a 'modern' statement has easily been mistaken[3] as a forerunner for modern declarations of independence, notably the American one of 1776, which is unlikely to be the case; all the same, the 1320 statement has a remarkably modern ring to it.

Shaping Scotland

Why should a sociologist bother to look at this early history of Scotland? Does it really matter? First and foremost, it establishes where, and when, 'Scotland' came to be thought of as a nation, and makes the point that the nation was an 'imagined community' (Anderson, 1996) as early as the thirteenth century. Being able to establish 'Scotland' in meaningful terms well before the modern period marks it as one of Europe's oldest nations. Second, this 'Scotland' derived from diverse peoples and territories, which were united under the authority of the Crown, and yet without ceding absolute legitimacy to that institution. To be sure, all nations have diversity in common, even though it behoves them to claim unity in diversity. From such a reading of Scottish history derived the belief in the 'sovereignty of the people', set against the sovereignty of parliament, otherwise the English Crown.[4] Third, and to reiterate the point, the Crown was imagined as a legal entity, as the *state*, and not the person of the monarch.

It was to take some time for the shape of Scotland to match its current contours. In the west, the Kingdom of the Isles fell to the Scots as a result of the Treaty of Perth in 1266. The northern isles of Orkney and Shetland were ceded to Scotland in the fifteenth century when the king of Norway failed to meet payment of the dowry promised to the king of Scots on the marriage of his daughter. In the far south-east, Berwick fell to the English in 1482, having changed hands between Scotland and England fourteen times in its history.

Thus were formed the modern boundaries of Scotland, which have not changed in more than 500 years. In Broun's words, 'Scotland was finally equipped with the essential elements of its modern identity as a nation, elements which have sustained its claim to be regarded as a nation despite the loss of independence three hundred years ago' (2013: 7).

Whether one is for or against independence in the twenty-first century, indubitably Scotland was an independent nation for much of its history.

Did people in the twelfth and thirteenth centuries actually think of themselves as 'Scots'? Surely this is to impose modern conceptions on a past we cannot know? The first thing to be said is that in modern Scotland we live quite happily with multiple meanings of what it means to be a Scot, by birth, descent and residence, and we know that each of these is sufficiently distinct from each other, but are also valid in their own right (McCrone and Bechhofer, 2015). Broun's point (1998: 11) about the thirteenth century, that 'Scotland and the Scots are, first and foremost, images which have been adapted and recreated according to the experiences and aspirations of the society to which they related', is just as valid in the twenty-first century.

Although it is a much more difficult task, especially for a sociologist, to know what the thirteenth-century peasant made of being Scottish, the historical consensus does seem to be that at least the 'middling folk' and foot soldiers of Scotland at that time certainly made something of it (Broun, 1998; Ferguson, 1998; Stringer and Grant, 1995). The concept of the 'community of the realm'[5] – *communitas regni* – appears to have been a sufficiently understood concept to rally the nation against the English foe, just as there is support for the existence of 'national' consciousness in England in the Middle Ages (Greenfeld, 1993; Hastings, 1997).

In short, the conditions for generating national awareness contra the 'other' were surely there for Scotland and England in mutual context, as Grant observes: 'in the two medieval kingdoms of the British Isles, the people were involved along with their elites in their countries' wars; in France, they were not' (1994: 95), which is why 'making Frenchmen' took so much longer (Weber, 1977). The point is also made by Adrian Hastings (1997) in his analysis of the development of national consciousness in these islands. Thus it was that the designs of the English state on its neighbours, particularly Scotland, helped to mould diverse peoples into a single nation in the face of this common threat.

Origin myth-stories

The Scots and English did not settle down contentedly into 'mutual other' status, especially as far as England was concerned. Bill Ferguson's monumental study *The Identity of the Scottish Nation* (1998) showed that the ideological battle raged as fiercely as the military one, and for longer. To twenty-first-century ears, debates about the ancient origins of peoples may seem arcane, even somewhat racist. The myth-stories, however, were deadly serious, because whether or not peoples had a right to exist depended on winning the ideological battle of origins. Much rested on whom the founding peoples were judged to be. Geoffrey of Monmouth's *Historia Regum Britanniae* ('History of the Kings of Britain') written in the twelfth century was long accepted as the standard history of that realm, and helped to promote feelings of Englishness to the considerable advantage of the state.

It was, in turn, judged by the Scots to be unacceptable because it appeared to reinforce English claims to the feudal overlordship of Scotland. This claim was based, to modern ears, on some far-fetched history. The medieval English appropriated the legend of Brutus, that the Trojan was the founder of the early kings of Britain. In Geoffrey's account, the descendants of Brutus carried sway over the entire island, the Picts were dismissed as late-comers, and the Scots were simply a mongrel race begat by Picts and Hibernians.

The Scots, in turn, mobilised their own origin-myth based on *Gaidel Glas*, who was either the husband or son of Scota, daughter of the Pharoah of Egypt, and who had come to Hibernia via Spain. We may wonder why any of this mattered. The point was the claim that the Scots, and the Irish, were deemed to have Greek, not Trojan, roots, and as a consequence could not possibly be of the same rootstock as the English.[6]

These claims to roots were deadly serious. They helped to shape claim and counter-claim among historians, and much focused on whether the founding peoples were the Scots (originally from Ireland) or the Picts. In the fourteenth century, John of Fordun minimised Pictish roots in favour of the Scots so as to counter English claims that Picts were 'really' Teutons ('Germans'), and hence Britons. Hector Boece, born in the second half of the fifteenth century, took the claim further by claiming that it was the 'Scots' who resisted the Romans, who had conquered the Picts, and held out against the Norse and the English. Boece also subscribed to the 'forty kings' theory, which purported to trace the lineage of Scottish monarchs (see Bruce and Yearley, 1989), and his view was shared by the Protestant reformer and historian George Buchanan in the sixteenth century, who argued that the Scots had come from Ireland. On the other hand, the Catholic priest and Jacobite, Thomas Innes, took a contrary view in the late seventeenth century, and preferred the Pictish theory of origins.

By the late eighteenth and early nineteenth centuries, Pictomania had come to serve the views of those such as John Pinkerton that the true aboriginals were the Picts – Teutons – and, ergo, English. James Macpherson, who claimed to have discovered the Gaelic poems of Ossian, fell foul of anti-Scottish feeling in the eighteenth century which was aimed at denying a distinct origin-myth to the Scots as they entered the British Union.

Lest we think that this sort of historiography was well and truly over, Ferguson reminds us that the English historian Hugh Trevor-Roper was still employing Celtophobic arguments in the 1970s to undermine the claims to Scottish autonomy. Ferguson, on the other hand, says that 'there can be little doubt ... that the national identity of the Scots sprang from an early Gaelic tribal root that first flourished in Ireland' (1998: 306).

It is almost impossible to avoid much of this historiography from becoming subordinated to one political claim or another. Ferguson, for his part, concluded: 'Scottishness was never exclusive, but, on the contrary, has always been highly absorptive, a quality that it retains even in the vastly different circumstances of today' (1998: 305). There are echoes here of Willie McIlvanney's claim that Scots are a 'mongrel nation', drawn from many roots, but primarily concerned with the future rather than the past; a concern, as Stuart Hall put it, with 'routes' rather than 'roots' (1992). Those who wish to argue that an ethnically diverse Scotland is the morally correct one, and no barrier to common identity, are thus able to mobilise history to considerable effect. This debate about origins came to matter significantly when issues of relations between the peoples of these islands became salient.

Understanding the Union

We can take it that 'Scotland' as a meaningful society existed at least from the fourteenth century, if not earlier, while accepting that it took a quite different form than the one we know today. While we can never be sure, its people would probably have thought of themselves as 'Scots'. How, then, do we understand the formal end of its 'independence' in 1707 when the Treaty of Union created the new state of Great Britain and brought the political existence of Scotland (and England for that matter) to an end?

The end of Scotland?

There is a conventional historiography, largely nationalist, which saw the Union in the words of the Earl of Seafield, one of the signatories to the Treaty document, as *ane end of ane auld sang* (see Figure 1.3).

Scotland would seem to have come to an end. Robert Burns took the view that its signatories to the Union were 'sic a parcel of rogues in an nation', bought and sold for English gold:

Fareweel to a' our Scottish fame, Fareweel our ancient glory!

Fareweel ev'n to the Scottish name, Sae famed in martial story!

FIGURE 1.3
The Downsitting of the Scottish Parliament, the only known illustration of the pre-Union parliament in session, illustrating the procession from Holyrood to Parliament Hall, and a view of the single chamber in session

Source: I am grateful to National Museums of Scotland for permission to reproduce this image

However, commented Lindsay Paterson, 'if it [Scotland] did end then, ... his [Seafield's] political successors did not notice' (1994: 2), and again, 'if Scotland was departing, it took a long time about it' (1994: 2). Paterson's arguments are worth examining in detail. He observed:

> The debate about whether union was inevitable or, to the contrary, was imposed on Scotland by the English and their Scottish agents is intricate and endless. There is, certainly, clear evidence that the proponents of union invoked the real threat of economic or military retaliation from England. They may also have used bribery, although this common claim is not well documented and is probably exaggerated. It might even be the case that the majority of the population were opposed: there were fairly widespread riots in lowland areas against union – most notably in Edinburgh itself, where the Scottish parliament met – and numerous burghs, counties, presbyteries and parishes petitioned against it too. (1994: 27–8)

The arguments in favour of union were, according to Paterson, three-fold.

First, *economic*: the dearths of the previous decade, and the failure of the Darien Scheme at the turn of the century, were pragmatic persuasions for union, and although, formally speaking, it was an incorporating union with a single parliament in London, arguably it created more economic opportunities than it destroyed.

Second, and relatedly, there was the *military* threat to England, and in Scotland's case, *from* England, in the context of the threat from the continental powers, France and Spain. Further, ensuring that the Stuarts did not succeed to the now-British throne (since 1603 when the Union of Crowns took place, James VI of Scotland becoming James I of England) was a major reason for union. Was English invasion of Scotland a real possibility? Paterson observes: 'The Scots concluded that it would be better to ally themselves with this power than risk its wrath' (1994: 29).

The third reason for union was *religion*: Scottish Presbyterians argued that British union safeguarded Protestantism against Catholic France and Spain. Thus, shared Protestantism, even though there were important internal diversities of belief, was a reinforcement of Scottishness, not its alternative. The Jacobite Wars (1715 and 1745) were as much about religion as about succession; indeed these were wholly intertwined. Paterson concludes:

> The Union which resulted was then a compromise. It contained safeguards for the continuing independence of Scots law, religion, education and local government, and offered to the merchants of the burghs some of the trading opportunities which they had long sought. The Scots knew they had struck a bargain, and this satisfaction – or indifference – extended beyond the elite groups who had done the negotiating. (1994: 31)

Above all, the British parliament was acceptable because it did not interfere, and thus guaranteed liberty, of both religious and civil sorts. The threat of an autocratic and Jacobite

Stuart regime was seen off, and the incorporation – 'pacification' – of the Highland *Gàidhealtachd*[7] after the Battle of Culloden in 1746 ensured Protestant supremacy. The forceable incorporation of the Highlands was one of the few instances of the British state using its considerable military muscle at home rather than abroad.

Union meant that Scots had a national right to be treated as equals, and it is to that belief, more often than not, which modern nationalists have appealed. The historian Colin Kidd (2008) has observed that in the ensuing centuries 'unionists' went to great lengths to assert the theoretical independence of Scotland, while 'nationalists' went to similar lengths to argue for equal treatment under the Union. Thus, much of unionism is tinged with nationalism, and nationalism with unionism, rather than being polar opposites.

What Scotland got out of this union, this *mariage de raison* (marriage of convenience), was a solution to many of its most pressing economic problems and a share in an expanding 'British' empire, so successful that many in England complained of 'Scots on the make'.[8] The defence of autonomous civil society with its institutions of law, education, religion and civil life was the achievement of union, and the reason why it lasted so long.

This independent civil society, however, as Paterson observes, was not a national expression in and of itself:

> The Scots could believe that they had won a great bargain because their culture could flourish and their economy could grow. This was their conception of liberty. It is not ours, nor that of nationalism: there was no mass franchise, nor even the nineteenth century icon, a national parliament. (1994: 45)

That was to come much later, and is quite another story, but without understanding the Union of 1707 for what it was, we cannot make sense of our politics in the twenty-first century. Even asserting that it was 'treaty' of union,[9] rather than conquest (as in Wales and Ireland), makes a historical point with much political force. It is the point which Kidd is making: that nationalists and unionists alike insist on the constitutional equality of Scotland with England.

Becoming British

In spite of popular opposition to the Union in the early years of the eighteenth century, it proved, in the nineteenth, to be relatively easy to refashion the Scots into British. The point was that Scots became British as well as continuing to be Scots, not despite that fact. The Jacobite legacy always had the power to be a potent nationalist myth, but, as Richard Finlay (1994) has observed, that was a step too far. In the first place, Jacobite ideology could not be moulded into the Scottish Presbyterian spirit: it was too Catholic and Episcopalian for that. In the second place, Jacobite adherence to the divine right of kings could not be worked into meritocratic and liberal ideology. And finally, it contradicted the notion of a bloodless Union. While Jacobitism has always had complex potential as an alternative Scottishness, although Smout judges that 'it is a sad misconstruction of Scottish history to see in the Jacobite movement some appeal to an archaic, anti-capitalist, anti-improvement, green past' (1994:110), it was too far removed from the experiences of most Scots for the connection to be made.

Rather, Scottishness in the nineteenth century was refashioned around three pillars of identity: church, state and empire. Protestantism helped to 'forge' the business of being British. Most people in Wales, Scotland and England, Linda Colley has observed, 'defined themselves as Protestants struggling for survival against the foremost Catholic power. They defined themselves against the French as they imagined them to be, superstitious, militarist, decadent and unfree' (1992: 5). That, in essence, is why most people in Ireland could not consider themselves British, nor were they permitted to be. Scottish Protestantism proved to be an important seedbed for the three dominant political creeds: Liberalism, Unionism and, latterly, Labourism.

The civilising mission: guns and God

Scottish military culture had a long pedigree in a country which relied on fighting other people's wars for a living (Wood, 1987). The Union, first after Culloden in 1746, and later in the imperial wars of the following century, offered new and improved opportunities for professional soldiering, and throughout the following centuries, Scots had disproportionately made a living, as well as a dying, in the ranks of the military (Smout, 1994: 106). It was no coincidence that Cliff Hanley's song 'Scotland the Brave' became an unofficial embodiment of the national character, to be succeeded in turn by another hymn to war, 'Flower of Scotland'.

The British Empire proved to be the battleground, both military and ecclesiastical, for what Graeme Morton (1999) has called 'unionist-nationalism'. In the nineteenth century, graduates from Scottish universities saw in empire new opportunities. In short, they believed that they had a mission to spread Scottish liberalism and Scottish Protestantism, and that only the Union could have given them the political influence to do that.

The missionary movement, in places like southern Africa and India – associated especially with David Livingstone and Mary Slessor – provided a powerful justification for empire, union and Presbyterianism. Tom Devine has commented: 'By underwriting the empire as a moral undertaking, religion helped to strengthen the union with England but also assumed greater significance as an important factor reinforcing Scottish identity' (2000: 367).

Scottish unionists in particular were able to draw together these strands of the Protestant ethic, and to infuse ideas of civic responsibility in the nineteenth century to their considerable political advantage. Not until the twentieth century did such an ideology lose its electoral power. Even by the 1920s, the Reformed tradition had begun to deteriorate into a 'preoccupation with the moral sentiment of patriotism and the preservation of a mythical Presbyterian racial identity' (Storrar, 1990: 47).

As we shall see in the next chapter, post-1945, the pillars, first of Protestantism, then imperialism and finally unionism, began to crumble, and a new edifice and a different sense of 'being Scottish' emerged. On the one hand, growing secularisation, but above all the moral economy of the welfare state, had transformed people's dependence on the church. On the other hand, demobilisation and the end of empire released the need for a standing army and a military attachment to the state. Finally, and not until the 1970s and 1980s, political unionism lost its appeal to Scotland's middle classes, while there was less reason for workers to be thirled (thirl means bound with ties of affection and loyalty. It has Old English roots like many Scottish words, but has died out in English, where 'thrall' is its closest cognate) to the Conservative Party.

The end of Scotland?

The third period in which the question 'when was Scotland?' became highly salient was the final quarter of the twentieth century. In the light of political developments in the twenty-first century, the recovery of a parliament and the rise and rise of the SNP, it might seem strange to suggest that Scotland 'died' as a meaningful entity after the Union of 1707. Nevertheless, a high degree of cultural pessimism has permeated Scottish thought for much of the last 150 years. This argued that Scotland was 'over' as a self-governing civil society and had thrown in its lot with England. Not for nothing did David Hume title his mid-eighteenth-century book *A History of England* (and not a History of *Britain*). He was not making a category error, but implying that 'England' was culturally and politically domi-nant because it was one of the most progressive societies on earth. England was conceived of a 'mature, all-round thought-world' (Nairn, 1977: 156–7) to which Scotland could only aspire to be part of.

Cairns Craig opened his essay on twentieth-century Scottish literature with this obser-vation: 'When TS Eliot, in a review in 1919, asked, "Was There a Scottish Literature?", the past tense perspective seemed all too appropriate to the possibilities of Scottish literature surviving into the twentieth century as an independent cultural force' (1987: 1). What Scotland was not considered to be was an 'organic whole', a vibrant literature and culture which sustained a sense of cultural identity, and which stimulated a greater political one. In short, much of the writing about Scottish culture and politics in the twentieth century assumed that 'Scotland' had effectively ceased to be; it had ended.

The supposed effect of this cultural incorporation was to fragment the Scottish story. The novelist Willie McIlvanney observed that we had inherited a 'pop-up picture' school of history, that moments in history seemed unconnected, that Scottishness existed in 'wilful fragments' (*The Herald*, 6 March 1999). Marinell Ash in her book *The Strange Death of Scottish History* likened modern perceptions of Scotland's past to a foggy landscape, 'small peaks and islands of memory rising out of an occluded background' (1980: 1). We will analyse this conception of Scottish culture and society in Chapter 17, but cultural pessimism has been a dominant trope in writing about Scotland. There seemed to be too *much* history in Scotland rather than too little, or perhaps too much of the wrong sort.

McIlvanney's own explanation was that 'when a country loses the dynamic of its own history, the ability to develop on its own terms, its sense of its past can fragment and freeze into caricature. For a long time this was Scotland's fate' (*The Herald*, 6 March 1999). In other words, there is a clear connection between Scotland's cultural and political development. It was as if, following the Union of 1707, Scotland was left with a deficit of politics, and a surfeit of culture, but one which was over.

A glance at the 'Scottish' shelves in any major bookshop might suggest that much of Scotland is 'over', for they are weighed down with accounts of the country's past. The conventional wisdom was that since Scotland lost its formal political independence in 1707, it could not have a 'national culture' worthy of the name. After all, it lacked distinctiveness as regards language and religion, being both English speaking and Protestant, and it had chosen to throw its political lot in with its richer and more powerful southern neighbour.

If proof were needed, the argument went, most of the inhabitants of Scotland had supported the suppression of the Gaelic-speaking and largely Catholic Highlanders after their defeat at Culloden in 1746. Furthermore, they became enthusiastic Unionists and Imperialists in the context of the British Empire, in contrast to the Irish and even the Welsh. The failure of political nationalism to emerge in the nineteenth century when it was the rage of Europe seemed to confirm that whatever form cultural identity and nationalism was taking at that time, it was not being mobilised in the cause of regaining Scottish statehood. Scottish history, the argument went, ceased to be important because it could not be reworked into a political programme for a separate state. Kidd (1993) argued that Scottish Whig historians looked to England for a progressive and liberating vision of society, and hence the absence of a nationalist historiography in the nineteenth century was because there was no real demand for one. Liberation and progress were to be achieved through the medium of the Anglo-British state.

Cultural pessimism

The strain of cultural pessimism ran deep among Scottish intellectuals. The perceived absence of a 'rounded' culture, reflecting the Scottish/British split, mapping as it does onto the culture/politics split, long had an appeal, and will be discussed more fully in Chapter 17. Writing in the 1930s, Edwin Muir saw a Scotland 'gradually being emptied of its population, its spirit, its wealth, industry, art, intellect, and innate character' (1935 (reprinted 1980): 3).

George Davie's *The Democratic Intellect* (1961), a powerful indictment of what he took to be the Anglicisation of Scottish culture and education in the nineteenth century, is one of the most influential books of the late twentieth century. Davie observed that 'when other neighbouring countries were becoming increasingly "history minded", the Scots were losing their sense of the past, their leading institutions, including the Universities, were emphatically resolved – to use the catch-phrase fashionable in the early twentieth-century – "no longer to be prisoners of their own history"' (1961: 337).

The most powerful and dominant analysis of Scottish culture was Nairn's *The Break-Up of Britain* published first in 1977. This is a view of Scottish culture, epitomised in Walter Scott, divided between 'heart' (representing the past, romance, 'civil society') and 'head' (the present and future, reason, and, by dint of that, the British state). There is the 'Caledonian Antisyzygy', a term borrowed by Hugh MacDiarmid from Gregory Smith's (1919) characterisation of Scottish literature as containing an antithesis of the real and the fantastic.

The image of Scotland as a divided and unhealthy society became a common one in Scottish literature, which acted as a key carrier of Scottish identity. In Douglas Gifford's words:

> Through recurrent patterns of a relationship such as father versus son, brother versus brother, or variants, a recurrent and shared symbolism states overwhelmingly the same theme; that in lowland Scotland, aridity of repressive orthodoxy, religious and behavioural, tied to an exaggerated work ethic and distorted notions of social responsibility, have stifled and repressed vital creative processes of imaginative and emotional expression, to the point where it too often has become, individually and collectively, self-indulgent, morbid and unbalanced. (1988: 244)

While Scottish civil society survived in the bosom of the British state, the Scottish 'heart' was split from the British 'head'; the 'national' with its over-emphasis on the past, was separated from the 'practical' with its emphasis on the present and future. This came about because, by the late eighteenth and early nineteenth centuries, the intelligentsia was 'deprived of its historic nationalist' role. Said Nairn, 'there was no call for its usual services' (1977: 154) of leading the nation to the threshold of political independence. Adam Smith, David Hume, James Mill (father of John Stuart Mill), William Robertson, Robert Adam and its other luminaries, Nairn argued, may have been Scots by birth and education, but they were universal men, and certainly, if anything, 'British' in orientation insofar as the term was meaningful.

Scottish culture could never, in this conventional wisdom, be an 'organic whole'. Instead, as Cairns Craig observes, it was common to see Scotland's as 'fundamentally a dead literature, the literature of a nation which once existed but now has no independent identity' (1999: 16). Much of the commentary was elegiac, as expressed in the work of critics like David Craig (no relation), which saw Scottish culture as doomed to failure, conspiring to produce a cultural wasteland. David Craig's book, *Scottish Literature and the Scottish People* (1961), covered the period between 1680 and 1830, presumably on the grounds that after that date there was little to say. Indeed, invited by the *London Review of Books* to reflect on the Independence Referendum in September 2014, David Craig wrote:

> A free Scotland would be founded on a nationalism roughly coterminous with race, and I grew up in a world where racist nationalism was the most abhorrent and dangerous tendency under the sun. ... I mistrust any party which is founded on nationhood as such – as a self-evident good – and for that reason, if I still lived in Scotland, I would vote No. (pp. 13–15)

Pessimism, it seems, runs deep.

Why should any of this matter to our question: when was Scotland? Because if, to all intents and purposes, Scotland was 'over', then the crucial link between culture and politics had been irrevocably broken. Does this matter? It does, because it seemed to explain why political nationalism in Scotland did not happen in the classic manner. In his book *Social Preconditions of National Revival in Europe* (1985), the Czech writer Miroslav Hroch argued that national movements went through three phases of development:

- Phase A, in which activists are engaged in small-scale scholarly enquiry into the cultural basis of the nation. This involves collecting linguistic, folkloric, historic and cultural fragments, and distilling them into a (cultural) national narrative.

- Phase B, which involves a new range of activists who seek to waken the nation from its slumbers by promulgating the national story of a distinctive people with their own culture.

- Phase C, the final or mass phase, which mobilises national identity for the purpose of achieving statehood. Hroch is careful to say that the phases do not need to happen sequentially, and, indeed, that phase C, the rise of the mass movement, often happens during phase A, and they feed off each other. Hroch is also careful not to put a time-scale on the shift from cultural to political nationalism, but it is fair to characterise it as occurring classically in nineteenth-century middle Europe, with the Czech lands being a good exemplar.

Scotland, manifestly, does not fit the model. The relationship between cultural and political forms of nationalism is quite different, and, in any case, entering a political union with England in the early eighteenth century obviated any need for the national bourgeoisie, the conventional carrier of national liberation elsewhere, to strike out for national independence. The British state and Empire provided the means for that to happen. (For a broad account of the sociology of nationalism, which sets Scotland within this literature, see McCrone, 1998.)

So here we have an intriguing puzzle. Scotland does not fit conventional accounts of the rise of nationalism, at least in terms of classical timings. It was not until the final quarter of the twentieth century that a strong Nationalist Party challenged for power. Furthermore, it seemed to be strong on 'politics' and weak on 'culture'. The fact that its leader Alex Salmond from the 1980s was a banker, not a poet, seemed to confirm that.

Back to our puzzle: why did Scotland not 'end', and, furthermore, what was the connection, if any, between culture and politics? Let us return to Davie's influential argument in *The Democratic Intellect* (1961) in which he argued that Scottish higher education underwent an unprecedented and fatal Anglicisation in the late nineteenth century, and with it Scottish society more generally.

Paterson describes Davie's argument as persuasive and usually undisputed, but quite wrong in its interpretation of events and processes (1994: 66). Paterson argued that change in the Scottish universities was not driven by English models, but by German and French ones which were judged to be more successful economically, and hence to be emulated. Scottish universities did not generate the same intensity when it came to nationalist campaigning compared with elsewhere (in Ireland and Wales, for example, or in Central Europe). The Scottish middle classes saw little need to mobilise in the pursuit of power; they were already in control over civil society and its institutions *within* the British state.

Thus, far from being divided, even schizophrenic, Scotland could be deemed 'normal'. That claim has been controversial for many decades now: at least since the nationalist cultural revival of the 1920s, the belief has gained currency that Scotland in the nineteenth century was subservient to England. This belief assumes that the only sure sign of not being subservient would have been a developed demand for an independent parliament. Paterson's argument is to the contrary: 'it is close to the image that middle-class Scots of the nineteenth century had of themselves. They had real autonomy' (1994: 70).

Scottish culture renewed

A further attack on the thesis that 'Scotland was culturally deformed' came from Cairns Craig. The quest for Scottish cultural independence from a culturally suffocating and homogeneous Anglo-British one ignored the fact that the latter had itself fragmented. Craig argued that the post-1918 period saw the collapse of the English cultural imperium, and thus, 'English culture' could no longer be equated with 'the culture of England'. In most English-speaking countries, there was a burgeoning of indigenous literature – in Canada, Australia, South Africa, New Zealand, the United States and Ireland. Craig comments: 'At no time in its history could Scotland have been described as "organic" or a "unified" culture: it could never have been envisaged as one "comprehensive" mind transcending the "prejudices of politics and fashions of taste" of particular periods' (1996: 15). The problem, he says, is that Scotland is not usually compared with Ireland or with Norway, but with England, deemed by T.S. Eliot and others to have a 'cumulative, unbroken history, supporting an organically growing literature' (Craig, 1999: 17).

The literary renaissance of the 1920s in Scotland expressed itself in the work of Hugh MacDiarmid, Lewis Grassic Gibbon, Eric Linklater, Fionn MacColla, Edwin Muir, James Bridie, as well as Violet Jacob and Naomi Mitchison. This renaissance was rooted in a pluralistic cultural and linguistic system in Scotland – in Gaelic (Sorley MacLean), in Scots (notably, MacDiarmid and Gibbon) and in standard English (Muriel Spark). These traditions survived and prospered, and ceased simply to be literary forms. Spoken language through radio and television also contributed to a multi-varied culture.

By and large, this was not an overtly 'political' literature. Writers such as these were not identifying a unique Scottish experience, but addressing the universal condition through day-to-day (Scottish) reality. The search for new images which express these experiences was no longer simply literary but artistic and cultural in the widest sense. As an exemplar of this, the folk music revival which itself became an important carrier of Scottish culture was cross-fertilised in terms of styles, tunes and instruments. The search for what is 'traditional' could no longer be taken as predating the nineteenth century; nor was it confined to oral conventions (Munro, 1996).

These ways of expressing Scottish culture are to be thought of as inclusive rather than exclusive, building on the erstwhile alternative ways of being 'Scottish' – Lowland and Highland, Protestant and Catholic, male and female, black and white. This involved borrowing and adapting what is available. In Cairns Craig's words:

> The fragmentation and division which made Scotland seem abnormal to an earlier part of the 20th century came to be the norm for much of the world's population. Bilingualism, biculturalism and the inheritance of a diversity of fragmented traditions were to be the source of creativity rather than its inhibition in the second half of the 20th, and Scotland ceased to have to measure itself against the false 'norm', psychological as well as cultural, of the unified national tradition. (1987: 7)

Borrowing the phrase 'being between' from the poet Sorley MacLean with reference to the mediums of Gaelic and English, Craig commented that: 'Culture is not an organism, nor a totality, nor a unity: it is the site of a dialogue, it is a dialectic, a dialect. It is being between' (1996: 206). What this condition signifies is not a divided but a diverse culture, which Scotland had to be from its earliest forms of statehood. It was neither feasible nor desirable to impose a single, uniform sense of culture.

Let us return to the question of the connection, or lack of it, between culture and politics in Scotland. The conventional wisdom has been to downplay the significance of 'culture' vis-à-vis 'politics' to explain the rise of nationalism in the late twentieth century. Scotland was certainly not 'over'. Many of us, however, while rejecting the notion that Scotland was culturally and psychologically damaged by being part of the British state since 1707, downplayed the cultural content of nationalism. Writing in 2001 shortly after the devolved parliament was established, I considered that Scotland was neither fragmented nor colonised, and in its journey to greater self-determination 'the Scots looked to see what was on offer, and have decided to travel light [in cultural terms]. No cultural icons need to be genuflected at, no correct representation needs to be observed in this journey into the future' (McCrone, 2001: 148).

Writing fifteen years later, I am less sure of that. Clearly, political and cultural revival have gone hand in hand. Compare, for example, the three major political events of the last thirty-five years: the referendums in 1979, 1999 and 2014. What marked the first of these, on a 'Scottish Assembly', while producing a small majority (51.6 to 48.4 per cent) was a failure to meet the imposed 40 per cent rule such that the proposal fell. The reaction had less to do with political chicanery and more with assumed psycho-cultural traits, as in the classic cartoon by Jimmy Turnbull (Figure 1.4).

FIGURE 1.4
Turnbull's feart lion (with acknowledgement to the Wizard of Oz)[10]

Source: John Bochel et al. (1981: 198)

Writing before the March referendum, Willie McIlvanney sensed defeat: 'Not to put too fine a point on it: I think a lot of us are feart. It's a feeling I share' (1991: 22). He too adopted the psychiatric trope: 'I think we've endured a condition analogous to that, one that has left us trapped in a weird psychic shuttle that runs from bleak and sterile self-doubt to wild declarations of arrogance and back again, with not a lot of stops in between' (1991: 20). His poem called *The Cowardly Lion* ended with the lines: 'Those who loved the lion had nothing to say / the lion had turned to its cage and slunk away / and lives still among stinking straw today.'

So why the turnaround in 1997, and even the 'No' vote in 2014? Why no recourse to psychiatric tropes after September 2014? There is something to be said for cultural change, as this comment from Cairns Craig makes plain:

> The overwhelming vote in favour of devolution in 1997 was not produced by the political parties – they were small boats rising on a tide of cultural nationalism that went from the rediscovery of the art of the 'Glasgow Boys' and the 'Scottish Colourists' to the music of the Proclaimers and Runrig, from the writings of Nan Shepherd to Ian Rankin's Rebus. … The Parliament was not an achievement of Scottish politics and politicians but the product of a cultural revolution that had given Scotland a significant past, a creative present and a believable future. (2015: 630)

Scotland may have danced to a different set of tunes than other nations; the relationship between culture and politics may be obtuse and complex, but that they are connected cannot be denied. Whatever else we can say, Scotland is not over.

Conclusion

In this chapter we have set ourselves a rather curious question: when *was* Scotland? To ask such a question is to try to establish Scotland as a suitable case for sociological treatment.

Chapter summary

What have we learned in this chapter?

- That 'Scotland' was a meaningful entity as early as the thirteenth century, reflected in the Wars of Independence, which helped to shape Scots as a people. In saying that, we are not implying that thirteenth-century peasants relate to Scotland in the same way as twenty-first-century Scots; how would we ever know? The most we can say is that, like many peoples in the world, war against an 'other' helped to make Scots. It is testament to the ideological success of a document like the Declaration of Arbroath in 1320 that many have seen it as the precursor for later such declarations (of independence), which may be historically dubious.

- That the second iconic moment was the Treaty of Union in 1707, at which point Scotland technically ceased to exist as a state; but then, for that matter, so did England. It mattered more to Scotland as the smaller country because the Union was, by and large, an incorporating one, although Scotland retained hold of its civil society institutions. These were to provide the bases for civil autonomy and, ultimately, the recovery of a law-making parliament in 1999. Indubitably, Scotland continued to exist after the Union. Its 'national' identity was underwritten by institutional autonomy; the recovery of 'stateness' came later. Whatever the outcome of the Union, Scotland was not over. As the oldest elected member of the 1999 Scottish parliament, Winnie Ewing opened the session with the words: 'I want to start with the words that I have always wanted either to say or to hear someone else say – the Scottish Parliament, which adjourned on March 25, 1707, is hereby reconvened.'

- That the final moment came in the late twentieth century. Despite claims that Scottish culture had ceased to exist, and hence could not underwrite the recovery of statehood, even short of independence, the reconnection of culture and politics could not be denied. What the future may hold in those respects is beyond us. Above all, much depends on the wager of history, and it is to the detail of Scotland's story in the twentieth century that we now turn.

Questions for discussion

1. Is it accurate to describe Scotland as a 'nation' in the thirteenth century? Where did the idea of Scotland come from, and why has it persisted?

2. To what extent was Scottish identity defined primarily vis-à-vis not being English?

3. Why does the Declaration of Arbroath in 1320 sound to many people like a 'modern' document?

4. If Scotland was governed from London after the Union of 1707, why did Scots retain a strong sense of national identity?

5. Why did 'cultural pessimists' fail to predict Scotland's future in the late twentieth century?

Annotated reading

(a) On medieval Scotland, see D. Broun, 'The origin of Scottish identity', in C. Bjørn, A. Grant and K.J. Stringer (eds), *Nations, Nationalism and Patriotism in the European Past* (1994); D. Broun, *Scottish Independence and the Idea of Britain* (2013); D. Broun, 'Rethinking Scottish origins', in S. Boardman and S. Foran (eds), *Barbour's Bruce and its Cultural Contexts* (2015); W. Ferguson, *The Identity of the Scottish Nation: An historic quest* (1998).

(b) On Scottish autonomy post-1707 Union, see L. Paterson, *The Autonomy of Modern Scotland* (1994); G. Morton, *Unionist-Nationalism: Governing urban Scotland, 1830–1860* (1999); M. Ash, *The Strange Death of Scottish History* (1980); C. Kidd, *Subverting Scotland's Past: Scottish Whig historians and the creation of an Anglo-British identity, 1689–c.1830* (1993); C. Kidd, *Union and Unionisms: Political thought in Scotland 1500–2000* (2008).

(c) On Scottish culture and politics, see Cairns Craig, *Out of History: Narrative paradigms in Scottish and British culture* (1996); Cairns Craig (ed.), *The History of Scottish Literature, Volume 4: Twentieth century* (1987); Cairns Craig, 'The literary tradition', in T.M. Devine and J. Wormald (eds), *The Oxford Handbook of Modern Scottish History* (2012).

Notes

1 The Welsh historian Gwyn Alf Williams wrote a book with the title *When Was Wales?* (1991) which explored the origin and idea of Wales. Asking 'When was Scotland?' has a similar focus in terms of 'imagining' Scotland, and is a tribute to Williams' approach.
2 See National Archives of Scotland (www.nas.gov.uk/downloads/declarationArbroath.pdf). The Latin text reads: *Quia quamdiu Centum ex nobis viui remanserint, nuncquam Anglorum dominio aliquatenus volumus subiugari. Non enim propter gloriam, diuicias aut honores pugnamus sed propter libertatem solummodo quam Nemo bonus nisi simul cum vita amittit.*

3   See for example Linda MacDonald-Lewis, *Warriors and Wordsmiths of Freedom: The birth and growth of democracy* (2009).

4   As in The Claim of Right, 1989 (https://en.wikipedia.org/wiki/Claim_of_Right_1989).

5   In the Middle Ages, the 'three estates' of prelates (bishops and abbots, nobles and burgh commissioners) were known as the 'community of the realm', a term which translated into the Estates of Parliament, or *Thrie Estaitis* in medieval Scots.

6   To twenty-first-century eyes, much of this debate can seem esoteric and irrelevant, but it had deadly import in the Middle Ages when English designs on Scotland were waged on the ideological as well as the military front. Ferguson's book *The Identity of the Scottish Nation: An historic quest* (1998) gives the best account of why such 'history' mattered.

7   The Irish term *Gaeltacht* refers to the west of Ireland where Irish (Gaelic) is spoken. The term *Gàidhealtachd* refers more broadly to the area of Gaelic culture in the Scottish Highlands and Islands.

8   See, for example, David Stenhouse (2004).

9   'Treaty' is preferred to 'Act' (of Union) because there were separate acts in Scotland and England in the respective parliaments.

10 Note the 'wound' of Argentina 1978, the Scottish footballing stramash [uproar] in the World Cup, on the lion's flank.

2

MAKING MODERN SCOTLAND: THE STORY OF THE TWENTIETH CENTURY

I n the first chapter we saw how 'Scotland' was a meaningful entity as early as the twelfth and thirteenth centuries; that the Union with England in 1707 did not spell the 'end' of Scotland; and that the 'recovery' of a Scottish parliament at the end of the twentieth century was the result of significant cultural as well as political and social changes.

In this chapter we focus on how modern Scotland was 'made' in the twentieth century. In the Appendix, you will find a timeline running from 1900 until 2015 to help you identify the main events in a historical sequence. Ask yourself: how important was the twentieth century in shaping Scotland? How much of the society would be recognisable to Scots of a hundred years ago? Supposing Scots of 1900 were able to project themselves forward to the end of the century, how much would be familiar to them?

Chapter aims

- To explore the social forces which made modern Scotland.

- To guide you through the complexity of social, economic and political forces by providing 'signposts' for 1900, 1950 and 2000.

- To characterise each of these signposts in terms of the broad motifs of, respectively, 'capital', 'state' and 'nation'.

Introduction

Our ancestors would probably be struck by how similar Scotland was to other West European societies of the present day. Compared with other Europeans, we live in similar houses, drive similar cars and eat similar food. We are educated in much the same way, work at the same kinds of jobs and produce the same kinds of products, and even work for the same companies. We have roughly the same number of children as they do, and we spend our money on similar products and cultural pursuits. We inhabit the same electronic world and have reduced geographical distance to negligible proportions when it comes to communicating with each other. We visit each other's countries, and while we enjoy the different ways of doing things that we find there, we are able to operate within them quite quickly and happily because so much is familiar to us.

Let us adopt, however, the perspective of our 1900 ancestors. Much that was familiar to them has disappeared:

- work no longer is the exclusive preserve of men in dungarees and bunnets, working in mass, noisy factories and yards;

- women make up almost half of the labour force, though many work part time;

- people no longer live in densely packed tenements which cluster round these work-places, close to city centres;

- it is harder to read off people's social class by the ways they dress and how they speak.

While the revolution which took place in the nineteenth century to create industrial Scotland was probably more profound, social change in the twentieth century has transformed the lives of people in Scotland.

Certainly, the pace of social and economic change altered the twentieth century in quite remarkable ways. Two world wars, the growing power of the state, the extension of the democratic franchise, growing and extensive affluence, albeit with pockets of abiding poverty, the move to the suburbs driven by the car – all were factors quite unknown to Scots of 1900. One thing, however, they would recognise was that their compatriots were living in a society structured overwhelmingly by the power of private capital. We can debate whether we live in a post-industrial rather than an industrial world, but no one can surely deny that it remains a capitalist one.

There is no doubting, however, that Scotland is a modern society because it has been transformed by the global processes of industrialism and capitalism from the late eighteenth century onwards. These shared processes, however, have not reduced the modern world to uniformity, even though the motors of change – economic, social, cultural – are largely the same. Each society is equipped with a set of cultural perspectives with which people make sense of these common changes. That is why our time-traveller from 1900 would still recognise Scotland as a familiar place. Its institutions and cultural systems provide the signposts, the means for understanding just how the common processes impact on place.

Motifs of change

Our journey takes us past three key dates, 1900, 1950 and 2000: stopping-off points which highlight the key determining features of the changing century. Our purpose is to use these as motifs which enable us to capture what was central at these times rather than describe the events in those years. For that, we can follow the timeline in the Appendix.

The year 1900 was dominated by *capital*, by unalloyed market power. This was an age of empire as well as of capital, and it was one on which the sun was beginning to set even though at the time it seemed never stronger.

Our second date, 1950, conveniently mid-century, captures a new set of processes, essentially political ones, in which the unrestrained market seemed to have caused more problems than it had solved: hence the motif of *state*, for this describes the ways in which the political system intervened in market forces to allocate jobs, housing, education, and play a greater role in determining people's life chances.

Finally, by the year 2000, we encounter a new motif – let us call it *nation* – which comes to play an increasing role in debates about Scotland. By *nation* we mean what Anderson called an 'imagined community' (1996), that social life in Scotland is framed by cultural factors rather than narrowly economic (capital) and political (state) ones. The debate at the end of the twentieth century was structured around Scotland's constitutional position in the modern world, in effect, by 'nationalism'. Scotland never ceased to be a 'nation', even when it gave up its statehood for a share in the economic and political gains of wider British union in 1707. What we encountered at the start of the twenty-first century was a reconfiguring of Scotland around its sense of being a nation, a way of explaining why it is the way it is, as well as a route-map for its future.

We should think of these motifs – capital, state and nation – like a piece of music in which new themes emerge, while previous ones submerge but do not disappear, becoming secondary and interweaving with the existing melodies, subtly changing their meaning. Each motif or theme helps to typify the mood of the times, even though the processes they symbolise were actually interacting with each other in complex and continuing ways.

Our task too is to explain why Scotland in the early decades of the twenty-first century has reached such an important conjuncture in its history, when no one can predict with any degree of accuracy where the restoration of even a devolved parliament is going to lead. Let us, then, begin our journey.

The world of capital: Scotland 1900

Scotland's people

What did Scotland look like at the start of the twentieth century? The Scottish population stood at 4.5 million in 1901, and a century later it was just over 5 million. That is an increase of just over 10 per cent, but it turns out that Scotland is unusual, for no other European country has had such *low* levels of population growth. While the population of Great Britain grew by 38 per cent between 1911 and 1991, Scotland's had a relatively stagnant growth rate of a mere 7 per cent. In comparison with other countries in the EU, this was a most unusual situation. As we shall see in Chapter 4, not a single national state has lost population in this period, only Denmark and Belgium have growth rates lower than England and Wales, and nowhere has a lower population growth rate than Scotland.

Scotland, like England, experienced a decline in infant mortality from 1900, although it was gradual and erratic. Girls had a better life expectancy than boys so that those born around 1910 could expect to live until they were 53, compared with age 50 for boys. Mothers too benefited from falling mortality rates. The chances of a woman dying in child-birth was 1 in 4000 by the 1970s, a hundred times better than it had been at the beginning of the century, a remarkable turnaround in the public health of the country. Childhood diseases like measles, scarlatina, whooping cough, diphtheria and croup accounted for as much as a third of deaths between the ages of 1 and 4 before the Great War. These had been all but eradicated by the end of the century.

Family life

Fertility, having babies, rather than mortality and migration was mainly responsible for much demographic change throughout twentieth-century Europe. Scottish marital fertility was for a considerable time higher than in England, while fewer women married. In the early part of the century, most Scottish men married when they were aged 28, and women at 26. Up until the Second World War and beyond, fewer women in Scotland compared with England were married. Indeed, in the early decades of the century, these low levels of nuptiality, the incidence of people getting married, put Scotland well below other coun-tries, with the exception of Ireland and Iceland. Levels of marriage were especially low in rural areas, but above all in the Highlands and Islands of north-west Scotland.

By the late nineteenth century, delayed marriage or permanent celibacy was a char-acteristic of these areas, largely because people had problems establishing and maintaining new families in the social and economic conditions which prevailed. These peculiar conditions around 1900 had the effect of depressing marriage patterns, which were not altered until well into the twentieth century when Scotland shifted from being a rural to an urban society.

The twentieth century saw a dramatic fall in family size. In 1911 it was common for completed families to have six or more children. Family size at this time was also class specific, for manual workers had almost twice the number of children as middle-class pro-fessionals. Broadly speaking, the lower your social class, the more children you had. Only in the second half of the century did these social class differences narrow significantly. The control of family size in Scotland as elsewhere was the result of a complex of factors includ-ing birth control and lengthening child dependency, especially for the middle classes. Not only did family size fall as the century progressed, but childbearing was concentrated into shorter periods of time.

Family size was also shaped by available housing. In 1911, over half of all Scottish households lived in houses with two rooms or fewer (compared with only 7 per cent in England). More than one in ten Scots lived in houses with only one room.[1] 'Overcrowding' remained a fact of everyday life in Scotland for much of the twentieth century.

In these desperate circumstances, it fell to women to keep the household economy going. Working-class women had the burden and responsibility for maintaining and sustaining the family in these conditions, in which there were few of the labour-saving devices we have grown used to: washing machines, vacuum cleaners or other household gadgetry. Women in the 1900s had responsibility for negotiating with the landlord, both on their own behalf and that of their sons and daughters looking for accommodation of their own.

The typical working-class family was chronically in debt. At the turn of the century, most found it impossible to survive from week to week on the money coming into the house, a reflection not only of the level of wages but of the nature of casual work. Family budgets had to take past and future debts into account, and thrift and savings were essential for the social security of the family as it negotiated its way around unemployment and illness.

Families relied on credit or 'tick' for day-to-day living. Most tenants required a 'character' or reference from the previous landlord before a new one took the family on. In Scotland at the turn of the century, the law underpinned the landlord's position in a quite remarkable way. The 'right of hypothec' in law gave the landlord the right to sequester the tenant's furniture and tools just in case they went into rent arrears.

To escape the dreadful and cramped conditions of intimate life, men spent much of their leisure time on street corners or in pubs. Women, meanwhile, given the drudgery of working-class life, had no option but to stay at home.

Town life

Life in Scottish towns and cities was atrocious. In desperation, authorities were forced to intervene in the housing market, and the cities in particular led the way in slum clearance by way of improvement Acts. They also developed the tradition of civic enterprise, known as 'municipal socialism'. Glasgow could boast of the Loch Katrine water scheme in 1859, the dredging of the Clyde in 1869 and 1893, the municipalisation of gas and public lighting, the pioneering of tramways, public baths and municipal wash-houses – the *steamies*, which became the subject of nostalgia later in the century. By 1902, Glasgow Corporation owned 2488 houses, 78 lodging houses, 372 shops, 86 warehouses and workshops, 12 halls, 2 churches and a bakehouse (Allan, 1965: 608).

This was an all-too-familiar world in 1900, notably the reliance on a complex mix of local private and public services in the political economy of Scotland's towns and cities. This was to be transformed from the 1920s by the 'nationalising' and politicising of these services:[2] by the rise of the state, both national and local, and the challenge to business at both levels.

Schooling

The most obvious state institution was the school. The 1872 Education Act and its aftermath had created the main features of the education system which were to last well into the century. The legacy of the nineteenth century had bequeathed to Scotland a universal elementary system of education, enshrined in the 1872 Education Act. The subsequent 1918 Act was, if anything, even more revolutionary in its purpose, for it asserted the principle of free secondary education for all in schools of a common type. It also brought Catholic schools into the state system, but allowed them to retain influence over parts of the curriculum and the appointment of teachers. The system of higher education was to remain virtually unchanged, apart from admitting women, until the middle of the twentieth century, and the proportion of the relevant age group at university did not rise until the 1950s. Teaching as a profession was highly gender segregated such that women dominated the primary schools and men the secondary system. Teacher training was the main form of higher education open to women, who had to suffer the 'marriage bar' whereby they had to leave teaching if and when they got married, a ban which was not lifted until after 1945.

The power of capital

With the exception of small landlords, Scottish capitalism in the early days of the twentieth century was self-confident and buoyant. Above all, it was local, not so much in its operations as in its ownership. Central to the structure of Scottish business were the railway companies and their interconnections with coal, steel and engineering. Nor was this simply a west of Scotland phenomenon, for regional clusters were also significant. In Dundee, for example, the juteocracy of the Cox, Baxter and Fleming families ruled. In Edinburgh, business clustered on the banks and the North British Railway, while the Glasgow segment focused on Tennants' companies, the Caledonian Railway and the Clydesdale Bank.

Scottish business at the beginning of the twentieth century was a complex network of interlocking ownerships and directorates within Scottish dynasties. It was fairly secure from external takeover, even from England. Nevertheless, by the outbreak of the Great War, its dependence on family control and family capital meant that it could not compete with the managerial and technological revolutions taking place in Germany and the United States. The further expansion of the banks and finance houses into Scottish business could not disguise the fact that they were ill-equipped to compete in a twentieth-century world in which imperial markets were being challenged. Scotland was undoubtedly well adapted to take advantage of Britain's highly advantageous structural position in the world economy, which was at that time shaped around Britain's own commercial interests. In the longer term, this proved to be a weakness rather than a strength. As these interests atrophied, so Scottish capital found it difficult to adapt to a world economy after empire.

Politics

The dominance of local capital in Scotland at the beginning of the twentieth century was reflected in politics. At the municipal level, power was in the hands of small-scale local capital, mainly small shopkeepers and local landlords. The 'Independent' label kept alive the view that local government was in essence 'non-political' – no politics in sewage, as the saying went – an enterprise in which individuals were elected on their merits rather than their political affiliation. There was resistance to the 'nationalising' of local politics; running the town was a matter strictly for local businessmen with proven experience.

At the national level, party preference was almost evenly split between Liberals and Conservatives (including their Liberal–Unionist allies). At the 1900 election Liberals were still able to win 50 per cent of the popular vote in Scotland, but ended up with two fewer seats than the Tories who won 36, for their 49 per cent vote share. The Liberal Party broke over the issue of Irish Home Rule, when a significant minority of pro-Union liberals sided with the Conservatives.

Religion

Here we see the power and importance of politics and religion in early twentieth-century Scotland. It was a society which saw itself as 'unionist', taking pride in empire, firmly imperialist, as well as Protestant in ethos and religious practice. 'The Bible: Basis of Empire Greatness' was the self-confident banner of the Bible Society at the Empire Exhibition of 1938. Being Scottish and British were complements of each other, shaped around being Protestant, unionist and proud of empire.

The beginning of the twentieth century also saw continuing migration from Ireland, both north and south. The arrival of the Irish exacerbated pressure among a developing urban proletariat already facing the social dislocations of rapid modernisation, and Catholic Irish labour was, on occasion, used by employers to depress local wage levels. These Catholic Irish were often seen as more than simply economic rivals: many viewed them as a root cause of various social evils. Integration would have been difficult enough, given the differences in speech, custom and religion which divided them from their new neighbours. Crucially, however, a sizeable minority of Irish arrivals were Ulster Protestants who brought their virulent anti-Catholicism with them.

These divisions were to prove significant for at least half a century in Scottish politics, with Catholics showing a solid propensity to vote Labour after 1921, while the Conservatives drew disproportionately on Protestant support, both native and immigrant. Only in the second half of the twentieth century did this link between religion and politics begin to fragment. This Scotland framed by Protestantism, unionism and imperialism was not short of internal divisions. Apart from the religious divide between Catholics and Protestants, and between the social classes, especially the working class and their bourgeois masters, Scotland inherited significant regional divisions, none more so than the Highland/Lowland one. Migration from north to south continued to erode the *Gàidhealtachd*, the region of Gaelic culture in the Highlands and Islands. By the 1901 census, around 5 per cent of Scots, almost a quarter of a million, were Gaelic speakers.

1900 overview

How best, then, to sum up Scotland at the beginning of the twentieth century? It was already a modern, mature industrial society built around imperial market opportunities. It was one in which most people – three out of four – belonged to the manual working class, with a much smaller but significantly more powerful middle class. This class ruled over different aspects of society and politics, leaving the provision of mass housing to its petite bourgeoisie, while self-confidently running its developing system of capitalism. The motif of the market ruled in housing as in much else, and it took the threat of social unrest in the second decade of the century before it was eroded by state action – rent controls, and then direct state housing in the 1920s.

The power of the state: Scotland 1950

If our Victorian predecessors would have felt comfortable in Scotland 1900, what would they have made of mid-century Scotland? The old locality-based systems of power were rapidly eroding in favour of central state power. While the world of empire was coming to an end, the impact of two world wars had helped to reforge a sense of Britishness among the Scots which was different from that older, imperialist sense they had been accustomed to.

Furthermore, by mid-century, Scots were confirmed in their Britishness. Scotland 1950 was part of an integrated all-British welfare state. If 'capital' was the defining motif of Scotland 1900, then 'state' defines its mid-century counterpart.

Being British

Why should mid-century Scots have felt so confidently British? Mass wars have the capacity to mobilise. The impact of the First World War on the population was unprecedented. In the UK, nearly 5 million men – some 22 per cent of the total male population – were recruited into the armed forces. Most of these were volunteers, some two-thirds, with the rest joining as conscripts after 1916. Imperialism and patriotism were virtually indistinguishable. The UK was still an imperial state, with colonies and dominions which embodied its identity, and to which migrants flocked in large numbers.

Why should war have such an impact? Almost a quarter of the male population had experience of military service, well over half of those of military age. But war was more important than that. It created the modern British state: warfare and welfare went together.

The extension of demands on the state had predated the Second World War, but war provided the catalyst for radical change, both with regard to the mobilisation of manpower and with the organisation of production. Translating this into practical changes, it meant greater state involvement in the economy, especially labour relations, housing and unemployment relief; a major extension of taxation; greater control of industry by managerially controlled corporations; the transfer of land to tenant farmers; and above all, the integration of the working class into the democratic process.

The other dimension of British national identity, alongside war and democracy, was social class. The Labour Party was the mechanism for enfranchising the manual working class. The party derived enormous benefit from this association which lasted until the final quarter of the twentieth century when de-industrialisation reduced the manual working class to less than 50 per cent of the workforce.

Politics

The Labour Party's role in mid-twentieth-century Britain was to deliver the manual working class into the democratic process, and to fix its politics into the British-national dimension of class. In comparison with continental Europe where religious – 'confessional' – politics was much more common, British politics was essentially about social class.

In Scotland in 1906, Labour took a mere 2 per cent of the vote, and two seats, in contrast to 65 per cent for the Liberals and 38 per cent for the Unionists. Labour's major break-through in Scotland came in the 1918 election when the party won 23 per cent of the vote against 33 per cent for the Tories with the Liberals already split between pro-coalition (19 per cent) and non-coalition forces (15 per cent). Labour held its share thereafter, never dropping below 33 per cent (in 1931) and winning 48 per cent (and thirty-seven seats) in 1945.

There was no room for explicitly 'nationalist' politics in mid-century Scotland, largely because the two main repertoires of Scottish politics squeezed it out. On the one hand, the Conservative Party mobilised the powerful nexus linking unionism and Protestantism welded together by a strong sense of British national/imperial identity. This version of Scottishness sat easily with Conservative rhetoric about being British. It was fostered too by a powerful strand of militarism which ran through Scottish society. Over half a million Scots enlisted in the army, over 40 per cent of all men between the ages of 15 and 49. One of the key and abiding icons of Scottishness was the Scottish soldier (Strachan, 2016).

Being Scottish and British were not at all at odds. The Scottish regiments were recruiting sergeants for British imperial and world wars, and helped to make Scottish and British national identities complementary. On the other hand, Labour politics made the Scottish (and the Welsh) working class safe for the British Union.

Emerging nationalism

Another – alternative – version of national politics was, however, slowly emerging. The inter-war period saw the first stirrings of modern nationalism in Scotland and Wales. Saunders Lewis founded *Plaid Cymru* (the Welsh Party) in 1925, and the Scottish National

Party (SNP) was formed in 1934, an amalgam of the National Party of Scotland and the Scottish Party. Indeed, the SNP won the seat of Motherwell at a by-election in 1945, but was unable to hold it at the general election in the same year.

While the SNP did not make an electoral impact until the late 1960s (it won just 30,000 votes in the eight seats it contested in 1945), it had begun its long political march. Ireland, Scotland and Wales were flexing their national muscles as the British Empire lost its force. What these fledgling political movements showed was that the British imperium was beginning to lose its power, first in the white Dominions, then in the Celtic countries, most noticeably in Ireland. The later threats from Scotland and Wales to secede from the UK undoubtedly have their roots in this period.

Shaping a new Scotland
Scotland's people

How had Scotland changed socially between 1900 and 1950? Scotland saw surges in the birth rate in 1921 and 1947 at the end of the respective wars, the baby booms. The national death rate bottomed out by mid-century, and falling death rates in the population were balanced by greater longevity. There were, however, still significant class differences in terms of mortality rates. In the 1950s and 1960s, working-class men and women had a mortality rate six times that of people in the top social class. Post-war babies in working-class families were three times more likely to die in the first year of life than their middle-class counterparts.

Fertility and mortality trends in Scotland mainly followed those in the rest of the UK. Where Scotland did differ was that far more people emigrated. This is the key to understanding why its population has been so static, compared with other Western European countries. Scotland in the 1920s saw the highest rates of emigration so that the small increase in improving birth over death rates was reversed by net emigration which totalled almost 400,000 in the decade, an enormous proportion in a country of only 5 million people.

The rates of emigration slackened in the 1930s, only to increase once more during the 1950s and 1960s when Scotland had a net loss of almost half a million people. There was no counter in-migration to Scotland such as occurred in England from new Commonwealth countries after the Second World War. Scotland, however, saw no major net incoming of population since the Irish arrived in the nineteenth century. This helped to reinforce the sense that Scotland was manifestly a society of emigrants, not immigrants.

Towns and cities

The post-war period did see a substantial redistribution of population within Scotland. Glasgow, whose population stood at over 1 million as late as 1961, tried to solve its overcrowding problems by exporting significant numbers to New Towns[3] via its overspill policies.

FIGURE 2.1
Redeveloping
The Gorbals in
Glasgow

Source: I am
grateful to The
Herald and
Times Group for
permission to use
this photograph
from their archive

Only later did it discover that those who went were disproportionately the younger and more skilled, and that it was retaining within the city's boundaries a disproportionately ageing and unskilled workforce. By 1911, 30 per cent of Scots lived in one of the four main cities, rising to 38 per cent by 1951, before falling back to 28 per cent in 1991.

After the Great War, the cities were slow to introduce council housing because it both undermined the market principle and threatened the livelihoods of the property men, the landlords and house factors, who sat on local councils. The solution to the housing question was tackled by the solidly Victorian 'deserving' principle. Those who could afford it and were judged morally able to look after good property (defined as 'General Purposes' housing) were allocated the best-quality council houses, while 'slum clearance' housing was confined to those on lower incomes, with uncertain jobs, and implied moral inferiority. 'Ordinary' housing went to those whom the housing visitor judged 'clean and decent', while those who failed this inscrutable test were given 'Rehousing' homes (see Figure 2.1).

Changing economies

By 1950, Scotland began to shift from an economy dependent on manufacturing to one based on services. Primary industry – agriculture, quarrying and mining – employed only one in ten workers compared with double that in 1900. These were trends which Scotland shared with the rest of the UK as well as other modern industrial societies. They involved the expansion of white-collar work, especially in the number of professional employees, people like teachers and clerical workers. By mid-century, Scotland was still a 'working-class' society, for over half of Scots were in manual work, a figure that was to drop significantly in later years. More women were in employment as 'family planning' allowed them to reduce the number of children, and new labour market opportunities opened up for women. In Scotland, however, the economic activity rate for married women was only two-thirds that of the rest of the UK until well after 1945, and it was not until the late 1970s that Scotland caught up. Just as more women were working, so certain occupations such as clerical work, hitherto a male preserve, shifted to being overwhelmingly female. The percentage of clerks who were female rose from about half in 1961 to three-quarters by 1981.

The transformation of Scottish business was also taking place. Even before the war, it was recognised that Scotland's economy needed to be restructured and diversified. In the inter-war period, the civil service was reorganised, Scotland was designated a separate area for industrial development, and the Scottish Economic Committee was created. This set off a dynamic in Scottish business which, with the aid of the state, was to have far-reaching effects. The old dynastic families may have retained control of traditional industry, but foreign and English capital came to play a much greater role in Scotland's economic affairs in the second half of the century.

Many of these initiatives had grown out of the activities of a much more proactive Scottish Office under the leadership of Tom Johnston, who was Secretary of State for Scotland during the Second World War, and who built it up into a formidable apparatus of economic development. The war had given a belated boost to traditional economic interests, but the fortunes of Scotland's traditional capitalists, the Colvilles, Tennants and Beardmores, were slipping away with new competition.

The post-war period saw the decline of this capitalist class. The dominant nexus in Scottish heavy industry of the 1930s, the Colville–Lithgow–Nimmo complex based on coal, iron and steel, disappeared with nationalisation. The links between financial companies and banks became more pronounced as the defining element of Scottish business.

By the mid-1950s, the 'managerial revolution' which had transformed American and English business had largely passed Scotland by, as did the establishment of the new automotive and white-goods industries. This crisis came to a head in the 1960s which forced on the traditionally dominant dynastic families a major crisis of confidence. In this vacuum, the government through the Scottish Office induced external capital to play a much greater role in Scotland. From the 1950s, new industries were set up, guided by state directive: the steel strip mill at Ravenscraig, the Rootes Car Company at Linwood, and new timber and aluminium plants in the Highlands. All were to fail in the cold market climate of the final quarter of the century.

Politics post-war

Along with its economy, Scotland's politics was also being transformed. Only Labour and the Unionists mattered at mid-century, and between them they took nine out of every ten votes in Scotland, just as in England. Two-party – all-British – politics ruled. There was virtually no difference between Scotland and England in terms of support for the parties.

Labour had an identical share of the vote north and south of the border, with the Tories in 1950 actually taking a marginally higher share of the vote in Scotland than they did in England (44.8 per cent to 43.8 per cent), and they were the only party to win a majority of the vote: 50.1 per cent in 1955. Seen from the vantage point of the end of the century, when they lost every seat they contested in the 1997 election, this seems almost incredible.

In large part the success of the Conservatives in mid-twentieth-century Scotland reflected their capacity to capture substantial sectors of the working-class vote. While they did not operate directly in local politics, they were able to wield influence through the diverse 'non-political' labels such as Moderate and Progressive in the major cities. These were loose coalitions of anti-Labour support designed to keep 'politics' out of local government.

The Scottish Unionist Party, as the Conservatives called themselves until 1965, captured a disproportionate share of the Protestant working-class vote. In the 1920s and 1930s, both Edinburgh and Glasgow saw militant Protestantism become a significant force in local politics. In Edinburgh, Protestant Action operated an informal electoral pact from the 1930s until the late 1950s with the self-styled 'Progressives' – basically an anti-Labour coalition. As late as the 1960s, working-class members of the Church of Scotland in Dundee were over six times more likely to vote Tory than Labour. This association was mirrored by Catholic support for Labour. Conservatives were also happy to play a Scottish card in the post-war period while in Opposition, complaining that Labour's centralising agenda at a UK level was eroding the autonomy of Scotland.

Religion

Religion continued to matter, and not only in politics. The Church of Scotland saw a significant growth in members between the early 1940s and mid-1950s when it reached an all-time high. This peak was not sustained, and by the early 1960s membership had fallen to its lowest level since the twentieth century began, and was to keep falling. Between the middle of the nineteenth century and the final quarter of the twentieth, attendance at Presbyterian churches fell by four-fifths, and as a result the Church of Scotland ceased to be a mass church. The Catholic share of total church adherents rose from about one-seventh in 1914 to more than one-fifth by 1970. This was a reflection of the major investment which Catholics put into building new churches in the new peripheral housing schemes, and in maintaining and extending Catholic schools in these areas.

The opportunities for that had been created by the 1918 Education Act, which had guaranteed Catholics influence over aspects of the curriculum and the appointment of teachers. Scottish schools generally saw only incremental growth between the 1930s and the 1960s, and the 1945 Education Act confirmed the distinction between 'senior' and 'junior' secondary schools. By the late 1950s over 40 per cent of post-primary pupils were in senior secondary schools. After the war, central government and local authorities had embarked on a programme of primary school building and curriculum reform, but only 5 per cent of the relevant age group entered university.

1950 overview

How had Scotland transformed itself in the first half of the twentieth century? It was still a society in which workers were mainly men, in many ways a turnaround from the war years when women took over many men's jobs. However, Scotland like almost all other Western European countries reverted back to a strict gender division of labour in which child-rearing and home-making were seen as primary female roles, and women's place became the home once more. This was both a reflection, and a cause, of the baby boom in the late 1940s and 1950s. Smaller family sizes, the fact that children survived infancy more successfully, and that there was a lengthening period of childhood and adolescence brought about by education, put greater focus on the family. A major programme of house-building sought to ensure that every nuclear family had its own domestic space, and helped to generate home-centredness – later to be called 'privatism' – which became the norm, or at least the ideal. The world after 1945 brought greater affluence and greater mobility, both geographical and social.

The 1950s were the highpoint of 'Britishness' in Scotland, as well as being a key turning point. That was reflected in the unprecedented similarity in voting behaviour in Scotland and England in the 1950s, and in the shared view that the state was a vehicle for transforming the economy, something desperately needed in Scotland. Despite the success of the Scottish Covenant in 1948 calling for Home Rule signed by 2 million people, the time was not right for a politically explicit nationalism in Scotland. The welfare state might have had a distinct Scottish dimension, but it was an all-British solution to the problem of social and economic reform.

The compromises reached in the inter-war years to strengthen the Scottish Office as the vehicle for transforming the Scottish economy helped to deliver an unprecedented level of prosperity to Scotland. While there were important differences within the UK (Scotland's unemployment rate was twice that of the UK, and out-migration to well-paid jobs in England was running strongly), there was little political pressure to detach Scotland from the British state. Two world wars in less than half a century, coupled with a new UK-wide welfare system, locked the Scots firmly into the British state. It was to take another twenty-five years before this contract began to lose its power, and an explicit Scottish political nationalism emerged. That was to be the running motif of the final quarter of the century.

Rediscovering the nation: Scotland 2000

The pace of social change in the late twentieth century has been bewildering, and most of the old certainties slipped away. The nature of work and the social relations around it were transformed. Employing people – overwhelmingly men – to make things in mass factories was no longer the norm. Women are no longer confined to the home. If, in 1900, the claims of the family took precedence over those of individuals, by the end of the century, the positions were reversed. Individualism ruled. Personal satisfaction and happiness took priority, and in a rapidly changing world which changes dramatically over people's life-times, new ways of meeting the individual's needs emerge.

Scots of 1900 would probably be quite shocked to find out what had become of the classical family. Families of six children or more were becoming exceptional by the time of the Great War and were rare by mid-century.

Scotland's people

Not only had the family shrunk dramatically in size – Scotland had the lowest birth rate in the whole of the UK in the 1990s – but new household types had become the norm. Less than a quarter of households now comprise the 'classical' family of two parents and dependent children. Almost one-third of Scottish households now contain only one person, and just over a quarter consist of couples with no children. By the end of the century, Scotland had, like other comparable countries, the lowest birth and death rates it had ever seen. The late 1990s also saw the lowest number of marriages in the century. Emigration too had diminished, but the lack of inward migration, coupled with low fertility rates, meant that the Scottish population was barely reproducing itself. In 1901 there had been 165 live births for every 100 deaths, and in 1951 the ratio was 138 to 100. By the end of the century, however, more people were dying than were being born.

The old killer diseases and epidemics which had been so familiar, the communicable infectious diseases caused by viruses and bacteria, had all but been eradicated. As we shall see in Chapter 5, people were dying mainly of cancers and ischaemic heart disease, and these alone were each responsible for around a quarter of all adult deaths in Scotland. Considerable class differentials remained, so that the death rate in eastern Glasgow, even allowing for age and sex differences, was more than three-quarters higher than middle-class Bearsden and Milngavie, and even considerably higher than in the Western Isles.

Family life

What brought about this dramatic improvement in health was less the discovery of new medical techniques and treatments, and more the impact of rising living standards during much of the second half of the twentieth century (see Figure 2.2). Only after 1945 did families expect all their children to survive into adulthood, and the death of a child became even more of a tragedy because it was so uncommon. Men could now expect to live until they were 73 and women 78.

While people were living longer, they were far less likely to remain with the same marriage partner. Marriages in the late 1970s had around five times more chance of ending in divorce than those of the early 1950s. By 1997, Scotland recorded the lowest annual number of marriages for over a century. Well over half of divorced people in Scotland, however, remarried within a year of divorce, and over a quarter of everyone marrying had been

FIGURE 2.2
The Broons

Source: I am
grateful to DC
Thomson for
permission to use
this illustration
(The Broons &
oor Wullie® © DC
Thomson & Co.
Ltd. 2016)

married before. High divorce rates coupled with lower rates of marriages were compounded by increasing rates of cohabitation.

There was also a rising level of illegitimate births, especially among cohabiting couples. By the end of the twentieth century, four out of every ten live births were to unmarried parents. In the early part of the century, illegitimacy had been a feature of rural areas like the north-east where cohabitation and births frequently preceded marriage as a response to prevailing economic and social conditions. By the late twentieth century, illegitimacy was mainly a feature of city life; 40 per cent of all births to unmarried parents took place in Scotland's four city areas.

Towns and cities

The cities and towns of Scotland were themselves transformed. Gone were the inner city slums of 'single-ends', lacking baths or inside toilets. The private landlord had been swept away in the process and by mid-century had been replaced by the state as urban landlord. By the 1980s, huge swathes of Scotland's housing were municipally owned, and in some areas in the major cities it was virtually 100 per cent. This represented the high tide of municipal ownership, for the Conservative government of 1979 set about selling off council houses and restricting the building of new ones. By the end of the century, over a third of all council houses in Scotland had been sold.

Scotland remained a country of 'city-states' with distinctive identities and cultures – Aberdeen, Dundee, Edinburgh and Glasgow – and while they were no longer as demographically dominant as they once were, the cities wielded considerable economic and cultural pull, and most of the Scottish population lived in their hinterlands. Like the United States, but unlike England, Scotland's main daily newspapers were city based. Over the course of the century, the fortunes (and populations) of Glasgow and Dundee have waned, and those of Edinburgh and Aberdeen have grown. Glasgow, erstwhile second city of empire, was twice the size of the capital city in 1900. By the twenty-first century, it was barely a third bigger. All the cities, however, had lost populations to smaller towns and to rural areas, where the phenomenon of counter-urbanisation has been strongest.

A changing economy

The end of the long boom in the early 1970s, coupled with the transformation of Scotland's economy from one dependent on heavy industry founded on imperial markets to a post-industrial one driven by foreign capital and global markets, ushered in a new economic era. As a by-product of these forces, many of the traditional repositories of labour solidarity were swept away. These were the occupational communities built around single industries like coal mining, the 'Little Moscows' of Fife and Ayrshire (MacIntyre, 1980).

A new genre of literature grew up as a panegyric to a declining way of working-class life. Willie McIlvanney, for example, invented 'Graithnock', an industrial town 'under siege from farmland' – a thinly disguised Kilmarnock. The image is one of communitarianism, 'where so little was owned, sharing became a precautionary reflex'. Even the sectarian rivalries of west of Scotland life are reduced to ritual conflict – 'the whole thing had the quality of a communal action, and had been conducted without rancour'. McIlvanney's novel describes Graithnock in 1914, and by the contemporary period (1985) its decline is obvious: 'When the money went, Graithnock turned funny but not so you would laugh.' The town becomes the past, somewhere to retreat to from the big city (Glasgow), and Graithnock is made to represent 'decaying industrialism', 'an aridity surrounded by the green world, a desert in an oasis'. That description resonated across much of post-industrial central Scotland.

Transforming social classes

It was also much more difficult to tell people's class simply by their lifestyle. Differences within classes rather than between them had become more important. People's lifestyle as well as their age frequently cross-cut matters of economic class so that reading off a person's social position becomes a much more complex and hazardous process than it ever was in 1900 or 1950. The essence of class – how people are connected into the system of production, consumption and exchange – had not disappeared, but class had undoubtedly changed its shape and form. Compared with the rest of the UK, Scotland had marginally fewer rich and more poor people, though the territorial similarities were much greater than the differences.

The overall shape of the social class structure in modern Scotland was now quite different. The traditional working class of manual workers were now about 40 per cent of the labour force, while professional and administrative workers – the 'service' class – were over 30 per cent. Around a quarter of workers were in 'intermediate' non-manual occupations, largely clerical, and mainly employing women. By the late twentieth century, there were far more people working in health and social work (around one in eight), while only one in fifty worked in agriculture, forestry or fishing.

By the end of the century, in occupational terms Scotland was a 'middle-class' society. It was also a much more open society, with considerable amounts of upward social mobility.

Since 1945, each generation had been able to count on being in better-paid jobs than their parents. Occupational mobility between generations was now commonplace, with a substantial proportion of the 'service class' drawn up from the manual working class. This made for a more socially diverse upper stratum, aided by the expansion in middle-class jobs in the second half of the twentieth century. The manual working class, on the other hand, in part because it was diminishing in size, was much more homogeneous and self-recruiting – and working class in its social origins.

Educational opportunities

The key reason for this social mobility was the expansion in educational opportunity. The abolition of selection for different types of secondary school had been much easier to effect in Scotland than in England, in part because 'comprehensive' schools had long been a feature of its towns in particular. It was, however, the expansion of higher education which was most marked. By the early 1960s under 10 per cent of the age group were in universities or colleges, compared with 25 per cent in the late 1970s, and almost double that by the end of the century. While social class differentials remained in terms of access to higher education, the expansion of the system led to a narrowing of these differentials by the end of the century as a result of rising family aspirations.

Social opportunities, however, were not evenly distributed. The chances of middle-class children remaining in their class of origin were disproportionately high. Middle-class families conferred on their children considerable cultural capital, in terms of educational skills and qualifications. Access to 'top jobs' continued to be class skewed, and for women especially the barriers are great. The 'glass ceiling' – the real but opaque barrier to women's mobility – as well as the 'double shift' – the fact that many women with families have domestic as well as employment responsibilities to handle in their lives – helped to explain why women in modern Scotland did less well than men. While it was true that Scotland had a slightly smaller middle class and a slightly larger manual working class compared with England, the processes of social mobility which had created these structures were very similar on both sides of the Tweed.

Religion

By the 1990s Scotland had survived the worst period of economic hardship since the 1930s without a return to the heightened ethno-religious tensions of that decade. It became difficult to talk meaningfully of a 'Catholic community' or a 'Protestant community': individuals of all faiths and none now worked together, drank together and, most significantly, married each other. For the majority of Scots, political sectarianism became an irrelevance. By mid-century the Conservatives were beginning to lose their hold on Protestant Scots. Processes of secular change and in particular the impact of the welfare state had loosened working-class attachments to traditional political associations. These processes speeded up as the century progressed.

Politics and nationalism

Just as religion had been losing its force as a key emblem of identity and political behaviour, so nationalism grew in importance. From the 1960s, the Scottish frame of reference figured more centrally as the key dimension in politics. The discovery and exploitation of North Sea oil opened up the political possibility of an alternative, and explicitly Scottish, future. It was no accident that the discovery of oil and the rise of the SNP coincided. From the 1970s, the SNP was in the right place at the right time, and provided a political alternative in the final quarter of the century when the British settlement began to fail.

At the height of its electoral success in the mid-1970s, the SNP took votes across all social classes, but especially among skilled manual and routine non-manual workers. The 'classless' appeal of the SNP allowed it to present itself as an alternative to the traditional class-based parties. Although the party did well among all social classes in Scotland, its particular appeal in the 1970s was to those who were socially and geographically mobile. The lack of a class connotation for the SNP was the key appeal to those people who came from working-class origins, but no longer did manual jobs.

Such people were susceptible to a kind of political perspective which was different from the one in which they had grown up. Increased affluence coupled with greater family-centredness as people moved away from traditional communities was not unique to Scotland. The rise of the SNP, however, gave these processes a particularly political resonance in Scotland. The party captured the generation who were beginning to vote in the 1970s and 1980s, and who, in England, gravitated to the Conservatives or the Liberals.

By the final quarter of the twentieth century, the crisis of Labourism, and its challenge by political nationalism, led to an abortive and half-hearted attempt by the government of the day to introduce a measure of Home Rule in the form of 'devolution'. This was too late, even too little, and was caught up in the incoming Thatcherite revolution which sought to sweep away state dependency and impose the iron rule of markets.

This curious amalgam of 'free market, strong state' had a particular impact on Scotland. On the one hand, the Scottish Office which had been founded in the 1880s and which had turned itself a hundred years later into a Scottish semi-state was in the front line of the New Right onslaught. In a country which had turned against the Conservatives as early as the mid-1950s, the attack on the state seemed as much an attack on Scotland itself. By the 1990s, only a quarter of Scots were voting Conservative, and by 1997 there were no Tory MPs whatsoever north of the border.

Alongside the decline of the Conservatives went a changing relationship between social class and politics. In the 1997 election, the professional middle class were more likely to vote Labour than Conservative. Manual workers still voted Labour, though the party's main challenger for the working-class vote was the SNP. In terms of how people defined themselves, however, Scotland still thought of itself as a working-class society. People in Scotland who had been born into working-class families and who had moved into middle-class jobs were much more likely than their counterparts in England to describe themselves as working class. Further, nationality seems for most people to take precedence over social class in determining identity, thereby confirming the importance of the Scottish national dimension.

In the final quarter of the twentieth century, a social–political agenda had emerged in Scotland at odds with the one in England. People in Scotland saw themselves as more socialist, liberal and less British-national than people in England. Scotland had evolved a different agenda, and one which seemed to be growing more different as the decades passed. Defining oneself as a Scot became a way of expressing certain political values. National identity and political values were connected in that saying you were Scottish was to say that you had left-of-centre values; and to say you were British was to assert distinctly more right-of-centre views.

2000 overview

By the end of the century, Scotland was renegotiating its place in the Union, or even considering whether the 'marriage of convenience' which had been negotiated in 1707 should hold at all. True, Scots had gained considerable economic and political influence within the imperial framework, but that had long gone. The ideological support systems of unionism, imperialism and Protestantism no longer functioned to bind Scots into the UK. Scotland's economy too had been transformed and reoriented towards Europe and a post-imperial world, reflected in the creation of a devolved parliament in Edinburgh (Figure 2.3).

The new variable geometry of territorial power involving the EU, the UK state and Scotland was becoming more significant. Like the Welsh, Scots saw in Europe a new union to augment or even replace the older British one. There were few of the English anxieties concerning the loss of political sovereignty in a country which had to trade off its independent parliament in return for a considerable measure of economic and political benefit. The long march from British imperial integration had come to an end.

FIGURE 2.3   The east elevation of the Scottish parliament building viewed across Horse Wynd. The public entrance to the building can be seen on the right-hand side of the image. Pic – Andrew Cowan

Source: Image © Scottish Parliamentary Corporate Body – 2010. Licensed under the Open Scottish Parliament Licence v1.0

Conclusion

What are we to make of this modern Scotland? Looking back over the century it is apt to repeat the novelist L.P. Hartley's line: the past is a foreign country: they do things differently there. Scotland 1900 and Scotland 2000 are, to all intents and purposes, foreign to each other. Consider the fictional words spoken by Lewis Grassic Gibbon's minister at the Kinraddie memorial to the dead of the Great War at the end of his novel, *Sunset Song*: 'A new generation comes up that will know them not, except as a memory in a song, they with the things that seemed good to them with loves and desires that grow dim and alien in the days to be.' The Rev. Mr. Colquhoun was referring to the 'old Scotland that perished then', the 'last of the peasants, the last of the old Scots folk'. The peasants, of course, had long gone, driven to the wall by economic and technological change of the twentieth century, but so too were the old certainties of working-class and bourgeois life.

Scotland at the end of the twentieth century remained a society which exported its people, but in nothing like the numbers of the 1920s, 1950s and 1960s. The lack of substantial in-migration in the second half of the century resulted in Scotland's population falling as a proportion of that of the UK. Only one person in a hundred living in Scotland in the 1990s belonged to an ethnic minority, compared with one in four in London. Around 10 per cent of the Scottish population was born elsewhere, of which the largest number – 7 per cent – came from England. The claim from some quarters that Scotland was becoming 'anglicised' foundered on the evidence that English incomers were likely to 'go native', and to end up sharing the political and social habits of native Scots.

So what had Scotland become by the twenty-first century? In essence, it was a northern European country which had outgrown its junior partner role in British imperialism. Empire no more. Possibly Britain no more. Feeling British became a descriptor of people of pensionable age who remember the Second World War and the creation of the welfare state. Feeling British was becoming a matter of memory, of history, rather than of the future. Being British had become a matter of speaking, not a matter of feeling.

Scotland in the new millennium: how are we to sum it up? It was a society transformed by the twentieth century, in economic, social, political and cultural terms. Its history left it the legacy of an open economy which started the century as the maker of ships and engineering for the world. By century's end, it was providing world markets with a share of its new technologies, but, unlike ships, it was not inventing them. Scotland remained a society shaped by class, but one in which it was easier than it had ever been to cross class barriers by means of education.

Scotland's masculinist cultures of work, politics and leisure were on the defensive. Workers were almost as likely to be women as men. Girls were outperforming boys in the classroom. The last redoubts of male leisure culture were under attack from a far less masculinist world and a more privatised family life. Scotland entered the millennium as a relatively affluent European society, semi-detached from the UK, and better able to sit with other European nations.

Chapter summary

In this chapter, we have sketched out the story of Scotland in the twentieth century. We have paid particular attention to:

- the key motifs of the century, of capital in 1900, of state in 1950, and nation in 2000;

- how Scotland in 1900 was a mature, industrial society locked in to imperial markets, with a predominant manual working-class population;

- the ways in which, by 1950, Scotland was transformed economically and socially by state intervention, thereby remaining British;

- the transformation of Scotland by 2000 such that its social structure and its politics were leading to a renegotiation of the Union, driven by nationalism.

In subsequent chapters we will elaborate the key theme by bringing it up to date by means of using the concepts and theories which sociology makes available to us. In the next chapter we identify the building blocks of sociology and try to erect an understanding of Scotland upon them.

Questions for discussion

1. What were the key features of Scottish society in 1900? To what extent were they the legacy of the nineteenth century?

2. How had Scotland been transformed by the middle of the twentieth century? What had been the main causes of change since 1900?

3. Compare and contrast Scotland in 1990 and 2000. Were the ways in which it had been transformed inevitable?

4. If you were to project Scotland forward to 2050, what would it look like, and what are likely to be the main forces which shape it?

5. In general terms, is it possible to isolate *social* change from economic and political change? What are the key features of social change which matter most?

Annotated reading

(a) For sociologically informed histories of Scotland, see T. Devine's wide-ranging *The Scottish Nation, 1700–2000* (2000); T. Devine and J. Wormald (eds), *The Oxford Handbook of Modern Scottish History* (2012), especially part V, which provides different accounts of social change.

(b) On the sociology of Scotland, see D. McCrone, *Understanding Scotland: The sociology of a nation* (2001), a shorter and early complement to this book.

(c) On the transformation of Scotland and its institutions, see L. Paterson's *The Autonomy of Modern Scotland* (1994); for statistical detail on transformations in the final decades of the twentieth century, see L. Paterson, F. Bechhofer and D. McCrone, *Living in Scotland: Social and economic change since 1980* (2004); and for a more 'political' account, see J. Mitchell's *The Scottish Question* (2014).

Notes

1   In Scotland the term 'house' includes flats.
2   For example, the 1924 Housing Act (known as the Wheatley Housing Act after the Labour minister John Wheatley, who introduced it) increased government subsidies for council house building.
3   These were designated under the New Towns Act of 1947, and catered for 'overspill' populations, mainly from Glasgow. They were East Kilbride (1949), Glenrothes (1948), Cumbernauld (1956), Livingston (1962) and Irvine (1966).

3

WHAT IS SCOTLAND?

Having spent two chapters examining Scotland's deep and more immediate history, it might seem facetious at this point to ask: 'What is Scotland?' It has, however, serious import. Our task in this book is to construct and give an account of a sociology of Scotland, but where to begin? One might, as we have, begin with 'history', because that purports to tell the story; and if we can tell the story reasonably coherently, then surely, we might say, Scotland must exist. It seems academic game-playing to say otherwise. That, however, is to dodge the question. So what *is* sociologically interesting about Scotland?

Chapter aims

- To ask whether Scotland is a meaningful topic for sociological analysis.

- To set out what we mean by 'society' using concepts such as 'state' and 'nation'.

- To examine whether the 'Scottish Enlightenment' provides a framework of understanding.

- To focus on 'civil society' as a way of understanding Scotland.

- To argue that, in the modern world, understated nations like Scotland reflect new ways of thinking about society.

Is Scotland a suitable case for sociological treatment?

When I was a young student, the first professor of sociology at Edinburgh, Tom Burns, gave an inaugural lecture (Burns, 1970). His purpose was to set out 'sociological explanation', framed by this statement:

> The purpose of sociology is to achieve an understanding of social behaviour and social institutions which is different from that current among the people through whose conduct the institutions exist; an understanding which is not

merely different but new and better. The practice of sociology is criticism. It exists to criticise claims about the value of achievement and to question assumptions about the meaning of conduct. It is the business of sociologists to conduct a critical debate with the public about its equipment of social institutions. (1970: 72)

In subsequent years, many have taken that as an excellent 'vision statement' for the discipline, even if they might cavil a bit at a sociological understanding being 'new and better', rather than simply 'different' from the ones which people themselves might have. It is always risky to try and explain what writers mean by such a statement after the event, but I read that as saying that people's accounts of what they do and why they do it may not square with what is actually going on. They are, after all, what sociologists call 'accounts'. Burns' famous book the *Management of Innovation* (Burns and Stalker, 1961) showed brilliantly just how managers' accounts in an electronics factory do not square with what they actually do.

This is close to the anthropologists' distinction between *emic* and *etic*; that is, the former relates to how social actors give an account of what they do, and the latter to the analyst's account of what they do. Michael Banton gives an excellent summary of the distinction:

An everyday example of the difference is that when a patient goes to a doctor for treatment, he or she reports his or her symptoms in ordinary language using *emic* constructs. The doctor makes a diagnosis, drawing upon technical knowledge expressed in *etic* constructs. In one formulation, *emic* constructs are accounts expressed in categories meaningful to members of the community under study, whereas *etic* constructs are accounts expressed in categories meaningful to the community of scientific observers. (2015: 85)

Can there be a sociology of Scotland?

In his lecture, Burns made the following statement: 'One cannot speak of the sociology of Scotland as one can of the Scottish economy, nor of the sociology of children as one can of child psychology' (1970: 58). Why not (we might ask)? Burns might have replied that sociology is defined by its perspective and not by its subject matter. That perspective focuses on the social determinants of human action, by a concern with 'society', big or small. It is not the only social science to define itself in terms of perspective: social anthropology focuses on culture; psychology on 'mind'.[1]

We can have a sociology of all sorts of institutional activities: for example, education, religion, economy, politics, which are in and of themselves obviously not the sole preserve of sociology. Nor necessarily is sociology a better perspective than, say, anthropology and psychology; merely different – even though, like cobblers who thought there is nothing quite like leather,[2] practitioners of our trade might find it superior to others. In the meantime,

what sociology studies – education, religion, economy, politics – are themselves analysed by practitioners defined by the subject matter: educationists, theologians, economists and political scientists. In practice, of course, there is considerable cross-over to mutual benefit, if, now and again, mutual incomprehension and disagreement.

Let us return to Burns' disclaiming of a sociology of Scotland. He did not think that a 'territory' could be the subject of sociological analysis. Similarly, his belief that one cannot have a 'sociology of children' has been overtaken by a wealth of studies focusing on how 'childhood' is sociologically constructed, and how it varies between different societies. Who is a 'child' and what is 'childhood' have become proper subjects for sociological study, with their own conferences publications, courses and degrees. For 'Scotland', patently this book, and its predecessors, *Understanding Scotland* (McCrone, 1992; 2001) have tried to do something similar.

The point, however, is not whether Burns was right or wrong in saying you could not have a sociology of Scotland, but how instructive it is to ask the question: what is sociologically interesting about Scotland? In any case, and especially for a student of Burns, his statement became the grit in the oyster. In the subsequent fifty years, much has changed in both sociological thinking as well as 'on the ground' in Scotland itself. To take the latter first, the assertion of Scottish 'difference' with regard to institutions, social values, political behaviour has become commonplace.

It would be unwise of sociology not to take that seriously, even if (possibly *especially* if) one wanted to argue that differences were superficial or unimportant. But compared with what, we might ask? Compared with other parts of the British state? Compared with other territories which shared common economic, political and social stages of development? The key word in those sentences is 'comparative'. Sociology takes seriously the comparative framework even when we are not making explicit comparisons (see Bechhofer and Paterson, 2000: chapter 1). In other words, if we make statements about this or that 'society', notionally freestanding, we are making implicit comparisons: it is *this* kind of place, rather than that; or again, you might expect *this* to be the case, but in fact it is that.

So what is 'society'?

You will notice in the last paragraph that the word 'society' has crept in again. This is because it is a central part of the sociologist's toolkit. If social anthropologists do 'culture', and psychologists do 'mind', then sociologists do 'society'. That begs the question as to what we mean by 'society'. In the early 1980s, the French sociologist Alain Touraine commented:

> The abstract idea of society cannot be separated from the concrete reality of a national society, since this idea is defined as a network of institutions, controls and education. This necessarily refers us back to a government, to a territory, to a political collectivity. The idea of society was and still is the ideology of nations in the making. (1981: 5; my translation)

Still, that leaves open the question as to what a 'national society' is, defined by a network of institutions, controls and education. Is that Scotland? The UK? Europe? Or what? When Touraine wrote in 1981, there was no Scottish parliament, so 'government' would be the UK, but arguably Scotland could be thought of as a 'political collectivity'. Touraine's final sentence about 'nations in the making' is perhaps the most intriguing statement of all. No doubt Touraine had no difficulty talking about French society, and possibly British society, but what he might have made of Scottish society is impossible to tell. In any case, he would have pointed out, Scotland is not an independent state, and hence less likely to be a society.

There is another way of expressing the puzzle. As Norbert Elias once observed: 'Many twentieth century sociologists when speaking of "society" no longer have in mind, as did their predecessors, a "bourgeois society" or a "human society" beyond the state, but increasingly the somewhat diluted image of a nation-state' (1978: 241). So we seem back to talking about 'British society', 'American society', and so on, for these are meaningful abstractions which short-circuit the analytical problem of what, in sociological rather than political terms, a society actually is.

This essentially modern view of society is somewhat at odds with an older meaning. The historic task of sociology has been to analyse 'society', to understand how social systems operate and lay down rules and procedures for its members. This is much closer to the way the term was used by writers such as Adam Ferguson in the eighteenth century, as we shall see later in this chapter.

Upper case 'Society' in this sense operates at a higher level of abstraction than the nation-state – which we might call lower case 'society'. The specificities of actual or 'real' societies can thus be ignored in favour of broad similarities between them. These are, of course, ideal types. Hence, as Elias comments, sociologists have talked about 'human society', or 'industrial society', or 'capitalist society', and so on. In this perspective, the common features of societies are deemed to have much more theoretical or predictive importance than their specific features.

Other sociologists have suggested that 'society' is far too problematic a term and should be jettisoned. Michael Mann went so far as to say: 'It may seem an odd position for a sociologist to adopt; but if I could, I would abolish the concept "society" altogether' (1986: 2). Using the term 'society', he says, brings two problems. On the one hand, as we have seen, most accounts simply equate polities or states with 'societies'. As a result, Mann comments: 'the enormous covert influence of the nation-state of the late nineteenth and early twentieth centuries on the human sciences means that a nation-state model dominates sociology and history alike' (1986: 2). On the other hand, the term 'society' implies a unitary social system, but, he says, 'we can never find a single bounded society in geographical or social space' (1986: 1). In other words, even nation-states are not 'bounded totalities'.

Clarifying concepts

Already we have stumbled into a thicket of competing concepts: society, nation, state, to which we might add for good measure, country. This is a crowded field, and before we choose which, if any, to apply to Scotland, we need to sort them out. Oddly enough, 'society' seems to present problems. Thus, Mann argues that society should be treated not so much as a unitary concept implying internal homogeneity, but a 'loose confederation', as 'overlapping networks of social interaction'.

Hence, a society is a unit within whose boundaries social interaction is relatively dense and stable, and while interactions will take place across these boundaries, those taking place within it are the most significant and consistent. John Urry also shares Mann's misgivings. In his book *Sociology beyond Societies* (1999) Urry came to the aid of Mrs Thatcher and her (in)famous statement that 'there is no such thing as society, only individuals and their families'. (We might note in passing that many cite Thatcher's assertion, but few contextualise it by quoting the *Woman's Own* magazine whence it came. Thatcher was bemoaning some people's desire that society should 'do something' to sort out their problems, only to point out that it was up to people themselves ('individuals and their families') to take responsibility. This does not excuse the statement, it contextualises it.)

In any case, it might seem an odd thing for sociologists to do, that is to abjure 'society', but Urry is making a point. Like Mann, he was arguing that sociology must abandon its practice of studying society as an assumed set of bounded institutions, the study of social structures, and instead focus on mobility: change over stasis. Urry observed: 'sociology may be able to develop a new agenda, an agenda for a discipline that is losing its central concept of human "society". It is a discipline organised around networks, mobility and horizontal fluidities' (1999: 3). He was arguing that we must seek a society of mobilities that disrupt a 'sociology of the social as societies' (1999: 4). Urry was making a plea for casting adrift from the relatively safe boundaries of functionally integrated and bounded societies bequeathed by its founders, notably Emile Durkheim.

In retrospect, this seems to be an expression of the time-old sociological puzzle of the relationship between 'structure' and 'agency': that is, the degree to which people are constrained by the social structures around them on the one hand, versus the capacity of individuals to make their own free choices on the other. In his later work on climate change, Urry (2011) appeared to have recanted his desire to jettison 'society', recognising that 'global governance' seems especially ill-placed to tackle this global issue. Only 'societies' seem able to put in place institutional levers and, above all, to legitimate social change to try and save the planet, or, more precisely, human life on planet Earth.

Mann, too, is a critic of the view that 'nation-states' have had their day, and is critical of 'globalisation' theorists who exaggerate the former strength of 'nation-states' only to exaggerate in turn their decline, and who, in any case, downplay relations between states (see Chapter 24 for a fuller account).

There are a number of concepts we need to clarify in that last paragraph, notably 'nation', 'state', as well as the hyphenated 'nation-state'. Following Benedict Anderson, we can define 'nation' usefully as an 'imagined community' having four dimensions:

- 'It is *imagined* because the members of even the smallest nation will never know most of their fellow-members, meet them, or even hear of them, yet in the minds of each lives the image of their communion.'

- 'The nation is imagined as *limited* because even the largest of them, encompassing perhaps a billion living human beings, has finite, if elastic boundaries, beyond which lie other nations.'

- 'It is imagined as *sovereign* because the concept was born in an age in which Enlightenment and Revolution were destroying the legitimacy of the divinely-ordained hierarchical dynastic realm.'

- '[I]t is imagined as a *community*, because, regardless of the actual inequality and exploitation that may prevail in each, the nation is always conceived as a deep, horizontal comradeship.' (Anderson, 1996: 6–7, italics in original)

It is important to stress that Anderson is saying that the nation is *imagined*, not *imaginary*. He rebukes Ernest Gellner for his famous line that 'nationalism is not the awakening of nations to self-consciousness; it invents nations where they do not exist' (1964: 169). Anderson points out that Gellner appears to be confusing 'invention' with 'fabrication' and 'falsity' rather than 'imagining' and 'creation'. That is why it would be more accurate to say that the nation is *imagined* rather than imaginary.

Anderson talks of nations being 'imagined communities' because they require a sense of belonging which is both horizontal and vertical, in place and in time. The 'nation' implies an affinity not only with those currently living, but with dead generations. The idea of the nation is to be conceived of, says B. Anderson, 'as a solid community moving steadily down (or up) history' (1996: 26). This idea of historical continuity is a vitally important part of the nation as imagined community. It implies links with long-dead ancestors, in such a way that Anthony Smith's words 'the nation becomes the constant renewal and retelling of our tale by each generation of our descendants' (1986: 208).

The question of social order

Why should sociologists be so concerned with the notion of 'society'? The short answer is to say that it is necessary because people are not simply driven by political concerns ('state') or cultural ones ('nation') or economic ones ('market'), but how they relate to each other, what is called 'social order'. In the words of the American sociologist Dennis Wrong, 'how are men capable of uniting to form enduring societies in the first place?' (1961: 184). Wrong's use of 'men' is grounded in the language of the 1950s, but he makes an important point. His concern was that the question focused overmuch on the way social norms were internalised, and so human behaviour conformed to the social expectations of others.

What this kind of sociology produced, said Wrong, was an over-socialised and deterministic conception of human behaviour, that people acted out the social roles allotted to
them. This is 'structuralism', simply reading off from social structures how people behave
and what they think, because that is what is expected of them. Subsequently, the pendulum swung a long way back towards a concern with 'social agency', whereby people were
treated as having much more awareness and influence over their actions and thoughts.
Truth to tell, the problem of 'structure and agency/action' is one of the most basic tensions
in sociology.

We have moved, in recent years, some way from Wrong's concern with what he called
the 'over-socialised conception of man', towards the view that human beings are responsible for their actions. This is to treat social actors as free agents whose social identities are
highly liquid, that we can be who we *want* to be by donning the appropriate garb. The rise
of methodological individualism complements the zeitgeist of our economic, political and
cultural worlds, and Wrong's central question (how is society possible?) no longer seems
central, even to many sociologists.

The question is as old as sociology itself. Despite being caricatured as *the* sociologist of
'structuralism', Durkheim sought to balance properly structure and action:

> The characteristic attributes of human nature ... come to us through society.
> But on the other hand, society exists and lives only in and through individuals.
> Extinguish the idea of society in individual minds, let the beliefs, traditions, and
> aspirations of the collectivity cease to be felt and shared by the people involved,
> and society will die ... society has reality only to the extent that it has a place in
> human consciousness, and we make this place for it. (2008 [1912]: 258)

So it turns out that while he is often seen as the supreme theorist of the 'social', Durkheim
had a proper understanding of the active role of the individual, and of social action.

Refining 'society'

At this point in our argument, we need to refine 'society' to make it clear that it is not
simply equated with the 'state', with 'political society', but rather with 'civil society'. Civil
society refers to these relatively dense networks of organisations and institutions resulting
from, and in turn framing, the day-to-day interactions of people. As Gellner (1994: 7–8) put
it, civil society is the social space located between the tyranny of kin and the tyranny of
kings; between the intimacy of family life and the impersonal power of the state. It is
related to the 'state', the political level, but is not coterminous with it. Neither does civil
society equate with the 'nation', for a sense of 'nation-ness' is sustained by institutional
autonomy, rather than the other way round (McCrone, 2010: 184).

We can see how the assertion of 'nationalism' derives not from elemental emotions based
on historic memories, but from the day-to-day contemporary social associations of people.
It arises from patterns of sociability structured by organisational life, with 'civility'. A nation
is an 'imagined community' *because* of its associational and institutional distinctiveness,

and, as a result, it follows Durkheim's definition that 'a society is not constituted by the mass who comprise it ... but above all by the idea it has of itself' (Fournier, 2013: 625–6).

This sense of being a 'nation' is sustained by its sociality, and, together, nation and society may encourage a quest for some kind of state-like characteristics even if these fall short of what conventionally is called 'independence'. There is considerable, and repeated, interaction between 'society', 'nation' and 'state', namely the social, cultural and political levels, but they remain distinct levels; we cannot subsume one into the other.

Thinking socially

The view that humans are thinking, sentient and, above all, *social* beings transcends narrow disciplinary boundaries and was usefully called the 'sociological imagination' by Mills in the 1950s (his book of the same name was published in 1959). The concept is not the preserve of sociologists: here are three non-sociologists employing it in all but words. The late Neil MacCormick, an eminent theorist of law, observed that: 'The truth about human individuals is that they are social products, not independent atoms capable of constituting society through a voluntary coming together. We are as much constituted by our society as it is by us' (1999: 163).

Second, the social philosopher Alisdair MacIntyre observed that:

> We all approach our own circumstances as bearers of a particular social identity. I am someone's son or daughter, someone's cousin or uncle; I am a citizen of this or that city, a member of this or that guild or profession; I belong to this clan, that tribe, this nation. Hence what is good for me has to be the good for one who inhabits these roles. As such, I inherit from the past of my family, my city, my tribe, my nation, a variety of debts, inheritances, rightful expectations and obligations. These constitute the given of my life, my moral starting point. (2007: 220)

And, third, the political philosopher Michael Sandel reinforces the point:

> If we understand ourselves as free and independent selves, unbound by moral ties we haven't chosen, we can't make sense of a range of moral and political obligations that we commonly recognize, even prize. These include obligations of solidarity and loyalty, historic memory and religious faith – moral claims that arise from the communities and traditions that shape our identity. Unless we think of ourselves as encumbered selves, open to moral claims we have not willed, it is difficult to make sense of these aspects of our moral and political experience. (2009: 220)

The descriptor 'encumbered selves' makes the point well. To paraphrase Karl Marx: we make ourselves, but not under conditions of our own making. Famously, Marx observed: 'Men make their own history, but they do not make it just as they please; they do not make it under circumstances chosen by themselves, but under circumstances directly encountered, given and transmitted from the past' (1937 [1869]).

So what are these non-sociologists telling us about 'society'? Each in their different way is arguing that there *is* such a thing as society; that we are not isolated, stand-alone, individuals, but that we are sustained by people around us. Without them confirming our social identities, we would not function at all.

Emerging civil society

We have reached the point in our argument where we focus more directly on 'society'. There is a particular Scottish dimension to this. We can even claim that sociology, the science of 'society' par excellence, had its origins in Scotland; that it was a pure case of civil society, because it was not formally speaking a 'state'. In other words, if we wish to understand what civil society is, then looking at somewhere like Scotland, which is a 'society' but not a 'state', might be just the place to find it. We can find examples of civil society operating at a micro-scale, as in Figure 3.1. It would, after all, be absurd to argue that Scotland had no sociological

FIGURE 3.1   This is the iconic photograph of local (male) decision making (in 1879), of the St Kilda 'parliament' before the island was evacuated in 1930. It represents the essence of 'civil society' on a micro-scale. Douglas Dunn wrote in his poem *St Kilda's Parliament*: 'You need only look at the faces of these men / Standing there like everybody's ancestors, / This flick of time I shuttered on a face.' (http://www.abandonedcommunities.co.uk/stkildaparliament.html)

FIGURE 3.2
Adam Ferguson,
by Henry
Raeburn,
courtesy of
University of
Edinburgh. This
portrait hangs in
the university's
Raeburn Room
in Old College

'It is in conducting the affairs of civil society that mankind find the exercise of their best talents, as well as the object of their best affections.' (Adam Ferguson, 1966 [1767]: 155)

meaning because it had ceased to be a state in 1707. Patently, it had assets of 'governing' institutions dealing with law, religion, education and local administration which were the foundations for further self-government in the following three centuries.

Adam Ferguson's *Essay on the History of Civil Society* (1966 [1767]) arguably provided the foundations for sociology as a discipline, or, better put, proto-sociology (Eriksson, 1993). Björn Eriksson argued that the Enlightenment, and in particular the Scottish Historical School, associated with writers such as Adam Ferguson (see Figure 3.2), Adam Smith, John Millar, Henry Home (Lord Kames) and William Robertson, was the general prerequisite for the emergence of sociological thinking.

Such writers shared a common question: how is society possible? The answer could not be found simply in adopting a rational calculative view, or one based on utilitarianism. Eriksson argued that a 'sociological' answer to the question is not based simply on economy or polity but on *society*, the emergence of organically emerging and maintained institutions and patterns of social action. Thus, 'society is possible because of the connection between the sociality of men, and the social patterns of institutions which are produced and reproduced in society' (Eriksson, 1993: 270). 'Rationality-based' answers are too superficial and cannot grasp the kernel either of human sociality or of social dynamics. Thus, he says: 'Ties between men and society … cannot be reduced to relations of individual advantage and individual calculation. They are much stronger and much deeper' (1993: 270).

The role of the Scottish Enlightenment

The Enlightenment was the general context for the emergence of sociological thinking, and Scotland was one of its key locales. Why so? Adam Ferguson, for example, was born and brought up on the cusp of the Highlands and Lowlands, at Logierait in Perthshire, and so appreciated that Scotland was something of a sociological test bed of stages and modes of social development. Further, in the eighteenth century Scotland underwent a 'professional revolution', among professionals such as churchmen, lawyers and academics who epitomised the 'spirit of the age of improvement', and who formed in a loose sense the Scottish 'Historical' School whose model of analysis mirrored the specific characteristics of professional life. Thus, concludes Eriksson, 'the sociological framework developed out by the Scottish Historical School fetched its variables from the very specific type of professional society in which they all lived, a society which differed markedly from that larger society outside their circles' (1993: 276).

This was not 'sociology' so much as 'proto-sociology', its emergent discourse before Auguste Comte in France formalised and was credited with the discipline's formation. To be sure, these 'proto-sociologists' did not call themselves sociologists, nor did they articulate a specific sense of 'Scotland' in their work. Rather, they were interested in what we might call 'Society' (capital S) through which actual societies 'on the ground' evolved through stages of social development. Scotland was simply the context, the exemplar, and the unusual social and cultural conditions to be found there in the eighteenth century meant that it was an appropriate testing ground. Above all, Scotland was not a 'state', an overtly political entity, and thus we could see the independent operations of (civil) society. Ironically, the debate over constitutional change in the late twentieth century, for example, evoked the distinctiveness of Scottish civil society and its capacity to frame economic and political issues independent of (central) state effects.

We can argue that the assertion of 'nationalism' in Scotland, of nation-ness in that period, derived not from some elemental set of emotions based on historic memories – ethnicity, if you prefer – but on the day-to-day contemporary social associations of people, on patterns of sociability structured by organisational life – in education, law, etc. – what might be called 'civility'.[3]

Civil society, then, comes to refer to the relatively dense networks of organisations and institutions resulting from and, in turn, framing day-to-day interactions of people. That is the meaning of Gellner's distinction, which we introduced earlier, between the 'tyranny of kin' (the familial, the intimate) and the 'tyranny of kings' (the state and its apparatus). 'Society' is the key intermediate realm, and is held together by the everyday relations of people and institutions as they go about their lives. It also invokes what is called *demos*, the sense that people are bound together by sharing common procedures and manners of thought, in contrast to *ethnos*, which places the focus much more on cultural homogeneity and 'tribal' identity.

Despite subsequently being hijacked in the cause of extreme individualism and private self-interest, Adam Smith was at pains to stress that much of the authority of the social order derived from 'society' rather than 'government'. As Jonathan Hearn observes: 'we can see the formation of a familiarly modern conception of "society" as a reality sui generis, as a system with its own emergent rules and order, not created from above, and also more than "the sum of its parts"' (2015: 410).

Thus, 'society' is not the state, nor, indeed, the economy, but sustains both state and economy because it operates on the basis of social trust between people. Society, then, precedes the political and the economic. Without 'social trust', state and economy cannot hold. Hearn observes: 'Very far from suggesting a world of individual atoms artificially bounded by constraining states, [Smith] suggests that "nations" and their states map onto the underlying principles of propinquity and sympathy, providing a certain intractable aspect of social structure' (2015: 402).

Doubting civil society

Some sociologists like Krishan Kumar are sceptical of the value of the notion of 'civil society', at least as used in modern contexts. He observed: 'Civil society sounds good; it has a good feel to it; it has the look of a fine old wine, full of depth and complexity. Who could possibly object to it, who not wish for its fulfilment?' (1993: 376). In short, civil society could be everywhere and nowhere, nothing beyond its reach, but specifying little. Kumar took the view that: 'Civil society is, no more than state power, a panacea. Its divisions and discontents remain a source of inequality and instability' (1993: 389).

The term 'civil society' with its *marxisant* overtones also evokes the contribution by Antonio Gramsci, 'the marxist de Tocqueville', as Kumar calls him (1993: 381): 'Civil society is the sphere of culture in the broadest sense. It is concerned with the manners and mores of society, with the way people live. It is where values and meanings are established, where they are debated, contested and change' (1993: 382–3). In short, 'the concept of civil society that is most widespread today is fundamentally Gramscian' (1993: 389).

In modern societies, it is difficult to find the dividing line between state and civil society, the distinction between 'civil society' – the arena of consent and direction – from 'political society' – the arena of coercion and domination (Poggi, 1978). Thus, the hegemony of the ruling class was expressed via the 'organic relations' between the two realms.

As Kumar observes, setting civil society in contradistinction to the state possibly overestimates the power of the state, and implies that civil society is anti-state. In his useful review of the concept, Jonathan Hearn comments: 'Civil society is almost always defined in opposition to the state, and yet much of what goes on in it is oriented precisely toward affecting the state, is guaranteed by the state, and at least two of its components – laws and markets – are substantially artefacts of the state' (2001: 342).

State and civil society

In truth, the line of demarcation between state and civil society these days is fuzzy. Gianfranco Poggi commented that civil society 'may need the state as ultimate guarantor, but their subsistence in a realm separate from that where the state predominantly operates is intrinsic to the very nature of the state, as a set of differentiated, specifically political institutions complementary to that realm' (2001: 145).

Reifying 'state' and 'civil society' gives a hardness to these concepts which they do not have, other than in theoretical, ideal–typical, terms. The philosopher Charles Taylor observed that, juxtaposed to 'political society', 'civil society ... exists over against the state, in partial independence from it. It includes those dimensions of social life which cannot be confounded with, or swallowed up in the state' (1990: 95).

Taylor argued that there were five roots to western 'civil society':

- society was not defined in terms of its identification with its political organisation;

- the church was a society independent of the state;

- feudal relations of authority involved quasi-contractual relationships of rights and obligations;

- civil society had its roots in the autonomous 'city-states' of Western Europe, something Max Weber identified in his essay *The City* (1966 [1921]);

- the autonomous social space of 'civil society' emerged out of those roots, 'not so much a sphere outside political power; rather it penetrates deeply into this power, fragments and decentralises it. Its components are truly "amphibious"' (1990: 117).

Is this distinction between civil society and political society meaningful any more in the modern age? It is noticeable that the concept 'civil society' has more currency in some places than others. It also has a curious history. Associated with the Scottish Enlightenment, it disappeared from view as sociology came to focus on self-contained 'societies'. In terms of actual social and political change, 'civil society' re-emerged in the 1980s and 1990s to account for the collapse of political communism in state socialist societies, notably where it provided a robust and alternative platform to state power, as in Poland where the Catholic Church had set up parallel social institutions to the communist state.

Civil society and nationalism

Closer to home, 'civil society' has been vested with normative and analytical significance to explain the rise of neo-nationalism, challenges to the British state (in Scotland and Wales), the Spanish state (in Catalonia and Euskadi (the Basque Country)), as well as in France, the classic bastion of the Jacobin state. Whether badged as 'nationalism' or 'regionalism', it became clear that the more developed and autonomous the associational structures in these territories, the greater the challenges to central state legitimacy.

Scotland – in contrast to Wales – had a framework of autonomous institutions, of law, religion, social governance dating from the Treaty of Union with England in 1707, and much developed subsequently. Since that Union, Scotland has continued its separate system of law, jealously guarded by its judges and legal establishment; also, of course, part of 'the state', or more precisely the 'semi-state', that collection of government and quasi-government departments in the Scottish Office, which was, at least nominally, until 1999 governed by ministers from the ruling party at Westminster.

Nowadays, Scotland has a parliament and its own directly elected ministers in control of the bureaucracy of state, if not a 'state' in the orthodox sense of the term, enough to describe Scotland as an 'understated nation', but a 'state' nonetheless in high degree. This might even suggest that there are *degrees* of state-ness, and Scotland has more of it than it used to have pre-1999, though not as much as most of its people would like. We can conclude that the precise dividing line between 'state' and '(civil) society' is unclear, but there is little doubt that they are not synonyms of each other.

If 'civil society' is not 'the state', neither is it simply to be equated with 'the market'. There is, as Sunil Khilnani (2001) pointed out, a distinction to be made between the 'liberal' position, which argues that the effective powers of civil society reside in the economy, in property rights and the market, and the 'radical' position, which locates civil society in 'society', independent of both the economic domain and the political apparatus of the state.

Furthermore, we construe civil society as the social hinge between economic capital and the political apparatus of the state. As Craig Calhoun observed: 'from the point of view of democracy, it is essential to retain in the notion of civil society some idea of a social realm which is neither dominated by state power nor simply responsive to the systematic features of capitalism (1993: 310–11).

In other words, people are determined neither by market relations and defined as economic actors, nor simply by the rights and obligations conferred by the state. Put another way, we are neither 'consumers' (still less 'customers') nor simply 'citizens' (of the state), which is why calling everyone from students to train passengers 'customers' is odd and inappropriate, and not simply because both universities and railways are imperfect markets.

If 'civil society' is neither 'state' nor 'market', is it simply a synonym for the 'nation'? Not quite. If anything, feeling and being 'national' are the *outcome* of the process of civil societalisation, sustained by patterns of sociability which teach us how to behave appropriately. The feeling of being a national, of belonging to a community, is the result of the channels and mechanisms which shape us and make us feel that way rather than the other way round.

There remains the point that civil society is difficult to define, or rather, as Sudipta Kaviraj observes, 'it is a minor curiosity that "civil society" appears to be an idea strangely incapable of standing freely on its own: it always needs a distinctive support (that is, support by being one half of a distinction) from a contrary term' (2001: 288).

- Civil society is usually defined vis-à-vis, in terms of what it is not, as much as what it is. Thus, in the works of Adam Ferguson, civil society is contrasted with *natural society*, that is the state of nature.

- Second, civil society is defined vis-à-vis the state, its counterweight as well as its complement. Kaviraj argued that all civil society arguments stem from some deep disillusion with the state and its mode of functioning: 'those calling for a re-assertion of "civil society" are basically calling for people to gather up all resources of sociability to form their own collective projects against the states' (2001: 319).

- Third, civil society is about sociability, not in the sense of intimate *Gemeinschaft*, the essence of community, but, vis-à-vis once more, as *Gesellschaft*, the ordering of relations between people not intimately connected, not of kin, but of sociability among strangers.

- Civil society is also defined vis-à-vis market and nation, closely connected, but not the same thing. Thus, civil society is more than market relations; in like manner, it is the 'cause' of national feeling, not its outcome.

Politics and civil society

Does this make civil society 'a good thing'? Can we ever have too much of it? It is important to remember that the concept has western roots, and thus is inherently ethnocentric. Kaviraj and Khilnani (2001) point out that colonial societies did not follow the same routes as their colonisers, that the relationships between state, society and economy are quite different. They argue too that civil society is best thought of, not as a substantive category, a distinctive entity, but as a set of enabling conditions.

It is best to see civil society as a set of human capacities, moral and political, and not a determinate end-state. One cannot, for example, assume a necessary association between civil society and a specific form of government such as liberal democracy. Just as one can have too much state power vis-à-vis civil society (compare East Germany and Poland pre-1989 state socialism, for example), so it is possible to have an overweening civil society vis-à-vis the state, at least in terms of party politics. Thus, for much of its history since 1921, the statelet of Northern Ireland generated very predictable politics, each so-called 'community', whether unionist or nationalist, squeezing out opportunities for the political arena to have an independent life. Whenever elections were held, so votes stacked up behind political parties which were creatures of these communities rather than of the political space within which negotiation could take place.

As Bernard Crick pointed out in his classic book *In Defence of Politics* (1992), there has to be a public sphere for negotiation between political organisations which are the hidebound creatures neither of the state nor of narrow social interests. In a telling comment, Crick observed: 'Democracy is one element in politics; if it seeks to be everything, it destroys politics, turning "harmony into mere unison", reducing "a theme to a single beat"' (1992: 73).

One can, then, have an overweening civil society, just as one can have an overweening state. Civil society presupposes a concept of 'politics' with an identifiable territorial and constitutional scope, a distinctive set of practices. It also requires, as Khilnani and Kaviraj observe, a particular type of 'self' – mutable, able to see interests as transient, and with changing political and public affiliations. This is not to reduce 'self' to a rational, interest-maximising self, guided by simple economic self-interest, as economic liberalism argues; neither is it to treat the 'civil' self as the 'citizen', the recipient of rights and responsibilities simply conferred by the state. Pushed to extremes, treating all rights as citizenship ones would enhance the power of the state, not circumscribe it. Thus, opposition to identity cards in the UK in 2006 arose because it conferred on the state the power to license people's identities, to bestow but also to rescind identities.[4]

Autonomous civil society

It should be clear by now that 'civil society' is related to, but not a creature of, the state, the market and the nation. It cannot be reduced to the level of the political (state), to the economic (market), or the cultural (nation). It stands in contradistinction to these even though it might appear to be their creature. Still less is civil society reducible to the 'private' sphere. Civil society can also claim to precede rather than derive from the state and political realm, and can unmake political authority and refashion it. That is why the concept was pressed into political service in Scotland (and Eastern Europe) in the 1980s and 1990s, and why doctrines of popular sovereignty in the 'People's Claim of Right' were reimagined.

Civil society and the Scottish dimension

Why should 'civil society' be an important part of current Scottish public discourse? As Kumar observed: 'If we wish to continue to use the concept of civil society, we must situate it in some definite tradition of use that gives it a place and a meaning' (1993: 390).

In late twentieth-century Scotland, it became plain that the political realm was at some odds with the informal and quasi-formal networks of civil society; in short, it was perceived to be unresponsive to its needs and demands, across the socio-economic spectrum, from professional bodies and voluntary groups to trade unions. This was in large part because of what was labelled the 'democratic deficit', the fact that no matter how people in Scotland voted at Westminster elections, they got a government elected by people in England; not unreasonable, given that they represented 85 per cent of the UK population.

The task was not to overthrow the state, but to refashion a state – parliament and government – more in keeping with the wishes of the electorate. Thus, people think of themselves as Scots because they have been educated, governed and embedded in a Scottish way. It is a matter of government, not of sentiment; and, if anything, the latter derives from the former.

The origins of Scottish civil society

As we saw in Chapter 1, there can be little doubting the ideological power of 'Scotland' as a nation in cultural terms. It implies that Scotland is not simply a collection of rocks, earth and water, but a transcendent idea which runs through history, reinterpreting that history to fit the concerns of each present. To be sure, it is not unique. To say that Scotland (or Wales, Ireland or England for that matter) are 'figments of the imagination' is not to imply that they are 'false', but that they have to be interpreted as ideas, made and remade, rather than treated simply as actual 'places'. Above all, as we saw in Chapter 1, they are places of the mind. In this regard, the term 'the Scottish people' implies a historical idea stretching back over centuries, implying that thirteenth-century peasants and twenty-first-century workers share some common identity.

If we accept that Scotland is a 'nation', nor is it a 'state', for it does not have a seat at the United Nations in New York. There is no seat for Scotland between Saudi Arabia and Senegal. Does that mean that Scotland is stateless – a stateless nation, perhaps? In the 1992 edition of *Understanding Scotland*, I so described it, but by 2001 it seemed that '*understated nation*' was a better term. This was because in the interim a devolved legislature, a parliament, had been set up, so Scotland possessed devolved statehood. In any case, as a number of reviewers of the 1992 book pointed out, there was sufficient institutional distinctiveness for Scotland to be considered a 'semi-state'.

Social institutions and civil society

Let us put some institutional flesh on those bones. Post-1707, day-to-day life in Scotland and its governance remained in the hands of Scots, consolidated in the 1832 Scottish Reform Act, and in the setting up of ad hoc governing boards to administer, among others, prisons, poor law, health, schools and the crofting counties (Paterson, 1994). These boards were incorporated into the responsibilities of the Scottish Office in 1886, ironically raising the complaint that the last vestiges of Scottish nationhood were thus being eroded.

The rights of a distinct society were jealously guarded by those who thoroughly approved of the Union. Thus, Walter Scott in the 1820s strongly objected to a London plan to abolish distinctive Scottish banknotes by invoking the loss of national identity. He wrote: 'I think I see my native country of Scotland, if it is yet to be called by a title so dis-criminative, falling so far as its national, or rather, perhaps, I ought to say provincial, interests are concerned, daily more into more absolute contempt' (Ash, 1980: 136).

Such nationalistic language did not contradict support for the Union, but rather under-scored the point that to the Scottish middle classes it was a union of equals, and that London interfered with both banknotes and Union at its peril (see Figure 3.3). The result was that Scottish banks retained the right to issue their own notes, something which strikes visitors to Scotland today as distinctive, even a little quirky. It is as if Scotland were an independent country but without an independent parliament or a national bank.

The Scottish semi-state

The remarkable growth of separate political administration for Scotland since 1886 has undoubtedly helped to reinforce this sense of 'Scotland'. It is easier to visualise what a separate Scotland would look like precisely because, by the 1980s, the Scottish Office had

FIGURE 3.3
Facsimile of Walter Scott's Malachi Malagrowther campaign to keep Scottish banknotes

Source: Courtesy of Bank of Scotland

become a Scottish semi-state with a powerful administrative apparatus. The proponents of devolution in the 1979 Referendum could set out their case for political autonomy in terms of the need to extend democratic accountability over this bureaucratic structure. Further, the emergence of a distinctively Scottish media agenda, which we will discuss in detail in Chapter 22, rested on the administrative apparatus governing Scotland from the 1960s to which the media could address political issues. Along with law, the church, education and banking, the media can be ranked as a key civil institution in Scotland which reinforces national identity. Thus, the press is the 'fourth estate', reflecting its role in social politics in modern societies.

Throughout the twentieth century, increased agitation for reform in Scotland resulted in increased responsibilities accruing to the Scottish Office to the extent that de facto Scottish self-government, or 'limited sovereignty' as Paterson called it, resulted. The demands for democratic accountability over this 'Scottish semi-state' in the late twentieth century represented recognition of the limits which bureaucratic devolution reached, and helped to bring about the devolved parliament in 1999.

At this level, Scotland plainly existed as a political–administrative unit, as a governed system defined by the remit of the Scottish Office. In just over 100 years of its existence, the Scottish Office had given a political meaning to Scotland. There is irony in this, because by treating Scotland as an object of administration, the Westminster government had to live with its political consequences. If the Scottish Office had never been created, it would have been much more difficult to address 'Scotland' as a meaningful political unit. The northern territory could have been handled as the North British regional province of the central British state, although the power and influence of civil society could never be ignored. It is significant that attempts to refer to Scotland as North Britain and England and Wales as South Britain after the Union of Crowns in 1603 came to nothing.[5]

This was reflected in the creation of the Scottish Office in 1885, and the building of St Andrews House in Edinburgh in 1939.

What of the hyphenated 'nation-state' which is in common currency in political as well as sociological thought? States are described as such in a fairly unthinking manner. Strictly speaking, however, the nation-state implies that the cultural concept 'nation' maps neatly onto the political one, 'state'; in other words, that a 'people' with a common culture and a sense of imagined community seek self-determination in having an independent state.

The exceptions prove the rule

In effect, there are few states to which the description applies. Even taking a simple linguistic measure, there is a distinct lack of correspondence between language and state. Thus, the same language will be spoken in different states (English, German, French to take but three), and within states there will be multiple languages spoken (Belgium, Canada, Spain).

The classic case is Switzerland, usually treated as 'an anomaly', the case which proves the rule that every state needs a cultural nation, or rather a dominant ethnicity.[6] Andreas Wimmer makes the point: 'Switzerland … presents a good example of a fully nationalised modern state built on an ethnically heterogeneous basis – contradicting the idea that industrialism or democracy demand cultural and linguistic homogeneity to work properly' (2002: 223). The point he is making is that matters of language and ethnicity never became politicised, and that Switzerland became a 'nation by will' (*Willensnation*). Wimmer comments:

> this small and somewhat bizarre country, surrounded by powerful states each ruling in the name of a single, distinct language community, was in fact revealing what these other states were hiding: the true nature of the national bond, made out of political spirit rather than cultural essence; out of the perception of commonality rather than objective distinctiveness. (2011: 720)

The point is not that Scotland is some analogue of Switzerland, but that similar principles applied as early as the thirteenth century as we saw in Chapter 1. It was territoriality, place, which defined the country, not ethnicity or tribe. Indeed, if a single ethnicity had been asserted by elites, it is unlikely that the state would have held, either in Scotland or in Switzerland. Monarchs were kings and queens 'of Scots' (plural), in contradistinction to kings and queens 'of England', not of 'the English'. Furthermore, the assembling of 'civil society' and diverse associational forms underpinned the state, even to the extent that when it was formally abolished, as in 1707, the 'society' held, and even deepened.

So why is the term 'nation-state' in such common currency? Largely because it represents an ideological claim, an aspirational one, that states which 'represent' nations are somehow natural. It does not take much effort to recognise that few are nationally cohesive, and that having made France, Germany, Italy, the United States, the UK, and so on, it was necessary to 'make' nationals. Even if we do not adopt linguistic criteria for 'nation-ness', it is hard to find the appropriate correspondence between nation and state. Thus, the UK is not a nation-state, for it contains distinct nations – England, Scotland, Wales and Northern Ireland[7] – and was constructed as a state-nation, rather than the other way round.

The best-known case of 'making nationals' is the US Pledge of Allegiance, considered necessary to socialise immigrants into a settler society. Following the end of the Cold War in the late 1980s it became plain that states in Eastern and Western Europe were far more fissiparous than they claimed, and that independence and secessionist movements have marked the geo-politics since then, including those in Scotland.

It is a reflection of the dominance of the nation-state idea, however, that it has such common currency in academic writing. Thus, critics like Wimmer and Glick Schiller argue that 'nationally bounded societies are taken to be the naturally given entities to study'; that 'methodological nationalism' abounds. Thus, 'the social sciences were captured by the apparent naturalness and givenness of a world divided into societies along the lines of nation-states' (Wimmer and Glick Schiller, 2002: 304). Note the unproblematic use of the term 'nation-states'. States have lost some of their power to transnational corporations and supranational organisations; they have been transformed by in-migration, and yet, the authors claim, social science continues to treat them as the unit of analysis.

This alludes to a set of arguments about 'globalisation' which we will explore in Chapter 24, but note for the moment that the critique is aimed at what is 'above' these 'nation-states' and not what is 'below' them, the sub-state level. Why does that matter? Because many of the key challenges derive from secessionist movements, which claim 'national' status for themselves. In other words, the 'nation-state' is undergoing a crisis of the hyphen (Anderson, 1996); Anderson might have added that it was far more of an aspiration in any case, than a reality. It is hard to think of many states which are homogeneous nations in cultural terms, and there are many 'nations' which are not states, including Scotland.

It is revealing that a critique of methodological nationalism (see Wimmer and Glick Schiller, 2002) focuses on external challenges to the legitimacy of the state, rather than its internal ones, which are, in any case, the other side of the same coin, arguably the hollow-ing out of the conventional state, which loses power and authority up and down to the supra- and sub-state levels.

Conclusion

In this chapter we have set out the arguments for studying Scotland. It is a 'civil society' in the sense that it is a cohesive institutional and cultural entity which can profitably be studied sociologically. We live in a world in which the conventional state (so-called 'nation-state') finds itself addressing challenges from above and below.

There is irony in the argument that we should avoid 'methodological nationalism' – which we should – on the grounds that the 'nation-state' has internal cultural and social unity. The irony rests on the fact that understanding 'sub-state' nationalism (in, for example, Scotland, Wales, Euskadi, Catalonia, Quebec) runs far less risk of 'methodological nationalism' than the implicit variety attaching to self-styled nation-states of Western Europe, the UK included.

One of the motivations for this book is the view that conventional 'British' sociology has failed to comprehend the fact that at best the UK evolved as a state-nation from the eighteenth century, and has never been a nation-state as such. That has not prevented sociologists from assuming that 'British society' is a meaningful and cohesive unity, when, strictly speaking, it has never been that.

British sociology, after all, emerged in the second half of the twentieth century out of a strong centralist and ameliorist tradition of social science, influenced heavily by Fabianist centralism and welfare statism. It is fair to say that the sociological project was bound up with British 'nation-building' post-1945. The underlying assumption was that the UK was a homogeneous 'nation-state' in which social class was the key determinant of life chances. 'State' and 'economy' rather than 'society' were the key dimensions. There is the comment made in 1970 by the French social scientist Raymond Aron that: 'The trouble is that British sociology is essentially an attempt to make intellectual sense of the political problems of the Labour Party' (Halsey, 2004: 70).

Granted that this is somewhat – but only somewhat – unkind, it does reflect much of the nature of British – or more accurately – Anglo-British sociology. In a telling definition, Anthony Giddens once remarked that 'a nation, as I use the term here, only exists when a state has a unified administrative reach over the territory over which its sovereignty is claimed' (1985: 119). The nation, he commented, is a 'bordered power-container' (1985: 120). There seems little room here either for more cultural diversity or for a purely social, that is societal, understanding, which may seem an odd thing for a sociologist to say.

One would never know that the UK is a complex multinational (and a multicultural) state by reading *British Sociology: Seen from without and within*, edited by A.H. Halsey and W.G. Runciman, published for the British Academy in 2005, thereby conferring state *imprimatur*.[8] It took a German sociologist, Wolf Lepenies, to observe: 'English (British?)[9] Sociology always remained curiously pallid and lacking in distinct identity' – quoted by Dominique Schnapper (who is also Raymond Aron's daughter) (in Halsey and Runciman, 2005: 110).

Societies which are not 'states' have a perceived fragility which conventional 'nation-states' do not have. Indeed, they are frequently deemed to be 'over', to belong to the detritus of history (see Norman Davies' excellent book *Vanished Kingdoms: The history of half-forgotten Europe*, 2011) with little or no future. That is often reflected in their accounts. Thus, Cairns Craig comments: 'From the 1920s to the 1970s, the analysis of Scottish culture was built around the assumptions of the terminal decline of Scottish culture that had supervened upon the end of the "golden age" of the 18th century' (2001: 17). For unionists this meant buying into the 'superior thought-world' of imperial Britain. For nationalists it meant reconstructing the nation from scratch. Either way, a new Scotland had to be invented. However, says Craig:

In academic terms, the re-imagining of Scotland took the form of the recovery of the sense of the Scottish past as precisely the opposite of the history of negation inherited from the early part of the 20th century. Scottish history and culture were reconceived in terms not of negations but in terms of fundamental continuities. (2001: 19–20)

Scotland, we can now see, never really 'ended', but survived and developed as a civil society within a state whose major focus was on imperial ventures in which Scots played a major part. The fact that this empire itself is now 'history' and new processes of cultural and political revival are transparent have made the old pessimistic order passé. The interweaving of social, political, cultural and economic processes means that studying Scotland is not the simple preserve of sociologists, political scientists, cultural historians and economists. It is the fruitful interaction of disciplines and perspectives which have reinvigorated the study of Scotland.

Chapter summary

What have we learned in this chapter?

- the conceptual tools for understanding Scotland sociologically;

- how the concept 'society', and in particular 'civil society', is useful in understanding Scotland;

- the historical and philosophical roots of this approach in the Scottish Enlightenment;

- how social institutions contribute to 'being Scottish';

- how our understanding of the term 'society' is extended by analysing Scotland sociologically.

In the first three chapters of this book we have set the scene for the rest of the book in terms of 'framing Scotland'. The first two chapters have used the rich and vibrant historiography of Scotland to locate Scotland in time. This third chapter has provided the conceptual tools for understanding Scotland sociologically.

The next part of the book is called 'People and Power' and explores the social structures and institutions which shape Scotland, starting with its population and demography. We then examine structures of power and what determines the life chances of people in Scotland.[10] The following chapters focus on key institutional aspects such as education, gender, social order, 'race' and ethnicity, and religion. The third part of the book examines 'cultural' dimensions: belonging, heritage and the uses of 'history', and national identity.

In the final part, we explore how Scotland is culturally represented. We do this by looking at the Scottish diaspora abroad, sport, the media, consumption and, finally, Scotland in the world. Just as history, economy, culture and politics are vital to a rounded sociology of Scotland, so too is our need to understand where we have come from, the people we used to be. Let us begin, then, with demography.

Questions for discussion

1. What do we mean by the term 'society'? How does it differ from terms like 'state' and 'nation'?

2. How did sociological thinking emerge from the Scottish Enlightenment? What impact, if any, did it have on the development of the discipline?

3. Does the concept 'civil society' help us to understand Scotland in a sociological way?

4. How meaningful is it to refer to 'British society', and in which contexts?

5. What are the key social institutions which make Scotland a 'society'?

Annotated reading

(a) On the sociological perspective, Tom Burns' essay is a good place to start: T. Burns, 'Sociological Explanation' (www.sociology.ed.ac.uk/tomburns/burns_inaugural196_sociologicalexplanation.pdf) (1970); see also C. Wright Mills, *The Sociological Imagination* (1959); P. Berger, *Invitation to Sociology: A humanistic perspective* (1963); E. Durkheim, *Elementary Forms of the Religious Life* (2008 [1912]); J. Urry, *Sociology beyond Societies: Mobilities for the 21st century* (1999).

(b) On the Scottish Enlightenment and the emergence of sociology, see B. Eriksson, 'The first formulation of sociology: a discursive innovation of the 18th century', *European Journal of Sociology*, 34(2), 1993; A. Ferguson, *An Essay on the History of Civil Society* (1966 [1767]); J. Hearn, 'Demos before democracy: ideas of nation and society in Adam Smith', *Journal of Classical Sociology*, 15(4), 2015.

(c) On 'civil society', see D. McCrone, 'Recovering civil society: does sociology need it?', in P. Baert et al. (eds), *Conflict, Citizenship and Civil Society* (2010); L. Paterson, 'Civil society and democratic renewal', in S. Baron et al. (eds), *Social Capital: Critical perspectives* (2000b); K. Kumar, 'Civil society: an inquiry into the usefulness of a historical term', *British Journal of Sociology*, 44(3), 1993; S. Kaviraj and S. Khilnani (eds), *Civil Society: History and possibilities* (2001).

Notes

1 For a lucid account, see Peter Berger's *Invitation to Sociology* (1963), now rather old, but influential for a generation of sociologists. It carried the subtitle 'A humanistic perspective'.

2 C. Wright Mills wrote: 'every cobbler thinks leather is the only thing, and for better or worse, I am a sociologist' (1959: 19n.).

3 That 'civil society' is a concept in use in Scotland is reflected in the fact that the Scottish Council for Voluntary Organisations (SCVO) edits and publishes a quarterly journal called *View: Policy Insights from Scottish Civil Society.*

4 The Identity Cards Act 2006, introduced by the Labour government, was to be linked to a database called the National Identity Register. The Act was repealed in 2011 by the incoming Conservative–Liberal Democrat coalition government.

5 Apart, that is, from the 'North British' Hotel in Edinburgh, opened in 1902, which had its name changed in 1991 to 'The Balmoral'. Thus ended the last vestige of 'North Briton'.

6 I am indebted to John Hall for reminding me of the Swiss case, and of Andreas Wimmer's work.

7 Northern Ireland is included to make the general point, even though its people are 'nationally' divided along political–religious lines, one owing allegiance to the UK and the other to the Republic of Ireland.

8 *Imprimatur* means the official seal of approval, and originally referred to books which had the approval of the Roman Catholic Church (*nihil obstat*, meaning that there was 'nothing in the way' of publication).

9 The question in parenthesis is his, not mine.

10 As far as possible, and without making it too tedious, I will use the term 'people in Scotland' rather than 'Scots' to make the point that not everyone living in Scotland considers themselves Scottish, and, indeed, many who do live furth of Scotland.

PEOPLE AND POWER

4

SCOTLAND'S PEOPLE[1]

I n this chapter we will explore Scotland's population and demography, and in the next pay particular attention to patterns of morbidity (disease) and mortality (death). Our focus in this chapter is mainly on the last hundred years, but it is important to situate changes in the context of Scotland's history as one of the first societies in the world to industrialise and urbanise.

Chapter aims

- To show how Scotland's population has grown in the long term, although relatively slowly compared with other societies.

- To examine the shape of Scotland's population structure, in terms of age and gender, over the last century.

- To chart how the key components of population, that is fertility (births), mortality (deaths) and migration (both outgoing and incoming), have shaped Scotland in the last century.

- To look at how population *within* Scotland has changed in order to appreciate how diverse Scotland is, that there are 'multiple Scotlands'.

- To establish population changes as a basis for understanding the 'sociology' of Scotland, and people's attachment to place, a theme which will be developed in later chapters.

How Scotland's population grew

Let us begin by looking at how Scotland's population has grown since the middle of the eighteenth century (see Figure 4.1).

The graph shows that the steepest rise in population occurred during the nineteenth century when Scotland was being transformed into an industrial society. At the beginning of that century, Scotland had a population of around 1.6 million, which in the next half-century increased by 80 per cent. By 1901, the population was just under 4.5 million,

FIGURE 4.1
Estimated
population
of Scotland,
1755–2013

Sources: Webster,
Censuses, five-
year means from
the *Registrar-
General's Annual
Review* (2005),
omitting 1943

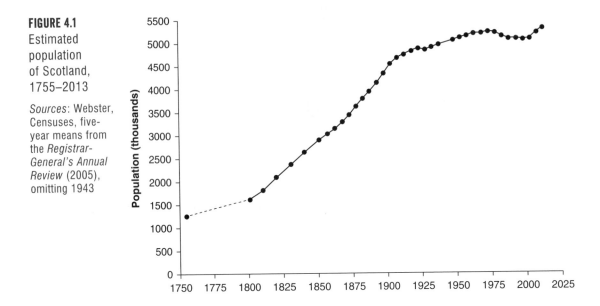

a rise of 55 per cent in the previous half-century. Thereafter, population growth levelled off such that growth in the next fifty years was only of the order of 13 per cent, reaching 5.1 million, marginally below where it stands today. Between 1900 and 2000 we can see that the growth line is more or less flat. Only post-2001 has Scotland's population risen significantly, by 5 per cent in the first decade.

International comparisons

But surely, we might think, Scotland was similar to other places, that slower population growth must also have occurred in comparable societies? It turns out not to be so. Of all the twenty-five EU states in 2001, only Scotland, Hungary, Latvia and Estonia had a smaller population than in 1971, and those last three underwent the major upheaval of post-communism, which had the dramatic effect of cutting populations substantially.

Indeed, Scotland has been one of the least demographically dynamic countries in north-west Europe, and, taking the long period from 1850 to 2000, only Ireland grew less, and it suffered the catastrophic effects of major famine in the middle of the nineteenth century. Nevertheless, as our second graph (Figure 4.2) shows, between 1951 and 2001, Ireland,[2] along with Sweden, Norway and Denmark, grew by more than 20 per cent and the Netherlands by well over 50 per cent.

British comparisons

Scotland is unusual, even within the British Isles, for in the second half of the twentieth century the populations of both England and Wales grew (by 19 per cent and 20 per cent respectively), while Scotland's fell by more than 30,000. Indeed, compared with England, Scotland's population

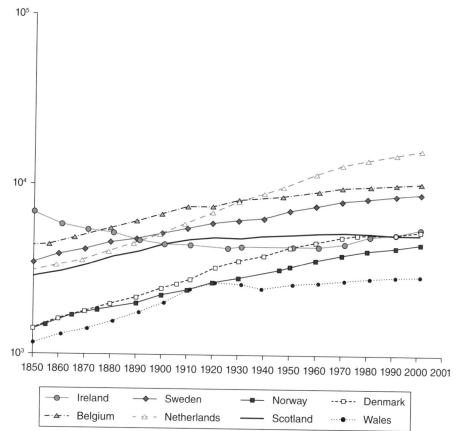

FIGURE 4.2
Population, selected small north-western European countries, c.1850–2001

Source: I am grateful to Michael Anderson for allowing me to use this graph from his forthcoming book on Scotland's population history. In subsequent graphs and tables, where the source is not given, they have been provided by him

Legend:
- ⊙— Ireland
- ◆— Sweden
- ■— Norway
- --□-- Denmark
- --▲-- Belgium
- - △ - Netherlands
- — Scotland
- ·····●···· Wales

growth has been slower in every decade for more than 200 years. In 1851 England's population was about six times that of Scotland, and by 1901, seven times. By 2011, the differential was ten to one, and population estimates suggest the gap between England and Scotland will grow. We can see (Table 4.1) how Scotland's population growth lagged behind other countries in these islands.

Since the middle of the nineteenth century, Scottish population growth has been much lower than England's and, compared with Wales, was lower throughout the second half of the twentieth century. While Ireland as a whole followed a very different pattern, reflecting famine and mass emigration in the second half of the nineteenth century, population growth since the 1960s has been far in excess of Scotland's. There can be little doubt, then, that compared with other countries, at home or abroad, and over the longer term, Scotland has significantly lower levels of population growth.

Predicted population change

On current population projections produced for the Registrar General's 2014 Annual Report, Scotland is close to the median, marginally above other EU countries, but significantly lower than England (see Figure 4.3).

TABLE 4.1 Intercensal rates of increase or decrease of population, component parts of Great Britain and Ireland, 1851–2011

Years	England	Scotland	Wales	Ireland[1]
1851–61	13.2	6.0	11.4	−12.9
1861–71	13.5	9.7	9.3	−6.7
1871–81	12.1	11.2	10.9	−4.4
1881–91	13.0	7.8	12.7	−9.1
1891–1901	12.1	11.1	13.6	−5.2
1901–11	10.3	6.5	20.4	−1.5
1911–21	4.7	2.5	9.7	–
1921–31	6.0	−0.8	−2.4	–
1931–9	4.7	3.4	−5.4	–
1939–51	5.3	1.8	6.0	–
1951–61	5.6	1.6	1.7	0.3
1961–71	5.9	1.0	3.3	3.9
1971–81	1.7	−0.9	3.0	10.5
1981–91	2.3	−1.9	2.1	2.8
1991–2001	3.3	−0.4	1.3	9.4
2001–11	7.4	4.6	5.3	14.1

[1] The 1921 partition of Ireland into the Irish Free State and Northern Ireland means that data were not available for the whole of Ireland between 1911 and 1951

Source: Michael Anderson, see Figure 4.2

FIGURE 4.3 Projected percentage population change in selected European countries, 2012–37

Source: National Records of Scotland, Office for National Statistics (ONS) (UK and constituent countries) and Eurostat

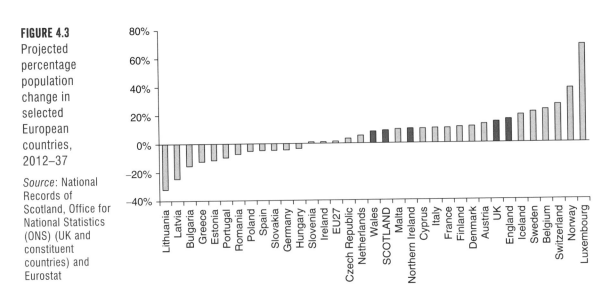

The changing shape of Scotland's population

So why has Scotland's population grown more modestly than elsewhere? The overall size of the population gives us an aggregate picture, for populations have three major components, namely births, deaths and migration, which determine the overall size and shape of the population. First of all, let us look at the shape of Scotland's population in terms of its age distribution at three time-points: 1911, 1951 and 2001.[3]

Early twentieth century: 1911

In 1911 there were far more young people than old people: the gradient (see Figure 4.4) is almost a straight line running from top left to bottom right. We can also see the lower proportion of men to women, especially in the 20 to 30 age group, reflecting the effects of the First World War, as well as post-war emigration by young men, a feature which had been evident from at least the middle of the nineteenth century. This meant, of course, a surplus of young women to young men, with implications for opportunities to marry. At the beginning of the twentieth century, there was a relatively high birth rate (25.7 live births per 1000) such that women who married aged 22 to 26 had on average six children, which today might seem extraordinary. In a population of 4.7 million, few people made it beyond the age of 50, and 113 out of 1000 babies died before their first birthday. The main cause of death in Scotland was infectious diseases, notably tuberculosis.

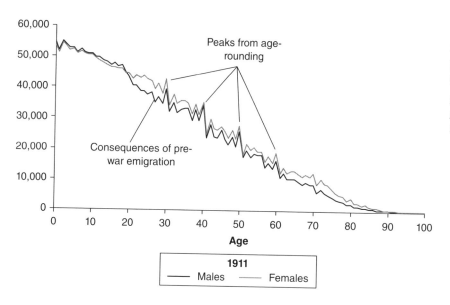

FIGURE 4.4
Scotland's population by age, 1911[4]

Source: Michael Anderson, see Figure 4.2

Mid-twentieth century: 1951

By 1951, the big fluctuations for men and for women reflect fertility patterns associated with the two world wars, with low birth rates during these wars and 'baby booms' which followed them. By mid-century there was no longer a simple gradient running from young

FIGURE 4.5
Scotland's
population,
1951[5]

Source: Michael
Anderson, see
Figure 4.2

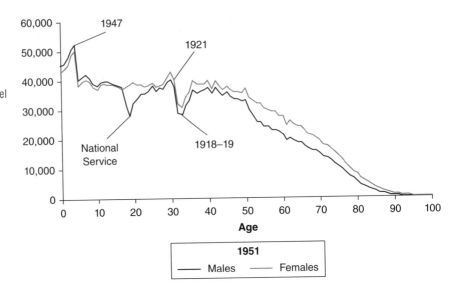

to old. The 'lumpiness' of the graph in Figure 4.5 reflects the disruption of wars on fertility patterns, and we can see the beginnings of longevity among people over 40. The 'straight line' effect, from young to old, which we saw in the 1911 graph, is diminishing.

The graph has broadened out in the middle, reflecting greater survival rates into middle age and the fact that life expectancy for women had risen to 72, and for men, to 66.[6] We can also see the longer term effects of wars and migration reflected in the lower numbers of men aged over 50. By 1951, Scotland's population had reached 5.1 million, but would have been significantly higher but for substantial net out-migration from Scotland in the inter-war and post-war periods, as well as losses in the two world wars (estimates put First World War losses at 100,000 (www.nrscotland.gov.uk/files//statistics/rgar-invited-chapter/rgar-2013-invited-chapter.pdf) and the Second World War at 50,000).

A post-war baby boom followed the Second World War, making up for a relatively low birth rate in the 1930s and early 1940s. The average number of children born to a woman over her lifetime was rising, in part due to a trend towards people marrying younger (in 1971, the average marrying age was 24 for men and 22 for women), which had the effect of extending childbearing years. Infant mortality rates had also improved, down from 82 deaths per 1000 in 1931 to 37 in 1951, and down further to 26 per 1000 in 1961. In addition, there was evidence of more active birth control practice across most of the population, with highly restricted fertility in the 1930s and also a falling off of fertility from its immediate post-war baby boom after 1947.

Twenty-first century: 2001

By the beginning of the twenty-first century, the patterns had changed once more (see Figure 4.6).

In marked contrast to the 1911 pattern, there were fewer children aged 0 to 4 than in *any* age group below the ages of 60 to 64. This reflected a marked restraint on fertility

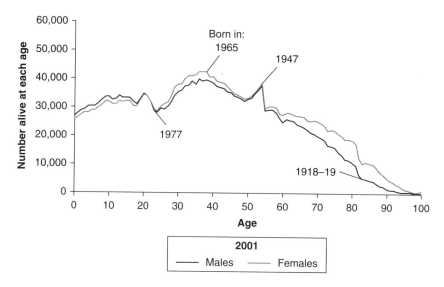

FIGURE 4.6
Scotland's
population, 2001

Source: Michael
Anderson, see
Figure 4.2

which had been continuing, with some fluctuations, for more than thirty years and especially, and with growing impact, since the late 1980s. The slumps in fertility during two world wars and their subsequent baby booms can still be seen among people who were in their fifties and their eighties at the turn of the century.

The medium-term consequences of the baby boom of the mid-1960s stand out, as do the subsequent reductions in births in the years around 1950 and especially the late 1970s. The gap between men and women in terms of survival rates continued to be evident: notice, for example, the gap (marked on the graph) between men and women born in 1918–19. The gender gap among those in the oldest age groups largely reflects the war and emigration losses of the first twenty-five years of the twentieth century. The effect is amplified by growing differences in death rates among older men and women, reflecting growing differential mortality, mainly from smoking-related cancers and heart and circulatory diseases, especially among men. We will explore this in detail in the next chapter.

Scotland's population today

By 2011, Scotland's population had risen to an all-time high of 5.3 million, but the obvious change related to Scotland's ageing population. In 1911, for example, only one person in twenty was 65 and older; 100 years later, it was one in six. People could expect to live to the age of 81 (for women) and 76 (for men), which meant that people in Scotland could expect to live at least twenty-five years longer than their 1911 ancestors. It was as if a whole generation span had been added to the population. Fewer children were being born: the **total fertility rate**, which is based on the age-specific fertility rates of women in their childbearing years, that is aged 15–49, was 1.7.[7] Infant mortality rates were down to only 4 deaths in 1000 (contrast that with 113 in 1911). There had also been a dramatic shift in age of marriage,[8] rising to 33 for men and 31 for women, an increase of two years in a decade (www.nrscotland.gov.uk/news/2013/more-marriages-in-scotland).

To be sure, such trends are broadly common to all advanced industrial countries reflecting greater affluence, more use of birth control, better medical care and improved social conditions generally. But all is not quite what it seems. True, what has happened in Scotland happened elsewhere, but not always in quite the same way or in the same mix. We have already seen that in terms of its population size, Scotland has failed to keep pace with comparable countries. All in all, we discover that Scotland's demography has unusual features, reflecting its particular economic and social history, and that even when comparing it with other countries in these islands, there are marked differences.

Understanding Scotland's demography

What, then, explains the peculiarities of Scotland's demography? In broad terms there are three key components of population: births (fertility), deaths (mortality) and migration; Scotland's 'difference' relates to how these work together to produce an overall pattern. Thus, in recent years, Scotland has a lower fertility rate than the rest of the UK; its death rate is something of a cause célèbre; and, above all, its historic flows of migration have been unusually high. We will explore these features in depth, but in this chapter we focus on fertility and migration. Scotland's 'way of dying' deserves a chapter in its own right.

Understanding the contexts

In order to make sense of Scotland's demography, we need to understand something of the historical background, changes in the context of its social, political and economic development, for demography is never context-free. Thus, Scotland's rapid transformation to an industrial and urbanised society in the early nineteenth century was important in shaping its population features.

Industrialisation

By mid-nineteenth century, Scotland, after England, was the second most urbanised country on earth, with half its population living in towns. Thus, between 1851 and 1911, the region of Strathclyde (excluding Argyll) grew from under 1 million to well over 2 million. In the next fifty years, Strathclyde grew by less than one-third of a million, and thereafter went into steady population decline. Michael Anderson comments: 'Strathclyde is a principal cause of Scotland's comparative demographic weakness in the twentieth century' (2012: 47). These changes were driven by early and rapid industrialisation in the nineteenth century, and by rapid de-industrialisation in the second half of the twentieth.

However, even if Strathclyde (which contained half of Scotland's population in 1961) is left out of the equation, the rest of Scotland managed only modest population increase

(11 per cent in the century after 1911). Nevertheless, rapid industrialisation in west–central Scotland helped to transform Scotland as a whole, and, in particular, Glasgow, which became a by-word for deprivation and overcrowding. Scotland has been living with the legacy ever since.

Regional differences

The second caveat reflects these regional effects. In truth, there is no single 'Scottish' pattern of demography, for Scotland is a highly diverse country, and there are 'multiple Scotlands' (Anderson, 2012: 46). For example, the changes in the islands and above the Highland line are not the same as those in the lowlands of Scotland; neither are they entirely independent of them. Migration from rural to urban, and from north to south, are interconnected, with rapid urbanisation in the Central Belt acting as a magnet for displaced populations. In short, aggregate Scottish demography is a mosaic of its constituent parts.

Climate and weather

A third contextual factor is an obvious one, but usually taken for granted: Scotland is a cold and wet country. Shetland, for example, is north of Oslo, Stockholm and Helsinki; and Wigtown in south-west Scotland is 500 kilometres north of Plymouth in south-west England. More than 60 per cent of Scotland's land surface is above 500 feet (152 m); this compares with 21 per cent of England's and 22 per cent of Ireland's. Its arable farming zones are few – around 11 per cent, compared with 28 per cent in England. Scotland has a cold and wet climate which marked out its topography and agriculture, and in the Middle Ages was prone to famine and 'dearth' (food scarcity) (see Dawson, 2009; Smout, 2012). Before 1700, in really bad crises, a third of a parish's population often died within a few months (Anderson, 2012: 41). The point is not that weather and climate 'determine' social and economic life in Scotland, but that they are the defining context within which such life (and death) takes place.

There is also an obvious connection between climate, diet and health: what can be grown in a wet and cold climate is limited. After the famine of the 1690s, there was no fall in population, because of agricultural improvement and better welfare support in bad years. We can argue about whether the depopulation of the Highlands, and notably the Clearances, was 'caused' by political and social exploitation post-1745, but we cannot ignore the underlying context of wet and marginal land unable to sustain substantial populations. Anderson has made the point that while sparsely populated places in Scotland have actually increased their populations, in proportional terms they have continued to decline. Furthermore, the availability of mineral resources – coal, iron, shale – which drove much of industrialisation in the Central Belt and marked out its geography helped to shift the balance of Scotland's population from east to west.

Summary

So how best can we summarise population change in Scotland over the last 150 years? In the late nineteenth century, the birth rate exceeded the death rate, but by the twenty-first century they were cancelling each other out. While the annual average number of births had fallen by half over the 150-year period (from 112,000 to 56,000), the number of deaths declined by just one-fifth (from 71,000 to 56,000). By contrast, the **net migration rate** (the number of emigrants minus the number of immigrants) was negative for much of the period, reflecting considerable out-migration, especially between 1901 and 1971. Only in the first decade of the twenty-first century did in-migrants outnumber emigrants, thereby reversing a centuries-old trend.

Let us now look in more detail at fertility, mortality and migration in turn.

Fertility

Changing fertility rates help us to explain Scotland's low level of population increase (see Figure 4.7). In crude terms, births in 2001 were only 40 per cent of what they had been a century previously. It is, however, not simply a question of absolute decline, but in the **general fertility rate**, a measure based on the number of women of childbearing age. The baby boom of the 1960s (see Figure 4.6, page 83 for 2001) fell away steeply in the 1970s and 1980s, and levelled off more gradually thereafter.

FIGURE 4.7
Seeing the Light

Source: Courtesy of David Hawkey

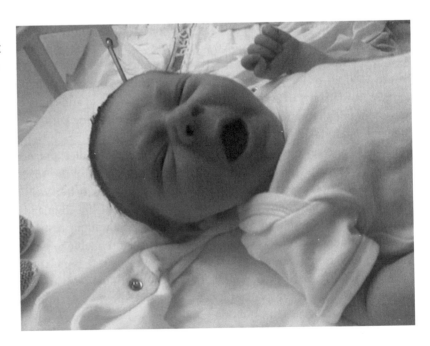

Ageing mothers

In recent years, the dramatic fall in fertility has occurred among women in their twenties, whereas births to older women have increased. Since the mid-1970s, there has been a trend towards women having children at older ages. Indeed, women aged 20 or less now account for 4 per cent of births, which is the same proportion as those born to women aged 40 or more[9] (*Registrar-General's Annual Review of Demographic Trends*, 2014: 23–4). Women over the age of 30 now account for just over half of all births in Scotland. These changes in fertility rates reflect the expansion of labour market participation for younger women, the use of birth control, as well as shifts in lifestyle, changes that Scotland shares with other countries in north-west Europe.

Marriage and fertility

Shifts in fertility are related to patterns of **nuptiality**, the percentage of people in a given population who marry. Indeed, for a century before the Second World War fewer women in Scotland than in England got married, but when they did so, they tended to have more babies. Anderson comments:

> The overall trend in fertility was markedly downward in the later twentieth century. However, this significantly reflected not a flight from childbearing altogether but the near disappearance of very large families, plus a general shift to later childbearing, which itself resulted in more very small families. As late as 1981–5 women's median age at childbearing was 25; by 2001–5 it was 29.3. In the same period, births to non-married mothers rose from 15 per cent to 45 per cent of all births. ... Most of this rise was directly linked to the growth in cohabitation. (2012: 56)

In social trends, we are accustomed to relatively smooth increases and decreases; consider, however, the data in Table 4.2 on the proportion of women at different time-points who were married.

By the beginning of the twentieth century, less than one in ten younger women were married, rising to almost six in ten in 1971 before falling back to one in four in 1991.[10] The figures for women in the second half of their twenties also shows a peak in 1971.

TABLE 4.2   Percentage of women married by age group

Age	1900	1971	1991
20–4	9%	58%	26%
25–9	37%	85%	65%

Source: Registrar-General for Scotland

Cohabitation

In modern times, **cohabitation**, which refers to unmarried couples who live together without formally registering their relationship as a marriage, was uncommon as late as the mid-1970s. There has been a sharp rise in the proportion of births to women who are not married but cohabiting. In 2014, more than half (51 per cent) of births were to unmarried parents, compared with 47 per cent ten years earlier, and 31 per cent in 1994 (*Registrar-General's Annual Review of Demographic Trends*, 2014: 21). At the same time, the proportion of births registered solely in the mother's name has fallen since the late 1990s to just under 5 per cent (it was around 6 to 7 per cent in the 1980s and 1990s), suggesting that the increase in births to unmarried parents has been to cohabiting couples rather than to 'single' mothers.

It is true that more people were cohabiting than ever before (among women aged 20 to 24, twice as many were cohabiting as were married), but young people chose to remain unattached rather than enter formal (married) or informal (cohabiting) relationships. Marriage seems to have become a minority pursuit among young adults, while a quarter of adults over 16 have some experience of having been married, but are no longer, at least to their original partner.

With these changes have come shifts in the composition of households. Single-adult households are already the most common form, projected to increase by a half in the next twenty years, closely followed by two-adult households, likely to increase by a quarter, changes with obvious implications for housing-stock needs. Concomitant decreases in household forms are likely among larger households (especially containing two or more adults with children), as well as three or more adults, all likely to decrease by one-third.

Mortality

To enable us to make sense of population change in Scotland, we need to explore patterns of mortality and morbidity, namely of death and disease (see Figure 4.8). We will do this in greater detail in the next chapter, but here we sketch out the major aspects. Figure 4.9 shows how Scotland's death rate has changed in relation to the birth rate since the middle of the nineteenth century.

Scotland's towns and cities in the nineteenth century were notoriously bad in terms of insanitary conditions and overcrowding, but twentieth-century improvements meant that the differences between urban and rural areas diminished. Nevertheless, improvements in survival rates in west–central Scotland slowed up, and there was a worsening of death rates from particular conditions such as heart disease.

In the 1980s, researchers began to talk about a 'Glasgow effect' (Carstairs and Morris, 1989) in which, like for like, and taking levels of multiple deprivation into account, living

FIGURE 4.8
Configuring death

Source: Author's photograph. It is striking that the fall in the crude birth rate is more dramatic than changes in the death rate. There are improvements in the death rate by around 20 per cent since mid-nineteenth century, but even by the early twenty-first century Scotland had the lowest life expectancy at birth in Western Europe, even though Scots were living much longer than their parents and grandparents

in Glasgow seems to have its own multiplier effect. In other words, if you lived in Glasgow, you were more likely to suffer from poor health and to have lower life expectancy than if you lived elsewhere. Indeed, the gap between local authority areas in terms of expectation of life actually worsened for women, and stayed about the same for men. Improvements were much slower for older people, especially those suffering from chronic conditions.

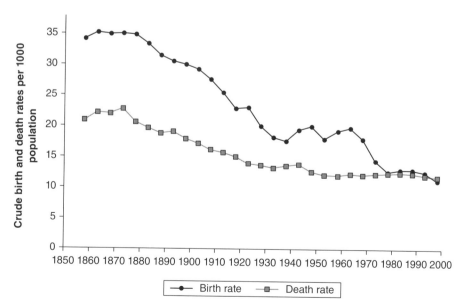

FIGURE 4.9
Crude birth and death rates, per 1000 population, Scotland, 1855–2000

Source: General-Register Office for Scotland GRO(S): mid-intercensal year population estimates

Anderson observed:

> By contrast, big improvements from improved sanitation and living standards impacted much earlier on deaths, especially from infectious diseases, of children and young adults. In the 1860s a fifth of baby girls died between their first and fifth birthdays, by the 1890s this was down to one in eight, and by the 1930s to one in eighteen; aided by antibiotics, by 2000–2 it was one in 200. And of women reaching 15 but dying before 45, the parallel figures were a quarter, a fifth, one in nine, and once mortality associated with childbirth and tuberculosis had been brought under control after the 1930s, one in fifty. (2012: 57)

Accounting for population change

So far in this chapter we have sketched out the key demographic components of Scotland's population, namely the birth and death rates and migration. **Natural change** is a simple measure subtracting the number of deaths from the number of births; and **net migration** is produced by subtracting the numbers migrating into Scotland less those migrating out. They provide a useful summary picture of Scotland's demography in the last sixty years (Figure 4.10).

Note two key features on this graph: first, that the excess of births over deaths, which was a feature of the two decades after the Second World War, had disappeared by the mid-1970s. Thereafter, births and deaths virtually cancelled each other out. Second, the historic pattern of out-migration which had been such a feature of Scotland's demography for at least the previous century had been reversed: by the late 1980s inward migration had exceeded outward migration for the first time in Scotland's modern history. Scotland's overall increase in population in the twenty-first century is the result of net inward migration, and not a substantial rise in the birth rate.

FIGURE 4.10
Natural change and net migration, 1951–2014

Source: Registrar-General's Annual Review of Demographic Trends (2014: figure 1.2, 12) (National Records of Scotland): 'Natural change' is births minus deaths; 'Net migration' is inward minus outward migration

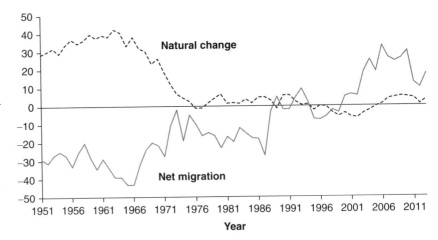

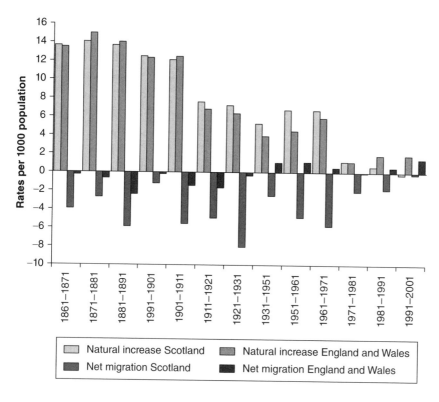

FIGURE 4.11
Natural increase and net migration per 1000 population, 1861–2001, Scotland, England and Wales

Source: Michael Anderson

In terms of differences within the UK, Scotland is much more similar to England and Wales with regard to 'natural increase' than on net migration. As we can see from Figure 4.11, England and Wales had a higher rate of natural increase in the late nineteenth century as well as the latter years of the twentieth, with Scotland having higher rates of natural increase between 1910 and 1960 as a result of its higher birth rate.

Taking births, deaths and migration together, what do the figures tell us about modern Scotland? That Scotland's population barely reproduces itself in terms of rates of natural increase (births over deaths), but that the major component of population growth is inward migration, both from the rest of the UK and from overseas. It is also clear that the very high rates of emigration, such a key feature of much of the twentieth century, have reduced significantly. Compared with England, the Scottish population grew much more slowly in every decade between 1801 and 2001 (Anderson, 2012: 45). While the differentials in 'natural increase' between Scotland on the one hand and England and Wales on the other are modest, what makes the difference is net migration rate, and it is to this topic that we now turn.

Migration

There is a long-standing tradition of Scots emigrating. In the sixteenth and seventeenth centuries, many traders went to continental Europe; Scots went as mercenaries serving in foreign armies, and many never returned; and crossing the North Channel to settle in Ulster was a feature of the late seventeenth and eighteenth centuries. In the seventeenth century about 200,000 Scots left the country, an average of 2 per cent of the population per year (Anderson, 2012). Graeme Morton observes: 'Between 1825 and 1914 it is estimated that 1.84m people left Scotland for non-European destinations, with around 44 per cent heading for America, 28 per cent Canada and 25 per cent Australia and New Zealand' (2010: 257).

The Highlands and Islands, which had a small population in any case, lost a higher proportion of their people. Anderson estimates that 20,000 emigrants to North America between 1765 and 1815 derived from a Highland population of well under 200,000, a serious loss of 10 per cent. Furthermore, 'between 1830 and 1914 about two million people left Scotland for overseas destinations and probably roughly similar numbers went to the rest of the UK, making Scottish emigration per head second in Europe after Ireland' (Anderson, 2012: 52). Dramatic though this was, there was an even older history, for in medieval Scotland, 'Scots were renowned in Europe as mobile people' (2012: 43).

Leaving Scotland

Many Scots had family and friends abroad, so that leaving Scotland became commonplace (see Figure 4.12, 'Lochaber No More', the classic emigration image). Indeed, it was common to follow them as a matter of course, and significant channels were established for people to do that, even to the point of sponsoring migrants by paying their fares and finding them jobs. We will examine the social and cultural significance of this 'diaspora', as it is called, in Chapter 20. Furthermore, people did not have to go 'abroad' to leave Scotland. Many simply crossed the border into England for work, such that even by 2011 there were over 700,000 Scots-born people who were living in England, and while that figure is just over 1 per cent of England's much larger population, it represents over 13 per cent of Scotland's resident population of 5.3 million. Anderson's observation that about 2 million left Scotland between 1830 and 1914 for overseas was probably matched by the same number going to the rest of the UK.[11] This marks Scotland out as a major exporter of people, second only to Ireland.

By the 1920s net migration was more than 8 per cent of Scotland's population, leading to absolute population decline. The pattern was repeated in the 1950s and the 1960s (roughly 6 per cent in each decade). By the 1970s, out-migration declined to about 3 per cent, in the 1980s to 2.4 per cent, and in the 1990s to a mere 0.3 per cent. Scotland contrasted significantly with England where net loss of population was much lower, around 1.7 per cent of the population between 1911 and 1921, just under 1 per cent per decade between 1921 and 1951, and again between 1981 and 2001.

Out-migration was not simply confined to the Highlands and Islands of Scotland. Anderson (2012: 53) calculates that nine out of ten parishes in the whole of Scotland had net out-migration from the 1860s, so that it was the ubiquitous experience for virtually *all* Scottish communities, and not just Highland ones. Most of the farming parishes in rural

FIGURE 4.12
'Lochaber No More', by John Watson Nicol, 1883

Source: I am grateful to The Fleming–Wyfold Art Foundation/ Bridgeman Images for permission to reproduce this image

Scotland – Perthshire, the north-east, the south-east and south-west in particular – suffered population losses far higher than the Highlands and Islands. So too did urban and industrial parishes. Anderson observes: 'in a UK or European context, after 1870 at least one of Glasgow, Edinburgh, Dundee and Aberdeen (by the 1900s all the four) experienced net outflow in every decade' (2012: 53).

Who were the migrants?

Scotland's story of demography is dominated by migration. It has been the ubiquitous experience for many people, and most families have immediate relatives living furth of Scotland. It has been an important safety valve in times of need, but emigration from Scotland was as much about aspiration as it was about necessity. By and large, Scots were more skilled and tended to be 'economic migrants', although the mix of 'push' and 'pull' factors is hard to estimate. On the one hand, lack of jobs at home drove many men, the unattached young in particular, to migrate, either to England or overseas. On the other hand, it tended to be people with skills, rather than the unemployed, who migrated in search of a better life.

Furthermore, it was much more a matter of using established contacts and channels, familial or community, than finding yourself cast adrift as a solitary individual on a foreign shore (see Harper, 2003). Skilled workers were significantly over-represented in the high emigration years of the early twentieth century. Scots' migration did not compare with the post-famine rates for Ireland in the decades after 1850, but as Anderson observes: 'overall, Scottish numbers per head of population exceeded those of any other country other than Ireland and probably Norway in this period [1860s–1880s] and was actually the highest of any of the Western European countries in the 1920s'. And he goes on: 'both in the 1900s and in the 1920s, Scottish emigration per head of population was markedly in excess even of that from Ireland' (from Baines, 1991: 10).

Post-war migration

In the period following the Second World War, Scottish emigration took up where it had left off before the war, broadly split between overseas and UK emigration (see Figure 4.13).

We can see from Figure 4.13 that, with a few exceptions, migration overseas matches that to the rest of the UK. The 1960s levels were particularly high in the light of economic restructuring post-war (see Chapters 8 and 9), and net emigration overseas continued until the 1990s. The net annual outflow of population from greater Glasgow in the late 1960s

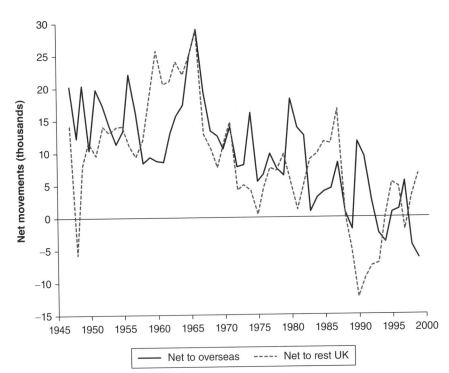

FIGURE 4.13 Net migration from Scotland, by destination/origin, 1947–99/2000

Note: Data for 1947–50 are for calendar years; from 1951 for mid-year starting in the year plotted

Source: Registrar-General for Scotland, Annual Reports

was particularly strong, representing almost 90 per cent of total net migration outflow. Reflecting what was to come later in the century, net emigration for Edinburgh and Aberdeen, and the more prosperous south-east, was less marked.

Reverse migration

It was in the 1990s that noticeable reverse migration began to occur, with immigrants outnumbering emigrants for the first time in Scotland's demographic history. Most immigrants came from the rest of the UK, notably from England. Thus, by 2011, nearly 13 per cent, or one in eight, of the Scottish population was born outwith Scotland, an increase of nearly 11 per cent on 1991, and most of them were born in England. By 2011, 8 per cent of people living in Scotland had been born in England, compared with 7 per cent in 1991 (Scotland's 2011 Census).

In this regard, immigration into Scotland differs from that into England, where most immigrants were born overseas. A significantly high percentage of 'British' immigrants to England came from Scotland. Only 2 per cent of the English population were Scots, but such people represented some 16 per cent of Scotland's own population, a higher proportion than fifty years before. Even by 2001, some 9 per cent of people living in England and Wales had been born outwith the UK, compared with about 4 per cent in Scotland. In this respect, Scotland's relationship to 'immigrants' is quite different to that of England's, with people born in England representing the largest proportion of immigrants to Scotland. Whether English-born people coming to Scotland thought of themselves as 'immigrants' is a moot point, given the racial connotations it conjured up.

By 2013–14, migration from the rest of the UK contributed most to Scotland's population growth, followed by net migration from overseas (see Table 4.3).

We can see that the inflows from the rest of the UK and overseas to Scotland are greater than the outflows, and so there are migration gains of 17,600.

TABLE 4.3 Migration between Scotland and rest of UK/overseas, 2013–14

	In	Out	Net
Rest of UK	49,240	39,660	9600
Overseas	33,200	25,200	8000
Total	82,440	64,860	17,600

Source: Registrar-General's Annual Review of Demographic Trends, 2014

Sub-national trends

To be sure, Scotland had long experience of immigrants, whether from near or far. Its major cities in particular reflected these trends. Thus, in 1851, a majority of the

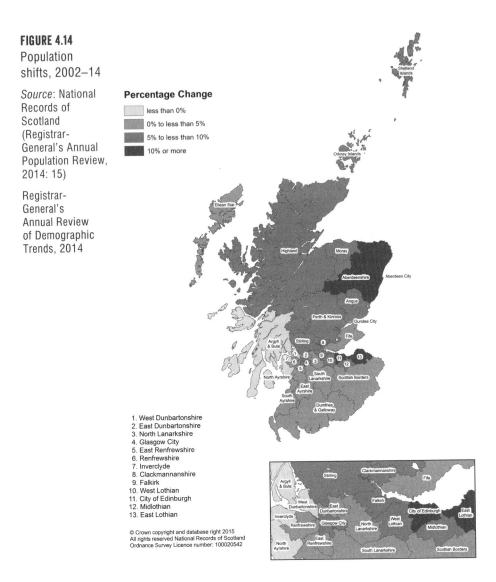

FIGURE 4.14
Population
shifts, 2002–14

Source: National
Records of
Scotland
(Registrar-
General's Annual
Population Review,
2014: 15)

Registrar-
General's
Annual Review
of Demographic
Trends, 2014

Percentage Change

less than 0%
0% to less than 5%
5% to less than 10%
10% or more

1. West Dunbartonshire
2. East Dunbartonshire
3. North Lanarkshire
4. Glasgow City
5. East Renfrewshire
6. Renfrewshire
7. Inverclyde
8. Clackmannanshire
9. Falkirk
10. West Lothian
11. City of Edinburgh
12. Midlothian
13. East Lothian

populations of both Glasgow and Dundee had been born outwith the cities (respectively, 56 per cent and 54 per cent), with Edinburgh (50 per cent) and Aberdeen (45 per cent) not far behind. By 1961, the figures for Glasgow and Dundee had fallen to around one-quarter, while 'non-natives' in both Edinburgh and Aberdeen were more significant (just over one-third).

By the beginning of the twenty-first century, a much higher proportion of the populations of Edinburgh and Aberdeen were born in England and Wales (13 per cent and 9 per cent), compared with 6 per cent for Dundee and 4 per cent in Glasgow. Glasgow's historic links with Ireland had diminished in terms of Irish-born residents, down from 3 per cent in 1961 to 1.7 per cent in 2001, but the city was home to overseas migrants, mainly from the Indian sub-continent. Thus, between 2001 and 2005, 9 per cent of births in the city were to Asian-born mothers, a figure which does not include people of Asian origin who had been born in the UK and had migrated to the city. This, however, continues the tradition of inward migration to Glasgow, even though, by 2001, only 10 per cent of the city's population had not been born in Scotland, compared with 22 per cent of Edinburgh's. Total net migration into Glasgow increased between 2001 and 2011 as the number of migrants arriving exceeded the number leaving, principally due to an increase in overseas migrants coming to Glasgow.

Shifting Scotlands

These variations in the ethnic mix of Scotland's cities remind us that 'Scotland' as such is an amalgam of different spatial features and experiences – that there are many Scotlands. In this section, we will explore some of the key ones. First of all, let us look at how Scotland has changed spatially in the decade since 2004 (see map of Scotland, Figure 4.14).

The largest percentage increases have occurred in the east of Scotland, in Aberdeenshire (+11.0 per cent), East Lothian (+10.7 per cent) and Edinburgh City (+10.5 per cent); and there has been population loss in Inverclyde (–3.4 per cent), Argyll & Bute (–3.2 per cent) and West Dunbartonshire (–2.4 per cent). The net gains and losses in population are not simply the result of more in-migration, but a complex outcome of differential births, deaths and migration patterns.

From the Registrar-General's Annual Population Review, 2014

In some areas where the population has increased since mid-2004, such as North Lanarkshire, Shetland Islands and West Lothian, the gain is attributable to both migration and natural increase (more births than deaths). East Lothian, Stirling and Dundee City have experienced a population increase because of in-migration combined with a relatively low (positive) natural change. In other areas, the population increase is due to in-migration, despite the number of deaths exceeding the number of births. These areas included Eilean Siar, Angus and Perth & Kinross. Inverclyde and West Dunbartonshire have experienced population decreases both from migration and natural change, whereas in Argyll & Bute the population decline is mainly attributable to more deaths than births. (Registrar-General's Annual Population Review, 2014: 14)

TABLE 4.4   Population changes in Scotland's four main cities, 2004–14

	Natural change	Net migration	Percentage population change
Aberdeen	1.8	8.4	10.2
Dundee	0.1	3.5	3.6
Edinburgh	2.3	8.2	10.5
Glasgow	1.0	4.3	5.3

Source: Registrar-General's Annual Review of Demographic Trends, 2014: 42

Table 4.4 shows how Scotland's four main cities have changed. Both Aberdeen and Edinburgh have higher levels of 'natural change' (more births than deaths) *and* of net migration, whereas Dundee and Glasgow have lower levels of both.

In the longer term there has been a shift of population from west to east, just as in the heyday of industrialisation in the nineteenth century when it was the other way round. In 1961 Glasgow had a population of over 1 million and by 2011 it stood at just under 600,000, a drop of 40 per cent. Edinburgh, with its population of just under half a million, is nowadays around 20 per cent smaller than Glasgow's, but in 1961 the capital was only half of Glasgow's size.

This, however, is not simply a debate between Scotland's major cities, but reflects the complex and historic diversity of the country: between islands and mainland; urban and rural; cities and hinterlands; as well as Highlands/Lowlands, north/south and east/west. These are not simply geographical distinctions, but places with meaning, imbued with cultural characteristics. We will explore this in Chapter 15 when we look at 'belonging' in Scotland. We will argue that people feel attached to place. 'Glasgow belongs to me' is not a legal statement, but a form of cultural claim. Similarly, if we were to say by way of short-hand that in the nineteenth century at least 'Glasgow killed people', we do not mean that literally, still less that the city fathers employed death squads. We mean that living in the city drastically shortened your life, such that regardless of your age, sex, social class and religion, your propensity to suffer disease, and possibly to die, was enhanced. This patently was because severe insanitary conditions in a city which grew rapidly in the early nine-teenth century (Glasgow trebled its population between 1851 and 1911) and horrendous overcrowding (densities were higher than anywhere else) increased drastically morbidity and mortality as we shall see in the next chapter.

If we assume that the characteristics of an area are also true for individuals who live there, we run the risk of what is called the 'ecological fallacy'. (We cannot assume that the characteristics of individuals are those of the place in which they live.) There is some link between spatial and individual characteristics, but we cannot impute one to the other. The demography of different parts of the cities of both Edinburgh and Glasgow contained, and still contain, huge contrasts in terms of mortality, fertility patterns and migration flows. 'Averages', especially for these two cities, are misleading, given the inter-nal variations they contain.

Understanding population

What could be more basic than a country's population? It is a litmus test of its strengths and weaknesses, how its economic and social fortunes wax and wane. We can 'read' these fortunes in its people. The social historian Christopher Smout has made the following startling statement:

> Scotland at the opening of the twenty-first century was apparently set on the road to environmental disaster. It could hardly be otherwise. It was a small but whole-hearted and generally successful part of a global economy growing out of control at an unprecedented rate. (2012: 33)

Given that Scotland's population had stabilised and begun to grow again after a long inter-lude, and its general rate of economic growth, that might seem a perverse judgement. But Smout is correct. Scotland's global footprint showed in 2009 that if everyone else lived as we do, we would need two earths simply to survive. It makes the point that our small, marginal, north-west European country is a major beneficiary of the world's resources – that we consume far more than we should do, per head of population.

The fragile land

When all is said and done, Scotland is a marginal land. It has two major disadvantageous features, altitude and slope (Smout, 2012). While it contains tracts of fertile low arable land, especially in the east, only 40 per cent of Scotland is below 500 feet (152 m) and almost one-third is above 1000 feet (305 m). Its second disadvantage is climate. It endures 'more wind and rain, more cold and shorter growing seasons than most other parts of the British Isles' (2012: 21). Even its valleys historically contained much low ground adversely affected by underlying clay soils and schists. This helped to generate crop failures, dearths and famines, especially before the eighteenth century.

Technological improvements and new forms of cultivation helped to banish these, and population growth showed this success, reflected by the mid-nineteenth century in the concentration of people in towns and cities where the work was. We treat these expansions as proof of success, but they reflect huge investment of time, money and technology, espe-cially as much of our historical geography was dependent on exploiting the mineral resources under our land and seas. The transformation of Scotland by agricultural improve-ments, but above all by industrial expansion, latterly driven by North Sea oil off our shores, has fuelled a new society, economy and politics, but the transformation remains fragile.

Furthermore, we are no longer the people we used to be. There are more of us than ever before; we live longer and healthier; we enjoy higher standards of living; we encourage others to come and live among us, at rates the highest in our modern history. This has meant that we are no longer a people defined by emigration but by immigration. To be sure, it is part of our story that there are far more people of Scots extraction living outwith Scotland than within it, although we cannot be sure how big the 'diaspora' is, dependent as it is on claims by others. Nevertheless, it helps to define how we see ourselves, as well as how others see us, and has become embedded in our sense of selves. We will return to these themes later (in Chapters 15 and 20 in particular).

New Scots

Scotland attracts far fewer 'immigrants' than other parts of these islands, notably England, but in a context of an ageing population this is broadly welcomed by the political classes. There is no sustained political movement or party which desires to restrict immigration, no 'little Scotland' movement. That this has occurred derives from an economic and social need to retain population in a country which as recently as the 1970s lost far more people than it gained. That such immigrants are encouraged to 'be Scots' is a mark of economic need as well as Scottish pride. As we shall see when we focus on 'national identity' (Chapters 18 and 19), claims to be Scottish are made regardless of birthplace and skin colour, although not all such claims are successful especially day to day and at 'street level' (see Chapter 13 on 'race' and ethnicity).

Population politics

Since the creation of a devolved parliament in 1999, the narrative on cohesiveness and 'integration' has gained pace. Talking the talk about social and ethnic cohesion is aided by the cultural diversity of Scotland. We have inherited a 'sense of place' rather than a 'sense of tribe' (Smout, 1994: 107), because we have had little option, but we have made necessity its own virtue. It would have been very difficult to hang a cohesive Scotland upon a single cultural marker – religion, language, geography – in a land so varied and so diverse. We would have excluded far too many people for our own good. And so we accept that there are many Scotlands, and different ways of being Scottish.

It is arguably to our benefit that there is no single dominant metropolis, like London, Paris or Dublin; no city region which sucks in so many resources, people and power. Even the tensions between the biggest city, Glasgow, and the capital city, Edinburgh, are advantageous such that no place becomes dominant. The tensions are healthy. Other cities such as Aberdeen, Dundee, Inverness and Perth are distinct in their culture and identity, with football teams, newspapers and social histories which ensure that these are jealously guarded. As the social anthropologist Anthony Cohen (2000) put it, there is a Glasgow way of being Scottish, and an Aberdeen way, and many other ways. Such a claim is also reflected in statements about Scotland being a 'mongrel nation', that the territorial claim outbids the lineage one. These are issues to which we will return later in the book.

Conclusion

So does population really matter? We might be tempted to see the study of population and demography as a technical and statistical exercise devoid of context; to think that it has little social and political meaning. In fact, population matters have a long and sometimes fractious political context: that the country is 'full up'; that there is a fear of being 'swamped' by a tide of incoming migrants;[12] that somehow we are diluted and diminished by incomers. In terms of domestic politics too, population matters to Scotland.

The **Barnett formula** determines the allocation of public spending and is derived from the older late nineteenth-century Goschen formula by which Scotland received 11/80ths of the allocation to England (Levitt, 2014). The relative size of the populations of the two countries matters, then, in terms of public money, and much of the debate about the formula hangs around the relative decline of Scotland's share of population. As the economic historian Jim Tomlinson observed: 'Insufficient recognition of the inadequacies of Barnett as a measure of "fair spending" helps us understand why the search for a "correct" formula for allocating spending was to prove as problematic after the 1970s as it had been for the previous century' (2015: 1456). So population matters – in terms of not only the allocation of public resources, but also the political economy of size (large countries have, broadly speaking, more power than small ones) and our conception of ourselves ('small and friendly' versus 'big and anonymous').

Chapter summary

So what have we learned in this chapter?

- That Scotland's population has grown substantially over the centuries, and while it has never been larger, it has lagged behind population growth in other countries, notably that in the rest of these islands.

- That Scotland's population is now older than it has ever been, not simply because people live longer but because the proportion of children and young people is smaller than it has ever been, something which has implications for the labour force, the housing stock and public services.

- Longevity is partly the result of improved health and social conditions, notably in Scotland's cities and principal towns, but the major influence on the rate of 'natural increase' is the fall in the birth rate rather than the death rate.

- The distinguishing feature of Scotland's demography, however, has been the long-standing patterns of migration. Historically, Scotland is a land of emigrants rather than immigrants, and its population stability has reflected its export of people, whether to England or overseas. Only since the 1990s have more people come to Scotland than have left it.

- Finally, whether we like it or not, population size matters. There is little doubt that Scotland's growing population is taken as a measure of its prosperity and economic growth, even though Scots consume far more of the planet's wealth and resources than our population share.

In the next chapter we shall see that Scotland matters in terms not simply of living, but of dying, for few things mark out Scotland more than what we have called the 'Scottish way of death'.

Questions for discussion

1. Why has Scotland's population grown more slowly than that of other societies?

2. To what extent are there distinctive features of Scotland's population?

3. What effects have higher rates of out-migration had on Scotland's social structure?

4. What are the social and cultural implications of having a higher proportion of people living in Scotland who were not born there?

5. What are the social, economic and cultural effects of de-industrialisation on shifts in Scotland's population?

Annotated reading

(a) For useful historical material on Scotland's demography, see T.M. Devine and J. Wormald (eds), *The Oxford Handbook of Modern Scottish History* (2012). In particular, the chapters by: M. Anderson, 'The demographic factor'; T.C. Smout, 'Land and sea: the environment'; T.M. Devine, 'A global diaspora'. See also M. Flinn, *Scottish Population History from the 17th Century to the 1930s* (1977).

(b) The best source of up-to-date data on Scotland's demography is National Records of Scotland, *Scotland's Population: The Registrar General's Annual Reviews of Demographic Trends* (www.nrscotland.gov.uk/statistics-and-data/ statistics/stats-at-a-glance/registrar-generals-annual-review/2014/). Check out the website for previous years, as well as invited chapters on key topics.

Notes

1   I am grateful to Michael Anderson for his help and advice with this chapter as well as Chapter 5, and especially for his generosity in allowing me to use key tables and figures.
2   That is, taking northern and southern Ireland together.
3   The three years are chosen as benchmarks, and the intermediate years simply confirm the pattern (see www.scotlandscensus.gov.uk/century-census).
4   'Age-rounding' (also known as 'age-heaping') refers to the tendency of census enumerators to 'round' up or down people's ages, notably that of babies aged 0 to 1, or for adults to ages such as 30, 40, 50 and 60.
5   National Service was compulsory military or public service in the UK for men aged 17 to 21. It ran from 1948 until 1963.
6   In 1931, life expectancy for women was 60, and for men, 56. Twenty years later, by 1951 (there was no census taken during the war), these figures had risen to 69 and 64 respectively.
7   The total fertility rate is the number of children a woman would have if she were subject to prevailing fertility rates at all ages from a single given year, and survives throughout all her childbearing years.
8   That is, for men and women marrying for the first time, and not including remarriages.

9   The percentage of births to mothers aged 20 or under has fallen from around 11 per cent in the second half of the 1970s to around 4 per cent in 2014.

10 This was an unusually high figure, for between 1851 and 1931 the figure was never more than 25 per cent.

11 Michael Flinn estimated that taking the period 1861 and 1930 as a whole, about half went to England and half overseas. The best figure for migration overseas from Scottish ports between 1853 and 1930 is about 2.1 million (gross figure), which represented 44 per cent of the Scottish population. See Baines (1991: appendix 5).

12 The former UK Prime Minister David Cameron was quoted on 30 July 2015 as saying 'because you have got a swarm of people coming across the Mediterranean seeking a better life, wanting to come to Britain because Britain has got jobs, it's got a growing economy, it's an incredible place to live. But we need to protect our borders by working hand in glove with our neighbours, the French, and that is exactly what we are doing' (www.theguardian.com/uk-news/2015/jul/30/calais-migrants-make-further-attempts-to-cross-channel-into-britain).

5

THE SCOTTISH WAY OF DEATH

Why devote a chapter to dying in Scotland? The short answer is that over the last few decades a view has emerged that health, morbidity and mortality[1] have figured far too prominently in Scotland's story. Plainly put, Scotland is deemed to be 'the sick man of Europe' (Whyte and Ajetunmobi, 2012) with rates of mortality and morbidity (Figure 5.1) far above the European average. Indeed, it is commonplace to find Scotland so described.

FIGURE 5.1
Memento Mori: Greyfriars Kirkyard, Edinburgh

Source: Author's photograph

In 1974 the *Glasgow Herald* used the headline 'Scotland – Sick Man of Europe', commenting that 'Scotland's health record compares unfavourably with other Western countries, with child health and morbidity an area of particular concern', and picking out spending on tobacco, tooth decay and high mortality from coronary heart disease from the published report of the health services in Scotland (*Glasgow Herald*, 19 June 1974). It is common to describe Scotland in this way, and newspapers, the media and political parties have all done so.[2] It is, then, a journalistic device, a shorthand, and is obviously meant to include women as well as men.

Chapter aims

- To see how rates of mortality have changed in Scotland over time.

- To see how particular causes of death have changed.

- To ask whether it is the case that mortality rates in Scotland are significantly worse than in the rest of Europe.

- To discuss whether we are able to explain Scotland's mortality rates in terms of social class and/or areas of multiple deprivation.

- To examine whether there are distinctive 'Scottish' and 'Glasgow effects' such that Scots, and especially Glaswegians, suffer premature disease and death; and if there are, how we might account for these.

Scotland's death rate in the long duration

Let us start by examining how mortality rates have changed over time. Has Scotland regressed, and might we even have reverted back to levels of death and disease not seen for 50 or 100 years? In fact, the Scottish **crude death rate (CDR)** has fallen from 23 per 1000 people in the mid-1870s to 12 per 1000 in the mid-1950s, and remained more or less at that level since then (see Figure 5.2). Broadly speaking the death rate in Scotland is about 10 per cent higher than for England and Wales. The figure shows the trend lines for the crude death rates for the countries of these islands since the mid-nineteenth century.

We can see that for much of the period Scotland was in the middle of the pack, but since the 1970s its position has worsened in relative terms. Nowadays, however, people die from different diseases and conditions than they did 100 years ago. This means that simply reading the trends and drawing conclusions about how 'worse' or, indeed, 'better' Scotland has become is not straightforward.

Measuring mortality

We cannot be sure, however, that the mortality trend line in the figure tells the 'real' story, because how data are recorded, diseases defined, classified and reported, and cause of death

FIGURE 5.2
Crude death
rates per
thousand
population:
Scotland,
Ireland, England
and Wales,
1850–2000

Source: Michael
Anderson

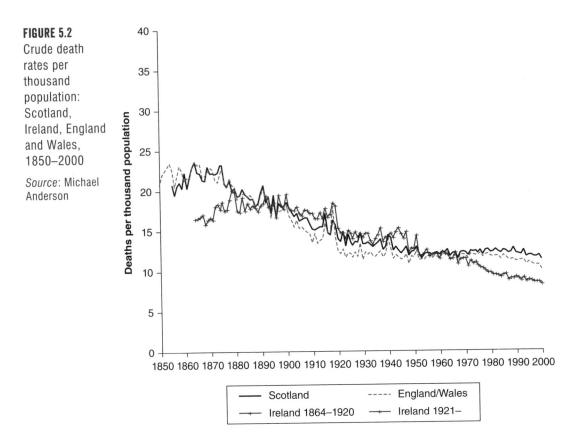

certified may well be reflecting different ways of doing things. Why, for example, in the figure, has Ireland a significantly lower crude death rate than, say, England and Wales, given the catastrophic famine of the mid-nineteenth century and its aftermath (and it does seem surprising that official figures show a *lower* crude death rate for Ireland after 1860, given the disaster of the famine).[3] The answer is that Ireland today has a much younger population, and by dint of that, a lower crude death rate.

This is a key point. There are now proportionately more older people in Scotland than a hundred years ago, and, by and large, most deaths occur in old age. To offset this 'age effect', statisticians use the **age-standardised rates (ASR)** to calculate like for like, comparing death rates among different age groups, which is essential if we wish to say something about how well, or badly, Scotland is doing in terms of death and disease. The age-standardised rate for a geographical area is the number of deaths, usually expressed per 100,000, that would occur if it had the same age structure as the standard population and the local age-specific rates of the area applied.

Contextual effects

We also need to take into account Scotland's economic and social history throughout the period. Scotland can be described as a *post*-industrial society, having been rapidly industrialised and urbanised in the nineteenth century with the health implications which that entailed, whereas southern Ireland[4] was, by and large, *non*-industrialised. So in Scotland we are dealing with a different historical context and the ensuing health legacy. In other words, history matters in that patterns of morbidity and mortality reflect the societies that generated them: we live with their legacy socially and medically.

Scottish towns and cities had very high death rates in the nineteenth century, and life expectancy at birth in Glasgow in the 1890s, for example, was almost ten years below the Scottish average. Michael Anderson has observed: 'Over the century up to 1950, marked improvements in sanitation and living conditions brought crude death rates down much faster in larger towns and cities than in smaller towns and the countryside, though this was helped by general ageing of rural populations' (2012: 57). Improvements in sanitation and living standards impacted much earlier on deaths, especially from infectious diseases, of children and young adults. His figures make the point nicely (Table 5.1).

TABLE 5.1   Proportions of girls in Scotland dying aged 1–5, and women dying aged 15–45, by time period

	Girls dying aged 1–5 years	Women dying aged 15–45 years
1860s	1 in 5	1 in 4
1890s	1 in 8	1 in 5
1930s	1 in 18	1 in 9
2000s	1 in 200	1 in 50

Source: Anderson (2012: 57)

Crude death rates are subject to all sorts of variations: whether people live in towns or in the countryside, the standard of sanitary provisions especially in Scottish towns and cities, the age of the population, and so on. The virtual eradication of childhood infectious diseases, coupled with the fall in family size, means that death has become mainly a feature of old people rather than a feature of all ages. 'Childhood' diseases such as smallpox, measles, scarlatina, whooping cough and diphtheria all but disappeared by the end of the twentieth century in the UK. The demise of tuberculosis (TB) and diseases ascribed to 'dirt' and sanitation in the nineteenth century were replaced in the twentieth by the predominance of circulatory diseases and cancers.

Causes of death

In any case, we cannot be sure about 'causes of death', still less be able to read those causes across time because in a large number of cases no cause of death was reported. Neither today would we accept 'old age' as a cause of death, nor 'convulsions' nor 'galloping consumption'[5] – descriptive rather than analytical categories – which appeared on many historic death certificates. There was also inconsistency, born out of ignorance of epidemiology,[6] but also because of social implications and legal niceties to be observed.

'Cause of death' had insurance implications; for example, pneumoconiosis, occupational lung disease, to which miners were susceptible, triggered compensation claims. If it was not diagnosed, you and your family did not get 'the comp'. Furthermore, social and religious stigma attached to some causes of death such as suicide, as Durkheim's classic sociological study *Suicide* published in 1897 made clear; hence, it is susceptible to under-reporting.

We have to be cautious, then, about the rise and fall of causes of death because so much depends on the historical context, which makes comparison *between* societies doubly difficult. Anderson makes the important point that comparing Scotland's expectation of life at birth with, for example, figures for Spain, Italy or Austria may not be very meaningful, especially in the nineteenth and early twentieth centuries. He argues that too little attention is paid to different climatic conditions, diet, levels of urbanisation, wealth and investment in sanitary infrastructure (drains, for example), which in turn generate different epidemiological regimes.

In fact, Scotland's mortality seems to have been *low* compared with many countries in the nineteenth century. Scotland, like England and Wales, was spared the worst ravages of war, famine and disease inflicted on many European societies since the middle of the nineteenth century, and so it avoided dramatic fluctuations in mortality. We can appreciate the huge disruption of two world wars in the twentieth century, coupled with the widespread improvements throughout continental Europe since 1945. Scotland too saw life expectancies rise in this period, but at a slower rate of improvement relative to other countries.

Climate and diet matter: they put diseases in context. Mediterranean countries, for example, have climates conducive to diseases of the gut and intestines, and proper sanitation systems came late. Anderson argues that Scotland, despite being one of the most industrialised and urbanised societies in Europe in the nineteenth century, had an **infant mortality rate (IMR)** better than any country apart from Scandinavian ones; the gap only began to close at the end of the century (Figure 5.3). One factor in explaining Scotland's low infant mortality in the nineteenth century was extended breast-feeding until the child was nine months, and the widespread use in children's diets of buttermilk with its slightly acidic content, offering protection against intestinal diseases (see Mitchison, 1977: 51–2).

By the end of the century the IMR gap between Scotland and the rest of Europe was beginning to close, but it held an advantage over England and Wales, whose IMR between 1896 and 1900 was 156 (per 100,000) compared with Scotland's 129.

Checking back to our population graph for 1911 in Chapter 4 (Figure 4.4 page 81) which showed high numbers of young children, if Scotland's babies were surviving longer, and there were more of them, then we understand better why the overall death rate was relatively low. The key point is that the overall death rate is a function, among other things, of the age structure of the population, which is why age-standardised measures of the death rate are preferred.

FIGURE 5.3
Close to death

Source: Glasgow
University
Library (special
collections)

History matters

Better sanitation and hygiene eliminated typhus (which was tick borne, effective in over-crowded slum conditions) and cholera (water borne), which effectively had disappeared by the late nineteenth century. Typhoid, a bacterial disease resulting from contaminated sewage, made a surprising comeback in the twentieth century, in Aberdeen in 1964;[7] and in Lanarkshire, E. coli in 1998 as a result of contaminated food.

Bronchial infections and related deaths peaked in the 1870s, and by the mid- twentieth century declined dramatically with improvements in environmental conditions (Clean Air Acts) and advances in antibiotics (see Figure 5.4). These, along with improving diet and social conditions, reduced the incidence of pneumonia, historically known as the 'old person's friend', which if left untreated with antibiotics was a precipitating cause of death among the elderly, although young children were also susceptible. Just as 'nineteenth-century' diseases waned, so twentieth-century ones such as cancers and heart disease became more prevalent. We can see that transformation in Figure 5.4.

There may have been historical under-reporting of cancer, but certainly on death certificates cancers have become more common. Crude cancer mortality rates for men between 1931 and 1956 rose from 140 to 227 per 100,000, and for women, from 155 to 193. By the early 1980s, rates had risen to 291 (for men) and 247 (for women). Over the next two decades, these rose, once more, to 316 and 281.

Cancer mortality rates for men more than doubled in fifty years, while those for women rose by a quarter. Once more, official reporting makes it more likely that cancer is selected as an official cause of death, and there is the fact that, with longevity, old people were more susceptible. If we use age-standardised measures, on the other hand, we find that the rate

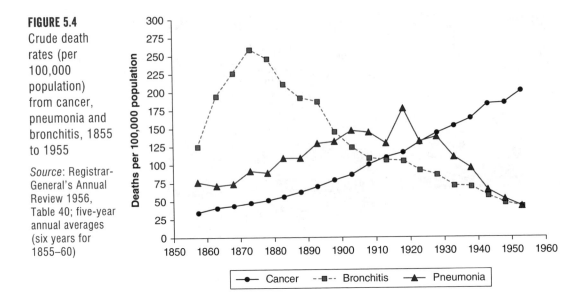

FIGURE 5.4
Crude death rates (per 100,000 population) from cancer, pneumonia and bronchitis, 1855 to 1955

Source: Registrar-General's Annual Review 1956, Table 40; five-year annual averages (six years for 1855–60)

for men actually fell after 1990, with more modest falls among women. Here is a good example of the ways in which we get different results if we standardise on age rather than relying on crude death rates.

Changes in mortality in the twentieth century

Taken together, Figures 5.5 and 5.6 show the overall picture as to how the major causes of death have changed since the middle of the twentieth century, looking at men and women separately.

The shape of these graphs is broadly similar for men and women (see Figure 5.6), and both show a major decline in rates of ischaemic heart disease (sometimes called coronary heart disease) and cerebrovascular disease.

Headline figures

Those diseases which have seen major *declines* in mortality rates over the period for both sexes are:

- stomach cancer: 84 per cent for men and 90 per cent for women;

- cerebrovascular disease: respectively, 82 per cent and 88 per cent;

- ischaemic heart disease: 72 per cent and 83 per cent;

- colorectal cancer: 56 per cent and 62 per cent.

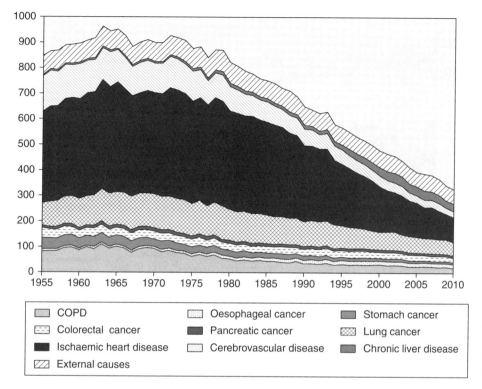

FIGURE 5.5
Age-standardised
mortality rates
for ten major
causes of death
among Scottish
men aged
15–74 years,
1955–2010

Notes: Horizontal
axis (*x*) indicates
year of death;
vertical axis
(*y*), the rate per
100,000 pa;
'COPD' is chronic
obstructive
pulmonary
disease;
'External causes'
include deaths
from injuries,
poisonings,
accidents, suicide
and homicide

Source: Whyte and
Ajetunmobi (2012)

Those which show *differential* rates for men and women are:

- chronic obstructive pulmonary disease (COPD): a fall of 74 per cent for men, but only 2 per cent for women;

- oesophageal cancer: 62 per cent for men, and virtually no change in the women's rate;

- suicide rates: an increase of 50 per cent for men, but a fall of 26 per cent for women;

- lung cancer: 23 per cent for men, but a major three-fold increase for women;

- pancreatic cancer: no change for men, but a 7 per cent fall for women.

To complete the picture, both sexes have shown a massive *increase* in deaths from chronic liver disease (six-fold for men and five-fold for women), while deaths from breast cancer for women show a fall of one-third. Over the piece, then, Scotland is a much healthier place than it used to be as measured by mortality rates for major diseases.

Gender and mortality

Why there should be different gender patterns, and how these interact with age, are interesting questions. The rate of lung cancer for older men, for example, tripled between

FIGURE 5.6

Age-standardised
mortality rates
for eleven major
causes of death
among Scottish
women aged
15–74 years,
1955–2010

Source: As
Figure 5.5

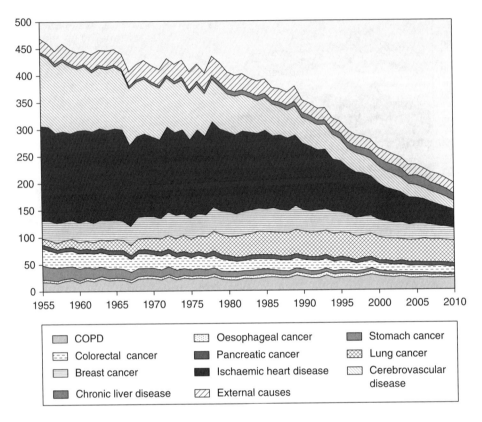

1950 and 1970 when it reached its peak before declining. For women, the rise began later, and peaked later. This reflected changing habits of smoking, whereby, on average, men began smoking in the first half of the twentieth century, whereas the rate for women did not peak until the second half of the century.

Smoking and lung cancer

The battle to prove the link between smoking and lung cancer was fought from the 1950s onwards, by Richard Doll in England, and by John and Elizabeth Crofton in Scotland from the 1960s. With regard to age, rates for stomach and bowel cancer in Scotland showed a steady fall, but a dramatic one for older men and women as diagnosis and treatment became more effective in the second half of the twentieth century. In both cases, however, the rate of improvement was greater in England and Wales than in Scotland. Throughout the second half of the twentieth century, Scotland lagged behind not only its British neighbours, but, as we shall see, much of the rest of Western Europe.

Cancer accounts

'Cancer' (known technically as malignant neoplasms) is not a single disease, and affects men and women differently, notably lung and breast cancers. For a brilliant account of the history of cancer diagnoses and treatments, see Siddhartha Mukherjee (2010). As far as we can judge, the cancer mortality rate in Scotland was and continues to be among the worst in Western Europe.

Knowing the connection between smoking and lung cancer is one of the greater certainties, although 'indirect' smoking raises another set of causal issues. Knowing what 'causes' higher rates of stomach and bowel cancer in Scotland is a more open question, and we can debate the role of diet – the Scottish lack of fruit and vegetable eating in particular – and why southern Mediterranean countries have much lower rates (but higher rates of other forms of cancer associated with gut diseases). And, in any case, propensity is one thing, treatment another. Early diagnosis programmes such as screening everyone for bowel disease between the ages of age of 50 and 74 in Scotland have had an appreciable effect on final mortality.

Heart disease

If 'cancers' are a major killer of people in Scotland, then so is ischaemic heart disease, and general 'circulatory' diseases such as cerebrovascular conditions (in common parlance, forms of 'stroke'). The number of deaths in Scotland, for example, ascribed to heart disease more than doubled between 1931 and 1956. Age plays its part, as does diagnosis, and we can never be sure that what was attributed to death by 'old age' in the inter-war period was not actually heart disease.

The mortality rate from ischaemic heart disease (IHD) for men over 65 shows a nice parabola, peaking in the early 1970s at around 200 per 10,000 deaths, whereas the comparable trend for women in this age group shows a much flatter curve (never more than half the men's rate). The Scottish female age-standardised IHD for ages 15–74 was almost continuously the highest among Western European countries, while male mortality was the highest in the later 1950s and after 1985, and the second highest to Finland in the remaining years.

Suicide rates

Suicide, as Durkheim (1952 [1897]) showed, is highly susceptible to definition, especially where there is social and cultural stigma involved. Dying from heart disease or cancer elicits sympathy rather than opprobrium. Scottish suicides rates, reasonably reliable from the 1950s, show little difference from those south of the border. From the mid-1970s there has been a rise, notably among young men, although the decline in deaths from other causes among this group throws the suicide rate into sharper relief. There is a strong association with areas of multiple deprivation (Leyland et al., 2007: 129).

Where there is rapid improvement in death rates for certain diseases, those which lag behind take on added significance. Young men, for example, may appear to die of suicide or homicide or substance abuse far more than previously simply because other causes of death have diminished. And it is not simply young men who end up dying of cirrhosis of the liver, a condition which both relatively and absolutely has become a much more significant cause of death in the last few decades.

Scotland in comparative context

How does Scotland compare with other European societies?[8] Let us look first at the aggregate ('all-cause') figures.

All causes

For both men and for women, Scotland is well above the mean throughout (Figures 5.7 and 5.8).

FIGURE 5.7
All-cause
mortality age-
standardised
rates among
men aged 15–74

Source: As
Figure 5.5

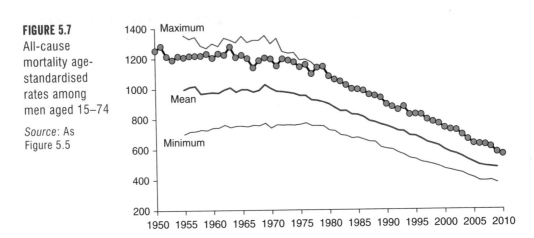

FIGURE 5.8
All-cause
mortality age-
standardised
rates among
women aged
15–74

Source: As
Figure 5.5

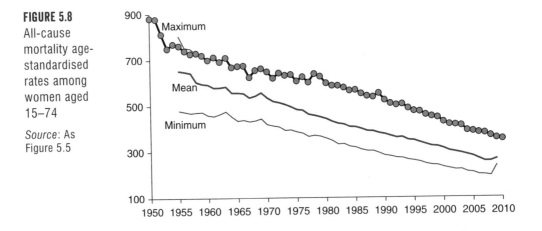

We find that:

- Both sexes in Scotland have seen falls in mortality rates since 1950.

- Since then, there has been a fall in mortality rates in most West European countries, and they have had consistently lower mortality rates than Scotland.

- For most years, Scotland has the highest mortality rates for men since 1978, and for women, since 1958.

- By the end of the first decade of the twenty-first century, the male Scottish rate was 21 per cent above the West European mean, and for women it was 30 per cent higher.

Oesophageal cancer

To make the point that 'cancers' have different trajectories, let us examine two forms: first, oesophageal cancer (Figures 5.9 and 5.10) and, second, lung cancer (Figures 5.11 and 5.12).

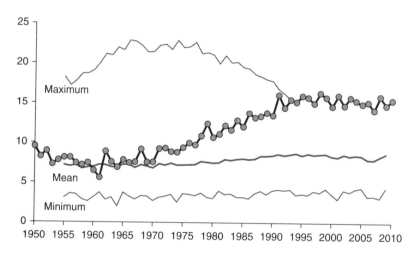

FIGURE 5.9
Oesophageal cancer mortality age-standardised rates, men 15–74

Source: As Figure 5.5

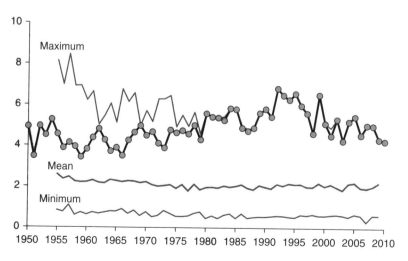

FIGURE 5.10
Oesophageal cancer mortality age-standardised rates, women 15–74

Source: As Figure 5.5

We see that:

- Until the 1970s Scottish rates for men were close to the West European mean. Scottish rates are now the highest, as much as 70 per cent above the mean.

- The rate for women fluctuates, but it is the highest among West European countries since 1981; by 2010 it is virtually double the European mean.

Lung cancer

As far as lung cancer is concerned, the rate for men has fallen, but that for women has risen, and for both sexes it is above the European mean.

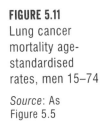

FIGURE 5.11
Lung cancer mortality age-standardised rates, men 15–74

Source: As Figure 5.5

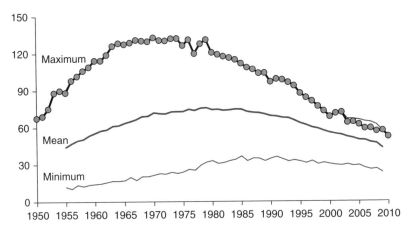

FIGURE 5.12
Lung cancer mortality age-standardised rates, women 15–74

Source: As Figure 5.5

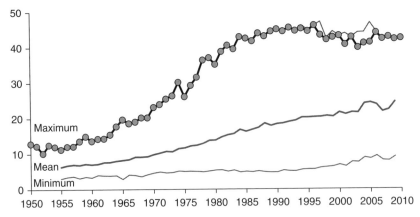

We see that:

- Lung cancer rates for men peaked in the 1960s, and by 2010 the rate was 23 per cent lower than in 1950. There is now a pronounced downward convergence to the West European mean.

- The rates for women, on the other hand, rose steadily from 1950, peaking in the 1990s, and the rate shows little reduction since. Women's rates are now more than three times that for 1950, and are 72 per cent higher than the West European mean.

Ischaemic heart disease

We now turn to IHD, the leading cause of death in Scotland, the UK and indeed worldwide. For men, see Figure 5.13.

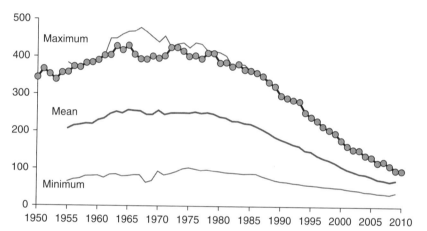

FIGURE 5.13
Ischaemic heart disease mortality age-standardised rates, men 15–74

Source: As Figure 5.5

For women, see Figure 5.14.

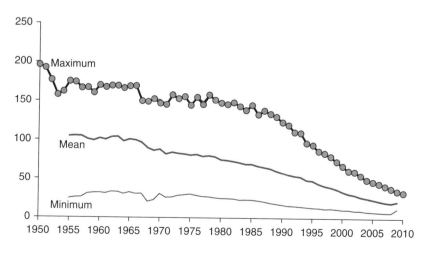

FIGURE 5.14
Ischaemic heart disease mortality age-standardised rates, women 15–74

Source: As Figure 5.5

We see that:

- The IHD rate for men, while remaining the highest in Western Europe, has been converging with the mean: in 1955, 73 per cent higher; and by 2010, 39 per cent higher.

- For women, the Scottish rate has also been converging with Western Europe since the early 1980s, but remains 64 per cent higher than the mean.

Chronic liver disease

If the falling rate of IHD in Scotland has been a good-news story, not so that for chronic liver disease (for men, see Figure 5.15; and for women, Figure 5.16).

FIGURE 5.15
Mortality from chronic liver disease, including cirrhosis, age-standardised rates, men 15–74

Source: As Figure 5.5

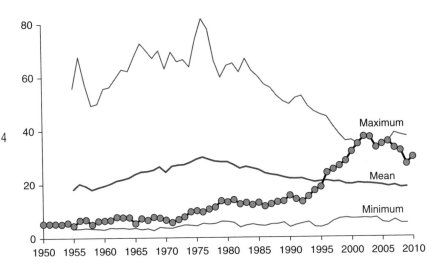

FIGURE 5.16
Mortality from chronic liver disease, including cirrhosis, age-standardised rates, women 15–74

Source: As Figure 5.5

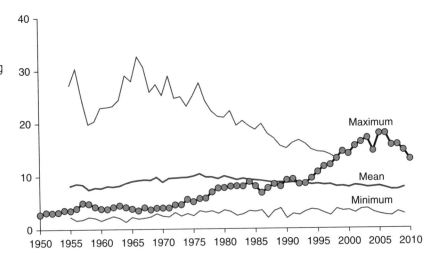

We see that:

- While the Scottish mortality rate for chronic liver disease was static between 1950 and the 1970s (at about 5 per 100,000), by 2000 the rate for men was *six times* what it had been in 1950, and for women, *five times*.

- The Scottish male mortality rate became the highest in Western Europe in 2001, while for women it was reached in 1998.

Even compared with England and Wales, Scotland was falling behind. For example, by the early twenty-first century the top seven local authorities in the UK for such age-specific mortality rates were all in Scotland, and Glasgow headed the league with 84 out of 100,000. Women too figured highly in this perverse league table. We might speculate that the increase was due to cheaper prices, easier availability and relaxed licensing hours, as well as the emergence of binge-drinking cultures among both sexes. (For a measured analysis of trends, see, for example, http://visual.ons.gov.uk/binge-drinking/.)

Relatedly, the emergence of soft and hard drugs cultures around easier availability, despite criminal sanctions, has propelled Scotland to the top of the table. There are also claims of under-reporting of drug deaths to the extent that between a quarter and two-fifths of the excess of Scottish over English and Welsh mortality in the early twenty-first century was attributable directly to the higher levels of drug-related deaths in Scotland (Bloor et al., 2008).

Accounting for the trends

Standing back a little, what do these figures tell us? First of all, the headline mortality rate conceals a considerable amount of 'churn', reflecting the variable mix of specific conditions and causes. Thus, the 'successes' relate to significant falls in IHD and 'failures' to increases in chronic liver disease. There are considerable improvements, as in the case of cerebrovascular disease rates which show major falls of over 80 per cent, but Scotland's rates are the second highest in Europe.

Second, some are gender specific: men's lung cancer rate has fallen much more significantly (–47 per cent) than the one for women (–15 per cent). Furthermore, the fall in generic cancer rates is greater for women than for men, and suicide is a significantly greater cause of death for men than it is for women, standardising for age.

On the other hand, rates for pancreatic cancer show little improvement since 1950, but for both sexes Scotland has comparatively low rates (respectively, twelfth for men and ninth for women). For most of the other mortality rates, Scotland ranks among the worst in Western Europe, notably for oesophageal cancer, IHD, COPD[9] and chronic liver disease, and in second worst place for cerebrovascular disease and lung cancer.

There has been a significant fall in mortality age-standardised rates for men (aged 15–74), from over 1200 per 100,000 in 1950 to less than half of that rate by 2010, and for women, from just under 900 to 350 per 100,000. Nevertheless, Scotland's trajectory remains around 20 per cent above the European mean, and hence Whyte and Ajetunmobi argue that Scotland can be considered still 'the sick man of Europe'. Even in terms of comparisons with the 'home countries' of England, Wales and Northern Ireland, where the data are available, Scotland has relatively high rates for IHD, liver disease and suicide, and the rates for COPD are high for women, and for oesophageal cancer, high for men. Whyte and Ajetunmobi conclude that:

> mortality in the working age population remains comparatively high and mortality for circulatory diseases and many cancer related diseases is higher than in most other Western European countries. However, there have been notable improvements in Scottish mortality for a range of major conditions – both in terms of absolute trends and in relation to Scotland's relative position in a Western European context. (Executive summary in Whyte and Ajetunmobi, 2012: 6)

What are we to make of international comparisons? We have made the point that we are inevitably drawn to compare Scotland with other countries, but that it is by no means straightforward and even at times misleading. The further back we go, the less valid the comparisons are, for making mid-nineteenth-century comparisons means that we are not comparing like with like, even less than we are today.

Thus, while we are on safer ground in doing comparisons from the middle of the twentieth century onwards, there remain issues of comparative differences in social and economic development. Most obviously, the southern and northern European countries differ in terms of their economic histories as well as in climate and diet.

Furthermore, the more we try to distinguish between 'lifestyle' diseases and 'structural' ones, we run the risk of saying that some conditions (often labelled 'behavioural') are people's 'own fault' (smoking,[10] obesity, and so on). Such judgements pay little or no attention to the role and influence of advertising and propaganda, and those associated with occupational cultures.[11] The authors of 'The Sick Man of Europe' report comment:

> The health and social patterns that emerged during the 1980s and 1990s are closely linked to behaviours harmful to health (e.g. excessive alcohol consumption) and that these behaviours are in turn heavily influenced and shaped by the social, cultural and economic disruption which were associated with abrupt changes in the political and economic policies of the UK from the late 1970s onwards. (Whyte and Ajetunmobi, 2012: 53)

Here we have an explanation in terms of the deleterious political–economic conditions arising from political policies of British governments since 1979, an account which the Scottish Public Health Observatory uses in its work (see in particular, McCartney et al., 2011).

Explaining differences

So far in this chapter we have focused on describing patterns of mortality in Scotland in two ways: changes over time; and in comparison with other countries. While, by and large, mortality rates have improved (but not always, see chronic liver disease), Scotland has improved at a slower rate than other West European countries.

We have referred previously to Michael Anderson's comment that longer term international comparisons pay too little attention to questions of historical life experiences, different epidemiological regimes, income and wealth configurations, and varying climatic conditions. He observes that rather superficial contrasts of changes in mortality in many European countries relative to Scotland can provide only very limited understanding of why Scotland became the West European country with the highest mortality by the 1980s.

Our task now is to account for these differences with regard to two dimensions: social class and 'geography'. Why these – are they not synonymous? Simply put, the former is a characteristic of individuals and their households; the latter is a characteristic of where people live. We might assume that occupational class is the more important cause, because that is how social class is conventionally measured, and what you do for a living is the key determinant of your life chances and hence the kind of housing you can afford. As we shall see in Chapter 7, however, where you live can have its own influences, especially if you live in an area of **multiple deprivation**.[12]

We will examine these issues more fully later in the book, but for the moment let us keep 'class' and 'geography' separate. In any case, 'Scotland' is not a social actor as such, but a territory in which social processes occur; hence, the health and death outcomes in aggregate need explaining. What, for example, are the social class differences with regard to mortality; and how are mortality patterns spatially distributed within Scotland?

Social class differences in mortality

These questions were tackled in a report by Alastair Leyland et al., called *Inequalities in Mortality in Scotland, 1981–2001* (2007). The study focused on men aged 20 to 64 on the grounds that attributing social class to older people and to women was difficult because they are less likely to be in the labour market. In addition, there was a major change in the classification of social class in the early 2000s (see Table 5.2).

We can see that the overall mortality rate among unskilled workers was more than four times greater than that for professionals, and that there are class gradients of comparable proportions (between three and five times) for each disease. Within the category of malignant neoplasms (cancers), the greatest class differences are those relating to lung and bronchus (more than five times greater for skilled and partly skilled than for professionals), with the lowest class differentials relating to cancers of the colon or rectum.

TABLE 5.2   Cause-specific age-standardised mortality per 100,000 population within each social class: men aged 20–59, Scotland 1990–2

		Cause of death		
Socio-economic group	All causes	Ischaemic heart disease	Cerebrovascular disease	Malignant neoplasms
I Professional	228	63	8	73
II Managerial and technical	233	68	10	68
IIIn Skilled non-manual	352	106	18	93
IIIm Skilled manual	463	144	22	131
IV Partly skilled	465	144	23	133
V Unskilled	987	288	43	222
All	385	113	18	104
Ratio of class I to V	**4.3**	**4.6**	**5.4**	**3.0**

Source: Leyland et al., table 3.4 (2007: 64)

In 2001, a new social classification system called NS-SeC (National Statistics Socio-economic Classification)[13] was introduced (Table 5.3), and while not directly comparable with the old system used in the previous table, it does confirm the class distributions of that table.

Despite the use of a new classification scheme for social class, we still find comparable orders of magnitude across the decade, suggesting that social class differences are endemic. Once more, cancers of the lungs, bronchus and trachea have the most pronounced rate of difference in class terms (the rate for routine workers being five times that of higher managers and professionals). The occupational gradients are less pronounced for cancers of the colon and rectum (2 to 1) but four times greater with regard to stomach cancers.

Mortality gradients are evident in both old and new classification systems. For example, mortality rates for partly skilled and unskilled workers were almost three times the rate for professional, managerial and technical occupations. Ten years later, and under a different classification system for social class, the ratio was 3.7. Furthermore, the authors of the study concluded: 'In 2001, the male mortality rate in each social class was higher in Glasgow than in Clydeside as a whole, and was higher in Clydeside than in the whole of Scotland. Differences in the social structure of the population clearly cannot explain the region's higher mortality rate' (Leyland et al., 2007: 2).

In other words, social class differences do not seem to be the only explanation of differential mortality rates; they also have something to do with where people live, an area factor, regardless of the social class they belong to. That there is a connection between social class and causes of death is clear, but it is far from clear what the precise mechanisms are which connect them up.

TABLE 5.3 Cause-specific age-standardised mortality per 100,000 population within each social class (NS-SeC)

NS-SeC	Cause of death			
	All causes	Ischaemic heart disease	Cerebrovascular disease	Malignant neoplasms
Higher managers and professionals	170	30	6	58
Lower managers and professionals	191	37	9	61
Intermediate	414	86	15	116
Small employers and own account	188	31	9	57
Lower supervisory and technical	411	78	14	113
Semi-routine	567	114	20	139
Routine	747	148	26	163
Never worked/long-term unemployed	73	8	2	8
All	356	65	16	37
Ratio of higher prof./managers to routine	**4.4**	**4.9**	**4.3**	**2.8**

Source: See Table 5.2

'Excess mortality'[14] in Scotland and Glasgow

Let us now consider the evidence in some detail for the linked phenomena, the Scottish effect and the Glasgow effect: that is, levels of disease and death in both Scotland and its largest city are such that they require explanation beyond what we might call social structural factors. Put simply, why does Scotland, and Glasgow, seem to suffer such levels of ill-health which cannot be accounted for in terms of factors such as age, social class and educational attainment? As we commented in a previous book:

> the notion of a 'Scottish effect' might be treated with some caution, designed as it was initially to identify differences in mortality between constituent countries and regions of the UK, and based on aggregate rather than individual level data. What we can say is that life expectancies have improved across the whole of the twentieth century, but that rates of improvement in the past 50 years have been slower in Scotland than in most western European countries. (Paterson et al., 2004: 24)

It is necessary to make some key methodological points, or, rather, to make more explicit those running through this chapter. In making spatial contrasts, whether of countries or of cities, we run the risk of the ecological fallacy which we introduced in Chapter 4. Simply put, the fallacy is to assume that we can determine the characteristics of the inhabitants from those of the area itself.

Michael Anderson gives the examples of occupational communities such as fishing and mining. High rates of mortality do not necessarily result from the disproportionate deaths of fishermen and miners directly. Thus, pollution from fish processing may contaminate the local environment (such as the water supply) and thus affect non-fishermen, who thereby die from contaminated water. Similarly, coal mining may also degrade the locality such that those who live there have higher death rates, while miners, historically highly paid, may be sufficiently well fed so as to avoid disease disproportionately. True, fishing and mining are dangerous occupations, prone to industrial accidents, but that is another issue which does not derive directly from the ecology.

'Area effects' and mortality

We can usefully broaden out the question. To what extent do the characteristics of an area, or a country for that matter, 'explain' the differential rates not simply of disease and death, but other forms of social practice? Thus, if we want to account for differential rates of morbidity and mortality, to what extent is it simply to be explained by what sociologists call social structure? If Scotland (or Glasgow, for that matter) is more 'working class' in that a higher proportion of the people are in manual work, or there are proportionately older people, and working-class people and the elderly have higher death rates, might this 'explain' the differentially high death rate?

We shall see in later chapters that this is not simply a matter relating to death and disease, for a similar question can be asked about, for example, how people vote, or what their social values are. If we can explain differences in outcomes in terms of the social characteristics of the population, then we call this a 'social structural' explanation.

So is Scotland simply different in respect to its social structures (social class, age, etc.) which then account for outcome differences, whether of differential mortality, voting habits, and so on? The short answer is, broadly speaking, no. We can say this if we find that the 'same' sort of people behave differently in different places; if, for example, people in the same social classes in Scotland and England behave (or suffer) differently. We might say that if the same kind of people behave differently in different places (country, city, and so on) then there is a 'contextual' effect.

This still leaves a large question mark over precisely what it is that generates 'difference', and it is this 'effect' which is the subject of debate vis-à-vis the 'Scottish effect' and/or the 'Glasgow effect'. We cannot simply jump to the other conclusion that the explanations are 'cultural', that there is something negative in people's beliefs and social practices which makes them behave in a particular way. There is added complication in this kind of research that the more we rely on directly comparing places rather than people, the more we run the risk of the ecological fallacy.

Let us return to the study by Leyland and his colleagues (2007). They compared age-standardised death rates by social class categories (NS-SeC) in the major cities of Scotland for the period 2000–2. They showed, unsurprisingly, that the four cities differed from each other and from the Scottish mean. As a ratio of the Scottish mean set at 100, they found that Edinburgh's rate was 92 per cent, Aberdeen's rate was 100, Dundee's 118 and Glasgow's 163 (table 3.16: 81). Perhaps that is not so surprising: Edinburgh and Aberdeen have higher proportions of middle-class people, and Dundee and Glasgow more working-class. It is, however, not the class composition of the different cities which makes the difference. The researchers found that age-standardised death rates for lower managerial and professional workers were 30 per cent *higher* in Glasgow than in Edinburgh, and for 'routine' manual workers, they were 70 per cent higher.

That is not the end of the story. If we compare Edinburgh and Glasgow, we find that the death rates for *all* the social classes are higher in Glasgow; for example, higher managerial and professional workers in Glasgow have a rate 60 per cent higher than Edinburgh's. In other words, there does seem to be a 'Glasgow effect' on mortality.

Not only that, as the authors observe:

> When considered in comparison with the mortality rates for Scotland as a whole, the rates for Clydeside [the wider conurbation] are higher in each of the occupational categories and especially so in the supervisory, semi-routine and routine groups: respectively, these rates are 34 per cent, 30 per cent and 48 per cent greater than the all-Scottish rate. (Leyland et al., 2007: 82)

Thus, the higher risk of death is a feature of the *populations* of Clydeside and Glasgow rather than the simpler explanation that a higher proportion of working-class people live there.

The point, of course, is that this raises more questions than it answers. We need to ask: what *is* it about 'Clydeside' or 'Glasgow' which has this effect? This question led researchers to break down the spatial units into small-area statistics (postcodes) and to attach 'deprivation' characteristics to them to try and tease out the factors. An early paper by Vera Carstairs and Russell Morris, in 1989, laid the trail.

Using the 1981 census data, Carstairs and Morris calculated deprivation scores for each postcode in Scotland (about 1000 in all) based on four measures: overcrowding, low social class, unemployment among men, and not having a car. The four standardised component variables were added together into a single score with a mean of zero and a standard deviation of one. These scores were divided into seven categories ranging from very affluent (1) to very deprived (7).

A Scottish effect?

The purpose of the analysis was to compare Scottish postcodes with 'wards' for England and Wales. Carstairs and Morris found that Scotland was considerably more deprived, notably on overcrowding. They defended their composite measure of deprivation on the grounds that 'social class' was not in and of itself having an explanatory effect. They concluded: 'These difficulties have led to proposals for alternative measures of social stratification and to the adoption of an area based method of analysis' (1989: 889). Carstairs and Morris followed up their *BMJ* paper with a book entitled *Deprivation and Health in Scotland* (1991).

Their aim was to compare Scotland's excess mortality with that of England and Wales, using 1981 census data (hence the choice of explanatory variables), and to explain it in terms of higher levels of deprivation north of the border, but above all in Glasgow. They estimated that around 62 per cent of the difference between Scotland and England and Wales could be attributed to their measure of deprivation. Replications in 1991 put the difference at 42 per cent, and for 2001 at 47 per cent.

Carstairs and Morris' research has had a major influence on subsequent work, notably in studies of the 'Glasgow effect' undertaken by the Scottish Public Health Observatory (ScotPHO) and the Glasgow Centre for Population Health (GCPH) based in the city. In particular, their work has shifted the focus from measures of social class based on individuals and households to area-based measures, as reflected in the Scottish government's Scottish Index of Multiple Deprivation (SIMD; http://simd.scotland.gov.uk/publication-2012/introduction-to-simd-2012/overview-of-the-simd/what-is-the-simd/). This is a much more sophisticated measure than the ones used by Carstairs and Morris, based on thirty-eight indicators of deprivation, reflecting the technical advances made since 1981.

Social vis-à-vis spatial inequalities

At this point, Carstairs and Morris' comments on 'social class' deserve comment. Social class is not simply a way of classifying occupations, even using the older 5/6-fold classification of 'socio-economic groups' (SEGs), which was updated and superseded by NS-SeC[15] which was introduced in 2001. True, occupational classification is still the basis of the new schema, but that is because for most people it is a proxy for their social class position, because what people work at, levels of pay and conditions, is the best predictor of social class. The point is that 'social class' attaches to individuals and households rather than to the areas in which they live. For most people their 'life chances' are determined by what they work at because it is the usual source of income for them. It characterises their life security, gives them access to housing, education, social capital, and so on.

On the other hand, *spatial* aspects of social inequalities, how these are played out, quite literally, on the ground, are important. Much depends on the size and scale of the spatial unit. Michael Anderson gives a good example. The town of Oban in north-west Scotland has a population of around 10,000 people and is divided into just two postcodes, extending far into the surrounding countryside. The 'average' for the postcodes comes out as having low deprivation scores even though the range within them is considerable.

Contrast that with the housing estate of Easterhouse in Glasgow, which has roughly the same size of population, and, like Oban, two postcodes. Each of the Easterhouse postcodes comes out at the extreme end of the deprivation scale. Because the analytical characteristics attach directly to the areas and not to the individuals within them, we cannot be sure that we are not dealing in social artefacts. This, to be sure, is not a matter of having to choose 'individuals' over 'areas', but of looking at how they interact. For example, similar individuals (or households, for that matter) may have their social position enhanced, or disadvantaged, according to where they live, and that is a matter for enquiry.

In any case, and contra Carstairs and Morris, we would not expect social class to explain more (or less) than an area-based analysis of social deprivation, for one measure is not a substitute for the other – they tell us different social things. Indeed, Leyland et al. comment:

> Deprivation accounts for most but not all of the regional differences [within Scotland] in mortality rates. In Glasgow and the Clydeside conurbation, male mortality rates tend to be comparable to those in the rest of Scotland in the more affluent areas but, in more deprived areas, they are higher than the Scottish rates at a given level of deprivation. Aberdeen City stands out as having, for the most part, mortality rates that are higher than in areas of comparable deprivation in Glasgow. (2007: 2)

That is a striking finding – that Scotland's most affluent city, Aberdeen, also contains areas of severe multiple deprivation comparable with those found in Glasgow.

A Glasgow effect?

Let us now examine in greater detail the 'Glasgow effect'. This has attracted considerable interest, notably for the finding that Glasgow contains a disproportionate number of Scotland's areas of multiple deprivation: in 2012, the city contained 36 per cent of the most deprived areas in Scotland, an improvement on 2004 when it contained almost half of them,[16] and that within the city, almost half of the city's population live in the most deprived areas. Using the SIMD categories, it seems that over half of the city's population (around 300,000 people) in 2001 lived in the worst quintile (i.e. the bottom fifth of data-zones), compared with 38 per cent in Dundee, 15 per cent in Edinburgh and 10 per cent in Aberdeen.[17]

This raises an important issue which makes the point about using different sources of evidence. Imagine two notional cities with identical proportions of individuals and households who are deprived, but in the two cities their spatial distribution is quite different: one (perhaps like Glasgow) in which 'poor people' are concentrated in certain areas; and the other in which they are more evenly spread throughout the city. We might expect that the former are subject to additional deprivation deriving from the area effect, whereas the others benefit from a more equal distribution of scarce resources because areas are more socially 'mixed'. As our knowledge stands, this remains hypothetical but worthy of further study. We will consider the implications in Chapter 7 when we examine poverty and inequality, whereas our focus here is specifically on mortality.

We have noted that Glasgow, and Clydeside, have markedly excess male mortality above any other city or local authority in the worst SIMD quintile. The age-standardised rate of 7.43 per 1000 for Glasgow, and 6.85 for Clydeside in 2000–2, compares with an all-Scottish rate for the *worst* quintile of 6.12, and the scores for Edinburgh, Dundee and Aberdeen at, respectively, 6.17, 6.01 and 5.96, make the point that there is a peculiarly 'Glasgow' (and Clydeside) effect.

Women in Glasgow, however, are much closer to the Scottish mean, even in the most deprived quintile (3.45 and 3.10 respectively), and the areas in Edinburgh which are in the worst decile actually have a marginally *higher* score (3.54) than Glasgow (3.45). For reasons we do not properly understand, Glasgow men who live in the most deprived areas do appear to have the worst mortality rates.

Comparing cities

What has attracted particular interest in the 'Glasgow effect' is that compared with English cities like Liverpool and Manchester, Glasgow has an appreciably higher mortality level. The Scottish Public Health Observatory which carried out the analysis explained it this way:

> Comparisons of area deprivation and mortality between Glasgow, Liverpool and Manchester showed that despite all three cities exhibiting very similar levels and patterns of deprivation, the mortality profile of Glasgow (in 2003–2007) was quite different. After adjusting for any remaining differences in 'income deprivation', premature mortality in Glasgow was 30 per cent higher than in Liverpool and Manchester, with mortality at all ages around 15 per cent higher. This excess was seen in all age groups except children, among both males and females, and in all types of neighbourhood (deprived and non-deprived). It does not appear to be explained by historical changes in levels of deprivation, nor by the population composition (e.g. ethnic profile) of the cities. The excess appears to be widening over time. Very similar results have also been shown for Glasgow relative to Belfast. (Excess Mortality in Scotland and Glasgow, ScotPHO: www.scotpho.org.uk/comparative-health/excess-mortality-in-scotland-and-glasgow)

Just why Glasgow should have such concentrations of deprivation is an open and interesting question. There have been attempts to explain Glasgow's excess mortality in terms of broad political–economic causes such as 'neo-liberalism' and the imposition of 'austerity' policies (McCartney et al., 2011; www.gcph.co.uk/assets/0000/1080/GLA147851_Hypothesis_Report_2_.pdf).

The difficulty with this as an explanation is that it is unclear why neo-liberalism and austerity should have a *specific* impact on Glasgow, as opposed to Liverpool, Manchester and Belfast. Nor does the research specify the precise mechanisms which bring about higher rates of mortality in Glasgow.

In a later report, the researchers argued that the 'key explanatory model for Glasgow is that the city, over time, was made more vulnerable to … particular socioeconomic and political exposures' (Walsh et al., 2016: 7), and listed a large number of factors which would make this plausible. Nevertheless, because something is plausible does not make it a sufficient explanation. There *are* a number of plausible, yet testable explanations: that the contiguity of deprived areas, notably in large housing schemes on the city's periphery, reinforce deprivation; and to make an obvious but important point, the high concentrations of the relatively powerless reflect the political geography which has built up over at least the last century if not longer. In his novel *Laidlaw*, Willie McIlvanney had his eponymous detective observe:

> You think of Glasgow. At each of its four corners, this kind of housing-scheme. There's the Drum and Easterhouse and Pollock and Castlemilk. You've got the biggest housing-scheme in Europe here. And what's there? Hardly anything but houses. Just architectural dumps where they unload people like slurry. Penal architecture. (1977: 32)

We will return to the issue in Chapter 16.

Out-migration

Another possible explanation for higher mortality in Glasgow relates to differential out-migration. The city embarked on extensive programmes of population overspill from the late 1950s, notably to new towns such as East Kilbride, Cumbernauld and Livingston. Those who left the city were younger and more occupationally skilled; if nothing else they had the material and social capital, leaving behind those less endowed. There is, then, the possibility that differential out-migration has left the city with a relatively unskilled population, and that people who remain are somehow more prone to disease than out-migrants. The problem with that as an explanation, however, is that it does not explain why higher rates of mortality attach to those in *higher* non-manual employment living in the city.

Epigenetic differences

More recently, an intriguing socio-medical line of research has emerged based on epigenetics. This focuses on possible ways in which environmental factors can affect the way in which elements of the genetic code in DNA are switched on or off, thus altering how these genes function (McGuiness et al., 2012). This research showed that even taking into account age and sex, and the interaction effects between variables, those living in deprived conditions showed markedly *lower* levels of DNA methylation. These low levels of methylation were linked to a number of predictors of poor health, notably those associated with enhanced levels of cardiovascular risk.

Why should this have a particular impact on Glasgow? Studies of the aftermath of famine showed that parental food deprivation, coupled with extreme switches between periods of glut and starvation, produced physical and mental long-term effects not only on those who suffered these conditions but also on their children. Thus, the famines of the mid-nineteenth century in Ireland (and the Highlands) and the seasonal fluctuations of food supplies had the potential to embed in subsequent generations 'epigenetic ageing' by accelerating factors which result in poor health, especially from such conditions as cancers and heart disease.[18]

Blame the ancestors?

To be sure, this remains in the realms of plausibility, but it is amenable to testing and research, and might help us to understand better why places such as Glasgow have had a long history of in-migration from Ireland and the Highlands. The plausibility of such an explanation also rests upon the common-sense notion that all of us inherit the genetic make-up of our ancestors, which do not determine patterns of morbidity and mortality, but are certainly an influence on them, which is why doctors ask us about family propensities to diseases and causes of death.

Our propensity to suffer (or avoid) certain medical conditions deriving from those of our parents and grandparents makes this an interesting line of enquiry, bringing together as it does genetic and social factors. As Michael Anderson observed, it does seem plausible to argue that much of the population will have had an unusually long and intense track record, going back several generations, of deprivation, disease, uncertainty and stress. If we add to this the fact of selective out-migration of skilled and healthy workers over several centuries, then we have an interesting line of research using new forms of long-term record linkage of health, census and vital registration data which is some way in the future.

Conclusion

In this chapter we have explored the fact that Scotland seems to have suffered, and continues so to do, differentially high levels of morbidity and mortality which seem to be well above the European average. Further, within Scotland, Clydeside, and notably Glasgow, appear to suffer levels of 'excess' mortality which cannot simply be explained by social class composition, or indeed small-area characteristics. The Scottish effect and the Glasgow effect have generated a considerable volume of research and speculation, which indicates that we currently have many more questions than we have answers. Here is a research field in which sociologists have a major role to play, for it reinstates questions of power and privilege which are then played out on the ground.

Chapter summary

So what have we learned in this chapter?

- That Scotland is a much healthier place in which to live in the twenty-first century than it was in the nineteenth and twentieth centuries as measured by rates of mortality.

- That causes of death today are significantly different than those in the middle of the twentieth century.

- Despite that, Scotland has higher rates of mortality than most other West European countries, and rates of improvement have been slower. There has even been a significant increase in some, notably chronic liver disease, in the last twenty years.

- Explanations for Scottish mortality rates have focused on social class effects which continue to generate significant inequalities in health.

- There also seem to be 'ecological' effects such that Glasgow, and Clydeside, do significantly worse in terms of 'excess mortality' than comparable cities and towns.

- Explanations for these effects are tentative and hypothetical, and include differential out-migration and epigenetic differences embedded in the population over time.

We will return to issues of poverty and social inequality in Chapter 7, but first we try to make sense of power in Scotland, and it is to that central topic that we now turn in the next chapter.

Questions for discussion

1. How have mortality rates in Scotland changed over the last century?

2. Which diseases now account for most deaths in Scotland, and why?

3. How does Scotland compare with other countries with regard to mortality rates, notably in Western Europe? How would you account for the differences?

4. To what extent has there been a shift from 'structural' to 'behavioural' causes of death, and why? How important are 'lifestyle' factors?

5. How effective have public policies been in affecting mortality rates? What more can and should be done?

Annotated reading

Michael Anderson, 'The demographic factor', in T.M. Devine and J. Wormald (eds), *The Oxford Handbook of Modern Scottish History* (2012).

Bruce Whyte and Tomi Ajetunmobi, *Still 'The Sick Man of Europe'? Scottish Mortality in a European Context, 1950–2010: An analysis of comparative mortality trends* (2012).

Alastair Leyland, Ruth Dundas, Philip McLoone and F. Andrew Boddy, *Inequalities in Mortality in Scotland 1981–2001* (2007).

See also the reports of the Glasgow Centre for Population Health (www.gcph.co.uk) including *Ten Years of the Glasgow Centre for Population Health: The evidence and implications*, October 2014; and *History, Politics and Vulnerability: Explaining excess mortality in Scotland and Glasgow*, May 2016.

Public Health Information for Scotland (ScotPHO) (www.scotpho.org.uk) including: 'Testing the fundamental causes theory of health inequalities in Scotland', October 2013.

Scottish Government, *Long-term Monitoring of Health Inequalities: Headline indicators*, October 2015 (www.gov.scot/Resource/0048/00487927.pdf).

Notes

1   As a reminder, *morbidity* refers to the incidence of disease, *mortality* to rates of death.
2   The 'sick man of Europe' tag has migrated from an entirely other source: it was the Ottoman Empire ('a sick man – a very sick man') which was so described by *The London Times* journalist John Russell in 1853 as a measure of political and not physical health. The handy term has been subsequently applied to most European countries at one time or another by political journalists, before becoming an epithet for Scotland's physical health in the late twentieth century.
3   We might speculate that post-famine chaos in Ireland in the 1860s made accurate recordings of deaths difficult if not impossible, just as they are in the famine conditions of modern Africa.
4   The north of Ireland, especially around Belfast's textile and shipbuilding industries, on the other hand, shared many of the industrialised characteristics of central Scotland, but still had proportionately more people working in agriculture (see Chapter 8).
5   'Consumption' (of the lungs) was an old term for tuberculosis, and 'galloping' simply indicated its rate of progress.
6   Epidemiology is the study of patterns, causes and effects of health and disease in particular populations.
7   The Aberdeen typhoid outbreak in 1964 led to virtual siege conditions in the city until traced to contaminated corn beef processed in Argentina. Schools and other public institutions were closed, much to the delight of school children, including the present author. No one in the city died directly from the disease.
8   I am grateful to Bruce Whyte and Tomi Ajetunmobi for permission to reproduce figures from their report *Still "The Sick Man of Europe"?* (www.gcph.co.uk/assets/0000/3606/Scottish_Mortality_in_a_European_Context_2012_v11_FINAL_bw.pdf) (2012).

9   COPD is the name for a collection of lung diseases including chronic bronchitis and emphysema. One of the main causes is smoking.

10 Arguably, the breakthrough in tackling lung cancer came when smoking was seen as addictive rather than freely chosen.

11 Such as journalism, hospitality trades and even medicine.

12 Multiple deprivation refers to the overlap and interlinking of deprivation in terms of, for example, income, employment, housing, education and health.

13 www.ons.gov.uk/ons/guide-method/classifications/current-standard-classifications/soc2010/soc2010-volume-3-ns-sec—rebased-on-soc2010—user-manual/index.html.

14 'Excess mortality' is a measure of the deaths which occur over and above those that would be predicted for a given population given its social and demographic characteristics.

15 www.ons.gov.uk/ons/guide-method/classifications/current-standard-classifications/soc2010/soc2010-volume-3-ns-sec—rebased-on-soc2010—user-manual/index.html.

16 See   http://simd.scotland.gov.uk/publication-2012/simd-2012-results/overall-simd-results/key-findings/.

17 There is no contradiction in saying that Aberdeen has the smallest proportion of the most deprived areas, and that living conditions within them are among the worst in Scotland.

18 See *The Annual Report of the Chief Medical Officer for 2011: Health in Scotland 2011, transforming Scotland's health* (NHS Scotland, 2012).

6

WHO RUNS SCOTLAND?

In this chapter we examine 'power' in Scotland by focusing on business, land and politics. Why those? The ownership of companies, and that of land, are basic to understanding material wealth; and 'politics' is conventionally thought of as power and control over such wealth.

The study of 'power', however, is not straightforward. And why does studying power matter if we are trying to understand Scotland sociologically? As Jonathan Hearn pointed out, 'power is not just one of the things that social scientists study, but the central thing' (2012: 3). He continues: 'What we normally encounter in social life, beginning with local social settings and all the way up to international relations, is a variegated multiplicity of centres of power, with their powers waxing and waning, in a web of relations with shifting combinations and alliances' (2012: 9). Power, then, is not a 'thing', something to be uncovered in one place. It refers to sets of relationships, many of which are opaque and subtle, operating most effectively in the form of a 'hidden hand' to use Adam Smith's metaphor, when it is unseen and taken for granted.

Chapter aims

- To focus on the changing patterns of ownership and control of the economy over the last century or so.

- To address the 'land question', who owns Scotland, and how, if at all, that has changed over a similar time period.

- To ask how 'political' power, in the broadest sense, has sought to reflect or stand up to economic interests.

Introduction

In essence, then, this chapter is about 'material' Scotland, the ownership and control of its economic and physical resources, in the context of debates about political autonomy. This is a necessary prelude to addressing issues of social inequality and power in the following chapter.

What is 'power' anyway?

We might take a literalist view that 'governments' run Scotland, because that is what politics is for: governments get elected, and they have power. It is, however, not so simple. Even if we acknowledge that power is shared between the Scottish and British parliaments (as well as Brussels), this may not get us very far, for governments have limited responsibilities and constricted control over economic affairs. We might even argue that multinational forms of capital are so dominant that governments are limited, even self-limiting, in what they can do.

Furthermore, 'power' has different dimensions (see Lukes, 2004). The most straightforward view is that people are aware of, and are able to express, their interests which are then manifest in overt conflicts. Critics point out there is the issue of agenda-setting such that some conflicts of interest remain submerged or diverted; not everything is out in the open. A third, more 'radical', view of power focuses less on actual decision-making and political agenda-setting, and argues that people may not even be aware what their 'real interests' are anyway.

A similar view of power is Pierre Bourdieu's concept '*habitus*'. He argued that social practices are 'objectively regulated without being in any way the product of obedience to rules, they can be collectively orchestrated without being the product of the organizing action of the conductor' (1984: 72). The secret, thought Bourdieu, lay in routinising practices, making them the 'normal' way of doing things, even though they have inbuilt benefits for some, and dis-benefits for others.

Economic vis-à-vis political power

In Scotland, there is a distinct conundrum. On the one hand, much of the ownership, and with it control, of the economy is no longer indigenous to Scotland, at least in the sectors which matter. Over the long term, we can see the dissipation of local ownership and control and certainly since the beginning of the twentieth century. On the other hand, our politics has never been more concerned with self-government.

This highlights the relationship between the economic and political spheres, reflected, for example, in arguments which surfaced during the Scottish Referendum campaign in 2014 about whether an independent Scotland could continue to use the (British) pound. The implication was that political independence might not deliver much by way of real control over the economy, except in terms of setting taxation levels and business rates. Unionists argued that formal independence meant little in the context of the lack of economic control, while nationalists argued for the powers to set taxation, and that Scotland was a good place to 'do business'. In short, this seemed to be an argument about where formal *political* control should reside, rather than about 'power' more broadly defined.

Changing forms of capital

So let us start with changing patterns of ownership and control. We are fortunate to have much excellent data on the Scottish economy, notably time-series analysis in a remarkable study by John Scott and Michael Hughes (1980) which provided snapshots of business interlocks at key points: 1905, 1921, 1938, 1956 and 1974. This research was updated by Sandy Baird, John Foster and Richard Leonard (2007). Taken together, we are able to see how Scottish capital developed over the century to the point that indigenous control was, to all intents and purposes, lost.

The hegemony of local capital: Scotland 1900

The beginning of the twentieth century marked a maturity in the Scottish economy, one which sought new commercial opportunities overseas and in England. At home, the Forth Rail Bridge, completed in 1890, was a monument to technological progress and the industrial bourgeoisie which had made it, much as the Eiffel Tower, completed one year previously, did for its French counterpart.

Overseas investment was also important. In 1900 it stood at £300 million, and by the outbreak of the Great War it had reached £500 million. Scottish money found its way into Australia, Canada and New Zealand, into the rebuilding of Chicago, into American ranches and real estate. The jute masters of Dundee had helped to create the investment trust as a vehicle for surplus profit, and lawyers channelled small and large funds into overseas opportunities.

None of this was deemed unpatriotic, and as the historian Bruce Lenman put it: 'It was a commonplace of late Victorian comment that Scotland invested abroad on a scale per head with no parallel among the other nations of the United Kingdom' (1977: 192). These levels of overseas investment by Scots were linked to the extent of Scottish migration abroad and their key roles in developing new territories.

Here is Sydney and Olive Checkland's summary of the period:

> By 1900, Scotland had produced a breed of major industrialists whose actions and prestige dominated the economic scene. They included such names as Colville, Baird, Yarrow, Tennant, Lorimer, Elder, Pearce, Neilson and Beardmore. These were the magnates of shipbuilding, heavy engineering, iron and steel and coal. They were autocrats, their decisions were made, conveyed and not discussed. They had a strong desire to keep everything in their hands. (1984: 178–9)

The analysis of the structure of business in 1905 showed the importance of the railway companies and their interconnections with coal, steel and engineering. Regional clusters were important, as in Dundee where the jute barons of Cox, Baxter and the Flemings held sway. Similarly, there was a clear distinction between Edinburgh clusters – centred on the banks and the North British Railway – and the Glasgow segment, focused on Tennants' companies, the Caledonian Railway and the Clydesdale Bank.

Central to the business interconnections were the banks, insurance companies and investment trusts, a system in which the landed gentry played a leading part. The Marquess

FIGURE 6.1
Scottish icons

Source: Courtesy
of Bank of
Scotland

of Linlithgow, for example, was a director of the Bank of Scotland and Standard Life; The Duke of Buccleuch, of the Royal Bank, Standard Life and Scottish Equitable; The Earl of Mansfield, of the National Bank and Scottish Equitable; and The Marquess of Tweeddale, of the Commercial Bank, Edinburgh Life and Scottish Widows. This interweaving of commercial and landed power (Figure 6.1) was one of the defining characteristics of Scotland at the beginning of the twentieth century.

This complex web of interlocking ownerships and directorates within Scottish dynasties at the beginning of the twentieth century helped the Scottish economy to remain fairly independent from England, although the takeover of indigenous companies by those from the south was underway. That Scottish business by the outbreak of war in 1914 still bore the signs of its origins as family concerns was both its strength and weakness. There had been few attempts at financial or technical reorganisation on the lines of American or German business, and few signs of a managerial revolution in this period.

The capacity of Scottish business leaders to wield personal control did not bode well for the future. Following the Great War, the expansion of the Scottish banks and the development of insurance companies led not only to a more interlocked system, but to one in which Scottish capital had less autonomy. Family control remained relatively strong, despite the fact that more resources and power had flowed outwith Scotland in the inter-war period, a feature which was to become even more marked after the Second World War.

Losing control: the inter-war period

Scotland's nineteenth-century prosperity had reflected its rapid adaptation to the market opportunities of empire, a habit which was to prove very difficult to shake off in the twentieth century. Locked in to imperial markets, once those markets declined, Scottish capital suffered. The fortunes of families like the Colvilles, the Tennants, the Beardmores and others had rested upon the earlier opportunities of steel, coal and engineering. The cold winds of economic change in the 1920s and 1930s left the social and political order, which they had built up, cruelly exposed.

The Second World War had given a belated boost to those unionist interests which remained, on condition they accepted an extension of state power. Nevertheless, demise was not far off, and as the historian Michael Fry put it, post-war saw the 'decline of the Scottish capitalist class, from the self-made local businessmen, to the dynasties of the Clyde' (1987: 193).

What had happened to the structure of Scottish business in this period? The dominant force in Scottish heavy industry in the 1930s, based on coal, iron and steel, had disappeared with nationalisation after the Second World War. The links between financial companies became a more pronounced part of a business network which 'was a mixture of family firms and firms controlled by financial interests. It was the financiers and members of the dominant families who welded these companies together into a densely connected system in which, nevertheless, certain spheres of influence could be identified' (Scott and Hughes, 1980: 153).

Post-war Scotland

In the immediate post-war period, there was little evidence of a 'managerial revolution' in Scotland, but by the 1960s the dominant dynasties which owned Scottish industry were in financial trouble. By the 1970s, 'family-owned' companies were predominantly Scottish, but those companies, growing in importance, which were controlled by corporate interests were far less Scottish.

The network of Scottish business interests was increasingly held together by the three banks, namely the Bank of Scotland, the Royal Bank of Scotland and the Clydesdale Bank,[1] each with their own clusters of related companies and spheres of influence. In spite of the fact that Scottish companies formed less and less of a distinct and autonomous entity in the face of external takeovers and amalgamations, 'family control remained a potent element in Scottish capital'. 'The major characteristic of the period studied [1904–5 to 1973–4] ... has not been a managerial revolution, but a managerial reorganisation of the propertied class' (Scott and Hughes, 1980: 153).

In the post-war period, Scottish dynasties continued to wield influence but in a diminishing sector of Scottish business. The problems of rapid industrial decline forced the state to play a more active role in diversifying the Scottish economy. Hence, government induced merchant capital to fund the building of a steel strip mill at Ravenscraig in the late 1950s, the Rootes Car Company to relocate to Linwood in 1963, a pulp mill at Corpach (also 1963) and an aluminium plant at Invergordon (1971). All subsequently closed down.[2] The influx of foreign-owned plants began to generate concern over Scotland becoming a 'branch-plant economy' (Firn, 1975; Young, 1984).

By the 1970s, the structure of economic power in Scotland was an amalgam of old and new wealth, the individual and the corporate, the indigenous and the foreign, the private and the public. Nevertheless, the financial journalist Chris Baur, who became the editor of *The Scotsman*, observed that in the 1970s Scotland's elites 'all know each other – a tight circle of politicians, businessmen, civil servants, lawyers, trade unionists, churchmen, academics, and a nostalgic sprinkling of titled gentry. They fix the nation's agenda' (*The Scotsman*, 18 September 1978).

In key respects, Scotland in the 1980s was a 'close-knit community where a high level of individual contact is possible' (Moore and Booth, 1989: 29), which helped to generate a 'pattern of policy networks' in which the values and culture of decision-making elites sustained a distinctive set of institutions and relationships which influenced bargaining and policy outcomes. Central to this policy network were bodies such as the CBI in Scotland, the Scottish Trades Union Congress (STUC), the Scottish Council (Development & Industry) and the Scottish Development Agency/Scottish Enterprise. Moore and Booth argued that Scotland represents a 'negotiated order' operating somewhere between corporatism and free-market pluralism, that the 'Scottish policy community' mediated through the Scottish Office represents a 'meso-level of the British state' (1989: 150).

The transformation of Scottish business in the twenty-first century

How well did that political–economic system survive into the twenty-first century? Sandy Baird, John Foster and Richard Leonard updated the analysis in 2007. Why, they asked, the relatively sudden conversion of Scotland's governing elite to neo-liberalism?

Business transformed

The answer lay in the changing structure of business. While in 1974, Scott and Hughes identified a specifically Scottish business network linking an array of Scottish-owned companies and financial institutions, nothing of that sort existed thirty years later. Director-level links between Scottish-registered companies became much weaker, and while some network groupings of multiple directors existed, they were fragmented and politically inconsequential. Thus:

> Major Scottish companies and financial institutions are now largely dominated by external institutional investors and their lines of accountability run principally outside Scotland. This is combined with two other structural changes: the increased size and centrality of the Scottish financial sector and, at the same time, its much closer integration with the City of London. (Baird et al., 2007: 3–4)

The mode of control of Scotland's largest non-financial companies identified by Scott and Hughes in 1974 (sixty-two in all) were followed up by Baird et al. (2007). First, the number of wholly owned subsidiaries[3] increased from seven in 1974 to twenty-six in 2004 (i.e. from 11 to 42 per cent) and to twenty-nine in 2010 (47 per cent).[4] There was also much greater central and dominating control by institutional investors. Exclusive minority companies, where one individual or family holds a dominating shareholding of less than 50 per cent, were a type largely populated by traditional Scottish firms in 1974. Their number was reduced to three by 2002, rising marginally to five by 2010, but this still represented a decline of three-quarters over thirty-six years.

The scale of the decline can be gauged from Scott and Hughes' list of non-financial companies recorded in 1974. Of the sixty-two, only eleven survived as Scottish-registered companies thirty years later. Firms that disappeared included Distillers (now Diageo), Coats Patons (Coats PLC, now headquartered in Middlesex), Burmah Oil (BP Amoco), Scottish & Newcastle (Heineken/Carlsberg), United Biscuits (HQ Hayes, Middlesex), and companies that no longer exist, such as Uniroyal (1999), Tharsis PLC (2006), Scottish Agricultural Industries (2008), Culter Guardbridge (2008), Inveresk PLC (2010). John Menzies is still family owned, while Weirs sold its Weir Pumps business to Jim McColl's Clyde Blowers PLC (now Clyde Pumps) in 2007.

We can sum up the key transformations in business ownership since the mid-1970s as follows:

- Families who were dominant for much of the last century lost position.

- They were replaced by career managers who were accountable to largely external institutional investors.

- Companies were far less interconnected, because the new generation of company directors were less linked by shared directorships to other firms in the Scottish economy.

- Externally owned firms had come to dominate the key sectors of the Scottish economy: manufacturing, oil and gas, business services, retail and most of the leisure industry.

Scotland's national drink: the transformation of whisky ownership

Nothing tells us more about the loss of indigenous ownership than what has happened to this iconic industry. In the decade between 2004 and 2014, sales of 'Scotch' whisky in general grew by 74 per cent and of single malt whisky by 159 per cent. At the same time, only 29 of the 102 distillers in Scotland are controlled by Scottish firms. Four out of ten are in the hands of overseas companies, and twenty-eight are owned by a single company, the multinational Diageo, based in London, created in 1997 out of the merger between Guinness and Grand Metropolitan hotels (GrandMet). As Baird et al. comment:

> Given that two thirds of the turnover in the Scotch whisky industry is externally controlled, can it properly be described as a Scottish whisky industry – and what will be the long term consequences for Scotland's most famous national brand if the majority of its output is controlled from outside Scotland? (2004: 49)

How that external domination has come about is instructive. The Distillers Company Limited (DCL) was formed in 1877 through combining six lowland grain distillers, with additional acquisitions over the next fifty years, such that by the late 1920s DCL had acquired the five largest blending firms and controlled more than forty distilleries (McKendrick and Hannan, 2014).

By the 1930s, the whisky market was dominated by seven brands of blended whisky of which five (Buchanan's, Dewar's, Walker's, Haig's and White Horse) were owned by DCL, as were all but two operating grain distilleries and about half of the malt distilleries. While foreign companies such as Hiram Walker and Seagrams (both Canadian) and National Distillers Products (US) entered the market in the 1930s, the post-war period saw new foreign entrants from Japan (Suntory), France (Pernod Ricard), Italy (Campari) and Spain (Pedro Domecq). However, the concentration of assets in DCL (by the mid-1970s, it sold six of every ten bottles) meant that when the Irish brewer Guinness took it over in 1986, and itself was amalgamated with GrandMet in 1997, the domination of Scotch whisky by a single owner, the London-based Diageo, was complete.

What is 'Scotch' about Scotch remains legally defined by the requirement that the cereal grains have to be grown in Scotland, and, for malt, the spirit bottled in the country. The long lay-down time required (around ten years), the loss of the 'angels' share' (around 2 per cent evaporates from the casks during maturation) and global product marketing mean that high amounts of capital are tied up for a considerable time.

Ironically, globalisation can trigger the re-emergence of local identities (see Chapter 24), particularly in the food industries where the *provenance* of food achieves cultural caché as well as legal protection (think of wine, cheese, seafood). There is market segmentation, malt whiskies alongside blended ones, and changing tastes (flavoured whiskies can be had as 'sons of liberty pumpkin spice', red stag black cherry, bird dog blackberry, and other concoctions appealing to new, and younger, markets for liquor).

There are surviving Scottish companies in the whisky market, notably William Grant (Glenfiddich, Balvenie), the Edrington Group (The Macallan, Highland Park) and the eponymous Glenmorangie. Baird and his colleagues make the point that the whisky industry is one of the few in which there is 'any significant presence of Scottish owned firms even among smaller companies', and that 'developments in whisky itself show that their presence there is precarious' (2004: 50). Furthermore:

> Of the 74 Scottish owned companies [among registered distillers] 27 were found
> to be either dormant or to have ceased trading. Of the remainder, 31 are so small
> that turnover is not recorded. Amongst medium and smaller sized companies
> with turnover of up to £30m a majority, 10 out of 15, are partially or wholly
> overseas owned. (2004: 49)

The strange tale of Whyte and Mackay

The globalisation of whisky can be gauged from the brief history of one company, Whyte and Mackay, founded in Glasgow in 1882. The brand was bought by Glasgow businessman Hugh Fraser's finance group SUITS (Scottish Universal Investment Trust) in 1971, which was acquired by multinational Lonhro in 1981, thence to Brent Walker in 1988, to American (Fortune) Brands in 1990, to Indian conglomerate United Breweries (who brewed Kingfisher beer), owned by United Spirits Ltd, who sold it on to Philippines-based Emperador Inc., which is owned by a holding company Alliance Global Inc. Meanwhile, Diageo gained control of United Spirits Ltd (USL)[5] in 2016, reinforcing its dominance of the world's whisky market.

While ownership of the Scotch whisky industry is multinational, all that 'protects' it is its local identity, and we will return to discuss this nexus of the 'global' and the 'local' in Chapter 24.

North Sea oil

The North Sea oil industry, which has transformed Aberdeen and much of Scotland, tells a similar story concerning ownership and control:[6]

> Oil development has been dominated by externally owned oil TNCs [transnational corporations]. Local firms have been restricted to supplying basic goods and services and have been unable to penetrate the more technically sophisticated parts of the industry such as engineering design, drilling services and downhole equipment manufacture. (Cumbers, 2000: 374)

Local business support is disproportionately high in such sectors as training, financial advice and staff recruitment, but disproportionately low in product development, production problem-solving, management consultancy and R&D support.

Cumbers concluded: 'there is little evidence (as yet) that the oil network is "localized" or "bedded" down in any deeper sense. If anything, networks operate through rather than within the local economy' (2000: 380). To quote a chapter title in Christopher Harvie's book *Fool's Gold* (1995): 'It's Not Scotland's Oil After All'; nor, for that matter, was it 'Mrs Thatcher's oil, to do with as she thought' (1995: 258). The tax revenues might have been, but North Sea oil was the property of the multinational oil companies.

Uncoupling finance

A remarkable story concerns the Scottish-registered financial companies, which hitherto were the linchpins which held Scottish capitalism together. Scott and Hughes had found strong interlinks among the financial companies and significant linkages, though less marked, between the financial companies and the non-financial companies (Figure 6.2). Writing in 2004, Baird and his colleagues observed that among the top fifty-eight Scottish-registered financial companies, there was at the time stronger survival of Scottish interests. However, not only had the total number of directors declined, but also there had been a

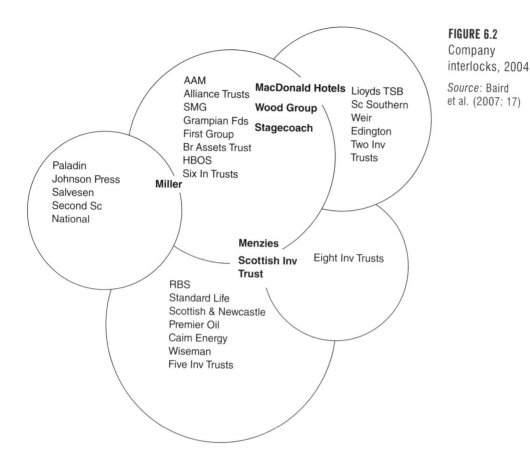

FIGURE 6.2
Company interlocks, 2004

Source: Baird et al. (2007: 17)

sharp decline in the number of multiple directorships. Further, there was a marked decline in the strength of directorship linkages.

Whereas in 1974 there were forty-five companies linked by more than one shared director, by 2004 there were just *three* linkages between companies and, of those, one was between the two Dundee Alliance Trusts, closely related companies (strictly speaking, Alliance Trust Savings and Alliance Trust Investments, both wholly owned subsidiaries of Alliance Trust PLC).

The Alliance Trust, founded in 1888, had, by 2015, £6.9 billion of assets under management, and had an unusually open ownership structure, with 70 per cent owned by around 60,000 shareholders. This open structure allowed so-called 'vulture' hedge funds (which took 12 per cent of ownership) to attack the company as too complacent and conservative. The chief executive, Katherine Garrett-Cox, had stressed her commitment to serving shareholders with a view to the long term, reflecting the Trust's heritage across generations of investors according to Douglas Fraser, BBC Scotland's business editor (www.bbc.co.uk/news/uk-scotland-scotland-business-35586754). In 2016, the CEO lost her job, her seat on the board, her business and investment strategies, along with her ally and chairwoman, Karin Forseke.

Her successor as Chair was the ubiquitous Lord Smith of Kelvin (of, and much else besides, the cross-party Smith Commission on devolution, and the Glasgow 2014 Commonwealth Games). The hedge fund Elliott Partners, who won the day, 'has a habit of getting in, getting ruthless and getting out fast', said Fraser. It seems like a lesson of our financial times.

In 1974, Scott and Hughes had found a cohesive network of top directors whose families had dominated business and finance over three or four generations, and this had virtually disappeared by 2004. By this date, while representatives of the old Scottish industrial and financial families were present in small numbers, they no longer dominated the commanding heights of the Scottish economy. There had also been a marked decline in the strength of linkages between companies, which indicates that they were far less networked and thus able to mobilise as and when required. Baird et al. concluded:

> We have found that every single comparison between the network of the 1970s and the network of today reveals a significant decline over time. The Scottish economy (at the highest level) is less inter-linked than in the 1970s and the links that do exist are also considerably weaker. A certain dominance of the financial sector remains but once again that dominance is not as widespread nor as strong. (2007: 20)

The banking crisis of 2008

Baird and his colleagues wrote this before the banking crisis of 2008, which swept into public ownership the Royal Bank of Scotland (RBS) and Halifax Bank of Scotland (HBoS) which had been at the centre of business networks for much of the preceding century. Nothing could have symbolised more the loss of indigenous ownership and control of the Scottish economy than this collapse of the 'Scottish' banks.[7] As long ago as 1981, the pivotal position of RBS was reflected in this submission to the Monopolies and Mergers Commission by McGilvray and Simpson:

> In terms of market capitalisation, the Royal Bank is the second largest company with its head office in Scotland. It is not putting it too strongly to say that if the Royal Bank goes, it will be the beginning of the end of the indigenous private sector in Scotland, with all which that implies for the regeneration of Scottish industry. (Young, 2015: 72)

The loss of power

Furthermore, the former public utility companies Scottish Power and Scottish Hydro (renamed Scottish and Southern Energy, SSE) were no longer owned and controlled in

Scotland. Scottish Power had fought off a takeover bid by the German power utility E.ON only to succumb in 2006 to the Spanish company Iberdrola based in Bilbao.

Writing before these events occurred, Baird et al. observed: 'political devolution has gone hand in hand with a sharply reduced ability to influence the economic basis of Scottish society' (2007: 34) – which takes us back to the conundrum we raised at the outset of the chapter, and echoes the observation in *Understanding Scotland* in 1992:

> At the turn of the century it was possible to identify a fairly self-contained pro-
> fessional class, a class of bourgeois owners of capital, together with a miniscule
> but powerful landed aristocracy, as Scotland's 'ruling class'; in the late twentieth
> century such an exercise becomes much more difficult. It seems the case that
> the operation of this power has become much more opaque, and that forms of
> ownership and control have become more impersonal, distant and less con-
> crete. (McCrone, 1992: 141)

Because the financial sector which previously had held the business networks together was now subject to external control, as well as ownership, it was now at the mercy of the Anglo-American model of company ownership which was mediated through short-term stock evaluation. By the beginning of the twenty-first century, takeovers and mergers, notably in the financial and banking sectors, resulted in the eclipse of the old Scottish business elite.

Much of what was happening to Scottish business mirrored what was going on at the British level, but there is nothing inevitable about the process: in Germany and France local economies were much more anchored in regional networks of ownership, and sustained by long-term strategic synergies in both manufacturing and services. This is because there is strong commitment to regional economies (what is known as Rhenish capitalism, or the social market economy in Germany) or because, as in France, the central state, by means of *dirigisme*,[8] defines 'the national interest'. Baird et al. developed the point:

> More often they derive from a corporatist coalition of dynastic capital and pub-
> lic bodies, banks and cooperatives established in the post-1945 period. In this
> respect there are some parallels with the previous situation in Scotland – except
> that these regional economies are still growing quite effectively in the environ-
> ment of the twenty-first century. (2007: 4)

It is the Anglo-American sphere of economic interest which is particularly prone to this kind of hollowing out of indigenous ownership and control.

Furthermore, whether Scotland had a 'branch-plant' economy, and, if so, what the implications were, was a serious topic for political debate and commentary at the end of the twentieth century. It is fair to say that since the hegemony of neo-liberal economics in the twenty-first century, this debate has largely ceased, even though the issue is if anything more pressing, especially in the context of political developments.

Writing his useful *Scottish Economy Watch* (www.scottisheconomywatch.com/brian-ashcrofts-scottish/2012/02/page/3/), Brian Ashcroft observed that: 'it appears that external

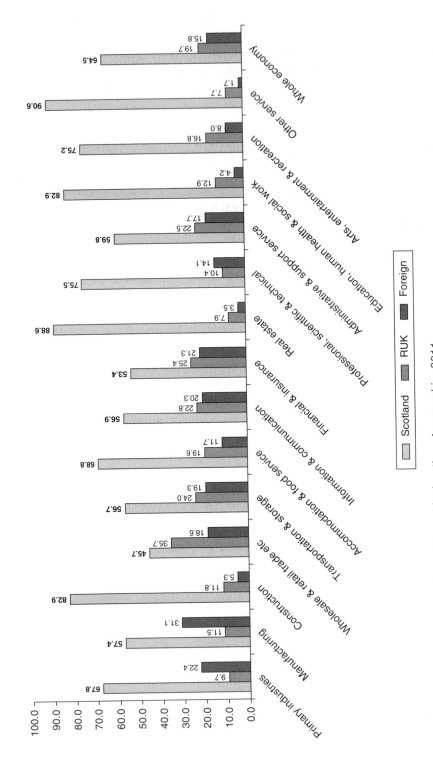

FIGURE 6.3 Scottish employment by sector and by location of ownership, 2011

Source: www.scottisheconomywatch.com/brian-ashcrofts-scottish/2012/02/page/3/

ownership and control of Scottish industry continues to grow. For example, in 1998 manufacturing employment in Scotland was 22 per cent foreign owned and controlled, by 2011 this had risen to 31 per cent.'

We can see from the chart in Figure 6.3 that foreign ownership is disproportionately strong in manufacturing, primary industries, finance and insurance, and information (all providing more than 20 per cent of employment). 'Rest of UK (RUK)' (largely English by definition) sectors are strong in wholesale and retail, transportation, information, and administration and support. Disproportionately Scottish-owned sectors are education and health, real estate and construction, as well as other services.

The share of manufacturing turnover that is foreign controlled also rose during this period from 41 to 62 per cent. Ashcroft comments that many economists who do research in this area think that a 'branch-plant' economy may not be healthy in the long term because the retention of HQ functions is a key issue. Writing in support of Scotland remaining in the British Union, Ashcroft commented that 'it is not improbable that Scottish independence would help to attract some HQ functions', and that while 'independence' of sovereign states in the modern age is heavily qualified, 'this is one argument which proponents of the UK union should put back in the locker in arguing against independence'.

This land is my land

We could be forgiven for imagining that with the sweeping away of local capitalist elites, older forms of power would have gone too. Not so. The remarkable concentrations of landed ownership in Scotland have altered very little. Earlier in the chapter we noted the insinuation of landowners into the fabric of power elites such that the landed aristocracy have played a historic role, notably in finance.

Let us remind ourselves that, at the beginning of the twentieth century, The Marquess of Linlithgow was a director of the Royal Bank of Scotland, as well as Standard Life; The Duke of Buccleuch, a director of the Royal Bank, Standard Life and Scottish Equitable; The Earl of Mansfield of the National Bank and Scottish Equitable; and The Marquess of Tweeddale of the Commercial Bank, Edinburgh Life and Scottish Widows. It might appear that having a lord on the board was simply a piece of presentational status-seeking, reinforcing the view, for investors, that banks and insurance companies had suitable bona fides, embedded in the land.

Indeed, the survival and prosperity of landed elites has been a feature of the integration of finance and industrial capitalism in these islands generally. Struggles between land and capital are the exception rather than the rule.

Times, however, change, but landownership patterns in Scotland are remarkably stable. Andy Wightman (1996, 2013), who has done more than anyone to document these changes, provides some startling statistics, thus:

- 97 per cent of Scotland consists of rural land;

- 83 per cent of rural land is in private hands;

- 12 per cent of private land is held by just ten owners.

Such a level of ownership concentration is unparalleled in Europe.

Who owns Scotland?

Let us document that pattern of landownership more precisely by drawing on Wightman's work[9] (Wightman, 2013). Just under 1000 landowners own 60 per cent of land in Scotland, with an average holding of about 10,000 acres. Wightman comments: 'what is revealing [about these figures] is the persistent pattern of very concentrated private ownership of land which has remained virtually static since the 1970s' (2013: 144). The number of land-owners holding this 60 per cent has marginally decreased (from 1180 in 1970 to 963 in 2012), largely due to the amalgamation of farms and multiple holdings. Thus, observes Wightman, 'today [writing in 2012] there are over 9.4m acres of land held by a mere 963 landowners, and over 10m acres are held by 1545 landowners in estates of 1000 acres or more' (2013: 144).

Despite the publicity given to community ownership, and not-for-profit ownership by conservation bodies, and the fact that such land holdings have doubled from under 500,000 acres in 1995 to just under 1 million acres in 2012, public land pales into insig-nificance compared with private land holdings. True, the 'state' in the form of holdings by 'Scottish Ministers' (whether of the British or Scottish governments) owns almost 10 per cent of Scotland's land area, but such holdings are largely passive in the sense that they are for use rather than for income generation. Adding land owned by the Ministry of Defence and Scottish Water brings the total to 2.3 million acres, or just below 12 per cent of land. Nevertheless, private landowners predominate. Table 6.1 shows the top ten land holdings in Scotland.

These estates total 1,221,000 acres and represent 12 per cent of private land. The list makes revealing reading, because it consists of 'old' and 'new' ownership. Thus, what the Checklands called the 'mighty magnates' are still represented by the houses of Buccleuch, Atholl, Seafield, Westminster and Sutherland.

There is 'new' money in the shape of Danish (Anders Povlsen, who made his money in the fashion industry) and Clyde Properties which, despite the name, is a Dutch holding company. It is continuity, not change, which is striking.

The insinuation of new wealth into old, however, is long standing. Wightman points out that by the end of the nineteenth century the Highland aristocracy had largely died out to be replaced by wealthy commoners such as James Morrison of Islay, who translated their capital into land to acquire social status. In fact, the traditional landed class survived in the Lowlands, notably in north-east, south-west and south-east Scotland. As regards the traditional aristocracy, Wightman observed:

TABLE 6.1   The major private landowners in Scotland

Estate	Acreage	Owner
Buccleuch Estates	241,887	Buccleuch Estates Ltd
Glen Feshie and other estates	159,274	Anders Povlsen
Atholl Estates	124,125	Trustees of Atholl Estates, Blair and Bruar
Invercauld and Torloisk Estates	120,685	Trustees of Captain Farquharson's Trusts
Alcan Estates	117,249	British Alcan Aluminium Ltd
Seafield Estates	95,815	Earl of Seafield
Westminster Estates	94,817	Trustees of the Duke of Westminster
Blackmount, Dalness and Etive Estates	92,141	Fleming Trustees
Sutherland Estates	87,898	Countess of Sutherland Trustees
Letterewe, Heights and Kinlochewe Tournaig Estates	87,066	Clyde Properties NV, Utrechtse Beheer Maatschappij

Source: Wightman (2013: 154–5)

A significant amount of land is still held by those families who succeeded in acquiring it many centuries ago. It is estimated that at least 25 per cent of estates over 1000 acres in extent have been held by the same family for over 400 years and the majority of the aristocratic families that owned land in 1872 still do so today. (2013: 162)

While institutional owners such as insurance companies (notably Eagle Star and The Prudential) have sold most of their estates, there are around eighty estates (of some 905,000 acres) held by overseas individuals and offshore trusts, including Anders Povlsen, Clyde Properties NV, Glenavon Ltd and Andras Ltd, Smech Properties, ArgoInvest Overseas.

Of 246 private estates, 6 per cent have changed hands since 1995 (less than 6 acres in total); of these two have changed hands by inheritance (the Dunvegan Estate on Skye being one) and 13 by sale, including those by Anders Povlsen. In a curious 'land swap' with the Forestry Commission, his Glenfeshie Estate was enlarged by 1000 acres in exchange for land in the Borders (see *The Herald*, 5 June 2013). Povlsen bought Glenfeshie in 2006, and is estimated to be worth around £4 billion, the wealthiest person in Denmark, only out-ranked by the Maersk shipping dynasty.

Why own land?

Why does Scottish land hold such an attraction for buyers? In his book *The Scottish Nation*, Tom Devine commented: 'Merchant bankers, stockbrokers, captains of industry, pop stars, oil-rich Arabs, and wealthy purchasers from Holland and Denmark are among the groups that have acquired Scottish estates in the past few decades' (2000: 458).

In his earlier account, *Who Owns Scotland?* (1996), Wightman gave the explanation. Speaking of sporting estates, by far the most favoured form of land use, he commented:

> Not only do they fail to make economic sense but the hundred years of their existence have perpetuated a state of affairs whereby no real investment has been made which by now might have expected to have secured some more economic return. Such money as has been poured in is better categorised as conspicuous consumption which has little local multiplier effect and is entirely dependent for its generation on a continuing stream of wealthy external interests. (Wightman, 1996: 173)

Wightman, borrowing his book title from a pioneering study by John McEwen (1977), made the point that 'power' is not a narrow 'economic' concept, dependent on profit-and-loss accounting.

Our own work on landed elites (McCrone et al., 1995) argued that the ideological claim to be 'keepers of the land' (see Figure 6.4) reinforced 'social' power and status. Max Weber had argued that (economic) class distinctions are linked in complex ways with (social) status distinctions. Hence: 'Property as such is not always recognised as a status qualification, but in the long run it is, and with extraordinary regularity' (Weber, 1978: 932).

In practice, as Weber argued, the three key dimensions of power – economic, social and political – are intertwined in such a way that they 'naturalise' social inequalities and help to

FIGURE 6.4
Land restrictions

Source: Image Copyright Hugh Venables. This work is licensed under the Creative Commons Attribution-Share Alike 2.0 Generic Licence. To view a copy of this licence, visit http://creativecommons.org/licenses/by-sa/2.0/ or send a letter to Creative Commons, 171 Second Street, Suite 300, San Francisco, CA 94105, USA

make any alternative distributions of power unthinkable. It is an easy step to conclude that there is nothing untoward about concentrations of property; it is the 'natural' order, and we will have more to say about this in Chapter 16 when we discuss Scotland as a 'country'.

Reforming land

The legislation by the Scottish government in 2016 to charge sporting estates business rates generated concerted reaction and protest, even though it came as a surprise to many people that these were not levied already, just as they would be for any other business in Scotland.

In fact, landowners of sporting estates had stopped paying business rates only in 1994 when the Conservative government of John Major gave them exemption. Further, although there has been an extension of community buyouts of land in The Hebrides, Assynt and Knoydart among others, the doubling of land in such ownership since 1995 started from a very low base, and is so hedged about with legal and financial constraints as to make such modest political action a long way from 'land grabbing' as caricatured by its strident opponents (critics are fond of the phrase 'Mugabe-style land grab'; see e.g. www.spectator.co.uk/features/9534022/should-we-fear-a-mugabe-style-land-grab-in-rural-scotland/).[10] As Tom Devine observed, there has been a remarkable continuity of landownership which the economic malaise in land prices between the 1880s and the 1930s had obscured:

> The nation still has the most concentrated pattern of landownership in Europe with 75 per cent of all privately owned land in the 1970s held in estates of 1000 acres or more, and more than one-third in estates of more than 20,000 acres. By the 1990s, this remarkable level of concentration had, if anything, increased further. (2000: 457)

Taking a historian's viewpoint, he points out that the continuities in landownership are deeply significant, as the core of estates have owned most of the land in Scotland over the past nine centuries: 'among the owners of great estates are several families who have been in hereditary occupation for more than thirty generations' (2000: 458).

We might assume that such a state of affairs is 'natural', that, in any case, there must be something in the argument that the traditional landed estate requires so much external investment that landowners are being public spirited in taking it on. Devine observes that there is nothing 'natural' about existing patterns, and points out that private landownership virtually disintegrated in Ireland as the 'mincing machine of land reform', as Thompson called it, destroyed the system of great estates in the space of a few years.

Indeed, in Scotland, the tax burden on landownership is slight, and ironically, it is public money, notably via the Common Agricultural Policy (CAP) and tax exemptions which make estate ownership viable, and even profitable. The extension of the 'heritage industry' which insinuates the 'private' life of the family with the perception of public 'stewardship', most notably in the form of the stately homes business, has stabilised landowners as 'keepers of the land'.

The nexus of politics and power

In our study of the heritage industry in Scotland (McCrone et al., 1995), we commented:

> Between the years 1900 and 1975 when local government was reformed, the
> Dukes of Buccleuch and of Roxburghe between them held the convenership of
> Roxburgh County Council for forty-three years. The Border landowners could
> also exercise their influence indirectly through the offices of Sheriff Depute
> (held once by Walter Scott), Commissioners of Supply, Lords Lieutenancies, and
> as Justices in the Commission of the Peace. By 1975, the year that Roxburgh
> County Council was abolished, the Duke of Buccleuch opened Bowhill [one of
> his houses] to the public. (1995: 127)

The involvement in politics of landowners like Buccleuch (the previous duke was
Conservative MP for North Edinburgh in the 1970s) has been a feature of Scottish, and
British, society, and as 'independents' they had a significant role in local government until
its reform in 1974. Much of this was not done for immediate material advantage, but out
of a sense of *noblesse oblige*, as something expected of a person, usually a man, of power
and privilege.

More generally, the connections between land, property, capital and politics defined
Scotland for most of the twentieth century. There is good example of that in George
Younger, the scion of the brewing and business family of McEwen/Younger (see Figure 6.5).

The connections between business, banking and politics are nicely captured by the family tree. Sir William McEwan Younger was the managing director of the company which
merged McEwan's and Younger's, and had been a prominent member of the Scottish
Conservative Party along with many of his kinsmen. His wife was related to A.J. Balfour,
Prime Minister between 1902 and 1905. Two members of the dynasty were Secretaries of
State for Scotland, Sir John Gilmour (1924–9) and Sir George Younger (1979–86). Having
been Scottish Secretary of State for Scotland in Mrs Thatcher's Conservative government
from 1979 to 1986, and Secretary of State for Defence from 1986 to 1989, Sir George
Younger resigned from politics to take up a directorship with RBS, and became its chairman
in 1992. Such were the connections between property and politics.

The gentry were marked off from the industrial and commercial bourgeoisie by their
association with *country* rather than city. Culturally too they were distinct, for the lairds
and nobles sent their children to be educated at English public schools, a feature which also
marked them out from the bourgeoisie which had set up Scottish independent and mer-
chant-company schools in Edinburgh and Glasgow. They spoke with 'English' accents
('Received Pronunciation' (RP), as it was called), rather than 'Scottish' ones.

By the last quarter of the twentieth century, the hegemony of the class coalition
which united bourgeois and gentry had weakened, driven by the loss of local economic
control and the transformation of Scottish business. The traditional alliance was
described by the Checklands thus: 'Scotland became endowed with great commercial

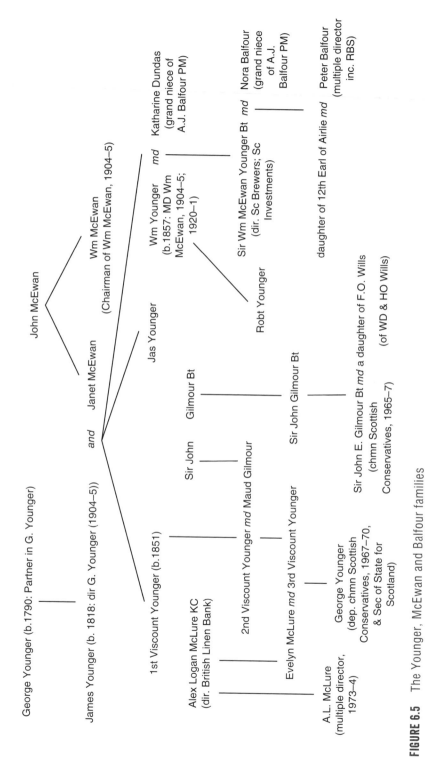

FIGURE 6.5 The Younger, McEwan and Balfour families

Source: Scott and Hughes (1980): Figure 4.7 Intermarriage of Younger and Balfour families

and industrial families, taking their place alongside the landed nobility, and to some extent linked together by marriage' (1984: 175). The alliance had also been political.

The lairds had provided leadership of the Conservative Party (strictly speaking, the Unionist Party, as it was called in Scotland until 1965). The Liberal–Unionists who had broken away from the Liberals over Irish Home Rule in the 1880s tended to be businessmen rather than lairds. They drew their original strength from the imperialist-inclined capitalist class concentrated in west–central Scotland. The transformation of business we have described in this chapter destroyed the class coalition which had dominated Scottish politics at local and national level until at least the late 1950s. Its political–ideological base also fell away as the Protestant working class, especially in the west, began to put class before religion from the 1950s. Effectively, the old 'ruling' class was no more.

Who runs Scotland today?

We might even ask: is there a ruling class any more, or has the transformation of its economic base into an international and globalised one meant that the question is no longer meaningful? Perhaps we should ask the question in a different way: not so much whose material interests are being promoted and defended; rather, who are the key decision-makers? In Chapter 2, we introduced the idea of the Scottish policy community which coalesced around the Scottish Office in the post-war years in order to bring about economic and social change in Scotland. This has been described as the 'Scottish lobby', which

> was a coalition of interests around The Scottish Office and its agencies including political parties, trade unions, and business seeking more resources for Scotland. They were able to cooperate in securing favourable treatment over public expenditure, regional policy and other issues without putting aside their distinct class, sectoral and party interests. (Keating, 2010: 21)

Pre-devolution, the key person was the Secretary of State for Scotland, whose remit was to fight Scotland's corner in the (Westminster) Cabinet, and to let it be known that he was doing so on behalf of the nation in the Union. This was not a party political issue, and Secretaries of State pre- and post-war, notably Walter Elliot, Tom Johnston, Willie Ross, George Younger, Malcolm Rifkind and even the neo-liberal Michael Forsyth fought Scotland's corner to good effect. The 'Scottish lobby' included the STUC, CBI (Scotland), Scottish Council (Development and Industry) – what Moore and Booth (1989) called 'meso-corporatist' organisations.

Managing Scotland

The Scottish style resembled a system of negotiated policy-making extant in other small European democracies, even though it fell well short of comprehensive social partnership. Thus it was that, since 1999 when the Scottish parliament was established, Scotland 'followed a more traditional social democratic ethos of public service delivery, based on universalism, egalitarianism and cooperation with public service professions' (Keating, 2010: 206).

The greater the political differences in policies and ethos north and south of the border, the more the 'Scottish lobby' focused on support for devolution and greater self-government. So it was that Labour, which had inherited the mantle to speak for Scotland in the 1970s, did so successfully until it was edged aside by the nationalist party in the context of devolution. Furthermore, public opinion (reflected in Scottish Social Attitudes surveys) swung behind this new way of doing politics, both in terms of judging who *has* most influence in governing Scotland as well as believing that the Scottish government *ought* to have most influence (Figure 6.6).

The shift towards seeing the Scottish government as the prime institution of influence, coupled with the complementary view that it should have sufficient powers to do that, has been a feature of post-devolution Scotland. By the late 1980s, political unionism which had helped to put together the 'Scottish lobby' notably pre-war had grown thrawn (that is, stubborn) and defensive, reduced simply to carrying out the UK government's wishes post-1979, and could no longer provide the game plan for Scotland and its leading classes.

Elite transformation

The transformations in Scottish politics can be gauged from the changing social compositions of MPs (Keating and Cairney, 2006). Post-1945 and before devolution in 1999, both Conservative and Labour MPs conformed closely to class stereotypes:

> Labour MPs were more likely to be working class, trade unionists and former councillors who entered Parliament as the culmination of a career in municipal politics. Few of them made it to high office, especially outside of their reserved domain of the Scottish Office. Scottish Conservative MPs, for their part, were disproportionately upper class, public-school educated and with military backgrounds. Indeed this tendency increased during the 1950s and 1960s with the decline of urban Toryism. (Keating and Cairney, 2006: 44)

It is devolution and the Scottish parliament which have transformed the social composition of each party. Labour representation at Holyrood moved sharply away from a manual working-class base to a professional middle-class one, in terms of the occupational backgrounds of MSPs. Conservative representation has moved in a similar direction.

Indeed, the 'formative' occupations of MSPs in the 2011 parliament were fairly evenly split between those from 'professional' occupational backgrounds (33 per cent) and 'politics-facilitating' backgrounds (28 per cent), that is roles in assisting elected politicians (referred to as SPADs, short for **Sp**ecial **Ad**visors).[11] This 'professionalising' of politics is as prominent at Holyrood as it is at Westminster. Cairney and his colleagues observe: 'The rise of legislators with a formative experience in narrowly defined "politics-facilitating" roles is

FIGURE 6.6

Who runs
Scotland?

Source: http://
whatscotlandthinks.
org/questions/
which-institution-
ought-to-have-
most-influence-
over-how-
scotland-is-run-
5#line (accessed
August 2015)

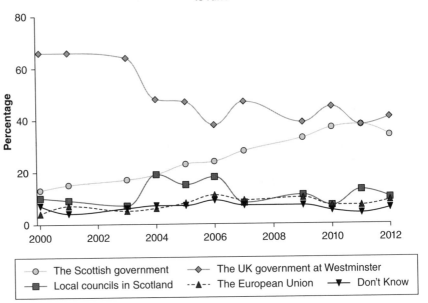

Which institution do you think has most influence over how Scotland is run?

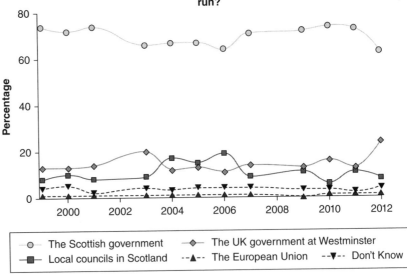

Which institution ought to have most influence over how Scotland is run?

a common feature of the devolved legislatures where they now challenge the professions
as the primary recruiting ground' (2015: 18).

   This shift in occupational backgrounds among elected politicians does not imply that
they 'represent' the occupations, still less the wider social class interests whence they came.
Rather, it is that the 'professionalising' of politics at all levels, in the sense that a much
higher proportion both have university degrees (especially at Holyrood) as well as 'training'

in politics as a trade, leading to accusations that the modern political class have little experience of life beyond politics (see Cowley, 2012).

There is an added Scottish dimension to this, for as Lindsay Paterson argued, 'civic Scotland', those interest groups and civic associations which played a major part in agitating for, and helping to set up, the Scottish parliament in the 1990s, was led by people with similar backgrounds and perspectives (see Paterson, 2002b). Keating and Cairney comment:

> It would be an error to read off political attitudes directly from the backgrounds of politicians, but the presence of public-sector professionals is also consistent with the greater consensus in Scotland around traditional models of public service provision and the lesser enthusiasm for the forms of privatisation, quasi-privatisation and competition found in England. It is also consistent with the greater emphasis on consensus and negotiation in public policy-making, in consultation with service providers. (2006: 57)

It is, perhaps, less a matter of a separate 'policy community' so much as a 'Scottish policy style' which has two dimensions: how policy is made in consultation with 'pressure participants' such as interest groups; and how it is implemented in partnership with local authorities and such groups (Cairney, 2014). In other words, 'there is often a distinction between the way that governments engage with groups when making policy and the "policy tools" they use to implement it' (Cairney, 2014: 308). If nothing else, the language and vocabulary of policy-making and implementation in Scotland (arguably a feature of all Scottish governments since 1999, Labour–Liberal Democrat and SNP) is one of 'partnership' and negotiation, in contrast to a more confrontational style associated with Westminster (Keating, 2010). Scottish governments emphasise social partnership, which draws in any case on the long-standing Scottish policy community, geared up over much of the past century to 'speak for Scotland' with one voice.

Conclusion

In this chapter we have addressed the key question of who runs Scotland, locating our answers in the *longue durée* of Scottish economy and politics, notably in the context of Scotland's membership of the British state. In doing so we encounter a particular conundrum. On the one hand, there is little evidence of the pattern of concentrated and interconnected ownership of Scottish business which Scott and Hughes found for much of the twentieth century. On the other hand, the political demands for greater self-government have grown, even to the point of Scottish secession from the British state becoming a real possibility.

There are, in truth, different ways of squaring that circle: notably, that Scotland has an open economy because that is the way the world is, and it is the role of governments to maximise those economic opportunities which matter by inducing footloose capital to invest here. Be that as it may, there seems to be little debate these days about owner-ship and control of the Scottish economy. Baird et al. made the point: 'When John Firn undertook his research on ownership in the 1970s his main conclusion was to warn against undue reliance on branch plants. Unfortunately, this warning proved only too correct' (2004: 51).

To return to the point we made at the beginning of this chapter, power is all-encompassing when there appears to be no alternative. How can one change things if it seems to be an impossible task, if people see it as the way of the world?

On the other hand, we can make two points. First, the deregulation of capital markets was driven not by economics but by politics, in the context of the rise of the political ide-ology, neo-liberalism, since the 1970s. Second, it cannot be inevitable if there are real alternatives on the ground. Rhenish capitalism, with a focus on non-market social coordi-nation between business, labour and governments, is a feature of some Northern European states, most notably Germany (see Crouch, 2013; Keating and McCrone, 2013). Furthermore, there is nothing inevitable about 'globalisation', as we shall see in Chapter 24. And as Baird et al. observe: 'Britain's very dispersed, fluid and externalized form of institutional com-pany ownership is itself not typical. It is largely restricted to this country [the UK] and the USA' (2007: 31).

Running alongside the fragmentation of 'Scottish' capitalism is the continuing concentra-tion of landownership in Scotland. This has changed very little over the past century, and is itself a reflection of the ease with which Scottish land can be bought and sold. As Andy Wightman pointed out, most of the landowning class who owned land in the 1870s still do so today. Somewhat unusually, the land reform legislation proceeding through the Scottish parliament in the early months of 2016 was strengthened by Scottish government to make it more 'radical', in the light of public representations. Nevertheless, the Scottish government rejected the proposal from Wightman and the Scottish Greens to disallow ownership through tax havens (www.bbc.co.uk/news/uk-scotland-scotland-politics-35353760). In the light of the 2016 Scottish election results, and the potential balance of power held by the Greens, it remains to be seen whether this is set in stone.

Faced with an 'open' economy in terms of ownership and control of Scottish business, and patterns of landownership which have changed little over the previous century, it might seem that there is little for governments and politicians to do. This might seem especially piquant in the context of strengthening political powers since devolution in 1999. What, we might ask, are they for, if economic power is located elsewhere?

There is, however, a wider agenda. The task, even of nationalist politicians hitherto, has been less to break that Union, as win concessions from it. It is not a zero-sum game, or at least has not been so up to now. The long complaint was that Westminster did not take Scotland seriously enough if it was a true partner in the Union, rather than that it was a small put-upon addendum to greater England.

Paterson has made a similar point in a different way. He argued that the creative ten-sions between a radical and reformist vision for Scotland's future have depended upon mobilising 'the Scottish interest', and claiming its authority (Paterson, 2015a). 'Parliament', he says, 'could never have avoided becoming civil society incarnate', for not only was it dependent on civic elites for ideas, but various interest groups were built in to consultation and implementation of policies which they themselves were instrumental in creating. We might take the view of Keating in the final sentence of his book *The Government of Scotland*: 'Scotland cannot, any more than other small nations, determine its future on its own, but it can shape its own adaptation to these powerful forces' (2010: 262).

Chapter summary

So what have we learned in this chapter?

- That the tight systems of ownership and control which characterised business in Scotland in the heyday of empire have been transformed.

- That even in the 1970s the structure of economic power was an amalgamation of old and new wealth, but since then business takeovers have significantly weakened local ownership and control.

- That iconic Scottish businesses – whisky, North Sea oil and Scottish finance – are no longer in Scottish hands to any degree that matters.

- That landownership in Scotland is highly concentrated in a few hands and that a mere ten owners hold more than 10 per cent of private land.

- That, nevertheless, much of it is owned by 'traditional' landowning families going back more than a century.

- That the nexus of power and politics has nevertheless changed, notably in transforming the social character of Scotland's political classes.

- That the key conundrum for Scottish politics is decision-making in the context in which so many material assets are not amenable to local control.

In the next chapter, we will shift our focus from 'government' and 'economy', and look at who gets what in modern Scotland, at how the material means of survival and prosperity are distributed.

Questions for discussion

1. How would you account for the transformation in patterns of business ownership in Scotland in the last century?

2. Does it matter in the twenty-first century that so much of Scottish business is externally owned and controlled? Can anything be done about it?

(Continued)

(Continued)

3. Why is landownership in Scotland in relatively few hands? Why do landowners hold onto it? Is land reform legislation likely to make a difference?

4. How have the links between property and political power changed over the last century? Why has there been a transformation in the social and class backgrounds of politicians in Scotland?

5. Can politicians and governments do much to change who owns business and land?

Annotated reading

(a) Business in Scotland: The classic study by J. Scott and M. Hughes, *The Anatomy of Scottish Capital* (1980), is the benchmark for understanding how patterns of ownership and control have changed. There are updated studies by S. Baird et al., notably 'Scottish capital: still in control in the 21st century?', *Scottish Affairs*, No. 58, 2007; in *Quarterly Economic Commentary*, 49, November, 2004; and further data updates in *Scottish Left Review*, Issue 64, 2011.

(b) Landownership in Scotland: A. Wightman's work is essential reading, notably *The Poor Had No Lawyers: Who owns Scotland?* (2013); and previously *Who Owns Scotland?* (1996).

(c) On politics and power, see M. Keating's *The Government of Scotland*, 2nd edition (2010); M. Keating and P. Cairney, 'A new elite? Politicians and civil servants in Scotland after devolution', *Parliamentary Affairs*, 59(1), 2006; P. Cairney, 'The territorialisation of interest representation in Scotland', *Territory, Politics and Governance*, 2(3), 2014.

Notes

1 The Clydesdale Bank was taken over by the (English) Midland Bank in 1920, and sold to National Australia Bank in 1987. By 2016, it was being floated on the London Stock Exchange.

2 The Proclaimers' hit song 'Letter from America' (1987) had the refrain 'Bathgate no more. Linwood no more. Methil no more. Irvine no more.'

3 These are Scottish-registered firms which are wholly owned subsidiaries of external holding companies (Baird et al., 2007: 8).

4 Baird et al. added the 2010 figures in *Scottish Left Review*, Issue 64, 2011.

5 For an account of the rise and fall of USL and its owner, see www.bbc.co.uk/news/uk-scotland-scotland-business-35681740.

6 The definitive account of North Sea oil and gas is Alex Kemp's *The Official History of North Sea Oil and Gas*, in two volumes (2011; 2012). Earlier, and less 'official', accounts include:

Christopher Harvie's *Fool's Gold: The story of North Sea oil* (1995) and Charles Woolfson et al., *Paying for the Piper: Capital and labour in Britain's offshore oil industry* (1997).

7   While their formal headquarters were in Scotland ('brass plate' HQs), it is a moot point as to whether these banks were owned and controlled in Scotland in any meaningful sense.

8   *Dirigisme* (from the French *diriger*, to direct) refers to an economic system where the state exerts a strong directive influence over investment.

9   Andy Wightman was elected as a Member of the Scottish Parliament (MSP) for the Scottish Green Party in May 2016.

10   Andy Wightman commented: 'it will probably take a generation before Scotland's land governance is set on anything like a modern footing' (www.andywightman.com, 13 August 2015).

11   At UK level, David Cameron, Ed Miliband and Nick Clegg had all worked as SPADs (see www.theguardian.com/politics/2015/apr/19/spads-special-advisers-took-over-british-politics).

7

INEQUALITY, POVERTY AND POWER

So much for looking at who runs Scotland. But who gets what? How are wealth and income distributed in Scotland? Note too our use of 'power' in the title. It is not an alliterative afterthought to poverty and inequality, but central to understanding Scotland, indeed any society. Nor is power a zero-sum game which you either possess or not, and, in any case, it works most effectively when it is opaque. In capitalist societies, money makes the world go round. Martin Wolf, the economics commentator, observed: 'In a society dominated by wealth, money will buy power' (*Financial Times*, 15 April 2014).

Chapter aims

- To analyse the distribution of wealth and marketable assets in Scotland, and how it has changed over time.

- To focus on what the most and least wealthy own, if anything, and how particular kinds of assets are distributed.

- To examine how income is distributed in Scotland, given that for most people it comes from wages and benefits.

- To review poverty in Scotland, treating it as the other side of the coin of 'affluence', and asking who is most susceptible to being poor, and in what senses.

- To treat 'poverty' not simply as something which attaches to individuals and households, but which has spatial dimensions.

- To explore the extent to which Scotland has particular features with regard to wealth and income, and set our understanding of these in a wider, global, context.

The power of money

By looking at how material assets, specifically wealth and income, are distributed, we are assuming that money, in the form of wealth, assets or income from labour, is what makes the world go round. In his influential book *Capital in the Twenty-First Century*, Thomas Piketty commented:

For millions of people 'wealth' amounts to little more than a few weeks' wages in a checking account or low-interest savings account, a car and a few pieces of furniture. The inescapable reality is this: wealth is so concentrated that a large segment of society is virtually unaware of its existence, so that some people imagine that it belongs to surreal or mysterious entities. (2014: 259)

For most people in their everyday lives, real wealth is unimaginable, beyond the few objects they own, perhaps a car, some furniture and, if they are lucky, a house they nominally 'own', or rather the share of the property not mortgaged to the bank or building society.

Wealth, for most of us, consists of *things*, what the social anthropologist Daniel Miller called 'stuff' (see Chapter 23). Even *what* we own has only a hazy value, because we have little sense of what it is worth in monetary terms. Thus, assessing the market value of objects by 'experts' makes for popular television, often to the surprise of their owners, for, truth to tell, most of us value objects for their *use-value* and not their *exchange-value*. This distinction is based on the idea that most of us use or consume the things we own, rather than treating them primarily as saleable commodities in the marketplace. A good example is the house people live in, and 'use', which may (or may not) also have tradable value in the marketplace as a commodity, but for most of us is secondary.

Piketty makes the point: 'Housing is the favourite investment of the middle-class and moderately well-to-do, but true wealth always consists primarily of financial and business assets' (2014: 260). Only when such assets are commercially valued, on divorce, or death, do we find out what they, and we, are 'worth on the market'.

What we are worth in financial terms is also tied up with how we come to possess wealth, and why. We can more easily comprehend that 'earnings' relate to what we are paid in income for our labour, that is our salaries and wages.[1] The tax authorities have stopped using the term 'unearned income' because it implies a judgement that the owner has not earned it. Most people whose taxes are deducted at source (in the UK, this is PAYE, 'Pay As You Earn') are more aware of net rather than gross 'earnings', that is their disposal income. For those who are self-employed, or who receive income from shares, savings or property, 'income' and 'wealth' are less distinct. Taxing income at source is easier than taxing wealth, and there is a measure of redistribution relating to income levels with differential tax rates, and thus the distribution of incomes is less unequal than that of wealth.

Wealth in Scotland

So how is wealth distributed in Scotland? We are fortunate in having good data on the ownership of wealth and assets since 2006, rather than relying on data distributions for the UK as a whole, which was the case until then.[2] Data collected by the Office for National Statistics (ONS) provides information on individuals and households in a **longitudinal sample**[3] for three waves:[4] (a) 2006 to 2008; (b) 2008 to 2010; and (c) 2010 to 2012.

We are able to chart how the same individuals fare over time, even though over a six-year period we would not expect a great deal of people's wealth to alter very much.

The Wealth and Assets Survey (WAS)[5] has some methodological restrictions: the measure of net wealth, for example, is based on personal private wealth of households, and not business assets, nor rights to state pensions (private pensions are included). Second, only 'private' households are included in the WAS, and not people living in residential institutions,[6] nor homeless people. Estimates of wealth are calculated at current values at the time of interview and have not been equivalised to take account of differences in household size or composition.[7] Nevertheless, the available data are much better than what we had previously, so we can be more definitive about what people in most of Scotland[8] are 'worth', and we can compare how wealth is distributed compared with elsewhere in the UK.

Wealth and assets

The WAS identifies four main types (Figure 7.1):

- *financial* wealth pertaining to financial assets minus the value of all non-mortgage borrowing;

- *property* wealth, that is value minus debt such as a mortgage or loan against the property;

- *private pension* wealth, namely occupational pension schemes;[9]

- *physical* wealth, that is the financial value of such things as cars and household goods (televisions, computer, jewellery, etc.).[10]

So what are people in Scotland worth?[11]

Total household wealth in 2010–12 was £714 billion, an increase of 2.4 per cent on 2008–10, but a flatter rate of growth than the one which occurred between 2006–8 and 2008–10. By far the two main components of wealth were private pension wealth (£302 billion) and property wealth (net worth of £277 billion), representing between them over 80 per cent of total household wealth. Physical wealth (£97 billion) and financial wealth (£87 billion) respectively made up the rest. Clearly, the overall balance of wealth depends on the fluctuations of the different elements, with increases in pension and physical wealth accounting for the overall increase in wealth between 2006 and 2012. Financial and property wealth did not appreciate in value to the same degree in that period.

Wealth distribution in Scotland

How are forms of wealth distributed in Scotland? In 2010–12, the wealthiest 10 per cent owned 44 per cent of all wealth, the top 2 per cent of households owning 17 per cent of total wealth and the wealthiest 1 per cent owning 11 per cent. There is, then, considerable concentration *within* the most wealthy top decile.[12] The least wealthy 50 per cent, on the other hand, owned a mere 9 per cent of wealth, with the least wealthy 30 per cent owning hardly any wealth at all (a mere 2 per cent).

Most of us, to be sure, would be quite unable to say what we are 'worth' in terms of wealth. The WAS study was based on three waves of interviews with samples of individuals who provided information on their households. Technical details of the surveys are given in the WAS report, and especially Appendices 1 and 2 (www.gov. scot/Resource/0047/00473432.pdf).

Some forms of wealth were far more unequally distributed than others. Table 7.1 shows the distributions for the wealthiest 10 per cent and the least wealthy 50 per cent.

Put another way, the wealthiest 10 per cent owned almost five times as much as the least wealthy 50 per cent combined, and over twenty times as much as the

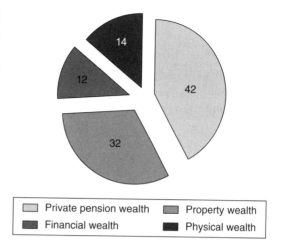

Private pension wealth Property wealth
Financial wealth Physical wealth

FIGURE 7.1   Components of total wealth, 2010–12 (percentages)

Source: Scottish Government, 'Wealth and Assets in Scotland, 2006–2012' (2015: 6)

bottom 30 per cent. Even where the least wealthy 50 per cent owned financial assets, these had a median value of only £500, compared with a median for the Scottish population as a whole of over £5000.

Wealth over time

How has this distribution changed over time, if at all? Compared with 2006–8, the share of wealth owned by the wealthiest 10 per cent fell from 49 to 44 per cent, largely due to falls in the value of pension wealth between 2006 and 2012, a period which included the post-2008 financial crisis. Unsurprisingly, the contrasts are greatest between the top and bottom deciles such that the top 10 per cent owned over 400 times more than the bottom 10 per cent, but such contrasts are volatile because the latter have no assets to speak of.

TABLE 7.1   Wealth distributions by type

2010–12 Type of wealth	The wealthiest 10% owned	The least wealthy 50% owned
Financial wealth	74%	Less than 1%
Pension wealth	55%	Less than 3%
Property wealth	43%	6%
Physical wealth	33%	20%

Source: 'Wealth and Assets in Scotland, 2015'

Only when it comes to physical wealth (such as cars and household goods) are assets at all spread out, and even these are still unevenly distributed. While the wealthiest 10 per cent owned around a third of such assets, this was far more than the whole of the bottom 50 per cent, who owned around one-fifth.

The most unequally distributed kind of wealth was financial wealth, where the wealthiest 10 per cent owned 3.4 times more than the rest of the population put together. At the bottom, it is even possible to 'own' negative amounts, with the least wealthy 20 per cent having more debts than assets owned.

Private pension wealth, the next most unequally distributed, was highly concentrated among the wealthiest, with the top 10 per cent owning twenty-two times more pension wealth than the bottom 50 per cent. Indeed, the bottom 20 per cent had no pension wealth whatsoever. Just under half (43 per cent) of the Scottish population have private pension wealth, which has dropped marginally as shares lost their value after the 2008 crash. Nevertheless, the worth of pension wealth to the richest 10 per cent was almost 100 times more than what the bottom 30 per cent owned.

A useful summary measure of distributional inequality is the **Gini coefficient**, which has the merit of being easy to comprehend: a coefficient of 1 indicates perfect inequality (where one person owns everything), while 0 is perfect equality (where everyone owns the same amount). We can then place distributions on a scale of 0 to 1, which allows us to compare how different forms of wealth are distributed; the higher the coefficient, the greater the inequality. The Gini coefficients for each type of wealth are given in Table 7.2.

Key points

First, age makes a difference. The longer you live, the more you accumulate, and hence, person for person, old people are worth more than young people. This has led to speculation that, for example, 'generational' inequalities are greater than 'class' inequalities. While it is true that households in the wealthiest 10 per cent are ten times more likely to

TABLE 7.2   Gini coefficients by wealth type

2010–12 Type of wealth	Gini coefficient
Financial wealth	0.93
Pension wealth	0.74
Property wealth	0.64
Physical wealth	0.45
All wealth	**0.61**

Source: Wealth and Assets Survey (2015: table 4.1, p. 19)

be headed by an older person, and, for example, are much more likely to own their property outright having paid off the mortgage, simply living longer makes you wealthier, all things being equal.

However, as Piketty observes, 'contrary to popular belief, intergenerational warfare has not replaced class warfare' (2014: 246), for the concentrations of wealth are in fact greater *within* each age cohort than between them. As far as property wealth is concerned, it is less likely to be the case that the lowest decile, who are unlikely to be home owners, has the lowest levels of debt than the next two or three deciles, because buying a house will incur substantial debt in the early years with no offset for positive value.

The second point is that wealth inequality in Scotland mirrors the distribution in the rest of the UK with 44 per cent of total wealth owned by the wealthiest 10 per cent – unsurprising, given the common tax system. The top 10 per cent own about five times more than the bottom 50 per cent taken together. Scotland was somewhat more equal than the rest of the UK in 2010–12, the ratios between the top two and the bottom two deciles being 87 in Scotland and 105 in the UK as a whole, a difference which is statistically significant.

The ONS report comments: 'The fall in inequality in Scotland over the three survey waves means that it has gone from being more unequal to be slightly less unequal than Great Britain as a whole over the last six years on these [ratio] measures' (ONS, 2015: 12). We can only speculate as to why this should be so. It is unlikely to be due to direct political intervention, because taxation policy remains largely under the control of the UK government.[13] It has more to do with where individuals and households, and especially the wealthy, choose to register their base for tax purposes (more live in London, for example). In other words, it is likely to be an artefact of taxation practices than of policy decisions by governments.

The least wealthy

People in the bottom 30 per cent of households have very few assets and own as little as 2 per cent of total wealth in Scotland. Indeed, they have no financial wealth to speak of, no private pension wealth, own only 6 per cent of property wealth and 7 per cent of physical wealth. In demographic terms, the bottom 30 per cent are likely to contain disproportionately more single-adult and lone-parent households, as well as the young, reflecting the fact that wealth tends to accumulate over the life cycle. Unsurprisingly, they are more likely to be economically inactive, but, more surprisingly, almost half of those in the least wealthy 30 per cent were headed by someone in work, indicating that being employed is no guarantee of being able to build up wealth. They are also more likely to have few or no educational qualifications, and to live in rented housing.

What do the bottom 30 per cent of people in Scotland own by way of assets, if any? Only a quarter of them have a savings account, but almost eight in ten have a bank current account in credit, an increase of 10 percentage points since 2006. This may simply reflect the fact that having a bank account has become essential to receive wages and benefit payments in the digital age. Wages and benefits no longer come in hard cash across the counter.

That the bottom 30 per cent are in credit may reflect the parlous statement of household finances that staying in credit, however modest, is necessary for financial survival. To those with little wealth, avoiding debt is necessary to 'getting by'. Neither are the bottom 30 per cent more likely to use alternative sources, such as savings in cash (keeping money 'under the mattress'), nor do they depend on informal loans from other people or give other people their money to look after. Few of the least wealthy have credit card balances in the black, and while debt is not a particular feature of their lifestyle, they are three times more likely to be in arrears on debt. This reflects their lack of financial muscle such that they are unable to borrow against any assets owned, not having many of those in the first place.

Having assets worth only £500 does not provide much of a financial cushion, and few own other financial assets such as ISAs (Individual Savings Accounts), while none own shares. What is significant is that highest levels of debt, and the greatest increase proportionately, relate to student loans, which have grown from a median of just over £4000 in 2006–8 to over £14,000 in 2010–12, massively dwarfing any other form of debt (hire purchase (HP) agreements, for example, are valued at less than £2000).

Changing wealth patterns

We might have been able to gauge asset values from simple cross-sectional surveys which give us a snapshot of what people own, but the particular value of the Wealth and Assets surveys lies in their longitudinal character. Interviewing people at three time-points tells us something about change and stability in terms of asset ownership.

Change and stability

So just how much stability or movement is there across the decile categories? Do people move up or down or stay in the same decile? Just how much volatility is there? The simple answer is that around half of households remained in the same wealth decile between 2008–12 and 2010–12, roughly about a quarter moved up and a similar proportion moved down. Nevertheless, there is less mobility in more recent years (2010–12) than previously (2006–8), possibly reflecting recession and financial austerity. Those deciles with the highest amount of 'retention' are the richest (76 per cent of whom remain where they were) and the poorest (61 per cent), with middle cohorts showing some modest movement across deciles but only into the adjacent ones. This is not surprising, given the relatively short time-span (six years at most), for rapid shifts are unlikely to occur in terms of asset ownership outwith unusual circumstances such as personal bankruptcy.

Movement between wealth bands is more likely to occur with regard to financial wealth, such that less than one-third (31 per cent) of households stayed in the same wealth band between 2008–10 and 2010–12. There was a slight downward movement, with proportionately more households moving down (37 per cent) than up (32 per cent), but this possibly reflects the fact that many of the wealth bands are narrow.[14]

Property wealth

As far as property wealth is concerned, the vast majority of people (eight out of ten) stay in the same decile, reflecting retrenchment in the housing market, and even in some cases a paper loss of market value if house prices fall. Almost everyone (over 90 per cent) without property wealth in 2008–10 was still without any in 2010–12, and the little movement that there was simply moved people into adjacent bands. Physical wealth (such as cars and household goods) is more volatile, reflecting people's changing economic circumstances; in recessionary times, with greater job insecurity, few people go in for further wealth acquisition (changing your car, for example). As with most other forms of wealth, two-thirds of both the top and the bottom deciles (respectively, 66 per cent and 68 per cent) simply remained where they were.

Laying out wealth

What do these surveys tell us about wealth ownership in Scotland? The WAS report comments that Scotland, like the rest of the UK,

> faces stark realities in wealth, with the wealthiest 10 per cent owning nearly half of all financial, property, pension and physical wealth in Scotland. In comparison, the least wealthy 30 per cent of the population owned no financial or pension wealth, and only 6 per cent of property wealth and 7 per cent of physical wealth. (2015: 47)

Any fall in wealth inequalities has more to do with the fall in the monetary value of assets owned by the wealthiest 10 per cent than any significant improvement among the non-wealthy. Those who are particularly at risk in the assets register are younger households, especially those on low wages and unable to get a foothold on the housing ladder, and single-adult and single-parent households who have a high risk of low wealth and much greater propensity for household bill arrears and are unable to use wealth as a buffer against unforeseen economic circumstances.

As we shall see when we discuss distributions of income, having a job is no longer a protection against low income and low wealth. As the ONS study observes:

> Households need sufficient income to be able to accumulate wealth. Those in low wealth households in employment are more likely to be headed by someone without qualifications, in routine or manual occupations. Often this employment is low paid, and can be temporary, and the experience of low pay can be long lasting. This increases the risks of low income, meaning households do not have the capacity to accumulate wealth. (2015: 47)

This nicely makes the point that 'income' and 'wealth' are not independent of each other, and while the wealthy also tend to have higher incomes, and vice versa, we cannot always assume that they do.

Distributions of income

Income is far less unequally distributed than wealth. For example, in 2011–12, the top 10 per cent of households in the income distribution earned about twice what the bottom 30 per cent earned, whereas for wealth the top decile owned about twenty times more than the bottom three deciles (Wealth and Assets in Scotland, 2006–12: ii). The distributions of income and wealth both show a spike such that those in the top deciles earn and own far more than lower deciles, but whereas the top 10 per cent of households have about 25 per cent of income, the wealthiest decile has 44 per cent of the wealth (see Figure 7.2).

Why wealth should be far more unequally distributed than income is not difficult to explain: it is far easier to tax income at source via PAYE. While it is true that income disparities have grown in the last few decades, taxation levels on income, while far less progressive than previously, continue to have a mildly redistributive effect.

Another way of looking at the distribution is to take weekly household income by deciles (equivalised for household size). Figure 7.3 shows the weekly household income for each decile for selected years since the mid-1990s. The income ratio of the richest to the poorest deciles remains stable at roughly four to one. This translates into a median income for the richest 10 per cent of about £800 per week, and for the poorest, of about £200 per week.

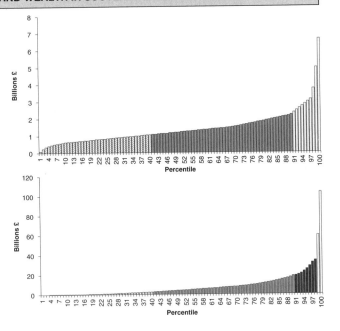

THE DISTRIBUTION OF INCOME AND WEALTH IN SCOTLAND IS HIGHLY UNEQUAL

Income is unevenly distributed in Scotland

The chart to the right shows the distribution of household income at each percentile. The distribution of income is dominated by a small proportion of very high income households.

In 2012/13, the bottom 40 per cent of households (blue bars) had around 20 per cent of total household income; the 'middle' 50 per cent (black bars) had half of all income – this is consistent over time. **The top 10 per cent of households (dotted bars) had around 25 per cent of all households income.**

Wealth inequality is far more unevenly distributed

Despite the majority of the population being distributed across a narrow band of income, this is enough to make it extremely difficult for much of the population to acquire wealth. In the period 2010 to 2012, the least wealthy 40 per cent of households (dashed bars) in Scotland owned less than 5 per cent of wealth; the 'middle' 50 per cent (black bars) owned around half of wealth; and the wealthiest **10 per cent of households (dotted bars) owned 44 per cent of wealth**. The top 2 per cent alone owned 20 per cent of all personal wealth in Scotland.

FIGURE 7.2   Comparing wealth and income distributions in Scotland

Source: 'Wealth and Assets in Scotland' (2015: 8)

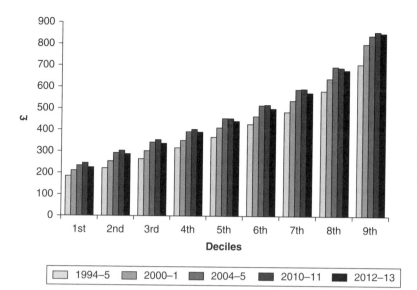

The stability of the ratio is not simply among the richest and poorest income groups, but more broadly. For example, if we compare the top 30 per cent with the bottom 30 per cent, the income ratio is 3.6:1. Put another way, the top 30 per cent have just over half of all income, and the bottom 30 per cent get about 14 per cent[15] (see 'Poverty and Income Inequality in Scotland, 2012–13', chart 6, p. 21 (www.gov.scot/Publications/2014/07/9247)).

By the second decade of the twenty-first century, median incomes actually *fell* by £400 pa, to £23,000 pa, and 2012–13 was the third consecutive year in which median incomes in Scotland did so (Figure 7.4). We can see that this downturn occurred both before housing costs were taken into account (BHC) and after (AHC).

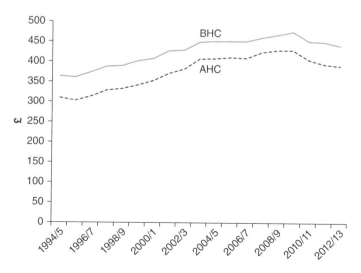

FIGURE 7.4
Median weekly
household
incomes, 1994–5
to 2012–13

Source: 'Poverty
and Income
Inequality in
Scotland, 2012–13',
derived from table
A6, p.39

Shares of income

The fall in incomes, however, affected the lowest deciles most (Figure 7.5). Indeed, in 2012–13, only the top two deciles saw an increase in income; all other income deciles saw their incomes fall, possibly the result of shifts in the labour market together with more regressive taxation policies introduced by the incoming Conservative–Liberal Democrat government elected in 2010. We can see how the lowest deciles lost out disproportionately in terms of income, while the top two deciles gained (see Figure 7.5).

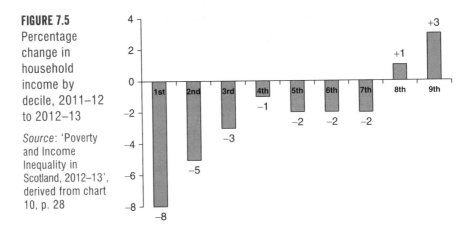

FIGURE 7.5
Percentage change in household income by decile, 2011–12 to 2012–13

Source: 'Poverty and Income Inequality in Scotland, 2012–13', derived from chart 10, p. 28

Put another way, the annual income in real price terms for the top, bottom and middle deciles are, respectively, £44,300, £23,000 and £11,500. Thus, the top 10 per cent get twice the income of the middle decile and four times what the bottom decile earn (see Figure 7.6).

FIGURE 7.6
The distribution of weekly household income across Scotland in 2014–15 by decile

Source: 'Poverty and Income Inequality in Scotland, 2015', chart 11, p. 37

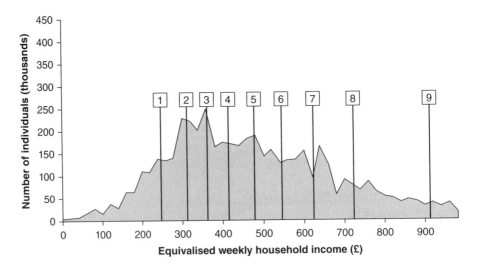

The figure marks where each decile falls. It shows that most of the lower deciles cluster together, but that the higher income deciles are more spread out. This reflects higher inequalities at the top end of the distribution. Note too the extent to which the top 10 per cent have incomes well above the median fifth decile: indeed, the gap between the seventh and the ninth percentile is in income terms as great as that between the lowest decile and the sixth.

Social characteristics

What kind of people, socially and demographically, fall into these bands? Single-adult households are over-represented in the bottom income deciles, especially single parents, who are clustered in the bottom three deciles, as well as single working-age adult house-holds. Pensioners tend to be disproportionately clustered in the lower deciles, but *not* in the lowest one. As we might expect, over half of people in the bottom three deciles are in households with no one in employment; and at the other end of the income distribution, over 80 per cent of those in the top three deciles are in full-time employment.

In Figure 7.7, we can see the distribution of incomes (before housing costs) and how they cluster at the median, with the long tail at the higher end reflecting the greater ine-quality of incomes at the top. The 2013–14 income distribution is included as a line for comparison and shows little variation from the 2014–15 shaded area.

The way to comprehend this graph is to imagine one in which there were as many poor people as rich ones. In that event, the graph would be 'bell shaped' (what is called a 'normal distribution'), with most people clustered in the middle. What we see in practice, however, is that there are proportionately few people at the top end of the

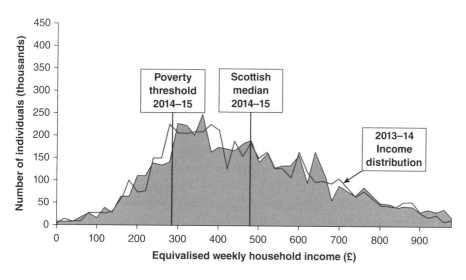

FIGURE 7.7

Distribution of weekly household income, 2014–15

Source: 'Poverty and Income Inequality in Scotland, 2015', chart 12, p. 38

distribution, but that they have *much* higher incomes than the rest. The median mark represents what the 'middle' household gets (the point at which there are as many households above as below the line). The official poverty threshold line, however, is much lower than the median, and this shows that there is a significant proportion of households who are not defined officially as 'poor', but have incomes much lower than the median one.

Poverty in Scotland

So far, we have looked at distributions of wealth and income, and now we turn to people at the bottom end of the distribution, to 'poverty', which can be measured in different ways.

Relative and absolute measures of poverty

Relative poverty is officially set at 60 per cent of the median income. The median, that is the 'middle' income in the distribution, is preferable to other measures of 'average', notably the mean,[16] because it is far less susceptible to extreme values and, as we have seen, income (and especially wealth) are not distributed normally (see Figure 7.7), but have a small number of high-income earners at the upper end of the distribution.

Absolute poverty, as opposed to relative poverty, measures the extent to which the lowest income households fall behind the rate of inflation. This has also shown an increase, from 15 per cent of the population in 2011–12 to 17 per cent in 2012–13. People are said to be in *absolute* poverty if they live in households whose equivalised income is below 60 per cent of the inflation-adjusted median income. Because absolute poverty is based on the 2010–11 poverty threshold, and because real incomes have decreased since then, this means that *absolute* poverty rates have overtaken *relative* rates.

In 2012–13, one in six people in Scotland were in relative poverty before housing costs (BHC) are taken into account. This was an increase on the previous year of 2 percentage points and translates into 820,000 people, 110,000 more than in the previous year. This is a significant increase in statistical terms and represents a move away from previous and long-term declines in relative poverty. If we take housing costs into account, the proportion in relative poverty in Scotland rises to one in five (19 per cent), which is a 3 per cent increase on the previous year. Thus, in 2012–13, we can say that there were 1 million people in Scotland living in relative poverty, 140,000 more than the previous year. Indeed, the decrease which had occurred between 2009 and 2011 was reversed.

Why should relative poverty rates have increased? It is likely to be the result of UK government welfare reforms, still ongoing, the freezing of benefits and tax credits, as well as changes in the labour market and employment patterns. While personal tax allowances have been modestly adjusted at the bottom levels, the overall effect is an increase in relative poverty. Coupled with a fall in the median income in Scotland of around £400 a year, the poorest households have increased in number. Taking the longer view, over the previous decade, relative poverty had declined from around 20 per cent in 2002–3 to 14 per cent in 2011–12. The decreases in relative poverty at the end of the first decade of the twenty-first century resulted from the fall in median incomes rather than a rise in people's economic circumstances.

Child poverty

Poverty, however, is not all of a piece. In terms of child poverty, the percentage of children in combined material deprivation[17] and low income rose from 9 to 11 per cent, representing an increase of 20,000 children on the previous year. This rise reflects low wage growth, restricting eligibility to benefits and tax credits under welfare reform, and deteriorating labour market conditions, especially for unskilled workers.

The major gains which had been achieved since 1998 and held up to the middle of the next decade have gone into reverse. The report, 'Poverty and Income Inequality in Scotland' comments:

> The increase in child poverty in the latest year [2012–13] is driven by a fall in household incomes for working households with children. For households in employment, the reduced entitlement to tax credits has contributed to a fall in household incomes for those with lower earnings who were unable to increase the number of hours worked. (2014: 11)

In April 2013, at the start of the new fiscal year, there was a 26 per cent decrease in the number of households receiving in-work tax credits, compared with the previous year.

Adult poverty

Working-age adult poverty has also increased to 15 per cent in 2012–13. This means that almost 500,000 working-age adults were living in relative poverty in Scotland in that tax year, reversing the decadal decline since the turn of the century. The household income for working-age adults without children fell, although at a slower rate than for households with children. As elsewhere in the UK, the number and proportion of low-paid jobs in Scotland decreased between 2004 and 2013. In particular, those in low-paid work saw no real increases in earned income. The balance between earnings and benefits rates has reversed because earnings have not kept pace with inflation, while out-of-work benefits have risen in line with prices. In other words, the cuts in child benefits and tax credits since 2010 have had the overall effect of cutting incomes for working-age households.

Pensioners gain ...

If working-age adult households have been the losers, then pensioners have been modest gainers. In particular, the fall in absolute poverty rates, and to a lesser degree relative poverty rates, have been the most significant change among them. Whereas almost 40 per cent of pensioners were in absolute poverty in 1998–9, the proportion fell to 15 per cent by 2012–13. During the first decade of the century, the proportion of pensioners in relative poverty fell from 23 per cent in 2002–3 to 15 per cent in 2012–13. Thus, the fall in pensioner poverty has been steeper than that for children and working-age adults.

... and workers lose

What is a feature of modern Scotland is *in-work* relative poverty. Thus, over half of working-age adults in poverty suffer from in-work poverty, representing 250,000 working-age adults. Concomitantly, the number of children living in such households has also increased. Six in ten children in poverty in Scotland in 2012–13 were living in households where at least one adult was in employment. The assumption that being in work is the best route out of poverty no longer applies. The recent changes in the social structuring of poverty in Scotland have been summed up by Scottish government researchers as in Figure 7.8.

FIGURE 7.8
Types of poverty in Scotland

Source: www. scotland.gov. uk/Topics/ Statistics/Browse/ Social-Welfare/ IncomePoverty

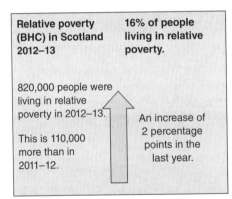

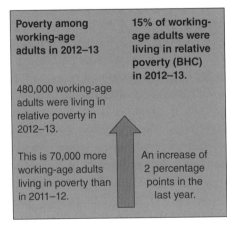

Deepening poverty

There is no doubt that poverty in Scotland increased in 2012–13. While the rate of poverty increased for all groups, the largest increase was in the rate of child poverty.

We have already made the distinction between absolute and relative poverty, the latter referring to people whose household incomes are below 60 per cent of the UK median value. There are two further official definitions which are useful in making sense of poverty in Scotland: *severe* poverty, which refers to people whose household incomes are below 50 per cent; and *extreme* poverty, where the threshold is 40 per cent (see 'Severe Poverty in Scotland', March 2015 (www.gov.scot/Publications/2015/03/4673)).

The number of people in Scotland in 2012–13 in relative poverty was 820,000, of whom 510,000 were in severe poverty (less than £11,500 pa), of whom, in turn, 230,000 were in extreme poverty (with incomes of less than £9200 pa). Thus, just over 60 per cent of people in relative poverty were in the 'severe poverty' category, and of the latter, 45 per cent fell into the 'extreme poverty' category.

Put in terms of the Scottish population as a whole, the proportions are, respectively, 16 per cent (*relatively poor*), 10 per cent (*severely poor*) and 4 per cent (*extremely poor*). Factoring in housing costs increases severe poverty to 14 per cent, and extreme poverty to 10 per cent, of the Scottish population. When we do this, working-age adults with children were most likely to suffer severe poverty (unlike pensioners), while working-age adults were the group most likely to live in extreme poverty after housing costs.

Over the first decade of the twenty-first century, while relative poverty has fallen, a higher proportion of Scots are now in extreme poverty than in 2002–3. If we look at those in extreme poverty (with equivalised incomes of less than £9200 pa, being below 40 per cent of the UK median income), nearly *half* of those in poverty are in this lowest category. In other words, the poverty of people who are nearest the median line has been ameliorated, leaving the 'extreme' poor as a higher proportion of the poor. Thus, working-age adults are most likely to be extremely poor, while pensioners tend to be in the low-income category between 50 and 60 per cent of the UK median.

Changes over time

In the decade between 2002–3 and 2012–13, relative poverty fell, but most of this fall occurred in the most marginally poor group. This means that poverty became far more a matter of *kind* than of degree. The Scottish government report Severe Poverty in Scotland comments: 'the picture in 2012/13 is very different from ten years previously. In 2002/3, 36 per cent of people in poverty were living in extreme low income after housing costs, compared with 50 per cent in 2012/13' (2015: 17 (www.gov.scot/Publications/2015/03/4673)). Such households are likely to be reliant on benefit and tax credit income. Restrictions on housing costs seem to fall mainly on tenants than landlords (see Figure 7.9).

To get a sense of the proportions in each social group in poverty, and particularly the extent of that poverty, we can make the comparisons shown in Figure 7.10.

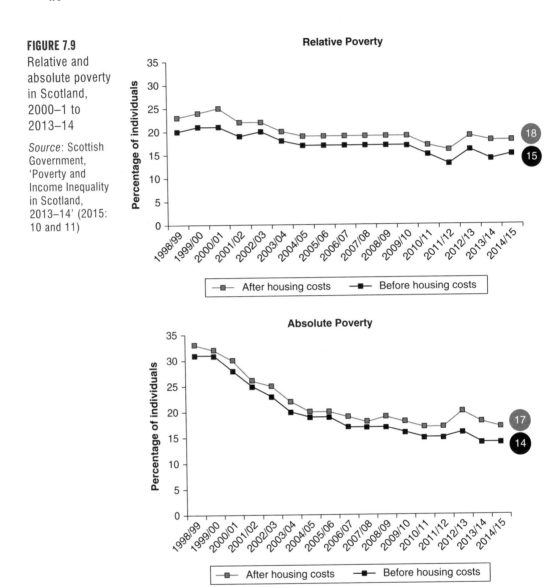

FIGURE 7.9

Relative and absolute poverty in Scotland, 2000–1 to 2013–14

Source: Scottish Government, 'Poverty and Income Inequality in Scotland, 2013–14' (2015: 10 and 11)

These data show that poverty is now deepest among working-age adults (more than half are in the extremely low-income category), while pensioners are least likely to have extremely low incomes (i.e. below 40 per cent). The merit of defining poverty in relative terms is that it avoids assuming that it is an all-or-nothing affair, and we can see that the depth of poverty is as significant as its spread.

Who are the poor?

So what sorts of people are most likely to be poor in Scotland today? The first decade of the twenty-first century has certainly seen a change in the nature of poverty. Getting a job still remains the best route out of being poor, but we have seen that the proportion of the 'working poor' has grown significantly, reflecting low levels of skills and wages. It remains true that the risk of severe poverty increases if households move into unemployment. Employment reduces the risk of poverty, but only if it is full-time work, and if more than one member of the household is working, even part-time, then the household's ability to escape poverty increases.

The rise in zero-hours contracts[18] even if working status is given as 'employed' manifestly does not reduce risks. While single-parent households have the greatest risk of relative poverty, those suffering the greatest risk of severe or extreme poverty are single-person households without children. For families with children, the risk of poverty, including extreme poverty, is heightened where the mother is young, that is, under 25, which doubles the risk compared with other age groups.

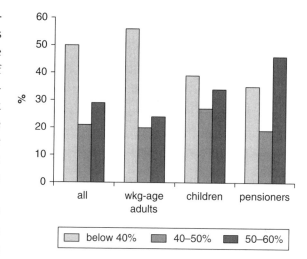

FIGURE 7.10   Percentage in relative poverty, after housing costs, 2012–13

Source: 'Severe Poverty in Scotland', extracted from charts 2, 4, 6 and 8 (www.gov.scot/Publications/2015/03/4673)

Nor do large families run an undue risk of extreme poverty, for people with three or more children are not significantly poorer than smaller families or people with no children at all. Minority ethnic groups, notably those who are defined as 'mixed, black, Chinese and other', have a higher risk of severe and extreme poverty compared with the white British population, although the number of cases is small.

Getting to be poor

What drives people into poverty, however, is not simply the size and security of their income. The rising costs of food, heating, water and housing are reflected in the fact that 60 per cent of the income of the poorest 10 per cent is spent on these, compared with half that figure for the richest 10 per cent. In other words, a much higher proportion of the income of the poor goes on 'basics'. Furthermore, poverty in Scotland is changing:

> Work is no longer a guarantee of a life free of poverty; people in poverty face increasing costs; and those in receipt of benefits and tax credits – which of course includes many in work – are finding their incomes squeezed. While policies targeted at reducing poverty have reduced relative poverty over time, the depth of poverty has not improved. Those in poverty are now more likely to

be further away from, not closer to, the poverty threshold. It is these poorest children and adults who are likely to live in prolonged financial and material deprivation, with the poor outcomes associated with persistent poverty. (Scottish Government, 'Severe Poverty in Scotland', March 2015: 42 (www.gov. scot/Resource/0047/00473036.pdf))

Deprivation and poverty

We have focused thus far on whether or not individuals and households possess the requisite material resources, especially wealth and income. There is another important aspect of **deprivation** which is a feature not simply of people themselves, but of the areas in which they live.

We saw in Chapter 5 that measuring deprivation has become much more sophisticated since Carstairs and Morris derived their measures based on 1981 census data. In 2003, Oxford University produced the Scottish Indices of Deprivation. Since that publication, the Scottish government has published indices of multiple deprivation in 2004, 2006 and 2009, referred to as the 'Scottish Index of Multiple Deprivation' (SIMD).

The SIMD uses data relating to multiple aspects of social and economic life to construct a broad and comprehensive picture of deprivation across Scotland. Seven different aspects are identified – the seven SIMD domains – and data from these domains are combined to produce the index. The seven SIMD domains relate to employment, income, health, education and skills, access to services, crime and housing (Figure 7.11). The latest SIMD analysis relates to 2012, which uses the same domains as in 2006 and 2009.

Multiple deprivation

The SIMD is constructed by dividing Scotland into 6505 small areas, called datazones, each containing around 350 households. The index provides a relative ranking for each datazone, from 1 (the most deprived) to 6505 (the least deprived). Each datazone has on average 800 people living in it.

Because they are population based, datazones can vary hugely in geographical size. For example, datazones might be confined to a few streets in towns and cities where people live close together, while in rural areas datazones are sparsely populated, and can cover many miles. In Chapter 5, we noted that comparing datazones in, for example, Easterhouse in Glasgow and Oban in Argyll may produce different results simply because they are drawn to have roughly the same size of population rather than for their meaningful social geography. Furthermore, physical datazone boundaries have stayed the same since they were created in 2004, but we cannot assume that the people who live within each datazone are the same people who were there in 2004.

The key to understanding datazones is to remember that they are measuring the characteristics of *areas*, not of individuals. The SIMD identifies multiply deprived areas; this

SIMD Scottish Index of **Multiple Deprivation**

Indicators in the SIMD 2012 domains

Income	Access	Education	Housing	Crime	Employment	Health
Adults receiving Income Support or Income-based Employment and Support Allowance (2011)	Drive time to a GP (2012)	Pupil performance on SQA at stage 4 (2008/9–2010/11)	Percentage of people living in households which are overcrowded (2001)	Domestic housebreaking (2010–11)	Working age unemployment claimant count averaged over 12 months (2011)	Standardised Mortality Ratio (2007–10)
Children dependent on a recipient of Income Support, or Employment and Support Allowance (2011)	Drive time to retail centre (2012)	School leavers aged 16–19 not in education (2009/10–2010/11), employment or training (2010 & 2011)		Crimes of violence (2010–11)		Comparative illness factor (2011)
	Drive time to a primary school (2012)		Percentage of households without central heating (2001)	Common assault (2010–11)	Working age Incapacity Benefit recipients or Employment and Support Allowance recipients (2011)	Emergency stays in hospital (2007–10)
	Drive time to a secondary school (2012)	17–21 year olds enrolling into fulltime higher education (2008/09–2010/11)		Sexual offences (2010–11)		Estimated proportion of population being prescribed drugs for anxiety or depression or psychosis (2010)
Adults receiving Jobseeker's Allowance (2011)	Drive time to a post office (2012)			Drugs offences (2010–11)	Working age Severe Disablement Allowance recipients (2011)	
	Drive time to a petrol station (2012)	School pupil absences (2009/10–2010/11)		Vandalism (2010–11)		Proportion of live singleton births of low birth weight (2006–09)
Children dependent on a recipient of Jobseeker's Allowance (2011)	Public transport travel time to a post office (2012)	Working age adults with no qualifications (2001)				Hospital stays related to alcohol misuse (2007–10)
Adults and children in Working Families Tax Credit households whose income is below 60% of median (i.e. below £198 per week) (2010)	Public transport travel time to a GP (2012)					Hospital stays related to drug misuse (2007–10)
Adults (aged 60+) receiving Guarantee Pension Credit (2011)	Public transport travel time to a retail centre (2012)					

Criteria for selecting indicators

Direct as possible measures for the given aspect of deprivation

Up to date

Capable of being updated on a regular basis

Statistically robust

Measure widely relevant features of deprivation (not conditions just experienced by a small number of people or areas)

Weights for each domain

Employment	28%
Income	28%
Health	14%
Education	14%
Access	9%
Crime	5%
Housing	2%

FIGURE 7.11 Indicators in the SIMD 2012 domains

Source: Scottish Goverment: Communities Analytical Services (http://www.gov.scot/Topics/Statistics/SIMD)

means that not everyone living in a deprived area is individually deprived, and not all deprived individuals live in multiply deprived areas. So what kind of correspondence is there? In Scotland, with a population of over 5 million, about 700,000 (13.4 per cent) are 'income deprived' on the SIMD income domain, and about 740,000 people live in the 15 per cent most deprived datazones on the overall SIMD. The SIMD study shows that one-third of 'income-deprived' people live in the 'worst' 15 per cent datazones, and that two-thirds of them do not.

So why not simply rely on individual/household measures, and why bother with SIMDs? They are useful planning devices for local authorities and governments – in locating public facilities, for example – but knowing how people are clustered is sociologically meaningful. To reinforce the example we used in Chapter 5, we might imagine two notional communities which had the same mix of people in terms of their social and demographic characteristics, but had quite different social geographies. In area A, for example, people might be spread evenly throughout the community, whereas in area B there are distinct clusters of rich and poor, of advantaged and deprived. We would expect that the different social geographies might well produce different outcomes; that material resources and social facilities are distributed differently. In other words, the 'political geography' of the two communities might differ. On the other hand, of course, they might not, which would tell us something about the political processes 'on the ground'.

What is more likely to happen in practice is that 'deprived areas' come to be stigmatised, as zones of avoidance; that deprivation and stigma get attached to people from the area regardless of their own personal characteristics. Sean Damer (1989) has written eloquently about this stigmatising process in Glasgow, pointing out that if you are identified by your postcode, your life chances, including getting a job, are that much poorer. In other words, you become, in the eyes of the authorities, one of 'those people'.

Methodological issues

It is important to reinforce key methodological points: that because the SIMD is a ranking exercise, from the most to the least deprived, we cannot say that one area is more deprived than another by a specified amount; for example, area A is twice as bad as area B. There is no fixed and definitive point on the scale below which areas are considered 'deprived' in an absolute sense.[19]

Furthermore, the SIMD is a measure of relative *deprivation*, not of affluence, because it has been designed to measure multiple deprivation; in any case, the indicator mix does not permit us to conclude that some variables are much more significant than others. It is also worth pointing out that the SIMD is a measure designed for *Scottish* government purposes and cannot be extended to England, for example, where the construction of spatial units is different (we saw in Chapter 5 that there are methodological difficulties in comparing Glasgow with English cities such as Liverpool and Manchester).

Changing geographies

So much for methodological difficulties. What does the 2012 SIMD report tell us about the distribution of deprived areas within Scotland, and to what extent have they changed since the previous exercises starting in 2004?

- The SIMD 2012 report showed that multiple deprivation in Scotland has become marginally *less* concentrated over time. In SIMD 2004, nearly *half* of all datazones in the most deprived 10 per cent across Scotland were in the city of Glasgow. In SIMD 2012 this has dropped to 36 per cent, with corresponding rises in other local authority areas.

- Second, the areas identified as multiply deprived by SIMD 2012 were similar to those identified by previous editions of the index (SIMD 2009, 2006, 2004). Of the 976 datazones in the 15 per cent most deprived in SIMD 2012, about three-quarters (77 per cent) were also in the 15 per cent most deprived in all the previous editions of the index.

Where in Scotland are these most deprived areas, and have they changed over the period of the exercise? The most deprived area in 2012 was Ferguslie Park in Paisley, which was ranked second in 2009. The other datazones in the list of top five most deprived datazones in SIMD 2012 in order of ranking are: Possil Park, Glasgow Keppochhill, also in Glasgow, Paisley's Ferguslie area, and Parkhead West and Barrowfield area in Glasgow, which was the most deprived datazone in SIMD 2009. In SIMD 2012, this datazone is now ranked seventh. North Lanarkshire, Fife, Renfrewshire and East Ayrshire have seen relatively large *increases* in their share of datazones in the 15 per cent most deprived areas in Scotland between SIMD 2009 and SIMD 2012.

Glasgow, Edinburgh, West Lothian, Aberdeen and South Lanarkshire have seen relatively large *decreases* in their share of datazones in the 15 per cent most deprived areas in Scotland between SIMD 2009 and SIMD 2012. Over half (57 per cent) of Scotland's 15 per cent most deprived datazones are located in only five local authorities: Glasgow (29.6 per cent), North Lanarkshire (10.2 per cent), Fife (5.9 per cent), Dundee (5.6 per cent) and Edinburgh (5.5 per cent). These five local authorities contain 37 per cent of Scotland's population. The five local authorities with the largest *local* share of Scotland's 15 per cent most deprived datazones are Glasgow (41.6 per cent), Inverclyde (40.0 per cent), Dundee (30.7 per cent), West Dunbartonshire (26.3 per cent) and North Ayrshire (25.7 per cent).

These are the same five local authorities as appeared the worst in SIMD 2009; indeed, the 2012 index is still strongly correlated with the 2009 index. The correlation between the individual domains is also strong, particularly for the four domains with the highest weights (employment, income, health, education). We can conclude that despite the changes SIMD 2012 is strongly comparable with SIMD 2009.

The sociology of deprivation

What is sociologically interesting about the SIMD? It provides an alternative way of measuring deprivation, and more generally the distribution of resources and life chances, than simply basing our analysis on individual or household data. In other words, the data tell us different and useful things. This opens up the possibility that living in a deprived (or indeed a non-deprived) area has differential effects on people's life chances.

Relatedly, it has the possibility of telling us something about people's own experiences of deprivation in the context of where they live and what they experience. One of the classic pieces of British post-war sociology was Garry Runciman's study of 'relative deprivation' (1966) in which he showed that people tended to judge their own social position in terms of 'people like themselves', rather than in the abstract. In other words, poor people compared themselves with their peers, including those living close by. If your close neighbours are 'people like you' and you live in an area of multiple deprivation, then that has the possibility of providing a different way of seeing than if you live with people who are in socio-economic terms a lot less like you.

Indeed, this may not work to your psychological advantage, for you may feel even more deprived if you live in a 'mixed' area if all around you is greater affluence and advantage. For example, the city of Aberdeen has a number of highly deprived datazones in what is a sea of prosperity and plenty. As in much of sociology, it is far less who is like you in 'objective' terms than who you actually compare yourself with, who your 'reference group' is. Social solidarity, or the lack of it, is based on judgements such as these.

Making sense of inequality

Let us now broaden our discussion of income and wealth. We could be forgiven for seeing deprivation, poverty and inequality in local and immediate terms and as a technical exercise, but it is manifestly a much wider issue. Piketty's magisterial work *Capital in the Twenty-First Century* (2014) is the latest, and most comprehensive, analysis of what is a global trend, or at least has such implications. He observed:

> Global inequality of wealth in the early 2010s appears to be comparable in magnitude to that observed in Europe in 1900–1910. The top thousandth seems to own nearly 20 percent of total global wealth today, the top centile about 50 percent, and the top decile somewhere between 80 and 90 per cent. The bottom half of the global wealth distribution undoubtedly owns less than 5 percent of total global wealth. (2014: 438)

A major change over the century, according to Piketty, has been the emergence of the 'patrimonial middle class' or 'super-managers' earning 'super-salaries' who fuse capital and income, a phenomenon especially of the Anglo-Saxon countries such as the United States, the UK, Canada and Australia. Income inequality in these societies, which had been high until the 1940s, began to rise again from the 1980s such that distributions of wealth and income are as unequal as they were in the early part of the twentieth century. Piketty's point is that it took world wars to force down extreme inequalities such that societies became more equal, and more solidaristic, places. He comments: 'To a large extent, it was the chaos of war, with its attendant economic and political shocks, that reduced inequality in the twentieth century' (2014: 276).

The economist Tony Atkinson (2015) has also reinforced the point by citing the Pew Research Center's Global Attitudes project in 2014, which found that inequality in the United States and Europe was deeply corrosive of the social order (2015: 1). Atkinson's point is that simply tackling poverty at the bottom is inadequate, because the issue is one of the *distribution* of resources more generally: it is a matter of relating income groups to each other. Nor is this an inevitable outcome. He points out that the UK belongs in the same quadrant as the United States and Canada in having high poverty and high inequality (2015: 26), in contrast to societies like the Netherlands and the Nordic countries, which have flatter income distributions and, as a consequence, lower levels of poverty.

International bodies such as the OECD (Office for Economic Co-operation and Development), not known for their radical stance on social issues, have also warned against rising inequalities. In its 2011 report 'Divided We Stand: Why Inequality Keeps Rising' (www.oecd.org/els/social/inequality) it notes that 'income inequality among working-age persons has risen faster in the United Kingdom than in any other OECD country since 1975'; that the share of the top 1 per cent of income earners increased from 7.1 per cent in 1970 to 14.3 per cent in 2005, hence doubling their share.

Further, transfers and taxes have become less redistributive, as have benefits. Despite being targeted at the poor, taxes have become less equalising, and, at least until the end of the decade, public services were deemed to be mildly redistributive. It is significant that the OECD report was based on data collected before the 2008 financial crisis, and before the election at UK level of centre–right governments in 2010 and in 2015.

The academic and political revival of interest in, and analysis of, economic inequality is not simply to be found among those on the centre–left (see Stiglitz's *The Price of Inequality'* (2012), and Pickett and Wilkinson's *The Spirit Level* (2010)) but on the centre–right. The economic commentator Martin Wolf, who writes for the *Financial Times*, published a book in 2014 called *The Shifts and the Shocks*. He attributed the 'huge shift' in the distribution of income from wages to profits, and, within wages, from bottom and middle to top, to globalisation, technological changes, financial liberalisation, changes in social norms, and 'particularly corporate governance' (2014: 322). He concluded:

> the past three decades have seen the emergence of a globalized economic and financial elite that has become ever more detached from the countries that produced them. In the process, the glue that binds democracy – the notion of citizenship – has weakened. The narrow distribution of the gains of economic growth risks exacerbating this development. (2014: 352)

In other words, this is much more about social order than it is about market values. Indeed, market values, at least as practised in Anglo-Saxon countries, may well be corrosive of the social order on which they so depend.

The inefficiencies of inequality

Furthermore, there is now more general concern about the economic inefficiencies of inequality. The global credit rating company Standard and Poor's issued a report in early 2016 on quantitative easing and its impact on economic inequality in the UK. Standard and Poor's commented: 'We believe [that] high levels of income and wealth inequality can hamper economic growth over the longer term' (see GlobalCreditPortal, 'QE and economic inequality: the UK experience').

What is remarkable about that statement is that it emanates from a company whose task it is to monitor the workings of capitalism. It documents how the richest 20 per cent have experienced the largest income gains between 1977 and 2014. As regards wealth, Standard and Poor's conclude:

> financial wealth in the UK has increased considerably in the aftermath of the global economic and financial crisis. The share of net financial wealth (net of financial liabilities) held by the wealthiest 10 per cent of UK households has increased ... from 56 per cent in 2006–8, to 65 per cent in 2012–14. (2016: 5)

Standard and Poor's objection to increasing inequality is not derived from a concern with social justice, but because they see it as harming longer term economic growth prospects. The causes are long term and structural: a more flexible labour market, financial market deregulation, lighter taxation of the top incomes and wealth. Furthermore, the Bank of England's monetary policy, notably of 'quantitative easing (QE)' aimed at financial wealth, boosted the assets of the wealthiest few, coupled with what they call a 'jobs-rich, pay-poor' recovery since 2008.

Is Scotland different?

And what of Scotland? Having a degree of self-government, albeit as yet one without substantial control of the levers of macro-economic power and taxation, would appear to put it in a very weak political position. Thus, the similarities between Scotland and the UK have been determined by UK Treasury decisions and not the Scottish government's finance department. Given the UK common tax system, one might take the view that support for redistributive policies in Scotland is little different from those in the rest of the UK; that differences in social attitudes between Scotland and England are differences of degree rather than of kind.

What do Scots think?

Let us examine briefly this assertion, because it has implications for political action, at least in the longer term. How much support is there for redistributive policies in Scotland, and how different are they from the rest of the UK? The Scottish Social Attitudes surveys and the British Social Attitudes surveys have carried similar questions for the last decade and provide useful data. Thus, when asked 'Do you agree or disagree that government should redistribute income from the better-off to the less well-off', we find the responses shown in Figure 7.12.

While support for redistribution in both Scotland and the rest of the UK dipped in the mid-2000s, by the end of the decade, notably in Scotland, it had risen. We can see that in virtually every year, there is proportionately more support for redistribution in Scotland.

As regards the gap between high and low incomes, people both in Scotland and in the UK consider it to be too large by a significant margin, and support is strongly for the 'progressive' option (Figure 7.13).

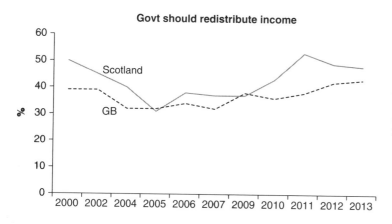

FIGURE 7.12
Attitudes to redistribution in Scotland and GB

Sources: Scottish and British Social Attitudes, 2000–13

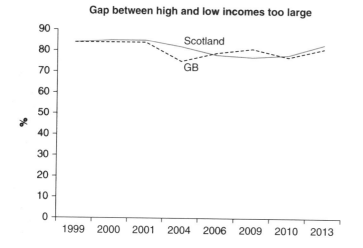

FIGURE 7.13
Attitudes to income distribution

Source: As Figure 7.12

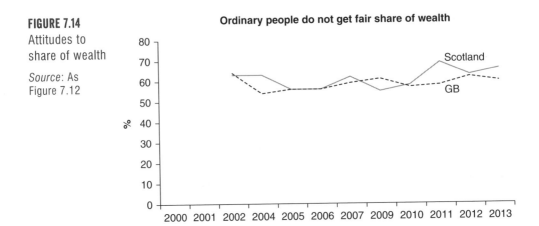

FIGURE 7.14
Attitudes to
share of wealth

Source: As
Figure 7.12

Similarly, there is consensus that 'ordinary working people do not get a fair share of the nation's wealth', with both Scotland and the UK on the 'progressive' side of the argument (Figure 7.14).

There is also strong support for the 'progressive' view that there is one law for the rich and one for the poor, with little significant difference between Scotland and the UK (Figure 7.15).

Only with regard to attitudes to benefits for the unemployed has public opinion moved to the right over the past decade, notably after 2005. Nevertheless, we can see that, up to 2003, the 'progressive' view prevailed in Scotland but not in the UK, and that after mid-decade, public opinion moved somewhat to the right,[20] but less strongly in Scotland than in the UK (Figure 7.16).

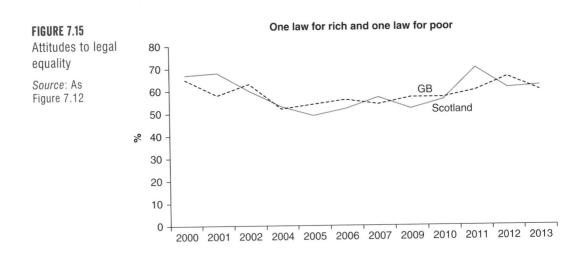

FIGURE 7.15
Attitudes to legal
equality

Source: As
Figure 7.12

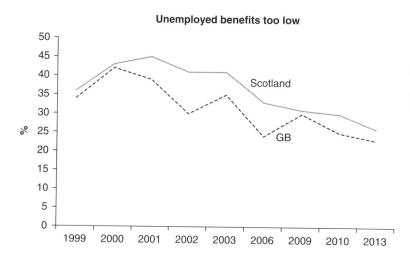

FIGURE 7.16
Attitudes to
unemployment
benefit

Source: As
Figure 7.12

Taken together, these survey findings show us that:

• Scotland is not radically out of line with the rest of the UK;

• Scottish public opinion in particular is consistently in favour of policies which are more redistributive.

If anything, the puzzle is why England elects right-wing governments committed to austerity and concomitant greater economic inequality, when public opinion remains on the centre–left.

Conclusion

In this chapter we have explored the distributions of income and wealth in Scotland and found that the balance of resources and power has shifted significantly in favour of the wealthy. Why this should have happened is an important question, because it gets to the heart of Scotland's economy and society. We might take the view that despite the existence of a devolved parliament, the key decisions about taxation continue to be made by the UK government, which is significantly more centre–right than those in Scotland. It also raises the question that even in the event of independence whether or not Scotland can buck the neo-liberal consensus.

That position, however, assumes there is no alternative, as Mrs Thatcher once remarked: that economic liberalism is so hegemonic that no state, especially a small one, can buck the markets. The problem with that assumption is that empirical evidence does not support the view that it is impossible, notably in Western Europe, where there are diverse 'political economies'. In any case, as both Piketty and Atkinson note, Scandinavian states are able to operate flatter economic distributions of both income and wealth with far fewer people falling into poverty. Writers like the economic liberal Martin Wolf believe that Piketty's argument in favour of substantially higher taxes on high incomes, and a global wealth tax, 'is unquestionably too ambitious' (2014: 352), but that movement in this direction is desirable. If social order is to be maintained, and indeed economic growth is to be pursued, perhaps there is no alternative.

And what of Scotland? It has followed the distributive trends of the rest of the UK, but public opinion is, if anything, more in favour of redistribution and greater equality. The point is not that it diverges markedly from its British counterparts – indeed, we might conclude that they are further to the left in public attitudes than the governments they elect – but that there is groundswell support for more redistributive policies among the political classes in Scotland.

And in any case, the centre of political gravity north of the border has consistently been to the left in terms of party competition. One of the major trends since the Scottish parliament was established in 1999 is the degree to which policies have evolved to meet Scotland's distinctiveness and difference. At a point where the so-called neo-liberal consensus is fragmenting, issues of who gets what, basically who has power, are firmly on the political agenda.

Chapter summary

So what have we learned in this chapter?

- That the distribution of wealth in Scotland mirrors that in the rest of the UK and has moved towards greater inequality since the economic crisis of 2008. Indeed, the winners have been those with financial wealth in particular, and the losers are those with nothing at all.

- That income inequality, which is less unequally distributed than wealth, has also seen increased concentrations of resources at the top and relative impoverishment at the bottom, reflecting changes in taxation and welfare policies, as well as labour market policies. The reasons are long term and structural.

- That the number of people in poverty – about 1 million, or 20 per cent of Scotland's population – has grown in the second decade of the twenty-first century. While there has been a lessening of geographical concentration of 'deprivation', by and large these are changes at the margin, and the continuities are much greater than the differences.

- That these structural changes which produce greater inequalities of wealth and income run against public opinion in Scotland, indeed as they do in much of the rest of the UK.

- That we can locate these changes in a global framework that has generated greater economic inequalities, which even the supporters of market capitalism view as threatening economic growth and social order.

Questions for discussion

1. How has the distribution of wealth in Scotland changed over time, and how does it compare with the rest of the UK?

2. To what extent does the distribution of incomes in Scotland mirror that of wealth, and if not, why not?

3. How have patterns of poverty changed in Scotland over the past decade? Does the concept of 'deprivation' change how poverty is to be understood?

4. What, if anything, can be done to redress the growing levels of economic inequality in Scotland, and is this redress socially and economically desirable?

Annotated reading

(a) For data and analysis of changes in the distributions of wealth and income in Scotland, see www.gov.scot/Resource/0047/00473432.pdf and http://news.scotland.gov.uk/News/Wealth-and-Assets-in-Scotland-179c.aspx#downloads. Also http://scotgov.publishingthefuture.info/publication/poverty-and-income-in-equality-in-scotland-201314.

(b) For comparative discussion of rising inequality levels, see OECD's 2011 report 'Divided we stand: why inequality keeps rising' (www.oecd.org/els/social/inequality). Standard and Poor's paper, 'QE and economic inequality: the UK experience', is available at their Global Credit Portal www.globalcreditportal.com.

(c) For discussions of the wider context within which these data can be understood, see T. Piketty's *Capital in the Twenty-First Century* (2014); and A. Atkinson's *Inequality: What can be done?* (2015); J. Stiglitz, *The Price of Inequality* (2012); K. Pickett and R. Wilkinson, *The Spirit Level* (2010); M. Wolf, *The Shifts and the Shocks* (2014).

(d) The Scottish Centre for Social Research (ScotCen) has collated over time results on social attitudes to income and wealth distributions at http://whatscotland thinks.org/.

Notes

1   The distinction between 'salaries' and 'wages' historically differentiated white-collar workers who were paid monthly directly into bank accounts and manual workers who received a weekly wage packet in cash. This distinction had much to do with status differences between 'middle class' and 'working class', but in the days of bank transfers has fallen into abeyance.

2   When we wrote *Living in Scotland: Social and economic change since 1980* (Paterson et al., 2004), we had to rely on UK-level data; see Chapter 5.

3   A longitudinal study samples the same respondents at different time-points, allowing us to identify any changes in people's behaviour or attitudes. Cross-sectional surveys sample different people at different times, are cheaper to run, but do not tell us how the same people fare.

4   The first sample had 6199 cases, the second 4390 and the third 4540.

5   Details of the survey and report are available at www.gov.scot/Publications/2015/03/2333.

6   Such as retirement homes, prisons, barracks or university halls of residence.

7   For example, we might expect that larger households would 'own' more than smaller ones simply because they lived in bigger and more costly houses.

8   People living north of the Great Glen or in the Scottish islands were not included in the WAS.

9   This includes pension schemes in the 'public sector', such as for teachers, health workers, etc. Only the state pension is excluded.

10 The WAS also includes financial assets such as bank deposits, shares and bonds, cash in hand, and non-mortgage borrowing such as HP debts, overdrafts and loans.

11 We will rely on the most recent analysis for 2010–12, and give changes over time where these are relevant.

12 Deciles are derived by dividing the population into 10 per cent 'slices' according to how much wealth or income they own. We can then compare each decile in terms of how assets or incomes are distributed.

13 Scottish governments will be able to make marginal changes to the rate of income tax, but not on wealth taxes, which remain the preserve of Westminster (www.scottish.parliament. uk/FinancialScrutiny/How_income_tax_revenue_will_change_in_Scotland.pdf).

14 Wealth is highly concentrated at the top, so there is little remaining to go round. If what is left is then divided between remaining decile bands, shifts of small amounts may make any movement between deciles rather meaningless.

15 Comparative data are for 1998/9, and 2012/13.

16 To find the mean income we would divide total income by the number of people, but high incomes would skew the mean unduly.

17 'Material deprivation' uses the Family Resources Survey to calculate people's ability to afford certain items and to participate in leisure and social activities. It is applied to households with incomes below 70 per cent of UK median income to create a combined 'material deprivation and low-income' measure. See 'Poverty and Income Inequality in Scotland', 2012–13, Annex 2, p. 50.

18 The Office for National Statistics reported that the number of people saying they work on contracts without a minimum number of hours climbed to 744,000 from 624,000 in 2014, a rise of 19 to 2.4 per cent of the total UK workforce of 31 million (see ONS, 2 September 2015 (www.ons.gov.uk/ons/dcp171776_415332.pdf)).

19 The 2012 SIMD report comments: 'Of the seven domains, four are based on absolute values (e.g. number of people claiming specific benefits) and can therefore be used to identify the proportion of the population affected by that particular kind of deprivation. This applies to the Income, Employment, Housing and Crime domains. The remaining three domains (Health, Education and Access) are not straightforward counts, but are constructed using weighted scores. As a result, these three domains can only be used in the same way as the overall SIMD ranking – i.e. to compare relative levels of deprivation.'

20 The percentage points difference between those agreeing that 'benefits are too low and cause hardship', and those agreeing that 'benefits are too high and discourage finding jobs' were, for Scotland between 1999 and 2003, +3, +15, +19, +10, +9; and between 2006 and 2013, respectively, –6, –11, –13 and –26. British opinion was significantly more to the right throughout the period.

8

MAKING A LIVING

Oh dear me, the warld is ill divided. Them that works the hardest are aye wi' least provided. But I maun bide contented, dark days or fine. For there's no much pleasure livin' affen ten and nine.[1]

In the previous two chapters our focus has been on how power is structured in Scotland and how wealth and income are distributed. In this chapter we will explore patterns of employment, in short how people make a living. In the following chapter we focus on social class and social opportunity, dimensions based on people's occupations, but with wider implications for social relations in Scotland. Taken together, these four chapters (6 to 9) provide an account of Scotland in terms of its 'social stratification', which refers to the ways that individuals are distributed among the levels or layers ('strata') of a social hierarchy, mainly on the basis of their economic position. Our task, then, in this chapter is to outline how patterns of employment, making a living, have evolved and continue to change, with economic effects which benefit some and disadvantage others.

Chapter aims

- To review debates about Scotland's economic development, in particular the degree to which Scotland was 'dependent' on England.

- To examine the changing shape of Scotland's industrial structure, specifically the occupational transition from a manufacturing to a service economy.

- To describe the impact of this shift on employment, in particular the rebalancing of the ways occupations are gendered.

- To focus especially on the impact of the 2008 financial crash on work and employment in Scotland.

- To assess the impact of the loss of ownership and control in the Scottish economy.

Explaining Scotland's economic development

We will start with the thesis that Scotland's economy was shaped, possibly determined, by the Union of 1707. There have been claims that since Scotland became part of Great Britain in 1707, it could only develop economically as part of the British state; that it underwent 'development by invitation'. This kind of argument implied that Scotland developed a regionally specialised economy in such a way that it fitted the wider requirements of an expanding British imperial economy.

This has evident implications for Scotland's industrial and occupational structures, and it has been assumed that these structures were specialised to reflect what Scotland was *allowed* to do, as part of the imperial command and the global order. If Scotland was indeed a junior partner in British imperialism in the nineteenth century, surely its political economy reflected what was required of it in helping to run that empire?

Between 1750 and 1850, Scotland became not simply an industrial society, but also one of the world's foremost examples. In particular, as Christopher Smout pointed out:

> The central belt of Scotland became ... one of the most intensively industrialised regions on the face of the earth. By 1913, Glasgow, claiming for herself the title of 'Second City of the Empire', made, with her satellite towns immediately to the east and west, one-fifth of the steel, one-third of shipping tonnage, one-half of the marine-engine horsepower, one-third of the railway locomotives and rolling stock, and most of the sewing machines in the United Kingdom. (1987: 85)

Given that prosperity (for a few) rested upon a small number of industries, it is plausible to assume that Scotland's development depended on its becoming regionally specialised.

The dominant image of Scotland's industrial structure was, in the words of the historian Bruce Lenman, that 'by the 19th century, Scotland had developed a *very specialised regional branch* of the British economy, heavily oriented towards the manufacture and export of capital goods and coarse textiles' (1977: 204; my italics). One book in the early 1980s by Tony Dickson and colleagues made the nexus between the economic and the political orders its central theme:

> In relation to Britain as a whole, what were to emerge in Scotland were complementary rather than competitive forms of capitalism, their interdependence being regularised under the political domination of Westminster. Such were the roots of the dependent or client status of the Scottish bourgeoisie. (1980: 90)

Development 'by invitation'

That notion of 'complementary' capitalism implied that Scotland's economic and industrial structures took unusual forms so as to fit in with the demands of the British imperial order of things. Hence, we find the attraction of the idea of economic development 'by invitation', which was associated with the writing of the American economic sociologist Immanuel Wallerstein in the 1970s.

Wallerstein had developed a general theory which treated capitalism as a 'world-system' which was driven by 'under-development' and 'dependency', such that a world economy emerged as early as the sixteenth century rather than as an integral part of the process of industrialisation in the nineteenth century. Accordingly, Wallerstein saw capitalism as a 'world-system' rather than a feature of a national economy, and in the late 1970s this was an attractive way of explaining how Scotland's economy developed.

In 1980, the house journal of world-system theory, *Review*, published a debate between the Scottish historian Christopher Smout and Immanuel Wallerstein. Smout expressed scepticism that describing some territories as 'dependent' in economic terms meant that they ultimately failed to develop economically, and thus were confined to the periphery, and not at the core, of the world capitalist economy. He pointed to Australia, New Zealand and Denmark, which began by trading primary products to 'developed' countries, but which eventually 'made it' to the core.

Thus, said Smout, historic 'dependency' did not turn out to be a barrier to economic development:

> Early 18th century Scotland was, indeed, as much a dependent economy as any country could be in that age, tied specifically to England in commerce and decision-making, more generally to the core countries of England, the Netherlands and France in technology and culture, and tending to look to the same countries on the rare occasions when it needed exceptional capital inputs. (1980a: 612)

It turned out, however, that Scotland was not doomed to permanent under-development. By the nineteenth century, it had a level of capital exports per capita greater than England's, and thus 'dependent' status in the early eighteenth century was simply a stage of economic development.

Smout concluded that 'dependency' did not block economic development in Scotland, but was benign, even beneficial. Wallerstein dissented. He replied to Smout that 'Scotland was a classic case ... of "development by invitation", the privilege (or the luck) of a very few, a case which offers few policy lessons for other states since it cannot be imitated at will' (1980: 633). Wallerstein insisted that the choice to develop or not was not made by Scottish elites, but at the behest of the English, thus:

> Scotland's secret was not structural but conjunctural. The Lowlands were in a position after 1745 [the failed Jacobite rising], in Hobsbawm's phrase 'to take advantage of the exceptionally favourable European and British conjuncture of the end of the eighteenth century'. (1980: 639)

It cannot be denied that Scotland's 'conjunctural' position was important in economic development, being in the right place at the right time, we may say, resulting from its position as a component part of the British state, and hence its wider empire. On the other hand, terms like 'core' and 'periphery' are ambiguous, for it is not clear whether they are simply metaphors, images or fundamental to the theory (for a critique, see Claval, 1980). Smout was critical of notions of core and periphery:

> Neither the old slums nor the new got there because Scotland was a *periphery*; they were the consequence of the nature of Scottish Victorian capitalism and twentieth century planning, just as the problems of Detroit or New York ... are the products of the history of American capitalism and planning, not of any peripheral relationship within the USA. (1980b: 269–70, italics in original)

World-system theory proved to be a creature of its times, of the 1970s and early 1980s, and especially of its author, Immanuel Wallerstein. In retrospect, its value lay in the argument that there was a single capitalist world economy, but a multiplicity of political and cultural systems. We can now see that it was a forerunner of 'globalisation' theories which date from the 1990s, with their focus on the spatial distributional effects of capitalism (we will discuss these in Chapter 24).

The limits of 'under-development'

With the benefit of hindsight, the focus in world-system theory on systematic and deliberate 'under-development' now seems inappropriate to Scotland, which in any case shared
'core' status with England in the Industrial Revolution. World-system theory belonged to a
revisionist or neo-Marxist perspective which defined capitalism as a system of market
exchange, rather than as a mode of production. It also suffered from inherent tautology:
that dependent countries lacked the capacity for autonomous growth; and they lacked this
capacity because they were dependent.

The intellectual climate in the early 1970s was receptive to such theorising, notably in
Latin America where Andre Gunder Frank (1967) showed that the *latifundia* (plantations)
were capitalist because they produced primary products for a world market, even though
they used slave labour, and hence did not conform to the conventional Marxist notion that
'free' labour finds its price in the marketplace.

It had resonances in Scotland because 'colonialism' seemed to fit the context whereby
the traditional economic base was being hollowed out and replaced by 'branch-plant'
factories, where ownership and control were located elsewhere (see Chapter 6). The stirrings of nationalism in the mid-1970s, seen as the local reaction to global forces, and
particularly the rise electorally of the SNP in the 1974 elections, chimed with theories
of under-development, and made them plausible. Scotland, it seemed to many, must be
a colony.

Internal colonialism

This idea was given momentum by the American sociologist Michael Hechter in his
book *Internal Colonialism: The Celtic fringe in British national development, 1536–1966*
(1975). Hechter saw Scotland, Wales and Ireland as 'ethno-nations', locked into a
'cultural division of labour' in which they were allocated subordinate – cadet – roles in
British imperialism. Hechter's book was an ambitious attempt in both conceptual and
methodological terms to apply an explicit Wallersteinian framework to the UK, and he
acknowledged: 'It would not even have been attempted without his [Wallerstein's]
example' (1975: xvii).

Hechter argued that orthodox 'diffusionist' models of development implied that strong
core regions, through powerful central governments, were able to establish one national culture. To the contrary, an 'internal colony' model argued that a spatially uneven wave of
modernisation creates relatively advanced and less advanced social groups and territories. The
stratification system which emerged out of modernisation generated a 'cultural division
of labour'. Thus Hechter saw 'Celtic nationalism' as the political response to regional inequalities and the sidelining of national elites in favour of English hegemony. While industrialisation
in Scotland and Wales, according to Hechter, did allow a degree of 'integration', its effects
were limited:

> Though the partial industrialisation of Wales and Scotland did permit the struc-
> tural integration of these regions into the national society, principally through
> the establishment of national trade unions and the Labour Party, persisting
> economic stagnation in the periphery has shaken much confidence in the class-
> based political organization. (1975: 265)

Hechter's analysis generated considerable interest and controversy, not simply on the
'periphery'. Historians, however, pointed out that Scotland was a poor fit for the theory
because large parts of central Scotland were heavily industrialised. While at times careful
to refer only to the *Gàidhealtachd*, the Highlands and Islands, at other times Hechter
implied that his theory applied to the whole of Scotland.

Scotland, he later admitted, provided a 'more complex' case than Wales and Ireland. He
tried to get round the problem by saying that: 'Because the rulers of the Scottish state were
themselves culturally anglicised, their English counterparts felt it unnecessary to insist
upon total control over Scottish cultural institutions, as they had done in Wales and
Ireland' (1975: 342–3). In other words, he argued that local elites were 'allowed' to participate in imperial activities only as and when permitted (thus, 'development by invitation').

Hechter underscored Wallerstein's notion of 'dependent development' accordingly:
'Industrialisation did not diffuse into the peripheral areas in the same form as it had developed in the core. When industrialisation did penetrate the periphery, it was in a dependent
mode, consequently production was highly specialised and geared for export' (1975: 345).

By the 1980s, Hechter (1982) had modified his account of the 'Celtic fringe' in the light
of criticism. He redefined the industrialised lowlands of Scotland as an 'overdeveloped'
rather than an 'underdeveloped' region, but he held onto his notion that a cultural division of labour existed, such that ethnic groups (notably Jews) who retained a degree of
occupational autonomy, even of institutional autonomy like the Scots, generated what he
called a 'segmental cultural division of labour'.

His revisionist interpretation of Scotland as an 'overdeveloped peripheral region' does
not easily explain why 'overdevelopment' should better account for the rise of such neo-
nationalisms. Tom Nairn was critical of 'analytical Third-Worldism' when applied to
Scotland (Nairn, 1977). To describe Scotland as 'underdeveloped' because it failed to become
an industrial society, which patently it was, does not make analytical or empirical sense.

What cannot be denied, however, is the powerful imagery which 'dependency' and
'colonialism' brought to academic study as well as to political practice in the 1970s and
1980s. Its power lay in being a metaphor rather than an explanatory concept, and it is in
this context that such assumptions have shaped academic work on Scotland, by both historians and sociologists alike.

Understanding occupational transitions

Why, then, discuss such 'dependency theories' by Wallerstein and Hechter if they fail to meet
analytical and empirical tests? Should they not be consigned to the dustbin of intellectual

history? With hindsight we can see that they represented efforts to theorise understandings of Scotland's economic development which are well worth pursuing; in particular, how its industrial and occupational structures developed and changed over time. We might say that asking the questions was more important than coming up with answers.

Even those who did not buy into 'dependency' theories saw mileage in trying to explain key occupational transitions (see, for example, the debate between Geoff Payne and Trevor Jones on understanding occupational transition (1977b)). Payne, for example, in his 1987 book observed that Scotland, as well as England, and Wales, are all

> countries with similar forms of capitalism and a shared recent history. However, we would not expect precisely the same patterns of [social] mobility because Scotland has not shared an identical history. *Its separate culture and historically subordinate relationship to England mean that its employment opportunities have been distinctive.* (1987: 2; my emphasis)

Comparing industrial structures

So what evidence is there that the three British countries, England, Scotland and Wales, have different industrial and occupational structures which might have proved Payne (as well as Wallerstein and Hechter) correct? While it is true that simply comparing the industrial structures of Scotland with those of the rest of Great Britain will not of itself tell us whether or not Scottish capitalism was 'complementary' or 'dependent', such an exercise does give us a much more accurate guide to industrial development in Scotland vis-à-vis England and Wales. If, for example, the structure of industrial employment in Scotland was historically and significantly different from Great Britain as a whole, for example, we might conclude that it had a more specialised economy, fitting into the broad parameters of the British one.

Nineteenth century

In the period between 1851 and 1911 it is clear that while there were differences between Scotland and Great Britain, they were nowhere as great as those between Wales and Great Britain. For example, while 37 per cent of total employment in Wales in 1851 was in mining and quarrying, and a massive 52 per cent in 1911, the figures for Scotland were 9 per cent and 17 per cent, respectively, and Great Britain as a whole, 10 per cent and 15 per cent. In other words, Wales was far more 'specialised' than Scotland, and Great Britain as a whole.

The simplest way to compare industrial employment structures is to construct an 'index of dissimilarity', to take the positive percentage differences between Scotland and Great Britain.[2] To calculate this index in 1851, we add together the differences between the

British and Scottish percentages for those industries for which the British figure is higher. If the structures were identical, the index would be zero. If there were no overlap at all, the index would be 100.

In 1851, the index of dissimilarity between Great Britain and Scotland was 12.3, and in 1911, 10.2. The comparable index for Great Britain and Wales, on the other hand, was 37.6 in 1851 and 41.9 in 1911. If we calculate the indices of dissimilarity between the industrial structures of the ten Standard Regions of Great Britain, in both 1851 and 1911, Scotland is closest to the overall British structure. In 1851 the mean value of the index between the regional structures and that of Great Britain as a whole was 25.4 compared with the figure for Scotland of 12.3, and in 1911 the mean was 25.7 compared with 10.2 for Scotland.

On these figures, there is little evidence for saying that in the second half of the nineteenth century Scotland had an industrial structure which was particularly specialised with respect to the British economy. Scotland mirrored Great Britain's industrial structure and was, if anything, more 'British' than other economic 'regions' (see McCrone, 1992: chapter 3). The key point is that Scotland became an industrial capitalist society within the context of a laissez-faire British state.

Scotland was, of course, a country within the British state with a high degree of civil autonomy within that state, and could not be compared with a region of England (like the north of England, for example). Scotland was especially well adapted to benefit from Great Britain's highly advantageous structural position within a world economy, itself shaped around Great Britain's interests, and Scotland's capitalists took advantage of the economic opportunities which the Empire afforded. As Maurice Kirby put it:

> The distinctive nature of Britain's industrial structure was in fact one of the most outstanding features of the pre-1914 economy. In 1907 the old-established staple trades of textiles, coal mining, iron and steel, and general engineering accounted for approximately 50 per cent of net industrial output and employed 25 per cent of the working population. Most were heavily dependent upon an increasingly narrow range of export markets located mainly within the British Empire, South America and Asia, and coalmining, textiles and iron and steel alone contributed over 70 per cent of the country's export earnings. (1981: 3)

The inter-war period

Scotland was so well adapted to imperial opportunities in the nineteenth century that the collapse of the economy after the First World War was catastrophic for Scotland. We can explain the roots of Scotland's decline in the *surfeit* of imperialism rather than because of clientage or dependence. When the international order collapsed, Scotland, locked firmly into it, suffered in the way experienced by Great Britain as a whole.

The extreme localisation of the effects of this collapse within Scotland in the 1920s and 1930s stemmed from the degree of regional specialisation which had occurred *within*

TABLE 8.1 Indices of dissimilarity between Scotland and Great Britain

Year	Index of dissimilarity
1931	15.4
1951	16.1
1961	18.2
1971	14.6

Note: The larger the index, the greater the difference between Scotland and GB

Source: McCrone (1992: 72)

Scotland prior to the war. Significant specialisation had taken place within Scotland in the nineteenth century. Thus it was that counties dependent on engineering and shipbuilding, such as Lanarkshire, Renfrewshire and Dunbartonshire, suffered most from the economic downturn, as well as the coalmining communities of West Lothian, Fife and Stirlingshire (see McCrone, 1992: chapter 3).

In the four decades in the middle of the twentieth century, from 1931 to 1971, the industrial structure of Scotland was marginally more differentiated from that of Great Britain as a whole than was the case in the nineteenth century. The indices of dissimilarity between Scottish and British industrial employment structures showed remarkably little variation between 1931 and 1971 (Table 8.1).

In 1931 and 1951, Scotland was the economic region with the industrial structure closest to the British mean, and in 1961 and 1971, only north-west England was closer. In general terms, we can conclude that the other British regions were converging with Scotland. Nevertheless, the general process of convergence in the industrial regions of Great Britain in the twentieth century is not mirrored (at least up to 1971) within Scotland. In most respects, industrial differentiation *within* Scotland has been greater than the industrial differentiation of Scotland from the rest of Great Britain; the traditional specialisations of the nineteenth century remained in key industrial regions of Scotland well into the twentieth century (McCrone, 1992: 72–3).[3]

We can argue, then, that far from being a specialised 'region' of Great Britain, Scotland throughout its industrial history has shared a very similar profile to Great Britain as a whole, while containing considerable internal specialisation, reflecting its position as a distinct country within the UK. If we compare Scotland with Wales and Northern Ireland in the 1950s, its industrial structure continued to be much closer to the UK mean. Wales at that point had proportionately eight times the number of workers in mining and quarrying compared with the British mean. In terms of people working in the agricultural sector, Northern Ireland had fourteen times the British mean. Scotland, meanwhile, was within 1 per cent of the British mean in terms of both industrial sectors.[4] In 'industrial' terms, Scotland was British.

Industrial and occupational change

It would seem to follow, then, that Scotland underwent industrial and occupational change along the lines of the rest of the UK and western societies generally. The 'occupational transition' – the shift from manufacturing to service employment – occurred in advanced industrial societies in the post-war period, but accelerated from the 1970s.

The increase in the share of jobs in the service sector – from 24 per cent in 1951 to 33 per cent in 1971, 66 per cent in 1991 and 70 per cent by the turn of the century – is undoubtedly the greatest single shift in sectoral employment which Scotland has experienced in modern times. The growth of the service sector has been by far the greatest single driver of social change in Scotland since 1945. The changes in occupational structure, patterns of female employment and social mobility right through to household structure, demographic behaviour and political orientations can be traced back to this single transformation.

Industrial change

So what does Scotland's industrial structure look like today, and how similar or different is it in comparison with the rest of Great Britain? Using the 2011 census, we can make the following comparisons (Table 8.2). The greater the difference, the larger the index of dissimilarity, which is calculated simply by adding together the differences between Scotland, and England and Wales, for each industrial sector.

The index of dissimilarity between Scotland, and England and Wales, is 13.7, roughly the same as it was in the final quarter of the twentieth century. The largest differences relate to health and social work (+),[5] education (–), professional, scientific and technical services (–), information and communication (–), mining and quarrying (+). Nevertheless, it is the similarities between Scotland, England and Wales which are striking, rather than the differences. If we disaggregate Wales from England, using the 2011 census figures we find a measured difference across all sectors in Wales of 16.2, compared with 13.7 in Scotland. The demise of mining and quarrying in Wales has brought it into line with the rest of the UK in terms of its industrial structure; de-industrialisation has done its work.

Occupational change

In sociological terms, occupational distributions are more relevant than industrial orders, in that what people work *at*, rather than what they work *in*, tells us more about their social and economic relations. Table 8.3 contains the comparative occupational distributions using the 2011 census data for Scotland compared with England and Wales, once more calculating an index of dissimilarity.

TABLE 8.2   Employment in industrial sector, Scotland, and England and Wales, 2011

Industrial sector	Scotland	England and Wales	Percentage point difference
Agriculture, forestry and fishing	1.7	0.9	0.8
Mining and quarrying	1.4	0.2	1.2
Manufacturing	8.0	8.9	−0.9
Electricity, gas, water	1.6	1.3	0.3
Construction	7.9	7.7	0.2
Wholesale and retail	15.0	15.9	−0.9
Transport and storage	5.0	5.0	0
Accommodation and food services	6.3	5.6	0.7
Information and communication	2.7	4.0	−1.3
Finance and insurance	4.5	4.3	0.2
Real estate	1.2	1.4	−0.2
Professional, scientific and technical	5.2	6.6	−1.4
Administration and support	4.3	4.9	−0.6
Public administration and defence	7.0	6.0	1.0
Education	8.4	9.9	−1.5
Health and social work	15.0	12.5	2.5
Other	4.8	5.0	−0.2
Index of dissimilarity			**13.7**

Sources: Scotland's Census 2011 (QS605SC); England and Wales 2011 (KS605EW)

The index of dissimilarity for occupational distributions is smaller than the one for industrial orders, which is partly a function of the smaller number of categories. The biggest difference relates to the proportion of managers and directors in Scotland (−2.4), followed a long way behind by skilled trades (+1.0), but the overall message is once more that Scotland is far more similar to England and Wales than it is different.

In summary, however, with regard to neither industrial orders nor occupational orders does Scotland differ very much from England and Wales, which is well in line with historic trends. Once more, Wales has a somewhat larger index of occupational dissimilarity (11.5) than Scotland, but compared with previous decades the similarities far outweigh the differences.

TABLE 8.3   Occupational distributions, Scotland, and England and Wales, 2011

Occupation	Scotland	England and Wales	Percentage point difference
Managers and directors	8.4	10.8	–2.4
Professionals	16.7	17.4	–0.7
Associated prof. and technical	12.6	12.7	–0.1
Admin. and secretarial	11.4	11.4	0
Skilled trades	12.5	11.5	1.0
Caring, leisure and other services	9.7	9.4	0.3
Sales and customer services	9.3	8.4	0.9
Process, plant and machine operatives	7.7	7.2	0.5
Elementary*	11.6	11.1	0.5
Index of dissimilarity			**6.4**

* The ONS *Standard Occupational Classification 2010* defines 'elementary' occupations as follows: 'occupations which require the knowledge and experience necessary to perform mostly routine tasks, often involving the use of simple hand-held tools and, in some cases, requiring a degree of physical effort. Most occupations in this major group do not require formal educational qualifications but will usually have an associated short period of formal experience-related training' (2010: 237).

Sources: Scotland's Census 2011 (QS606SC); England and Wales 2011 (KS608EW)

Explaining occupational change

What is sociologically more interesting is how industrial and occupational orders relate to each other: that is, how occupations are structured within industrial orders. For example, our image of mining and quarrying might conjure up manual workers with picks and shovels, although the use of advanced cutting equipment transformed the deep-mine industry long before its demise in the 1990s. In other words, technical change within mining is likely to reduce the number of workers and replace them with machinery which is operated by fewer, and skilled, operatives.

We can think of occupational change being driven by two sets of forces: what happens to *industrial* sectors; and how *occupations* are organised within these sectors. Thus, to continue our example, a decline in the number of coalminers might be the result of fewer people employed in the coal industry generally, or it might result from a remix of skills within the industry itself, or both. There may have been changes in the skills mix required in the industry, such that re-skilling took place as machinery replaced labour.

Mining is a good example. In 2011, we find that employment is split between manual trades (described as process operatives, skilled trades and 'elementary' (unskilled) workers) and non-manual occupations (managers, science and technology professionals, and

FIGURE 8.2
Cutting coal

Source: Courtesy
of Scottish Mining
Museum

associated professionals). In other words, the image of 'pick and shovel' mining and quarrying has become history (Figure 8.2).

The old mainstream industries of manufacturing and construction (now employing around one in twelve people in each sector) have also undergone fundamental change. The image of masses of semi- and unskilled workers is also a redundant one. Both industries are still 'manual', but manufacturing is now evenly split between skilled trades and process, plant and machine operatives (roughly 25 per cent each), and only one in ten are in unskilled, what the census calls 'elementary', occupations. The majority of construction workers are now 'skilled' (56 per cent), and less than one in ten are defined as unskilled. There are few 'navvies' left in the construction trades.[6]

Why should this sort of analysis matter? We retain images of occupational trades conjured up from a previous age, and these inform our social sense of occupational 'worth'. To say you are a miner might still conjure up for us an image of a face worker armed with a pick and a Davey lamp, but nowadays you are much more likely to be operating heavy machinery in an open-cast mine. Old images, however, die hard.

How can we sum up occupational and industrial change over the last few decades?

- First, there is little evidence of de-skilling, notably in sectors such as manufacturing and construction.

- Second, there are many more managerial and administrative jobs in such industries, while agriculture is split fairly evenly between skilled trades (28 per cent) and elementary and operative trades (31 per cent).

- Third, many sectors, public and private, have developed occupational skills specific to their needs, such as in education, health and social work (23 per cent work in 'caring, leisure and other service occupations', and one-third are in 'professional occupations' in this sector).

Indeed, the highest proportions of what are called 'elementary' or unskilled workers are in 'distribution, hotels and restaurants' (39 per cent), or in finance or real estate (15 per cent), or in public administration, education and health (14 per cent). The association of unskilled manual labour with factory work (in manufacturing, it is only 7 per cent) or with building trades (construction, a mere 6 per cent) is long gone.

Here is a summary of how occupations are distributed within industries:

- Most 'professional' jobs are now in public administration, education and health (60 per cent).

- A majority of managers, directors and senior officials work either in distribution, hotels and restaurants (37 per cent) or in finance and real estate (18 per cent).

- Administrative and secretarial occupations are in public administration, education and health (40 per cent) or finance and real estate (27 per cent).

- 'Skilled' trades are nowadays to be found in construction (36 per cent) or distribution, hotels and restaurants (21 per cent) or manufacturing (16 per cent).

- The most occupational concentrated industries are *distribution, hotels and restaurants* where 74 per cent are in sales and customer service occupations, and in *public administration, education and health* where there is a preponderance of caring, leisure and other service occupations (72 per cent).

Accounting for change

So what explains overall occupational change? Is it the result of the decline, even demise, of certain industrial sectors, or has there been a process of de-skilling (or even re-skilling) within the *same* industrial sector? Coalmining is a good example: we think of deep mining having ended and, with it, the demise of pick-and-shovel mining, while on the other hand, open-cast mining requires skilled operatives to drive machinery.

It turns out that changes in the industries in which people work do *not* account for most of employment change. Rather, 'structural' change *within* industries, that is changes in the demand for and the nature of labour, accounts for much more. In a review of occupational change in Scotland between 2001 and 2008, followed up with an analysis of the labour market in Scotland in 2013, John Sutherland confirmed the finding that the process of 'sectoral' change (industry) plays a minor role in accounting for changes in employment.[7]

Re-skilling work

In general terms, then, there has been a process of 'up-skilling' within firms and organisations, rather than 'de-skilling'. For the 2001–8 period Sutherland concluded that proportionately more people were employed as managers or senior officials or in professional occupations, and significantly fewer as process, plant and machine operatives, and elementary workers.

Employment in elementary occupations fell marginally between 2001 and 2008, from 12.8 to 11.7 per cent. This, however, was a period of economic expansion in Scotland, as elsewhere, reflected in the net increase in the number of workplace jobs by 264,000. There was, however, a lot of 'churn' beneath that figure. For example, while manufacturing lost jobs overall, there was net job creation in other sectors such as human health and social work activities; education; professional, scientific and technical activities; and administrative and support service activities. Fifty-six per cent of the net new jobs created went to women, and 40 per cent went to those with part-time contracts of employment (Sutherland, 2013: 30).

In contrast to the period between 2001 and 2008, post-2008 saw an overall job loss of 154,000 in Scotland, notably in construction, manufacturing, wholesale and retail, human health and social work, in public administration and defence. Net job creation occurred in professional, scientific and technical activities. Men suffered most, accounting for 60 per cent of the total net job losses. During this period of net job destruction, the number of part-time contracts of employment increased. In short, there are clearly gender implications attached to job creation and destruction.

Gendering work

Both industrial and occupational structures are heavily gendered, reflecting labour market segmentation. On the one hand, men predominate in construction (90 per cent), agriculture, energy and water (80 per cent), transport and communication (76 per cent) and manufacturing (74 per cent). On the other hand, women predominate in public administration, education and health (71 per cent), distribution, hotels and restaurants (53 per cent). Finance and real estate has a rough gender balance, with 51 per cent male and 49 per cent female.[8]

The apparent balance between male and female jobs, however, masks considerable differences with regard to employment status. While men mainly work full-time (73 per cent), women work part-time (52 per cent), but a significant minority of women (40 per cent) are in full-time employment.[9] Men in part-time employment are most likely to be found in sales and customer service jobs (40 per cent) or in caring, leisure and other service occupations (24 per cent). Women, on the other hand, are most likely to work full-time in the professions (69 per cent), as process operatives (68 per cent) or as managers, directors or senior officials (64 per cent).

In terms of broad socio-economic groupings, men and women are distributed as in Table 8.4. We can see that men are more likely than women to be in higher status jobs, as managers and professionals, and that women occupy lower managerial and administrative jobs. Men are disproportionately represented among the self-employed, and lower supervisory and technical trades, while there are more women in semi-routine, but fewer in routine, manual work.

Predominantly *male* occupational groups are lower supervisory and technical where men outnumber women by almost three to one, and small employers (just over two to one).

TABLE 8.4   Socio-economic group by gender

Socio-economic group (NS-SeC)*	Male	Female	Difference (F − M)
Large employers and higher managers	2	1	−1
Higher professionals	9	5	−4
Lower managerial and professionals	18	23	+5
Intermediate	7	18	+11
Small employers and own account	11	4	−7
Lower supervisory and technical	12	4	−8
Semi-routine	12	19	+7
Routine	16	10	−6
Index of dissimilarity			49

Source: Scotland's Census 2011, table KS612SC

* For details of NS-SeC, see Rose and Peralin, 2005.

Inversely, the most *female* occupational groups are in 'intermediate' (almost three to one) and 'semi-routine' jobs (almost two to one).

The financial crisis of 2008 turned out to be a major watershed in dividing job growth and job destruction. Between 1996 and 2008, there was a net *increase* in jobs (approximately 23,000 per annum), and of those jobs more went to men than to women, as well as to full-time than to part-time work (Sutherland, 2013). Between 2008 and 2011, on the other hand, there was a net *decrease* of approximately 50,000 jobs per annum, and disproportionately more men's jobs were lost than women's.[10] The number of part-time jobs in the period increased, and net job destruction occurred among full-time jobs.

There was little evidence that the share of jobs held by women changed significantly over the period as the economy moved from net job creation to net job destruction. Two features of the change were noticeable: first, that more men than previously were working part-time; and second, there was an increase in the percentage of jobs held by women working part-time. Both were the result of non-standard contracts becoming more common. Sutherland sums up the change as follows:

> The period 1996–2008, therefore, was one of net job creation, when more of the jobs created went to men than women; and more to those working full time rather than working part time. In contrast, the period 2008–2011 was one of net job destruction, when the jobs lost were associated more with males than females; and more with full time workers than part time workers. (2013: 22)

As many as 40 per cent of jobs lost between 2008 and 2011 had been done by women, notably in three sectors: health and social work activities (where 62 per cent of the decrease were 'women's' jobs); finance and insurance (78 per cent); and wholesale and retail.

Part-time working became more common in professional, scientific and technical work, in wholesale and retail, and in public administration and defence. Many employers began to use part-time employment as a way of cutting costs and increasing labour flexibility, most notoriously in the use of **zero-hours contracts**. (ACAS (Advisory, Conciliation and Arbitration Service) defines zero-hours contracts as one where the employer is not obliged to provide any minimum working hours, nor is the worker obliged to accept any work offered.) Because workers were defined as 'employed', the unemployment rate appeared to fall, coupled with labour retention ('hoarding') as some companies sought to retain scarce skilled labour.

Restructuring labour

The crisis year of 2008 was a key watershed in transforming labour. In his review of labour market changes for Fraser of Allander Institute Economic Commentary, Stephen Boyd observed that: 'Some six and a half years after the start of the Great Recession in the spring of 2008, neither employment nor unemployment has yet attained its pre-recession rate. Employment[11] may well be at its "highest ever" level in Scotland but that is not uncommon' (2014: 63).

These trends are not as impressive as political narratives would suggest. Rather, the apparent rise in self-employment is not the result of greater entrepreneurship, but because 'a large new cohort of self-employed workers who currently work less hours and earn less by doing what they used to do as employees' (2014: 66). The use of insecure forms of contract, notably zero-hours, as well as 'illusory' forms of self-employment, is designed to depress wages and offload tax burdens onto employees. Boyd, the assistant secretary of the Scottish Trades Union Congress (STUC), estimated that 120,000 workers in Scotland were on zero-hours contracts.

There has also been a rebalancing of the age distribution such that the employment rate of workers aged over 65 increased by 4.7 per cent between 2008 and 2014, while that for young workers aged 16–24 fell by 2.9 per cent. Boyd commented:

> An optimistic account of these changes would stress that people are living healthier, longer lives and therefore wanting to work for longer. A more pessimistic account might highlight pension reforms and falling real wages, forcing people to work for longer when their own and/or partner's pension entitlements are eroded or wages fall. (2014: 69–70)

The considerable slack in the labour market is reflected in the fall in real median wages, which in Scotland fell by 7.6 per cent (an annual loss of £1760 in 2013) between 2009 and 2013. Female part-time workers saw the biggest fall in real wages at a time when the number of people working part-time has increased. Similarly, the biggest fall in real wages (10 per cent) has occurred among young workers, and people in 'elementary' occupations suffered a 14.8 per cent fall during the period.

In contrast, the gross wages of the top 10 per cent of corporate managers and directors has risen by more than £14,000 pa over the same period (Boyd, 2014: 71). Boyd concluded: 'The shift towards the "hour glass" labour market is likely to continue and possibly accelerate; a labour market characterised by increasing opportunity (and rewards) at the top and growing employment in low pay, low skill, low productivity sectors at the bottom' (2014: 71).

The 'hour-glass' labour market

The image of the changing shape of the labour market is an interesting one in which 'middle' jobs are squeezed, while jobs which are high skill/high wage[12] at the top and low skill/low wage at the bottom have increased in number. Middle-ranking jobs either increased less rapidly or fell, and this has become a recognisable feature of the labour market in Scotland and elsewhere (what is known as the 'hour-glass' effect (Figure 8.3); see Paul Sissons, 2011 (www.theworkfoundation.com)).

In an analysis of the Scottish labour market, Rogers and Richmond observed that 'in terms of share of total employment, the proportion of all jobs in the middle deciles (deciles 3–6) declined by 4 percentage points, the proportion in the top three deciles rising by 3 percentage points and that in the lowest two deciles falling by 1 percentage point' (2015: 85).

Over the period, the number of 'standard jobs' (defined as full-time and permanent) has declined among occupations in the middle deciles (in terms of wages), while non-standard jobs (defined as part-time, self-employed or temporary) have increased. Job polarisation is also the result of 'offshoring', whereby firms take advantage of lower labour costs in other countries to 'offshore' part of their production process or service provision to cheaper locations.

Jobs likely to be offshored are lower skilled technical production jobs or administrative tasks (such as customer call centres), activities that tend to be mid-paid occupations. Longitudinal data[13] from the British Household Panel Study (BHPS) suggest that about a third of the bottom 10 per cent of earners in the UK in 2001–2 were still there in 2008–9, and that more than 60 per cent remained in the bottom three deciles.

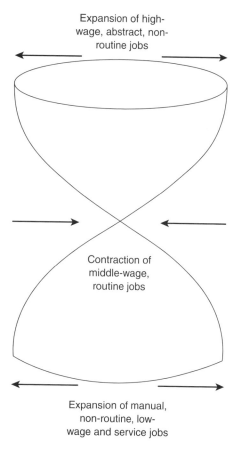

Expansion of high-wage, abstract, non-routine jobs

Contraction of middle-wage, routine jobs

Expansion of manual, non-routine, low-wage and service jobs

FIGURE 8.3 The hour-glass effect

Source: Author's drawing, adapted from http://www.theworkfoundation.com

Those most likely to be stuck at the bottom are women, young people and those with no educational qualifications. More commonly, they move sideways into other poorly paid jobs with few prospects. The authors, who are attached to Scottish Enterprise, provide the following forecast trends for Scotland by 2022:

- Jobs *growth* in each of the highest skilled (and so highest paid) occupations (manager, professionals and associated professional/technicians).

- A *decline* in the number of jobs in some of the more intermediate skilled occupations, such as skilled trades, process and plant operatives, and admin./secretarial.

- A *fall* in the number of jobs in some lower skilled occupations (elementary and sales/ customer services) with a *rise* in others (e.g. caring, leisure and other service occupations where jobs increases are expected).

They concluded:

> Job polarisation appears to have a disproportionate effect on already disadvan-taged groups – specifically young people and women as they tend to make up a higher proportion of workers in low wage, low skill occupations. It also has impli-cations for potential career progression for those in lower paid occupations, due to the decline of mid-range occupations (although there may be increasing opportu-nities for those in mid-range occupations to progress into higher ones). (2015: 93)

Thus, while jobs at both the upper end and the lower end of the wage scale have increased proportionately, the number in intermediate and skilled occupations has fallen, contribut-ing to job polarisation and blocked career mobility. What we see is a 'hollowing out' of medium-skilled work. Scottish government analysis confirms this process of job polarisa-tion between 2001 and 2010 (see Figure 8.4).

This graph shows the change in share of total full-time jobs (left axis and bars) and share of total full-time hours worked (right axis and line), for occupation types, between 2001 and 2010. Occupations are ordered in terms of typical income level (low to high). The report comments:

> Over the decade up to 2010, there was overall growth in the share of jobs amongst the lowest and highest paid occupations and reductions in middle income occu-pations' share of jobs and hours. This polarisation increases inequality. This is partly due to factors like computerisation of middle-income routine tasks and structural shifts away from manufacturing towards low-income services. (www. gov.scot/Resource/0048/00485433.pptx)[14]

While the number of jobs rose across all deciles, the highest increases were in the top and the bottom deciles. Lower paid occupations had a higher proportion of part-time and

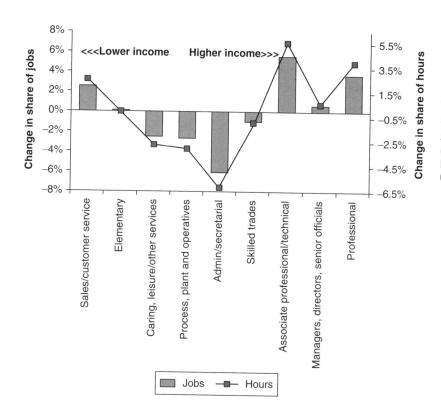

FIGURE 8.4

Job polarisation: shifts in lower income and higher income jobs, 2001–10

Source: www. gov.scot/ Resource/0048/ 00485433.pptx

self-employed workers especially in elementary, sales and customer services, and a higher percentage on zero-hours contracts, notably for cleaners, care workers, those working in call/customer centres, and in food and accommodation occupations.

The driving down of wage costs, cuts in welfare and the tightening up of eligibility for benefits have created a highly segmented labour force in Scotland, as in the rest of the UK. This is reflected in the association with educational qualifications. Thus, while three-quarters of people in higher managerial, administrative and professional occupations were educated to degree level, half of those in 'routine' occupations had no educational qualifications whatsoever (Scotland's 2011 Census, table LC6502SC).

Furthermore, unionisation rates in Scotland (and the UK generally) have fallen by over 20 per cent since the mid-1990s. Whereas 39 per cent of Scottish employees were members of trade unions in 1995, by 2014 this had fallen to 30 per cent (in the UK generally, the fall over the period was from 32 to 25 per cent). The public sector has had a much higher rate of unionisation than the private sector, but in both there has been a decline in the proportions covered by collective agreements: from 74 per cent in 1995 in the public sector, down to 61 per cent in 2014, and from 23 to 15 per cent in the private sector over the same period. This decrease in union density has led to downward pressure on wage rates as workers' bargaining power has weakened.

Scotland: similarities and differences

In key respects, Scotland is far less 'different' from the rest of the UK than we might imagine, or than some writers have claimed. Over the long term, its industrial and occupational structures have been much closer to the British mean since the nineteenth century, and certainly more so than particular English regions, or Wales and Northern Ireland. Its employment and wages structure reflects a common UK labour market.

We can conclude that whatever drives 'political' differences from the 1970s, it is not 'structural' differences in occupational and industrial terms, or at least in any straightforward way. This is a theme we will raise again in the next chapter when we look at social class and social opportunity, for it raises the puzzle in a more direct way: that is, how can Scotland's politics have diverged so dramatically when its social class structure is so similar to England's?

We might go further and say that 'similarity' has its own social and political dynamic. Take, for instance, unemployment rates. For much of Scotland's twentieth-century history, its rate of unemployment was well above the rest of the UK. As Alf Young observed: 'Had there not been massive net out-migration from Scotland in the fifties and sixties, one wonders how much bigger these adverse Scotland/UK unemployment ratios might have been in that period' (2015: 6).

In the mid-1960s the Scottish rate of unemployment was twice the UK rate, and ten years later it was 1.7 times the UK rate. In recent years, that differential has reduced significantly, and at times Scotland has even had a lower rate of unemployment than the rest of the UK. In terms of the seasonally adjusted unemployment rates comparing Scotland and the UK since 2005, the similarities far outweigh the differences (Scotland is represented in Figures 8.5 and 8.6 by the darker trend line and the UK by the lighter line).

The employment rate, that is the percentage of the eligible population who are in employment, stood at 74.1 per cent, and the Scottish rate was marginally above the UK rate for virtually all of the previous decade.

Indeed, Scotland has one of the lowest rates of 'economic inactivity' in the EU, some 22.1 per cent, marginally better than the UK (at 23.6 per cent) and only surpassed by Denmark (21.7), the Netherlands (20.5) and Sweden (19.1) (http://ec.europa.eu/eurostat/data/database).

Nevertheless, we have seen that there is considerable *under*-employment, which means that there is considerable spare capacity in the labour market. The under-employment rate

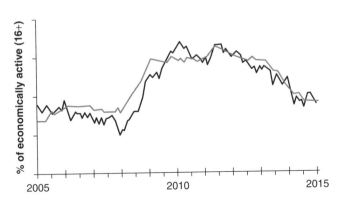

FIGURE 8.5
Unemployment rates, Scotland and UK, 2005–15

Source: Quarterly Labour Market Briefing, August 2015 (www.gov.scot/Resource/0048/00484492.pdf)

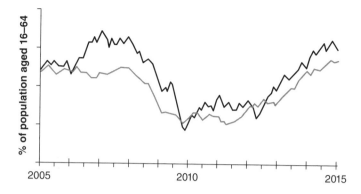

FIGURE 8.6
People in employment, Scotland and UK, 2005–15

Source: www. gov.scot/ Resource/0048/ 00484492.pdf

is around 10 per cent, an increase of just under 3 per cent since the beginning of the recession in 2008–9. This means that a substantial number – as many as six in ten under-employed workers – were looking to increase the number of hours worked, by as much as ten hours per week; and seven in ten of part-time workers wanted to work between five and twenty hours more per week, reinforcing the point that choosing to work part-time is by no means a lifestyle choice, but forced on workers by labour market conditions.

Furthermore, real wages have not increased since 2008, and the 'recovery' is largely driven by increases in part-time working and 'self-employment'. The weakening of trade unions and the fall in their membership since the 1980s have fundamentally reduced union influence over pay rates, thereby depressing sustainable growth in wages.

Being in employment is not a guarantee of prosperity, as we saw in the previous chapter. The phenomenon of the 'working poor' has become much more common. Research by the Rowntree Foundation (https://www.jrf.org.uk/report/referendum-briefing-child-poverty-scotland) shows that raising the minimum income standard (MIS) to £7 per hour does not produce a statistically significant increase in the percentage of income going to the bottom three deciles.

This is because less than half of the income received by people in these deciles derives from employment, and that households liable to benefit from the 'living wage' in the public sector are not confined to the bottom 30 per cent. In any case, any increase in wages is likely to be offset by a reduction in benefits and higher tax payments; in other words, what is called the 'poverty trap'. To take an example: if a single adult living in council housing and working thirty-seven hours per week went from a minimum wage of £5.73 per hour to £7, this 22 per cent increase would be offset such that their net income before housing costs would rise only by 9 per cent (Low Pay and Inequality in Scotland, 2008–9 (www.gov.scot/Resource/Doc/1034/0100962.pdf)).

The rise and fall of Silicon Glen

> Bathgate no more, Linwood no more
> Methil no more, Irvine no more
> Bathgate no more, Linwood no more
> Methil no more, Lochaber no more
> (The Proclaimers, 'Letter from America')

Writing his account of economic change in Scotland, Douglas Fraser, business correspondent of BBC Scotland, commented:[15]

> The post-war period in Scotland saw sustained effort to restructure the economy, and in particular to induce foreign capital to come to Scotland. Governments and a succession of development agencies were proactive in attracting inward investment, and 'persuading' employers to set up plants and facilities. The 1960s wave of such facilities included the Hillman car plant at Linwood in Renfrewshire, the BMC/Leyland truck factory at Bathgate, the steel strip mill at Ravenscraig in Lanarkshire. By 1992, all these had closed.

With the benefit of hindsight, we can see that these factories were built for 'political' reasons, induced by UK governments to come to Scotland.

The business journalist Alf Young in his 2015 review of post-war industrial history pointed to the importance of personal connections. The US company Singer, for example, which came to Clydebank in the 1880s,[16] and which was the world leader, producing a staggering 36 million sewing machines, more than all the other makers added together, just happened to have a senior US executive who came originally from the town. IBM set up in Greenock, Young implies, because the man who founded it was of Scottish extraction. Why Greenock? The town's MP, Hector McNeil, was Secretary of State for Scotland in the 1950s. By the end of the twentieth century, many of these foreign companies had moved on, closing their Scottish plants: Singer in 1980, Massey Ferguson in Kilmarnock in 1978, British Aluminium's smelter at Invergordon in 1981, and the closure of 'traditional' industries such as shipbuilding (Upper Clyde Shipbuilders (UCS) went into liquidation in 1971).

The inward investment strategy pursued by the Scottish Development Agency (later, Scottish Enterprise) since the mid-1970s, following the Highlands and Islands Development Board (HIDB) a decade earlier, came to a halt. Both Labour and Conservative Parties, albeit with slightly different political twists, had supported state intervention up until this point. The election of the Thatcher governments from 1979 sounded its ideological death-knell, but not before the last hurrah – Silicon Glen.

Successful more as a slogan than a long-term reality, this footloose industry found bigger incentives, cheaper labour and more nimble fingers in the Far East, and post-1989, in Eastern and Central Europe. Young spells it out:

> Motorola had built a massive complex to assemble mobile phones at Bathgate which opened in 1990 and employed more than 3000 people. By 2001 it was closing down and shipping the assembly work off to cheaper host economies in eastern Europe. In 1996 the Taiwanese group Chungwha arrived at Mossend in Lanarkshire promising even more jobs, 3300, assembling cathode ray tubes. But that was yesterday's technology. The advent of flat screens changed all that and Chungwha was gone in six years. The Korean group Hyundai agreed to come

to Fife to fabricate silicon chips. A hugely expensive wafer fab was built, with lots of support from Scottish Enterprise and government. But Hyundai changed its mind. And with other established wafer fabs, like the Japanese group NEC's plant at Livingston, also closing, the Fife site never produced a single wafer. It has since been demolished. (2015: 24)

Only the moniker, Silicon Glen, remained, imitated by other versions of the original Silicon Valley in California: *Silicon Bog* (Ireland), *Silicon Allee* (Berlin), *Silicon Wadi* (Israel) and *Silicon Plateau* (India): what we might call a tribute slogan to the original, but far less embedded in local economies. What they had in common was the idea that the slogan prefix 'Silicon' resonated progress and prosperity. In 2002, exports of computer, electronic and optical goods from Scotland were worth nearly £5.6 billion. By the end of the decade, they were worth under £1.4 billion, precisely a quarter of their value ten years previously.

Perhaps, though, all was not in vain. *Computer Weekly* reported in 2015 (8 August) that Scotland's technology sector had seen a large growth in start-up companies of the order of 32 per cent IT start-ups since 2009, only marginally behind the 38 per cent increase in tech start-ups in London. Such companies focused far less on electronics manufacturing and more on software development and services, which required far less set-up capital.

Conclusion

The message of this chapter is that we do not have to import theories of dependency and colonialism to account for Scotland's economic development. With hindsight, what lay behind such a search was the notion that political and cultural divergence from the rest of the UK seemed to require it. How else, the argument went, were we to explain such dramatic political and social developments from the 1970s and 1980s unless they were underpinned by structural economic shifts?

With further hindsight, we know that these were not necessary to account for political change. Indeed, this has implications for understanding Scotland's class structure, as we shall see in the next chapter. The key point, however, is that structures in and of themselves are far less sociologically significant than how people see them and relate them to their lives. There is nothing fixed and automatic about that relationship, and that is what we will examine in the following chapter on social class and social opportunity.

Employment, and making a living, have been transformed, and what remains is a small and highly globally dependent economy, one which ironically has carried over those characteristics from the old imperial days. 'Work' is no longer the preserve of men with heavy hammers. Scotland is no longer a 'working-class' society in terms of its employment structure. Roughly one-third of people are in managerial and professional jobs; one-third in administrative and services jobs; and one-third in manual labour. How this maps onto Scotland's social class structure and the system of social opportunity is the topic of our next chapter.

Chapter summary

So what have we learned in this chapter about 'making a living' in Scotland?

- That none of the theories claiming that Scotland was a colony of England, and suffered from systematic under-development in its economic history, stand up to much scrutiny.

- That Scotland's industrial structure, how the economy was organised in terms of production, is much more similar to the rest of the UK than different, and it has been this way for well over a century.

- That, in terms of occupational structure, once again similarities with the rest of the UK far outweigh the differences. Furthermore, there has been a process of 'up-skilling' rather than 'de-skilling' in paid employment. Even jobs in classical heavy industry, like mining and construction, have been transformed by technology and new labour processes.

- That while a much higher proportion of the labour force is female, a process of labour market segmentation marks out women's and men's employment.

- That a process of job polarisation has separated high-wage, high-skill jobs, from low-wage, low-skill jobs, while there has been a growth in employment in both. Middle-range jobs have suffered most in terms of deteriorating pay, conditions and prospects. Women and young people have most to lose from this process.

- Finally, that Scotland has moved inexorably to depend on jobs in businesses which are externally owned and controlled, and its economy is subject to considerable global shifts in economic fortunes, typified by the rise and fall of 'Silicon Glen'.

Questions for discussion

1. Why was it argued in the 1970s that Scotland was a colony of England, and how convincing were the arguments?

2. What accounts for the transformation in employment patterns in the last two decades? To what extent are patterns of employment determined by shifts in industrial structures and/or occupational shifts within sectors?

3. To what extent are women's and men's employment patterns and experiences in Scotland different from each other? How would you explain that?

4. How is Scotland's employment structure being affected by the 'hour-glass' effect? Who benefits and who loses out, and why?

5. What explains the rise and fall of 'Silicon Glen'? With the benefit of hindsight, was it worth encouraging foreign capital to invest in Scotland in the first place?

Annotated reading

(a) While attempts to argue that Scotland was a 'colony' and suffered from economic and political under-development have not stood tests of time, the debates which they instigated are worth revisiting. See, for example, M. Hechter's *Internal Colonialism: The Celtic fringe in British national development, 1536–1966* (1975) and his defence and revision of the thesis. The debate between Immanuel Wallerstein and Christopher Smout is enlightening (see *Review*, 3(4), 1980). T. Dickson's *Scottish Capitalism: Class, state and nation from before the Union to the Present* (1980) was an interesting attempt to write a history in this context.

(b) There is careful and valuable empirical analysis of trends in industrial and occupational structures, notably by J. Sutherland, in *Scottish Affairs* ('Occupational change in Scotland, 2001–2008', 2009; 'The labour market in Scotland', 2013). The *Fraser of Allander Economic Commentary* has been published for forty years, and is an excellent source of analysis and commentary on economic trends (see https://www.strath.ac.uk/media/departments/economics/fairse/Latest-Fraser-of-Allander-Economic-Commentary.pdf). In particular A. Young's 'Forty turbulent years: how the Fraser Economic Commentary recorded the evolution of the modern Scottish economy' is a valuable and readable account of the trends (www.strath.ac.uk/media/1newwebsite/departmentsubject/economics/fraser/Forty_Turbulent_Years_Booklet.pdf).

(c) Finally, Scottish Government and the Office for National Statistics continue to produce analysis of social and economic trends, making excellent use of census data. See for example, 'Low pay and economic inequality in Scotland' (www.gov.scot/Resource/Doc/1034/0100962.pdf). The Scottish Parliament Information Centre (SPICe) produced a useful briefing note, 'A brief overview of Scottish, UK and international labour market statistics', by Andrew Aiton, in 2013.

Notes

1 Mary Brooksbank, 'revolutionary, poet and songwriter' wrote the Jute Mill Song, of which this is the last verse (Figure 8.1). The iconic status of Mary Brooksbank's song is reflected in its place on the Canongate Wall at the Scottish parliament of which this is a photograph. 'Ten and nine' refers to the weekly wage of the mill lassies at the turn of the century – ten shillings (paid as a gold half sovereign) and nine pence; about 55p in today's money.

2 A fuller account of the methodology for this analysis appeared in the first edition of my book *Understanding Scotland* (1992: chapter 3). The key source for the data was Clive Lee's book *British Regional Employment Statistics, 1841–1971*, published in 1979.

3 See McCrone (1992), in particular figure 3.4, which shows how employment structures in twelve Scottish industrial areas changed between 1931 and 1971.

4 These data are taken from DC Cairncross Papers 104/1/1 'Industry and Employment in Scotland, 1962–3'. For 2011 census data, see Northern Ireland Statistics and Research Agency (NISRA), and for Wales, https://statswales.wales.gov.uk/Catalogue/Census/2011.

5   A plus sign indicates that Scotland has proportionately more than England and Wales, and a minus sign, proportionately fewer.

6   Data are from Scotland's Census 2011, table DC6604SC, occupation by industry, 2014.

7   Sutherland (2013) uses National Online Manpower Information System (NOMIS) data, which are provided by the Office for National Statistics (ONS) giving online access to labour market statistics (www.nomisweb.co.uk). The previous data used in the chapter are from the 2011 census and use slightly different categories.

8   These data are taken from Scotland's Census 2011, table LC6118SC.

9   The figures do not add up to 100 per cent because the rest are self-employed.

10 There is, of course, no such thing as a 'man's' job or a 'woman's' job, and gender composition of jobs is fluid (think of clerical work over the last 100 years, which shifted from 'men's' to 'women's' work). The loss of full-time manufacturing jobs, for example, has affected men most.

11 'Employment' refers to the number of people in the labour force.

12 The methodology involves ranking jobs into wage deciles such that lower waged, lower skilled jobs are in elementary, sales and customer services, and caring, leisure and other services; higher waged, higher skilled jobs are in associated professional and technical, professional, and managers, directors and senior officials; and people in mid-level jobs are in process, plant and machine operatives, admin. and secretarial, and skilled trades operatives.

13 Longitudinal data are those collected on the *same* people on more than one occasion. Such studies are also referred to as 'panel studies'.

14 Scottish Government: Communities Analysis Division, 'Economic inequality brief – drivers of inequality', September 2015.

15 See www.bbc.co.uk/news/uk-scotland-scotland-business-24509655 (2013). Fraser used The Proclaimers' song to make the point.

16 See www.singersewinginfo.co.uk/kilbowie/.

9

SOCIAL CLASS AND SOCIAL OPPORTUNITY

Is Scotland a class society? It would be hard to argue otherwise, and yet how social class operates, and crucially what it means, are not straightforward. There are apparent contradictions. Thus, in Scotland there is a long history of class action, a tradition of radical politics, all of which seeming to indicate that class particularly matters in Scotland. Furthermore, as we saw in the previous chapter, describing Scotland as an ethno-class colony of England was fashionable in the 1970s, such that writers like Hechter and Wallerstein attributed oppressed status to Scotland.

At the same time there is a stubborn belief that Scotland is a more egalitarian country than England, where people relate to each other in terms of merit and not status. This 'egalitarian myth' is a powerful one. Writing in the mid-1970s, the nationalist Stephen Maxwell observed:

> The idea that Scottish society is egalitarian is central to the myth of Scottish Democracy. In its strong nationalist version, class division is held to be an alien import from England. In the weaker version, it describes the wider opportunity for social mobility in Scotland as illustrated in 'the lad o' pairts' tradition. (1976: 5)

Chapter aims

- To set out what we mean by 'social class'.

- To explore how structures of social class in Scotland have changed over time.

- To examine processes of social mobility whereby people end up in the social classes that they do.

- To explain why, if class structure and patterns of social mobility are similar throughout the UK, Scotland's culture and politics of social class are different.

Social class: structure and ideology

Let us begin with Maxwell's point about the 'myth' of Scottish democracy. Describing egalitarianism as a 'myth' is not to imply that it is false, but that it takes on implicit truth status. It shares many similarities with the American Dream, the narrative that hard work and native ability will shine through, surmounting any human obstacles in the way.

It is not too difficult to prove that the American Dream does not 'work'; that the structuring of social privilege and transmitted wealth reinforces deep and abiding inequalities which make it very difficult for the child of poor parents to rise to positions of power and privilege. We know, after all, that the best way to become rich is to have rich parents. Life is not a race in which everyone starts from the same baseline; as a consequence, we cannot assume that the 'winner' of the race is the most able.

Nevertheless, that does not invalidate the American Dream, which is not, at the end of the day, meant to be proved or disproved. This is because it is, in those famous American words, a truth held to be self-evident. In that respect it is a 'myth' in an anthropological sense of the term. It is an active and contemporary force which provides a reservoir of legitimation for belief and action. It says who 'we' are in identity terms, who we aspire to be, a narrative running back into history and on into the future. Above all, it demands reconciliation of reality with belief, and as such is a stimulus to social and political action.

At the opening of the Scottish parliament in 1999 when the singer Sheena Wellington sang the Burns' song, 'A Man's a Man for A' That',[1] this was not to be taken as a statement of fact, that social inequalities did not matter, still less that they applied to men and not women. It was a statement of aspiration, of belief, of what it meant to be Scottish. The ambiguity and ambivalence of the 'myth' help to account for its persistence. As the historian Allan MacLaren observed: 'The belief that Scotland was an open society whose fundamental egalitarianism was gradually eroded, in part by contact with its more powerful neighbour is not just a piece of popular nationalism but has penetrated and been propounded by works of academic scholarship' (1976: 2). The myth becomes the grit in the oyster, pressing for resolution such that it brings practice into line with aspiration.

The ubiquity of social class

Like many concepts in social science, 'social class' is part of the currency of everyday life. People use it as part of their common vocabulary, but not necessarily in ways used by social analysts. At its most basic, a 'class' (of things) is akin to a category, objects which share common characteristics, but this dictionary definition is of little help in understanding social class. In any case, social classes do not exist in isolation from each other.

The English historian Edward Thompson in his classic *The Making of the English Working Class* (1968) remarked that 'class is a relationship and not a thing. ... "It" does not exist, either to have an ideal interest or consciousness, or to lie as a patient on the Adjustor's table' (1968: 11). By this he meant that any social class could only be understood vis-à-vis other social classes; that, for example, working class and middle class were in juxtapositional relationship such that one could only be understood in relation to the other.

Thompson called his book 'The Making of the *English* Working Class', and apologised to Scottish and Welsh readers in the preface, saying that he did so not out of chauvinism, but out of respect. He made a key point, explaining why he had apparently neglected the Scottish and Welsh working classes: 'It is because class is a cultural as much as an economic formation that I have been cautious as to generalizing beyond the English experience. ... The Scottish record, in particular, is quite as dramatic, and as tormented, as our own' (1968: 13–14). In saying this, Thompson is pointing to the record of class conflict in Scotland, without implying that the 'egalitarian myth' invalidates it.

That social class is cultural, and not simply economic, is vital to our own story and, as we shall see, does much to explain why 'structure' (what Thompson calls 'economics') does not explain how people experience social class, and why they act accordingly.

Social class: structure, consciousness and action

We can think of the concept of 'social class' as having three dimensions: structure, consciousness and action. By *structure* we mean how class is 'objectively' formed and re-formed – that, for example, the industrial system, or the economy more generally, shapes occupations in terms of working and market conditions, as we saw in the previous chapter. Such structures stand outside people's understanding of them, although, to be sure, people may have explanations and accounts as to why they belong to a particular social class.

This raises the second element of social class, *consciousness*, the general awareness that you have something in common with others, and that you 'belong' in some indefinable way. 'Consciousness', however, cannot simply be read from 'structure'. Karl Marx famously took the view that people with similar social characteristics but lacking class solidarity were simply 'homologous magnitudes, much as potatoes in a sack form a sack of potatoes' (from *The Eighteenth Brumaire of Louis Bonaparte* [1869]) in the sense that they shared common objective experiences, but were largely bereft of common awareness that they had much in common.[2]

Furthermore, if people wish to do anything to improve their social conditions by banding together as a group with common interests, to act together, common consciousness is a necessary requisite for social *action*, the third component of social class.

Thus, 'social class', properly worked out, will have three separate but related dimensions:

- *structure* – what people have objectively in common, whether this is a similar relationship to the means of production (Marx) or shared similarities of work and market conditions (Weber);

- *consciousness* – common levels of culture and meaning which people share to explain their lot in life;

- *action* – on the basis of common interests, objective and subjective, stimulating action to defend and extend common interests.

'Social class' can exist at any or all of these three levels, although it is uncommon for all three to operate together, either because people are prevented from seeing what their common interests are, or because, should they do so, they are unable to do anything much about it. Furthermore, social classes are not static. The metaphor of 'social strata' (hence, social stratification) is a common one in social science, one borrowed from geology and signifying layering. It is often used to broaden social differences beyond those of the narrowly 'economic', but it is a metaphor with limitations. Thus, as Göran Therborn observed, 'classes must be seen, not as veritable geological formations, once they have acquired their original shape, but as phenomena in a constant process of formation, reproduction, re-formulation and de-formation' (1983: 39).

'Social class', then, refers to the ways power is structured, largely but not exclusively with reference to the economic realm, which differentiates people in the marketplace according to the skills and resources they have, as well as the rewards they derive from it. All advanced industrial or capitalist societies share similar features, namely the private ownership of economic resources coupled with the capacity to transmit such property by sale or by inheritance, and this determines the power structures within them.

For most people their 'life chances' are determined by what they do for a living, what they work at, because that is the source of their income. This is why we discussed industrial and occupational change in the previous chapter. The jobs people do characterise their life security, give them access to housing, education, social goods, and so on, not only in terms of levels of earnings, but in terms and conditions of employment.

In modern market societies, there tend to be three main classes: a dominant class whose power is based on the capital they own; an intermediate class whose power derives from the educational or organisational skills they possess; and a subordinate class whose power, such as it is, tends to be based on their physical or routine labour. It is this relationship to the labour market which determines which social class people belong to.

In their classical *Affluent Worker* study (1969), John Goldthorpe and colleagues distinguished between 'market', 'work' and 'status' situations.[3] 'Market' indicates the price (wage) you get for your labour depending on its scarcity value or otherwise; 'work' refers to how much (or how little) control you have over the labour process; and 'status' is about how much (or how little) social standing and prestige attach to your occupation. Garry Runciman (1990) adopted a similar distinction, arguing that three key criteria matter: 'control' – an ability or otherwise to control or organise the work process; 'ownership' – the legal title to some productive property; and 'marketability' – the institutionally recognised possession of an attribute, skill or asset with income-generating powers.

That the UK is a quintessential 'class' society has long been part of popular consciousness. The conventional image of the UK's traditional class structure was nicely captured by a comedy sketch in the TV satirical comedy show *The Frost Report* (7 April 1966), where the three classes are caricatured. The class images were captured by the height and dress of each 'class' character.[4]

Fifty years later, the sketch arguably would not 'work' in the same way because the class symbols (clothing, and especially the hats (see Figure 9.1)) have lost their capacity to typify.

FIGURE 9.1
Images of social
class

Source: BBC Photo
Archives library
(www.bbc.co.uk/
programmes/
p00hhrwl,
5 June 2011)[5]

We will examine the apparent classlessness of contemporary dress codes in Chapter 23. This is not to say, of course, that social class no longer matters; simply that we cannot 'read' it in the ways we used to.

Measuring social class

In modern times the conventional rankings were those of the Registrar-General whose socio-economic groups (SEGs) were 'differentiated by life-style' (Marsh, 1986). These were later revised by David Rose (Rose and Pevalin, 2005) and became the National Statistics Socio-Economic Classification (NS-SeC for short). A related schema was derived by Hope–Goldthorpe bringing together 'market' and 'work' situations (Runciman's marketability and control aspects respectively), and described by Goldthorpe as:

> Occupational categories whose members would appear, in the light of the available evidence, to be typically comparable, on the one hand, in terms of their sources and levels of income and other conditions of employment, in their degree of economic security and in their chances of economic advancement; on the other hand, in their location within the system of authority and control governing the processes of production in which they are organised. (1987: 40)

Such occupational classifications are the common currency of social science and have to do with social relations generated around the means of economic production. In any case, so many data are in the form of official statistics as to make occupational analysis using these essential if we wish to chart how structures alter over time.

Some sociologists like Mike Savage have included cultural markers such as consumption tastes and social activities in their definition of social class (Savage, 2015), but critics argue that this is to confuse causes and effects. As one sociologist puts it: 'Do you really believe that changing one's social class can be a matter of getting out of bed and making a serious effort to like Brahms or to attract a few more Facebook friends?' (Mills, 2014: 444). In this chapter, we will adopt the more 'orthodox' view of social class: that it derives, by and large, from relationships to the means of economic production, notably through occupations.

Scotland's changing class structure

So how has Scotland's class structure changed? One hundred years ago around three-quarters of the labour force were in manual jobs, and roughly one in seven in white-collar work, with the rest under- or unemployed. Alistair Gray's image in *Lanark* of men going to work captures the times (Figure 9.2): 'Hundreds of thousands of men in dirty coats and heavy boots were tramping along grey streets to the gates of forges and machines shops' (1981: 223).

FIGURE 9.2
Traditional work: leaving work at Glasgow shipyards, 1944

Source: Imperial War Museum (D20847)

Hence the pyramidal shape of the Scottish class structure, with the bulk of the labour force in manual work, a much smaller group than today in white-collar work, and at the top a small, self-contained elite (see Chapter 6).

To be sure, there were crucial internal differences of skills, pay and status in all classes, not least among manual workers where status divisions between skilled 'labour aristocrats' and unskilled residual labour were far more important than they are today, and usually cross-cut against religious and other cultural differences. It was claimed that getting a job in a Clydeside shipyard, for example, depended far more on your religion, which foot you happened to kick with,[6] than it did in the second half of the twentieth century. By that time, in Scotland as a whole, manual workers represented less than half the labour force, and the rise in white-collar work had grown significantly, reflecting the occupational transition to service employment.

Gender and social class

By the twenty-first century, around three-quarters of people worked in services, although such 'services' were transformed over the previous hundred years, from jobs in domestic service to office work, whether as a state functionary or in the private sector such as banking and finance. The growing trend for women to participate in the labour force has been a feature north and south of the border. Until some time after 1945, the economic activity rate for married women in Scotland was only two-thirds that of the rest of the UK, and it was not until the late 1970s that Scotland caught up. By 1981, 57 per cent of married women in Scotland aged under 60 were economically active.

The expansion of new occupations for women involved the feminisation of certain occupations such as clerical work, in which the proportion of clerks who were female rose from about half in 1961 to three-quarters by 1981. Women were not, however, becoming 'middle class' by dint of being in non-manual jobs, because female pay and conditions still remain consistently poorer than those of men. In any case, many 'white-collar' jobs such as those in call centres, and in care work, are poorly paid and badly provisioned, despite being labelled 'non-manual'.

In the previous chapter we compared the distributions of men and women in each socio-economic group (NS-SeC). We saw in Table 8.4 that men predominate in higher managerial and professional jobs (+5), small employer and own account work (+7), lower supervisory and technical (+8), and routine manual work (+6). There are more women than men in lower managerial, professional and intermediate jobs (+16), such as clerical workers and nursing auxiliaries, and in semi-routine manual work (+7), receptionists and catering assistants, for example (for a full account of how the NS-SeC system was constructed, see https://www.iser.essex.ac.uk/archives/nssec).

However we choose to group these occupations will depend on what social class schema we have in mind and for which purposes, but broadly speaking around one-third of men and women are in 'professional' occupations, about one-third are in 'manual' jobs (routine or semi-routine) (roughly the same proportion of women), and one-third of both men and women are in lower level white-collar work. Whichever way we look at it, the pyramidal shape of the class structure has been transformed from what it was a hundred years ago.

Social class in Scotland and England[7]

By the 1970s, Scotland, and the UK generally, saw the expansion of white-collar work, notably the growing number of professional employees, and intermediate non-manual workers (such as teachers and non-managerial workers). Manual workers declined as a percentage of those in employment, from just over 50 per cent in 1961 to 40 per cent in 1981, and by 2011 around one-third did 'manual' work. In comparison with the rest of the UK, while Scotland had a marginally higher share of manual workers in employment, the general decline was in line with that in the UK.

In comparison, Scotland had a lower share of non-manual workers, notably in the private sector, and of own-account workers. In broad terms, however, the similarities far outweigh the differences, for the forces shaping the occupational and class systems north and south of the border are comparable. This is because the agrarian revolution in the eighteenth century marked the end of the peasantry, and early industrialisation created a manual working class. Thereafter, differences between Scotland and England were of degree rather than of kind, although, as we saw in the previous chapter, industrial specialisation as in South Wales' coal, iron and steel works marked that country out as distinctive with regard to class structure.

Here we encounter the puzzle which we will deal with later in this chapter: if England and Scotland have not dissimilar class structures, why are they appreciably different as regards both class consciousness and political action? The short answer is that structure does not in and of itself determine how people respond; they do so in terms of the cultures in which they are embedded, and which they use to make sense of who they are, and why they are there. In that respect, it is culture that matters more than structure, even where territories like Scotland and England have been part of the same state for over 300 years.

Transforming social class

What is it that has transformed the occupational, and hence the class, structure? In the previous chapter we showed that there is a complex interaction between industrial structures and occupational structures. Thus, because far fewer people now work in manufacturing, it might seem logical to assume that as a result there are far fewer manual workers. The process of de-industrialisation is an obvious candidate to explain the decline of the working class, historically understood. We saw, however, that even within the same industries, such as manufacturing, proportionately fewer are employed nowadays in manual trades. Thus, whereas in 1981, 41 per cent of the manufacturing labour force were skilled manual workers, twenty years later the proportion was down to 35 per cent.

More generally, manual jobs as a proportion of those employed in manufacturing declined from 73 to 60 per cent over the period. In a previous analysis of occupational and industrial change in Scotland over this twenty-year period, we observed that:

> the fall in the size of the working class, and the growth of professional and managerial employment, is due mainly to change in the nature of the work processes within nearly all sectors – more automation, more supervision and more professional autonomy. Sectoral change, such as the decline of manufacturing, has played a much less significant role. (Paterson et al., 2004: 87)

The proportion of professional and managerial workers in manufacturing more than doubled between 1981 and 2001, from just under 10 per cent to 22 per cent. It is undoubtedly true that the decline in manufacturing has removed a tranche of manual jobs from the economy, but the transformation of the occupational, and hence the class, structure is not simply driven by changes in industrial sectors. We saw that even in coal mining, the iconic working-class manual occupation, there are now more technicians and managers, reflecting the automisation and technical investment in coal mining machinery. The virtual demise of deep mining in the UK, and its replacement with open-cast mining, has not only reduced the scale of the industry, but also transformed the labour process within it.

We can conclude, then, that changes in the work processes across all industrial sectors have been a more important cause of transformation than simply the rise and fall of such sectors. Thus, sectoral change per se is not the key factor leading to the growth of the professional and managerial class, or to the decline of the manual working class. It is what happens to the labour process *within* these industrial sectors which makes the most difference to the class structure.

Social mobility

So far in this chapter we have focused on what the class structure looks like and how it has changed over time. Our next question is: how do people come to be in the class positions they are in? To what extent, for example, do people remain in the social class of their parents, or move into a different class?[8] Social mobility studies in the UK have a long history, and in recent years the topic has attracted political interest. For example, the Conservative-led government set up in 2010 the 'Social Mobility and Child Poverty Commission' (https://www.gov.uk/government/organisations/social-mobility-and-child-poverty-commission) led by the former Labour MP Alan Milburn. He wrote in the *Daily Telegraph* just after the British general election of 2015: 'progress from the bottom to the middle of society is stalling. It is becoming harder to climb the social ladder' (www.telegraph.co.uk/news/politics/11627719/Social-mobility-has-come-to-a-halt.html). The Commission might more appropriately have been called the Social *Inequality* and Child Poverty Commission, as it seems to have little expertise in social mobility as such. For that we need to turn to a series of academic studies.

Social mobility studies

We are fortunate to have successive generations of academic studies, by John Goldthorpe in the 1970s and 1990s, and by Cristina Iannelli and Lindsay Paterson in the present century. As with occupational structures, it is the similarities, not the differences, in social mobility patterns of Scotland and England which are striking. Goldthorpe commented: 'On the basis of such comparison, it would seem clear enough that, had our enquiry been extended to Scotland, no substantially different results would have been produced so far at least as the pattern of de facto intergenerational rates is concerned' (1980: 291).

He concluded that the mobility model for England and Wales had a tolerably good fit with the Scottish data, the model accounting for over 95 per cent of the association between class of origin and class of destination. Social mobility is conventionally measured by comparing people's social origins (the social class of their parents) with their own social class positions as adults (their 'destinations').

The 1970s

In his social mobility study, Goldthorpe had this to say about the Scottish experience in the wider context of other industrial nations (England and Wales, France, West Germany, Republic of Ireland, Sweden, Hungary and Poland): that relative rates of mobility in

> England and Wales, together with France, turn out to be the most central nations with the configuration that emerges. Scotland and Northern Ireland, along with Hungary, fall into the intermediate band, and it is Poland, Sweden, West Germany and Ireland which, in that order, represent the most outlying cases. (1987: 309)

Goldthorpe is making the point about *relative* rates of class mobility, that is patterns of social fluidity. In that regard, the British nations are unexceptional. However, they are distinctive with regard to *absolute* rates of mobility, in terms of distinctive historical and structural effects. Scotland, England and Wales shared common characteristics by virtue of early industrialisation and the demise of the peasantry. Hence, in terms of comparative inflow rates, Scotland, as well as England and Wales, had the highest percentage in the top social classes who originate from manual working classes, and the lowest recruitment from farm origins (unlike the Republic of Ireland, for example). On the other hand, the British nations showed the highest proportions of self-recruitment into the manual working classes, with Poland and Hungary the lowest. These patterns were the result of a shared economic history of industrialisation. In Goldthorpe's words:

> Britain's early industrialisation and the unique path that it followed can be rather clearly associated, first, with a service class recruited to an unusual degree from among the sons of blue collar workers, and secondly with a broadly defined

industrial working class which is to an unusual degree self-recruited or which, one could alternatively say, is highly homogeneous in its composition in terms of its members' social origins. (1987: 316)

Britain, he concluded, did not possess any kind of historical legacy or institutional barriers (reflected in these data) either to impede or to promote social fluidity. In this context, Scotland together with England and Wales were the nations in which the distributions of social origins and destinations differ least.

We should not be surprised at this finding, because Scotland, England and Wales share common features as industrialised countries. Plainly, it would be perverse to conclude from the general data on social mobility patterns that Scotland had taken a different mobility route from the rest of the UK. Historically, Scotland had a slightly smaller middle class, and a slightly larger manual working class, but the processes of upward and downward social mobility which created these structures of opportunity are remarkably similar to those in England.

The picture of inter-generational social mobility in Scotland in the 1970s, then, was of a society similar in many ways to England and Wales, with a substantial proportion of the service class drawn up from manual working-class backgrounds. As many as one-third of the top 'salariat' (what Goldthorpe called the 'service class') had fathers who had been in manual jobs, and for class II ('subaltern or cadet levels of the service class'), the figure was 43 per cent.

On the other hand, the manual working classes (respectively skilled manual and semi-skilled manual workers, including those in agriculture) were much more homogeneous and self-recruiting. In other words, while there was considerable upward mobility into the social classes at the top, there was little corresponding downward mobility into social classes at the bottom. This lack of correspondence was due to the fact that while the size of the manual working class had shrunk, that of the service class had grown, thus allowing those who were already in that class to remain, but permitting considerable upward social mobility from lower levels. Thus, the changing shape and size of social classes was allowing for class retention at the top and class mobility from the bottom.

The 1990s

Studies in the 1990s using the British election surveys replicated those in the 1970s. Once more, the similarities between Scotland, and England and Wales, were more striking than the differences. It is not possible to sustain an argument that somehow Scotland and England were diverging in terms of social, that is occupational, mobility. The structural similarities between the component parts of the UK were following similar trends.[9] Hence, looking at people who have been upwardly mobile in 1975 (men) and in 1997 (men and women), we find almost identical percentages in Scotland compared with England and Wales (Tables 9.1 and 9.2).

TABLE 9.1 Inter-generational social mobility: percentage who had been upwardly mobile

	1975 Men*	1997 Men	1997 Women
Scotland	42	47	48
England and Wales	43	45	50

* The data were only available for men in Goldthorpe's earlier (1980) study

Sources: Goldthorpe (1980: 289 and 290); British Election Survey 1997

TABLE 9.2 Inter-generational social mobility: percentage who had been downwardly mobile

	1975 Men	1997 Men	1997 Women
Scotland	29	27	30
England and Wales	28	27	31

Sources: Goldthorpe (1980: 289 and 290); British Election Survey 1997

These data clearly show not only that Scotland and England and Wales do share virtually identical patterns of social mobility, but also that people are far more likely to be upwardly rather than downwardly mobile.

We might expect that different generations may encounter different patterns of mobility, and Iannelli and Paterson in their later work calculated rates of mobility for cohorts born in different decades: 1937–46, 1947–56, 1957–66 and 1967–76.[10] Analysing the 'origin' and 'destination' classes in the four cohorts for 1999, they showed that the professional classes drew on very diverse class origins, for, in terms of 'destination', only one-third had come from a similar professional background, and almost half (47 per cent) came from working-class backgrounds. They concluded:

> The idea that society is socially open is sustained by the high proportion of the service class (senior professional and managerial occupations) who have come from lower down the social scale, even though it is partly a result of changed class structure rather than openness itself. In other words, there are simply more service class jobs, and expanded opportunity because of that, rather than greater opportunity to move up the occupational ladder at the expense of other people moving down. (Paterson et al., 2004: 95)

Nevertheless, about one-third of the working class end up in working-class jobs. There is, then, little downward mobility in the sense that people moving up are replaced by those moving down, for fewer than one in five of the working class come from middle-class families. In other words, the expansion of professional and managerial jobs in the post-war period has permitted upward movement into those jobs as educational opportunities have expanded, while at the same time the sons and daughters of the middle classes manage to remain in their class of origin.

Further analysis by Iannelli and Paterson (2003, reported in Paterson et al., 2004: 95) showed that upward mobility was the result of the professional classes expanding their proportionate share, rather than because of changes in the relative chances of mobility from a certain starting point. They concluded:

> people who had a service class origin were more likely to end up in a service class job than people who had a skilled manual origin. But for both these origin groups the proportion in a service class job had risen across the cohorts. So the inequality in opportunities for mobility associated with class of origin had remained fairly stable, but all classes had benefitted from a higher level of overall opportunity. (Paterson et al., 2004: 95–6)

Absolute and relative social mobility

The distinction between absolute and relative social mobility is an important one. The former refers to the changing experience of individuals, while relative mobility focuses on inequalities of opportunity *between* different social classes. Put another way, one can have absolute mobility, in that the expansion of service-class jobs gives working-class children greater opportunities to move away from their origin class (mainly through education); and yet the *relative* differential between middle-class and working-class children remains unchanged as there is a considerable degree of service-class retention by virtue of their class of origin.

In Britain, as well as in Scotland, studies of social mobility show that absolute mobility has increased, and that for the past forty years upward mobility has been more frequent than downward mobility. This has led to a socially more *heterogeneous* service class, while a diminishing working class have remained relatively socially *homogeneous* in terms of people's class of origin. Thus, of those adults of working age at the turn of the twenty-first century, two-thirds have been socially mobile, and more than two-thirds of this mobility has in turn been upwards. Iannelli and Paterson conclude that the association between origin and destination has changed very little over the past half-century.

Furthermore, patterns of both absolute and relative mobility between men and women differ little. We saw earlier that women are more likely to be in lower non-manual jobs and men in skilled manual ones. Among younger people, women are marginally more likely to occupy service-class positions. While it is the case that educational opportunity is the main driver of social mobility, middle-class children who do not reach the highest levels of educational qualifications have other forms of social and cultural capital (finance, social networks) which are an aid to remaining in their social class of origin.

Much depends too on an expanding service sector, both in public services (education, health) and in the private sector (finance, property), for upward mobility is greater in this sector than it is in manufacturing or primary industries (agriculture, fishing and extraction) which are in structural decline (Paterson and Iannelli, 2007).

There has been greater downward mobility among the cohort born between 1967 and 1976, a change induced by the occupational structure itself; in other words, available service-class jobs have now been filled. While this might plausibly be attributed to economic recession, Iannelli and Paterson argue that a more likely explanation is *saturation*: that is, as the middle class gets larger, the chances of further mobility are reduced because in essence there is no room to expand; the system seems to have stopped growing. They conclude that 'the unchanging patterns of relative mobility ought to give pause to those policy makers who are currently trying to expand social mobility … it seems difficult to bring about an increase in fluidity by political means' (Paterson and Iannelli, 2007: 15). Indeed, the only way to increase absolute upward mobility would be to promote further growth of the service class.

While Scotland and England have grown more alike in terms of mobility processes, Paterson and Iannelli suggest that Wales has *not* converged with the other British nations. Thus, the proportion of destinations in the routine non-manual class and in the lower grade professional class is lower for Wales than for Scotland or England (Paterson and Iannelli, 2007: 8), and that more people in Wales than in England or Scotland moved downwards from origins in the middling classes. The absolute mobility rates for Scotland and England[11] converge, but not in Wales, suggesting that Wales' historic reliance on industrial and extractive employment, which has collapsed since the 1980s, holds the key. We can think of it as a lasting legacy of the old industrial structure.

Social mobility in the twenty-first century

The convergence between Scotland and England in terms of absolute mobility rates means that we can safely extrapolate the findings of a later paper by Goldthorpe and his colleagues (Bukodi et al., 2015). They take issue with the assumption established within political circles that social mobility in Britain is in decline or has even 'ground to a halt – despite the evidence for such a view being slight and the evidence going contrary to it far more substantial' (Bukodi et al., 2015: 94). The processes they describe are far more subtle, namely 'that among the members of successive cohorts, the experience of absolute upward mobility is becoming less common and that of absolute downward mobility more common; and class-linked inequalities in relative chance of mobility and immobility appear wider than previously thought' (2015: 93).

If there is a mobility problem today, it is not that mobility has fallen, but that the balance of upward and downward mobility in the experience of successive cohorts is moving in an unfavourable direction (2015: 99). Thus, the experience of downward mobility may, under current economic conditions in the second decade of the twenty-first century, become more common among successive cohorts. On the other hand, younger cohorts are at an early career stage, and hence we cannot be definitive about shifting processes of social mobility in the longer term. Nevertheless, people born in the 1980s may eventually experience less upward mobility, and more downward mobility, given economic and occupational stasis.

Education and social mobility

And what of education? Lindsay Paterson will address this more fully in the next chapter of the book, but his conclusions vis-à-vis social mobility are worth highlighting here. Despite Scotland's distinctive educational system, it appears to have no independent effect on rates of mobility, which resemble those of Britain as a whole. Iannelli and Paterson conclude:

> the intermediary role of education between origin and destination has not grown over time leading to a more 'meritocratic' society as the modernisation theories had predicted. These similarities between Scotland and the whole of Great Britain testify that different education systems and rates of educational participation may yield similar results in terms of the association between education and social mobility patterns. (2007a: 230)

What seem to be operating are forms of **cultural capital** available to the middle classes, especially in times of recession and competition for jobs. Cultural capital refers to non-monetary social assets such as social contacts, education, styles of dress and speech – what Pierre Bourdieu called 'symbolic goods' (Bourdieu, 1986). Iannelli and Paterson observe: 'if the main influence on success is the cultural capital that students acquire in the family, and if cultural capital is correlated with class position, then class differences in educational outcomes will be similar everywhere' (Iannelli and Paterson, 2007b: 350). If middle-class children acquire the acumen from their parents which teaches them how to negotiate various systems, then 'education' is much more than school or 'book' learning.

Educational institutions themselves are important channels for transmitting social mobility. Raffe and Croxford (2015) concluded that there is a stable hierarchical relationship among higher education sectors within Scotland as well as England such that the institutional hierarchies in standing remain much as before. They conclude: 'we find no evidence that the status distinctions associated with the former binary line, the Russell Group or the golden triangle [Oxbridge, and the London universities] have become less important; if anything, they have strengthened – especially at the top end of the hierarchy and towards the end of the period [2006–10]' (2015: 331).

Furthermore, the institutional stratification of higher education in Scotland has been almost as stable as that in England. Nor has 'marketisation' of higher education in either country eroded their institutional status hierarchies, or, perhaps we might say, they are incorporated into what is perceived as the 'market value' of institutions. Here, if we needed it, is further proof that 'the market' does not operate in a vacuum but confers 'value' upon what already has high status conferred upon it. Thus, the 'market' ends up compounding inequality rather than counteracting it.

Religion and social mobility

One other important feature of social mobility in Scotland relates to religion, and in particular to the assertion that Catholics have suffered significantly lower levels of social mobility historically (see e.g. Williams and Walls, 2000). Paterson and Iannelli show that 'in younger cohorts, there is no religious difference in social status, and that in older cohorts Catholics are generally of lower status than Protestants, and the non-religious' (2006: 374). The historic difference had far less to do with discrimination and sectarianism than with immigrants lacking capital and economic skills, and corroborates Bruce's conclusion that Catholics worked their way out of poverty at broadly the same rate as non-Catholics of similar social status (Bruce et al., 2004).

The extension of Catholic schools since they were incorporated into the state system in 1918 has removed historic mobility differences. The expansion of educational opportunity for Catholics, and in particular the availability of a full range of secondary schooling since the 1930s, meant that the life chances of Catholics became largely determined by social class, *not* religion (McPherson, 1992). Paterson observes:

> Because the remaining educational disadvantage of the Catholic population in the 1950s had been due to social disadvantage, a reform that extended opportunities for a full secondary education to all social class groups had disproportionate effect on Catholics. The result was that, by the 1980s, the attainment of pupils in Catholic schools was better than would have been expected from their social status alone. (2015a: 238)

Just as Catholics now take up their share of service-class occupations, so it is likely that more recent immigrants such as Asians, whose younger members have entered higher education, will rise accordingly. Paterson et al. observe: 'Asians are very likely to become prominent in the leadership of Scotland as people of Jewish, Italian or Irish family origins were in the second half of the twentieth century' (Paterson et al., 2004: 101).

How is Scotland different?

Let us return to our question. If Scotland and England now have very similar class structures *and* share similar processes and outcomes of social mobility, why should we think they are 'different' with respect to social consciousness and social action? To assume that is to invest structures with too much influence. Marx's distinction between '*klasse an sich*' and '*klasse für sich*' (roughly translated as 'class in itself' and 'class for itself') is a useful one: that is, the existence of classes objectively does not determine how their members see themselves. Whether or not people use class categories and what they mean when they do so depends on an array of social and cultural forces impacting upon how they see and make sense of the world around them.

We are drawn back at this point to important matters of *culture* which are under-pinned by institutional differences. Supposing that we are interested in studying social class in different societies, in Germany and France, say. We would have little quarrel with the view that their class structures were quite similar, and yet we would accept that the *meanings* of class, generated by distinct political cultures and histories, were differ-ent. We would acknowledge, for example, that these cultures are historically constructed and refracted through, for example, the institutional differences and political agendas in the two countries.

While this might seem an obvious point to make, it is frequently unobserved when looking at differences within the societies within the same state such as the UK. Put simply, we should not expect that social class in Scotland (or Wales, or Northern Ireland, for that matter) will be interpreted and explained in the same way as in England, because key insti-tutions such as the legal system, religion and the education system will evidently mediate structures and experiences to produce different political and social outcomes. In other words, culture mediates structure.

Class identity in Scotland and England

Let us take a look at a striking version of that. British and Scottish Social Attitudes surveys have asked the following question over the years: *'Do you ever think of yourself as belonging to any particular class?'*, where respondents are given the following options: 'yes, middle class'; 'yes, working class'; 'yes, other'; 'no'; and 'don't know'. If we cross-tabulate with respondent's own social class in terms of NS-SeC categories, we find the results for 2013 in

What these data show is that:

- employers, managers and professionals in Scotland are far *less* likely to describe them-selves as 'middle class' (a difference of 16 percentage points), and that they are *more* likely to say that they do not belong to any social class;

- semi-routine and routine manual workers in Scotland and Britain differ little in class descriptions, almost half saying they do not belong to a social class, and four in ten say-ing they are working class;

- both intermediate and lower supervisory and technical workers are *more* likely to say they are working class in Scotland (respectively, percentage point differences of +9 and +12);

- comparing those who say they are 'middle class' with those saying they are 'working class', we find there is parity among Scottish employers, managers and professionals (1:1), but a ratio of 1.76:1 among their British counterparts;

- in all the other class categories, there is a greater propensity for Scottish workers to self-describe as 'working class'.[13]

TABLE 9.3   Objective social class by subjective social class, 2013

% by column	Employers, managers and professionals	Intermediate occupations	Small employers and own account	Lower supervisory and technical	Semi-routine and routine workers
Yes, middle class	21 (37)	11 (14)	11 (15)	6 (17)	7 (10)
Yes, working class	22 (21)	33 (24)	28 (34)	43 (31)	40 (39)
Yes, other	1 (2)	1 (1)	1 (5)	1 (1)	1 (2)
No	56 (40)	55 (61)	60 (45)	50 (51)	52 (49)

Source: British and Scottish Social Attitudes surveys, 2013

Table 9.3 (Scotland, with GB in brackets).[12]

The striking finding from these surveys is how *few* people describe themselves as 'middle class' in Scotland, even among employers, managers and professionals, a majority of whom (56 per cent) deny that they are members of any class (compared with 40 per cent of their British equivalents).

Corroboration of these Scottish/English differences is found in the British Election Survey of 1997, which compared self-assigned class by own class and father's class as in Table 9.4.

While those in non-professional jobs (rows I and II) are equally likely to describe themselves as 'working class', those who are mobile out of the working class into the professional classes in Scotland (row III) are significantly more likely to describe themselves as 'working class' than similar people south of the border (+9), while even those who are professionals from professional origins are more likely than their counterparts in England to call themselves 'working class'. This suggests that the culture or meaning of class operates differently: that people in Scotland are much more likely to say they are working class, regardless of either their class of origin, or their class of destination.

TABLE 9.4   Self-assigned class, by own social class and father's social class, 1997: percentage describing self as 'working class'

	Respondent's objective class	Father's objective class	Scotland	England and Wales
I	Not professional	Not professional	85	76
II	Not professional	Professional	49	53
III	Professional	Not professional	59	50
IV	Professional	Professional	28	25

Source: British Election Survey 1997 (note that 'professional' = classes I or II)

The Scottish myth revisited

How are we to explain these different perceptions? We return to the conundrum we raised at the beginning of this chapter: the Scottish egalitarian myth. Myths of this sort, and this includes its comparator, the American Dream, are not designed to be open to proof or disproof, but held as truths to be self-evident. In other words, they help to frame how we think about things. The notion that hard work coupled with ability will lead to achievement unless you are particularly unlucky is a powerful value in the United Sates. It is a story, a narrative, of considerable power which helps to define Americans to themselves and, they hope, other people. It is an identity-myth, saying who they are and who they are not.

Similarly, the Scottish myth – with interesting parallels with the American one – is a truth held to be self-evident: that all people are created equal, that 'we're a' Jock Tamson's bairns', that 'a man's a man for a' that'. 'Myth' here does not refer to something which is manifestly false, but to a perspective, a guide for helping to make sense of social reality. As guides, myths are of little help in predicting or explaining actual features of the social structure. Like 'traditions', they have an active, contemporary significance (Williams, 1977: 115). Like traditions, myths connect with past realities. They draw selectively from the past, a process which involves selective exclusion and inclusion. In so doing, myth becomes a contemporary and an active force providing, in most instances, a reservoir of legitimation for belief and action. There is the famous saying by Marx (1959: 320): 'Men make their own history, but they do not make it as they please; they do not make it under self-selected circumstances, but under circumstances existing already, given and transmitted from the past' (*The Eighteenth Brumaire of Louis Bonaparte*).

The Scottish myth makes much of the inherent egalitarianism of the Scots and operates in different ways and at different levels. The system of education and forms of democracy are judged to have contributed to the relatively open and democratic ethos of seventeenth-century Scotland, but the myth of egalitarianism has at root an a-sociological, almost mystical element. It is as if Scots are judged to be egalitarian by dint of racial characteristics, of deeper social values. Man (or at least Scots-man) is judged to be primordially equal; inequality is man-made, created by the social structure he (for the myth has historically been about men) erects, or which is erected by others around him.

The myth is ambivalent, and it lends itself to two interpretations. The first, the activist interpretation, takes the co-existence of man-made inequality and primordial equality and argues for an active resolution of this anomaly in favour of social equality; that we are not trying hard enough to achieve our 'natural' state. A second, 'idealist', interpretation adopts a more conservative response. If man is primordially equal, social structural inequalities do not matter, so nothing needs to be done. In this way, the egalitarian myth lends itself to conservative as well as radical interpretations.

Although egalitarianism is, in essence, a set of social values, a body of sacred truth, it is usually connected with features of the social structure, and above all with social institutions

such as education. The debates about educational change in the 1960s took on a particular
Scottish flavour with the publication in 1961 of George Davie's *The Democratic Intellect*,
which, observed Andrew McPherson, 'served, in the context of English debates of the time
about social class inequalities of access to educational opportunity in England, only to confirm to Scottish opinion the egalitarian pedigree of the national institution that Scotland had
substituted for English gentility' (1983: 225–6). Despite evidence that structures of social
mobility are similar to those south of the border, how these are interpreted – culturally – in
Scotland are undoubtedly different.

The Scottish myth, then, is kept alive not simply because people believe it to be
founded in fact, but also because there are institutional mechanisms, like the education system, which provide sufficient affirmation of validity, and these are reinforced
by the accounts people like Davie give of it. In many respects, egalitarianism was a key
element in a conservative ideology which congratulated itself on the openness of
Scottish (essentially rural and small town) society and its social institutions. The myth
had its own social agent, the lad o' pairts, described by Robert Anderson and Stuart
Wallace as

> the boy from a relatively obscure background who rose through education
> to professional success. This was one of those powerful and enduring images
> which turn complex realities into national myths. The 'lad o' parts' was in part
> a literary construction, and the term itself did not appear until 1894 but the idea
> was an old one. It was a very masculine ideal, and also a very Protestant one,
> seeing the Reformation as the source of modern Scotland's vigour and identity.
> (2015: 267)

The egalitarian myth is 'old' because it is premised upon the existence of a hierarchical
social order, not a classless society. It described ideal conditions in the typical pre-capitalist
and pre-industrial community, often rural. Said Allan MacLaren: 'There is some evidence
to suggest that the "Scottish Myth" is a product of a former rural paternalism rather than
an urban industrialism in which class identity and economic individualism overruled a
declining concern for communal and parochial obligations' (1976: 9). The image of social
identity which is held up for praise is of *community*, rather than class, but it entered Scottish
consciousness in a less precise fashion.

Much of the reason for the relative success of Scottish education lies in the fact that
the progressive coalition of educators has held together better than in England.
Believers in economic efficiency made sufficiently common cause with popular educators and humanists who argued for universal education, reinforced by a more
widespread nationalistic belief that Scottish education was one of the defining characteristics of the nation. The role of the 'Scottish myth' has been to translate national
distinctiveness into institutional characteristics, reinforced by relative success in
improving access to cultural capital.

Politics, class and identity

So far in this chapter we have focused on social class in terms of social structure and social mobility. There is no strong case for saying that Scotland is significantly different in both respects from the rest of the UK, and notably England. How, then, are we to explain important political differences between Scotland and England? What, indeed, has 'politics' to do with social class?

The simple answer is that there is no straightforward translation of social class into politics. Scottish political differences, notably those relating to ideas of Scottish self-government, are connected to social class in an interesting way. In 1979, when the first devolution referendum took place, the vote, while won in the sense of getting most votes (by 52 per cent to 48 per cent), was defeated because it failed to meet the 40 per cent rule whereby this percentage of the total electorate was required to vote 'Yes' for the Act to proceed. The Scottish middle classes voted against devolution in 1979, but by 1997, when the vote to set up a Scottish parliament took place, they backed it overwhelmingly.

In the 1997 British general election, Scotland's service class, professional and managerial workers, were far less inclined than their British/English counterparts to vote Conservative: 23 per cent did so, compared with 37 per cent in the rest of Britain. Writing of that 1997 election, Paterson commented: 'It is clearly no longer the case, if it ever was, that voting behaviour can be explained solely in terms of class location. Amongst the salariat in England and Wales equal proportions voted for Labour and the Conservatives, whilst in Scotland a higher proportion of the salariat voted Labour than Conservative' (Paterson, in Brown et al., 1999: 53).

By the 2015 British general election, the pattern had changed even further: 38 per cent of the Scottish salariat (i.e. employers, managers and professionals) voted SNP, twice the proportion who voted Labour in 2015, and compared with only 17 per cent who voted Conservative. Furthermore, 37 per cent of the salariat said they had voted 'Yes' in the 2014 Scottish Independence Referendum (2015 Scottish Social Attitudes election survey). The salariat had shifted to supporting a more powerful Scottish parliament, with one-third supporting one which would make *all* decisions about Scotland, and a further one-third who supported 'devolution-max', meaning that only defence and foreign affairs would be left with Westminster, and all other decisions made by the Scottish parliament.

Furthermore, Paterson (2015b) has argued that the 'Yes' movement was led by left-leaning middle-class people, and thus support was the result of interaction between political ideology and social class. He observed that, among those who had made their minds up in mid-summer 2014, the 'Yes' percentage in the left-leaning middle class was 47 per cent, higher than the 42 per cent in the working class as a whole.

Using evidence from the 2013 Scottish Social Attitudes survey, Paterson showed that the percentage intending to vote 'Yes' was highest among people who identified with Scots, even those belonging to a different class, rather than those in England who share the same class position: 46 per cent and 41 per cent respectively among such working-class and middle-class people, and significantly ahead of their respective classes as a whole (36 per cent and 31 per cent). Paterson concluded:

> not only may we conclude that the Yes intention was strong among left-leaning middle-class people; it was strongest among those left-leaning middle-class people who identified with working-class Scots, and among left-leaning working-class people who did not show much solidarity with working-class people across the border. (2015b: 42–3)

While a majority of the Scottish salariat said they had voted 'No' to independence in 2014 (the 2016 Scottish Social Attitudes survey put the split at 57 per cent 'No' to 37 per cent 'Yes'), those supporting a 'No' vote during the campaign were criticised for remaining unduly quiescent. The journalist Hugo Rifkind (son of the former Conservative politician, Malcolm Rifkind) admonished people he called 'timid posh folk' in Scotland who were keeping their heads down during the referendum. He commented: 'They know what they think. They have grown accustomed, insidiously, to avoid stating it. … These are the missing voices from the independence debate. This is the source of the No campaign's terrible insipid bloodlessness, and its palpable lack of fire' (*Spectator*, 22 February 2014). Rifkind was writing to inform and to entertain, but his comment does pick up the point that Scotland's middle classes do not behave politically in the same way as their counterparts south of the border, and, in particular, that they have, relative to England, deserted the Conservative Party, the party of their parents and grandparents.[14] That as many as 38 per cent of the salariat voted SNP in 2015 reflects once more that 'politics' cannot be read off social class in a simple manner. More to the point, politics is refracted through Scottish culture and society in a manner which would have been unthinkable, a hundred or even fifty years ago.

Conclusion

This chapter reinforces the point that culture matters. It is not simply enough to draw a straight inference from structure to consciousness to action, as if one neatly follows the other. To assume so is to indulge in structuralism, to assume that simply by pointing to similarities in socio-economic condition, we can read off how people see themselves and others, and above all that this will lead to similar forms of social action. To repeat E.P. Thompson's comment, class is a cultural as much as an 'economic' formation.

Scotland has followed the trajectory of western (post)-industrial societies in its employment patterns, and its social class profile, and a similar process of social mobility. To say this is not to imply that we can expect to know how people define themselves in class terms, for that is the outcome of culture and history, meanings set within the context of the society in which they are embedded. In that respect, culture matters. The 'Scottish' framework of understanding is not totally at odds with a 'British' one, but is carried by institutional differences and shared expectations. We will develop that important point when Lindsay Paterson explores the role of education in Scotland in the next chapter.

Chapter summary

So what have we learned in this chapter?

- That 'social class' derives from systems of economy and industrial production, but that as well as 'structure', it has important and independent effects relating to 'consciousness' and social and political 'action' which are framed by cultural experiences.

- That 'social mobility' is about the ease or difficulty people have in moving up (and down) the social ladder, particularly across generations.

- That with regard to both social class structures and patterns of social mobility the similarities between Scotland and England are greater than the differences between them.

- Nevertheless, how people relate to social class and to social mobility, what sense they make of these, has far more to do with the cultural and historic understandings. Such understandings in Scotland are different from those in England.

- This is reflected in how people self-describe their social class and relates in particular to how they do their politics.

Questions for discussion

1. How has the structure of social class in Scotland changed over the last fifty years, and why?

2. Is Scotland a 'class society', and, if so, in what senses is that the case?

3. How does social mobility in Scotland operate? How easy or difficult is it to change your social class?

4. Does education make a difference to your social class, and, if so, why?

5. What is the relation between class structure and class identity and how people do politics? How would you account for contemporary political change in Scotland in these terms?

Annotated reading

(a) On the different dimensions of 'social class', see F. Bechhofer, B. Elliott and D. McCrone, 'Structure, consciousness and action: a sociological profile of the British middle class', *British Journal of Sociology*, 29(4), 1978; and L. Paterson et al., *Living in Scotland: Social and economic change since 1980* (2004), chapters 6 and 7.

(b) On cultural dimensions of social class in Scotland, see R. Morton, 'Class in a "classless" society: the paradox of Scottish egalitarianism', *Scottish Affairs*, 75, Spring, 2011.

(c) On patterns of social mobility, see C. Iannelli and L. Paterson, 'Social mobility in Scotland since the middle of the twentieth century', *The Sociological Review*, 54(3), 2006; and E. Bukodi, J.H. Goldthorpe, L. Waller and J. Kuha, 'The mobility problem in Britain: new findings from the analysis of birth cohort data', *British Journal of Sociology*, 66(1), 2014.

(d) On the role of education, see A. McPherson, 'Schooling', in A. Dickson and J. Treble (eds), *People and Society in Scotland, 1914–1990* (1992); L. Paterson, 'Democracy or intellect: the Scottish educational dilemma of the 20th century', in R. Anderson, M. Freeman and L. Paterson (eds), *The Edinburgh History of Education in Scotland* (2015c); and D. Raffe and L. Croxford, 'How stable is the stratification of higher education in England and Scotland?', *British Journal of Sociology of Education*, 36(2), 2015.

(e) On social attitudes relating to social class in Scotland, see Scottish Centre for Social Research, 'What Scotland Thinks' (http://whatscotlandthinks.org/questions/do-you-think-of-yourself-as-belonging-to-any-particular-class), 1999–2013.

Notes

1   The last stanza makes the point:
    'Then let us pray that come it may (As come it will for a' that,)
    That Sense and Worth, o'er a' the earth, shall bear the gree, an' a' that.
    For a' that, an' a' that, it's coming yet for a' that,
    That Man to Man, the world o'er, shall brothers be for a' that.'

2   The full quotation is as follows: 'Thus the great mass of the French nation is formed by the simple addition of homologous magnitudes, much as potatoes in a sack form a sack of potatoes. Insofar as millions of families live under conditions of existence that separate their mode of life, their interests, and their culture from those of the other classes, and put them in hostile opposition to the latter, they form a class. Insofar as there is merely a local inter-connection among these small-holding peasants, and the identity of their interests forms no community, no national bond, and no political organization among them, they do not constitute a class' (Book VII).

3 This distinction was first developed by David Lockwood in *The Blackcoated Worker* (1958).

4 The actors spoke the lines: *Barker* [middle class]: 'I look up to him [*Cleese* – upper class] because he is upper class, but I look down on him [*Corbett* – working class] because he is lower class'. *Corbett*: 'I know my place.'

5 The reader might like to play the YouTube video provided by the BBC to get the full flavour of the exchange.

6 The metaphor as to which foot one kicked with is obscure, but possibly derived from the type of spade Irish peasants used to dig peat, hence 'left-footer' as befitted the implement. Hugh Cheape of the National Museums of Scotland commented: 'the two-sided spade of Ulster was generally used with the left foot whereas the one-sided spade tended to be used with the right foot. Instinctively, the "wrong foot" of the Catholics has come to be thought of as the left foot' (http://tywkiwdbi.blogspot.co.uk/2013/11/these-are-left-footed-spades.html).

7 The convention used here is to compare Scotland and Great Britain, rather than England per se. This is because (a) the statistics vary, sometimes Britain (GB), at others England and Wales, and England; (b) England is such a large proportion of the British population (over 80 per cent) that, for England, read Great Britain in terms of general trends. The comparator with Scotland will be specified as appropriate.

8 The conventional way of assessing social mobility is inter-generationally: that is, comparing social class positions of parents and their children. *Intra-generational* mobility refers to comparing an individual's social mobility over their own working lifetime.

9 Fuller versions of the tables here appear in McCrone's *Understanding Scotland* (2001: 88).

10 This is more fully described in Paterson et al.'s *Living in Scotland* (2004: 91–8).

11 The data refer to place of birth, not current residence; see Paterson and Iannelli (2007: 15).

12 We have used GB figures here because British Social Attitudes surveys do so. If 'England only' figures had been available, the differential would have made little difference, given the size of the 'England' component of GB.

13 The respective ratios of working class to middle class in Scotland are: for intermediate workers, 3:1 (GB 1.7); small employers, 2.5 (GB 2.3); lower supervisory and technical, 7.2 (GB 1.8); semi-routine and routine workers, 5.7 (GB 3.9).

14 We will have more to say on the outcome of the 2016 Scottish parliament election in subsequent chapters, notably about the relative revival of Conservative fortunes (up 8 percentage points from 2011 to 22 per cent of the constituency vote).

10

SCOTTISH EDUCATION AND SCOTTISH SOCIETY

LINDSAY PATERSON

S o often has it been claimed that education is an icon of Scottish identity that the very claim itself has become a cliché. When, during the referendum on independence in 2014, the two sides of the debate sought to attach themselves most legitimately to an authentic past, they looked for metaphors of opportunity, of an educated culture, and – if not of equality – then of what the American sociologist R.H. Turner called as long ago as 1960 'contest mobility', the right to be treated as equal in potential, the right to compete for recognition by those in power, and the right for the criteria of evaluation to be defined in a meritocratic way.

Chapter aims

- To describe the structure of provision – for example, the schools, universities and other institutions which are responsible for education, and how these have changed over the twentieth century.

- To assess education as leading to social success or failure – for example, the extent to which education has been a route to social mobility.

- To consider education as a form of culture: how has education shaped Scottish ideas about the nation?

Introduction

The old claim that education is an icon of Scottish society cannot have stood still. In Scotland, as elsewhere, it is over a century since the very meaning of a worthwhile education came to be defined in the measurable terms of examinations approved of by the state.

The Scotland of the middle of the twentieth century was led by the professional products of that first wave of mass measurement, a leadership class that remained firmly in charge of Scotland's place in the Union until the government of Margaret Thatcher challenged it in the 1980s. The beginnings of the rebellion against the unreformed Union, in the 1970s and 1980s, was provoked in part by the same effects of wide educational opportunity as underlay the revolt against old authority that underpinned her quite different kind of political project in England: a society where nearly everyone had completed secondary education was no longer willing to be told what to do.

Thus the emergence of pressure for self-government was in part the rebellion of mass education against the old complacency of Scottish professional education, against what Tom Nairn has called the Scottish subaltern class. And then, from the late 1980s, a new professional class emerged out of mass higher education that was on the left and national-ist, placing itself at the leadership of the political movement which – seen in historical perspective – came remarkably close to winning in the referendum of 2014.

Educational expansion

These three phases of educational expansion – elite professional education, mass secondary education and then mass higher education – may be taken as one way of characterising what has happened to Scottish society in the past century. The first way to tell that story is structurally – an account of what kinds of institutions were created or reformed, and what segments of the population they served. That is on the whole how the sociology of education in Scotland has been told, and it is the bedrock of everything else.

The second type of understanding is also well represented in Scottish research – the investigation of what being educated leads to. This raises questions about social class and social mobility, and indeed sometimes the characteristic myth of Scottish education is reduced to only that – to the claim that poor children were encouraged to progress in Scottish education as in no other, and the resulting political aim, when that claim is shown to be not true, that such a myth ought to inspire action to make it more true.

There is also a third way of looking at the same processes – by considering how educa-tion related to Scottish culture: what was taught and learnt; what ideologies and beliefs were acquired through that; and what were the relationships of these to other belief sys-tems in society, notably to the ways in which Scotland conceived of itself as an autonomous nation within the UK. On the whole, that way of looking at the history has not been attended to as systematically in Scotland as the other two. When Scottish culture is men-tioned in connection with education, the connotation is rather more often of overtly Scottish content – novels or poems or plays or history that mark Scotland as different.

Rarely has it been considered whether a more important cultural question might be whether curricular topics that Scottish education shares with many other places – including with England – might have distinctive implications here. Does, say, reading the essays and poetry of T.S. Eliot on cultural tradition mean something different in a society such as Scotland's from the meaning in the stable core culture of England to which he thought he belonged, or from the anarchically capitalist culture of the United States from which he came? Might reading Eliot thus not inspire an intellectual rebellion in Scotland all the more profound for being thus acquired through the distancing effects of Eliot's deeply conservative but subtly original intellect? This third way of considering education then can tell a story that emphasises continuity even while the structural approaches find much change.

In each of the three phases of expansion, some version of liberal education has been asserted against utilitarianism, a belief – sometimes almost utopian in its intensity – that education ought not to be only for personal or social advancement, but also to be to make better people and thus a better society. That belief has close parallels in all other developed education systems, but without paying attention to its strong presence in Scottish arguments about educational reform, we cannot understand the cultural effects of curricular ideas in Scotland. It is certainly not enough, when trying to understand these cultural effects, simply to pay attention to overtly Scottish curricular content.

This chapter considers all three ways of thinking about education – institutions, social structure and cultural content. In these three respects, educational expansion has modified Scottish society as well as been shaped by it. What we call Scottish culture in the twentieth-first century is a product in large measure of educational influences, but not, mostly, of educational programmes that have been, in their cultural content, distinctively Scottish. Education in Scotland, as elsewhere, can have distinctive effects because it interacts with a distinctive environment, even though, in most respects, education in all developed countries does much the same kinds of things and relates in much the same kinds of ways to its local context.

Institutions and participation

The main structural changes affected what we now call secondary schooling and, much later, higher education, though at the beginning of the century these terms overlapped to indicate everything beyond elementary schooling. The structural changes to primary education had mostly been completed by the 1880s, as a consequence of the Education (Scotland) Act of 1872, which brought into one national and compulsory system most of the schools that had previously been managed by the various Presbyterian Churches. The schools of the Catholic and Episcopal Churches followed after the Education (Scotland) Act of 1918, the main purpose of which was, however, to lay the basis for a proper system of secondary education. That goal was achieved by the eve of the Second World War, and in most respects the structure of secondary schools which Scotland still has today is that which was bequeathed by the 1918 Act. For the conditions of 'traditional' schooling see Figure 10.1.

The main changes in the meantime were the ending of selection for different kinds of secondary education in the 1960s and the rapid expansion of secondary education by the

FIGURE 10.1
Scotland Street
School Museum

Source: www.
glasgowlife.org.
uk/museums/
scotland-street/

We are grateful
to the museum
for permission
to reproduce this
image

1990s, such that, at the end of the century, the proportion completing at least five years of secondary schooling (67 per cent) was nearly seven times what conservative officials in the governing Scottish Education Department (SED) had thought possible in the early 1920s (Paterson et al., 2004: 105–7).

These developments of secondary schooling were fairly inevitable corollaries of the advent of compulsory primary education after 1872. The Act of that year left the question of post-primary schooling unresolved. On the one hand, there were about forty or so endowed schools, the terms of whose endowments required some kind of public purpose of a charitable kind even though legislative adjustments to these specifications had enabled the schools to become, in effect, the property of the urban middle class: they remained public largely in the sense that various bursary schemes allowed able poor children to be recruited into them in a meritocratic way (Anderson, 1983: 168–201).

On the other hand, there were about a dozen secondary schools managed by the new school boards which the 1872 Act had set up to oversee the primary schools. These schools, too, had some endowments, but not generous enough to survive independently of public authorities, and indeed the boards gradually took over more such poorly endowed schools up to the 1920s. The problem of finance after 1872, however, was that the boards were not permitted to use local taxation to fund secondary education, and so their secondary schools had to charge fees.

All of this changed from the beginning of the new century, when a new category of higher grade schools was founded and funded by the SED. At first these were intended to provide only a technical education for a minority of post-primary pupils, but the SED lifted such restrictions from 1902, after which they grew to provide a full liberal curriculum for the five years that secondary education then normally lasted. The schools inspectors used the Leaving Certificate that they had founded in 1888 to regulate the quality of secondary courses in the various kinds of school.

Details of the curricula of the courses which led to the certificate are considered below, but the essential structural features were that nearly all subjects were offered at two grades – higher and lower (the former term not to be confused with the terminology of the schools) – and that, to achieve the full certificate, it was necessary to pass a specified combination of subjects with a specified number at the higher grade. The specifications varied over the years, but they were the main structural means by which breadth of study came to be a defining feature of Scottish secondary schooling. The higher grade courses came to be referred to simply as 'the Highers', a name that has stuck.

There were 196 higher grade schools by 1918, educating 60 per cent of secondary pupils who were in publicly financed schools (Anderson, 1983: 243; Paterson, 2004; 2011). Places in them were free or cost only low fees, and there were enough of them to make free secondary education available in all districts throughout the country. They were mostly situated in areas populated by the lower middle class or by the skilled working class, and so this quintupling of secondary education promised a social revolution. From an SED led by Sir Henry Craik, who was later to become a Unionist MP representing the Scottish universities, that was quite remarkable, but unionism was then in one of its most creative phases, and Craik had acquired through his own education in the principles of British social idealism the belief that the state was a force for good (Paterson, 2015b).

Restrictions in public expenditure in the mid-1920s ended this period of expansion, and ended also the SED's encouragement to schools to organise the five years of secondary education into two phases: three years to an intermediate Leaving Certificate (consisting only of lower grade passes) and five to the full Leaving Certificate (Stocks, 1995). This was a serious pause, increasing again the cost of attending secondary education, but did not reverse most of the results of what had been achieved, and laid the basis for developments up to the late 1950s.

From 1935, all post-primary education was recognised as properly secondary education, funded and staffed to the same standard, though, from 1935, divided between junior secondary courses, lasting three years, and senior secondary courses, lasting five. In urban areas this became a distinction between schools offering only three-year courses and those which offered both kinds; the resulting approximately 400 junior secondary schools were generally thought to be of poor quality, and were certainly much inferior to the 250 or so senior secondary schools. Allocation between these was mainly on the basis of tests of intelligence and of attainment at the end of primary education, the best known of which was widely known as the 'qualifying exam' (analogous to what in England was called 'the eleven plus'). The proportion entering senior secondary courses was always a minority – around one-third (Paterson, 2003: 65 and 131).

Processes of selection

The next structural change was then provoked by the growing evidence that the selection processes were not as effective at picking out talented pupils as all shades of political opinion – even the political left – had hoped in the 1930s (Paterson, 2003: 130–6). Thus able working-class children were being denied opportunities that meritocratic criteria indicated they ought to have, and society was being denied what ought to be their resulting economic and civic contribution.

The distinction between the senior secondary and junior secondary courses was abolished between 1965 and the mid-1970s, so that all secondary schools in the public sector became comprehensive in the sense that they took all children from a local catchment area (McPherson and Willms, 1987; Paterson, 2003: 136–42). Although this was modified in the 1980s when parents were given quite thorough rights to choose the school which their children would attend, the general principle of neighbourhood comprehensives remained intact.

Only about 5 per cent of secondary pupils attended independent schools, most of which were the direct descendants of the endowed schools of the late nineteenth century. They charged fees and continued to select their pupils on the basis of entrance tests. They had the largest presence in the city of Edinburgh, where they educated around 20 per cent of pupils. Over the system as a whole – including independent schools – Scotland retained, by international standards, a low level of social class segregation among schools (Croxford and Paterson, 2006; Smith and Gorard, 2002). Oscar Mazaroli's famous photograph of 'The Castlemilk Lads' taken in the 1950s conveys something of post-war change (see Figure 10.2).[1]

FIGURE 10.2
'The Castlemilk Lads' by Oscar Marzaroli

Source: I am grateful to National Galleries of Scotland, and the Marzaroli trustees, for permission to reproduce this photograph

The debates around these structural changes indicated the importance of the relationship between institutional structure and social segmentation, insofar as questions of affordability recur. The widened provision in higher grade schools of a common standard of secondary education extended opportunity in relation to social class, gender and religion.

Social class

On class, not much specific can be said in this respect until the late 1940s, apart from the general point that the new schools served communities where secondary education had previously been unavailable. But evidence from surveys of school pupils in the late 1940s confirms that the former higher grade schools truly were far more successful than the older secondary schools in serving a nationally representative segment of society (Paterson et al., 2011). The proportion of pupils in these schools in 1947–50 who were from semi-skilled and unskilled working-class families (Registrar-General classes IV and V) was 28 per cent, not far short of the 34 per cent of children nationally who were in these classes. The old secondary schools, by contrast, had only 14 per cent. At the other end of the social scale, in classes I and II, the proportion in the old schools was 38 per cent, far more than the 12 per cent nationally or than the 13 per cent in the former higher grade schools.

Gender

The reforms from early in the century to the 1950s also benefited girls (Paterson, 2011). By as early as 1911, girls made up as many as 57 per cent of candidates for the Leaving Certificate. This fell somewhat with the restrictions after the mid-1920s, but remained at 40 per cent in the mid-1930s. In 1947–50, girls and boys were equally represented on the senior secondary courses. Throughout, girls were disproportionately served by the newer schools: in the mid-1930s, girls made up around 45 per cent of Leaving Certificate candidates in the newer schools, but 36 per cent in the old (though even that figure of over one-third indicates an opening up of a system that had been very closed to girls). These gender differences were similar in 1947–50 (Paterson et al., 2011). In the later 1950s, although the employment opportunities which this schooling led to were differentiated by gender, young women were certainly not denied opportunity: by 1963, among people who had left school around 1951–4, 55 per cent of men and 39 per cent of women had acquired some kind of post-school certificate, mostly in trade skills for men and in secretarial skills for women (Paterson et al., 2010). We return shortly to look at gender differences in the curriculum.

Religion

On religion, one effect of the 1918 Act was to enable public funding to build up a system of Catholic secondary schools. These were wholly public schools, insofar as they were funded in the same way as all the other secondary schools, had the same staffing standards and building standards, and followed the same curriculum except in connection with religion itself. The result was another kind of social revolution: by 1935, the proportion of candidates for the Leaving Certificate who were Catholic was 11 per cent, not far short of the national proportion of pupils who were Catholic (14 per cent), and a gap that was relatively much smaller than two decades before (5 per cent compared with 11 per cent in 1911) (Paterson, 2004).

The remaining difference was due to the continuing socio-economic disadvantage of Catholic families: among those children who left school in 1951–4, attainment and progression in the labour market can be entirely explained by measured ability on entering secondary school and by social class of origin, in other words by the same deeper sources as explain inequality among children of other faiths or of none (Paterson et al., 2015). Thus by the 1950s, and probably as early as the 1930s, religion as such was not an impediment to educational opportunity.

Nevertheless, despite this widening of opportunity in the first half of the century, the old schools remained more effective than the newer ones. One long-term follow-up of children who left school in 1951–4 found that there were lasting effects of the type of school that they had attended, effects that were not merely a reflection of intelligence, gender, paternal social class or parental education. The older schools that dated from the nineteenth century and earlier were particularly effective at enabling pupils of well-above-average ability to have high attainment after leaving school and thereby to have high-status careers (Paterson et al., 2014; see also McPherson and Willms, 1986).

In that sense, the older schools were probably more competitively meritocratic than the newer ones. They had no effect beyond their capacity to encourage high attainment: there were no hidden networks promoting social status, no old boys' networks. In that sense, the system that had been put in place by the 1950s was a success. But it had not overcome the effects of social class, merely reproduced that effect in many more schools than previously. In any case, and affecting far more pupils, the three-year junior secondary schools were very ineffective compared with either the new or the old senior secondary schools.

The hope by campaigners for comprehensive schools was that they would at least end these divisions among different kinds of school, and possibly also overcome some of the background effects of social class. With respect to religion and to gender, the system set up after 1965 led to the ending, or even the reversing, of old inequalities. The most striking change was for gender (Croxford, 2015: 122–4; Paterson, 2003: 147). For example, whereas among school leavers in 1951–4, 10 per cent of boys but only 6 per cent of girls had gained the equivalent of three Highers, that proportion was equalised a quarter of a century later (at 18 per cent in 1975) and was reversed before the end of the century (27 per cent and 34 per cent in 1997).

On religion, the building of comprehensive schools was particularly beneficial to Catholic pupils despite there no longer having been any discrimination against them in the school system. Because Catholic families still lived disproportionately in poorer districts, and because – despite the progress – such districts were served disproportionately by junior secondary schools, the upgrading of these schools had an inadvertently beneficial effect on working-class Catholic pupils. By the 1990s, for school leavers of the same class, there was no religious difference in attainment: for example, in 1994, the proportion gaining three or more Highers was 21 per cent among working-class leavers from Catholics schools, and 19 per cent among working-class leavers from non-Catholic schools. The respective proportions for middle-class leavers were 50 per cent and 51 per cent (Paterson, 2000a).

These proportions also illustrate, however, that social class remained a source of wide social inequality, addressing which had been the main original aim of comprehensive schooling. The initial move to a non-selective system was accompanied by a small fall in class inequality (McPherson and Willms, 1987), but only for school leavers with middling or low attainment. McPherson and Willms (1987) speculated that reducing inequality at higher levels of attainment would take much longer, and it did indeed happen slowly. Thus immediately before the ending of selection, among leavers in 1960–3, 25 per cent of middle-class leavers passed three or more Highers, five times greater than the 5 per cent among working-class leavers.[2] In 1978, the proportions were 38 per cent and 9 per cent, a ratio now of just over 4:1; in 1994 it was about 2.5:1 (51 per cent and 20 per cent) (Paterson, 2003: 148). The slowness of this change – which may, indeed, have come to a halt altogether in the new century (Croxford, 2015: 125–8) – is likely to reflect a commonly observed phenomenon in other countries that social class inequalities tend to reduce more as a result of general expansion than of specifically targeted measures (Lucas, 2001; Raftery and Hout, 1993).

Higher education

It took a long time for the expansion of secondary schooling to have much of an impact on participation in higher education, and indeed there was no deliberate structural change at all between the beginning of the century and the 1960s. Scotland had four universities that had been founded in the fifteenth and sixteenth centuries, which in the 1950s were educating around 15,000 full-time undergraduate students (Paterson, 2003: 156). This was no more than about 3–4 per cent of each age cohort.

Alongside the universities were technological institutions, several of which had been founded by the SED in the late nineteenth and early twentieth centuries as an attempt to emulate German success in developing technological higher education. They had about 3500 undergraduate students, and there were also about 4500 students training to be primary school teachers (and who had not previously taken a university degree). So in the middle of the century there were about 23,000 undergraduate students in the whole of higher education. That was perhaps double the number of such students in the 1930s (Paterson, 2003: 81) and about quadruple the number at the beginning of the century: the new secondary schools were slowly having an effect in enabling school leavers to pass the Leaving Certificate that would give them entry to these higher courses.

It is not then surprising that the steady expansion of secondary schooling after the 1950s created pressures to expand higher education as well. Structural change was in two phases, the 1960s and the 1990s. The Robbins report of 1963 (http://www.educationengland.org.uk/documents/robbins/robbins1963.html) – dealing with university expansion across the UK – led to the setting up of four new universities in Scotland, but two of these – Strathclyde and Heriot-Watt – had been among the technological institutions established earlier, and the new Dundee University had been a college of St Andrews University; thus only Stirling University was wholly new. Numbers of full-time undergraduate students rapidly grew, more than tripling to 86,000 in 1990.

Thereafter, the second structural change brought together into a single system of higher education all the eight universities with the remaining technological institutions, the colleges for educating teachers and various specialist colleges of music and of art. The number of students reached around 150,000 just after the end of the century – a six-fold increase in 50 years and more than a twenty-fold increase in 100 years. There were about as many undergraduate students in higher education at the end of the century as there had been in full secondary education in the 1930s (calculating the latter as five years of about one-third of each age group of around 90,000 pupils). As a proportion of each age cohort, this was a rise from about 1.5 per cent in the early years of the century, through about 3 per cent in the 1930s, to 6 per cent in 1960, 18 per cent in 1980 and 50 per cent in 2000 (Gray et al., 1983: 204–5; Paterson, 2003: 17; Paterson et al., 2004: 108).

As with the expansion of secondary education, there was also a narrowing of inequalities in access to higher education. The gender difference reversed in the last two decades of the century: in 1980, 19 per cent of men and 16 per cent of women entered by age 21; in 2000, the proportions were 45 per cent and 56 per cent (Paterson et al., 2004: 108). Religious differences vanished (Paterson and Iannelli, 2006: 368): among people born around the Second World War, the proportions who had gained a higher education qualification by the end of the century were 22 per cent among people with no religion, 12 per cent among Protestants and 13 per cent among Catholics. Among those born in the early 1970s, the proportions were 25, 24 and 26 per cent.

Social class differences remained, but, following from the narrowing at secondary school, they too started to decline: in 1960–3, 16 per cent of middle-class school leavers entered higher education, but only 3 per cent of working-class school leavers. The ratio was still about 5:1 in the late 1970s (23 per cent and 4 per cent in 1978), but after the unification of higher education in 1992 they narrowed (51 per cent and 25 per cent in 1993) (Gray et al., 1983: 204–5; Paterson et al., 2004: 189). Although, in the first phases of the resulting expansion, inequalities widened with respect to entry to the old universities, they narrowed again by the early years of the twenty-first century (Iannelli et al., 2011).

Education and Scottish culture

The structural patterns, measured by statistical indices, tell us only in broad terms how education has had an influence on Scottish society. In order to understand that, we must also consider what students learnt. In the debate about the meaning of the curriculum, the most influential text, by far, has been George Davie's *The Democratic Intellect*, published in 1961.

It is often cited as a source for what he saw as a narrowing of access to the universities between the late nineteenth century and the 1930s, but he adduced no statistics in this connection, and the evidence – as we have seen – does not sustain any such claim. But the book is in fact much richer in connection with two further aspects, one on what happened to the old curriculum of the universities and the other on the kind of leadership class which that curriculum prepared. We come back to that second question later; in this section, we summarise the evidence relating to Davie's view that the old academic attachment to a kind of ethical intellectualism declined.

There is no doubt that the cultural role of the universities changed between the late nineteenth century and the 1920s. From being essentially the training schools of the old liberal professions – mainly ministers of religion, lawyers, doctors and to some extent school teachers – they became the main route into a much wider range of professions as the extent of professional employment grew in the twentieth century. This rise of professional society, as Perkin (1989) calls it, was a common experience in the rest of Europe and in North America.

The curriculum

In order to be able to fulfil the new role of professional education, however, the universities had to make their undergraduate courses more specialist, and it was essentially that process to which Davie was objecting. The breadth of the liberal education which used to be found in the Scottish undergraduate curriculum could no longer be fitted in around necessary advanced study. What Davie misses, however, is that the old curriculum migrated to the senior years of the secondary school, being formally enshrined in the new Leaving Certificate which became the defining feature of what Scotland would regard – from the 1920s onwards – as a proper secondary education for all (Paterson, 2004; 2011).

The secondary curriculum was not identical to the former university curriculum, notably in that – unlike in France, for example – philosophy was not included. Nevertheless, that place was taken by the study of literature, which was treated almost as a branch of moral philosophy, and which included the subject matter of what later became history and geography. It included also – through the study of contemporary literature – attention to politics and the nature of society. Every candidate for the Leaving Certificate had to study English literature, just as formerly every student who wanted to graduate from a Scottish university had to take philosophy.

From 1908 until 1950, candidates had to pass a broad range of subjects if they were to be awarded any certificate at all: passes in individual subjects did not count. Thus everyone with a Leaving Certificate had to have studied not only English but also a language (which was usually Latin or French), and a science or mathematics. And everyone who was admitted to a university or to the training courses for any of the professions had to have the Leaving Certificate. This curriculum became the distinctive feature of Scottish secondary education in the first half of the century, with a legacy long after the formal grouping requirements were removed: the combination of subjects that still commanded greatest prestige at least until the 1980s, and which provided access to university courses, was that which would have satisfied the grouping requirements.

The characteristic Scottish curriculum of the middle of the twentieth century was then still a selection of culture that mattered – still what Matthew Arnold had called the best that has been thought and said. Indeed, in adhering to these principles so thoroughly in defining the new secondary schooling, Scotland was somewhat more faithful to Arnold's ideas than was England to which, in the second half of the nineteenth century, he directed most of his proposals for reform.

This curriculum was available in the same way in the new kinds of secondary school in most respects as thoroughly as in the old. There was no sense, for example, that French was socially inferior to Latin, since French was taken as widely in the old schools as in the new. Because English was compulsory, there was no sense that it was less important than Latin. But because Latin was taken almost as widely in the new schools as in the old, there was also no sense that it belonged to a social elite. Furthermore, the curriculum of female candidates for the Leaving Certificate was much the same as that of males, with the exception that girls took natural science in lower proportions than boys. The main reason for this gap in science is that the number of girls-only schools grew in the 1920s and 1930s, and such schools were less likely to provide scientific laboratories than mixed schools.

The curriculum in Catholic schools was also very similar to that in non-denominational schools, aiding the incorporation of Catholics into a common citizenship. In particular, Latin was not more common in Catholic schools than elsewhere, which would perhaps be surprising unless we remember that almost none of the Scottish Catholic schools were in any sense preparatory for seminaries: they were just public schools serving Catholic communities. By the end of the century, this sense that Catholic schools were drawing upon the same educational culture as non-denominational schools was reinforced by there being a large minority of non-Catholic teachers in Catholic schools: in a survey of 1996 (Paterson, 1998), 28 per cent of teachers in Catholic schools were not Catholic.[3]

Throughout the century, the curriculum in the colleges which trained teachers for Catholic schools was essentially the same as in the colleges for non-denominational schools, and almost all teachers in secondary schools, of whatever denomination, had to have a specialist degree from a Scottish university or higher education college, none of which were denominational (Paterson, 2004; 2011). Little systematic evidence is available at any point in the century on the proportion of pupils in Catholic schools who were not Catholic, but a report of the Bishops' Conference of Scotland in 2006 suggested that 'while it is impossible to be precise with these figures, approximately 5 per cent of Catholic students attend non-denominational state schools and around 10 per cent of students in Catholic schools are not baptised Catholics' (Bishops' Conference of Scotland, 2006: 2).

Curricular breadth

So the new professional classes that grew to dominate Scottish society in the second half of the century continued to have an educational grounding in a modernised version of liberal education. The prestige of that programme then shaped the thinking about the curriculum in the new system of comprehensive schools after the 1970s until the 1990s.

Indeed, in the main policy development of that period – the reform in the mid-1980s of the curriculum in the middle years of secondary school – the same principles of curricular breadth were adopted as had informed the development of the Leaving Certificate a century earlier. The resulting standard grade courses then finally overcame girls' lower participation in science at that age (their participation rising from 50 per cent in 1977 to over 90 per cent in 1991) (Croxford, 1994). Social class differences in access to a broad curriculum also fell as part of this reform (Gamoran, 1995).

That was, however, the last time in the twentieth century that the old curricular philosophy was embodied in an official reform of the curriculum, since principles of choice and of direct vocational utility dominated the changes to the Highers which took place in the late 1990s. The coherence of the old liberal curriculum was set aside rather than explicitly rejected, so that breadth as such was no longer given any attention and English – far from the moral philosophical role which it had officially had in earlier schemes – became merely learning about language.

There was also in these reforms the sharp assertion of ideas from child-centred education that had come to dominate primary schooling in Scotland (as elsewhere), especially after the 1960s. No longer was a curriculum to be a selection of culture, as the Scottish curricular tradition had taken from Matthew Arnold: choice, enjoyment and usefulness were overriding criteria guiding the selection of curricular material. This same approach also pervaded the reform to the curriculum for all ages 3–18 that was put in place from 2010 onwards (under the title of 'curriculum for excellence').

A further consequence of the rise of choice and vocational purposes was that, when higher education grew rapidly from the late 1980s, there was no prospect at all that the universities might take on again the responsibility of liberally educating what was now a vastly expanded professional class. The last vestiges of the liberal requirements of the university curriculum had vanished between the 1960s and the 1980s – when philosophy was finally removed from any central place in programmes of study, and when breadth beyond a student's main programme became entirely voluntary.

The consequences of educational expansion

Thus education expanded massively in the twentieth century, first at secondary level and much later in higher education. Secondary education grew to include girls as extensively as boys, and Catholics on the same terms as Protestants or those with no attachment to institutional religion. Although social class inequalities remained wide, they did slowly narrow during the century. At the same time, until the 1980s, what was taught and learnt in the new and reformed institutions continued to adhere to modernised versions of liberal education. By the 1980s, its principles were being extended to embrace almost all pupils, and so liberal education was becoming no longer merely the preparation of the professional classes, but now the civic foundation of the whole society.

The most long-lasting influence of these principles was through the professional classes, where growing proportions had passed through the Leaving Certificate courses and the universities. Their share of the labour force grew from 1.8 per cent in 1921 to 3.2 per cent in 1971, and to 6.2 per cent in 2000 (Paterson et al., 2004: 85; Payne, 1977a: 16 and 27); in 2011, the occupations classified (since 2001) as high professionals made up 9.3 per cent of the labour force.[4] By the 1920s, because all new entrants to these careers would have passed the school Leaving Certificate with its basis in liberal education, all would have been exposed to the ethical intellectualism that these courses were intended to imbue.

The educational foundation of professionalism grew more formal in the last part of the century, as entry to professions came to be predominantly through higher educational courses: the proportion of professionals who had a higher educational qualification was 74 per cent in 1981, and was 84 per cent in the high professions in 2011. Moreover, they were recruited from a wide social range, especially through the mechanism of upward social mobility facilitated by education: at the end of the century, 62 per cent of people with a higher educational degree had been upwardly mobile to a higher social class than their parents (Paterson et al., 2004: 193). At the same time, 47 per cent of people in the professional and managerial social classes had been upwardly mobile from working-class origins (Paterson et al., 2004: 94), a percentage that was similar to that in the early 1970s (McCrone, 1992: 109). That wide recruitment could not have happened without the educational expansion and partial democratisation that we have traced here.

If upward social mobility is now becoming somewhat less common (though still far more common than downward mobility), that is not due to any change in access to education (Iannelli and Paterson, 2007a). The contraction is because of a slowing in the growth of the relative number of high-status and low-status jobs: the number of professional positions cannot expand indefinitely, and the lowest status jobs have contracted almost out of existence. The contraction of opportunity may also be because some high-status jobs that used to require merely school leaving qualifications now ask for degrees: thus, among people born around the Second World War and who left full-time education with only Highers, 36 per cent entered jobs in the top two social classes (Goldthorpe classes I and II); this had fallen to 33 per cent among people born between the mid-1960s and the mid-1970s. By contrast, the proportion entering such jobs among people who had a university degree was 80 per cent for both birth cohorts (Iannelli and Paterson, 2007a: 227).

Insofar as Scotland in the Union was led by the professional classes, here was a way in which the reformed educational system shaped the leadership class of the second half of the century. If there was an ethical ideal behind the development of the welfare state in Scotland it came not only from religion or from social democracy, important though these influences were, but also from a modernised version of what Davie called the democratic intellect. It is often forgotten that Davie's main interest in writing *The Democratic Intellect* was not in the universities as such, but in the appropriate way of preparing people for leadership in a democracy (Paterson, 2015a). Is it right, he asked when technocracy might have appeared to be a way to resolve political conflict, that political control should belong to the experts? Anticipating in 1961 the populist rebellions against professional leadership – revolts that were sometimes of the left, in the 1960s, and more powerfully of the right in the 1980s – he noted the countervailing tendency to believe that the 'consensus knowledge of the many entitles them to have full control' (page 262).

The Scottish tradition, however, was, rather, a matter of perpetual discussion, as if the seminars in which the professionals had been educated were carried over by them into a form of educative leadership, on the basis of a belief that, as Davie put it, 'the limited knowledge of the many, when it is pooled and critically restated through mutual discussion, provides a lay consensus capable of revealing certain of the limitations of interest in the experts' point of view' (1986: 262).

This understanding of professional leadership as being based on dialogue may be one consequence of a professional class that has been recruited in large measure from below through education; but that has been true in all developed countries in the same period of time, and it may be that it required the Scottish mythological belief in the necessity of a democratic professionalism to strengthen the inclination to educated dialogue in Scotland.

Something of an awareness of the always uneasy relationship between expertise and popular views lies behind Scottish views of professionalism. It is one reason why professionals were trusted to lead the political discontent with the Conservative governments of the 1980s, then to lead the Scottish Constitutional Convention of the 1990s that yielded the consensus for a Scottish parliament, and finally to take charge of the networks of consultation and consensus around the parliament (Paterson, 2009). Despite the views of radical critics of professional leadership, whether from the New Right or from the nationalist left, trusting professionals still seems to be the Scottish preference; and if that is because professionals acquired their sense of social duty from their education, the educational reforms which we have considered here could be said to have shaped the new Scotland quite profoundly.

Education and the twenty-first century

Nevertheless, education's influence was not only that, and not only through highly educated professionals. There are two further ways in which the educational expansion of the twentieth century has shaped the Scotland of the new century. One is common to many countries. An educated electorate no longer were willing to accept largesse from the state uncritically: education had led them to want choice and influence, and also to want the high standards that the burgeoning free market was offering to them as increasingly wealthy consumers.

These discontents were indeed the sources of both the left-wing and right-wing challenges to professionals that Davie wrote about, and one of the ironies of Scottish resistance to Margaret Thatcher was that this same revolution, inspired in part by education, was the basis both of her power, in England, and of the challenge to her power in Scotland. When she challenged the power of professionals in Scotland, she was taken to be anti-Scottish – a sentiment that itself indicated the intimacy of the links between professionals and democracy in Scotland – and yet at the same time the radical nationalist intellectuals of the left, such as Tom Nairn (1995) and Stephen Maxwell (2013 [1991]), were challenging these same professionals from a quite different direction. They alleged that the professions lacked imagination in response to a post-industrial age, although Maxwell was rather more optimistic than Nairn in discerning an emerging middle-class self-confidence in response to the policies of the Thatcher government.

Education and social capital

Scotland thus exemplified a link between education and civic engagement, sometimes described in the international research writing on this as the educational basis for social capital, for the norms and networks that constitute a working democracy (Paterson, 2000b). In many ways, this is best illustrated, again, by the example of professionals from far back in the century, acquiring from their education an attachment to the value and duty of social leadership.

The difference which educational expansion made was simply to extend these beliefs more widely beyond the middle class. For example, in the Scottish Social Attitudes survey of the year 2000, being civically active in various ways was more common among people with higher education attainment than among those without: 32 per cent as against 21 per cent active in a charity, 34 per cent against 17 per cent a member of a community group of some kind, 73 per cent against 54 per cent active politically (for definitions, see Paterson, 2002a: 9–15). In Scotland, as elsewhere, educated people tend to be more liberal and more respectful of diversity (Paterson, 2014).

It is education as such which seems to have these effects, not the institutional form which it takes (Paterson, 2013): people educated in comprehensive school systems are no more liberal or active than those educated in divided systems, despite some of the beliefs of the campaigners for comprehensive schools (in Scotland as strongly as anywhere: Murphy et al., 2015). Indeed, what matters more than anything is the social milieu in which a person lives. Thus people become liberal when they become middle class, regardless of whether their origins are working class or middle class (Paterson, 2008): in a mobile society, it is destination that matters, not origins. But education still matters because, to reach these destinations, people have had to pass through the kinds of educational programmes which we have discussed in this chapter.

Education and self-government

Yet the tension between experts and lay people expressed by Davie, and directed in Scotland at the unionist elites by radical critics, has not been resolved, and is still politically potent. The second way in which educational expansion is still shaping Scotland is through the emergence of a left-wing and nationalist segment of people who have a higher educational qualification that is without precedent in Scotland and which led the campaign for independence in the referendum of 2014. This is seen in evidence from the Scottish Social Attitudes surveys of 2013 and 2014. Ideological position can be defined according to an index of views in reply to survey questions about inequality, the role of free enterprise and the role of the state.[5] Over the whole population, in 2014, 40 per cent were on the left, 21 per cent on the centre–left, 24 per cent on the centre–right and 15 per cent on the right, but a similar distribution was found among people with a higher educational qualification: 34, 20, 26 and 20 per cent. Of all eight groups defined by ideological position and by whether or not the respondent had a higher educational qualification, the highest proportion intending to vote 'Yes' to independence in the referendum (among those who had made up their minds in July 2014) was 54 per cent among people who had a higher educational qualification and who were on the left. The 'Yes' proportion was almost the same (52 per cent) among those on the left without a higher educational qualification, but there was a larger gap associated with education for those on the centre–left: 40 per cent 'Yes' among those with a higher educational qualification and 30 per cent among those without.

Another way of putting this is that 28 per cent of all people intending to vote 'Yes' were people on the left or centre–left who had a higher educational qualification. This segment of educated opinion was a source of intellectual leadership for the 'Yes' campaign that was as important as the more general leadership of Scottish society in the middle of the twentieth century by highly educated professionals. It is a new way in which the educational revolution is having an impact on the country's development.

Conclusion

Education in Scotland has expanded massively and is now the dominant organised experience of a majority of people until their early twenties. It has become the route by which people have gained good jobs, in particular have been upwardly mobile socially, and it has also been the way in which access to social power has been diffused. Large minorities of social groups which have high status and strong influence have reached these positions through upward mobility, and that has been feasible because of expanded opportunities in education.

All of this has been achieved as a result of deliberate policy, under political regimes of all kinds. The expansion in secondary education early in the century was led by conservative officials and guided by liberal politicians. The expansion of the middle of the century may have been legitimated by the post-1945 Labour government, but the basis for it, too, was laid down by officials in the SED in the 1930s. Comprehensive education was inaugurated by a Labour government in 1965, but provoked much less political controversy than in England, and the consequent democratising reforms to the curriculum and assessment in the middle years of secondary school were put in place by the government of Margaret Thatcher. It was then John Major, another Tory much reviled in Scottish debate, who presided over the massive expansion of higher education in the 1990s, though he, too, was building on the earlier expansion that had been pushed forward under Labour in the 1960s.

All these policy changes show, moreover, that the Union could be more creative in policy than is often alleged, and could build upon Scottish practices that could be presented as distinctive traditions. The main policy change in school education which the Scottish parliament has brought about is a fundamental challenge to these traditions, moving away from the particular version of liberal education that had been at the core of Scottish school education throughout the twentieth century.

It is too soon to assess the likely long-term effects of these changes, or even whether they will persist against the continuing potency of the original traditions. But what we can say, looking back, is that the content of education in Scotland throughout most of the century is best interpreted as a recurrent attempt to make liberal education of a quite traditional kind available widely, democratising access to the sort of intellectualism that used to be offered only to undergraduate students in the universities.

Whatever may have been lost at university level from the late nineteenth century onwards, the shifting to the new secondary schools of the core principles of the democratic intellect – the breadth, the attention to ethical matters, the sharing of a common framework of learning – laid the basis for a much more radical influence than had ever previously been possible. An entire leadership class in the middle of the twentieth century had been educated in these ways, and so education can make a reasonable claim to have shaped Scotland's modern character within the Union.

That professional leadership also educated, in turn, those who challenged the Union more insistently towards the century's end. People who entered school teaching between the 1920s and the 1980s would have followed a secondary school curriculum that had the liberal education characteristics that we have discussed. Allowing for forty-year careers, these people would have become a majority of teachers by about the 1940s, and would still have constituted a majority in the 1990s; the youngest of them will not retire until the late 2020s. So almost every campaigner for a Scottish parliament who was educated in Scotland, and almost every member of the parliament (a large majority of whom were educated in Scotland),[6] will have been taught by school teachers who were themselves shaped by the democratised version of liberal education that grew to dominate Scottish school education in the twentieth century.

Liberal education, as interpreted in Scotland, may have been conservative and only slow to admit more than quite small social groups to its benefits. But that caution may be why it survived through the very great changes of economy, society and politics that the twentieth century brought, and why its solid intellectual basis could equip successive generations to dissent. It is perhaps always one of the ironies of education's place in the process of social change that today's reformers have been taught in some of the very institutions against which they rebel.

Chapter summary

So what have we learned in this chapter?

- That education has expanded massively over the past century.
- That it has become an important means by which people have been socially mobile.
- That it has shaped Scottish society as well as been shaped by public policy.

264 PEOPLE AND POWER

Questions for discussion

1. What does the Scottish case tell us about the question of whether social equality can be achieved through education?

2. To what extent does concentrating on education as a route to social mobility or economic success help a society to achieve its social goals, or does it detract from the true purposes of education?

3. Is higher education any longer a means of 'getting on' in society?

4. Do most students today find liberal education of the traditional Scottish kind intrinsically alienating, or view it as a means of emancipation for everyone?

Annotated reading

(a) Anderson, R.D., M. Freeman and L. Paterson (eds) (2015) *The Edinburgh History of Education in Scotland*, Edinburgh: Edinburgh University Press. A collection of essays by leading historians of Scottish education, telling the history of Scottish education since the Middle Ages.

(b) Paterson, L. (2003) *Scottish Education in the Twentieth Century*, Edinburgh: Edinburgh University Press. An account which goes into much greater detail than in this present chapter, paying particular attention to the structure of provision – the first aim of this chapter.

(c) Paterson, L., F. Bechhofer and D. McCrone (2004) *Living in Scotland: Social and economic change since 1980*, Edinburgh: Edinburgh University Press. Chapters 6 and 7 deal in detail with the second aim of the chapter: what opportunities has educational expansion offered?

(d) Paterson, L. (2015d) *Social Radicalism and Liberal Education*, Exeter: Imprint Academic. A development of the third aim of the chapter, discussing liberal ideas on culture and the curriculum, and thus setting the Scottish approach to these matters in context.

Notes

1 The National Galleries of Scotland who hold this photograph describe it thus: 'The "Castlemilk Lads" is one of Marzaroli's best known photographs. Shot on one of the growing housing estates on the outskirts of Glasgow during the 1950s, it speaks of a city altered by town planners beyond all recognition. The provocative stare of three of the boys and the angst of the one looking away, give us a clear idea about the unfriendly environment which they inhabit.'

2 'Middle class' is defined here to be class I, II and III non-manual of the Registrar-General's classification scheme. 'Working class' is defined to be classes III manual, IV and V.

3   In a sample of 74 teachers from Catholic schools.

4   Calculated from economically active respondents age over 16, resident in Scotland, in the Labour Force Survey of January–March 2011. See also Paterson et al. (2004: 209–10).

5   The questions asked whether people believe that 'big business benefits owners at the expense of workers', 'management will always get the better of employees if it gets the chance', 'there is one law for the rich and one for the poor', 'ordinary working people do not get their fair share of the nation's wealth' and 'the government should redistribute income from the better off to those who are less well off'. Responses to each item were on a five-point scale from 'strongly agree' to 'strongly disagree'. The average of each respondent's replies then gave an index of their position on this left–right scale, which runs from 1 to 5, and the whole population was divided into four segments: left (values 1 to 2, corresponding to agreement with left-wing positions), right (values 4 to 5), centre–left (values above 2 and not above 2.5) and centre–right (values above 2.5 and not above 4).

6   In 2015, of the 104 (out of 128) sitting MSPs who declared their education, 75 had been educated in a Scottish university and 16 in another Scottish higher education institution; a further 9 listed their education as finishing in a Scottish secondary school (compiled from the Scottish parliament website, 14 July 2015). Similarly high levels of Scottish education were found for sitting MSPs in 2005 (Paterson and Bond, 2005: 29).

11

GENDERING SCOTLAND

I n this chapter, we will focus on gender in Scotland. This is not simply a chapter 'about' women in Scotland rather than men. That may seem an obvious point, but 'gender' is frequently used as a code for 'women', because women are on the receiving end of inequality rather than men, and partly as a consequence women are the focus of gender issues.

Chapter aims

- To provide a sociological understanding of gender relations and gender inequalities in Scotland.

- To examine whether there is a specific Scottish focus on gender, particularly in terms of cultural assumptions and reflected in public images.

- To analyse how women and men construe their social identities, and in particular focus on how they relate national and gender identities.

- To provide a 'gender audit' in terms of inequalities between men and women, and explore how these may have altered over time.

- To ask whether the key to gender inequalities lies in the domestic division of labour, in the intimacies of family life.

- To focus on gender in politics in Scotland, in the context of the Scottish parliament and constitutional change.

How are we to understand gender relations and in particular gender inequalities in contemporary Scotland? At the time of the Scottish Independence Referendum campaign in 2014, the campaigning group Engender issued a report called 'Gender Inequality and Scotland's Constitutional Futures' (www.engender.org.uk/content/publications/Gender-equality-and--Scotlands-constitutional-futures.pdf). The report was hard-hitting. Its authors commented:

> Gender inequality is caused, perpetuated and masked by cultural norms. Gender stereotyping and segregation shape girls' and women's lives from early years and are key factors in determining life chances. Scotland's culture tolerates the

widespread abuse of women and the normalised objectification of women in the media and popular culture. Women's economic inequality is both stigmatised and socially accepted as a fact of life. (2014: 33)

The point of that comment was to argue that gender inequalities are not easily addressed simply by public policies, by passing legislation or enforcing equal pay, important though these are. It is what lies behind those material inequalities, how they are sustained and practised in what we might call the materiality of social relations.

The sociology of gender relations

Let us look at what sociologists call the interactive effects of gender inequality. To take an example, because far more women than men work part-time and do different kinds of jobs (what is called occupational and industrial segregation), there are abiding pay differentials between men and women. 'Women's work', therefore, is often more poorly paid than men's.

Or again, because women have children, and their employment patterns are different and fragmented, they are less likely to get promoted and have poorer access to occupational pension schemes. Similarly, women are expected to be the prime carers for children and sick or aged relatives; their duties of caring are different, and their capacity to earn over their lifetimes is reduced.

This does not rule out the possibility that there are not systematic and deliberate attempts to discriminate against women in a straightforward way. By and large, it is more complicated than that, otherwise simply banning discrimination would have had an effect. Because of the complexity of inequalities which attach to gender, women may well suffer not 'because' they are women, but because they perform certain roles in society in a way which is different to those of men.

This is 'institutional sexism', which has its parallel in institutional racism, which we will explore later in Chapter 13. The point about these being 'institutional' is that, built into how the economy, the family, education, health systems, and so on operate, women are on the receiving end of inequalities. In other words, this is not because there is necessarily deliberate sexism by intent, but because the way institutions operate puts women in disadvantaged positions.

Furthermore, the impact of separate institutions on women's lives – as well as men's – is interactive, and as a result there are liable to be unintended consequences which compound inequalities. Nor does this imply that women are on the 'receiving end' every time: they are not systematically at the bottom of the heap. To take an example, in recent years, females are attaining much higher examination grades at school than males. Why? We cannot be sure. And, we might wonder, with what impact? Does that put them in much better positions to get better jobs in the future, and, if so, why is it that pay differentials between men and women remain stubbornly unequal?

We might even take the sanguine view that women's superior exam performances will eventually feed through into better paid jobs and positions of power; we cannot count on that, because gender inequalities (like other social inequalities) are much more insidious and basic. Such is the complexity of modern life that changes in one institutional sphere will have an impact on another, often in unexpected ways.

There is a related point. We live in times where social structural explanations are dis-favoured. If something happens, it must be *someone's* fault. We seek out the culprit. Or we decide that the victim is to blame, for not working hard enough, having the wrong qualifications or even the wrong set of attitudes. We have been duped into explanations for failings where the onus falls on the individual. If only, it is claimed, people had the proper mentality, the right set of attitudes, they would achieve greater things: the will to win is all.

Here is cultural hegemony in operation: we live in individualistic times in a manner in which our parents and grandparents would find bewildering. High unemployment, or sim-ply a lack of jobs in an area, is plainly not the fault of 'the individual': it is structural – the demise of certain industries, international cost-cutting by global capital, cheaper imports from China, or whatever.

What does this have to do with gender? Quite a lot, as it happens. Simply telling women that they are as good as men, if not better, cannot be enough. Feeling good about yourself runs up against the lack of opportunities, and if your gender, race, social class, age or what-ever is against you, life is that much harder. There is an important gender aspect to this. If we define the problem as changing attitudes rather than structures, we will fail. That is not to say that structures themselves will do the trick. People will not act like puppets on a string, simply carrying out the social roles allotted them. Life is far more complicated.

It follows, then, that focusing unduly on changing attitudes, whether of men or of women, will not rid us of sexism and gender inequalities. Urging men to be fair to women is not enough: there has to be a level playing field. Typifying men or women as being distinct kinds of people, with different interests, proclivities, even different brains, somehow all deriving from their biologies, will not get us very far either. The 'fact' that pink is for girls and blue is for boys, or claiming that men come from Mars and women from Venus, may help sell books, but it does not amount to proper social science even of the most elementary kind. We might, of course, ask why these typifications exist, where they come from, and in whose interests they operate, and that is sociologically much more interesting.

Given the complexities, and the intransigencies, of social relations one can under-stand why people might reach for simplistic nostrums about the 'inherent' differences of the sexes, but they are sociologically misinformed. In this chapter, we will talk about 'sex' and 'gender' without being too precious about the distinction. While 'sex' in essence refers to biology, and 'gender' is a social/cultural phenomenon, it is easy to get bogged down in terminological distinctions when in the 'real world' people tend to use them interchangeably.

It is true that 'gender' can attach to the 'wrong' sex, that men can act in a 'feminine' way, and so on, but in this chapter we will confine ourselves to relations, and differences, between men and women, which, in any case, are terms which fudge the sex/gender distinction. Social life is complicated, but that is no excuse for not trying to change social institutions and relations between people. In any case, if we start out with simplistic notions, we are bound to become disillusioned quite quickly. If we appreciate what we are up against, we will know that we have several mountains to climb, and that meaningful social change is hard to achieve.

Scotland and gender

What, you might ask, is the Scottish take on all this? Is there much which is specific to Scotland, and are Scots any better or worse at gender relations than anyone else? There is not some international league table in which to place Scotland; rather, we will address the issues as we find them, as they are described and explained by writers on Scotland.

There is a view that Scotland is inherently a male chauvinist country – Mac-His-Mo, we might say – fairly unreconstructed with regard to relations between men and women, but like many typifications it is hard to quantify, especially as most of these belong to the 'everyone knows' category of social thought. Readers of this book, the author hopes, will by now have become sceptical of the taken for granted.

Scotland and misogyny

Writing in *Feminist Review* (1998), Esther Breitenbach and her colleagues observed that: 'Women's role in Scottish society was paid scant attention in the past, as exemplified by Hugh MacDiarmid's notorious line: "Scottish women of any historical interest are curiously rare"' (1998: 44). The authors comment: 'Scotland has few female icons (leaving aside the question of whether it is desirable to have icons), and those that she has, such as Mary Stuart and Flora Macdonald, appear romantic and doomed as participant's lost causes' (1998: 45).

Some trace the lack of female icons far back in history. Armel Dubois-Nayt (2015) argued that the medieval poet and reformer George Buchanan set out not simply to criticise Mary Queen of Scots (Mary Stuart), but to argue that all women were not fit to be monarchs. Dubois-Nayt argues that Buchanan's *History of Scotland* 'is a framed narrative on the harmfulness and "unScottishness" of female rule' (2015: 20). Leslie Hills, writing in the Scottish literary journal *Chapman* (1994), claimed that: 'Attempts to celebrate identity in Scotland fall foul of a deeply misogynist society – a society demonstrating its misogyny in its press, its public life, its politics and the daily lives of women' (1994: 47).

Finally, this extended quotation from Barbara Littlewood locates this misogyny deep in Scotland's history and culture:

In the popular imagination, Scotland is often conceived of as a sexually repressed and repressive culture, with much of the blame put on the special tradition of Protestantism which took root here. Closely linked with this is a misogyny manifest in both violent and non-violent ways, in the burning of witches and the writing out of women from Scottish history. The heroes and villains of our popular histories, with the exception of Mary, are invariably male, and alternatives only replace kings, lairds and politicians with the equally male dominated roster of the Red Clyde heroes. Scottish socialism offered no relief from the puritanical ethos of Calvinism; a good socialist could be just as much a patriarch in his private life as any Kirk elder, with no sense of contradiction with his principles. Currently, ... popular representations of Scottish men continue to celebrate the inarticulate (except, if drunk, or discussing football), physically competent (except if drunk, or dealing with the weans), man's man. This representation, like that of his female companion, is also as yet invariably white. (Quoted in Breitenbach et al., 1998: 45–6)

The task of this chapter is not to accept these accounts as given, nor to treat them as fixed products of history, hard-wired into our culture and consciousness, but to ask sociological questions about gender inequalities and gender relations in contemporary Scotland. It is, however, worth noting that much of this writing took place in the 1980s and 1990s, and that much of its critical energy was funnelled into the campaign for a Scottish parliament and the proper representation of women therein, as well as making the new institution women- and family-friendly.

Who do people think they are?

We might read into such representations of women in Scotland that they do not think of themselves as 'Scottish' at all, given the dominant maleness which is implied. We might say that if there is *Mac-His-Mo*, there is unlikely to be *Mac-Hers-Mo*.

So who do women (and men) in Scotland think they are? Using Scottish Social Attitudes surveys, in 2003, and again in 2006 and 2009, we included questions on social identity as follows:

People differ in how they think of or describe themselves. If you had to pick just one thing from [this] list to describe yourself, something that is important to you when you think of yourself, what would it be?'

We gave people a list of over twenty social identities including being: a man/woman; wife/husband/partner; a mother/father; working class/middle class; a working person; and descriptors on religion, age, ethnicity, employment status, and allowing for none. We gave respondents the chance to select multiple identities by asking them to choose their first, second and third choices from the list.

The point of the exercise was to see how, if at all, 'national identity' – whether being Scottish, British, English, and so on – fitted into people's sense of their *own* social identity.

TABLE 11.1 Most important social identities by gender (2003 survey)

1st, 2nd and 3rd choices (1st choices in brackets)	Men	Women	Difference between men and women
Parent	33% (13%)	62% (34%)	−29
Husband/wife/partner	30% (8%)	29% (5%)	+1
Man/woman	18% (5%)	34% (14%)	−16
Working person	32% (12%)	28% (5%)	+4
Working class	26% (14%)	16% (5%)	+10
Scottish	53% (19%)	47% (15%)	+6

Source: Scottish Social Attitudes Survey, 2003

Surely if being Scottish was, in essence, a *masculine* identity, we would not expect women to buy into it? When we asked the question in 2003, the identities given in Table 11.1 were the most frequently mentioned ones (first, second or third).

The most obvious point to make is that men and women construe their social identities differently. Thus, women place much greater emphasis on being a parent and on their gender than men do. What is also striking is that both genders think it is important to be Scottish, and while men are more likely to do so, almost half of women do the same. Table 11.2 shows them in rank order for each gender.

TABLE 11.2 Rank order of social identities by gender

Men	Rank order	Women
Scottish	1st	Mother
Father	2nd	Scottish
Working person	3rd	Woman
Husband/partner	4th	Wife/partner
Working class	5th	Working person
Man	6th	Working class

Source: Scottish Social Attitudes Survey, 2003

We can sum up these identity choices as follows:

- Being Scottish is very important for men (first in the list) but it is *also* important for women (second in their list).

- Being a parent is significantly more important for women than for men, along with gender identity.

- Nevertheless, being Scottish is mentioned more frequently by women than gender.

- Working-class identity, and employment status ('being a working person'), are more important for men than for women.

We repeated the exercise in 2006 and 2009, setting a much tougher test for territorial identities. In these surveys we did not include 'Scottish' (or 'British')[1] in the long list of social identities, and subsequently asked respondents whether if being Scottish (or British) *had* been included, they would have chosen them as one of their three identities.

We *still* found that 'being Scottish' figured prominently in the identity rankings for both men (43 per cent) and for women (42 per cent).[2] Once more, we found that women ranked 'being a parent' much more highly than men (65 per cent to 44 per cent), just as they ranked their *gender* more highly than men did (37 per cent to 19 per cent).

We can be confident, then, that both men and women identify strongly with 'being Scottish': for men, it is on a par with being a parent and a partner; and, for women, it is ranked second to being a parent, and, as in the 2003 survey, *above* gender. Over the three survey points, 2003, 2006 and 2009, women were roughly twice as likely as men to choose their gender identity, but only marginally less likely to say they are Scottish. We will return to 'national identity' in greater detail in Chapter 18, but it is useful at this stage to know how being Scottish relates to other identities, and for women and men.

Here we have a good example of using survey findings to check up on the assertion that 'women don't feel Scottish', but one which turns out not to have much evidence to back it up. Furthermore, by repeating the question, and tightening up the format to make it harder for respondents to choose national identity, we can now be quite certain that people in Scotland rank it highly, without forcing them to choose one identity over another. Being Scottish matters, to women and to men, and certainly not at the expense of other social identities. Representing your country is not something only men can do.

Auditing gender

So let us begin with some statistical data on relations between men and women – a gender audit on modern Scotland.

2007

Esther Breitenbach and Fran Wasoff carried out the most comprehensive 'audit' to date in 2007. The stimulus for this research was the introduction of the Gender Equality Duty which was enacted in the UK Equality Act 2006, and which applied to a range of public bodies including the Scottish government (then called the 'executive'). Such bodies were required to comply with the Equal Pay and Sex Discrimination Acts.

Here are their key findings:

- There is a gender pay gap of 15 per cent, based on average hourly earnings for full-time staff. The gap in weekly earnings of full-time workers has diminished over time. In 1970, women earned only 54 per cent of male full-time workers' average earnings. By 2003, it stood at 77 per cent of men's, and between 1998 and 2005, women's weekly earnings as a proportion of men's increased from 72 per cent to 81 per cent.

- Women's earnings are significantly affected by the fact that most women were in part-time jobs, which we explored in Chapter 8. While women's hourly rates of pay compared reasonably well with similar males in part-time work, the disparity in hourly pay rates between men and women was of the order of 63 per cent in 2005.

- Working in the public rather than the private sector makes a difference: men and women were far more likely to get equal pay in the former (97 per cent) than the latter (80 per cent).

- Even comparing like with the like, gender matters. For example, male high-income earners have significantly higher incomes than similarly placed females.

- Women are far more likely to be benefits claimants than men, notably dependent on state pensions and pension credits.

- The most obvious difference in terms of employment is that far more women work part-time. As we saw in Chapter 8, women and men work at different things in different industries, with far more women than men in public administration, distribution and catering, and in banking and finance. Women are more likely to work in personal services, administrative and secretarial occupations, and in sales and customer services. Because of these structural differences, settling equal pay for equal work is much harder to achieve. Far more women than men lack pension provisions: for example, in 2004–5, 60 per cent of women part-time workers had no pension provision whatsoever.

- In terms of care provision, women are more likely not only to provide care, but to receive it. Thus, 64 per cent of those providing care outwith the home were women, and women were 62 per cent of those receiving regular help and care. About three-quarters of long-stay residents in care homes are women, in part reflecting their greater longevity than men.

- While at school, girls have overtaken boys as regards educational performance and qualifications; this has not (yet) worked its way through into the labour market, if it ever will.

- Those who leave school with few or no qualifications also take different gender paths: girls are more likely to find their way into low-skilled and low-paid jobs with little prospect of training or advancement, while boys are more likely to end up unemployed. Breitenbach and Wasoff commented: 'poor levels of educational attainment is one factor often associated with offending behaviour, as are health problems such as drug and alcohol abuse, and this is the case for both sexes, though rates of offending are much higher for males' (2007: ix).

The point about this gender audit is not simply listing the inequalities between men and women, but observing the complex interactions between different kinds of inequality. Thus,

> patterns of family change both affect and are affected by employment patterns and levels of income. These influence both decisions about childbearing and about childrearing, and they also influence the capacity of individuals to care for others at different stages in their life-course and to ensure that they themselves will be adequately cared for in old age. (Breitenbach and Wasoff, 2007: 308)

And they conclude:

> In indicating ways in which aspects of gendered experience are inter-related, it becomes clear that many factors interact to reinforce patterns of gender inequality. There is not one simple cause of gender inequality, but rather disadvantage in one area often contributes to disadvantage in another area. (2007: 310)

2014

But surely, we might assume, things have improved since the establishment of the Scottish parliament? In considering the relationship between gender equality and constitutional futures, Engender, the gender equality organisation in Scotland, noted in 2014 the continuation of women's inequality:

- *Care gap*: 62 per cent of unpaid carers are women. Twice as many female carers as their male counterparts receive benefits at a rate of £1.70 per hour.

- *Freedom gap*: every 13 minutes a woman in Scotland experiences violence.

- *Income gap*: twice as many women as men rely on benefits and tax credits. Women are 95 per cent of lone parents who receive income support.

- *Pay gap*: women earn 13 per cent less than men as full-time workers and 34 per cent less than men part-time. Female-dominated occupational and industrial sectors are low paid and undervalued.

- *Power gap*: only 15 per cent of senior police and 25 per cent of Senators of the College of Justice in Scotland (senior judges), 10 per cent of UK national newspaper editors and 8 per cent of directors of top companies (FTSE 250) are women.

- *Representation gap*: only 36 per cent of MSPs, 17 per cent of MEPs, 24 per cent of councillors, 3 per cent of council leaders and 26 per cent of trade union leaders are women. (Engender, 2014: 4)

This report was written in the run-up to the 2014 Scottish Independence Referendum, a period of heightened politics in Scotland. Engender were endeavouring to raise the profile of gender issues in that context. Taking the 2007 and 2014 'gender audits' together, we can conclude that not a significant amount has changed in this heightened context of Scottish political change. So why are gender inequalities so abiding?

Power relations

The 'distributional' aspects of gender inequalities in Scotland are well documented. Not only do women have lower incomes, and less secure ones, than men, but also their relationship to positions of power is different. This does not imply that nothing can be done about that; rather, the complex nexus of economic, political and cultural power which embeds women in subordinate positions is difficult to resolve.

Violence against women

That figure in the Engender report, that every thirteen minutes a woman in Scotland experiences violence, deserves highlighting, for it would be easy to overlook it in the context of the other 'gaps' which the researchers point to. Research for Scottish Government (2005: www.gov.scot/Topics/People/Equality/violence-women/Key-Facts) highlights the following:

- Violence against women is widespread, affecting women of any age, class, race, religion, sexuality or ability.

- Women are most at risk from men they know.

- Factors like age, disability and poverty increase women's vulnerability to some types of violence.

- Violence involves patterns of abusive behaviour and repeat victimisation, rather than discrete assaults.

- Women experience violence at different points in their lives, and significant numbers of women experience more than one type of violence.

This is, in the main, the territory of 'domestic abuse', defined by the Scottish government as follows:

> gendered based violence … perpetrated by partners or ex partners and can include physical abuse (assault and physical attack involving a range of behaviour), sexual abuse (acts which degrade and humiliate women and are perpetrated against their will, including rape) and mental and emotional abuse (such as threats, verbal abuse, racial abuse, withholding money and other types of controlling behaviour such as isolation from family and friends). (National Strategy to Address Domestic Abuse in Scotland, Scottish Partnership on Domestic Abuse, Edinburgh, November 2000: http://www.gov.scot/Topics/People/Equality/violence-women/Key-Facts)

In 2009–10, over 50,000 incidents of domestic abuse were recorded by the police in Scotland, with over 80 per cent of cases involving a female victim and a male perpetrator. Undoubtedly, these figures underestimate the degree of violence, because many women do not report abuse to the police, which, in any case, may not be 'physical' as such, and hence does not constitute a 'crime'. Furthermore, a study of almost 1400 young people aged 14 to 18 found that a third of young men, and a sixth of young women, thought that using violence in an intimate relationship was acceptable under certain circumstances (Burman and Cartmel, 2005).

What this points to is the routinisation and 'normalisation' of violence against women. Arguably, there are contexts in which such violent behaviour is the by-product of other aspects of life. One such is football, and in particular the fallout of 'Old Firm' matches between Rangers and Celtic. It would be easy to surmise that domestic abuse is simply associated with sport and football generally, but in a remarkable piece of research, Damien Williams and colleagues have shown that it is specifically Old Firm matches which are associated with such violence. Looking at reported domestic incidents for the twenty-four-hour period following all twenty-one Old Firm matches between 2008 and 2011, they found that:

- the number of reported incidents associated with Old Firm matches was significantly greater than the number of incidents recorded seven days later (non-Old-Firm days);

- there was no difference in the number of reported incidents associated with Scotland international matches hosted in Glasgow and the number of incidents reported seven days later;

- there were significantly more reported incidents associated with Old Firm matches than Scotland international matches.

The authors concluded:

> the Old Firm effect is not merely due to the presence of a high-profile football match in the city (and potentially the excessive alcohol consumption and expression of hegemonic masculinity that is often associated with such events), or seasonality, or weekday effects. (Williams et al., 2013: http://sgo.sagepub.com/content/ 3/3/2158244013504207.full)

The authors are careful not to speculate as to what the precise mechanisms might be which associate domestic violence specifically with Old Firm matches, but undoubtedly the relationship is a significant one. The fact that Rangers were relegated in season 2012–13 meant that Old Firm fixtures became rare, and presumably associated domestic abuse declined. The club's promotion to the Premier League for season 2016–17 does not bode well for violence against women,[3] especially as there was a year-on-year increase of 67 per cent between 2002 and 2012 of incidents of domestic abuse reported to the police (mainly Strathclyde). And as if on cue, Police Scotland confirmed that more than 200 incidents of domestic abuse occurred on 17 April 2016 when Celtic and Rangers played each other in the Scottish Cup, an increase on 'normal' reporting of 43 per cent.[4] Here are 'power relations' in operation in their most brutal form, and it is to relations within the household to which we now turn.

The late Ailsa McKay (2013), a leading feminist economist, wrote:

> Although much progress has been made in recent decades in promoting greater gender equality, at least with respect to 'equality of opportunity' within the labour market, the same cannot be said of change in the domestic economy. This asymmetric nature of change has resulted in significant gains for women in the world of work – equal pay legislation, improved maternity provision and flexible working practices, greater career opportunities – but progress towards actual gender equality has been hampered by a lack of commensurate change in the household. Persistent patterns of gender-based divisions of labour within the household mean women continue to perform the majority of household determined duties and tasks, including – most significantly – childcare. Thus, it is precisely because women do care that they have less time and resources to commit to other activities. (https://www.opendemocracy.net/ourkingdom/ ailsa-mckay/debate-over-scotland's-future-do-women-care)

McKay's point is a good one in sociological terms, and moves the focus away from the narrowly 'economic' and, indeed, the formally 'political' and on to the personal and the cultural, the implication being that inequality, like charity, begins at home. So that seems a good point to focus on at this stage in our argument. What do we know of gendering within households? To what extent are the 'intimate relations' of gender determining the broader macro-economic and political pictures?

The domestic division of labour

Let us look, then, at how people do domestic labour in Scotland, or, rather, at their accounts of how they do it.[5] We have good data from the 2005 Scottish Social Attitudes Survey which asked people about family life. For later data, we will look at British Social Attitudes survey trends over time, and extrapolate these to Scotland on the grounds that these surveys provide the best approximate data we have.

The Scottish evidence

The most striking finding from the Scottish survey data is how strong the 'sharing' ideology is. When asked 'Who should be mainly responsible for ensuring that the housework is done in a family, the man, the woman or both equally?', eight out of ten people say 'both equally', with no difference between men and women. Among people aged 18–49 (for men) and 18–45 (for women) the sharing ideology is even stronger.

However, and as we might expect, women are in practice far more likely to *do* the housework than men. Thus, over half of men[6] (54 per cent) admit that their partners do all or most of the housework, and two-thirds of women (68 per cent) say that *they* do it all or most of the time. Furthermore, significantly more men (34 per cent) than women (22 per cent) claim that they actually share the housework equally.

While we might expect differences by age, social class and educational levels of respondents such that young people, the middle class and the more highly educated would be more likely to have 'sharing' arrangements, this turns out not to be so. Broadly speaking, twice as many men as women believe that they share the housework, and yet in every case a majority of women, regardless of age, class and education, believe that they do most of it.

What *is* consistent is the belief among men that they have 'sharing' arrangements, a belief which women do not verify. Once more, the ideology of sharing housework is consistent, regardless of age, class or education, and yet these beliefs do not accord with reported practice, even though men like to think that they do far more than their partners say they do.

We can be fairly certain, then, that these beliefs and practices derive from relations of gender, rather than from age, class or educational characteristics. In other words, being male or female is a far more significant factor than any of these, and young, middle-class and highly educated people are very little different than anyone else when it comes to sharing domestic chores.

We can sum this up as in Table 11.3.

Family life

Even if women work, do people think that men should still be the main income earner in the family? The notion of the male 'breadwinner' is no longer the dominant view, either among men or among women. Equal proportions of both men and women (respectively, 44 and 45 per cent) dissent from the traditional notion, with only half of those proportions (22 and 23 per cent) supporting it.

TABLE 11.3 Responsibility for housework, by gender

	Men 18–49 living with partner	Women 18–45 living with partner
Who *should* have responsibility for housework?	86% say both should be equally responsible	86% say both should be equally responsible
Who *does* the housework?	65% say their partner does all or most housework	70% say I do all or most of the housework

Source: Scottish Social Attitudes Survey, 2005

Nor is there support for the view that most women need children to feel fulfilled: 40 per cent of women disagree, and only 20 per cent agree with that proposition. Men split 28 per cent and 26 per cent, respectively, that women need children. On the proposition that men need children to be 'fulfilled': 30 per cent of men think they do, broadly balanced against 27 per cent who do not. Women, on the other hand, split 42 per cent who agree that men need children, compared with 15 per cent who disagree. Having and rearing children is still seen as 'women's work'.

'Working mothers'

There is virtually no difference between men and women in terms of attitudes. Asked if mothers of pre-school children should work, and if so how much, men and women are in agreement. Only 17 per cent think they should not, and similar proportions of men and women think they should work if they want to – part-time (35 per cent of women and 32 per cent of men) and a larger proportion full-time: respectively, 41 per cent and 39 per cent. All in all, the traditional notions of male and female family roles in relationship to work and childcare no longer seem to apply.

British evidence

How does Scotland compare with the rest of the UK? The British Social Attitudes surveys have the merit of asking questions about family roles more frequently so we can see change (or lack of it) over time. They too show that support for a traditional division of gender roles has declined over time (Scott and Clery, 2013). Whereas in the mid-1980s almost half of respondents agreed that 'a man's job is to earn money; a women's job is to look after the home and family', twenty years later, only 13 per cent took this view. Compared with 1989 when almost two-thirds of people thought a mother should stay at home with children under school age, by 2012 this had fallen to one-third, and working part-time was the most acceptable option.

This change in attitudes is largely because of 'generational replacement': that is, those who did subscribe to it have been replaced by subsequent generations who take a more 'equal' view of gender relations. In other words, each successive generation or cohort is being replaced by one which is less likely to support a traditional division of gender roles compared with the previous one. Furthermore, there is very little difference between men and women in terms of such attitudes.

As regards household behaviour, however, there *are* major gender differences, and along the lines suggested by the Scottish data. British Social Attitudes surveys reported that, in 2012, men spent an average of eight hours a week on housework, whereas women spent thirteen hours. In terms of caring for family members, women spent twenty-three hours per week and men only ten (Scott and Clery, 2013).

Over the past two decades, there has been very little change as to how couple-households divide household tasks. Women still claim they do the laundry (70 per cent) and men that they do 'small repairs' around the house (75 per cent), two areas of 'traditional' gendered activity. So not that much has changed in almost twenty years (between 1994 and 2012): 'women are much more likely than men to always or usually care for sick family members, shop for groceries, do the household cleaning and prepare the meals' (Scott and Clery, 2013: 127).

Furthermore, there is little sign of a revolution in gender roles in terms of who does what around the house. The proportion of women reporting that they did more than their fair share changed very little in the decade between 2002 and 2012 (at around 60 per cent). Men are unlikely to say that they do more than their fair share (10 per cent in 2002 and 15 per cent in 2012), as are women to say they do *less* than their fair share (respectively, 4 per cent and 6 per cent). Around half of men and a third of women think that they do roughly their fair share of housework.

Even where women and men are doing comparable amounts of paid work (whether full-time or part-time), the inequities in household work are the same. Scott and Clery concluded:

> Gender equality in terms of who does the bulk of the chores and who is primarily responsible for looking after the children has made very little progress in terms of what happens in people's homes. Men's uptake of unpaid domestic work is slow, and women continue to feel that they are doing more than their fair share. Whether women's 'double shift' – both doing a paid job and the bulk of family care and housework chores – is sustainable is an important question for the future. (2013: 134)

Comparative trends

A further piece of comparative research on the domestic division of labour in relation to women's employment reinforces the point that what people do at home is not (simply) a matter of having the 'correct' attitudes. Rosemary Crompton and her colleagues did cross-national analysis – in the UK, Norway and the Czech Republic – in 1994 and again in 2002 (Crompton et al., 2005). In 1994, Norway, as a Scandinavian social democratic state, the Czech Republic as a post-war dual-earner economy reflecting the Soviet era, and the UK somewhere in between, were selected as ideal types. Norway had the most generally liberal attitudes, the Czech Republic the least liberal and most stereotypical in respect of gender roles, with British attitudes somewhere in between. The earlier survey demonstrated a significant association between more 'liberal' gender role attitudes and a less traditional division of domestic labour in all three countries.

By 2002, however, this association had actually weakened in the UK and Norway. The dislocation between attitudes and behaviours is the intriguing aspect, given that the conventional wisdom is to assume that what people do comes into line with what they believe. However, there appears to have been a process of 'lagged adaptation' such that men were doing more household tasks in the domestic division of labour. The data for 2002, however, suggested that this process of lagged adaptation had actually stalled. While the partners of women working full-time were still doing more at home, the rate of change had slowed down, and there was hardly any change among those whose partners worked part-time or not at all.

In the UK and Norway, the link between gender role attitudes and the division of domestic labour had disappeared. Crompton and her colleagues commented: 'a man with "liberal" gender role attitudes may nevertheless carry out little by way of household work, particularly if his partner's working hours are shorter' (2005: 223). So despite the fact that women make a greater contribution to household finances and are increasingly likely to be in employment when they have young children, the rate of change in the division of domestic labour is minimal.

So why do gender attitudes *not* lead on to greater equalities of domestic practice? Crompton et al. concluded: 'Increasing individualization in careers and employment relations, together with the introduction of "high commitment" management practices, are leading to more work intensification as employers struggle for competitiveness in an increasingly global market' (2005: 229).

In other words, we find that there are limits of attitudinal change leading on to behavioural practice precisely because the 'household economy' is embedded in the wider one. Simply insisting on the proper attitudes as regards gender relations has very little impact on behaviour when the pressures to perform in paid employment are so pressing, and women will be subject to the 'double shift', in paid work and at home. In short, it is the 'materiality' of social relations which affects practice, and insisting on the primacy of 'attitudes' has little effect other than to reinforce feelings of inadequacy and stress under the intensification of paid labour.

Family and society

In truth, it is easy to lose sight of the bigger picture if we dissociate the household from wider society and focus instead on immediate family relationships. Here is a good example of the connection. Katherine Botterill (2014) studied Polish migrants to Edinburgh, as well as those who had returned to Poland. She is critical of the false dichotomy between 'family' on the one hand and 'individual mobility' on the other, because it fails to take account of the central role of the family in the process of mobility itself. She comments: 'The family performs ideological, practical and affective roles that shape individual mobility across the lifecourse' (2014: 233). In particular, she points to three ruptures: 'moving out' of family life via mobility; 'keeping in touch' with the family while away; and 'coming back' to the family and associated responsibilities. Mobility represented new opportunities and freedoms from which 'habits of home are recalled as an immovable irritation' (2014: 238).

It seems obvious, then, that the family is not a sealed silo in which social relations are internally determined and played out, but rather are embedded in a much wider political economy which has its own imperative drivers and determinants. Relations between the sexes are nested perforce within that. Furthermore, there are powerful 'narratives of return' which are 'guided by gendered economic rationalities for care in later life, and unwillingness to "sacrifice" familial intimacy for household gains' (2014: 240).

Household narratives

Nor are these 'narratives' confined to long-distance migrants. In the 1990s, we carried out intensive interviews with couples aged 25–45 with one or more children, living in Kirkcaldy, as part of wider research on the social and political economy of the household (see Anderson et al., 1994). We were interested in people's 'household strategies', by which we meant 'more or less rational principles which actors can articulate and describe: higher order constructs which form general prescriptions for actions leading towards desired medium- or long-term goals' (1994: 65). Take, for example, these contrasting comments from people we interviewed:

> I'm no' really a planner. Just whatever comes, comes. I think that things change that much nowadays [that] ye canna plan too much ahead.

And:

> I think most people in life have a set plan, and ye try to achieve yer aims. But again, a lot o' things that actually happen … best thing is to have a long-term outlook, and short-term planning towards it.

The second respondent tries to behave strategically (having a 'set plan', a 'long-term outlook'), while the first person recognises that planners exist, but does not think of himself in that way (McCrone, 1994).

Far from the case that very few people had such things as household strategies, we encountered well-worked-out 'strategies' which applied to the worlds of work as well as the family and household. In essence, strategies were constructs which people used to make sense of their world. Most people have them, and nowhere did we find that the few without them were socially or economically incompetent. Indeed, such strategies were frequently reviewed and amended in the light of events. Women usually subordinated their own plans to those of men, for example uprooting the family to follow the male career, or adapting working hours and practices to fit in with routines of work.

In the course of our research we found many women with fragmented and diverse work histories, avoiding full-time work because of upheaval, and downgrading their own career and long-term plans. Examples of serendipity abounded, such as one woman who 'solved' her childcare problem by setting up a playgroup, developing the skills, and then embarking on a social work career as a result. While 'planning' was the background to family life, few talked explicitly about actively 'planning' to have children. Women 'fell pregnant', children 'just came along', as if the practice of 'family planning' was implicit and unspoken. For most people, 'strategies' were not blueprints, but ways of imposing some order and signposting for life, frequently revised and adapted to circumstances which 'came up'.

Intimate lives

Perhaps, spelling it out like this, it seems surprising to connect the intimacies of family life with wider opportunities (or the lack of them). After all, most people can articulate similar narratives in their lives, just as Polish migrants to Edinburgh did in Botterill's research. This teaches us that we cannot derive an understanding of people's lives simply by reading these off from their structural circumstances, still less from their array of social attitudes. Even in what are apparently the most constraining circumstances, we find leeway and serendipity.

So how do women handle such demands in everyday life? In an analysis of marriage, children and choice in a Scottish fishing community (which they call 'Fisherton'), Andy McKinlay and Chris McVittie interviewed a small number of women married to fishermen. While describing their lives in relation to the constraints they experienced as fishermen's wives, they spoke of the freedoms and opportunities which arose from being married to fishermen. Gender identities needed 'to be examined in context for their relevance to the participants themselves rather than assumed to be self-evident features of a broader social landscape' (McKinlay and McVittie, 2011: 176).

Above all, social life is negotiated through talk, open to negotiation in a variety of ways. The authors show that

> when the women of Fisherton describe their lives, they take up, develop or introduce particular gendered ways of talking. In their talk, they describe themselves in terms which emphasize marital status, child-rearing and the importance of the husband's occupation – an occupation which is presented, in matter-of-fact terms, as imposing constraints on their own lives. (2011: 183)

Thus, commented one: 'We think we've got the ideal situation where we ... have a man part-time and the rest of the time we have complete liberty to come and go as we like' (2011: 183).

McKinlay and McVittie describe this as 'hybrid identity' because the women negotiate markedly different versions of themselves, and the consequences their marriages have for their lives. On the one hand, the fact that the fishermen are away from home places the responsibilities for home and children on the women; on the other hand, this feature of their lives allows them to lead their lives in ways that they see fit. Thus, 'gender and its meanings can indeed be seen to be "situated accomplishments of local interaction"' (2011: 187). This reinforces our general point that gender relations and, with them, gender identities are not simply derived from structures of opportunity (or the lack of them), but are worked out by people themselves 'on the ground', both metaphorically and literally.

Gender and politics

Earlier in this chapter, we noted that in the 1990s there were major critiques of the role of women in Scottish history and society. Scotland was portrayed as a sexist society, driven by its culture and its history, and reflected in its iconography as a 'men's society'. In retrospect, this critique can be seen as a stimulus to improve gender balance in Scotland, a case of stepping back to make a leap forward.

Gender and devolution

The presenting opportunity for this was the long campaign for a Scottish parliament which stretched back into the 1980s, but which was propelled forward in the early 1990s by the failures of the political classes to implement greater self-government. As part of this pressure, the women's movement established the 50:50 campaign (www.women5050.org) to press for equal representation between men and women in political office (see Breitenbach and Mackay, 2001; Brown, 1996).

The Scottish Constitutional Convention became the main vehicle in the 1990s for working out what sort of parliament Scotland should have, and gender balance was a key aim, set within an electoral system of proportional representation. The convention's report in 1995 commented: 'We believe that a new Scottish parliament is a great opportunity to improve radically the representation of women in Scottish politics, but the new parliament should represent the whole community and reflect the priorities of the people of Scotland' (for the report 'Scotland's Parliament: Scotland's Right', see https://paulcairney.files.word-press.com/2015/09/scc-1995.pdf).

In the first Scottish parliament in 1999, 37 per cent of MSPs were women, more than double the proportion of female MPs at Westminster (in 1997, 18 per cent of MPs were women, actually twice the proportion elected in 1992). As Meryl Kenny observed, 'on 6 May 1999, more women were elected to the Scottish Parliament in one day than had been elected to represent Scotland in the House of Commons since 1918, when women were first eligible to stand for political office' (www.democraticaudit.com/?p=1392).

Describing such a proportion as reaching 'Nordic levels of women MSPs', Kenny comments that this was not achieved by accident, but

> was the result of a sustained struggle by a diverse coalition of women's organizations, grassroots activists, female trade unionists, party women and gender experts. Framing their demands within wider calls for a 'new politics' in Scotland, women working inside and outside the main political parties pushed for equal representation in the new parliament.

Much of this was due to the policy of the Labour Party in Scotland at the time to implement 'twinning' for constituency and for list seats to ensure women's representation.[7] The SNP used informal measures to place women high on the list, but a proposal to formalise

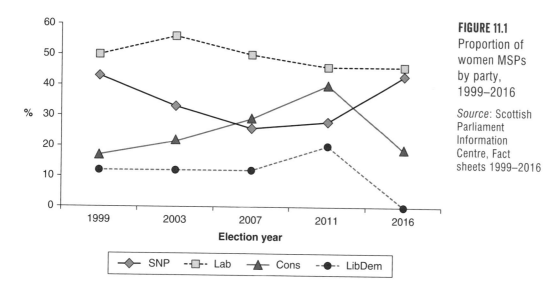

FIGURE 11.1
Proportion of women MSPs by party, 1999–2016

Source: Scottish Parliament Information Centre, Fact sheets 1999–2016

twinning was rejected at the party conference. Nevertheless, both Labour and the SNP ensured a high proportion of women were elected, with Labour's representation about 20 percentage points higher than the SNP's since 1999 (Figure 11.1).

Following the 2016 Scottish parliamentary election, 43 per cent (27) of the SNP MSPs were women, 46 per cent of Labour MSPs (11), six Conservatives (or 19 per cent), one Green (out of six MSPs) and no Liberal Democrats (see Table 11.4).

If we take the total number of MSPs elected for each party in the five elections since 1999,[8] Labour comes out best with 50 per cent of its MSPs female, followed by the SNP (34 per cent), the Conservatives (24 per cent), the Greens (22 per cent)[9] and the Liberal Democrats come last with 12 per cent over the seventeen years of the Scottish parliament. Over the period, there have been sixteen MSPs elected as independents or for other small parties, half of whom were women.[10]

While just over one in three (35 per cent in 2011 and 2016) is a long way from gender balance, it is significantly higher than the representation of female MPs at Westminster,

TABLE 11.4 Proportion of women MSPs by election year

Election year	% of women MSPs
1999	37.2
2003	39.5
2007	33.3
2011	34.8
2016	34.9

Source: Scottish Parliament Information Centre (SPICe)

where the 2015 election resulted in 29 per cent, the highest proportion of women ever elected.[11] On the other hand, women's representation in local government has been woefully low. While there was a slow but steady increase in the number of women candidates and councillors between 1974 and 1999, progress since then has stalled. The authors of the study commented that 'there is no inevitability about further improvements in women's representation at council level' (Bochel and Bochel, 2016: 182).

In Scotland, the increasing proportion of women MPs at Westminster mirrors that of the rest of the UK, but still falls short of the number in the Scottish parliament. Following the surge in female Scottish MPs elected to Westminster in 2015, women are now 34 per cent of Scottish MPs (twenty out of fifty-nine, a net gain of seven since 2010).

This reflects the domination of the SNP, despite the party not using formal gender quota measures. The party has struggled to be women-friendly, despite a history of high-profile female nationalists such as Winnie Ewing, Margaret Bain (Ewing), Margot MacDonald and Nicola Sturgeon (for an analysis, see Mackay and Kenny, 2009). Nicola Sturgeon acknowledged their iconic contribution, in the foreword to a report on the status of young women in Scotland: role models matter.

> When I first thought about entering politics, seeing other women blazing a trail encouraged me to believe I could do the same. What aspiring female politician growing up in Scotland could help but be inspired by Winnie Ewing or Margo MacDonald? (www.ywcascotland.org/wp-content/uploads/2015/03/Status-of-Young-Women-In-Scotland.pdf)

Demonising women

During the 2015 British general election campaign, Nicola Sturgeon was the most prominent of all the women party leaders and, as Kenny observes, much of the media attention was highly gendered:

> Sturgeon was decried as 'the most dangerous woman in Britain' by the Daily Mail (which she later noted was 'possibly one of the nicest things the Daily Mail has ever said about me'). Her appearance was a particular focus – the Times responded to the launch of the SNP manifesto with an extended analysis of her hair, makeup, fashion and weight loss … while the Daily Mail noted that she had become 'sexier with age, income and office'. (2015: 396)

Sturgeon's salience, and demonising, is reflected in the poster issued by the Conservative Party during the campaign (see Figure 11.2).

Perhaps only Mrs Thatcher evoked such fascination and hostility, possibly in equal measure.

FIGURE 11.2
British general
election 2015

Source: The
Conservative Party
used this as a
poster in England

The relationship between gender and nationalism, however, is part of a bigger puzzle: why are women less likely to vote for the SNP than men?

That they do so in significant numbers cannot be doubted (see Figure 11.3). For example, since 1974 there has been a consistent gender gap in SNP voting, as large as 8 and 9 percentage points in the constituency and list votes for 2007 (Johns et al., 2012). By 2011, the SNP's best performance to date, final opinion polls were putting the gender gap at between 3 and 9 percentage points (www.scotcen.org.uk/blog/will-the-gender-gap-narrow-findings-from-2011-and-quebec).

FIGURE 11.3
Women for
Independence,
2014

Source: Scottish
Independence
Referendum,
2014. I am grateful
to 'Women for
Independence' for
permission to use
this photograph

The gender gap and Scottish politics

Analysing the 2007 election data, Johns and his colleagues concluded that while the gender gap was partly to be explained by the relative popularity among men of Alex Salmond as leader, women are no less likely to feel Scottish than men are. What does seem to explain the gender difference is that women are more reluctant to support independence than men, or rather that there are more 'undecideds' among women. Johns et al. conclude:

> Just as gender gaps in voting vary according to the way gender and related issues are presented and discussed at different elections, it seems probable that the gender gap in support for independence will depend on the framing of that policy in party and media discourse. In other words, a greater appeal to men is not intrinsic to the policy of independence but is the result of the way that policy has been defined and discussed. (2012: 596)

Women and independence

Johns and his colleagues were writing that on the basis of analysis of the 2007 Scottish election. The obvious point is to explore that further in the context of the 2014 Independence Referendum. The Scottish Centre for Social Research (ScotCen) carried out analyses in 2013 and 2014 to try and explain the gap.

First of all, the 2013 survey confirmed that it was long-standing: since 1999 up to 2012, the gender gap in support of independence was around 6 or 7 percentage points ('Why don't more women support independence?', www.scotcen.org.uk/media/176043/gender-and-indep-paper-final-2012.pdf).

The researchers ruled out the possible explanation that women's policy priorities are substantially different from men's, nor was an apparent lack of focus on gender equality. Alex Salmond's relative unpopularity among women (or, put more accurately, his greater popularity among men) was not an explanation, and in any case the gap existed when he was *not* leader (between 2002 and 2004). Women were just as likely as men to say they were Scottish in national identity terms.

What did appear to make the difference was that women were significantly more likely to be uncertain of the consequences of Scottish independence, and that this uncertainty about its consequences appeared to be a factor in explaining lower support for independence among women. Replicating the questions a month before the referendum itself, the researchers concluded:

> What continues to matter rather more is the greater level of uncertainty among women compared with men about what independence will mean for Scotland. Women are less likely to feel sure about what the consequences of independence

will be. And this greater uncertainty appears to be a key part of the explanation why women are currently less willing than men to say they will vote Yes. (Ormston, 2014)

They rejected the view that women were more feart or risk averse than men, but that 'uncertainty is an understandable reaction to an inherently complex debate in which opposing claims are frequently stated as fact by the two sides'. We will give the late Ailsa McKay the last word:

> No, women voters are not fickle, but yes they remain largely undecided. Yes, women are concerned about what independence will mean for them and their families on a whole range of practical and personal financial levels but that does not mean they do not care about the wider constitutional issues. In fact it is precisely because women 'care' that they remain undecided. (2013)

Conclusion

More than most, this is an interim conclusion, for gender issues in Scotland are far from 'settled'. Rather, there is an ongoing debate. We only have to look backwards to see how far gender relations have come since our parents' and grandparents' days; we can look forward to see how much there is still to do to create a more gender-equal Scotland.

Nor is this a zero-sum game in which if men lose, women win. Recalibrating gender relations in Scotland has far more winners than losers. McKay once more:

> The point being made is that women and men occupy very different spaces in advanced capitalist economies and these 'spaces' serve to influence their access, participation and voice in political life. However, whilst the space they occupy may restrict and limit their ability to participate, women remain resourceful in finding alternative spaces to organise, influence and ensure their voices are heard. (2013)

We can argue about how 'different' these gender spaces actually are, but undoubtedly creating a Scottish parliament was both the expression of the search for 'alternative spaces' as well as the means to expand them further. Scotland's vibrancy as a political community has been greatly aided by this forum, reflected in the rise and rise of formidable politicians: for the nationalists, Winnie Ewing, Margot MacDonald and Nicola Sturgeon; for Labour, Wendy Alexander, Johan Lamont and Kezia Dugdale; for the Conservatives, Annabel Goldie and Ruth Davidson.[12] We only have to compare their presence with their relative absence at Westminster to see how the cultures of gender politics in the two parliaments have diverged. Indeed, the fact that Margaret Thatcher was Prime Minister from 1979 to 1990 is the classic exception which proves the rule that Westminster remains a man's club.

What is to be done? The Engender report written in the context of the independence campaign in 2014 commented: 'Gender roles and relations are not the natural order, but social constructs that have evolved over time to deny women rights, citizenship and power. However, gender inequality is so ingrained in the cultural psyche and social institutions in the UK that it is rendered invisible' (Engender, 2014).

Chapter summary

So what have we discovered in this chapter?

- That gender discrimination and inequality is as much about the roles women and men play in society as it is about prejudice and bias.
- That the assumption that Scotland is an especially chauvinist society is often asserted, and less reliably proven.
- That while women in Scotland are more likely than men to emphasise their household and gender roles as key to their social identity, they are just as likely to say they are Scottish.
- That economic and social inequalities based on gender are deeply resistant to change, especially where they operate in the domestic sphere.
- That political and constitutional change, notably the creation of a Scottish parliament, has altered the ways politics and gender are done in Scotland.

Finally, we might take issue with the notion that gender inequality remains invisible, even more that it is ingrained in the 'cultural psyche', for the transformations of Scotland's economy, politics and society are such as to make the issues more explicit and more pressing, and as a result more amenable to social and political action. In the next chapter, we will consider related issues of social order.

Questions for discussion

1. What, if anything, is distinctive about gender inequalities in Scotland? Is Scotland a particularly chauvinistic society?

2. What evidence is there that women and men 'do social identities' differently? Why should this be the case?

3. Have gender inequalities in Scotland diminished since the Scottish parliament was established in 1999? What impact, if any, has 'politics' had on wider gender relations?

4. What are the connections between the domestic division of labour and gender relations in Scotland? How are the two connected?

5. Is the number of prominent women politicians in Scotland likely to make a difference to gender relations in the public sphere in Scotland?

Annotated reading

(a) The most comprehensive 'gender audit' was carried out for Scottish Government in 2007 by E. Breitenbach and F. Wasoff, 'A gender audit of statistics: comparing the position of women and men in Scotland' (www.gov.scot/Resource/Doc/172901/0048232.pdf). A successor audit was done by Engender, 'Gender equality and Scotland's constitutional futures', 2014 (www.engender.org.uk/content/publications/Gender-equality-and--Scotlands-constitutional-futures.pdf).

(b) For survey data on attitudes to the domestic division of labour in Scotland, see Scottish Social Attitudes Survey, 2005 (www.gov.scot/Publications/2006/12/05122049/0); and for British Social Attitudes survey data on gender roles, see J. Scott and E. Clery, 'Gender roles: an incomplete revolution?', *British Social Attitudes*, 30, 2013. For comparative studies, see R. Crompton, M. Brockmann and C. Lyonette, 'Attitudes, women's employment and the domestic division of labour: a cross-national analysis in two waves', *Work, Employment and Society*, 19(2), 2005. And on migrants' lives, see K. Botterill, 'Family and mobility in second modernity: Polish migrant narratives of individualization and family life', *Sociology*, 48(2), 2014.

(c) On women and Scottish politics, see F. Mackay and M. Kenny, 'Women's political representation and the SNP: gendered paradoxes and puzzles', in G. Hassan (ed.), *The Modern SNP: From protest to power* (2009); E. Breitenbach and F. Mackay (eds), *Women and Contemporary Scottish Politics: An anthology* (2001); and A. Brown, 'Women and politics in Scotland', *Parliamentary Affairs*, 49, 1996.

(d) On the 'gender gap' in support of the SNP and of independence, see R. Johns et al., 'Gendered nationalism: the gender gap in support for the Scottish National Party', *Party Politics*, 18(4), 2012; M. Kenny, 'Women and the 2015 general election: shattering the political glass ceiling?', *Scottish Affairs*, 24(4), 2015; also www.democraticaudit.com/?p=1392; and R. Ormston, www.scotcen.org.uk/blog/will-the-gender-gap-narrow-findings-from-2011-and-quebec (2011).

Notes

1 We did include 'being British' in our list, but in 2003 this was only chosen as one of their three choices by 19 per cent of men and 8 per cent of women. In 2009, the figures were 14 per cent of men and 10 per cent of women.

2 The data reported here are for the 2009 Scottish Social Attitudes survey. The 2006 scores were much in line with those.

3 This is not to suggest that Rangers FC are to blame for domestic violence; merely that their relegation from the Premier League removed the presenting condition whereby the 'Old Firm' played each other regularly.

4 Reported in *The Herald*, 27 April 2016 (www.heraldscotland.com/news/14461385.Old_Firm_domestic_abuse_soared_by_43_per_cent_on_derby_day/).

5   Relying on people's accounts of their actions and attitudes runs the risk of taking their word
    for it. Nevertheless, in long experience of survey research, it is striking how honest and open
    people are, especially as regards gender relations, especially when partners are present to set
    the record straight.

6   The subsequent analysis focuses on men aged 18–49, and women aged 18–45, in relationships.

7   Twinning involved pairing winnable seats such that men and women candidates had a more
    equal chance of being elected.

8   These figures are calculated on the total number of MSPs elected for each party at each elec-
    tion, and ignore the fact that some MSPs are re-elected.

9   The Greens are not included on the graph because the number of MSPs returned at each
    election is too small to express as a percentage; a total of eighteen Green MSPs have been
    elected since 1999, including four women.

10 The Scottish Socialist Party did best with four women out of six MSPs in the 2003 election.

11 Not until 1997 did the number of women MPs reach double percentage figures at Westminster
    (18.2 per cent), while up to the late 1980s it was fewer than 5 per cent, that is one in twenty
    (www.ukpolitical.info/FemaleMPs.htm).

12 The Liberal Democrats are missing from that list because they have never had a female leader
    and consistently a lower proportion of women MSPs (see Figure 11.1). Neither have the
    Greens had a female leader in Scotland.

12

SOCIAL ORDER: CRIME AND JUSTICE IN SCOTLAND

SUSAN McVIE

This chapter explores the changing nature of social order in Scotland, both in terms of its trends and patterns of crime and the wider context of its policies on crime control and institutional structures of governance (Figure 12.1). It takes a historical perspective, although arguably the events since devolution mark this as one of the most active periods of both social and political change. As Keating observes, 'Crime is one of the most complex of public policy issues to define, to measure and to control' (2010: 249). Little surprise then that it has proven to be so controversial in the settlement of the post-devolution landscape.

FIGURE 12.1
Parliament Hall
(Supreme Courts
of Scotland)

Source: Courtesy
of the Scottish
Courts and
Tribunals Service

Chapter aims

- To review the evolution of criminal justice policy in Scotland in the context of other historical developments.

- To examine key changes in the governance of criminal justice and penal policy, and outline the role and structure of Scotland's key crime control institutions.

- To explore the range of data sources used to measure crime and map out Scotland's crime problem at a national level.

- To study two forms of crime in Scotland – crimes of dishonesty and non-sexual crimes of violence – in specific detail, paying close attention to trends and patterns of change over time, the geographical spread of these crime types and how Scotland compares internationally.

- To conclude with some tentative speculations as to the future of crime, law and order, and what it means for Scottish society.

A brief history of crime

For most of the last 300 years, Scotland was a nation locked together with the rest of the UK in a political and bureaucratic union, subject largely to the same social and economic changes, and exposed to a common set of global influences that have gradually pervaded the developed world. And yet the institutional structures and the philosophical underpinnings of law and order in Scotland have remained largely intact and maintained a certain distinctiveness, setting it apart from its closest neighbours in both nature and approach.

Following the Act of Union in 1707, the integrity and independence of Scotland's legal system (along with the education system and the church) were preserved, allowing it to maintain an autonomous criminal justice and penal system from that of England and Wales (Young, 1997), but more than this, it has a very idiosyncratic history in terms of both its crime rates and its crime control and penal policy. Arguably, both have been strongly influenced by Scotland's wider civil society, powerful elites and indigenous political culture which have largely resisted the neo-liberal policies of prevailing UK governments.

One of Scotland's greatest triumphs is that key aspects of its justice system have adhered staunchly to a set of welfarist principles even in the face of significant pressure to buckle under populist punitivism, with the exception of a relatively short-lived crisis of penal identity which was at odds with the partial emancipation from UK control shortly after devolution. It has been argued that, in the immediate post-devolution period, Scotland's crime control and penal policy agenda was developed principally as a mechanism for building political capacity rather than developing radical Scottish social policy (McAra, 2008). Moreover, aspects of policy development have often ignored the evidence on trends in crime or misrepresented them for political purposes, which has led to a lack of clarity on the situation as regards Scotland's crime problem and its impact on the Scottish public – particularly those subject to the greatest excesses of poverty, deprivation and social injustice (McAra and McVie, 2010).

The evolution of Scottish criminal justice and penal policy

Scots criminal law and the Scottish legal system have a long and complicated history. Dating back to the medieval era and developing originally from Roman Dutch law, they have been strongly influenced by the legal traditions of various different cultural groups that inhabited the country (including the Gaels and the Norse) and have evolved as a hybrid legal system based on both civil and common law. Following the Act of Union in 1707, the constitutional settlement allowed Scotland to retain a separate legal system from that of the rest of the UK, even though it was subject to the rule of the UK parliament and the Union did exert English influence on Scots law. Although it continued to share some elements with England and Wales and Northern Ireland, the distinctiveness of the Scottish legal system was fiercely protected by the legal profession and institutions of Scotland (Smith, 2005).

In more recent times, Scots law has been further influenced by European law under the Treaties of the European Union and by the requirements of the European Convention on Human Rights. However, the reconvening of the Scottish parliament following passage of the Scotland Act 1998 marks the most significant event in recent legal history as this transferred to Scotland the power to pass legislation within all areas of domestic policy not reserved to Westminster, including law and order (the exception being national security, which remains a reserved matter).

While the run-up to devolution in Scotland marked a period of radical institutional transformation in political terms, it caused relatively little disruption to the architecture of the various institutions and organisations tasked with delivering criminal justice (McAra, 2005). This has been attributed largely to a degree of 'cultural continuity' which has its origins in the creation of the Scottish Office and the appointment of the first Secretary for Scotland in 1885 (becoming the Secretary of State for Scotland in 1926). Sitting as a member of the UK Cabinet, the Secretary for Scotland gradually took on greater responsibility for the administration of domestic policy, including the development and implementation of Scottish criminal justice and penal policy. According to McAra (2006), the Scottish Office enjoyed considerable autonomy from the Westminster government and was able to develop and preserve distinctive policies that were tailored specifically to the needs of Scotland.

Over time, the key elites representing the institutions that comprised the various components of the criminal justice system (including the police, the prosecution service, the judiciary, the prison service and criminal justice social work) played a powerful role in shaping crime control policies and penal practice in Scotland and protecting it from the worst excesses of penal punitivism evident in England and Wales. When pressure began to build for constitutional change in Scotland, therefore, debates around crime and justice policy were largely subdued because distinctive aspects of the criminal justice system, such as a prominent welfare-based ethos and a strong commitment to non-custodialism, were already embedded deeply within an uncontested historical and cultural context, and this helped Scotland to avoid the more populist, punitive policies associated with England and Wales (Cavadino and Dignan, 2006; Croall, 2006).

Not all commentators, of course, agree that Scottish justice policy – either pre- or post-devolution – has been imbued with such an ideological notion of distinctive collectivism and insulation from wider influences (see Mooney and Poole, 2004; Mooney and Scott, 2005). Mary Munro et al. argue that the welfarist ideology of Scottish criminal justice is somewhat mythological and that political governance in Scotland was severely constrained prior to devolution as a result of the '"democratic deficit" of the union settlement which allowed for the anachronistic dominance of values associated with liberal elitism' (2010: 269).

This point of view contradicts the picture that Garland (1999) paints of an 'internationalised' criminal justice in Scotland arising from a century of critical engagement in transnational debate and reform and the development and implementation of path-breaking interventions and philosophies. And there are many specific examples of sharply juxtaposed Scottish and English dogma, including the evolution of Scottish juvenile justice policy which is built on stronger welfare-based principles and philosophies compared with that south of the border. Nevertheless, there is widespread agreement that the period following devolution has marked one of the most significant periods of change within Scottish criminal justice and penal policy in its history (Scott, 2011). It is to these changes that we now turn.

Governance of crime and justice post-devolution

Criminal justice and penal policy has arguably been one of the areas of Scottish public policy that has been subject to the greatest debate, scrutiny and reform since devolution. Previously, domestic crime and justice issues were under the jurisdiction of the Scottish Office Minister of State for Home Affairs, while the Lord Advocate was chief legal advisor to the UK government for both civil and criminal legal matters in Scotland. Following the Scotland Act 1998, the Advocate General for Scotland took on the advisory role to the UK government and a specific position of Minister for Justice was created by the new Scottish Executive, taking over responsibility for all aspects of law and order with the exception of prosecutions, which remained under the control of the Lord Advocate as the head of criminal prosecution in Scotland.

The incumbents of the role of Minister for Justice under the Labour–Liberal Democrat coalition were the Liberal Democrat's Jim Wallace MSP (1999 to 2003) and Labour's Cathy

Jamieson MSP (2003 to 2007). According to Lesley McAra, this period marked a significant transformation in crime and justice policy, especially in the case of youth justice, as a result of 'the greater ideological congruence' (2006: 133) between Scotland's coalition government and the New Labour government at Westminster.

In building a new polity, crime control was a good place to start – as Keating (2010) notes, crime is a popular issue for politicians to play up or down according to their political needs. The incoming Scottish Executive created a new administrative structure consisting of a Justice Department, which had responsibility for all matters relating to crime, justice and policing, and was accountable to the Minister for Justice. In a process that McAra (2006; 2008) has labelled 'detartanisation', the Justice Department gradually introduced a raft of new policy documents, legislative powers and targeted interventions which were underpinned by a managerialist approach to law and order that brought it in line with more punitive practices in England and Wales. This is most clearly evidenced in the Criminal Justice (Scotland) Act 2003, which had major symbolic and practical impacts on Scotland as it incorporated several elements that introduced essentially English practices (see Eski et al., 2011).

There was, as Hazel Croall puts it, a 'lack of "political will" to depart from the influence of the "Blair orthodoxy" of New Labour' (2006: 592) which constrained the Scottish Executive in terms of pursuing a range of more radical policies. Responsibility for strategic planning and target setting around offending was devolved to myriad local multi-agency and cross-sectoral groups in an effort to improve efficiency and effectiveness. Meanwhile, two Justice Committees were established by the Scottish parliament to scrutinise an increasingly complex landscape of activities and ensure that criminal justice issues were central to the political agenda.

This period was marked by a 'sudden and dramatic politicisation' of criminal justice (McNeill and Batchelor, 2004: 9) and populist rhetoric was evident in the emergence of new legislation targeted at low-level disorder and poorly performing parents. In the case of youth justice, aspects of public protection, risk management and effective practice began to take precedence over existing welfare-based principles centred on the best interests of the child. A target-driven culture led to a dangerous new performance-based discourse aimed at tackling the 'problem' of persistent young offenders, despite a lack of evidence about the nature or extent of such a problem, and ultimately failed to deliver as a result of misconceived policies and poorly implemented interventions (see McAra and McVie, 2010). According to McAra (2008), this period of criminal and penal policy in Scotland largely reflects an attempt to shore up a weak government by building political capital based on a highly politicised law and order agenda.

Following its election in 2007, the SNP government rationalised the Justice Committees to one, and reconfigured the governance structure, introducing several new roles to oversee penal policy. The Minister for Justice became the Cabinet Secretary for Justice, a position held for seven years by Kenny MacAskill MSP (2007 to 2014) before passing to Michael Matheson MSP; and the position of Director-General for Learning and Justice was created to oversee the portfolio containing all aspects of civil, criminal and youth justice policy.

The work is currently split across three separate directorates. The Justice Directorate has responsibility for policies relating to the justice system, including both civil and criminal law, the reform of courts and legal services, the management and rehabilitation of offenders, and support for victims and witnesses of crime. The Safer Communities Directorate has responsibility for policies relating to police service reform, operational policing, and reducing violent and anti-social behaviour; while the Children and Families Directorate contains the policy teams with responsibility for youth justice and the Children's Hearing Unit. This new structure reflects the SNP administration's aim to construct a joined-up approach to governance by bringing crime policy together with other aspects of safety, health and education; however, in the wake of the Christie Commission report (http://www.gov.scot/resource/doc/352649/0118638.pdf) on the future delivery of public services, there remain questions as to the extent to which different areas of government policy are truly 'joined up'.

The new Scottish government demonstrated a significant determination to 'improve' the Scottish criminal justice system (Scott, 2011). MacAskill spearheaded a major programme of reform and legislative change during his time as Cabinet Secretary for Justice (although much of this built on work that was established by the previous administration). For example, taking forward the recommendations of an extensive review of the summary justice system that had been commissioned by Jim Wallace (McInnes, 2004), MacAskill forged ahead with significant legislative change to improve the efficiency and effectiveness of justice system processes and procedures. The Criminal Proceedings etc. (Reform) (Scotland) Act 2007 made eight key changes to the operation of the summary criminal justice system, including: widening the range of alternatives to prosecution available to courts; increasing the sentencing powers of summary courts; increasing the efficiency of collection for monetary penalties; and a broad review of the courts' structure and administration.

The Criminal Justice and Licensing (Scotland) Act 2010 was another significant piece of legislation, especially in the areas of prosecution and sentencing, as it introduced presumptions against prison sentences of three months or less and against the prosecution of children aged under 12 in court (although it stopped short of increasing the age of criminal responsibility from age 8). It also established a new sentencing disposal, the Community Payback Order, which was seen as bringing 'together elements of restorative justice and rehabilitation as well as more punitive elements' (Nugent and Loucks, 2011: 364).

MacAskill's time in office marked a new phase of justice history, and penal reform took a distinct change of direction from that of the previous administration. In the area of youth justice, for example, which had been highly politicised under the Labour–Liberal Democrat coalition, there was a renewed emphasis on prevention and early intervention based on the identification of 'risk factors', and the whole area of youth offending became much less politically charged (McAra and McVie, 2010).

A new model of justice, premised on 'getting it right for every child', promised a vision of high-quality services for all children that was at odds with the previous punitive rhetoric. That is not to say that penal policy moved to a predominantly welfarist paradigm; both Keating (2010) and McAra (2010) have pointed to an uneasy mix of welfarist, actuarial and retributive impulsions driving justice policy during this period. Nevertheless, the new administration did abandon many previously unpopular policies and there was evidence of a more compassionate approach to justice (which attracted worldwide publicity over the release of the convicted Lockerbie bomber Abdelbaset al-Megrahi from prison in 2009). The election of the Conservative–Liberal Democrat UK coalition government in 2010 undoubtedly helped the SNP administration to highlight its distinctiveness from the English system of justice yet again; however, it has by no means been an untroubled period, especially in relation to policing reform.

Institutions that form the Scottish criminal justice system

The day-to-day work of dispensing justice in Scotland is the role of the criminal justice system; however, most commentators would agree that it is inappropriate to describe it as a 'system', as this implies some element of rational coordination or one principal governing organisation. For the purpose of completeness, the following sections will briefly summarise some of the major changes since devolution in the structure, role and administration of the main organisations that constitute this system. It is interesting to consider these changes because, as noted earlier, the institutional elites in Scotland have historically played a significant role in the development and direction of penal policy. However, as McAra (2008) has noted, major changes since devolution have had consequent repercussions on the justice system and the society it serves.

Police

The first police force in the UK was founded in Glasgow in 1800, and an Act of Parliament stipulated that every town and county in Scotland should have their own police force by 1857. Not surprisingly, this proved unwieldy and the number of forces was gradually reduced to eight by 1975 (see Jackson et al., 2015). The period from then until devolution involved relatively little change, with chief constables experiencing a high degree of autonomy and a very low political profile even though they were subject to regular scrutiny by local police boards and the Inspector of Constabulary (HMICS).

The creation of the Scottish parliament shifted the responsibility for policing fully within the remit of the new government, with chief constables now accountable to the Minister for Justice and the Justice Committees. According to Kenneth Scott (2011), the devolution settlement created a 'moving landscape' for Scottish policing that was to mark one of the most turbulent periods in policing history. Over one-third of all the Acts passed in the first ten years of the Scottish parliament involved criminal justice issues, many of which expanded policing powers in ways that could potentially impact on people's human rights. In addition, the continued freedom of the chief constables to exercise their discretion with regards to policies and procedures enabled certain practices to develop unchecked.

Concerns about the ability of the existing system to ensure the accountability and governance of the eight Scottish police forces were raised by the Scottish parliament's Justice Committee in 2008, although there were conflicting views as to how police boards were operating at the local level (Fyfe, 2010). The role of the Scottish government gradually became more interventionist over time, such as directing HMICS to undertake specific thematic reports on policing and establishing the Scottish Police Services Authority (SPSA) to oversee various core aspects of the service.

The constitutional context of Scottish policing became much more politicised following devolution and the degree of interaction between the police and politicians increased significantly, largely as a result of the importance of law and order to the Scottish electorate (Scott, 2011). The decision to establish a single national police force in Scotland marked one of the most radical public sector reforms in a generation (Fyfe and Henry, 2015). Following a consultation period, in which various chief constables and others argued vigorously against the idea, MacAskill announced in 2011 that a single police service would be created. Presented very much as a modernising development, it was claimed that the single service would 'protect the future of police and fire and rescue services in Scotland ... [and ensure] our vital services are fit to face the challenges of the 21st century' (Scottish Government, 2012a).

The Police and Fire Reform (Scotland) Act 2012 established the new Police Service of Scotland and Stephen House (then Chief Constable of Strathclyde Police) was appointed the first Chief Constable of the new national service. At the same time, the Scottish Police Authority (SPA) became the main scrutinising body for Police Scotland, although it was widely reported that there were disagreements about the powers and responsibilities between the heads of these two organisations from the start.

Police Scotland (Figure 12.2) officially came into being on 1 April 2013, but its first two years were beset by problems and controversy. One of the most high-profile issues was that of stop-and-search, a procedure that has until recently been undertaken on the basis of both statutory powers and voluntary consent (see Murray, 2014). Predicated on the ability of the public to give their 'informed consent' in the face of authority, it became clear that non-statutory searches were being used to discriminate against children, young men and those from Scotland's most impoverished communities. Following a widespread review, a Scottish Government Advisory Board recommended cessation of the practice (Scott, 2015).

The inception of Police Scotland proved difficult for not only the police and the politicians involved, but also the various scrutiny bodies who came in for criticism in the light of poor operational accountability mechanisms. Concerns about armed officers on the streets of Scotland and the ability of the single force to keep Scotland safe in the wake of extensive budget cuts and police station and control room closures dogged the chief constable, who eventually resigned from office in September 2015.

FIGURE 12.2 Police Scotland

Source: Author's photograph

In a recent governance review, the SPA issued a thinly veiled critique of the government's interference in policing matters which acted to blur lines of responsibility and accountability following the establishment of the new force (Flanagan, 2016).

Prosecution

The Crown Office and Procurator Fiscal Service is Scotland's independent public prosecution service. The Lord Advocate is the head of criminal prosecutions, a position which was protected by the 1998 Scotland Act. Uniquely for a senior prosecutor, the Lord Advocate became an *ex officio* member of the Scottish Executive in 1999, regularly attending weekly cabinet meetings. Following the 2007 election, however, the new SNP First Minister, Alex Salmond, decided to 'depoliticise' the role and the Lord Advocate was no longer invited to attend cabinet meetings.

This unique position of Scottish Minister and independent head of the system of criminal prosecutions caused further controversy in 2008 when the Calman Commission raised concerns about the possibility that the Lord Advocate, acting in her capacity as head of the system of prosecutions, might give rise to devolution issues under the Scotland Act. Following a consultation process overseen by an Expert Working Group, and led by the Advocate General, a legislative amendment was proposed to remove certain responsibilities from the Lord Advocate that were incompatible with the European Convention on Human Rights and to introduce a right of appeal in relation to cases where this was felt to have occurred, thus bringing her in line with other UK prosecutors. While the chief prosecutor in Scotland retains a very unusual role in governance terms, therefore, the political nature of the role has been watered down somewhat since the inception of the Scottish parliament.

Courts and sentencing

Sentencing is the preserve of the judiciary of Scotland, who sit in a variety of courts and make decisions on both civil and criminal cases. Each case is overseen by a judge who makes sure that cases are dealt with within the parameters set out by Scots law and hands down judgments and sentences.

Unique to Scotland, there are two forms of trial and three levels of criminal court. More serious cases are heard under solemn procedure where the verdict is decided by a jury of up to fifteen citizens and the judge decides the sentence, although by far the majority of cases are heard under summary procedure by a judge sitting alone. The lowest level of criminal court is the Justice of the Peace Court (known prior to 2008 as the District Court) where the judges are lay persons called Justices of the Peace (or JPs), although in Glasgow there is also a Stipendiary Magistrate Court which is presided over by a professional lawyer. Only summary procedure cases are dealt with in the JP Court.

Sheriff Courts may hear either summary or solemn cases, and are presided over by a Sheriff who is an experienced lawyer. At the highest level, the High Court of Justiciary is the supreme criminal court and deals only with the most serious solemn cases and appeal cases from the other courts.

The type of court does place some restrictions on the sentencing powers of judges; however, legislation is often piecemeal and Scottish judges have historically enjoyed a very wide level of discretion in their choice of sentence (Hutton, 1999). The most senior Scottish judge, the Lord President, has responsibility for all of Scottish civil and criminal court business. In reality, however, all judges exercise their powers independently of others, including government and parliament. Scottish judges have traditionally maintained a strong defence of the principle of judicial independence which, until very recently, prevented them from participating in any significant programme of sentencing reform. This resistance to change has set Scottish sentencing apart from that of other western jurisdictions (Ashworth, 2005), especially during the decade prior to devolution when sentencing reform was developing apace elsewhere.

Cyrus Tata (2010) provides a powerful illustration of the ability of the Scottish judiciary to stave off change and resist external interference. In the early 1990s, concerns were raised about inconsistency in sentence decision-making both between sentencers and across courts. This led the then Conservative government to introduce plans for mandatory minimum custodial sentences for certain types of serious crimes. Rejecting this proposal, senior members of the judiciary recommended instead the introduction of a Sentencing Information System (SIS) for the High Court in an effort to improve consistency in sentencing through self-regulation.

With the assistance of academics from Strathclyde University, a sophisticated electronic system was developed and phased in during the 1990s before being handed over to the Scottish Court Service in 2003. However, political pressure on the judiciary weakened and enthusiasm for the system waned. Following devolution, ministers commissioned a review of Summary Justice in Scotland aimed at improving effectiveness and efficiency, and recommended that the SIS be extended to Sheriff Courts (McInnes, 2004). However, this recommendation has not so far been pursued and the SIS has essentially fallen into disuse.

Since the election of the SNP government in 2007, some progress has been made towards changing sentencing practice. The Criminal Justice and Licensing (Scotland) Act 2010 introduced a presumption against short-term custodial sentences of three months or less; and, in October 2015, a new scrutiny body, the Scottish Sentencing Council, was established to improve consistency and transparency in the decision-making of the Scottish judiciary. According to Tata, however, the judiciary remains staunchly protective of its status and power, and the story of the SIS signifies 'the ability of the Scottish judiciary, at least so far, to head-off, at least temporarily, the threat of "interference"' (2010: 211). The extent to which it can continue to stave off interference in the context of a highly politicised justice agenda remains to be seen.

Prisons

Relative to other parts of the Scottish criminal justice system, the Scottish prison system is modern, as imprisonment was not used as a form of judicial sentence until the early nineteenth century. Prior to this, Scottish courts generally used banishment or transportation, monetary fines or hanging to deal with those they found guilty, as the expense of keeping and feeding a prisoner was considered unpalatable (Cameron, 1983). The modern Scottish prison system developed from the 1930s to deal with long-term and other categories of prisoners as transportation gradually diminished.

The Board of Directors of Prisons in Scotland, which was tasked with imposing uniformity and efficiency in Scottish jails, recorded in 1839 that there were 178 buildings functioning as prisons, including mostly lock-up houses, tollbooths and small burgh jails, which were often insecure and unfit for purpose. There were only twenty larger prisons maintained at borough or county level. Over the period from 1839 to 1877, central government gradually took over the management of Scottish prisons and rationalised the number of prison buildings in response to their 'shocking conditions' (Smith, 1983: 309), although centralisation was resisted by both the Board of Directors and local authorities which wished to retain local control. The number of prisons gradually reduced as centralisation prevailed. In 1860 the number of prisons had reduced to seventy-two and by 1898 there were just fourteen prisons in Scotland. In 1886, with the establishment of the Scottish Office, the Scottish prison system formally came under the jurisdiction of the Secretary (of State) for Scotland.

The modern-day Scottish Prison Service (SPS) has existed as an executive agency since 1993, headed by a chief executive and funded by the Scottish government with direct accountability to Scottish ministers. It operates a service framework with each of the thirteen public sector prisons and manages two private sector providers of prisons and custodial services under contract arrangements.

One of the most contentious issues facing the SPS prior to devolution was the scale of the prison population. Over the period from 1950 to 1994, the prison population rose three-fold from 1800 to 5600 (Young, 1997). This meteoric rise could not be easily explained by the rise in crime or changes in population demographics, leading James McManus to conclude 'that imprisonment has become an increasingly popular option for the courts and that this tendency is likely to continue unless some positive steps are taken to alter it' (1999: 235). In particular, the rise in the prison population seemed to be driven by an increase in remand (un-sentenced) prisoners and those sentenced to either very short-term sentences (of thirty days or less) or long-term sentences. Despite severe criticism of the use of imprisonment in Scotland, on grounds of both social and financial costs, the prison population grew at an even more meteoric rate from the early 1990s to peak at a figure of 8178 in 2011–12 before declining slightly (Scottish Government, 2015a).

Like other parts of the Scottish justice system, the SPS came under the spotlight in the period since devolution, mainly as a result of the spiralling prison population. There were calls from the Scottish Prisons Complaints Commission (SPCC) to deal with the chronic conditions in Scottish prisons (many of which were built during the Victorian era) caused by overcrowding and poor sanitary regimes (SPCC, 2004). There were numerous poor reports from Her Majesty's Chief Inspector of Prisons and an increase in the number of complaints from prisoners citing violations of their human rights under the European Convention on Human Rights, which placed a strain on prison resources. Concerns were also raised about the high concentration of prisoners from the poorest council estates in Scotland (Houchin, 2005).

Of particular concern over this period was the increase in the number of prisoners serving short-term sentences which were perceived to be both costly to society and of little benefit in terms of reducing reoffending (Audit Scotland, 2012). A high-profile report commissioned by Scottish Government and undertaken by the ex-Lord Advocate, Dame Eilish Angiolini, was particularly critical of the large increase in low-level offenders with significant mental health and substance abuse problems being dealt with in Scotland's women's prison and recommended a significant reduction in the number of women in prison (Commission on Women Offenders, 2012).

The response from the Scottish government to increasing pressure around imprisonment rates was to introduce a presumption against short-term custodial sentences of three months or less in the Criminal Justice and Licensing (Scotland) Act 2010. This was in line with recommendations set out in a review of 'what works to reduce re-offending', advocating greater use of community disposals to replace short-term prison sentences (Sapouna et al., 2011). However, even as recently as 2012 the Scottish government was still projecting a continued increase in the average daily prison population from 8300 in 2012–13 to 9500 in 2020–1 (Scottish Government, 2012b). The sudden downturn in prisoner numbers since 2011–12 appears to have moderated this thinking, as the most recent projections suggest that the daily prison population will remain stable at around 7800 until 2021–2 (Scottish Government, 2015b). At the time of writing, the Scottish government has put out to public consultation a proposal to increase minimum sentence lengths further (potentially to as much as one year). It remains to be seen whether the recent reduction in prisoner numbers will be sustained in the longer term.

Crime policy and the referendum

Given the turbulent nature of change within this area of public policy post-devolution, one might reasonably have expected criminal justice and penal policy to play a significant role in the debates running up to the 2011 Scottish elections. Alas, issues around social order in Scotland were largely eclipsed in the context of wider debates about the constitutional future of Scotland and the demand for greater powers. Similarly, the debates surrounding the referendum for Scottish independence in 2014 barely touched on issues of crime control, focusing instead on the dominant themes of national security and economic stability.

As Gerry Mooney and Gill Scott (2015) observe, criminal justice is just one of a number of equally important, and intertwining, issues such as inequality, social justice and poverty that have been neglected amid the landscape of political, media and public discussion on Scotland's future. Of course, one wonders whether criminal justice policy may have been higher up the political agenda within these debates if crime trends had been rising during this period (which they were not) – particularly in the context of severe austerity and significant welfare reform. Indeed, the interest in Scotland's crime trends among all but a small sector of the criminological community has been notable by its absence in recent years – a sad testament considering the very significant shift in crime which indicates that Scottish society is indeed getting safer, as will be discussed in the next section.

Crime in Scotland

The aim of this section is to provide an overview of crime in Scotland drawing on the most recent evidence from a range of sources of data. It is important to note that crime data sources are not always completely accurate or comparable, due to the technicalities of how crimes are defined and recorded; however, the objective will be to provide as comprehensive a picture as possible of how crime has impacted on Scottish society.

It is worth noting that efforts to measure and quantify crime are not without their critics. Some scholars have rejected a technocratic or positivist approach to identifying and labelling crime as a series of discrete 'events' because this abstracts it from the context in which it occurs and, therefore, the *reality* of the incident (Skogan, 1986). Indeed, the application of quantitative methodological approaches to the study of crime has created one of the greatest schisms within criminology, with positivist approaches being described as outmoded, crude and dehumanising (see McAra and McVie, 2012). Nevertheless, the production of crime statistics is a major industry and such data are used by governments and a host of criminal justice and other organisations on which to base public policy, operationalise practice, and target resources and services within Scottish society.

Data sources on crime

The primary, and most long-standing, measure of crime in Scotland is police-recorded crime statistics. First published in 1871 as part of the 'Judicial Statistics of Scotland', recorded crime statistics provide an enduring record of the changing nature of crime as measured by the police; however, crime is not an uncontested social fact. As stated by David Smith and Paul Young, 'it arises from moral judgements, from a legal code, and from a multitude of decisions taken by officials and citizens about whether to invoke the legal process on a particular occasion' (1999: 15). As a result, fluctuations we observe in the official measures of crime over time do not necessarily reflect changes in the underlying behaviours that we consider to be criminal or anti-social acts – they also reflect a variety of social, legal, operational and policy processes that impact on the way in which the police respond to and record incidents of crime.

There has long been scepticism over the reliability and validity of police statistics in measuring the totality of crime because they are, in essence, a by-product of the administrative process through which contraventions of our legal code are dealt with – a barometer of police activity rather than criminal behaviour (Kitsuse and Cicourel, 1963). Crimes are often not reflected in recorded crime figures, mainly because they go unnoticed; they are explained away; or they are not reported to or recorded by the police (Soothill et al., 2002). Any interpretation of police-recorded crime statistics must, therefore, take account of their idiosyncrasies and limitations (Maguire, 2012).

Largely in response to the perceived inadequacies of police-recorded crime statistics to reveal the so-called 'dark figure of crime' in the UK, a new measure of crime – the national victim survey – was introduced in the early 1980s. Pioneered in the United States as part of President Johnson's National Commission on Crime, victim surveys were implemented in a number of countries before the first British Crime Survey (BCS) was established by the Home Office in 1982 (Mayhew, 2000). Its introduction, according to Simon Anderson (1999), was the result of several factors: increasing pressure from the academic community; a feeling that the UK was lagging behind other countries; the influence of a new strand of 'administrative criminology'; and a climate of 'law and order' politics in the wake of the inner cities riots in England in 1981.

The BCS was designed to provide a picture of crime that could be directly compared with that of the recorded crime statistics, thus allowing the scale of the 'dark figure of crime' to be estimated. The responses to a range of questions on people's experiences of household and personal crimes are recorded in a 'victim form' and then coded using police recording rules, so as to match up as far as possible the survey definition with that of the police (Mayhew, 2000). By scaling up these responses using a population weighting factor, the number of crimes committed at the national level can be estimated and the gap between this and recorded crime figures can be compared. In addition, large-scale surveys offer the opportunity to identify a wide range of factors that are related to victimisation, including the characteristics of the household and the individual, as well as a wealth of information on people's wider experiences, attitudes and perceptions of the criminal justice system.

Like recorded crime statistics, however, victim surveys have limitations in terms of their ability to provide a 'true' measure of crime. They exclude certain types of crime (including crimes against businesses and 'victimless' crimes like drug use) and they exclude certain types of victims (such as victims of murder and those who do not reside in private households). In addition, the approach to coding responses to match recorded crimes can only be applied to a limited number of 'comparable' crimes recorded by the survey, which means that crime estimates are restricted.

This goes against the beliefs of criminologists who approach crime from a 'left realist' perspective, who place less emphasis on finding comparable measures to recorded crime and more on establishing the full extent of crime and disorder as experienced and defined by members of the public, especially those from the most deprived and marginalised communities (Lea and Young, 1984). This tension is neatly summarised by Anderson who observes that 'in some ways, crime surveys have been used to challenge the "official" picture of crime presented by the police statistics, in other ways they have served to reinforce the categories and definitions of formal criminal justice' (1999: 40).

For two of the earliest sweeps, in 1982 and 1988, the BCS included central and southern Scotland; thereafter, a decision was taken to launch an independent Scottish Crime Survey (SCS), mainly so that the government in Scotland could exert more control over the design and content of the survey, including extending it to cover the whole of Scotland (McVie et al., 2011). To date, there have been thirteen large-scale victim surveys in Scotland; however, these surveys have been known by four different names and have varied in terms of geographical coverage, survey design, sample size and frequency.

In comparison with the BCS (which was at long last accurately renamed the Crime Survey for England and Wales in 2012) Scottish crime surveys have been very much the poor cousin, under threat at various times due to cuts in public funding and subject to political expediency as governments have used them to measure performance targets rather than to improve our understanding of victimisation. Therefore, while these surveys provide an important alternative measure of crime in Scotland to police-recorded crime statistics, they are not an uncontested methodology and, like other measures of crime, should be subject to critical scrutiny.

Overall crime in Scotland

Trends in police-recorded crime statistics in Scotland, like those of many other developed countries (except Japan), showed a dramatic increase in the years following the Second World War (Smith, 2004; Smith and Young, 1999). This is illustrated in Figure 12.3, which shows the number of recorded crimes and offences in Scotland from 1930 to 2008–9 (the last year for which data going this far back were published).[1] Looking at the overall trend in both crimes and offences, things remained relatively stable during the 1930s and 1940s (with the exception of a short-term increase in recorded offences in the late 1930s). During the 1950s, the crime rate started to increase slowly (mainly due to another rise in offences) and from the 1960s onwards there was a year-on-year increase, in both crimes and offences, which continued until the early 1990s. Smith (2004) notes that there was an increase in all crime types between 1950 and 1980, including a three-fold increase in housebreaking, a five-fold increase in theft and a nine-fold increase in violent crime.

Precise comparison of post-war crime trends between Scotland and other countries is hampered by a lack of comparable data and the frequent publication of 'UK' data that do not differentiate their constituent jurisdictions. However, a very clear linear, or even exponential, rise in crime since 1955 or 1960 has been observed in almost all West European countries (van Dijk and Tseloni, 2012). Smith (2005) compared crime trends in Scotland with those in England and Wales and found that, while both showed a significant rise, they differed in terms of scale and timing.

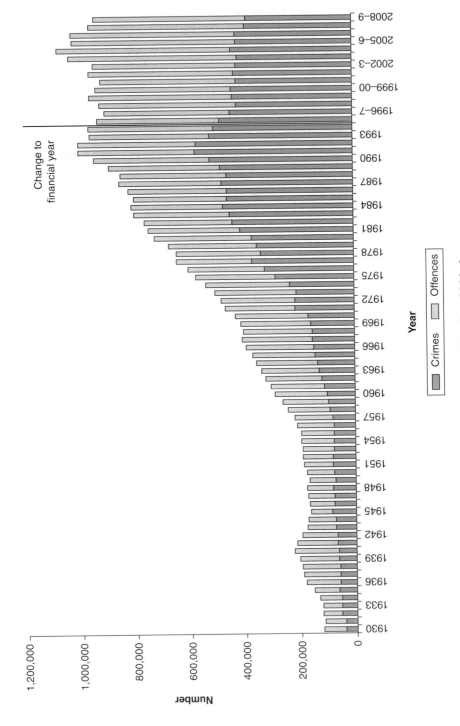

FIGURE 12.3 Crimes and offences recorded by the police, 1930–94 and 1995–6 to 2008–9

Source: Scottish Government (2009)

Overall, the rise in recorded crime was substantially lower in Scotland than in England and Wales. For example, the three-fold increase in housebreaking in Scotland compared with a thirteen-fold increase in England and Wales; and the number of recorded robberies increased by fifteen times in Scotland compared with sixty-seven times in England and Wales. In Scotland, crime increased the most over the period from 1950 to 1971, whereas the increase in England was greater from 1972 onwards. Similarly, the crime surveys for Scotland showed a flat trend from 1981 to 1992, then a falling trend from 1999, whereas in England and Wales there was a continued rise up to the mid-1990s.

It is highly likely that the dramatic rise in crime in both jurisdictions during this period was explained to varying degrees both by an increase in criminal behaviour and by technical factors (such as changes to counting rules, the introduction of new crime categories and generally better recording practices) (see Maguire, 2012).

Smith (2005), however, attributes the more subdued rise in crime in Scotland, at least in part, to the different political culture and civic values that developed in Scottish society after the war (see McAra, 2008). Smith notes that the divergent trends in crime between Scotland and England and Wales are unlikely to have been the result of different social and economic conditions that may have impacted on crime because most of these were shared over this period. For example, absolute levels of unemployment, poverty and income inequality were similar, and there were analogous changes in indices of deprivation, rates of illegal drug use and shifts in family structure. Smith suggests that informal social controls which are known to reduce the risk of crime may have survived the post-war social and economic transformations better in Scotland, and that the emphasis on penal welfarism within Scottish policy (such as rehabilitation and reintegration) may have protected Scottish society against the worst excesses of punishment witnessed south of the border which may have exacerbated crime rates there.

From the 1990s onwards, the pattern of crime in Scotland shows a distinctly different trajectory. This is illustrated in Figure 12.4, which separates out the trends for recorded crimes and offences over the period from 1980 to 2014–15. Despite being at almost identical levels in 1980, there was a distinct difference in the trends for crimes and offences over the next three decades. The number of recorded crimes increased fairly steadily until 1991, before declining in two distinct phases: initially between 1992 and 1997–8; and then between 2004–5 and 2014–15. The decline in crime since the early 1990s bears a remarkable similarity to crime trends in North America and a number of other European countries which, as will be reported below, have experienced a dramatic and continued drop in crime as measured using official crime statistics since the early 1990s (Farrell et al., 2010; van Dijk and Tseloni, 2012).

Such similarities have led to claims of a global crime drop (Levitt, 2004), but as yet there is no consensus as to what the main drivers for this might be and important differences have been found between trends in different countries (Aebi, 2004; Morgan, 2014) which mitigate against claiming a global effect at the expense of ignoring important local differences. In addition, there is a lack of well-validated modelling approaches to exploring causal explanations (Zimring and Fagan, 2000) including very little consideration of the possibility that

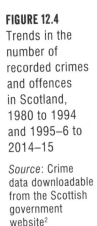

FIGURE 12.4

Trends in the number of recorded crimes and offences in Scotland, 1980 to 1994 and 1995–6 to 2014–15

Source: Crime data downloadable from the Scottish government website[2]

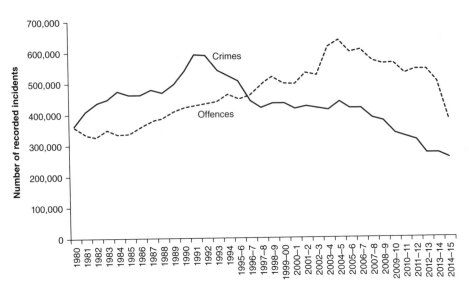

explanations for crime change may vary over time (Humphreys et al., forthcoming). This could be potentially important in Scotland, given that crime dropped over two distinct periods, one prior to devolution and the other several years after.

Turning to the trend in police-recorded offences, Figure 12.4 shows a slight decline after 1980 before a slow and steady increase from 1985 to 2002–3, followed by a sharp peak, and then the number of recorded offences starts to decline from 2004–5, more or less in parallel with the trend in crime. There is a particularly sharp drop in offences in the last three years (although changes in the classification of offences from 2013–14 onwards prevent direct comparison with earlier statistics). For around fifteen years, then, when the rate of crime was falling or remaining stable, the offence rate was continuing to increase.

These very different trend lines provide little support for the theory of a unified crime drop; or at least, they suggest that if some global factor or set of factors impacted on crime over this period, they did not have a commensurate effect on less serious forms of social disorder. In fact, it is highly probable that trends in lower level offences were subject to more localised influences over time since it is these types of crime that have been most subject to operational and legislative changes in Scotland. For example, a new Scottish Crime Recording Standard (SCRS) was introduced in 2004–5 aimed at establishing a more consistent and victim-centred approach to recording crime, which included ensuring that all low-level crimes reported to the police were formally recorded (Police Scotland, 2015).

It appears that the SCRS did have some effect (especially on low-level incidents like public disorder and petty assaults), as evidenced by the large spike in recorded offences between 2003 and 2005, although the exact impact cannot be independently verified (Scottish Government, 2005). It is also very clear that motor vehicle offences were driven up by more widespread enforcement of speeding offences and the use of speed cameras from this period.

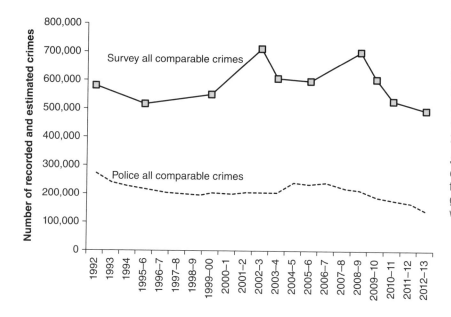

To assess whether the police-recorded figures reflect those of the Scottish crime surveys, Figure 12.5 compares both sources of data from 1992 to 2012–13. Six comparable crimes are included in this analysis: vandalism, theft of a motor vehicle, housebreaking, bicycle theft, assault and robbery. Like Figure 12.3, the police-recorded figures show a fairly steady downward trend over time, although there is some evidence of a slight increase in the mid-2000s. Over the entire period, the Scottish crime surveys also suggest that crime has reduced, although not to the same extent as the police data. There are also some periods of increasing crime that have been measured in the survey that do not appear in the police data. Note, in particular, the sizeable gap between the two lines, which highlights the vast number of crimes estimated to occur in Scotland that are not recorded by and reflected in the police figures. As noted above, caution is needed when interpreting any crime data; however, it appears from Figure 12.5 that the significant downward trend in crime witnessed in the recorded crime data is not as straightforward as first imagined.

To get a more detailed picture of how crime has changed over time, it is necessary to examine trends in specific types of crime. It is not possible within the scope of this chapter to investigate all crimes and offences in Scotland; therefore, attention will be restricted to two crime categories: crimes of dishonesty (which include housebreaking, vehicle theft, fraud and various other forms of theft or deception) and violent crime (which includes homicide, attempted murder, serious assault and robbery). These are two of the most important crime types, both in terms of their trends over time and because of their impact on Scottish society. They are also the categories of crime that have been most studied in the international literature, and therefore it is possible to compare trends in Scotland with a wide range of countries.

Figure 12.6 shows that the overarching trends for crimes of dishonesty and non-sexual crimes of violence were very similar until the early 1990s, where both peaked; however,

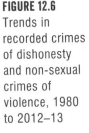

FIGURE 12.6

Trends in recorded crimes of dishonesty and non-sexual crimes of violence, 1980 to 2012–13

Source: Crime data downloadable from the Scottish government website

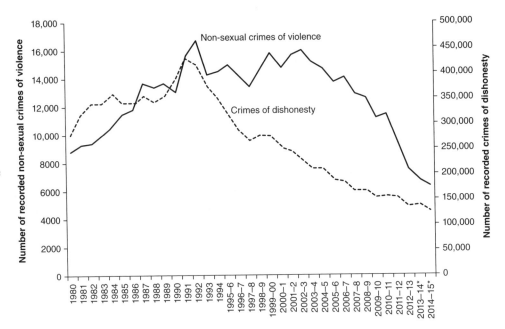

crimes of dishonesty have shown a dramatic and sustained period of decline since that time, whereas violent crime remained high for another fifteen years before declining significantly during the last decade. Note the very different scales of the y-axes in Figure 12.6, however. The scale on the left, for non-sexual crimes of violence, is much smaller in magnitude than the scale on the right, for crimes of dishonesty. In other words, crimes of dishonesty are a much bigger problem in volume terms than crimes of violence. We will now consider each of these crime categories in more detail.

Crimes of dishonesty

As illustrated in Figure 12.6, crimes of dishonesty have fallen by a massive 71 per cent since they peaked in 1991. This represents the largest reduction in any crime category in recent history and is the primary reason behind the overall drop in crime. Indeed, the percentage share of all crimes and offences that is contributed by crimes of dishonesty more than halved from 42 per cent in 1991 to 20 per cent in 2014–15. Almost all types of crimes of dishonesty have declined since the early 1990s, making it one of the most consistent crime categories in terms of its underlying trends. Figure 12.7 reveals the underlying trends for the crime groups that contribute to crimes of dishonesty.[4]

There are two groups which show the largest drops overall since 1991 and are more or less identical in terms of trend and scale after that period, although they show very different prior trends. These are theft by opening a lockfast place (OLP) (which includes theft and attempted theft from motor vehicles and other lockable places), which fell by

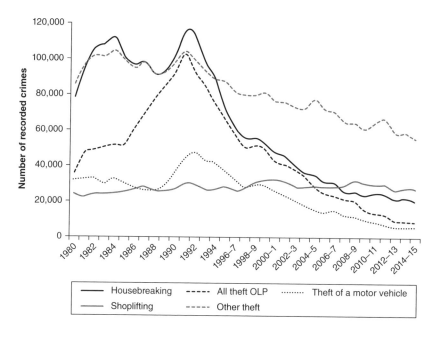

FIGURE 12.7

Trends in the crime groups that contribute to crimes of dishonesty, 1980 to 2014–15

Source: Crime data downloadable from the Scottish government website

92 per cent; and housebreaking (the Scottish equivalent of burglary, which includes domestic and non-domestic properties), which fell by 82 per cent. Theft of a motor vehicle and other forms of theft (which includes bicycle theft and various other forms of property theft) also declined significantly over this period (by 89 per cent and 47 per cent, respectively). The only group to show a small but steady increase over this period was shoplifting (although this could be due to better in-store detection and recording).

This national pattern of decline in crimes of dishonesty was replicated across most parts of the country. Between 1996–7 and 2014–15,[5] crimes of dishonesty fell in all thirty-two local authority areas. The average drop in crimes of dishonesty over this period was 56 per cent nationally, but this varied from 78 per cent in East Renfrewshire down to 22 per cent in Clackmannanshire. One local authority stands out as having very little change during this period: in Midlothian crime reduced by only 1 per cent overall, bucking the trend compared with other parts of Scotland. In absolute terms, the four largest cities (Glasgow, Edinburgh, Aberdeen and Dundee) benefited most from the reduction in crimes of dishonesty. Overall, however, most parts of Scotland benefited to some degree from this crime drop.

Police-recorded crimes of dishonesty can be compared with crime survey data for two of these groups, housebreaking and theft of a motor vehicle (MV), as shown in Figure 12.8. Looking at motor vehicle theft, there is a remarkably similar pattern between the two data sources over the period from 1992 to 2012–13, which indicates that the fall in recorded vehicle thefts was caused by a real decline in underlying crime. The two lines map so neatly because it is very rare for a vehicle to be stolen and not reported to the police (for insurance purposes); therefore, the survey provides very similar estimates to the recorded crime figures.

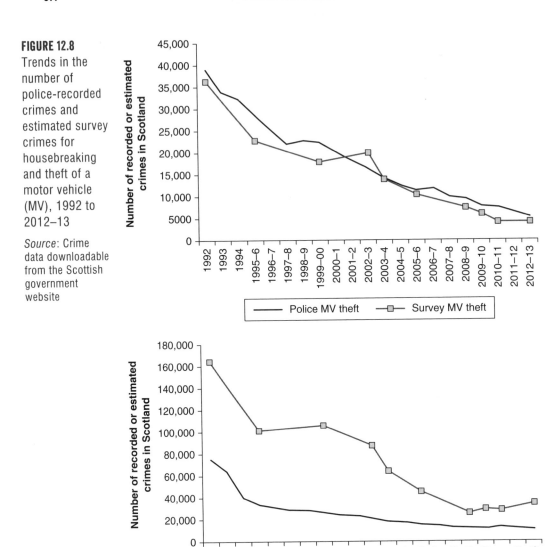

FIGURE 12.8

Trends in the number of police-recorded crimes and estimated survey crimes for housebreaking and theft of a motor vehicle (MV), 1992 to 2012–13

Source: Crime data downloadable from the Scottish government website

Looking at housebreaking, however, there is a significant gap between the two trend lines. This indicates that the vast majority of incidents of housebreaking that occurred in Scotland in the last two decades were not recorded by the police. Nevertheless, both data sources show a significant fall in housebreaking over time, and the gap between the two trend lines has closed dramatically, which indicates that far fewer housebreaking incidents have gone unrecorded in recent years. Note that the most recent surveys suggest a small rise in housebreaking, although this is not reflected in the recorded crime statistics.

This fall in property crime is not confined to Scotland. Similar declines have been observed in New Zealand (Mayhew, 2012), Canada (Ouimet, 2002), the United States (Zimring, 2007, 2012), Australia (R. Brown, 2015) and much of Western Europe (Aebi and Linde, 2010). A number of comparative studies have focused on burglary (known as housebreaking in Scotland) as this is a good indicator of overall volume crime. For example, Jan van Dijk and Andromachi Tseloni (2012) compared five nations, including Scotland, and concluded that, despite some differences in scale and timing, all showed a significant downward trend between 1990 and 2010.

More recently, the *European Sourcebook of Crime and Criminal Justice Statistics* (HEUNI, 2014), which examines crime trends from 2007 to 2011 across forty-one countries, confirms that motor vehicle crime has continued to decline consistently over time in almost all countries. Rates of vehicle theft in Scotland were around 1.5 times higher than the mean when compared across countries; however, Scotland had the fourth biggest drop in motor vehicle theft over this period.

Scotland's burglary rates were considerably lower than average when compared internationally, and it fell from twelfth to seventeenth in the rankings over this five-year period. The report notes that while burglary decreased between 2003 and 2007 in most countries, it had started to increase again in most countries thereafter, which suggests that the recent rise in Scotland's survey data may be reflecting a wider trend.

A range of explanations has been put forward for the dramatic fall in property crime, including demographic changes, immigration patterns, legalised abortion, increased police officer numbers, smarter policing practices, increased imprisonment, changing drug markets and consumption, economic recession and reductions in exposure to lead pollution (for comprehensive reviews, see Blumstein and Rosenfeld, 2008; Farrell, 2013; Levitt, 2004).

As yet there is no theoretical consensus as to what has caused this phenomenon and few of the theories have been properly tested. The most promising explanation for the fall in car crime rests on the 'security hypothesis': that is, improved security within the vehicle industry has significantly reduced opportunities for all forms of property crime across all countries (Farrell, 2013; Fujita and Maxfield, 2012). Causal explanations for the decline in burglary have been harder to pin down; however, there is evidence that changing economic conditions, consumer confidence and reductions in black market economies played some part in driving down burglary in the United States and Europe (Aebi and Linde, 2012; Rosenfeld and Messner, 2012).

Violent crime

While crimes of dishonesty are a bigger problem for the Scottish public in volume terms, it is as a violent country that we have gained an unenviable reputation. In truth, the problem has mainly been localised to specific parts of the west of Scotland and even recent research has shown that the legacy of Glasgow's old gang culture lives on (Bannister et al., 2010; Williams and Carnochan, 2015).

Following the publication of a UN report in 2005, Scotland was dubbed the most violent country in the developed world and Glasgow was awarded the unflattering title of homicide capital of Europe by the UK media. More recently, the UK Peace Index ranked Glasgow as the least peaceful major urban centre after comparing its rates of homicide and violent crime with ten other areas, including London and Belfast which were ranked second and third, respectively (Institute for Economics and Peace, 2013), while the UN Global Study on Homicide revealed that Scotland's use of knives and other sharp objects in homicide cases was consistently higher since 2005 than every other country in Europe for which data were available (UNODC, 2013).

Non-sexual crimes of violence only represent about 1 per cent of the overall crime count per year. As illustrated previously in Figure 12.6, overall trends increased during the 1980s, remained high and fairly stable until the mid-2000s, and then declined sharply. However, trends for the four underlying categories of violence were quite different. Figure 12.9 shows that the largest group, attempted murder and serious assault, showed a steady increase throughout the 1980s and remained at a high level until the mid-2000s, whereas robbery remained relatively stable throughout the 1980s, only showing a distinct spike in the early 1990s before falling steadily thereafter. In fact, the trend in robbery was more similar to crimes of dishonesty than other types of violent crime – which is perhaps appropriate given its potential link to similar causal factors.

The trend in homicide is very hard to discern from Figure 12.9 because the numbers are so small; however, the most recent statistics published by Scottish Government (2015c) indicate that homicide has shown a pattern of decline similar to that of attempted murder and serious assault. In fact, the Scottish homicide rate is at its lowest level since 1976, the earliest point at which data can be reliably compared.

The final group, 'other violence' (which includes threats, extortion, cruel and unusual treatment of children, and abduction) increased steadily from the early 1980s to the early 2000s before falling. However, most of this increase was driven by a rise in the reporting of child cruelty cases which is most probably due to better reporting and recording rather than a real rise, although it does coincide with a rise in reports of rape and attempted rape (not shown here) which suggests there could be some connection between sexual and non-sexual violence. Nevertheless, this significant and consistent downward turn in all types of violence throws into question whether Scotland's violent reputation is still justified.

There was considerable variation across the country in terms of the local authorities that had benefited from a reduction in violence from 1996–7 to 2014–15 (Figure 12.9). In absolute terms, the city of Glasgow saw the largest reduction in non-sexual crimes of violence. Indeed, it is notable, given its troubled reputation, that Glasgow and most of its neighbouring local authorities in the west of Scotland witnessed the largest relative drop in violence. Of the ten local authorities where crime had fallen the most, nine were from the Strathclyde region and all of them had seen a fall of over 60 per cent in violent crime (the average was 55 per cent). A few local authorities, mainly very small ones, had seen a small drop in violence or even (in the case of the Islands) an increase over this period. Overall, however, most parts of Scotland saw some reduction in recorded violence.

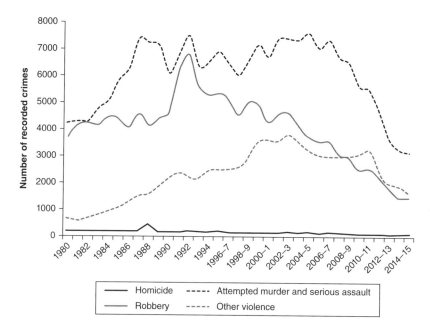

FIGURE 12.9
Trends in the crime groups that contribute to non-sexual crimes of violence, 1980 to 2014–15

Source: Crime data downloadable from the Scottish government website

Crime survey data for violence include robbery, serious assault and petty assault, the latter of which is recorded in the police statistics as an offence.[6] Distinguishing between serious and petty assault is important because they appear to show very different trends over time. The charts in Figure 12.10 highlight a large and growing gap in overall violence as measured by the police and the crime survey, although a recent decline is reflected in both data sources. The lower chart, however, indicates that this widening gap largely reflects a growing difference in the amount of petty assault recorded by the police in comparison with survey crime. Indeed, the survey data suggest that serious violent crime declined significantly over time but there was a large growth in low-level, petty forms of violence within Scottish society. Emerging evidence suggests that while violent crime has declined for many, it has not reduced among those who are at the highest risk of repeated victimisation and who live in the most deprived communities in Scotland (McVie et al., 2015).

International research on the crime drop suggests that rates of property crime fell first and were followed by modest falls in violence at a later stage (van Dijk and Tseloni, 2012). Indeed, some theories about the fall in property crime have been extended to cover violent crime, including the debut or keystone crime hypothesis which suggests that reductions in property crime (arising from improvements in security) may have had a knock-on effect on violence by eliminating the natural progression from property crime to violence (Farrell et al., 2011). However, the steady and constant downward trend in property crime has been less clearly mirrored internationally in the findings on violence, where the picture has been described as heterogeneous (Clarke, 2013: 2). The work by van Dijk and Tseloni (2012), for example, indicated that the downward trend in violence may have only persisted over time for some countries.

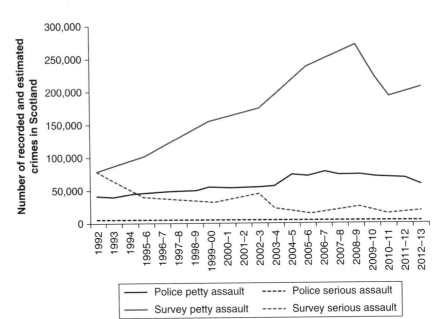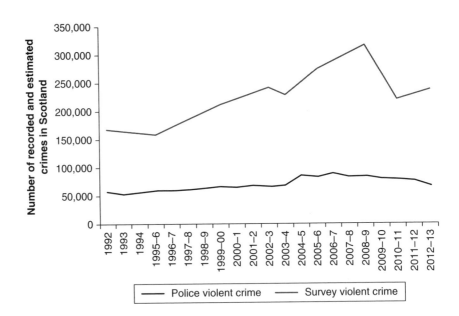

FIGURE 12.10

Trends in the number of police-recorded crimes and estimated survey crimes for all violence, and petty and serious assault, 1992 to 2012–13

Source: Crime data downloadable from the Scottish government website

As noted earlier, comparisons between Scotland and other countries make for stark reading. The 2012–13 Scottish Crime and Justice Survey reported that the rate of violence (including assault and robbery) was 543 per 10,000 adults in Scotland compared with only 420 per 10,000 adults in England and Wales. This indicates that the violence rate was 29 per cent greater in Scotland than England and Wales during that twelve-month period. The *European Sourcebook of Crime and Criminal Justice Statistics* found that homicide rates varied significantly between countries in a way that could not be explained by different definitions (HEUNI, 2014).[7]

Scotland showed one of the biggest declines in its homicide rate (27 per cent from 2007 to 2011); however, it was still ranked between first and third highest each year – between two to three times higher than the international mean. Similarly, Scotland was consistently ranked first in terms of its rate of assault across all years. Even though it showed a 10 per cent drop over time, this was far lower than for most other countries and Scotland was consistently five times higher than the mean in terms of its assault rate.

The reasons underlying Scotland's violence problem are complex and difficult to tease out – they link to a wide range of economic, social, cultural and historical factors and are deeply rooted in poverty and social deprivation (McAra and McVie, 2015). Violence in Scotland has also been linked to drug markets, alcohol consumption and an increase in the use of knives and other weapons, especially in the west of Scotland where violence has historically been highest (Bannister et al., 2010). The very large drop in serious violence since the mid-2000s coincides with a particularly intensive period of policing activity, including the establishment of the Violence Reduction Unit (Burns et al., 2011) and a dramatic growth in the use of stop-and-search in the Strathclyde area (Murray, 2014). Both of these have been credited by the police as reducing serious violence; however, this has not been subject to rigorous evaluation and there were reductions in violence in many areas of Scotland where these policies were not operating.

In addition, there have been a number of government-led educational and preventative initiatives introduced in Scotland to tackle violence, including the No Knives Better Lives campaign, the Medics Against Violence preventative programme and Mentors in Violence Prevention training introduced in some Scottish secondary schools (Scottish Government, 2015e). Without proper evaluation, it is almost impossible to disentangle the relative impacts of one or more of these initiatives on violent crime in Scotland. It is notable, though, that England and Wales have seen similar reductions in violent crime over the same time period (ONS, 2015), which reduces the likelihood of localised causation.

What next for social order in Scotland?

Scotland has always prided itself on having a distinctive and independent justice system that is predicated on principles of social welfare and driven by a strong civic and political agenda that set it apart from its UK neighbours and largely protected it from wider challenge prior to devolution. This chapter has highlighted a radical programme of reform to the Scottish system of crime control and penal policy in the years following the Scotland Act 1993, driven largely by increased political involvement and interference in both organisational and operational matters. Some of these changes have called into question the notion of a distinctive Scottish penal identity and undermined certain aspects of its administrative structure and philosophical underpinnings. More recently, the pendulum appears to have swung back in the opposite direction; however, competing rationales make it difficult to see exactly how distinctive Scottish justice is compared with other nations.

Interestingly, trends in crime over this period have changed dramatically and it is almost certain that some of these changes have been driven in part by systemic forces (especially at the less serious end of the offending spectrum) such as better recording and more intensive policing practices. However, there have been major changes in both crimes of dishonesty and non-sexual crimes of violence that appear to reflect real and widespread behavioural change and which are largely in line with changes in other, similar developed countries.

To most of us who live here, Scotland does not feel like a particularly violent society and, indeed, we are at little risk of violence. However, within small communities and pockets of Scottish society the spectre of violent crime is as prevalent today as it has been in decades past. Despite a continuing reduction in homicide and serious assaults, we continue to sit at the top of a number of international league tables that make it difficult to shake off our unenviable reputation for violence.

Conclusion

At the time of writing (April 2016), another set of Scottish elections looms. It is clear that criminal justice and penal policy should be at the heart of debates about the future of Scotland and its people, especially because it interlinks so closely with wider public policy concerns about welfare, inequality and social justice. Despite being a small nation, Scotland deserves to be as proud of its low crime rates as it is of its other remarkable achievements in recent years. Indeed, it is because we are a small nation that we should be able to identify and eradicate the perennial wicked problem of violence in those small nooks and crannies where it still resides.

Maintaining social order is neither art nor science, it is a carefully balanced set of decisions made on the basis of available evidence and within the constraints of the prevailing resources, circumstances and social context. Criminal justice policy in Scotland is not delivered by one system, but by a collection of autonomous and closely connected organisations, each with their own agendas, pressures and priorities, but with one common goal. The future of social order in Scotland must be concerned with ensuring that each of these organisations work as effectively as possible in achieving this goal and that political influence is provided only to support and sustain those efforts.

Chapter summary

So what have we learned in this chapter?

- That Scotland's criminal justice system developed relatively autonomously from that of the rest of the UK following the Act of Union in 1707. Pre-devolution, there was relatively little disruption to the criminal justice system in Scotland, arguably because its distinctive underlying principles, such as a prominent welfare-based ethos, were already deeply embedded.

- That the period following devolution marks one of the most significant periods of change within Scottish criminal justice in terms of both institutional transformation and penal policy development.

- That the post-devolution period marked one of the most turbulent periods in policing history, with the establishment of a new single police force which was subject to major controversy, intense public scrutiny and political intervention.

- That, according to both police-recorded crime statistics and Scottish crime surveys, there were significant falls in most crime types, but especially crimes of dishonesty and non-sexual crimes of violence.

- That Scotland has gained a particular reputation for violence so the fall in violent crime was welcome, although it mainly consisted of a drop in serious forms of violence, whereas there is evidence of an increase in low-level petty assault over the same period.

- That, in international terms, trends in violence have seen less consistent patterns of change than for crimes of dishonesty, and while Scotland has seen a drop in violent crime it still tends to be high in comparison with other countries.

Questions for discussion

1. What factors peculiar to Scotland enabled it to retain an independent legal system following the Act of Union in 1707?

2. In what ways did devolution mark a significant shift in crime control policy and governance?

3. Why did Scottish policing become more politically charged after the establishment of a single police force?

4. How might we explain rising imprisonment rates during a period of falling crime?

5. Why might the very large drop in crimes of dishonesty in Scotland have been mirrored in many other countries?

6. What factors might be responsible for Scotland's reputation as a violent country?

Annotated reading

(a) There have been several useful overviews of crime and criminal justice in Scotland which are worthy of more detailed examination. In particular: P. Duff and N. Hutton, *Criminal Justice in Scotland* (1999); H. Croall, G. Mooney and M. Munro, *Criminal Justice in Scotland* (2010); and H. Croall, G. Mooney and M. Munro, *Crime, Justice and Society in Scotland* (2015).

(b) For useful statistical information on crime and justice in Scotland, Scottish Government 'Crime and Justice Statistics' webpages provide a high-level summary of statistical trends in crime and disorder, policing, violent crime, drugs and alcohol, and criminal justice processes including sentencing, imprisonment and criminal justice social work. Additional links on each page will take you to more detailed statistical bulletins and spreadsheets containing raw data that allow further analysis. These can be accessed on the Scottish Government website at: www.gov.scot/Topics/Statistics/Browse/Crime-Justice?utm_source=website&utm_medium=navigation&utm_campaign=statistics-topics.

(c) To conduct more detailed secondary analysis of the Scottish Crime and Justice Survey datasets for research purposes, see the data from the UK Data Service, which also contains details of the survey questionnaires, technical reports and metadata. You will also find a wide range of other crime datasets here that may be of interest, including both survey data and administrative data sources. To register to use this service and access the crime datasets, visit the UKDS website at: https://www.ukdataservice.ac.uk/get-data/themes/crime.

Notes

1   Scottish crime recording reflects a subtle distinction between 'crimes' which are more serious criminal acts, including violent crimes, sexual crimes and crimes of dishonesty, and 'offences' which are less serious incidents, such as motor vehicle and public order offences (see Justice Analytical Service, 2014). The distinction is made primarily for statistical reporting purposes, and the seriousness of the crime generally relates to the maximum sentence that may be imposed by a court (Scottish Government, 2015c).

2   Changes to the statistics for offences from 2013–14 onwards (see Scottish Government, 2014: 2–3) prevent direct comparability of offence groups.

3   The police-recorded crime data were provided by Scottish Government on request. Data have been adjusted to make them as comparable as possible with the survey data (i.e. excluding non-domestic incidents). Police data for all years are shown; however, survey data are only available for the years indicated by markers, so it is possible that trends in between these points were different. In addition, the number of crimes measured by the survey are estimates and, therefore, subject to confidence intervals (not shown here). Even accounting for this, a sizeable gap remains between the two sources.

4   For reasons of clarity, two groups have been excluded from the chart: 'fraud' and 'other crimes of dishonesty'. These are the two smallest groups and both also showed a decline over time.

5   The starting point of 1996–7 has been selected here as this marks the last period of significant local government reorganisation in which the boundaries of the current thirty-two Scottish local authorities were revised.

6   Serious assault is defined as 'an assault or attack in which the victim sustains injury resulting in detention in hospital as an inpatient, for the treatment of that injury, or any of [a list] of injuries whether or not detained in hospital' (Scottish Government, 2015e: 89). All other assaults are defined as common or petty assaults.

7   Concerns have been expressed by Scottish Government over the comparisons of violence rates in the *European Sourcebook* statistics due to differences in definition and measurement.

13

'RACE' AND ETHNICITY IN SCOTLAND

How does Scotland relate to 'race' and ethnicity? Here is how we like to see ourselves, and how we hope others see us (see Figure 13.1).

As sociologists, we should be properly sceptical of claims that anyone can be accepted as a Scot so long as they behave in a 'Scottish' way. Simply flag-waving is not enough to be accepted as 'one of us'; and would such a claim be accepted in any case? This chapter is about how racial and ethnic relations operate in Scotland, and we ask whether the assumption that Scots are more liberal and tolerant than others, notably the English, stands up to scrutiny.

FIGURE 13.1
Scotland against Racism demonstration, 2010

Source: Author's photograph

Chapter aims

- To examine the assumptions and assertions about 'race' and ethnicity in Scotland.

- To review what is meant by terms like 'race' and ethnicity.

- To assess what Scotland looks like today in terms of multiculturalism and multi-racialism, especially in comparison with the other 'home nations' of England and Wales.

- To analyse what 'being Muslim' means in contemporary Scotland, and whether you can be Muslim and Scottish.

- To survey the extent to which 'native' Scots are willing to accept non-white people as Scottish.

Conventional wisdoms

In addressing these issues, much depends on assumptions. Broadly speaking, there are two competing accounts of 'race' and ethnicity in Scotland. On the one hand, there is the view reflected in the image in Figure 13.1: that anyone can be Scottish if they want to be; that, in the words of the government, there is one Scotland but many cultures (see Figure 13.2).

Others take the view that this is too sanguine; that there is a dark side to Scotland, reflected in street-level racist attacks, and drawing upon older habits of religious sectarianism. See Elinor Kelly's comment: 'Scottish devolution has failed as abysmally as its Welsh counterpart in achieving inclusion and participation by its black and minority ethnic population but, as in Wales, the curtain of nationalist struggle cannot be drawn across the stage in the same way as before' (2004: 83).

The task of this chapter is not to come down on one side or the other, for social reality is much too complex to come to simple conclusions, but to review the evidence as best we can. Let us begin, then, by reviewing the terms we are using.

FIGURE 13.2
Scottish Government's 'No Place for Racism' campaign, 2015

Source: I am grateful to Scottish Government for permission to use this

'Race'

Why is the term 'race' in inverted commas in the chapter title? The sociologist Robert Miles argued that 'race' cannot operate as a meaningfully analytic concept because the particular biological features of human beings were 'racialised' in such a way that social and psychological attributes were attributed to people by others, notably the powerful. In any case, modern science has discredited the supposed existence of biological differences between 'races'. As Miles observed:

> The idea of 'race' no longer had a 'real' object. What remained was the common-sense idea that 'races' existed, an idea sustained by the unquestionable reality of somatic and cultural differences between people. If social scientists retain the idea of 'race' as an analytical concept to refer to the social reproduction and consequences of this belief, it necessarily implicitly carries the meaning of its use in the everyday world. (1994: 2)

The social anthropologist Michael Banton used the concept *phenotype*, or physical appearance. He says: 'No one has ever seen another person's race. People perceive phenotypical differences of colour, hair form, underlying bone structure and so on' (Banton, 1997: 16). He goes on to say: '"Race" is often used as if it were an objective, scientific and culture-free designation of differences of appearance. It is not. The very use of this word to identify such a classification brings with it a host of cultural associations deriving from the historical circumstances in which the word acquired special meanings' (1997: 16).

In the middle of the nineteenth century, 'typologists', as they were called, believed that each racial type had inherent psychological characteristics which enabled them fit for tasks, that 'races' had inherited dispositions for thought and action. Two such theorists were the French Count Arthur de Gobineau (*Essays on the Inequality of Human Races*, 1853–4) and the Scottish anatomist Robert Knox (*Races of Men*, 1850) who achieved notoriety by purchasing, for purposes of dissection, the cadavers stolen by the 'body snatchers' in Edinburgh, the notorious Burke and Hare, as in the ditty: 'Burke's the butcher, Hare's the thief, Knox the boy who buys the beef.' In later life, Dr Knox contented himself with drawing up theories of human nature on the basis of anatomical differences. His notoriety was reinforced in the 1930s by the playwright James Bridie in *The Anatomist*, based loosely on Knox.

Few people these days accept 'racial' theories of human behaviour, except on the fringes of far-right politics. Nevertheless, a yearning for more simple 'biological' explanations of human behaviour is never far away, such as believing that there is a bit of the brain which makes us do what we do, that our social behaviour is somehow determined by our biology, as we saw in our previous discussion of gender.

If 'race' is properly employed by social scientists to account for human behaviour, it is because it is a concept in common use, the inverted commas alerting us to its problematic status, and the fact that others use it to account for their actions. Thomas Eriksen, the Norwegian anthropologist, argued for putting 'race' in inverted commas 'to stress that it has dubious descriptive value. Social science studies "race", not because it believes people can be divided into "races" biologically, but because the object of study is the social and cultural relevance of the *notion* that race exists' (1993: 5, italics in original). Thus, if influential people developed a theory about the personality traits of people with red hair, it might become a field for academic research for similar reasons, even though we might view such a theory as nonsense in social scientific terms. There is W.I. Thomas' famous dictum (1928), the 'definition of the situation', that if people believe something to be true, they act out its consequences, whether they are 'mistaken' or not.

'Ethnicity'

If the notion of 'race' is too problematic, then its cognate, 'ethnicity', seems a better term, and in common usage in academic and public policy writing. The language of 'ethnic groups' and 'ethnic minorities' is common currency. The census, for example, provides relevant data (see below), and Scottish Government has published an *Ethnicity Evidence Review* (Scottish Government, 2013). 'Ethnicity', however, does not really solve the problem. Eriksen observes:

> In everyday language the word ethnicity still has a ring of 'minority issues' and 'race relations', but in social anthropology it refers to aspects of relationships between groups which consider themselves, and are regarded by others, as being culturally distinctive ... majorities and dominant peoples are no less 'ethnic' than minorities. (1993: 4)

The term 'ethnicity' is credited to the American sociologists Lloyd Warner (1941) and David Riesman (1953), but, surprisingly, does not appear as an entry in the *Oxford English Dictionary* until the 1970s. Given the salience of 'ethnic groups', notably in US cities as described by the Chicago School in the 1920s and 1930s, this may seem hard to believe, but Robert Park's classic Chicago study *The City* (Park and Burgess, 1984 [1925]) contains no index reference to 'ethnicity'. To be 'ethnic' was to be 'other', 'not-us', and hence the term 'minus-one ethnics' has been used to describe white Anglo-Saxon Protestants – Digby Balsell's WASPs – the 'us' against which 'they' were defined as 'ethnics'.

Closer to home, Banton observes:

> In Britain, the English have regarded Scots, Welsh, Gujeratis, Afro-Caribbeans, Poles etc., as groups defined by ethnic attributes. They [the English] have not regarded themselves as possessing an ethnicity, because, being the largest group and the dominant element in the population, there has been no pressure upon them to distinguish their group from the society as a whole. (1997: 17)

If Banton is correct, the English are *minus-one ethnics*, the implicit benchmark against which 'ethnic others' are to be measured, and usually found wanting. 'Minus-one' is the norm from which others are deemed to deviate. This brings us to a key point in our discussion of 'race' and ethnicity in Scotland; it is based on comparisons especially with England.

To be sure, there is a tension running through the analysis of 'ethnicity', because it has a social scientific-*etic* which runs up against a public discourse-*emic*.[1] We might take the view that ethnicity can only be talked about in the former, strict, sense, but that would be to rule out a lot of official statistics, as well as people's own accounts of themselves and others. And in any case, it is not sensible to treat official census data as having the same truth status as that of the person in the street. After all, the Office for National Statistics, and the Office for Censuses and Populations in particular, have invested considerable resources in getting academics to refine the concepts and categories they use. It is arguably better to take the view that 'ethnicity' should be understood in the round so that we can properly comprehend its use and meaning in the wider society.

Are Scots 'ethnics'?

Before we examine what official statistics tell us about ethnicity in Scotland, we have to tackle a basic issue: are 'Scots' an ethnic group as implied in Banton's comment above?[2] And if our answer is 'no', are they possibly 'minus-one ethnics'? We could fall back on the conventional wisdom that 'ethnics' are 'not us', but others who are different and possibly inferior in some respects.

Furthermore, are 'ethnics' not incomers, immigrants, who have settled here, bringing their own cultures and ways of life with them? That is closer to the conventional wisdom but still does not get us very far. For example, are people who were born in England and now live in Scotland 'ethnic'? They probably would not consider themselves to be such, nor in truth would many 'Scots', which itself is in inverted commas to flag that even such a term is problematic.

Who is a Scot?

Who, we might ask, is a Scot anyway? Someone born and living in Scotland? Or perhaps not even living in Scotland – an *émigré*? And if you are not born in Scotland, can you ever *become* 'Scottish', that is to consider yourself such, and be treated so by other people? In any case, it is almost unheard of to describe Scots as a 'national minority' in the British state, even though technically they are a numerical minority, and Scotland is thought of as a nation.

Language matters. Here is a comment from the UK report on the Council of Europe Framework Convention for the Protection of National Minorities:

'National Minority' is not a legally defined term within the UK. Our report is based
on the definition of racial group as set out in the Race Relations Act 1976 which
defines a racial group as 'a group of persons defined by colour, race, nationality
(including citizenship) or ethnic or national origins'. This includes our ethnic
minority communities (or visible minorities) and the Scots, Irish and Welsh,
who are defined as a racial group by virtue of their national origins. Gypsies (and
Travellers in Northern Ireland) are also considered a racial group under the Act. It
should be stressed, however, that these historic national identities within the UK
are in no way ethnically exclusive. Members of ethnic minority communities, just
as much as the rest of the UK population, may feel an identity with one or other
of the UK's constituent parts. Being Welsh, for example, does not depend upon
being white. (http://webarchive.nationalarchives.gov.uk/20120919132719/www.
communities.gov.uk/documents/communities/pdf/152275.pdf)

What is interesting about that observation is that 'the Scots, Irish and Welsh ... are defined
as a *racial group by virtue of their national origins'*. Presumably the English are excluded
because they are a statistical majority in these islands, but it is a nice example of the (con)
fusion of 'race' and 'nation', despite the coda that non-white people can be Welsh too.

These are big questions, which we will address fully later in the book when we discuss
'identity' (Chapters 18 and 19), but they are relevant to our discussions here. We might, of
course, be rather impatient of such issues, preferring the taken-for-granted assumptions
'out there' in the society around us, but we cannot be sure precisely what they are. Does it
matter? Surely it does, because who 'we' are thought to be determines the norm, accepts
more or less unthinkingly what it means to be Scottish, except when there is dispute about
'real' Scots. Claims that 'my granny was a McTavish' may not matter much to those born
and living in Scotland, but diasporic claims to 'belonging' on the basis of an ancestral claim
may be food and drink for much of the tourist industry (see Chapter 20).

The distinction between 'ethnic group' and 'nation' is, in any case, complex, even fuzzy.
Richard Jenkins refers us to Max Weber's observation that the belief in common ancestry is a
consequence of collective political action, rather than its cause. In other words, we feel a common inheritance *because* we act together; collective action generates the feeling of belonging.
Jenkins observes that a sense of 'ethnic commonality is a form of monopolistic social closure:
it defines membership, eligibility and access' (2008: 10). This is what Max Weber defined as a
'status group', and, thus, the possibilities for collective action rooted in 'ethnicity' are indefinite
and flexible. Furthermore, Jenkins comments 'ethnic groups are what people believe or think
them to be; cultural differences mark "group-ness", they do not cause it (or indelibly character-
ize it); ethnic identification arises out of, and within, interaction between groups' (2008: 11).

Concepts like ethnicity and nationalism are closely linked; they draw 'on the same analytical breath', for each is a matter of cultural definition, of shared meanings, of
identification, both collective and individual, and they are malleable. Thus, says Jenkins,
'the "nation" and "national identity" or "nationality" are, respectively, varieties of ethnic
collectivity and ethnicity, and are likely to be historically contingent, context-derived, and
defined and redefined in negotiation and transaction' (2008: 148); as a result all nationalisms are in some sense 'ethnic'. The distinction mark, according to Thomas Eriksen, is that

nationalism has to do with the *state*, actual or aspired to; that it is overtly 'political'. Ethnic and national categories are closer as analytical concepts than we think.

We might take the view, however, that being 'Scottish' is a matter of territory (*demos*) rather than ethnicity (*ethnos*), that it is a matter of 'place' and not 'tribe'. Here we encounter the distinction between 'civic' and 'ethnic', one of the staple antinomies in the study of nationalism, and we will discuss the distinction once we have explored more fully what 'ethnicity' means in Scotland.

In practice, however, the distinction between civic and ethnic is hard to sustain analytically. As Hearn pointed out, 'we should bear in mind that what these conceptual pairs [such as civic/ethnic] ultimately define is opposing styles of arguments about what nations are, and how social values are created, rather than actual types of nations, or societies' (2000: 194). Hearn doubts whether Scottish nationalism is as 'civic' as it claims, as it draws upon cultural histories and identifiers because the political pay-off is greater. Nevertheless, the ideology of 'civic' Scotland, that being Scottish is defined territorially, has particular relevance to our arguments in this chapter about 'race' and ethnicity conventionally defined, and it is to that we now turn (see Figure 13.3).

FIGURE 13.3
'Refugees Welcome Here'

Source: STUC publicity for March and Rally against Racism 2015. Reproduced with their permission

One Scotland, many cultures?

The most comprehensive source of data on ethnicity in Scotland derives from the decennial census, the latest in 2011. The relevant question in that census asked people a simple question, 'What is your ethnic group?', according to their own perceived ethnic group and cultural background.[3] There followed a series of tick boxes for categories such as 'white Scottish', 'white other British', 'white Irish', 'white Polish', 'white other'.[4] The point of the exercise was to get straightforward information on how people chose to self-describe;[5] no more, no less, and only one choice was possible. Fully 96 per cent described themselves as 'white', the vast majority as 'white Scottish' (84 per cent), with 'white other British' (largely being born in England) at 8 per cent. 'Non-British white' (4 per cent) comprised 'white Polish' (61,000) or 'white Irish' (54,000), while 4 per cent were 'minority ethnic', mainly 'Pakistani' (49,000), 'Chinese' (34,000) or 'Indian' (33,000).

Scotland's ethnic mix

These are the key points from the 2011 Scottish census data:

- While Scotland in 2011 was a much more diverse country than ten years earlier (the numbers in the minority ethnic group had doubled over the period), Scotland's 'minority ethnic' population, at 4 per cent, is much lower than England's (15 per cent). The proportion in Wales is similar to Scotland and twice that in Northern Ireland (2 per cent).

- Scotland's 'Asian' population is the largest minority ethnic group (3 per cent) and has doubled in number since 2001.[6] The largest proportion is 'Pakistani' (35 per cent), whose numbers have increased by over 50 per cent in the decade. The numbers of 'Chinese', 'Indian' and 'Bangladeshi' have more than doubled, and 'other Asians' more than three-fold, albeit from a low base. The 'African, Caribbean or Black' population increased more than four-fold, by 28,000 since 2001.

- The 'non-British White' group has also increased, from 3 to 4 per cent (127,000, to 222,000), and includes 'white Polish', 'white Irish' and 'other white', mainly other East European, other West European, North American, Australian/New Zealand. The numbers of Polish-born people in Scotland increased twenty-fold (from 3000 to 55,000), a proportionately greater increase than in the rest of the UK where it was ten-fold.

- More than 5 per cent of the populations of the four main cities belong to 'ethnic minorities', with Glasgow having the highest share (12 per cent), followed by Edinburgh and Aberdeen (8 per cent each) and Dundee (6 per cent).

- Edinburgh has the highest proportion of 'white other British' (mainly English) at 12 per cent, and both Edinburgh and Aberdeen have the highest percentage of 'white Polish' (3 per cent each).

- All local authority areas (excluding Eilean Siar (Western Isles) and Orkney) have at least 1 per cent of their populations belonging to 'ethnic minorities', a relative transformation since 2001 when, with the exception of Aberdeen, only the Central Belt had that share of population.

Plainly, Scotland is a much more ethnically diverse country than it was at the turn of the century. We might assume that how people define themselves is simply a matter of where they were born, and that is the most common criterion that most people use (see McCrone and Bechhofer, 2015: 30–1). It is not, however, straightforward, as we can gauge from the misuse of the term 'immigrant' in everyday speech. To use 'immigrant' as a synonym for 'non-white' is to commit a category error.

Consider the following numbers: 60 per cent of self-describing 'Asians' living in Scotland were born in the Middle East or Asia, 31 per cent in Scotland and 7 per cent in England.[7] Among 'Africans', more than three-quarters (77 per cent) were born in Africa, 15 per cent in Scotland and 5 per cent in England. Among 'Caribbeans and Blacks', the proportions are fairly evenly divided between 29 per cent born in the Americas or Caribbean, 31 per cent in Scotland and 22 per cent in England. We can see these differences in Figure 13.4.

Three in ten, then, of 'Asians' and 'Caribbeans and Blacks' were born in Scotland, and thus are 'native' to the country in terms of birthplace. Step migration from England to Scotland is highest among 'Caribbeans and Blacks' (22 per cent), but relatively low among the other two ethnic minority groups (7 and 5 per cent, respectively). Plainly, the relationship between where people were born and how they describe themselves is quite complex.

In terms of living conditions, and as measured by the Scottish Index of Multiple Deprivation (SIMD) (see Chapter 7), 'Africans' and 'white Polish' are twice as likely to live in areas of deprivation as the average population, and one-quarter of 'Caribbean and Black'.[8] In contrast with England, where 'minority ethnic

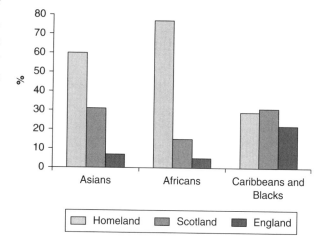

FIGURE 13.4 Ethnic identity by birthplace

Source: Census Scotland 2011, table LC2205SC

groups' are more likely to live in 'deprived' areas, proportionately fewer in Scotland do: less than 10 per cent of people describing themselves as Pakistanis or Bangladeshis live in officially deprived areas, in contrast to more than 30 per cent in England.

Ethnicity and identity

Statistics such as these can seem a little dry, but they tell us vital things about who lives in Scotland. What is sociologically interesting about them? The most obvious point is that most people living in contemporary Scotland describe themselves as 'white' and are born in Scotland. A much lower percentage belong to officially designated 'minority ethnic groups' (around 4 per cent) than in England (15 per cent). So whom do people identify with in terms of national identity? The 2011 census also gives us basic 'national identity' data, which will be the topic of later chapters, but they are worth flagging up here (see Figure 13.5).

'White Scots' are overwhelmingly 'Scottish only' (73 per cent), and only one in five say they are 'Scottish and British only'. 'Other British' (who are overwhelmingly English-born)

FIGURE 13.5
Ethnic group by
national identity

Source: Census
Scotland 2011,
table DC 2202Sc

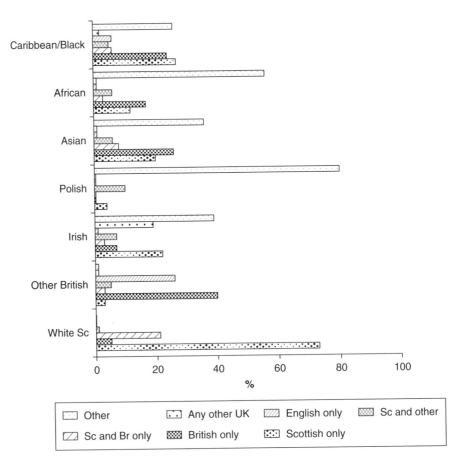

are split between saying they are 'British only' (40 per cent) or 'English only' (26 per cent), and only about one in ten make any claim to being 'Scottish'.[9]

The 'Irish' are spread across 'Other' (39 per cent), presumably citizens of the Irish Republic, 'Scottish only' (22 per cent) and 'Any other UK' (19 per cent), presumably Northern Ireland. The 'Polish' mainly self-define as 'Poles' (80 per cent), while 'Asians' divide 36 per cent 'Other', 26 per cent 'British only' and 20 per cent 'Scottish only'.[10] 'Caribbeans and Blacks' split almost evenly between saying they are 'Scottish only' (27 per cent), 'British only' (24 per cent) or 'Other' (26 per cent). 'Africans' are 56 per cent 'Other', 17 per cent 'British only' and 12 per cent 'Scottish only'. In short, we see a complex kaleidoscope of self-ascribed 'ethnicity' and 'national identity', even using something as rough and ready as census data categories. It is not a simple task to read off how people construe their ethnic and national identities from how they describe their 'ethnic group'.

Behind these statistics lie much more complex political and cultural agendas: who is thought to be 'one of us'?

Understanding ethnicity

Social categories such as 'ethnic groups' are not 'neutral', but resonant with cultural and even political meanings. Think, for example, of the term 'Muslim'. We might simply treat it as a synonym for a follower of 'Islam', but especially since the events of 9/11 it has become a 'racialised' and politicised category, replete with threat (Meer, 2015; Virdee, 2014). Indeed, the 2011 census records that since 2001 there has been an 80 per cent increase in the numbers of people in Scotland describing themselves as 'Muslim'. Furthermore, 90 per cent of 'Asian Pakistanis', the largest ethnic group in Scotland, give their religion as 'Muslim'. This is now the second largest religious group in Scotland after 'Christian'.[11]

We might describe Islam (and Christianity for that matter) as a 'politicised religion', and in truth all major religions can be considered such (see Chapter 14). Indeed, what gives Islam added piquancy in Scotland is that it nestles into other erstwhile 'politicised' forms of religion such as Catholicism and Protestantism, of which there is a long, and not always honourable, history. In truth, in talking about 'religion' it is impossible to separate out the narrowly theological sets of beliefs from the social practices which surround religion.

They are bound up with how religion is practised, and by whom, how it fits into social and cultural mores, how willing the 'host' society is to accommodate its practices. We only have to think of reactions to forms of dress, notably the hijab and burka, to grasp that point. How people choose to express their beliefs is inextricably bound up with forms of social and cultural identity, and there is a complex interaction between faith and behaviour. Further, given that linguistic and cultural practices are part and parcel of religious identity, they cannot be separated.

Given the heightened political tensions since 9/11, and 7/7,[12] there are claims that 'Muslims' cannot be trusted to be 'British' in the UK, even though academic research (in England) shows that there are very high levels of belonging to the UK among minority ethno-religious groups, contrary to political rhetoric (Heath and Demireva, 2014; Karlsen and Nazroo, 2015; Platt, 2014).

South of the border, it is in relation to 'being English' which is more problematic. Steve Fenton and Robin Mann observed that 'with respect to the distinction between Englishness and Britishness, whiteness appears important' (2013: 226–7). This has generated a debate in England as to whether ethnic minorities are excluded from being 'English' or *choose* not to be. Thus, Charles Leddy-Owen claims that 'large numbers of the English population who identify – or wish to identity – as English feel actively excluded from the category because they are not white' (2014: 1464). On the other hand, Susan Condor and her colleagues argued that any reluctance to identify as English among people from ethnic minority backgrounds should not be interpreted as 'exclusion' but as an 'autonomous ethnic preference' (2006: 140).

The key debate, then, emerges around 'national' identities, being English, Scottish or Welsh, vis-à-vis being British. There is a complex variable geometry of identity in these islands, into which 'ethnic minorities' add a further level of complexity. Our specific question in this chapter and in this book relates to 'being Scottish', but this cannot be dissociated either from 'being British', or indeed in comparison with the other home nations, notably England. This is because many of the assertions about being Scottish (vis-à-vis British) are made in the implicit contrast with being English (vis-à-vis British).

The difficulty is that it is hard to get at the views of ethnic minorities through standard sample surveys because there are too few cases to hand. In a survey size of 1500, more or less a standard, we would only encounter around sixty cases, and the sampling errors[13] would be too great to allow us to draw definitive conclusions. However, analysis by Ross Bond using the 2011 census micro-data, a random 5 per cent sample of census returns for Scotland, England and Wales (National Records of Scotland 2014, and Office for National Statistics 2014, respectively), generates sufficient sample sizes to overcome the conventional problem that there are too few members of ethnic minorities in normal population samples to allow statistical analysis (see Bond, 2016).[14]

Bond found that there is significant variation in identifying as 'British' among non-white minorities in the home nations, ranging from a majority in England to little over one-third in Scotland, with Wales lying in between. Furthermore, non-white minorities are much more likely to identify with being Scottish than comparable identities in England or Wales. Nevertheless, a higher proportion of ethnic minorities in Scotland identify as British than as Scottish. Bond concludes:

> The analysis supports previous research in suggesting that those in minority ethnic and religious groups are particularly unlikely to identify as English, and that in England and Wales ancestry is a key marker of sub-state national identities while being less important for British identification. Scotland does offer a

contrast to some extent, in that Scottish identity is *relatively* inclusive of minorities, but this is not true to the extent that we might have expected from previous research in Scotland, and overall people in minority groups in Scotland are still much less likely to identify as Scottish than are the white majority. (2016: 20, italics in original)

He concludes that Scottish national identity is relatively inclusive of minorities, but does not extend to ambitious claims to 'multicultural nationalism'. Ethnic minorities in Scotland are less likely to identify as 'Scottish' than the white majority, even when key identity markers such as birthplace are taken into account. What gives added weight to Bond's findings is that they are based on adequate sample sizes to enable him to carry out statistical modelling (in this case, logistic regression), as well as comparative analysis of Scotland, England and Wales.[15]

Being Muslim in Scotland

Seventy per cent of Scottish Muslims live in Scotland's four main cities, mainly in Glasgow, which has 42 per cent, and Edinburgh (16 per cent), with Aberdeen (6 per cent) and Dundee (5 per cent). In Glasgow, many live in Pollokshields on the south side of the River Clyde, which 'has become a distinctively Pakistani and Muslim place: shops have dual signs (English and Urdu), Asian clothes shops display mannequins dressed in *shalwar kameez*, and there are beauty salons for women only' (Bonino, 2015: 84). In Edinburgh, the Muslim population is much smaller (12,500, compared with Glasgow's 32,000), and is more widespread and diverse. Ali Wardak's study (2000) of Edinburgh Pakistanis in the 1990s, who accounted for about half of the city's Muslims, found that they lived in inner city areas such as Gorgie, Leith and Broughton, and that most were Sunnis of the Barelvi tradition. Edinburgh had eleven known mosques, nine catering for Sunnis and two for Shi'as.

Despite the diversity of traditions, the events of 9/11 had a major impact on social acceptance. One of Stefano Bonino's respondents,[16] a Somali man in his mid-fifties who had lived in Edinburgh for over twenty years, commented: 'At the beginning, Muslims were treated as a racial group: people would say to you "Paki" as it happened to me a number of times. Then, 9/11 changed things. If you have a beard and wear a *khamis*, they will call you "Bin Laden"' (2015: 86). Bonino comments: 'Scottish Muslims have undoubtedly found an overarching unifying religious and ideological identity banner in their belonging to Islam' (2015: 88). He goes on: 'Muslimness appears to be part of a more complex and fluid process of external categorization and internal self-reflection that has emerged within post 9/11 societies as a result of global events that have threatened the socio-psychological identities of Muslims' (2015: 89). Because 'Muslimness' has been promoted by global negative categorisation and essentialisation, 'Islam has served as a tool of individual and collective survival through which Muslims can find a sense of in-groupness and sharedness in the face of threat and uncertainty' (2015: 92).

'Dangerous aliens'

Muslims have responded to 9/11 by developing stronger internal cohesion on the basis of Islam as both religion and ideology. Treated as 'dangerous aliens', they have sought solidarity in 'religion'. In this respect, there seem to be many similarities with Catholics emigrating from Ireland in the nineteenth century. Much of the debate about 'sectarianism' in Scotland has focused around whether it is a 'religious' question or a wider social and political issue (see the excellent analysis carried out by the Advisory Group on Tackling Sectarianism in Scotland (www.gov.scot/Publications/2013/12/6197)). Michael Rosie has commented that 'Scotland's Catholics have been grossly simplified and stereotyped as "Irish" and "working class"' (2014).

He comments that the assumed orthodoxy on Catholics in Scotland is that 'because of the (in particular Irish) migrant heritage of many of Scotland's Catholics and because of the hostility, or at least coolness, with which such migrants were received historically, Scotland's Catholics have proved suspicious of "Scotland"' (Rosie, 2014: 128). Rosie cites the historian Tom Gallagher who asserts:

> Working-class Catholics in particular found it difficult to relate to the symbols of Scottish nationhood (and many still do). The custodians of Scottish national identity have tended to be bourgeois institutions like the law, the Presbyterian religion, and the higher reaches of education which are uncomfortable entities to many working-class Catholics. (1991: 32)

While recognising that the experiences of Irish and Asian immigrants to Scotland are different (the Irish came as a reserve army of relatively unskilled labour; Asians came originally as small traders and pedlars), Rosie is making the important point that external stereotyping, notably seeing the incomers as a cultural and social threat, helps to reinforce the accounts and narratives they themselves adopt.[17] Whether or not 'Muslims' (or Catholics for that matter) feel threatened by the 'host' society, and, indeed, do not identify themselves as 'Scottish', as Gallagher implied for Catholics, is contentious.

First, what evidence is there that people in Scotland see Muslims, and other 'immigrants', as a threat? There seems, on the face of it, to be evidence of growing hostility to migrants since the turn of the century (McCollum et al., 2014). The authors point out that Scotland is much more dependent on migration in order to maintain and grow its population than other parts of the UK.

The research relied on two sets of questions from Scottish Social Attitudes surveys for 2002, 2006 and 2010. One asked for responses on a five-point scale ranging from 'strongly agree' to 'strongly disagree', with a 'neither' mid-point, to the statement: 'People from ethnic minorities take jobs from Scottish people'. In 2002, 20 per cent agreed, and 42 per disagreed, a ratio in the direction of the 'liberal' option of around 2:1. By 2006, the proportions were 27 to 37 per cent (ratio of 1.4:1) and, by 2010, 31 to 37 per cent (ratio of 1.2:1).

Put another way, over the period there had been an increase from 20 to 31 per cent in the proportion agreeing that ethnic minorities were taking jobs from 'Scots'.[18]

A second question (in 2006 and 2010) asked if respondents thought there was a threat to Scotland's identity from increased numbers of migrants, once more using the five-point scale from 'strongly agree' to 'strongly disagree'. This time there were three putative 'migrant' groups: Muslims, Black/Asians and East Europeans. There was little change between 2006 and 2010, but almost half thought that there was a threat to Scotland's identity (49 per cent and 50 per cent, respectively), with 31 per cent in each year disagreeing with the statement. Furthermore, the perceived threat to identity from 'Muslims' was greater on both occasions than from 'Blacks/Asians' (respectively, 46 per cent and 45 per cent), or 'East Europeans' (45 per cent and 46 per cent).

McCollum and his colleagues showed that the more education people received, the more 'liberal' they were, a finding more broadly acknowledged in the literature. Furthermore, those in favour of independence for Scotland were more likely to see 'migrants' as a threat to jobs though not identity:

> Seeking independence, as opposed to further devolution, is associated with greater agreement that ethnic minorities take jobs from other people in Scotland. However, constitutional preference is not a statistically significant determinant of the propensity to believe that ethnic minorities pose a threat to Scotland's identity. (McCollum et al., 2014: 95)

Further analysis of the data for 2010[19] indicates that the more 'Scottish' respondents feel, the more likely they are to think that 'ethnic minorities' take jobs from Scottish people, and to see Muslims as a threat to Scotland's identity.[20] There are, however, two important provisos: factors such as national identity, age and education have an effect, and we know that education is a major predictor of attitudes; and second, feeling strongly that you are a member of a 'club' (in this case, being Scottish) means that you care more about 'member-ship' than people who do not feel strongly.

In other words, people who do not feel very Scottish are far *less* likely to care whether 'Scotland's identity' is under threat. This is reflected in the fact that those who say they are Scottish and not British are also more likely say that 'East Europeans', and not simply 'Muslims', are a threat to jobs and identity. We will develop this point later in the chapter.

Let us take stock of our argument. Scotland is a somewhat more homogeneous society in terms of ethnicity than England, but since the beginning of the twenty-first century has become much more diverse than previously, not simply in terms of 'race', but also in terms of in-migration more generally. Furthermore, as we shall see in more detail in Chapter 18, people's sense of 'being Scottish' is highly developed. This 'ethnic' sense of identity is purported by some to reflect a more 'exclusivist', even a 'racist', sense of Scottishness: hence Gallagher's comment about Catholics/Irish not being privy to the symbolism of Scotland. Might we then assume that 'ethnic minorities', and especially Muslims, feel similarly alienated from a sense of Scottishness?

How Scottish are Muslims?

Much of the research on Muslims in Scotland has used either 'purposive' samples aimed at minorities, or small-scale qualitative work.[21] Thus, Peter Hopkins (2007) studied around seventy young Muslim men in Glasgow and Edinburgh, and found that Scottish Muslims, while possessing a strong Islamic affiliation, also had strong links to Scottish culture and society. Saeed and colleagues (1999) talked to 63 pupils from Pakistani backgrounds, aged 14–17, as part of a larger study of over 200 school pupils on Glasgow's south side.

They found that while almost all respondents described themselves as 'Muslim' (97 per cent), as many as 63 per cent said they were 'Scottish Pakistani' when bicultural labels were offered. Writing in the context of the setting up of a Scottish parliament in 1999, Saeed et al. concluded: 'It is perhaps within the chemistries of identity created by the most radical shift of political power within the UK for three hundred years that the possibility of a new kind of Scottish-Pakistani identity may require to be grasped' (1999: 840).

We have made the point that 9/11 events were a watershed for Muslims, and as Hopkins comments, based on his 2002–3 interviews: 'Exploring young men's religious identities … demonstrates how the young men's narratives tended to focus on doing Islam and being Islamic' (2007: 78). Nevertheless, Rosie's conclusion would seem sound: 'Studies of Black and Ethnic Minorities generally (Bond, 2011), and more specifically on young Muslims (Hopkins, 2004, 2007) and ethnic Pakistanis (Saeed et al., 1999; Hussain and Miller, 2006; Amir et al., 1999) all suggest widespread Scottish identification' (2014: 130). For that matter, Rosie also showed that being Muslim, or being Catholic, has no statistically significant effect on whether people claim to be Scottish or not.[22]

Multicultural nationalism

The most comprehensive survey of public attitudes to Muslims in Scotland was carried out by Asifa Hussain and Bill Miller using the 2003 Scottish and British Social Attitudes surveys, and reported in their book *Multicultural Nationalism* (2006). As well as collecting data on 'Islamophobia', Hussain and Miller also explored 'Anglophobia', allowing us to see whether there is any relationship between them; whether, for example, people prejudiced against Muslims are also prejudiced against the English.

Their study also has the merit of comparing Scotland and England using comparable survey questions in, respectively, Scottish and British Social Attitudes surveys. They concluded that 'Islamophobia is significantly lower in Scotland than in England – despite the growth of Scottish national identity and the advent of a separate Scottish parliament' (2006: 49). Furthermore, they found a significant difference between 'exclusive Scots' and 'exclusive English' people,[23] thus:

> Compared to those who identify equally with Britain and England/Scotland, the exclusively English are 27–30 per cent more likely to cite race … as a necessary condition for being 'truly British' or 'truly English'. Yet in Scotland the

exclusively Scottish are scarcely any more likely (only between 2 and 4 per cent) than those who identify equally with Britain and Scotland to cite race as a necessary condition for being 'truly British' or 'truly Scottish'. (Hussain and Miller, 2006: 62)

'Exclusive Scots', then, do not display as high levels of Islamophobia compared with 'exclusive English', which appears more closely tied to English nationalism south of the border than to Scottish nationalism north of it.

Nevertheless, Scotland does not come out of this analysis with an entirely clean bill of health. Anglophobia exists in Scotland, albeit at a fairly low level, and somewhat lower than Islamophobia. In other words, Scots have *different* phobias from the English, not simply lesser ones. Hussain and Miller explain the difference using the helpful metaphors of 'wall' and 'bridge':

> For English immigrants culture is the bridge and identity the wall. Their culture is close to that of the majority Scots and more important, it is flexible ... but English migrants can't easily or quickly adopt a 'Scottish' identity.
>
> For ethnic Pakistanis, culture is the wall and identity the bridge. They identify quickly, easily, and in large numbers with Scotland; but they want to change Scotland by adding to the variety of Scottish culture and traditions. (2006: 169)

Thus, Muslims can claim to be 'Scottish' (the bridge) whereas the English may share symbolic repertoires of culture with the Scots (shared understandings) but cannot think of themselves as 'Scottish', nor for that matter be accepted as such (the wall).

Validation of Hussain and Miller's findings comes from a different kind of study by Satnam Virdee et al. (2006), of fifty-two people, split between white and non-white, in south Glasgow. They concluded that 'whiteness is an unstable identifier of Scottishness; and Scottishness is an unstable identifier of whiteness' (www.socresonline.org.uk/11/4/virdee.html: 1). Thus, a negative view of Islam as antithetical to imagined conceptions of being Scottish cannot easily be sustained, at least in areas of relatively high racialised minority settlement. Thus, 'a Scottish accent disrupts the suggested relationship between skin colour and behaviour. Cultural codes of belonging identified through accent provide an authority such that the subject legitimises himself with regard to this hybridised cultural code of Scottishness' (Virdee et al., 2006: 6).

In that respect, the religious beliefs of Muslims do not place them beyond the limits of national identity, such that the Scottish nation cannot easily be imagined as 'white' by definition. Accent is a key code of Scottishness, and culture cannot operate unproblematically as a homologue of 'race', at least as soon as people open their mouths to speak.

Women, on the other hand, have a harder time of it, according to Akwugo Emejulu (2013).[24] The problem, she argues, is embedded masculinity in being Pakistani in Scotland which de-emphasises women's interests in public spaces and essentialises women's domestic roles in private spaces. The effect is to leave them in a contradictory position between public and private spaces 'for which they have the burden of attempting to negotiate, challenge and transform' (2013: 59), and as a result they are unable to be empowered or to advance their interests.

Being Scottish

In our research on national identity, we used both qualitative and quantitative data, one supplementing the other (McCrone and Bechhofer, 2015). The survey data gave us breadth; the intensive interviews, depth. These intensive interviews with people born and living in Scotland (whom we called 'natives'), as well as people born in England and living in Scotland, together with 'Scots' living in England, and English 'natives', gave us a basis for understanding the criteria people used to decide who was 'one of us'.

To what extent, we wondered, would people accept or reject claims to be Scottish (and south of the border, to be English) based on 'race', as measured simply by a putative claimant being white or non-white?[25] Manifestly, skin colour is not necessarily the only criterion, and we varied questions according to an array of other criteria, such as accent, birthplace, ancestry and residence. If 'race' mattered in being accepted as Scottish or English, then to what extent could it be offset by criteria such as these? If, for example, you were non-white, could that be outweighed by where you were born, for example, or who your parents were, or where you lived?

Our questions were systematic, designed to get at the 'tipping point' at which rejecting a claim flipped over into accepting it, by adding new criteria. An example will make the point. One such question was:

> I'd like you to think of a white person who you know was born in England, but now lives permanently in Scotland. This person says they are Scottish. Would you consider this person to be Scottish?

Which was followed up with:

> What if they had a Scottish accent? Would you consider them to be Scottish?

And again:

> And what if this person with a Scottish accent also had Scottish parents? Would you consider them to be Scottish?

The point of the exercise was to introduce new criteria (accent, parentage) in order to see if that made a difference to accepting or rejecting the claim. The same set of questions was asked about a 'non-white' person, which enabled us to check whether skin colour ('race', for our purposes) made a difference, all things being equal. Could we find a measurable premium, in Scotland as well as in England, which would allow us to say that 'race' mattered?

The effect of lowering the barrier to acceptance by introducing appropriate markers like accent and parentage was clear for whites and non-whites alike. Less than half of respondents in both countries were prepared to accept a national identity claim based solely on residence alone. Introducing 'accent' and then 'parentage' improved acceptance up to around 80 per cent. Nevertheless, about one in six people rejected even the strongest claim if place of birth was the 'wrong' country, even though no one has any say in where they are born (as in the phrase, 'accident of birth').

Broadly speaking, the figures for the hypothetical non-white person are similar, though, when all is said and done, there is a 'premium' difference of about 9 per cent greater acceptance if the notional person making the claim is white. Ostensibly, then, we find a modest degree of racism. When we did this exercise in Scotland and England in 2006, we found quite similar results between the two countries.

There were further questions: would people be prepared to accept claims to be Scottish/English *simply* on the basis of birth and residence? And would they be less willing to accept the claim if the person was non-white? We called this the 'default' question, and it led to an acceptance rate of 99 per cent in Scotland and 97 per cent in England for a putative white person, and 88 per cent and 83 per cent respectively for a non-white person. In other words, the 'race' premium was of the order of 11 percentage points in Scotland and 14 in England. Put another way, 12 per cent reject the claim by a non-white person who was born and is living in Scotland, albeit that this is 5 per cent lower than in England.

We know, however, that Scots have a stronger sense of national identity than the English, and we might expect those who are 'exclusive' Scots ('Scottish not British') to be more rejectionist (see our discussion of Hussain and Miller's work above). The patterns in the data are complex, not least because so few Scots put themselves at the 'British' end of the scale, which makes comparison with England – where far more do – difficult.

It seems, however, that national identity does not have a major effect on accepting or rejecting claims, but that is possibly because other social and demographic factors such as education, age, social class, even gender, are operating. We repeated the exercise in the 2009 survey, and found that national identity was a weaker determinant of accepting or rejecting claims than it had been in 2006.

Why that should be is a matter for conjecture. On the one hand, the Scottish political climate is one in which, and certainly since 2007 when the SNP was elected to government, national identity figures prominently. Having a public debate about inclusion/exclusion, and what it means to be Scottish, has been a much more explicit part of the Scottish agenda, whereas in England, the England–Britain dimension is significant, in the sense that being 'British' is a matter of citizenship, and being 'English' is – currently, at least – not.

One straw in the English political wind is the emergence of UKIP, the United Kingdom Independence Party, which carries an appeal to 'English' rather than 'British' sensibilities (Ford and Goodwin, 2014; Kenny, 2014). Michael Kenny's point that in 2014 Englishness was something of an 'empty signifier', which could mean what social and political movements wanted it to mean, is a good one. Perhaps it is less that Scotland is moving away from a 'British' norm than England is, confronted by a rich mix of social forces such as Euroscepticism, populism, opposition to migration, and economic and social pessimism, refracted through UKIP and Conservative politics.

Islamophobia in Scotland and England

Let us return to a question we raised earlier: are Scots 'civic' or 'ethnic', and what implications do these have for 'race' and ethnicity? Recall Hussain and Miller's valuable work and the survey question 'Scotland would begin to lose its identity if more Muslims came to live in Scotland', asked in both Scottish form, as above in 2003, and in English form[26] in the British Social Attitudes survey of the same year.

Those data showed that a majority of English natives (people born and living in England) – 55 per cent – took the 'ethnic' response to this question by agreeing or strongly agreeing with the statement. In Scotland, the relevant figure was 41 per cent. The respective 'liberal' or civic responses, based on those disagreeing with the proposition that Muslim in-migration would lead to a loss in national identity, are 25 per cent in England and 39 per cent in Scotland. So whereas Scots split almost equally between ethnic and civic (41 to 39 per cent), the equivalent English split is roughly 2:1 (55 to 25 per cent). In terms of a similarly worded question about the in-migration of English people in the 2003 Scottish survey, around 33 per cent of Scottish natives gave an 'ethnic' response and 46 per cent a 'civic' one.

If we combine this with the answers to the question about Muslims coming to live in Scotland, we have a good measure of the proportion who take an overall 'ethnic' or a 'civic' view of the impact on Scottish identity. We find strong associations in the responses people give: thus, 29 per cent of Scottish natives have 'ethnic' views and 36 per cent 'civic' ones. The 'ethnics' tend to be older, of a lower social class, have no educational qualifications and are slightly more likely to be 'exclusive Scots'. 'Civics' on the other hand tend to be younger, more highly educated, but, perhaps surprisingly, national identity is not an explanatory factor.

Taking all these possibilities together, we find that it is level of education, rather than age, sex, social class or national identity, which differentiates the 'ethnics' from the 'civics' in Scotland. Furthermore, when asked who should get a Scottish passport, namely only those 'truly Scottish', or 'anyone permanently living in Scotland', there was a strong association along the ethnic/civic divide: 73 per cent of 'civics' thought everyone living in Scotland, but only 18 per cent would restrict it to 'true Scots'. The figures for 'ethnics' were respectively 46 and 43 per cent, showing that even a small majority of 'ethnics' were prepared to issue a passport on the basis of residence alone, rather than to those they consider *echt* Scots.

Is Scotland a 'racist' society?

When we ask these kinds of questions, it obviously depends what we mean. More people feel that 'jobs' and 'identity' are threatened if 'foreigners' come to settle in Scotland, notably Muslims. Furthermore, they are less willing to accept claims from non-white people to be 'Scottish' than from white people, all things being equal – which, of course, they rarely are in real life, and often contested.

In truth, context is all. In 2010, Steve Reicher, Nick Hopkins and myself wrote a research report for the Equality and Human Rights Commission (www.equalityhumanrights.com/sites/default/files/documents/research/national_identity_viewpoint_research_report_62.pdf). Drawing upon Reicher and Hopkins' social psychological research, we wrote:

> Consider this experiment. Young Scots are approached by a researcher and asked to read a passage which purportedly summarises what Scots in general take as the criteria for being Scottish. For some, this provides what we have called an 'ethnic definition': to be Scottish is to be born in Scotland of Scottish parents. For others, it provides a 'civic definition': to be Scottish is an act of choice and of commitment. Then, as they leave the researcher's company, they see a young woman of Chinese origin wearing a Scotland football top. She is struggling by, carrying a pile of files on top of which is perched precariously a box of pens. She stumbles, the box falls to the floor and the pens are scattered about. How do the young Scots react?
>
> In her appearance, the woman is ethnically non-Scottish, and those who have been exposed to the ethnic definition pick up relatively few pens. By her shirt, however, she is civically Scottish, and those who have been exposed to the civic definition pick up relatively more pens. This study suggests three things. *First*, there are many competing ways to define an identity and people are willing to accept different definitions. *Second*, the ways we draw the boundaries of our identity define who is and who is not seen as 'one of us'. *Third*, whether we see someone as one of us or not affects how we behave towards them and whether they benefit from those various acts of civility which so shape our everyday experience.

If Scotland is or is not 'racist', whom do we compare it with? The usual comparison is with England. In an essay on ethnicity and Britishness, Tariq Modood and John Salt make the following statement:

> A confident Scottish nationalism has achieved devolution, which looks set to go further and in the estimation of some people threatens the very existence of Britain, accompanied as it is by similar if currently lesser developments in Wales. The English, who for so long had to suppress their own sense of

nationality for the sake of the greater prize of being an imperial power, find themselves having to find or invent national symbols and narratives. Scotland and Wales could conceivably get away with thinking of nationality as ethnicity writ large over a territory and a state but England cannot. Not only is there no such state, England being governed by the UK parliament without any remainder. But urban England is multi-ethnic in a way not yet fully experienced by the rest of Britain. (2011: 262)

What do we make of this lengthy statement in the light of our discussions in this chapter? First of all, it implies, properly, that political–constitutional developments in Scotland (and Wales) provide an important context within which migration and ethnicity are framed. Second, there is an odd statement that Scotland and Wales can 'get away with' equating nationality and ethnicity, but England cannot, on the grounds that it is an 'imperial power'.

Leaving aside any distinction between 'England' and 'Britain', and ignoring the fact that Westminster effectively doubles up as the 'English' parliament (English MPs are over 80 per cent of the House of Commons), it is hard to know in what respects 'the English' suppress their own national identity to accommodate the Scots and the Welsh.

Our research in England, qualitative and quantitative, does not suggest that English people are confused about the English/British distinction. Modood and Salt assert that urban England is multi-ethnic in a way 'not yet' experienced by the Scots and the Welsh. This implies that England leads and Scotland and Wales follow, but the statement takes no account of quite different historic and contemporary patterns of migration, as well as cultural understandings, and is not simply a reflection of 'numbers', which in any case does not figure in their account. Nevertheless, the statement by Modood and Salt is useful in spelling out a form of conventional wisdom, revealing as it does a *mentalité* about misplaced uniformity.

Conclusion

On the basis of the evidence of this chapter, we need to treat the experiences of Scotland/ Wales and England as regards migration and ethnicity as different. Being 'English' has not figured prominently hitherto in the 'politics' of identity in these islands. Its mobilisation by the political right is one of the more interesting features of modern politics (see Ford and Goodwin, 2014; Kenny, 2014).

It is also something of a truism that 'ethnic minorities' in England are far less willing/ able to call themselves 'English', and more likely to say they are 'British' by a factor of almost 3:1[27] (Centre on Dynamics of Ethnicity, 2013). In Scotland, comparable figures for 'ethnic minorities' put 'British only' on 26 per cent, and 34 per cent included some form of Scottish identity.

The key to understanding 'race' and ethnicity has as much to do with relations 'on the ground' as with national dimensions, and this is as true of England as it is of Scotland. We cannot assume that 'race' and ethnicity operate 'on the ground' in the same way. For example, Sandra Wallman (1986) compared Bow and Battersea in London. In Bow, networks seemed to be closed and dense, with people interacting with the same partners in different contexts. In Battersea, people belonged to different groups with only partially overlapping membership, with clear implications for ethnic as well as wider social relations.

To make an obvious point, 'Muslims' in Scotland, indeed in Glasgow compared with Edinburgh for that matter, operate in different contexts and meaning frameworks (recall Bonino's evidence on Edinburgh which resembled Battersea rather than Bow), and while there will be common identifications of a religious and cultural sort with Muslims in England, we cannot assume that the latter will be dominant, anymore, perhaps, than Catholics in Glasgow will primarily identify with Catholics in Birmingham.

Above all, it is what Satnam Virdee calls the 'racialisation' of the political process which is the touchstone of difference between Scotland and England. Put simply, in Scotland it is the lack of political oxygen for 'race' politics to flourish, and the fact that the Scottish political system squeezes out 'ethnic' politics which makes the difference, aided by the iconic presence of a Scottish parliament system distinctive from Westminster.

It is not the case that Scotland plays 'catch-up' with England; its politics are simply different. This is not to deny that the 'raw materials' of racism in the form of people's attitudes to incomers and ethnic minorities have the potential to ignite under the right conditions, but the political 'sparks' are absent. As in many other matters, Scotland is not better, merely different. That is why in the next chapter Steve Bruce explores religion.

Chapter summary

So what have we learned in this chapter?

- That 'race' and ethnicity are terms in common currency in popular discussion as well as academic debate, but have different significations in each.

- That debates about Scottishness, as well as Englishness and Britishness, have particular implications for issues of 'race' and ethnicity.

- That ethnic minorities in Scotland are, by and large, more likely to say that they are Scottish than equivalents in England, but more claim to be British in both countries.

- That non-white people are less likely to have their claims to be Scottish accepted than white people, but, nevertheless, 'Scottish' is treated as a more inclusive category than 'English'.

- That 'race' and ethnicity in Scotland are not pale imitations of those in England, but are constructed and maintained within different cultural and political frameworks.

Questions for discussion

1. What do sociologists mean by the terms 'race' and ethnicity? How do the terms differ from the ways they are used in everyday speech?

2. In what ways, and why, does Scotland differ from the rest of the UK as regards 'race' relations?

3. How easy or difficult is it for non-white people to be considered Scottish?

4. Does being Muslim in Scotland differ from being a Muslim in England, and, if so, why is that?

5. What is the relationship, if any, between 'Islamophobia' and 'Anglophobia' in Scotland?

Annotated reading

(a) For general understandings of 'race' and ethnicity, see R. Miles, *Racism after 'Race Relations'* (1994); M. Banton, *Ethnic and Racial Consciousness* (1997); R. Jenkins, *Rethinking Ethnicity* (2008); and N. Meer, *Citizenship, Identity and the Politics of Multiculturalism: The rise of Muslim consciousness* (2015).

(b) On ethnicity and national identity, see D. McCrone and F. Bechhofer, *Understanding National Identity* (2015), chapter 7; A. Hussain and W. Miller, *Multicultural Nationalism: Islamophobia, Anglophobia and devolution* (2006); R. Bond, 'The national identities of minorities in Scotland', *Scottish Affairs*, 75(1), 2011; M. Rosie, 'A' the bairns o' Adam'? The ethnic boundaries of Scottish national identity', in J. Jackson and L. Molokotos-Liederman (eds), *Nationalism, Ethnicity and Boundaries: Conceptualising and understanding identity through boundary approaches* (2014).

(c) For empirical data on 'race' and ethnicity, see the 2011 Scotland census (www.scotlandscensus.gov.uk), especially 'Ethnicity, identity, language and religion' (www.scotlandscensus.gov.uk/ethnicity-identity-language-and-religion); D. McCollum et al., 'Public attitudes towards migration in Scotland', *Scottish Affairs*, 23(1), 2014.

(d) Ethnographies of ethnic minorities include P. Hopkins, '"Blue Squares", "Proper" Muslims and transnational networks', *Ethnicities*, 7(1), 2007; A. Saeed et al., 'New ethnic and national questions in Scotland', *Ethnic and Racial Studies*, 22(5), 1999; S. Virdee et al., 'Codes of cultural belonging: racialised national identities in a multi-ethnic Scottish neighbourhood', *Sociological Research Online*, 11(4), 2006; S. Bonino, 'Scottish Muslims through a decade of change: wounded by stigma, healed by Islam, rescued by Scotland', *Scottish Affairs*, 24(1), 2015.

Notes

1   A reminder: *emic* refers to people's own explanatory terms, and *etic* to those used by analysts.
2   Banton is not claiming any such thing by his comment, merely that this is a piece of conventional wisdom in England.
3   Everyone was officially deemed to have an 'ethnic group', including 'white Scottish' people.
4   The 2011 census options were as follows: A. White: Scottish, Other British, Irish, Gypsy/Traveller, Polish, and other (write in). B. Mixed or multiple ethnic groups (write in). C. Asian, Asian Scottish or Asian British: Pakistani, Pakistani Scottish or Pakistani British Indian, Indian Scottish or Indian British; Bangladeshi, Bangladeshi Scottish or Bangladeshi British; Chinese, Chinese Scottish or Chinese British, Other (write in). D. African: African, African Scottish or African British, Other (write in). E. Caribbean or Black: Caribbean, Caribbean Scottish or Caribbean British Black, Black Scottish or Black British, Other, (write in). F. Other ethnic group: Arab, Arab Scottish or Arab British, Other (write in).
5   It is important to put these self-descriptions in inverted commas to remind ourselves that they are self-chosen categories from within the options available.
6   By 69,000, to 141,000 over ten years.
7   There is a telling joke which makes the point. A non-white person was asked, during an unusual heatwave in Scotland, 'I bet this weather reminds you of where you come from.' 'Dunno,' said the person, 'the weather in Wolverhampton is much like it is here.'
8   The SIMD has 15 per cent of the Scottish population living in deprived areas. The proportion of 'white Polish' people living in such places is almost 30 per cent, and for 'Africans' around 35 per cent. The three most numerous 'Asian' groups, namely 'Pakistani', 'Indian' and 'Chinese', all have proportions living in deprived areas lower than the 15 per cent mean.
9   That is, they say they are 'Scottish only' (3 per cent), 'Scottish and another identity' – presumably 'English' – (5 per cent), or 'Scottish and British only' (3 per cent).
10 The distribution used here refers to people saying they are 'Asian', 'Asian Scottish' or 'Asian British'. There are complex distributions depending on how 'Asians' are grouped, notably whether 'Pakistani', 'Indian' and 'Bangladeshi' are treated separately (see census table DC2202SC for full details).
11 Among 'white Scots', 37 per cent give their religion as Church of Scotland, 15 per cent as Catholic, 3 per cent as 'other Christian', and 37 per cent say they have no religion (table DC2201Sc).
12 On 7 July 2005 four suicide bombers with rucksacks full of explosives attacked Central London, killing 52 people and injuring hundreds more. It was the worst single terrorist atrocity on British soil.
13 Sampling error arises from the fact that samples deviate from the population from which they are selected. The smaller the sample, the greater the deviation or 'error' is likely to be.
14 A minor complication is that in England and Wales people were asked: 'How would you describe your national identity?', and in Scotland, 'What do you feel is your national identity?' To compare answers, we have to assume the question was interpreted more or less the same way.
15 Northern Ireland was not included in his analysis because the total numbers of ethnic minorities are much smaller than in Scotland, England and Wales, and in any case ethnicity in the Province only distinguished between 'white' and 'other'.
16 Bonino's data are drawn from thirty-nine interviews and participant observation conducted with Muslims in Edinburgh between 2011 and 2013.
17 One notorious example related to the alleged report of the Church of Scotland Assembly in 1923, and associated with the Rev. John White, entitled *The Menace of the Irish Race to our Scottish Nationality*, which described Catholics as a threat to the social and biological fabric of Scotland. For more measured accounts of this report, see Rosie (2004) and Bruce in this volume.

18 Marginally more people thought that the threat to jobs came from 'East Europeans' than from 'ethnic minorities': respectively, 31 per cent in 2006 (27 per cent said 'ethnic minorities') and 37 per cent in 2010 (31 per cent said 'ethnic minorities'). This possibly reflects how respondents perceive labour markets where 'Polish plumbers' have become culturally iconic if empirically thin on the ground.

19 McCollum and colleagues used a simple 'Scottish' or 'British' distinction which they refer to as 'self-declared citizenship'. Subsequently, I carried out this analysis using the five-point 'Moreno' national identity scale.

20 For example, 45 per cent of people who say they are exclusively Scottish ('Scottish not British') think ethnic minorities take jobs away from Scots compared with 23 per cent of 'Brits', that is people who say they are 'British more than/not Scottish'. Similarly, 57 per cent of 'Scottish not British' think that Muslims are a threat to Scotland's identity, compared with 46 per cent of 'Brits', a difference, however, which is not statistically significant.

21 Such as Bonino's work on Muslims in Edinburgh (thirty-nine interviews) referred to earlier in the chapter. See also Amir et al. (1999) For a study of Glasgow Muslim Teenagers.

22 In his analysis of the annual Population Survey focusing on that question, 'What do you consider your national identity to be?', Ross Bond found that in the relevant regression model Muslims were just as likely to say they were 'Scottish' as the rest of the population (2011).

23 By which is meant those who say they are 'Scottish/English not British'.

24 The author interviewed nine men and fourteen women in Edinburgh and Glasgow (2013: 43 for details).

25 Simplifying the distinction between 'white' and 'non-white' seemed to us a straightforward way of getting at 'racial' meanings, given that it is based on judgements about skin colour. Whether people are able or willing to differentiate within 'non-white', and even 'white', is not the issue here.

26 'England would begin to lose its identity if more Muslims came to live in England.'

27 In the 2011 census for England, 38 per cent of 'ethnic minorities' described themselves as 'exclusively British', compared with 14 per cent of the white British population.

14

RELIGION: HAVE SCOTS BECOME A GODLESS PEOPLE?

STEVE BRUCE

Scots have a reputation for being more than usually religious, but stereotypes outlive their realities as much as they exaggerate them. The image of 'Scotland as a land where people and church are in unique alliance' (Henderson, 1969: back cover) remained current long after that alliance had collapsed. At the end of the twentieth century, the queen's summer holiday attendances at Crathie Kirk were still reported on the evening news, the popular magazine the *People's Friend* often featured a rural church on its front cover, and every profile of the Labour Chancellor and then Prime Minister Gordon Brown mentioned that he was 'a son of the manse'. Minority Christian communities could, with little difficulty, be pressed into the same stereotype. The Highlands and Islands were either the 'last stronghold of the pure gospel' (as a Lewisman put it) or a grim Puritan wasteland where nothing moved on a Sunday, but their eccentricity was distinctly Scottish. And even the much exaggerated sectarian conflict of Catholics and Protestants in Glasgow could be treated under the same general rubric: England's hooligans were modern; Scotland's refought the Reformation.

Chapter aims

- To describe the current religious affiliations, beliefs and behaviour of Scots.

- To consider the part played in secularisation by Presbyterian factionalism and schism.

- To assess the contemporary importance of sectarian conflict.

- To explain why the national identity of Scots no longer features a religious component.

It is common for the fringes of countries to be more religious than their cosmopolitan centres (Figure 14.1 and 14.2). The social forces that undermine religion strike the industrialised, wealthy and socially diverse core first and most forcefully (Bruce, 2011). The people of the

FIGURE 14.1 Incoming religions. St Patrick's Roman Catholic Church in Edinburgh, which began life as an Episcopalian chapel, was bought in 1856 by the Catholic Church to accommodate the growing Catholic population from Ireland in the Old Town

Source: Author's photograph

FIGURE 14.2 Incoming religions. Less than a mile away is the Edinburgh Central Mosque, opened in 1998

Source: Author's photograph

peripheries then compensate for supposed backwardness by emphasising their godliness as a claim to moral superiority over the decadent centre.

It is certainly the case that for most of the twentieth century Scotland, like Wales, was markedly more churchgoing than England. In 1980 only 13 per cent of English adults were church members; the comparable figures for Wales and Scotland were 23 and 37 per cent. But by the end of the twentieth century English church membership had fallen to 9 per cent while Welsh and Scottish figures had fallen faster: to 12 and 25 per cent respectively.[1] And if we consider church attendance rather than membership we find the differences further eroded. In 2000 both Welsh and English church attendance was at 8 per cent and the proportion of adult Scots who attended church was 13 per cent (Brierley, 1999: figure 2.7.1 and tables 2.12.1, 2.12.2 and 2.12.3).

Current affiliations and attitudes

The 2011 Scottish census asked: 'What religion, religious denomination or body do you belong to?' Just under half of Scots identified with some Christian church. Those disclaiming any religion or refusing to answer amounted to 43.6 per cent and non-Christians accounted for the small gap between those figures. The largest group of Christians (32.4 per cent) identified with the national Church of Scotland (or Kirk). Roman Catholic identifiers were 15.9 per cent and the smaller Christian bodies amounted to 5.5 per cent. The growth of the avowedly non-religious has been spectacular. Even in the 1960s a church affiliation was assumed by the armed forces, schools and hospitals: those who had no particular affiliation were logged as Church of Scotland for chaplaincy purposes. By 1974, 24 per cent of Scots described themselves as having no religion; in 2001 it was 37 per cent, and in 2011 just over half of Scots said they had no religion (Field, 2013).

The growth of indifference has not been haphazard. A large sample survey conducted in 2001 asked both for current religious identification and for religion of upbringing. We can thus map the general patterns of change over the second half of the twentieth century (Bruce and Glendinning, 2003). The Catholic Church was most successful in retaining at least nominal attachment: three-quarters of those raised as Catholic still described themselves as such, while almost all the rest were now 'No religion'.

Two-thirds of those raised in mainstream Protestant churches (such as the Kirk) still described themselves as such: almost all the defectors had gone to 'No religion'. The conservative Protestant churches had apparently fared worst, in losing two-thirds of their children: one-third to 'No religion' and one-third to mainstream churches. Before we take this to mean that the Catholic Church was vastly more successful at retaining its children, we should note that we are comparing nominal attachment, which is always higher for the large mainstream churches than for the small and marginal ones. But that observation does not prevent us drawing two conclusions. First, acquiring religion in adulthood is rare: only 7 per cent of those raised with no religion later claimed a religious identity. Second, almost all the movement between childhood and adulthood had been in a liberal direction: either from conservative to more mainstream churches or from some religion to none. There was almost no flow in the other direction.

A slightly better sense of religious attachment can be gained from church membership figures. In 2000, 40 per cent of Scots aged 16 and over were members of some Christian church, with the Catholic Church (at 20 per cent) and the Church of Scotland (at 15 per cent) accounting for most of them. This represents a major decline since 1950, when some 60 per cent of Scots adults were church members (Currie et al., 1977).

Church attendance

If those figures seem high it is because we are still looking at what may be quite nominal identification. As all Christian churches require their people to gather together to worship God, church attendance is a more acute measure of allegiance. A 1994 count of actual attendance found that about 16 per cent of adult Scots then attended church: 6 per cent in Catholic churches and 5 per cent in the Church of Scotland (Brierley and Macdonald, 1995). This represents a considerable change from the middle of the nineteenth century. In 1851, when between 40 and 60 per cent of Scots were churchgoers, more people attended church than were members. This is still true of the smaller Protestant groups such as the Baptists and the Brethren, but for the larger churches attendance declined faster than membership, and now only about half of those who are interested enough to keep their names on some church roll of members actually attend.

Rites of passage

One way in which churches connect with people beyond their core adherents is by blessing rites of passage. In 1900 almost all Scots were baptised, married and buried by a Christian church. By the end of the century a considerable part of those 'hatch, match and dispatch' functions had been lost. In 1930 the Church of Scotland baptised about 40 per cent of children aged 1 or less. In 1970 it baptised only a third of such children and in 2010 the figure was a mere 7 per cent. Even allowing for the growth of the Catholic and non-Christian populations, that is a serious decline.

The changes in weddings is also notable. In the years immediately after the Second World War, 84 per cent of Scots weddings were religious. By the late 1960s this had fallen to 74 per cent. In 2010 it was less than 40 per cent. Remarkably, in 2012 there were more humanist than Catholic weddings.[2]

Baptism and marriage are optional but we all die. Funerals are almost invariably occasions of great sadness and, even for those who cannot really believe it beyond the context of the service, the promise of eternal life can be a great consolation. Hence we would expect that the disposal of the dead is more likely than welcoming new members into society or celebrating marriages to remain church business, but even here we see a considerable change over the twentieth century. There are no reliable statistical records but there is no doubt that the rapid rise in cremations has, especially since the 1980s, been accompanied by a clear shift from traditional religious services which commend both the dead and the mourning to the care of God to secular celebrations of the life and personality of the deceased.

Thus far, we have been looking at Scots in general. One of the most striking changes in Scottish religion has been the disappearance of men. In thoroughly religious societies men and women are equally likely to be religious because being religious is more a property of the society and its shared culture than an individual preference. In largely secular societies few people of either gender are religious. But between the two extremes there is a common pattern of women being more religious than men. As churchgoing has declined, women have come to make up an ever-greater part of the congregations (see Figure 14.3). By the 1960s, women were between 60 and 70 per cent of most congregations. By the end of the century 80/20 splits were not uncommon (Trzebiatowska and Bruce, 2012).

There is no doubt that the Christian churches were far less popular at the end of the twentieth century than at the beginning. What is less easily agreed is the significance of that decline. The obvious reading is that we are less religious than our forebears, but it could be that modern Scots are really as religious as ever they were and that the change

FIGURE 14.3
Kirking Online

Source: I am
grateful to Steven
Camley for
permission to use
this cartoon which
appeared in *The
Herald* on 13 May
2016

represents simply a decline in confidence in the churches as institutions. That is, Scots may now be 'believing but not belonging' (Davie, 1994). Surveys suggest otherwise (Voas and Crockett, 2005). A large majority of Scots – almost three-quarters in 2001 – still say they believe in God, but only a quarter choose the conventional Christian God. Roughly similar numbers preferred 'There is some sort of spirit or life-force' or the remarkably vague 'There is something there.' A very large number of surveys all point to two conclusions: traditional Christian beliefs (e.g. about the nature of the Bible, Jesus, or heaven and hell) have been declining steadily and that holding such beliefs is closely related to both churchgoing and age (Field, 2001). Churchgoers and those who are old enough to have been children in the heyday of Sunday School are much more likely than non-church young people to hold conventional religious beliefs.

Unconventional beliefs

As Christianity has declined there has been a coincidental (but not compensating) rise in the popularity of claiming to be spiritual rather than religious. In some cases it represents a sincere commitment to non-Christian forms of spiritual enlightenment. In more it seems a rhetorical device designed to pre-empt accusations of shallowness and insensitivity.

Such nominal claims to spirituality have been tested with survey questions that asked if people had ever tried a variety of 'New Age' activities and how important they felt them to be (Bruce and Glendinning, 2003). Topics were divided into four: reading the sorts of horoscopes published in papers and magazines; consulting more serious forms of divination; practising yoga and meditation; and using various forms of alternative medicine. Under each heading respondents were asked if they had ever tried X, if they had tried it more than once, if they had paid for it, and how important it was 'in living your life'. That may sound clunky but it has been used by pollsters for years and it produces responses that fit with other patterns.

The results are displayed in Table 14.1. Not surprisingly, 41 per cent of Scots had read their horoscopes and 45 per cent had tried some form of alternative or complementary medicine. Only 30 per cent had ever tried any serious form of divination and only 22 per cent had tried yoga or meditation. But as we see in the top row of the table, across the board few respondents thought these things very important.

TABLE 14.1   Experience and salience of the New Age

	Horoscopes[1] (%)	Divination[2] (%)	Yoga or meditation (%)	Alternative medicine[3] (%)
Very important	1	2	3	5
Quite important	4	4	7	15
Not very important	21	13	9	20
Not at all important	15	11	4	5
Never tried	59	70	78	55
Sample size	1605	1605	1605	1605

[1] Consulting horoscopes in newspapers and magazines

[2] Consulting a tarot card reader, fortune teller or astrologer (excluding horoscopes in papers and magazines)

[3] Alternative or complementary medicine, such as herbal remedies, homeopathy or aromatherapy

Source: Scottish Social Attitudes Survey, 2001

The decline of Christianity may dismay the Christian but a close look at what people do believe may equally dismay the committed atheist. While religion in the sense of coherent packages of beliefs about the supernatural, embedded in organisations and expressed through group rituals, has declined, many Scots continue to hold supernatural or non-materialist beliefs. Many of those who have given up the churches have also given up belief in an afterlife and other non-material entities, but, as we can see from Table 14.2, more Scots than those attending church still entertain the sorts of ideas that were traditionally packaged and presented by the churches: they just freestyle.

Just over a third of respondents claimed to have had an answer to prayer and more than a quarter thought there was some sort of life after death. We need to be cautious of making too much of survey data on beliefs. Questionnaires are always more useful, the more concrete the matter in hand. There is little ambiguity in the question 'How many toilets are there in your house?' and, unless we can think of a good reason why respondents should lie, no difficulty in interpreting the replies. Obviously what is heard in the question 'Have you ever experienced an answer to prayer?' and what is meant by a positive answer are not so simple. When we analyse such answers by church

TABLE 14.2 Church attendance and non-materialist beliefs

Church attendance

Percentage of those in each attendance category which:	Non-religious	Never attended regularly	Attended regularly; definitely stopped	Attended regularly; stopped but might go again	Regular churchgoer	All Scots
Have had answer to prayer	8	18	28	43	68	34
Have sense of having lived previous life	19	17	16	27	14	17
Have had actual contact with someone dead	20	23	23	32	21	23
Think there is another existence after death	33	37	37	63	68	46

Source: Scottish Social Attitudes Survey, 2001

attendance we find the expected. Regular churchgoers are much more likely to assent (68 per cent) than those who never attended regularly (18 per cent) or who say they have no religion (8 per cent). Nonetheless, that 8 per cent of the avowedly non-religious have had an answer to prayer raises an interesting question about to whom they were praying.

On the question of whether we cease to exist at death, or have some sort of further existence, we again find a clear pattern according to church adherence or background: 68 per cent of regular churchgoers and 63 per cent of those who once attended regularly and then quit but have considered going back believe that there is another existence after death. What might be surprising is that a third of each of the other categories (including those people who disclaim any religious identification) also believe in some sort of life after death. Equally significant is the high proportion of these respondents who believe they have lived a previous life: 19 per cent of the non-religious, 17 per cent of those who have never attended church regularly, and 16 per cent of those who were socialised in a church but then quit. Even more noteworthy is the high proportion of respondents who feel they have had contact with the dead: about a fifth of people in all categories of religious practice, from those who attend church regularly to those who say they have no religion, claim to have had such an experience.

One further observation reinforces the point that the growth in religion indifference has not been caused by wholesale conversion to atheism. Most Scots have a considerable sympathy for religion in the abstract. The 2001 survey asked if people were in favour of daily prayers in state schools: 48 per cent were in favour; 40 per cent were against. Those who favoured public prayers actually outnumbered the 25 per cent of respondents who believed in a God; to whom or what did they want school children to pray?

Overall, we can summarise the views of most Scots as being positive towards religion in the abstract – so long as faith is relatively undemanding it is a good thing because it makes people nicer – but the first decade of the twenty-first century has threatened that benign indifference. A series of sex abuse scandals in the Catholic Church climaxed in February 2013 with its most senior official, Cardinal Keith O'Brien, being sacked after admitting that he had used his institutional authority to force young priests into gay sex acts. And although Scotland's Muslim communities have been largely immune to the appeal of jihadi radicalisation, the international spread of violent Islam has contributed to a general sense that religion taken seriously is just too much trouble (Bruce, 2016).

Religious diversity and secularisation

It is often assumed that the gradual secularisation of the state and of such important social institutions as education, social control and social welfare is a result of political pressure from secularists (i.e. people who promote the secular). French secularity was indeed a result of a power struggle between revolutionary forces and defenders of the old order. But Scotland shows a very different route to the marginalisation of religion: the fragmentation of a once-dominant church into a series of competing fragments, each denying legitimacy to all but itself and only gradually accepting toleration once it became clear that it had not defeated its competitors.

Historical trends

The Reformation that began in the sixteenth century split the Western Christian church into the Roman Catholic Church and very many Protestant churches. Central to Protestant innovations were rejection of the idea that a professional clergy was necessary to represent humankind to God and vice versa; rejection of the notion that religious merit could be transferred from one person to another (as when the living pray for the dead); denial of the claim that the clergy had the power to forgive sins (so out goes confession, penance and absolution); and rejection of the pope's claim to the spiritual direction of the church. In came an insistence that all people had to be equally pious: it was no longer enough for lay people to support a small core of religious professionals who worshipped God on their behalf. So that ordinary people could know what God required of them, the Reformers translated the Bible and the texts spoken in rituals into local languages and taught the people how to read.

In Scotland the Reformation was a genuinely popular movement. Small pockets of Catholicism survived in Moray and Aberdeenshire, but the most modern parts of the country – the English-speaking lowlands – were converted and the Presbyterian Church of Scotland was a genuinely national church, with few dissenters. To the right were Episcopalians who preferred the English model of rule by bishops to the more democratic rule by presbyter or elder, largely reformed Protestant in doctrine but episcopal in structure and retaining liturgies for worship that were similar to those of the Church of England. To the left were radical Presbyterians who agreed that the one true church should be imposed on the nation but did not think the Kirk sufficiently reformed to merit that status.

Over the century from the 1730s to the 1840s there were a number of departures from the Kirk, mostly over patronage. In Presbyterian theory all believers are equally able to discern the will of God, which translates into the claim that all members of a congregation should have an equal say in the choosing of their minister. But the church was funded, not by its members, most of whom were far too poor, but by a tax on landowners, who, not surprisingly, wanted to select the minister they were paying for.

The issue was compounded by political significance. A state church was assumed to be an important source of social integration and stability. By promising reward in the next life to people who placidly accepted their conditions in this life, the national church bolstered the status quo. After the laird or his resident agent, the minister was often the most influential person in any parish, so those who had a large stake in the status quo had good reason to wish to control church appointments. Hence Presbyterian democracy and the rights (or burdens) of the heritors were always in tension.

In 1740 a number of ministers led by Ebenezer Erskine were expelled for objecting to patronage. Their heritage was the Secession Church, which recruited from the growing middle classes and the top end of the working class: the people who matched independence of mind with financial independence. Within a decade the Seceders had split over the Burgher Oath, which required holders of public office to affirm the religion 'presently professed in this kingdom'. Then both Burgher and Anti-Burgher factions divided over theology. In both churches there was a gradual move away from the strict Calvinism of Presbyterianism's founding Westminster Confession of Faith (in which only some people had been 'pre-destined' since eternity to salvation) and toward a more generous (or Arminian) view of the offer of salvation. That argument became institutionalised as both Burghers and Anti-Burghers split into liberal and conservative options. Thus was created the wonderfully named 'Auld Licht Anti-Burger' Church and three competitors.

The biggest blow to church unity came in 1843 and again involved the principle of patronage. In what was rather euphemistically called 'the Disruption', one-third of the Church of Scotland's clergy left to form the Free Church. At the time of the split, the Free Church was classically Presbyterian in believing that the state should impose the true religion on the people but, because it had to be self-funding, it gradually came round to the idea that religious affiliation should be a matter of free choice.

That ideological shift was no more than a recognition of social change. A publicly funded state church that managed the nation's education system and disciplined people's behaviour made sense when everyone belonged to the same church. But various types of coercion had not stemmed dissent. The state had tried to maintain religious conformity with the bayonet and that had failed. It then coerced conformity with legal disabilities such as barring dissenters from public office and that had failed. Accepting the inevitable was made easier by the gradual realisation that religious uniformity was not a necessary condition for political stability. The British state did not collapse as ever-larger numbers of its subjects decided that their faith should be a personal choice rather than a condition of citizenship. And the Disruption itself hastened the separation of church and state because, after 1843, there were more Scots outside the Kirk than in it.

At the same time as the notion of choosing one's religion was becoming more popular, the tone of what was being chosen was changing. Calvinism was well suited to harsh times when most people had little or no say over anything, but ill-suited to a world in which material conditions were improving and ordinary people were gaining more control over their lives. Impotent serfs may find reasonable the idea of a dreadful all-powerful God whose providence was as likely to mean pain as comfort: that just reflected their lives. Skilled tradesmen and affluent businessmen think better of themselves and will prefer a more benign faith which flatters more than it challenges the believer.

In part the growth of religious diversity reflected Scotland's geological divisions. When the Lowlands became Protestant in religion, Anglophone in language and capitalist in economic organisation, the Western Highlands and Islands, insulated from modernisation by geology, remained Catholic, Gaelic and feudal. A number of related changes radically altered the Highlands after 1745. The near success of the second Jacobite Rebellion gave the state good reason to suppress the clans and to open up the Highlands. In the old order, a clan chief's power rested on the number of men he could mobilise to fight.

With the British state determined to pacify its peripheral badlands, the chiefs gave up their military pretensions and recast themselves as landlords pure and simple, taking rents in cash to buy status in Edinburgh and London. Now large numbers of subsistence farming retainers were a liability rather than an asset, and the agricultural changes that had occurred very slowly in England and the Scottish Lowlands were imposed on the Highlands and Islands in a few decades. The clearance of people from their traditional homelands to the barren fringes created great hardship and resentment. It also coincided with vigorous attempts to convert the Highlanders to evangelical Protestantism, an endeavour that worked spectacularly well. A few pockets of Catholicism remained (Barra, South Uist and Benbecula, for example) but at the same time as the people of the Lowlands were giving up enthusiastic religion, large parts of the Highlands and Islands were embracing it.

That division between Highlands and Lowlands explains the contours of subsequent divisions. As the Free Church in the Lowlands gradually became more liberal and merged first with the Seceders and then with the national Church of Scotland, Highlanders broke away. The Free Presbyterian Church was formed in 1892; the Free Church legacy was reclaimed in 1900. At its 1901 Assembly it had twenty-five ministers and around sixty-five congregations, mostly in the Gaelic-speaking parts of Scotland. Within two years the Free Church had more than quadrupled in size but it made no serious inroads into the religious culture of Lowland Scotland. Though its Glasgow and Edinburgh congregations were among its largest, they were émigré churches: a home from home for exiles from Lewis and Assynt.

To summarise, the first century after Erskine's expulsion in 1733 saw Scottish Presbyterianism fragment and the second century saw it reunite. But every reunion left behind at least one dissident minority. After 1929 the Church of Scotland was again the national church in reality as well as name, but its social power was fatally damaged by the very large number of dissenting alternatives. There were the Free Church and the Free Presbyterian Church in the Highlands and Islands. The Scottish Episcopal Church persisted, often as the option for the English in Scotland. One might have thought Scotland amply supplied with competing versions of Protestantism but branches of every sect found in England – Methodists, Independents, Baptists, Brethren – also found a foothold in Scotland. The nineteenth century saw the arrival of two American imports, but neither the Jehovah's Witnesses nor Mormons were terribly successful. In the 2001 census there were only 361 Witnesses and 177 Mormons in Scotland.

Religious fragmentation

By the 1950s Scotland had also acquired a small number of Pentecostal churches: the Church of the Nazarene, the Apostolic Church and the Elim Pentecostalists. These bodies were distinguished by their claim that certain 'charismatic gifts' – speaking in the tongues of men and angels, prophesying and healing – which most Christians think were a privilege of the disciples who literally, rather than metaphorically, knew Christ – were still available to the true believer.

Protestant fragmentation was complemented by Catholic resurgence. In 1795 there were only some fifty Catholics in Glasgow. By 1829 there were 25,000 and in 1843 almost twice that number. Edinburgh in 1829 had some 14,000 Catholics where thirty years earlier there had been no more than a thousand (Handley, 1964). This and subsequent growth were largely a result of migration from Ireland. In the 2001 census just over 800,000 Scots said they had been raised as Catholics.

This fragmentation had two profound consequences: the gradual acceptance of the idea that religious affiliation should be a matter of personal choice and the growth of the secular state. From the Reformation on, schools had been provided by the Kirk and then by the larger competitors. But the churches were unable to fund the expansion of schooling necessary to adjust to a growing (and increasingly urban) population. The state could have channelled tax funding through the Kirk (as its leaders naturally wished) but Scotland's religious diversity made such schemes politically unacceptable and the result was that the Protestant churches handed their schools to the state.

The national church also lost its role in social welfare. Having beggars licensed by each parish and supported out of such sources as fines on congregants for such offences as the wonderfully named 'haughmagandy' (or 'putting it about') worked well for a stable rural community where everyone belonged to the same church. The combination of religious diversity and urbanisation destroyed that capacity and forced the state to become increasingly the provider of social welfare. Anyway, fining miscreants only worked so long as their good standing in the community depended on their membership of the parish church. Once it became socially possible for people to leave the Kirk, it lost its role in disciplining personal behaviour.

Non-Christian religions

The Jews are Scotland's oldest non-Christian community. The earliest clear references come in the seventeenth century, but most Scottish Jews today are descended from Central European migrants who settled in Glasgow (and to a lesser extent Edinburgh, Dundee and Aberdeen) in the late nineteenth century. The community was increased by refugees from Nazism and reached about 80,000 in the mid-twentieth century (Daiches, 1997; Glasser, 1986). It subsequently declined drastically as many 'married out' and those who wished to remain orthodox moved to English cities with communities large enough to sustain an infrastructure (rabbi, kosher butcher and the like) and offer a wide choice of potential spouses. In 2011 there were only some 6000 Jews in Scotland, with almost 80 per cent of them in Glasgow.

Scotland's Muslims, Hindus and Sikhs are almost all recent immigrants, a potent reminder of the spread of the British Empire. In 2011 there were 77,000 Muslims in Scotland, just under 1.5 per cent of the Scottish population. Almost half of them were born outside the UK and two-thirds described their ethnicity as Pakistani; the rest were Bangladeshi, 'other South Asian' and African. Scots Muslims are highly concentrated: almost half live in Glasgow and 16 per cent live in Edinburgh.

Scotland's Hindu community (some 16,000 strong in 2011) is largely of Indian origin, although many came in a round-about route that involves a second part of our imperial history: African anti-colonialism. Many Indians worked for the British in other parts of the empire. In the 1890s, for example, over 30,000 Indians were sent to East Africa under indentured labour contracts to build the railways and about 7000 remained once the project was completed. By the 1960s, when the UK granted independence to most of its African possessions, Asians had established themselves as a successful commercial class, which made them ready targets for nationalist scapegoating. In 1969, Kenya expelled its Asian population and in 1972 Uganda followed suit. The Sikh history of migration, both direct and via East Africa, is very similar. In 2011 there were some 9000 Sikhs in Scotland, most of them in Glasgow: of the six gurdwaras in Scotland, there are four in Glasgow and one each in Dundee and Edinburgh.

Muslims, Hindus and Sikhs have added variety to Scotland's religious constitution. They have also made it a slightly more religious country than it would otherwise have been because they are typically more religious than the average Scot. But beyond that, they have had little impact on the natives. Conversion is rare. In the 2001 census, the proportions of those three traditions who said they were raised in that faith were respectively 95, 94 and 91 per cent. Only the Buddhists, with 54 per cent having been raised as something else, have grown much by conversion and their numbers are small. The Buddhists also differ in constituting a religious category but not a community. They come from a very wide variety of ethnic backgrounds and they have a low inter-marriage rate. While 80 per cent of Muslims and 76 per cent of Sikhs are married to co-religionists, for Buddhists the figure is only 30 per cent: Buddhists are more likely to be married to people who said they had no religion than to Buddhists.

Finally, in this brief review, we come to the new religious movements of the 1960s. Despite attracting a great deal of academic and press attention because they were exotic, their lasting impact on Scotland has been negligible. In 2001 there were fifty-eight members of the Church of Scientology and twenty-five members of the International Society for Krishna Consciousness (or 'Hare Krishnas'); they would all have fitted on one bus. There were no recorded members of the Unification Church (or 'Moonies'). There were also 1930 Pagans and Wiccans, 421 Baha'is, 47 Rastafarians and 53 Satanists.

The Irish and sectarian conflict

Generally lacking capital and industrial labour skills, the Irish entered Scotland at the bottom of the labour market (Handley, 1964) but initially through providing services to their own community they gradually increased in wealth and social status. As in Australia and the United States (and in contrast to the Netherlands, where separate trade unions and parties were part of a distinct Catholic 'pillar'),[3] the Irish in Scotland joined Protestants in a shared labour movement and unions, and Labour Party politics offered an important route to upward social mobility. Initial church opposition to what at times looked like socialism fell away once the Labour Party accepted denominational schools. The Labour movement allowed Irish Catholics and then their children considerable political power. Of seventy-six Labour councillors elected to the Glasgow Council between 1922 and 1931, a fifth were Catholic, well in proportion to Catholic support for Labour. By the mid-1980s over half of elected Labour members of the Glasgow District Council were Catholic, a considerable over-representation.

That Irish Catholics and native Protestants made common cause was important in preventing the immigrants being effectively scapegoated during the inter-war depression years. In the late 1920s and 1930s two sectarian Protestant parties – the Scottish Protestant League in Glasgow and Protestant Action in Edinburgh – did their best to recruit Protestants for a nativist movement. Their fortunes were identical: three years of spectacular success in local council elections, a year of councillors squabbling – because they shared no principles beyond anti-Catholicism and local councils had no jurisdiction over such matters as immigration which did unite them – and then sudden collapse. The demise of both parties was hastened by the failure of the Orange Order, the fraternal organisation that embodied popular Protestantism, to support them. And neither party had any support and hence legitimacy from the clergy of the major Protestant churches.

The one instance of the Church of Scotland trying to use anti-Irish sentiment to make itself more popular was a dismal failure. A number of ministers tried to persuade the church and, through it, Protestant Scotland that the Irish migrants posed a major threat to the Scottish 'race', but when in 1928 they were finally given an audience with the Secretary of State for Scotland, he dismissed their campaign as being based on inaccurate information and for good measure added that he could not prevent migration from the Irish Free State (as it was then) because, for purposes of population movement, it remained part of the UK.

That response would not have been surprising had it come from a radical Labour politician such as John Wheatley or Tom Johnston. It is highly significant that it came from Sir John Gilmour, a Presbyterian Unionist MP who was also a member of the Grand Lodge of the Orange Order. His preference for social harmony over what we must suppose were his private views of Catholicism was entirely typical of Scottish elites. On the same day, the even-handed Colonel Sir Thomas Moore, Unionist MP for Ayr, opened a Catholic Church bazaar in the Ayr town hall and addressed an Orange rally in Maybole.

The internal geological divisions of Scotland were an important accidental obstacle to the promotion of an anti-Catholic religio-ethnic identity. Those Scots who continued in the Calvinist Presbyterianism which gave them religious reasons to oppose Catholic interests were largely confined to the Highlands and Western Isles, where there were very few Catholics and hence little actual competition. When the 1918 Education Act brought Catholic schools into the national structure of funding and management, only one education authority in Scotland objected to the generous terms on which Catholic schools would be transferred. That was Caithness, where there were no Catholic schools!

When the 'Troubles'[4] began in Northern Ireland in the early 1970s, there were fears that the violence would spread to Scotland, but these proved unfounded. There was not a single politically inspired murder in Scotland during the Troubles, and the attempts of a small number people who supported Ulster unionist terror organisations to raise funds and collect weapons and explosives for shipment to Northern Ireland were dismal failures (Bruce, 1992: 153–65).

Such sectarian violence as there has been in Scotland in the last few decades has been entirely football related. The ritualised conflict of Celtic and Rangers (heightened by the fact that no other Scottish football clubs have ever been able to provide a long-term threat to their duopoly) occasionally spills out of the stadia but, contra the gross exaggerations offered by parts of the mass media, some politicians and a number of anti-sectarian campaigning organisations, 'Old Firm'-related murders were less than one-third of 1 per cent of homicides committed between 1984 and 2001 (Bruce et al., 2004: 133–50). Surveys suggested that people in Glasgow were more likely to be assaulted because of their residence, their sexuality or their ethnicity than their religion. And under that heading, Muslims and non-Muslim Asians were much more likely than Catholics to be the victims (Bruce et al., 2004: 89–91).

Religious discrimination?

It is sometimes claimed that Catholics continue to be the victims of sectarian discrimination in the labour market, but there is no evidence for this in data on the relative social class of Catholics and Protestants. We need to be clear that such patterns as we may find can only establish *relative* disadvantage. Of itself, disadvantage need not mean discrimination. It may well be that a particular population is disadvantaged by circumstances that have nothing to do with hostile actions of others. And some of those circumstances may result from choices made by members of the disadvantaged population themselves. So disadvantage does not prove discrimination. But it does work the other way round. Widespread labour market discrimination must result in a visible pattern of disadvantage. If there is no pattern, we can reasonably conclude that there is no discrimination.

In the twentieth century the problem for settling such arguments was the absence of reliable data, but the 2001 and 2011 censuses provided information on the religion and social class of almost the entire adult population of some 4 million. One study of the 2001 data concluded: 'For the younger cohorts there is no longer evidence that Catholics are at a socio-economic disadvantage compared to Protestants' (Raab and Holligan, 2012: 1950).

The following analysis of the 2011 census estimates the likelihood that people will occupy a middle-class socio-economic position, given their educational qualifications. For two reasons, the analysis is restricted to adults born in Scotland. As claims to sectarian discrimination mainly involve descendants of Irish immigrants, we did not want to disguise accidentally their fate by combining them with the very large number of young and well-educated recent Polish migrants. And as such claims often suppose that bigots use their having attended a Catholic rather than a state school as a way to identify potential victims, we wanted to focus on those schooled in Scotland. To clarify the problem further, only data for Greater Glasgow – which offers the greatest variety of religious backgrounds – are reported here.[5]

As their experience of the labour market is significantly different, men and women's social class is analysed separately. And because those under 35 may not yet have reached their career peak, while the social class of the elderly is complicated by illness and retirement, the analysis is confined to the middle age group of 35 to 54 year olds.

What is presented is the relative likelihood (or odds) that people of various religious identities will occupy a middle-class position given their educational qualifications. The odds are presented relative to those for Christians who are not Roman Catholic. The odds on an 'Other Christian' man (or later woman) age 35 to 54 years with an intermediate education occupying a middle-class position are set as 50:50 (i.e. an evens chance) and the fate of all other blocs is described relative to that reference point. To be clear, our analysis involves four identities: Roman Catholic, Other Christian (mostly Church of Scotland identifiers), Other Religion (mostly Muslim, Hindu, Sikh and Buddhist) and finally No Religion.

FIGURE 14.4

Likelihood of middle-class occupational status by religion and education, Greater Glasgow (men aged 35 to 54 years, born in Scotland)

Notes: Binary logistic regression with other Christians holding intermediate qualifications set as the reference category.
N = 219,947

Source: Census 2011

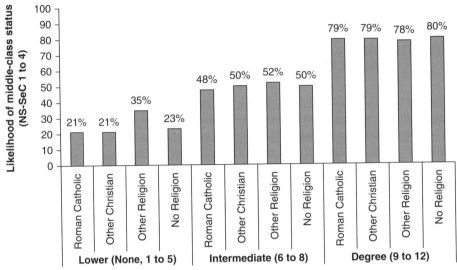

Figure 14.4 presents 2011 census data for men in three separate ranges of educational qualification. The first four columns of the figure show those who have the lowest level of credentials, the middle four columns are those with intermediate qualifications, and the final four are those with at least an undergraduate degree.

The key to interpreting the figure is to see how well the columns representing the four religious identifications match for each of the three levels of education. With one exception, to which we will return in a moment, the four columns are pretty much level. Catholic and Other Christian are the same for the lowest and highest education bands and Catholics are only slightly behind Other Christians in the middle level of attainment. Interestingly, those who say they have No Religion do marginally better than both Catholics and Other Christians. Nothing here suggests that Catholic men suffer systematic labour market discrimination.

The one column that does stand out is that for men of Other Religion, who have been far more successful than average in attaining middle-class status with the lowest levels of educational attainment. Further analysis shows that we are seeing the effect of self-employment and the family firm; only 14 per cent of less qualified men aged 35 to 54 years among the two Christian groupings are own-account workers or employers of small business as compared with 28 per cent of the Other Religion group.

Figure 14.5 displays the same analysis for women and again the obvious conclusion is that there are few salient differences between the columns representing Catholics, Other Christians and No Religion identifiers. At the lowest level of educational attainment, Catholics are marginally behind Other Christians but similarly ahead of those of No Religion.

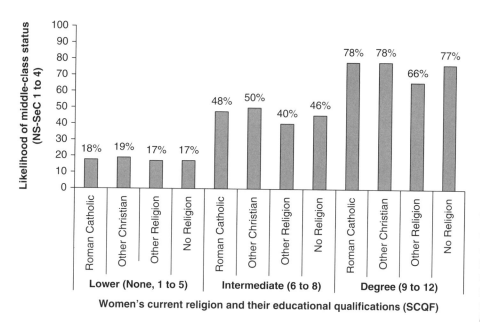

FIGURE 14.5

Likelihood of middle-class occupational status by religion and education (women aged 35 to 54 years, born in Scotland)

Notes: Binary logistic regression with other Christians holding intermediate qualifications set as the reference category. $N = 238,996$

Source: Census 2011

At the middling level, Catholics are behind Other Christians (48 compared with 50 per cent) but to the same extent ahead of those of No Religion (48 compared with 46 per cent). And at the highest level of educational attainment, Catholics and Other Christians are the same. In brief there is no compelling evidence that in the Greater Glasgow area Catholic women aged 35 to 54 are the victims of discrimination.

As with the data for men, Other Religion female identifiers stand out, but this time they are relative losers. Although very much at par for the lowest level of education (17 per cent compared with 18 per cent elsewhere among the less qualified), they fall considerably short of the other blocks for the middle levels (40 per cent middle class compared with 48 per cent elsewhere among those with intermediate qualifications) and even more for the highest level of attainment (66 per cent middle class compared with 78 per cent elsewhere among graduates).

Without further information, we can only guess what has caused this anomaly.[6] Such little research of the education and employment histories of Muslim women in Scotland as there is (El-Nakla et al., 2007; Kidd and Jamieson, 2011) has been of the focus group type and makes no claims to be representative. However, little of it claims discrimination. What we do know from 2001 census data is that women of Other Religion have distinctive work histories. While only some 6 per cent of Scottish women as a whole had never worked (meaning paid work outside the home), that figure for Muslim women was 45 per cent, for Sikh women 27 per cent, for Hindu women 20 per cent and for Buddhist women 18 per cent (Kidd and Jamieson, 2011: 76). Using the census data that we do have for 2011, we find that twice as many women of Other Religion had never worked, compared with 6 per cent of Scottish women in the 35 to 54 age group as a whole.

In brief, there is some connection between South and South-East Asian background and the possibility of a life of domesticity. It may be that reluctance to enter the formal labour market is in some part caused by anticipating negative reactions of potential employers, but more likely the distinctive occupational profile of the Other Religion identifiers represents a culture that prioritises the domestic sphere, the family and informal, unpaid work over the world of formal employment, even for women who are graduates.

To summarise, analysis of the 2011 census data on religion, education and social class offers no support for the claim that Catholics are the victims of labour market discrimination. The two clear outliers are both people of Other Religions: ill-educated men of Other Religion have done better than expected, while well-educated women of Other Religion have done less well.

Further evidence that Scotland is not a society deeply divided by religion can be found in marriage patterns. As the descendants of Irish Catholic migrants have improved their socio-economic status, they have increasingly 'married out'. Taking only the west of Scotland, where Catholics are concentrated, Raab and Holligan's analysis of 2001 data found that a quarter of marriages were Protestant–Catholic (2012: 1945). Considering that most Catholics were schooled apart from non-Catholics, this degree of intermarriage suggests that Scots pay little or no attention to religion in making the most important choice of their lives.

The gradual integration of the new Catholics has weakened the Catholic Church. The descendants of Irish migrants no longer form an identifiable community, loyal to the church which could regard them as 'our people'. Decline in mass attendance began later than the corresponding decline for the Church of Scotland and, as we have seen above, nominal attachment remains stronger, but Catholic religious participation is now around the Scottish average.

Religion and national identity

It was common for nation-states to support (and be supported by) a national church and minority nationalist movements have often invoked a shared minority faith as part of what distinguishes them. So long as most Scots were some variety of Presbyterian, it was possible, as we saw at the start of this chapter, for Scots to think of themselves as united by a common religion and divided from the English by the same. The secularisation of Scotland gradually reduced the salience of religion in national identity but it was decisively undermined by the growth of the Catholic community. There is some suspicion that Scots Catholics were reluctant to support devolution in the 1970s because they feared that a politically autonomous Scotland would be more unpleasantly anti-Catholic than one run from London. In the run-up to the 1997 referendum, Cardinal Thomas Winning very publicly announced that Catholics had nothing to fear from a Scottish parliament. Whether he led or merely announced a change is not clear, but in the event Catholics were as likely as Protestants to vote for a devolved parliament and less likely to have voted against.

Where religion and national identity were firmly linked was in support for the Scottish National Party. In the 1930s, Scottish nationalism often assumed it was addressing a Presbyterian audience (Brand, 1978). It is telling that the vehicle that John McCormick used to promote nationalism in the 1940s was called a 'Covenant', a reminder of a significant period in Presbyterian church history. In 1982 William Wolfe, who had been a senior figure in the party for over thirty years, publicly criticised the appointment of a papal nuncio (the Vatican's equivalent of an ambassador) to the UK. Following the outbreak of the Falklands War, he wrote to the press that the 'mainly Protestant and democratically minded Falklanders, mostly descendants of Scots' had to be protected from Argentina, a 'cruel and ruthless fascist dictatorship of a Roman Catholic state' ('Nationalist chief retires in religions dispute', *The Times*, 8 May 1982: 2). Twice the party's national executive disowned Wolfe's statements, a sign that the SNP now understood that it could not make serious inroads into the Labour vote in the urban Lowlands so long as its image of the nation excluded Catholics (and for that matter, non-Christians and the non-religious). The SNP set its face against the idea of the nation as a body defined by its shared religious background and instead promoted a 'civic' nationalism. The Scottish nation comprised all residents of Scotland, irrespective of religious or ethnic background.

That policy shift was eventually rewarded. In 1970 only 4 per cent of Catholics (as compared with 11 per cent of the population at large) voted SNP. In 1987 the figures were 9 and 14 per cent. Five years later the Catholic and general SNP vote were almost identical: 20 and 21 per cent. And the collapse of the Labour vote in 2011 and again in 2014 confirmed the end of any lingering religious tinge to Scottish nationalism.

In countries such as Poland and Greece where almost the entire population shares a common religion that divides them from their neighbours, national identity is bolstered by religion, which not only acts as a convenient badge of belonging, but also provides myths of election, of possessing some specially favoured status in the eyes of God. The religious diversity of modern Scotland, reinforced by the large and growing number of Scots who are religious indifferent, makes such an association impossible.

Conclusion

It is possible to extract from what may seem a bewildering mass of information, a single theme to Scotland's recent religious history and that theme is not 'decline', though it is hard to write about religion in modern Scotland without repeating that word. It is choice. In the seventeenth century it was thought perfectly reasonable to use the militia to coerce people to conform to the state's chosen church. Increasing civility saw violence replaced by more subtle discrimination. The 1829 Catholic Emancipation Act removed the last serious disabilities imposed on dissenters but positive privileging of the national church was still accepted until the end of land tax funding in 1925.

With a few exceptions – such as the state funding of Catholic schools or the honorific status accorded the Kirk – Scotland now has a free market in religion which offers the spiritual seeker a vast cafeteria of options. We now have all the major world's religions and every variety of Christianity. We also have a wide variety of new religious movements. And this range is not just available in the practical sense that we can find out about and participate in almost every conceivable kind of religion; it is also available in the social sense that minority religions are no longer stigmatised. Where witches were once burnt at the stake, the Aberdeen *Press and Journal* now prints large photographs of Kevin Carlyon, self-appointed head of Britain's white witches, performing rituals to protect the Loch Ness monster.

Many Scots still stay with the churches into which they were born: the most popular options remain the Kirk and the Catholic Church. But there are two other choices which are important for understanding religion in modern Scotland. First, there is the choice to ignore religion. By far the most significant change over the twentieth century has been the rise of religious indifference. The arguments that excited the Victorians and Edwardians now fall on deaf ears and even many churchgoers are indifferent to once-pressing theological differences.

Second, there is the choice to prefer choice itself. A sample of people who had moved from the Brethren to the Baptists were asked why they had shifted (Dickson, 1990). The main reason was narrowness: the Brethren were too narrow in discouraging contact with other churches, in rejecting new ideas and in prescribing conservative ways of behaving. Moving to the Baptists gave greater freedom.

We can understand much of what is happening across Scottish religion if we just generalise that preference. Liberty has trumped rectitude and personal autonomy has trumped obedience. We see it in the growth of the non-religious. We see it in the movement between generations from conservative to mainstream churches. We also see it in the way that those who have stayed attached to the churches in which they were raised have become more selective and assertive. Catholic cardinals and Presbyterian ministers complain that their adherents are no longer willing to accept their authority. Remarkably, Akong Rinpoche, the founder and head of the Samye Ling Tibetan Buddhist Monastery in Eskdalemuir, made the same complaint: too many of those who were interested enough to come to Samye Ling wanted to decide for themselves just what it was they would believe. Secularisation need not mean the end of religion, but it does undermine shared religion. With the state and the public sphere religious neutral, religion has become a thoroughly private matter, a sphere in which the individual consumer is sovereign.

Chapter summary

So what have we learned in this chapter?

- Christian churches were far less popular at the end of the 20th century than at the beginning. Scots are far less religious than their forebears.

- Most Scots remain positive towards religion in the abstract, but their prevailing attitude is one of benign indifference.

- Claims of the Church of Scotland to be the 'national' church have been fatally damaged by the large number of dissenting alternatives, and by religious indifference.

- There is no support for the claim that Catholics are victims of labour market discrimination.

- Religious diversity in modern Scotland has seriously weakened the association between religion and political identity.

Questions for discussion

1. Why can religion no longer form a part of Scottish national identity?

2. How significant is what is variously called 'New Age', contemporary, alternative and holistic spirituality?

3. Is sectarianism important beyond football fan rivalry?

4. Which of religious identification, church membership and church attendance is most useful for assessing the popularity of the Christian churches in Scotland?

Annotated reading

(a) C. Field, '"The haemorrhage of faith?": Opinion polls as sources for religious practices, beliefs and attitudes in Scotland since the 1970s', *Journal of Contemporary Religion*, 16, 2001. This article lives up to its title. It is the best short source for statistical information about changing religious beliefs and practices in modern Scotland.

(b) S. Bruce, *Scottish Gods: Religion in modern Scotland 1900–2012* (2014). *Scottish Gods*, which won the 2014 Saltire Society prize for best Scottish history book, is the source of much of this chapter and has the advantage of space to put historical, biographical and sociological flesh on the skeleton sketched here.

(c) S. Bruce, A. Glendinning, I. Paterson and M. Rosie, *Sectarianism in Scotland* (2011). This elaborates and tests all the various claims that are made for the relevance of sectarianism and concludes that most of those claims are social myths. But its conclusions are less important than its role as a compendium of relevant information.

Notes

1   Where no other source is cited the data come from Bruce (2014).
2   The Registrar-General's published statistics confuse the issue by classifying humanist ceremonies as 'religious'. My analysis corrects that mistake.

3   'Pillarisation' (*Verzuiling* in Dutch) refers to the political–denominational division into distinct 'societies', historically strongest in the Netherlands, with Protestant, Catholic and Socialist 'pillars'.

4   The 'Troubles' was the way of referring, somewhat euphemistically, to ethno-religious conflict in Northern Ireland dating from the late 1960s.

5   I am grateful to the Registrar-General for Scotland for supplying the data analysed here and to my colleague Tony Glendinning for the statistical work.

6   Because the Registrar-General takes the religion data to be unusually sensitive, very little is released on the website and any further analysis would require specially commissioned and approved outputs.

CULTURE AND IDENTITY

15

BELONGING: PLACING PEOPLE

The stanza next to Figure 15.1 is possibly the most famous part of a poem by Alexander Gray, simply called 'Scotland'. Gray, a civil servant and a professor of political economy, published it in 1928. Perhaps we marvel these days that a civil servant and economist could write such a poem, but such is its fame that the verse appears in stone on the wall leading to the Scottish parliament at the foot of Edinburgh's Canongate. The poem ends:

Yet do thy children honour and love thee.

Harsh is thy schooling yet great is the gain:

True hearts and strong limbs, the beauty of faces,

Kissed by the wind and caressed by the rain.

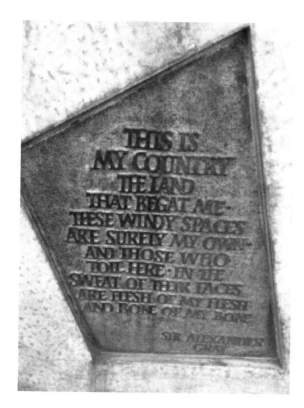

FIGURE 15.1
This is my country (and poem stanza)

Source: Author's photograph

This is my country, the land that begat me.

These windy spaces are surely my own, and those who here toil

in the sweat of their faces are flesh of my flesh,

And bone of my bone.

We know it is an elemental Scottish poem because it alludes to the weather, and because, to use a more modern expression, there is no gain without pain. It may seem odd to some to address poetry to a place rather than a person, but the country is personified in verse, and in this respect Scotland is not unusual. The late Norman MacCaig once said, tersely: 'I hate a man who calls his country *his*.' Replied Douglas Dunn, 'I don't call Scotland mine. I call it Scotland' (Dunn, 1992: 9).

We can see Scotland as having two dominant Scottish landscapes. It is a place of teeming towns, densely populated and dominated by tenements. In George Blake's words, Scotland appears 'overweight with cities'.[1] The other image, which we will focus on in the next chapter, presents Scotland as a 'people-less place', reflected in its rural, usually Highland, image of empty spaces as if no one has ever lived there. These are our two dominant motifs.

In this chapter, we will explore the expressions of 'belonging' and attachment to place, and not simply to Scotland, because there is another strain of writing which asserts the importance, even the primacy, of the 'local'. In the following chapter, we will extend our discussion to 'country', which can also be read as Country ('This is my country ...' as Gray wrote), or as 'land' or 'countryside'. Hence, both chapters should be read in conjunction.

Chapter aims

- To assess the significance of 'belonging', and ask what, if anything, is specific to Scotland.

- To examine the importance of locality and place in Scotland.

- To observe how jokes and humour reveal meanings of place.

- To apply the concept of 'cultural intimacies' and 'Kailyardism' to Scotland.

- To analyse the applicability of 'community' in a Scottish context.

- To show how ideas of person, place and nation apply to Scotland.

Where do you belong?

In Scotland, there is a common question which seems unique to this place: 'where do you belong?' This is neither a question about where you were born, nor whence you have travelled, but also more than a question about your attachment to place. It elicits your roots, your origins, reinforced by a sense of 'home'. Belonging, then, matters; nor is it unique to Scotland. It famously is celebrated in song: 'I belong to Glasgow', which ends, 'Glasgow belongs to me'. The social historian Bob Morris observes that there is a double meaning of 'belonging': 'Will Fyffe and others might sing *"Glasgow belongs to me"*, but Glasgow actually belonged to those whose property deeds were in Register House in

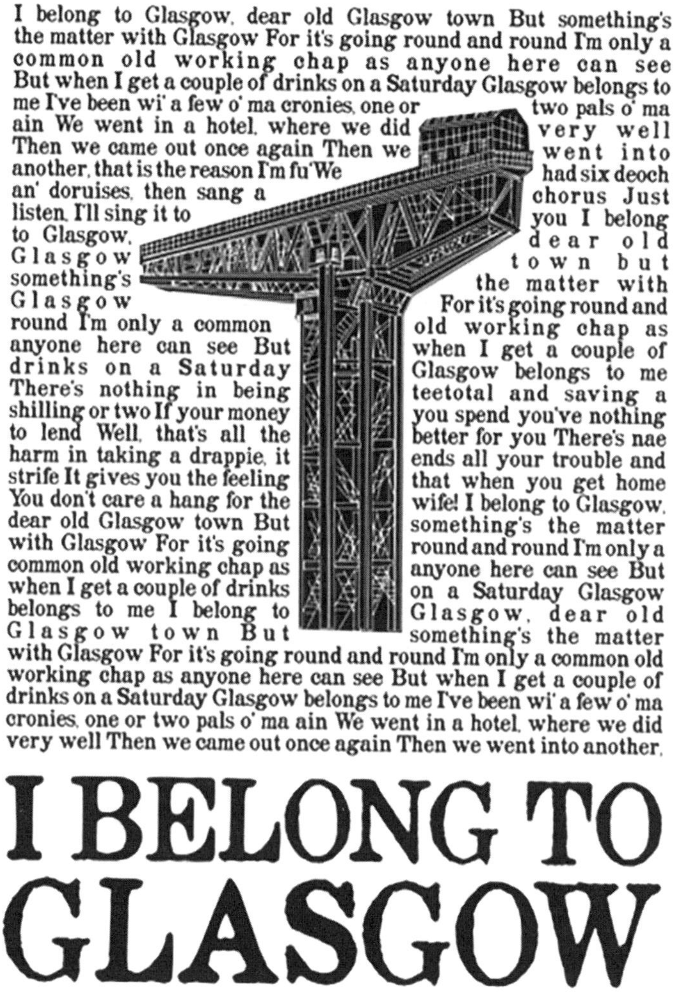

I belong to Glasgow, dear old Glasgow town But something's the matter with Glasgow For it's going round and round I'm only a common old working chap as anyone here can see But when I get a couple of drinks on a Saturday Glasgow belongs to me I've been wi' a few o' ma cronies, one or two pals o' ma ain We went in a hotel, where we did very well Then we came out once again Then we went into another, that is the reason I'm fu' We had six deoch an' doruises, then sang a chorus Just listen, I'll sing it to you I belong to Glasgow, dear old Glasgow town but something's the matter with Glasgow For it's going round and round I'm only a common old working chap as anyone here can see But when I get a couple of drinks on a Saturday Glasgow belongs to me There's nothing in being teetotal and saving a shilling or two If your money you spend you've nothing to lend Well, that's all the better for you There's nae harm in taking a drappie, it ends all your trouble and strife It gives you the feeling that when you get home You don't care a hang for the wife! I belong to Glasgow, dear old Glasgow town But something's the matter with Glasgow For it's going round and round I'm only a common old working chap as when I get a couple of drinks anyone here can see But on a Saturday Glasgow when I get a couple of drinks Glasgow, dear old belongs to me I belong to something's the matter Glasgow town But with Glasgow For it's going round and round I'm only a common old working chap as anyone here can see But when I get a couple of drinks on a Saturday Glasgow belongs to me I've been wi' a few o' ma cronies, one or two pals o' ma ain We went in a hotel, where we did very well Then we came out once again Then we went into another,

I BELONG TO GLASGOW

FIGURE 15.2

Glasgow iconography. Adrian McMurchie's graphic combines the image of the Finnieston crane with the words of the iconic song

Source: Graphic – Adrian B. McMurchie (www.amcmurchie.com)

Edinburgh' (Morris, 2000: 231). Morris was not implying that the song should properly be a testimony to title deeds, but that it is so ubiquitous that it became a, even *the*, Glaswegian theme tune. It was in many ways the first of many strap-lines and brand slogans whereby towns and cities promoted themselves: most famously in the 1980s 'Glasgow's Miles Better', to be followed by a succession to the most recent (from 2013), 'People Make Glasgow', which has the implicit inversion that 'Glasgow Makes People', a nice implicit twist on the Will Fyffe song[2] (see Figure 15.2). Other cities struggle to keep up. Dundee is clearly attached to being 'City of Discovery', Edinburgh, not very convincingly, promotes its capital status, and Aberdeen fails to reach the starting line on the branding stakes.

What is being played upon clearly is 'community', collective identity. In an essay entitled 'Glasgow's Miles Better', the symbolism of community and identity in the city, the social anthropologist Simon Charsley observed that:

the master identity, Glasgow itself, means different things to different people, but always complex and slightly ambiguous things, like the city's current slogan ['Glasgow's Miles Better']. ... There is a negative side, a stigma to be overcome, but also a plethora of embraceable symbols, particularly those which cluster round two polar conceptions, the working class city and the cultural centre. (1986: 171)

Like most cities, Glasgow has districts to which people adhere – hence, Charsley's comment about 'Glasgow' as the 'master identity'. But localities matter. He goes on to say:

Ties of kinship or friendship with particular ministers or priests, some variation in preparedness to marry people in different personal circumstances and the complexities introduced by 'mixed marriages',[3] as well as the attractiveness of particular churches as settings, are all factors in reducing the localisation of choice. (1986: 172)

These local identities and attachments are nested within the city identity, and reflect local roots and attachments, for many districts stood outside the city boundaries until well into the twentieth century. To be sure, few may remember the incorporation, but it seems firmly embedded in the local sense of place, reinforced by local institutions, newspapers, football teams, and public facilities like former town halls.

To be sure, Glasgow (see Figure 15.3) is not unusual in a Scottish or a British context, in terms of either its internal differentiation, or its 'master identity'. The writer James Meek commented: 'People who live in cities assume their city is a thing in the way they talk about it. They '"hate" London, they "miss" Bristol, they "adore" Belfast' (2016: 23).

Localism matters, as we shall see later in the chapter, and in the Glasgow case has been pressed into political service by the ruling Labour Party to counter the electoral successes of the Scottish National Party. Overtures are made to comparable English cities like Manchester and Liverpool on the grounds that Glasgow has more in common with them than with the rest of Scotland. In the run-up to the Scottish Independence Referendum, the-then Glasgow City Council leader, Gordon Mathieson, commented: 'The fact is that Glasgow has more in common with cities such as Liverpool and Manchester than we do with much of the rest of Scotland. I welcome this powerful intervention against separatism from my fellow city leaders' (*The Herald*, 8 May 2014).

Labour would not go so far as to say that Glasgow is not a *Scottish* city, although the Irish roots of many of its inhabitants lead some to infer that people of Catholic/Irish origin do not identify with 'Scottish symbols' (see Gallagher's assertion in Chapter 13 that 'Working-class Catholics in particular found it difficult to relate to the symbols of Scottish nationhood (and many still do)' (1991: 32)). The electoral success of the Glasgow Labour Party, against the odds, in holding onto council power in 2012, convinced many that it danced to a different political tune to the rest of Scotland, including its rival, Edinburgh. This was brought into sharp relief when Glasgow (and Dundee) voted 'Yes' for Scottish

FIGURE 15.3
Wellington Statue, Glasgow. The statue of Wellington with the traffic cone on his head stands outside the Gallery of Modern Art in Glasgow, and has become a Glasgow icon

Source: Graphic – Adrian B. McMurchie (www.amcmurchie.com)

independence at the September 2014 Referendum. And then the SNP swept the board in the city by winning all the Glasgow seats in the 2015 British general election and, in 2016, all the constituency seats in the Scottish parliament election. Maybe Glasgow turned out to be 'Scottish' after all.

'Local patriotism'

Like many places, local patriotism attaches to towns and cities in Scotland. Local libraries and history societies encourage local histories and delving in historical records. Local newspapers run features on 'place' in an effort to stay live in the modern age. Scotland is somewhat unusual in that the four main cities each have 'local' daily newspapers: *The Herald* (until 1992, called *The Glasgow Herald*), and in Edinburgh, *The Scotsman*, although each claims to be Scotland's 'national' newspaper. Their lack of success throws into relief the fact that the (Aberdeen) *Press and Journal* and *The* (Dundee) *Courier* are proportionately far more successful in holding onto subscribers than the two big-city papers (see Chapter 22 on media). Specialising in 'local' news provides a news service not covered by the 'new' social media, nor by the London-dominated media.

The celebration of the 'parochial' becomes mythical, as in the alleged headline following the sinking of the *Titanic* by the *Aberdeen Press and Journal*: 'North-East Man lost at Sea'. This most persistent myth in British newspapers has attached itself to the *P&J* or the 'Pressie', as it is known locally, for over a century. It turns out to be the headline that never was. The *Aberdeen Journal* (it only became the *Press and Journal* in 1922 when it incorporated the *Aberdeen Free Press*) carried a sober(ing) headline: 'Mid-Atlantic Disaster – Titanic Sunk by Iceberg – 1683 Lives Lost, 675 Saved – Increasing Race to Rescue'. Chris Holme in *The Scottish Review* (https://historycompany.co.uk/2012/01/25/the-headline-that-never-was/) points out that 'North-East man is a new epithet; the phrase of the day was "North Country" (man)'. Holme observes: 'He is a relative newcomer – although his ubiquity is the reason the myth sticks. Every day ["North-East man"] is killed in an accident, survives several more, appears in court, or he's involved in a stushie[4] somewhere else. Some guy.' It matters less that stories are inaccurate than that they seem to confirm who 'we' are.

Biding in the toon

There is a strong literary tradition of writing about 'the town' in Scotland (note the ubiquity of 'the town', rarely 'the city'; 'the toon' is where life really happens). The novelist Willie McIlvanney once observed:

> It seems to me that the thing Scottish writing would have to confront is the Scottish urban experience. Because the truth is for most of us that is where we have been. You take the nexus around Glasgow [McIlvanney himself was from Ayrshire] that's still the eye of the hurricane. I think that's where our understanding of ourselves resides. (Quoted in Idle, 1993: 56)

McIlvanney's toon is a firmly gender-segregated place. Writing of 'Graithnock' (a barely disguised Kilmarnock) in his novel *Docherty*, he commented: 'Wives looked in on one another without ceremony. The men gathered compulsively each night at the street corner' (McIlvanney, 1975: 32).

This gendering of place, as well of social relations, is a key theme in toon-writing. Leslie Mitchell/'Lewis Grassic Gibbon' describes Edinburgh as 'a disappointed spinster, with hare lip and inhibitions'; Dundee is a 'frowsy fisher-wife addicted to gin and infanticide'; Aberdeen 'a thin-lipped peasant woman who has borne eleven and buried nine'; and 'no Scottish image of personification may display, even distortedly, the essential Glasgow' (Gibbon, 1967: 82). Aberdeen held few delights for his alter ego, the journalist Leslie Mitchell:

Bleakness, not meanness or jollity, is the keynote to Aberdonian character, not so much lack of the graces or graciousness of existence as lack of colour in either of these. And this is almost inevitable for anyone passing his nights and days in The Silver City by the Sea. It is comparable to passing one's existence in a refrigerator. Aberdeen is built, largely and incredibly, on one of the enduring and indestructible and appalling building materials in use on our planet – grey granite. (Gibbon, 1967: 96–7)

Glasgow, where Mitchell was briefly employed, comes off even worse. It is indescribable: 'The monster in Loch Ness is probably the lost soul of Glasgow, in scales and horns, disporting itself in the Highlands after evacuating finally and completely its mother corpse' (1967: 82). One of Glasgow's own sons, Alasdair Gray, paints an unprepossessing picture of 'Unthank' (in his novel *Lanark*, 1981). His literary personum, Duncan Thaw, observes:

What is Glasgow to most of us? A house, the place we work, a football park or golf course, some pubs and connecting streets. That's all. No, I'm wrong, there's also the cinema and the library. ... Imaginatively Glasgow exists as a music-hall song and a few bad novels. That's all we've given to the world outside. It's all we've given ourselves. (Gray, 1981: 243)

Characterising toons

Scotland's cities are toons with character, possibly even Character. Here is Hugh MacDiarmid's account of them in his poem, *Midnight*:

Glasgow is null,

Its suburbs, shadows,

and the Clyde a cloud.

Dundee is dust

And Aberdeen a shell.

But Edinburgh is a mad god's dream,

Fitful and dark,

Unseizable in Leith

And wildered by the Forth,

But irresistibly at last

Cleaving to sombre heights

Of passionate imagining

Till stonily,

From soaring battlements,

Earth eyes Eternity. (Hugh MacDiarmid, *The Complete Poems*, 1978)

After 'The complete Poems, 1978', from D. Dunn (1992) *Scotland: An Anthology*, London: Fontang.

Cities with their hinterlands developed their own persona, and in Grassic Gibbon's imagery, as female, urban wombs; and the ubiquitous high street, a 'second mother' (McIlvanney, 1975: 34). Cities, and above all Glasgow, grew rapidly: in 1840, it held 10 per cent of Scotland's population; a century later, it had doubled to 20 per cent, before falling back to little over 10 per cent today. Scotland is an 'urban' society, and while strictly speaking about 30 per cent of Scots now live in one or other of the four cities (40 per cent did so in 1951), as many as nine out of ten Scots now live in 'urban' areas of 1000 people or more,[5] compared with eight out of ten in 1931, and less than 50 per cent in 1851. While England seems to have a hierarchy of city–town–village, Scotland makes do with the generic term 'toon'. Even Glasgow with 1 million people until the 1960s was described as a 'toon' (in Will Fyffe's 'I belong to Glasgow', 'dear old Glasgow city' would not have had much of a ring to it).

Above all, the toon is physically distinctive. It rose up out of its surroundings in an unmistakable way. The dominant image was the three-, four- or five-storey tenement in contrast to the low-density brick rows of England. Travelling by train from Scotland to England entails crossing a border in building styles. Edinburgh and Newcastle, Glasgow and Manchester, can only belong to different countries and cultures. One remarkable thing about Scottish towns and cities is that, despite the degree and rapid rate of urbanisation, there was no equivalent of English 'Coketown' in literary discourse. Scotland came to be defined by its urban space as much as by its rural ones.

Even when no city is named we know which is being talked about. We need to be in the know to get the allusions:

Nae knickers, all fur coat

Slurped Valvona and Crolla,

Tweed-lapelled, elbow-patched, tartan-skirted,

Kilted, Higgs-bosoned, tramless, trammelled and trammed,

Awash with drowned witches prematurely damned,

Prim as skimmed milk, cheesily floodlit, breezily,

Galefully, Baltically cold with royal

Lashings of tat and Hey-Jimmy wigs, high on swigs

Of spinsterish, unmarried malt ...[6]

Here are abundant in-jokes about 'cultural intimacy', to use Michael Herzfeld's notion (1997). Jokes are for *us*, but about *them*. 'Aberdeen man lost at sea' fits the bill. An empty Union Street is Aberdeen on a flag day when locals allegedly avoided giving to charity (see Figure 15.4).

Grassic Gibbon told a particularly savage version of the joke:

> An Aberdonian died and gave instructions in his will that his body be cremated. This was done. The day after the cremation the widow heard a knock on the door. She opened it and saw a small message-boy standing on the doorstep holding out a package towards her. 'What's this?', she enquired. 'Your husband, Mem', said the boy '– his ashes, you know.' Slowly the widow took the package in her hand. 'His ashes. Oh aye. *But where's the dripping?*'

Commented Grassic Gibbon, 'You laugh but (if you have any imagination at all) you have a slight qualm. The grisliness below the humour is insufficiently concealed' (Grassic Gibbon, 'Aberdeen', in *Scottish Scene*, 1934).

Legendary meanness makes for a laugh: *Scotland the What* made a good living out of recounting

ABERDEEN ON A FLAG DAY —

AND ON A HOUSE-TO-HOUSE COLLECTION DAY
SCOTS MAKE FUN OF SCOTLAND   COLLECTORCARD
A Valentine's Card c1920   Croydon CRO 1HW
C1813

FIGURE 15.4   Celebrating meanness. Aberdeen on a flag day: a Valentine's postcard *c.*1920

Source: Author's photograph of original postcard

in-jokes, always in Doric, which was more than half the joke. Edinburgh snobbery: *fur coat and no knickers* – keeping up appearances. 'You'll have had your tea', as a pre-emptive greeting to avoid feeding guests.[7] Dundee speech: known as a women's town in its jute-spinning days, and men called 'kettle-bilers', staying at home and making the tea. Pride in trade: 'ah'm no' a spinner, I'm a wyver [weaver]', the affronted woman addressed as a spinster by the wedding registrar; or a misunderstood compliment: 'You're stunnin'; no, ah'm stannin'; or a request for an accessory for the Dundee mutton pie (the *peh*):[8] 'an' ane wi' an ingin' an' a''. Glasgow jokes with a slight edge – *weegies* – but not to their faces; jokes about poverty and religion, always told carefully. Non-Glaswegians will tell weegie jokes, but safely out of earshot. Tom Leonard's 'this is thi six a clock news', makes the class point: 'if a toktaboot thi trooth lik wanna yoo scruff yi widny thingk it wuz troo. Jist wanna yoo scruff tokn' (1984; Dunn, 1992: 238). The use of language and dialect is a key device for separating out us and them.[9]

Joking relations

Truth to tell, mockery can be dangerous, even life-threatening: witness *Charlie Hebdo* in January 2015. 'Can you not take a joke?' is offered to women for sexist jokes, and Muslims for racist ones. Jokes are often not at all funny for those on the receiving end. Think, for example, of a word cognate to humour, ridicule. There is nothing funny about being ridiculed. Michael Billig observed: 'Rather than criticizing some types of humour as inappropriate, and commending others for meeting the requisite standards, it is possible to call into question laughter's assumed goodness' (2005: 1).

What is sociologically interesting about them is that they reinforce stereotypes; they are in- and out-jokes, told in the argot of 'the patter' in Glasgow, and the Doric in Aberdeen: words which signal you are an insider, because you get it (even 'an' ane wi' an ingin' an' a''). The 'edge' which jokes carry is that they imply insiders and outsiders; you either get it, or you do not. You are either one of us, or you are not. Georg Simmel made the point that 'The Stranger' is someone living in the midst of members of the group, but whose 'distance' is emphasised more than their 'nearness'; think about the cultural constructions of 'Muslims' in western societies (Wolff, 1950).

Then there are national jokes; about the Scots as mean, the English snobbish, the Irish less than intelligent (see C. Davies, 2011). Once more there are health warnings. Telling them about 'the other', and to their faces, can be dangerous. Magazines like *Punch* made a good living out of them since the mid-nineteenth century until it shut up shop in 2002.

There is something quite intimate about jokes. Think of trying to understand a joke in a foreign language. You may understand all the words but not get the joke, because you do not comprehend the allusions, the implied intimacies. He who laughs last fails to get the joke. How much insider knowledge do you need to understand The Broons: *jings, crivvens, help ma boab* (see Figure 15.5)? Do you need to 'place' them in mythical Auchenshuggle,[10] somewhere in cultural–geographical space between Dundee and Glasgow?

Cultural intimacies

Jokes are good examples of Herzfeld's 'cultural intimacies': 'the recognition of those aspects of a cultural identity that are considered a source of external embarrassment but

FIGURE 15.5
The Broons &
oor Wullie®

Source: © DC
Thomson & Co.
Ltd. 2016

that nevertheless provide insiders with their assurance of common sociality' (1997: 3). This often involves self-stereotyping which insiders express ostensibly at their own collective expense. As Herzfeld observes: 'The language of national or ethnic identity is ... a language of morality. It is an encoded discourse about inclusion and exclusion' (1997: 43). *We* find it easier to take the joke about ourselves; *you* cannot.

Cultural intimacy is above all familiarity with perceived social flaws which offer culturally persuasive explanations for distinctiveness. Nevertheless, Herzfeld comments, the stereotype is a double-edged sword; it is a discursive weapon of power.

> It does something, and something very insidious: it actively deprives 'the other' of a certain property, and the perpetrator pleads moral innocence on the grounds that the property in question is symbolic rather than material, that the act of stereotyping is 'merely' a manner of speech, and that 'words can never hurt you'. (1997: 157)

What does this have to do with Scotland? Scotland is replete with self-images; indeed, to use Raymond Williams' concept of 'cultural formations', they are over-abundant and usually deemed negative. Two such are 'tartanry' and 'kailyard', which we will discuss in detail in Chapter 17, and Scottish intellectuals were in the habit of explaining their distorting hegemony for the absence of self-government until the late 1990s.

The view was that Scots had internalised the stereotypes to the extent that they believed their own propaganda, and if Herzfeld is right, with deleterious consequences for self-esteem.[11] Sometime described as 'mythic structures', they seemed to offer only negative visions of Scotland. To say they were 'mythic' is not to imply that they were false, driven out by an injection of wholesome reality, but that they skewed our understanding of ourselves such that they were internalised as ways of seeing. We will discuss these in detail in Chapter 17. Andrew Blaikie has commented: 'While different groups with varying cultural or political agendas might "deploy the debris of the past for all kinds of present purposes", for those with an eye to the main chance the fruits of tartanry, the Kailyard, Clydesidism,[12] or Highlandism are continually rebranded and marketed' (2010: 13).

Kailyardism

'Kailyard', literally the cabbage-patch, was taken to mean parochialism, identification with inward-looking communities, with 'Scotland' the biggest kailyard of all. Old accusations die hard. When the Scottish government rejected the Trump Organization's objection to offshore wind farms in the north-east in 2015, Trump's executive vice-president reached for the standard comment: 'History will judge those involved unfavourably and the outcome demonstrates the *foolish, small-minded and parochial mentality*' (Mure Dickie, 'Trump loses Scottish wind farm battle', *Financial Times*, 16 December 2015; my emphasis).

The novelist and critic George Blake is credited with coining the term 'Kailyard' to describe its attributed values of domesticity, rusticity, humour, humility, modesty, decency, piety and poverty (Shepherd, 1988). It was a strain of writing associated with 'Ian MacLaren' (John Watson) (1850–1907), S.R. Crockett (1860–1914) and J.M. Barrie (1860–1937), and later couthy manifestations were captured by *The Sunday Post*, and *The People's Friend*,[13] published by DC Thomson of Dundee, who also publish *The Beano* comic; its stable partner *The Dandy* ceased publication in 2012.

The power and influence of the Kailyard School was thought to be hegemonic, dominating the cultural and literary representations of Scotland at least until the Great War, with its heyday at the end of the nineteenth century. Scotland was 'parochial', in both literal and symbolic forms, with a cultural significance beyond Scotland. The writer T.D. Knowles commented that the work of kailyard writers 'contained British Victorian elements as well as Scottish; they were regionalists, and there is influence from the gothic novel, the fairy tale, 18th century sentimentalism, and the Victorian penchant for death and dying' (1983: 64). Its influence took a long time in dying, particularly the view that it was responsible for the 'deformation' of Scottish cultural forms for much of the twentieth century, and even for the failure of the devolution referendum in 1979: Scotland was feart, and lacking self-confidence.[14] What Andrew Blaikie called the 'parish paradigm' (2010: 99) had progressive as well as reactionary features: a belief in a community spirit, and yet an unwillingness to step out of line for fear of public ridicule.

It was not necessary to 'prove' that such features were hard-wired into Scottish culture, simply that they defined the country a priori, in contradistinction to the 'mature, all-round thought-world' of England. Scots were deemed to be culturally schizophrenic, both inextricably attached to 'the land' and yet seeking an escape from it, nicely epitomised by Lewis Grassic Gibbon (who wrote *Sunset Song* in 1932 while living in Welwyn Garden City in the south of England – Gibbon had escaped):

> Two Chrissies there were that fought for her heart and tormented her. You hated the land and the coarse speak of the folk and learning was fine and brave one day. And the next you'd waken up with the peewits crying across the hills, deep and deep, crying in the heat of you and the smell of the earth in your face, almost you'd cry for that, the beauty of it and the sweetness of the Scottish land and skies. (1946: 37)

The point is not that this is about 'the land' narrowly defined, but the tensions between attachments and ways of life: two forms of belonging, the parochial and the universal.

The power of these tropes is less about how 'true' they are, or not, but that they were held responsible for keeping Scots in their place: haud'n doon.[15] It was the cultural power of the image which mattered, not its reality; it was taken to be a form of intellectual and cultural colonialism. In a country from which a disproportionate number had migrated over the centuries to 'get on' as economic migrants, to stay at home was somehow a retrograde step, to be what the historian Christopher Harvie (1977: 17) called being a 'black'

Scot ('demotic, parochial and reactionary') rather than the 'red' ('cosmopolitan, self-avowedly enlightened'). We will discuss this more fully in Chapter 17.

In these matters, representation, not reality, was all, and the traction afforded Carol Craig's books on (the lack of) Scottish self-confidence in political and cultural circles was testimony to that. Simplicities such as these became useful devices. As Herzfeld observes: 'Polarities are a convenience. They are useful for sorting out issues. But, like all classificatory devices, they can also become a substitute for thinking: they get essentialized, turned into fact' (1997: 165).

Place matters

There is another twist to this as regards Scotland. Place matters; not simply the locality, but the national territory. Christopher Smout famously observed that 'being Scottish' involved a sense of *place* rather than a sense of *tribe* (1994: 107). This is usually taken to signify living in Scotland, rather than belonging to a cultural, linguistic or religious tradition which defines who is Scottish.

Smout's point was that from its origins as a 'kingdom', such was the cultural (i.e. ethnic) diversity of Scotland that unification could only be achieved by uniting diverse peoples around 'place'; in other words, inculcating a sense of 'civic' or territorial Scottishness. We take that to mean that Scots were by and large non-tribal, but it also attributes particular power to 'place', whether at the national or local level (indeed, the 'parochial', which might well account for attributing negative connotations to attachment to place).

Writing is almost always 'placed' to be effective. To take a few examples: Neil Gunn, who had lived in Galloway, London and Wigan, returned to his native Caithness where he was 'overwhelmed with the vision of bleak greyness, with an aversion ... to touch the realities of life in his native place' (Hart, 1987: 87). Willa Muir wrote her first novel *Imagined Corners* (1931), loosely based on Montrose ('Calderwick'), to explore the oppression of women and restrictions on individual freedom in the 1930s.

As Blaikie has observed:

> When individuals connect [to places] in this way they are acknowledging something personally felt but also something beyond the personal in that they are only part of the imagined picture, and sometimes stand outside looking in. And this 'something' is akin to community in that memory acts as a catalyst for yearning, being the mechanism through which a trace of past identification is recollected. (2010: 246)

In truth, it is neither a matter of 'tribe' or 'place', but the ways they fuse together, how biography and place intermingle. Blaikie quotes the poet Norman MacCaig: 'The little plot – do I belong to it or it to me? No matter. We share each other as I walk amongst its flags and tombstones' (2010: 248). MacCaig was intimately connected to Achmelvich, near Lochinver in Wester Ross, as well as to Edinburgh where he lived and worked, and these places became mentally intertwined, as in his poem 'Assynt and Edinburgh':

From the corner of Scotland I know so well

I see Edinburgh sprawling like seven cats

On its seven hills beside the Firth of Forth.

And when I'm in Edinburgh I walk

Amongst the mountains and lochs of that corner

That looks across the Minch to the Hebrides.

Two places I belong to as though I was born

In both of them.

They make every day a birthday,

Giving me gifts wrapped in the ribbons of memory.

I store them away, greedy as a miser.

(From *The Poems of Norman MacCaig*, edited by Ewen McCaig, Polygon, 2005: 505)

Scotland and community

Scotland is not unique in this fusion of place, memory and identity, but it insinuates what Scotland is, and who Scots are, to themselves and ultimately to others. It conveys community. There are few concepts in social science which are so vexatious, and yet ubiquitous. 'Community' is used, and abused, in everyday speech. Interest groups are 'communities', and terms like 'the business community' abound, even though companies are in competition with each other.[16]

As the social anthropologist Anthony Cohen pointed out, '"Community" is not to be approached as a morphology, as a structure of institutions capable of objective definition and description' (1985: 19). The key feature is not 'what it looks like to us', but 'what does it look like to its members?' (1985: 20). In other words:

> 'Community' is a largely mental construct, whose 'objective' manifestations in locality or ethnicity give it credibility. It is highly symbolized, with the consequence that its members can invest it with their selves. Its character is sufficiently malleable that it can accommodate all of its members' selves without them feeling their individuality to be overly compromised. Indeed, the gloss of commonality which it paints over its diverse components gives to each of them an additional reference for their identities. (1985: 108–9)

Cohen's point is not that 'community' can be objectively and externally measured, but that it is symbolically constructed by its members, and reinforced in the telling. He gives the splendid example of 'Erte's greatcoat', a tale told on Whalsay in Shetland about a reclusive character, Erte, whose shabby greatcoat held the secrets of his life and, both metaphorically and practically, was a repository of its keys. The point of the story, told on certain occasions, was not that the listeners had not heard it before, but that they had heard it many times. It functions to reinforce 'community', for it cannot be understood outwith the symbolic context. Cohen observes:

> Members of a community can make virtually anything grist to the symbolic mill of cultural distance, whether it be the effects upon it of some centrally formulated government policy, or matters of dialect, dress, drinking, marrying or dying. ... People construct their community symbolically, making it a resource and repository of meaning. (1986: 17)

He also raises the important point of how symbolic constructions such as community are sustained over time. There is the problem of the 'objective correlative' in that some kind of external validation, some institutional support, is required (Cohen, 2000). We might think of the institutions of civil society as helping to provide validation, reinforcing but not determining the Scottish 'community' in question.

Placing community

It is in this context that we are able to understand jokes. They recount tales about ourselves and others, reinforcing both the senses of who we are and, crucially, who we are not. Jokes against others reinforce our sense of self, who we are as a people, as a 'community'. Graham Crow and Catherine Maclean remind us of Peter Willmott's distinction between 'place community', 'interest community' and 'community of attachment' (Willmott, 1986, in Crow and Maclean, 2013). 'Place community' is possibly the most commonplace, as it were: a geographically bounded locality, hence its association with city/town/village, bounded in space, whether this is Glasgow, or Whalsay. The politics of space are powerful.

Sean Damer's classic study of 'Wine Alley' reinforces the point that 'places' are often held together by reputation imposed by significant others. In the process of allocating new council housing in Glasgow in the inter-war period, the Glasgow Broomloan Road Rehousing Estate ('Scheme', in Scottish parlance) came to be known as 'Wine Alley', reflecting imposed stigma by those who had been excluded from new housing. The moral code was internalised by the inhabitants. Damer commented: 'Tenants distance themselves from the reputation of their scheme by differentiating themselves from the deviants. They tend to displace their fears and fantasies to the point in the scheme furthest from them. The animals are always in another zoo; the witch is always at the far end of the village' (1974: 238).

Thus did the tenants themselves come to believe the moral tales told about them by 'outsiders', including the 'authorities' (council officials, the police, housing officers and the rest). Damer pointed out that these tales could not possibly be true, for if they were, there would be more criminals than people like themselves in the schemes.

Communities can be read into places, such that 'we' become *'those* people'.[17] Communities also comprise *common interests*, of culture, politics, economics. The *soi-disant* 'business community' is one such, the assumption of common material interests being implied. Finally, there are *communities of attachment*, possibly the most common meaning because it implies that people have something in common and care about it. Crow and Maclean describe them as 'built around common identities. ... People in these communities come together through their shared culture, uniting around symbols that emphasise ... common ethnicity, shared difference from able-bodied norms, shared political visions, or aspects of lifestyle such as taste in music' (2013: 356).

Communities of the mind

In practice, communities of place, interests and attachment are interconnected; we assume that they are aspects of the same thing, even if we can think of many counter-examples. We cannot assume that people who live in a 'place' have much which is very meaningful in common (think of commuting suburbs), or that those we might expect to act in their common interests will necessarily do so (Marx's description of peasants as atomised 'potatoes in a sack of potatoes' (*Eighteenth Brumaire*)), still less that pragmatic interests necessarily demand common attachments ('instrumental' actions being a case in point).

The point about 'community' is to figure out, in Clifford Geertz's words, 'what the devil they [participants] think they are up to' (quoted in Pahl, 2005: 622). The key part of that comment is 'what *they think* they are up to', not what the analyst *assumes* to be the common interest. Here, once more, is Cohen's 'symbolic construction' of community, how people put it together for themselves, and possibly make common cause. Pahl makes a crucial point. Sociologists accept that people get their understanding of society from their day-to-day experiences ('on the ground'), but have 'tended at the same time to dismiss much of this as epiphenomenal' (Pahl, 2005: 630). This matters because, as we shall see in discussing globalisation (Chapter 24), the focus has swung firmly away from 'the local' and even from 'the national'.

Which places matter?

What does this tell us about Scotland? In the first place, there is an important question about which 'place' matters. To return to previous arguments: is being a Glaswegian more or less important than being Scottish? Do people really identify most with those they encounter every day, and not with people they have no hope of meeting? Is identifying with 'the nation' so much political froth?

We can explore people's commitment to 'place' through Scottish Social Attitudes survey data (Bechhofer and McCrone, 2008). We asked people to choose which of these they felt 'most important to you generally in your everyday life': The street in which you live/The local area or district/The city or town in which you live/The county or region, for instance Yorkshire, Lothian or Glamorgan/The country in which you live, for instance England, Northern Ireland, Scotland, Wales/Britain/The United Kingdom/Europe.

Asking similar questions in England and Scotland meant that we could test out the view that people in England were more likely to identify with city or region, and the Scots with Scotland. It turned out that only 7 per cent of the English and 17 per cent of Scots thought that 'the country' (i.e. England or Scotland) was the most important. Twenty-nine per cent of Scots opted for their 'local area or district', as did one-third of English people. The town or city was highly salient for Scots and English (31 per cent and 27 per cent, respectively), while 10 per cent of each nationality identified with 'the street'.

People, then, are emotionally attached to the localities in which they live. As many as 87 per cent of Scots and 81 per cent of the English felt very or somewhat proud of their *local* area. It seems that locality trumps 'nation', even for Scots, though in practice it is both/and, not either/or.

Another way to get at commitment to place is to ask: 'If you were abroad and someone who knew this country asked you "where do you come from?"', Scots were three times more inclined to choose 'country' (Scotland) than the English (52 per cent compared with 18 per cent), while similar proportions in the two countries gave their town or city. The 'place' which matters disproportionately to the English is county or region (21 per cent compared with 8 per cent for Scots). We did not find, however, that English people substituted city/county or region (as in 'I'm not English; I'm from Yorkshire') for their national identity. True, local and regional identities were strong in places like Yorkshire and in north-east and north-west England, but identification with 'England' was not significantly lower than elsewhere.[18]

There is nothing especially 'British' about this, one suspects, and 'placing' people, either locally or nationally, has always been vital in deciding who is, or is not, 'one of us'. Robert Louis Stevenson once wrote that, despite differences of 'blood and language', the Lowlander and Highlander 'when they meet abroad, they fall upon each other's necks in spirit; even at home there is a clannish intimacy in their talk'. They 'still have a strong Scotch accent of the mind' (quoted in Dunn, 1992: 17).

Truth to tell, in both Scotland and England, people identify both with their city/county/region and with their nation. Indeed, in talking about how they identify with 'place', people we interviewed as part of our national identity research programme wove the local and the national together naturally. Here are two examples:

> I do have my own images that, and again, it doesn't tend to be Angus Og[19] striding through the heather with his kilt on and a big muckle great coo trailing away at his back in the gloaming. I see and I hear Govan, as a child, hear all that clamour. We were talking about this just last week. I had to go for some supplies into Clydebank and I was with one of the workmen in the vans, and we were coming up through Scotstoun [in Glasgow] ... and I

had an aunt who lived there and I used to be mesmerised by the fact that I was in the west, north of the river but in the west end of Glasgow and I could see the south. Govan was directly across the water and I could hear the men coming out, on the other side of the water. I could hear them going in for their lunch and there used to be this mad clatter because they were running across these steel platforms. These men, it was Yarrow's and John Brown's [shipyards], it was just empty. And the streets were black on the Friday afternoon because they'd money in their pocket and they would come out and leave the staff canteen and go to the pub, the bakers or whatever. I can remember the noise and the smells and that's what I remember, that's Scottishness to me. All that industry and the smell hanging over the Gorbals, all the way when I was growing up. You would come in through across the bridges on the bus to come into town. You would go to work in the morning, the night shift workers would be coming off and you could smell the hops in the air because they had been blending over at Whyte and Mackays [whisky bottling plant]. That's what I remember.

This person 'roots' their Scottishness in specific localities – Clydebank, Govan, Scotstoun, Gorbals – and sees no contradiction: 'that's Scottishness to me', she says.

Here is someone else, living in a small town, who also connects up Scottish places from north to south:

R: Oh yes, I feel Scottish. That's something, I suppose, which I've always felt. I've fulfilled something this year, which I had been meaning to do for a long time previously and that was establish more about my family background, a not un-common pastime. There's many a person, especially as they get older, I think, maybe looks into that. I'd always grown up with a lot of information about my father's family, which I've always been fascinated in and I also had the links with going up, every year, to Morayshire. I've never known as much about my mother's side and there was a particular mystery about her grandmother. Nobody knew the name of her. Who was she? So it's been great fun. Along with my son, involving him in this, we've been into Edinburgh two or three times to dig through records. We've made journeys across ... down to the Borders, up to Morayshire and established lots of very interesting facts. I feel very much part of that. It's given me a sense, also, of not coming from just those two people or those two people, it gives you a sense of how very much everyone is ... there's such a range of people that you are generated from. They were all an incredible mixture.

Interviewer: And that, in some ways, has reinforced your sense of roots to Scotland?

R: Yes, uh-huh, it's been very interesting finding that ... I've got people who are from Ayrshire, the Borders, Glasgow, the Gorbals. The number of people I've found in the Gorbals and that's not just in my family, in loads. It was, I think, an incredible breeding ground. People, I think, flocked there at the end of ... moving out of Highlands and North, I think an awful lot of them ended up in the southside of Glasgow. They all eventually come from further north, whether it be up around Morayshire and west and also to the east, to Aberdeenshire. I never knew that my mother's side ... her mother all originated actually up in Aberdeenshire. And I found the grandmother as well.

So, once more, we find a litany of places associated with family members, as people describe what it means to them to be Scottish. There is no contradistinction between the 'local' and the 'national'. Cohen captured that nicely:

A man's awareness of himself as a Scotsman may have little to do with the Jacobite wars, or with [Robert] Burns, or with the poor state of the housing stock in Glasgow. It has to do with his particular experience as a farmer in Aberdeenshire, as a member of a particular village or a particular group of kin within his village. Local experience mediates national identity, and, therefore, an anthropological understanding of the latter cannot proceed without knowledge of the former. (1982: 13)

There is, by implication, a Glaswegian way, and a Shetland way, and lots of other 'ways' of being Scottish which reflect different ways and experiences of life in a tenement or a croft. Elsewhere, Cohen observes, 'people construct the nation through the medium of their own experience, and in ways which are heavily influenced by their own circumstances. The nation is mediated through the self' (2000: 146).

This is a key point in the arguments about 'belonging'. People construct who they are from the social and cultural materials around them. They derive meaning from what is familiar and connect up personal experiences in a meaningful way. 'Nation', after all, has been described memorably by Benedict Anderson as 'imagined community', *imagined*, because even in the smallest nation one could never hope to meet everyone belonging to it, 'yet in the minds of each lives the image of their communion' (1996: 6–7); *limited*, because it has finite, if elastic, boundaries beyond which lie other nations; *sovereign*, because 'the people' have the right of self-government even though they may not be able to practise it; and a *community*, because it is conceived as a deep, horizontal comradeship, despite unequal social and economic relations, whether of social class or gender as we saw in previous chapters.

It's personal

One of the key features of national identity is that it is 'personal'; in the celebrated phrase of Ernest Renan, it involves a 'daily plebiscite' (*plébiscite de tous les jours*), an implicit affirmation, captured in Michael Billig's telling notion of 'banal nationalism': '"*our*" particular world is experienced as *the* world' (1995: 50, italics in original). Nor do you have to salute the flag daily as in the US Pledge of Allegiance to affirm your identity, although in a nation of incomers that *is* the daily plebiscite.

Most of the time, however, 'the nation' is taken for granted as the 'way we do things'. Politicians who seek to go against the flow are spotted as frauds. Thus, the political ploy by a Conservative Secretary of State for Scotland to insinuate loyalty by having the Stone of Scone/Destiny returned to Edinburgh Castle on St Andrews Day in 1996 failed because there was nothing predictable nor magical about working the spell. Magic can only be performed when the magician has credibility.

The Norwegian social anthropologist Thomas Eriksen has observed that 'nation' is the metaphysical space in which people locate their personal histories, and thereby their identities (in Cohen, 2000: 152). A similar sentiment was expressed by Bruce Kapferer – that 'the person conceives of self as also the nation' (1988: 161). And Cohen has argued that the concept of the nation is

> [s]omething which simply does not require to be well defined, first, people presume that they know what they are talking about when they refer to it; and second, because the lack of definition allows them scope for interpretive manoeuvre in formulating or inventing or imagining the nation in terms of their selves for the purposes of personal identity. (2000: 166)

Thus, the nation is not 'out there' but 'in here', actively constructed and employed for the purpose of 'interpretive manoeuvres' in everyday life. Only in unusual circumstances, and when it is imposed or insisted upon, do people cavil with what is on offer, or where alternative conceptions of 'the nation' are on offer. We give our active consent to belonging such that what we choose to belong to is actively made and transformed.

Places of memory

Fundamental to this personalising the nation is 'memory'. The rising interest in 'memory' owes much to the French historian Pierre Nora and his massive series of research studies called *Lieux des mémoire* (published by Gallimard, in three volumes, in 1997, and running to over 1600 pages). Memory attaches itself to sites, while history attaches itself to events. Nora made a further distinction between memory and history, thus:

> Memory and history, far from being synonymous, appear now to be in fundamental opposition. Memory is life, borne of living societies founded in its name. ... History, on the other hand, is the reconstruction, always problematic and incomplete, of what is no longer. Memory is a perpetually actual phenomenon, a bond tying us to the eternal present; history is a representation of the past. (1989: 8)

FIGURE 15.6
Bannockburn
today: echoes
of 1979

Source: Bochel et al.
(1981: 198)

Of the two, memory is the active force, and it is sustained and amplified by 'sites'. Places – *lieux* – of memory are stimulated by the plethora of records, archives, anniversaries, celebrations of the modern age, which require commemorative vigilance lest history sweep them away. 'Memory' is sustained by what Nora calls the 'exterior scaffolding and outward signs' and above all by its 'new vocation to record'. The apparatus of memory cannot be left to chance, but requires structured remembering. New techniques for remembering are pressingly required, especially if the 'original' site cannot evoke the required response.

Thus, the iconic battle site of Bannockburn cannot carry us back to the fourteenth century because it is a twentieth-century housing scheme (see Figure 15.6).

Accordingly, the National Trust for Scotland has invested millions of pounds in a reimagining process involving three-dimensional imagery and an active battle game in which the enthusiastic taking part is what matters, not the accuracy of the outcome.[20]

Andrew Blaikie has commented: 'the "stories" of Bannockburn and Culloden cannot be disentangled from the battlefields themselves, any more than the meaning of, say, the scheme or farm where one grew up can be understood apart from the place itself' (2010: 242). Once more we return to the significance of 'place'.

Not all are convinced about 'memory', or at least the notion of 'collective memory'. Duncan Bell is critical of the commonly employed notion of collective memory as it operates in studies of nationalism (and in the work of Anthony Smith in particular) because 'memory' today has 'assumed the role of a meta-theoretical trope, and also, perhaps a sentimental yearning' (2003: 65). Memory, he says, can only be understood as the product of individuals and groups of individuals coming together to share memories of particular events they were part of; memory has to be anchored in common and shared experience.

Collective memory as such is 'mythical' and actually performs a 'totalising' function. Thus, says Bell, 'there is no singular, irreducible national narrative, no essentialist "national identity"' (2003: 73). The notion of a singular 'national memory' has to be challenged, and Bell replaces it with the idea of 'mythscape', 'the discursive realm, constituted by and through temporal and spatial dimensions, in which the myths of the nation are forged, transmitted, reconstructed and negotiated constantly' (2003: 75). Mythscape is not memory; the two are not synonymous. He comments: 'Memories may fall instead into the private, silenced tideways of time, or they could be employed as a site of opposition to myth' (2003: 77). It is interesting that Bell does not cite Nora's work, although by implication he seems critical of the notion of *mémoire*, of its implicit singularity. Thus:

> The memories that are privileged in the minds of individuals (whether they like it or not) or are recalled through ceremonies of collective remembrance may not be the ones which are privileged in mythology, conceivably due to the highly personal nature of the incident recalled, or because it happens to conflict with the self-image embodied in the various mythical narratives. (2003: 76–7).

Conclusion

> Blebo, Largo, Dunino
>
> Into Europe seem to go.
>
> Strangely Scottish, we may deem
>
> Auchtermuchty, Pittenweem. (Anon., in Dunn, 1992: i)

Place matters to people in Scotland. It is a fair point to say that it matters to other people elsewhere too; so what, if anything, is different? Such has been the attachment to place, local or national, that some see it as an *over*-commitment, an unhealthy connection to 'kailyard'. Why else would we be thought of as 'parochial', and seemingly in an unhealthy way?

We now know that the 'kailyard' was peculiar in time and place, an *émigré* literature for a wider British and American market in the late nineteenth century. Willie Donaldson's conclusion is worth highlighting:

> On the whole, popular fiction in Victorian Scotland is not overwhelmingly backward-looking; it is not obsessed with rural themes; it does not shrink from urbanisation and its problems; it is not idyllic in its approach; it does not treat the common people as comic or quaint. The second half of the 19th century [the heyday of 'kailyard'] is not a period of creative trauma or linguistic decline; it is one of the richest and most vital episodes in the history of Scottish popular culture. (1986: 149)

A concern with 'place' is not to be taken as proof that people in Scotland did not, or do not, engage with the wider world. After all, there are over thirty places called 'Aberdeen' around the world, the largest number in the Unites States and Canada, which we can take as a celebration of origins, rather than a desire to escape back home to the north-east.

Nor is attachment to 'community' in its diverse forms to be taken as proof that somehow we lack 'self-confidence', that we require a 'positive psychology' to be able to take our place in the world, which has been part of Scotland's universe since the Middle Ages. And, in any case, notions of 'country' and 'city' do not exist in isolation from each other.

Raymond Williams once observed that country and city are not so much social experiences as powerful images, symbols and archetypes. He comments: 'People have often said "the city" when they meant capitalism or bureaucracy or centralised power; while "the country" has at times meant everything from independence to deprivation, and from the powers of an active imagination to a form of release from consciousness' (1973: 289). Part and parcel of that is commitment to 'the land', and it is to this that we now turn in the next chapter.

Chapter summary

So what have we learned in this chapter?

- That there are strongly local commitments to place in Scotland and elsewhere which shape and direct our sense of identities. We belong to places to such an extent that accusations of 'parochialism' are strong.

- That these are reinforced in literary forms, and in cultural and jocular expressions in which person, place and nation are intertwined.

- That communities are multiplexed and nuanced because they are 'symbolic constructions'.

- That there is no necessary contradiction between the 'local' and the 'national'.

- That vital to our sense of belonging is 'memory', both individual and collective.

Questions for discussion

1. To what extent do people in Scotland prioritise 'locality' over 'nation'? Is it a meaningful distinction?

2. Compare and contrast 'local patriotism' in Scotland's major cities. How and why do they differ?

3. Are jokes to be taken seriously?

4. What is the 'kailyard', and what role does it play in Scottish literary culture?

5. Is 'community' all in the mind?

Annotated reading

(a) For discussion of the idea of 'community', see A. Cohen's work, especially *The Symbolic Construction of Community* (1985); *Symbolising Boundaries: Identity and diversity in British cultures* (1986); and *Signifying Identities* (2000). See also M. Herzfeld, *Cultural Intimacy: Social poetics in the nation-state* (1997).

(b) For different meanings of community, see G. Crow and C. Maclean, 'Community', in G. Payne (ed.), *Social Divisions* (2013); and R. Pahl, 'Are all communities communities in the mind?', *Sociological Review*, 53(4), 2005.

(c) On cultural and historical memory in Scotland, see A. Blaikie, *The Scots Imagination and Modern Memory* (2010).

(d) On the social and cultural significance of jokes and humour, see M. Billig, *Laughter and Ridicule: Towards a social critique of humour* (2005); and C. Davies, *Jokes and Targets* (2011).

(e) On memory and history more generally, see P. Nora, 'Between memory and history', *Representations*, 26, 1989; and D. Bell, 'Mythscapes: memory, mythology and national identity', *British Journal of Sociology*, 54(1), 2003.

Notes

1   George Blake was a novelist who lived from 1893 till 1961. He wrote *The Shipbuilders* (1935) and his novels mainly centred on Glasgow and Greenock as a counter to 'kailyard'.

2   Will Fyffe was a star of music hall in the 1920s and made the song his theme tune. It became a party piece for many. According to Albert Mackie's *The Scotch Comedians* (1973), Fyffe got the inspiration for the song from a drunk he met at Glasgow Central Station. The drunk was 'genial and demonstrative' and 'laying off about Karl Marx and John Barleycorn with equal enthusiasm'. Fyffe asked him: 'Do you belong to Glasgow?' and the man replied: 'At the moment, at the moment, Glasgow belongs to me.' Thus are iconic songs made. Fyffe himself belonged to Dundee.

3   'Mixed marriages' refers to those between Catholics and Protestants ('Non-Catholics' in RC parlance, a revealing distinction implying that, as far as the RC Church is concerned, there is a binary divide between Catholics and 'the rest'). According to Charsley, in the 1980s about 40 per cent of marriages in Catholic churches in the city were 'mixed marriages'.

4   A 'stushie' is a commotion or rumpus; more commonly, 'stooshie' in the west of Scotland.

5   In Scotland, the term 'town' can be used for quite small settlements. For example, a scattering of crofts in the crofting counties of the north-west are called 'townships'.

6   The title of Robert Crawford's poem, *Camera Obscura*, possibly gives the game away. This is Edinburgh, but only those in the know get the jokes (*London Review of Books*, 8 January 2015: 15). I am grateful to Robert for permission to reproduce the poem here.

7   *The Herald*'s Diary column is a good source of jokes about Edinburgh – the Other Place; such as 'Here is the "you'll have had your tea"-time News.'

8 In Dundee there is a 'classic' sound for recognising native Dundonians: *eh*. Billy Kay, in *Scots: The Mither Tongue* (2006: 152–3), gives a good example of this sound in the following sentence: 'Eh hud meh eh on a peh' (I had my eye on a pie). See www.scotslanguage.com/Scots_Dialects/Central/East_Central_North_uid821.

9 See, for example, the Scots translation by James Robertson of Julia Donaldson's children's classic *The Gruffalo*, which begins: 'A moose took a dauner through the deep mirk widd. A tod saw the moose and the moose looked guid.'

10 Auchenshuggle in fact is not mythical, but a real place in the east end of Glasgow (in Gaelic, 'the rye field'); it was made famous as a tram and bus terminus, and the name was on the destination board of the number 9 tram until 1962.

11 Scottish self-esteem and 'self-confidence' became a recognisable trope, reflected in writing from Edwin Muir in the 1920s to Carol Craig in the early years of the twenty-first century.

12 'Clydesidism' was an attempt to inject 'real' images of working-class life into representations of Scotland (Caughie, 1982), but was itself becoming a historic discourse even in its heartland, west–central Scotland, by the 1980s (Craig, 1983).

13 *The People's Friend*, founded in 1869, is still published weekly, and had a half-yearly circulation of just under 300,000 in 2013 (*Press Gazette*, 15 August 2013).

14 Carol Craig established the Centre for Confidence and Well-Being in the early 2000s, described on its website 'as a leading organisation in the field of Positive Psychology'.

15 Held down; that is, oppressed.

16 On the other hand, as Adam Smith said in *The Wealth of Nations*: 'People of the same trade seldom meet together, even for merriment and diversion, but the conversation ends in a conspiracy against the public, or in some contrivance to raise prices' (Book 1, 1827: 54).

17 The Belgian singer Jacques Brel once wrote a song called '*ces gens-là*' (1966), roughly translated as 'that lot there'.

18 For example, identification with city/county/region in Yorkshire, north-east and north-west England was high (respectively, 49, 48 and 43 per cent), but identifying with 'England' was only marginally lower in these regions (15, 14 and 17 per cent) than the English national average (18 per cent).

19 Angus Og was a strip cartoon character in *The Daily Record* newspaper in the 1970s and 1980s. Òg (which means 'young' in Gaelic) was a composite Highlander, hence the allusions to heather, kilts, cows and gloaming, and much given to saying '*ochone!*' ('oh no!').

20 When I visited the new heritage site in October 2015, the battle game was played with gusto between local primary school children divided into two teams. The fact that the English army 'won' on this occasion was neither here nor there.

16

'NOTHING BUT HEATHER':[1] SCOTLAND AS COUNTRY

That is the Land out there, under the sleet, churned and pelted there in the dark, the long rigs upturning their clayey faces to the spear-onset of the sleet. That is the Land, a dim vision this night of laggard fences and long stretching rigs. And the voice of it – the true and unforgettable voice – you can hear even such a night as this as the dark comes down, the immemorial plaint of the peewit, flying lost. **That** is the Land – though not quite all. Those folk in the byre whose lantern light is a glimmer through the sleet as they muck and bed and tend the kye, and milk the milk into tin pails, in curling froth – they are The Land in as great a measure.
(Lewis Grassic Gibbon, 'The Land', reprinted in *The Speak of the Mearns*, 1994: 152)

FIGURE 16.1
Norman
MacCaig, 'A Man
in Assynt'

Source: Author's
photograph

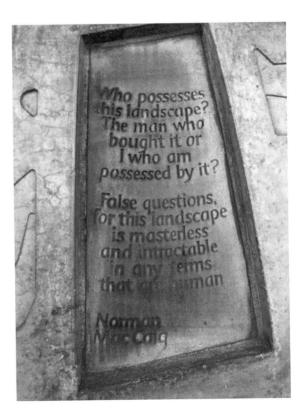

Scot-Land. It would seem that we are dominated by images of land and country, and yet most people in Scotland are urban, not rural, dwellers. Indeed, it is one of the most urbanised countries in the world, both in terms of where people live and how they make a living. We are not a country of peasants, nor have we been for at least a century and more.

Chapter aims

- To ask if we can be sure that 'the land' really matters to people, and, if so, why?

- To examine if Scotland is so different from other places.

- To discuss why there is such a focus on High-Land, on the *Gàidhealtachd*, when fewer and fewer of us live there.

- To see how relations of power with regard to land operate, both in material and in ideological terms.

We ended the previous chapter with the comment by Raymond Williams that the country – and the city – are not so much actual places, as powerful images, symbols and archetypes. The 'country' in particular has at times meant 'everything from independence to deprivation, and from the powers of an active imagination to a form of release from consciousness' (Williams, 1973: 289).

Williams observed that:

> 'country' can mean both a nation and part of a land; the 'country' can be the whole society as well as its rural area. In the long history of human settlements, this connection between the land from which directly or indirectly we all get our living and the achievements of human society has been deeply known. (1973: 1)

'Country', in other words, has come to stand for the essential values and images of place (Figure 16.1), hence the fusion of land and nation.

Land matters

Can we be sure that people, on this ground, actually place such importance on land in what is an urbanised society? When we carried out our research on national identity, we asked people in Scotland, and in England, to select which symbols of national identity they thought most important to Scottish/English culture.

We did not want people to relate their own *personal* sense of being Scottish or English to these symbols, nor to say whether or not they approved of a particular symbol.[2] We were trying to get at which symbols people thought typified the respective cultures and produced matching lists for Scotland and England to see whether they were similar or different. Did Scots and the English identify different things? We preferred the term 'landscape' in Scotland to 'countryside' as it seemed to us a more commonly used phrase north of the border, and we argued that the 'English countryside' and the 'Scottish landscape' are broadly equivalent.

We found that in Scotland 'landscape' is the most important national signifier, mentioned as first or second choices by almost half of people in Scotland (47 per cent), whereas in England 'countryside' was mentioned as their first or second choice by one-third of people, with '(English) language' by far the most important (68 per cent). The Scots placed 'landscape' at the top of their choices, followed on roughly equal par by 'music and the arts' and a 'sense of equality'.

The national flag (the Saltire) and Scots or Gaelic language were broadly equal, and sporting achievements were, as in England, the least important. Language was mentioned by three in every ten Scottish respondents, a considerable proportion, considering that only a minority of Scots speak Gaelic or the Scots language, though the vast majority speak with a Scottish accent.

Setting aside 'language' in both countries to see whether it made a difference to people's rankings, we found that among Scots 'landscape' was mentioned by over half (57 per cent) and 'countryside' by 45 per cent of people in England. There is no doubt, then, that Scots rank 'landscape' as the most significant Scottish symbol, and English people put 'countryside' second in their list.[3] To both it is an important signifier of the country.

Indeed, Scottish 'natives', that is people born and currently living in Scotland, were even more likely than those born elsewhere to rate 'landscape' highly (53 per cent compared with 45 per cent). We have, then, fairly incontrovertible evidence that Scots rate 'landscape' as the most meaningful symbol of being Scottish, even compared with its equivalent, 'countryside', in England. The point is not that this is unique to Scotland, but that it is a disproportionate signifier. In other words, land and landscape matter.

Land and country

Why should this be? Scotland is not unique in configuring 'land' with national identity, but there are particular cultural forms which bring this about. There is an obvious point to make: the term 'country' is nicely ambiguous. It can stand for rural areas, but it is also coterminous with 'nation'. On the other hand, 'Country' (capital C) has come to stand for the essential values and images of place: land and nation become fused.

There is a wider comparative context. The historian Simon Schama proposed that national identity would lose much its 'ferocious enchantment' without the mystique of a particular landscape tradition: that is, 'its topography mapped, elaborated, and enriched as a homeland' (1996: 15). Imagining the nation implies that it has a picture, and Schama argues that landscapes are 'culture' before they are 'nature', that they are constructs of the imagination projected onto wood and water and rock. German culture was rooted in its native soil ('*deutschtum*'), and such a vision drove Herder, the romantic nationalist, to view the essence of the nation as organically rooted in the topography, customs and communities of the local native tradition (Schama, 1996: 102).

In his book *Germany: Memories of a nation* (2014), Neil MacGregor quotes Steffan Markus: that in the nineteenth century German art and literature were inventing the German landscape.

> The German forests that we know today – huge woods with fir trees, and the other typical German broad-leaved trees – these are just as much an invention of Romanticism as were the fairy tales. Today's German forests largely originated through reforestation later in the nineteenth century, and this romantic woodland project became the backdrop for literature, for fairy tales and the like. The Grimms use the forest as a kind of double-edged sword. What happens in the forest in their fairy tales is often quite dreadful, quite cruel, and this is intended to frighten children, so that, at the end of the tale, they can be calmed and comforted by their mother's voice. (2014: 123)

In England the mythic memory of 'greenwood freedom' was prime material for nineteenth-century novels, including Walter Scott's *Ivanhoe* in which Anglo-Saxon rural liberties were contrasted with Norman tyranny. Schama commented: 'The forest as the opposite of court, town and village – the sylvan remnant of arcady, or what Shakespeare called the "golden world" – was an idea that would lodge tenaciously in the poetic and pious imagination' (1996: 142).

There is also an important and influential literature on rural pastoralism in England, dating back at least to Oliver Goldsmith's *Deserted Village* (1769): 'E'en now, methinks, as pondering here I stand, I see the rural virtues leave the land.' Eric Hobsbawm noted the widespread 'pretence that the Englishman is a thatched-cottager or country squire at heart' (quoted in Wiener, 1981: 42). Donald Horne contrasted competing metaphors in England:

> In the northern metaphor Britain is pragmatic, empirical, calculating, Puritan, bourgeois, enterprising, adventurous, scientific, serious, and believes in struggle. Its sinful excess is a ruthless avarice, rationalized in the belief that the prime impulse in all human beings is a rational, calculating, economic self-interest.
>
> In the southern metaphor, Britain is romantic, illogical, muddled, divinely lucky, Anglican, aristocratic, traditional, frivolous, and believes in order and tradition. Its sinful excess is a ruthless pride, rationalized in the belief that men are born to serve. (1969: 1)

We do not have to believe in the accuracy of these 'liberal' versus 'conservative' values so much as to see them as Horne intended: as metaphors, as *ways of seeing*.

Just as the idealised England is essentially a rural idyll, a place where country and Country come together, so the 'real' Scotland (as in Wales and Ireland) are in essence rural: 'Welsh Wales' and the *Gàidhealtachd/Gaeltacht* in Scotland and Ireland are deemed to be the heartland of the nation, and are promoted as such by their respective tourist industries.[4]

Central to identity is the sense of place: thus, we might ask, *where* is Scotland? We shall see later in this chapter that Scottish culture has adopted, or had thrust upon it, a 'Gaelic vision'. Malcolm Chapman (1978) has shown how, as Scotland was becoming industrialised in the late eighteenth century, and its Lowlands became much like other urbanised and industrialised regions, so the symbols, myths and tartans of the Highlands were appropriated by Lowland Scots, notably Sir Walter Scott, in a bid for some distinct culture.

The irony was that the part of Scotland which had been reviled as barbarian, backward and savage found itself extolled as the 'real' Scotland – the land of tartan, kilts and heather. Would Scots have attributed such significance to 'landscape' if there had not been such an exoticised, romantic and even tragic Gaelic vision? It made Scotland appear distinctive and unusual in the European, even global, scheme of these things, as we shall see when we discuss 'selling the nation' in Chapter 17.

A way of seeing

To understand 'landscape' we need to place it in context. Above all, we need to develop Schama's point that it is about 'culture' rather than 'nature'. By this he means that what we see is determined by the 'frame' through which we see, not by the object itself. We might even say that *what* we see is only meaningful in the context of our expectations. The analogy might be the contrast between a photograph and a painting, between the apparently 'naturalist' photo-image and the 'culturalist' creation. But even that is not what it seems. John Berger, the culture critic, in his classic account *Ways of Seeing*, made the more general point that photographs are certainly not 'natural':

> Every image embodies a way of seeing. Even a photograph. For photographs are not, as is often assumed, a mechanical record. Every time we look at a photograph, we are aware, however slightly, of the photographer selecting that sight from an infinity of other possible sights. This is true even in the most casual family snapshot. The photographer's way of seeing is reflected in his choice of subject. The painter's way of seeing is reconstituted by the marks he makes on the canvas or paper. Yet, although every image embodies a way of seeing, our perception or appreciation of an image depends also upon our own way of seeing. (1972: 10)

Berger's point is worth dwelling upon. 'Our own way of seeing' is not unique to us; it is a cultural expression. That does not mean that we cannot see things for what they are, but that what we see and where we 'place' them are culturally framed. Neither do we see just *one* thing, but the relationship between the thing and ourselves. Furthermore, we are also aware that we can in turn be *seen*; that we are objects as well as subjects.

Indeed, Berger made the important point that 'being seen' constitutes a particularly gendered way of seeing. As he put it: men *act*, and women *appear*. In art in particular, but in life generally:

Women *watch themselves* being looked at. This determines not only most relations between men and women but also the relation of women to *themselves*. The surveyor of woman in herself *is male: the* surveyed *female*. Thus she turns herself into an object – and most particularly an object of vision: a sight. (1972: 47, italics in original)

Berger was talking particularly about art nudes, but the point is a more general one. Paintings depict 'things', that is possessions, and in this regard, women were possessions: 'To have a thing painted and put on a canvas is not unlike buying it and putting it in your house. If you buy a painting you buy also the look of the thing it represents' (1972: 83).

When we 'see' a landscape, we situate ourselves in it; not the equivalent of a 'selfie', but certainly placing ourselves in its frame. We are part of the picture even when we are looking at it. Thus, pictures, and paintings in particular, often depict 'things', things which can be possessed, owned, even though art filters out the owner directly.

Art history and 'appreciation' conventionally treated the object in its own terms. There is a famous painting by Gainsborough of Mr and Mrs Andrews situated in their country estate in England[5] which convention interprets as reflecting their philosophical enjoyment of uncorrupted and unperverted 'Nature'. Berger's point is different and much more sociological. We can understand his point if we focus first on the close-up of the faces of Mr and Mrs Andrews (see Figures 16.2a and 16.2b).

How do you 'read' them? We do not get much sense of 'enjoyment' from their facial expressions, and possibly even of something more sinister. Both adopt the proprietorial stare, what was deemed the appropriate way to 'look' in this context. Berger's point is that they are not a couple in Nature, as Rousseau imagined Nature: 'They are landowners and their proprietary attitude towards what surrounds them is visible in their stance and their expressions' (1972: 107). We can now judge the full painting for what it is (Figure 16.3).

FIGURE 16.2A Mr Andrews

Source: © The National Gallery, London

FIGURE 16.2B Mrs Andrews

FIGURE 16.3
Thomas
Gainsborough,
*Mr and Mrs
Andrews*

Source: © The
National Gallery,
London

By studying their facial expressions and body language before looking at the painting, we got a different perspective on Mr and Mrs Andrews. We are better able to appreciate that the painting is an articulation of ownership, and that these are people not to be meddled with. Berger concludes:

> The point being made is that, among the pleasures their portrait gave to Mr and Mrs Andrews, was the pleasure of seeing themselves depicted as landowners and this pleasure was enhanced by the ability of oil paint to render their land in all its substantiality. And this is an observation which needs to be made, precisely because the cultural history we are normally taught pretends that it is an unworthy one. (1972: 108)

Berger's point about 'ways of seeing' is the key. Conventional art history sees the painted object as representational (high *Art* rather than *art*, what is 'made') and not sociological. He refers us to the comment by the French social anthropologist Claude Levi-Strauss, that: 'It is this avid and ambitious desire to take possession of the object for the benefit of the owner or even of the spectator which seems to me one of the outstandingly original features of the art of Western civilization' (Berger, 1972: 84).

Reading Scottish landscape

So what has this to do with Scotland, and with landscape? How do we 'read' what we 'see'? Surely we might think that eighteenth-century landscape is much like its twenty-first variant, if we are able to obtrude modern housing and roads? And presumably if our predecessors had available modern photo-technology they would see what we see? Not so. There is a famous pair of prints by the military historian Paul Sandby, one

FIGURE 16.4A Sandby, 1747   **FIGURE 16.4B** Sandby, 1780

Source: S. Schama, *Landscape and Memory* (1996: 468)

done by him in 1747 (shortly after the second Jacobite rising) and the other in 1780. We can see the prints, juxtaposed, in Figures 16.4a and 16.4b.

The key point is that Sandby was a military artist; not for him poetic licence, but the accurate and sober recording of what he saw. And that is the point: *what he saw*. We too can see a marked increase in the elevation of the mountains, lowering cloud-cover, and he intrudes a human figure – an iconic Highlander, naturally – into the foreground. James Holloway and Lindsay Errington, who provided commentary for the National Gallery of Scotland in the 1970s when these works were exhibited, remarked:

> The comparison of a view made by Sandby in 1747 with the print which was engraved after it over thirty years after reveals an interesting change of attitude to the Scottish landscape. Sandby's view shows the rich farming country of Strathtay as he saw it, in fact very much as it is today. But by 1780 the view was not thought to be sufficiently 'Highland' and several additions were made to dramatise the landscape; the mountains were heightened and their outlines made more rugged, fir trees and a kilted onlooker were introduced. (1978: 37)

Sandby was not practising deliberate deceit (he was a paid government surveyor; make of that what you will), but he was sketching what was in his vision; and expectations, and visions, had altered dramatically in the second half of the eighteenth century. Holloway and Errington describe the reactions of the painter Joseph Farington (1747–1821) who was taken to the Grey Mare's Tail in the Borders, and Cora Lynn on the Clyde:[6] 'To Farington, with a taste formed in picturesque principles, much of Scotland presented a diet of visual starvation. The empty moorland spaces bored and repelled him, "barren of strong Hedgerow the great ornament of great English landscape"' (1978: 87).

To us, Farington's reaction is well nigh incomprehensible, for we have been educated to 'see' landscape differently, at least in Scotland, although Constable's *Haywain* might contain sufficient hedgerows to suit Farington's taste. Holloway and Errington observe: 'the mountains of Scotland were never painted before the middle of the eighteenth century. Where possible they were avoided. When it was necessary to cross them travellers viewed the scenery with the greatest distaste' (1978: 3).

How our vision has altered. Thus, too, it is difficult these days to comprehend the artist and craftsman William Morris' dislike of the Forth Rail Bridge as 'the supremest specimen of all ugliness' (quoted in Wiener, 1981: 70). It all depends on the eye of the beholder.

Seeing Scotland

What did change, in the second half of the eighteenth century, was a revolutionary new way of seeing, the Romantic movement, which sought out 'unspoiled' places:

> Again and again one hears, on the lips of travellers in remote parts of the Highlands, echoes of the Ancient Mariner's astonished cry, 'We were the first that ever burst into that silent sea.' That the value of a place should reside in its complete rebuttal of all human values, its total innocence of human contact, is strange, but in the century of spoliation by mail coach, railway, and steamer, understandable. (Holloway and Errington, 1978: 111–12)

Knowing, as we do, the history of cultural and social repression which followed the 1745 Rising, the notion of elemental empty glens seems so much cant, given that 'the year of the sheep' (*Bliadhna nan Caorach*) – 1792 – had seen people evicted for a more profitable harvest than humankind. In its cultural place had intruded the notion of the primitive.

Peter Womack, in his book *Improvement and Romance: Constructing the myth of the Highlands*, commented: 'Botanically, no doubt, *calluna vulgaris* [heather] is exactly as it was in the 1730s. Semiotically,[7] it has been irrevocably hybridised' (1989: 2). He concluded:

> The Highlands ... are imaginary. It follows that the non-Highlands (the Scottish Lowlands or the metropolis or Anglophone Britain generally) are real ... to move back across the Highland line is to leave Fancy's hand and re-enter, sadly or thankfully but in either case inevitably, the realm of factual truth. (1989: 166)

In short, the Highlands are romantic because they have been romanticised.

Scotland as 'country', then, is a landscape of the mind, a place essentially of the imagination. This has made Scotland much easier to market by the tourist industry, as a 'land out of time', as an 'enchanted fortress in a disenchanted world' (Rojek, 1993: 181). The point is that tourist Scotland is essentially an *imaginary* place. There is little point in visiting a country that looks like the one back home: Milwaukee and Motherwell may have too much in common as declining industrial towns. Scotland has a major feature to play as 'country': its association with wilderness. 'Wilderness', as a version of 'nature', is the antithesis of 'culture'. We know, of course, that much of this conception of wilderness was actually fabricated, that it is a social construction of the late eighteenth century.

Take another look at the re-presentation of the Highland landscape by Paul Sandby. His second engraving, thirty years after the first, has higher mountains, more rugged terrain, and a figure in a kilt added to compound authenticity. What was seen as a barren and desolate landscape of mid-century becomes a romantic and tragic icon of the late eighteenth century. The re-presentation of the Highlands of Scotland as a people-less place, in spite of the lonely kilted figure, is the direct outcome of social forces which cleared people from the land in favour of sheep and deer, or simply nothingness.

By the end of the eighteenth century, the Highlands were reinvented as a scenic game park filled with 'nature' and its game, but removed of people. So powerful is this reinvention that we ourselves struggle to see the Highlands in any other way. They – and we – have been 'colonised by an empire of signs' (Womack, 1989: 1). The Highlands as we know them are the result of a process 'at an identifiable point in time, in response to specific requirements and contradictions which are both exhibited and disguised by its eventual form' (Womack, 1989: 2).

As Scotland was losing its distinctiveness and becoming industrialised and urbanised, it appropriated that which flourished in the currency of the late eighteenth-century Romantic movement – the *Gaelic vision*. These images have in turn become vital to the modern tourist vision of Scotland. Whereas in the eighteenth century the Highlands had been invested with the symbolism of the exotic, the foreign, so by the end of that century all Scotland was being colonised by that sign. Womack again:

> Processes which promoted capitalist accumulation in the lowlands through economic integration with England simultaneously exaggerated Highland difference. For the Scottish bourgeoisie, therefore, the Highlands had the aspect of a residual historical nation. So the Highlands acquired the role of representing Scotland 'for the English'. (1989: 148)

We might add the rider that Lowland Scots were also happy to acquire the role for themselves, to be associated with this romantic view of Scotland, despite the considerable irony that Highlanders had long been reviled by them as barbaric and savage (Hunter, 1999). Nevertheless, Scotland as a whole settled for a Celtic definition of itself in contradistinction to England, so that 'the face that Scotland turns to the rest of the world is, in many respects, a Highland face' (Chapman, 1978: 9).

The end of the eighteenth century, then, was a crucial period in the 'reinvention' of Scotland. The accoutrements of Highland imagery, which was reinforced by Walter Scott in the early decades of nineteenth-century Scotland, and the Highlands in particular, became the focus for the 'rediscovery' of the wilderness. By the 1880s, visitors were remarking that 'the farther we went, the more we were reminded that to travel in Scotland is to travel through the Waverley novels' (MacArthur, 1993: 23). Presumably no irony was intended.

In essence, we are dealing with 'terrains of power'. Dennis Cosgrove (1994) argued that nature, landscape and environment are semiotic signifiers, deeply embedded in the cultural constitution of individual European nations and integral to the distinctive identities of Europe's 'peoples'. Imagining the nation conjures up landscape signs of considerable cultural power (recall the association between forests and Germanness). Each nation has an 'imagined geography' which acts as a physical representation of the Country as country.

'Nature' and 'nation' are closely bound together. In particular, as Cosgrove points out, 'Welsh and Scottish nationalisms have constructed their own meaning from mountain landscapes, valleys and glens, drawing as heavily on the natural world as upon their separate language[8] to construct differences from England' (1994: 24). This imagining of Scotland and Wales as lands of mountain and flood has helped to foster different versions of community from England which nourish distinctive national feelings, and have both conservative and radical implications.

Gentrifying Scotland

Cosgrove's point about landscapes as terrains of power is key. On the one hand, the 'land' question in Scotland remains a live one, as we saw in Chapter 6, and issues of landownership and use have considerable power to mobilise political debate. On the other hand, the Eden myth, as Andrew Blaikie (2010) has called it, has been colonised and amplified by the powerful, notably the aristocracy and the monarchy. As Blaikie observes: 'the iconography of Scottish landscape overwhelmingly consists of images of empty places that are distant from where most Scots live' (2010: 137). The supreme irony is that the British state which was threatened by the Jacobites first in 1715, and more seriously in 1745, stole the enemy's clothes (tartan) and culture, and insinuated itself into its own version of Scottish, and Highland, culture.

In 1747, the Proscription Act was passed, and the kilt and tartan were appropriated by the British Army in its colonial wars – literally and metaphorically stealing the enemy's clothes. It set about inventing new tartans, notably darker shades of green, browns, blues and blacks more suited as camouflage in its wars on the North American continent. The Proscription Act itself was not repealed until 1782, under lobbying from the London Highland Society which had such establishment members as General Fraser of Lovat, Lord Chief Baron MacDonald, the Earl of Seaforth, Col. Macpherson of Cluny, and MP John Graham, Duke of Montrose – Highland gentlemen. It was a measure of the incorporation of Highland landed aristocracy into the British elite that they were able to effect such a change. In this respect, Trevor-Roper is correct to say that the development of (modern) tartans originated 'more often in the officers' mess than in the straths and glens of Scotland' (1984: 29).

The 'gentrification' of tartan was boosted considerably by Walter Scott, who, acting as impresario, persuaded George IV to visit Edinburgh in 1822, and set off the long sequence of royalist associations with Scotland, and the Highlands in particular. Queen Victoria's acquisition of her Deeside estate at Balmoral in 1848 gave the royal seal of approval to the tartan enterprise, and she and Albert had one of their very own tartans designed. The garb of rebels had become that of the establishment. The royal association, begun by George IV, 'German Geordie', helped to guarantee commercial success.

Behind all this was a considerable 'heritage' industry bent on authenticating the ancient designs for an anxious world eager to believe. The picture was completed by the Allen Brothers, John and Charles, who so fell in love with the mythology of tartan that they changed their names to the Sobieski Stuarts, claiming to be the grandsons of the Young Pretender (and to have a Polish connection into the bargain).

There is little doubt that they fabricated their most famous work, calling it, for effect, *Vestiarium Scoticum*, published in 1842 in Edinburgh, supposedly from a manuscript of 1721, compiled in 1571. This was soon denounced as a forgery (for a full account, see Stewart and Thompson, 1980) but did nothing to dampen the desire to accept the authenticity of tartan (www.tartansauthority.com/tartan/the-growth-of-tartan/vestiarium-scoticum/). Hugh Trevor-Roper describes the Sobieski Stuarts' *The Costume of the Clans* of 1844 as 'shot through with fantasy and bare-faced forgery' (page 22). John Telfer Dunbar is more relaxed in his assessment:

> [It] is, without doubt, one of the foundation stones on which any history of Highland dress is built. It cannot be ignored, and it is surprising how little it has been consulted by writers on the subject. We can think what we like about the ancestral claims of the Stuart brothers, but this does not reduce the value of their monumental books. (1962: 111)

The Romantic search for the 'noble savage', and the 'discovery' of the Ossian poems by James Macpherson in the 1760s;[9] the raising of Highland regiments after Culloden was a master-stroke by the British state, incorporating the symbols of its enemies into its own identity. By the early nineteenth century, the climate was right for Walter Scott's romantic tales to become bestsellers, the king effectively acting as literary agent by visiting Edinburgh in 1822, accoutred in the way Scott thought appropriate.

The self-styled Sobieski Stuarts simply took the whole thing to its logical extremes. The weaving company Wilsons of Bannockburn added the commercial element, and gave material expression to this fantasy. The whole enterprise was rounded off by royal seal of approval, first by George IV, and then by Queen Victoria in 1848.

There then followed the unmaking of the past and the invention of the present. Much of the royal association is imagined, if not imaginary, and reinforced by imagery and 'ways of seeing'. Take, for example, the following iconic paintings. First, the one of Lochnagar in the Cairngorms (now badged as 'Royal' Deeside) painted by the Bavarian artist Carl Haag, who presumably knew a thing or two about mountains. The point is not to take a rather precipitate horse ride in mountainous country, but to conquer it. Gentry on horseback, with Highland ghillies on hand to guide the horses, added to the new landscape (see Figure 16.5).

The best-known icon is the *Monarch of the Glen* by Edward Landseer, whose painting became a popular emblem of Highland Scotland, and was described by Cosgrove as a

FIGURE 16.5
Morning Highlands: Royal Family Ascending Lochnagar by Carl Haag (1853)

Source: Royal Collection Trust/© Her Majesty Queen Elizabeth II 2016

'pastiche of the sublime'. Landseer's painting (1851) has a curious history. It had been commissioned for the Refreshment Rooms in the House of Lords, but the House of Commons refused to pay the commission fee of £150, and it was sold to a private collector. It was eventually bought by the Pears soap company in 1916 and used in advertising before being sold on to John Dewar and sons, whisky distillers, who did the same, using it on some of their products. Dewar's is now part of the Diageo group, and the painting is on loan to the National Museum of Scotland in Edinburgh (see Figure 16.6).

FIGURE 16.6
Monarch of the Glen by Edward Landseer (1851)

Source: I am grateful to Diageo PLC and National Museums Scotland for permission to reproduce this image

FIGURE 16.7
Queen Victoria landing at Loch Muick by Landseer (1850)[10]

Source: Royal Collection Trust/© Her Majesty Queen Elizabeth II 2016

The point, of course, was not simply to admire the wildlife and the landscape, but to conquer it, along with the natives. This world was heading for a fall, and so it came about (see Figure 16.7).

Here, the stag is no longer at bay, but dead, set out for the admiring gaze of an alighting Queen Victoria at Loch Muick, along with Albert adopting a suitably conquering poise, foot on carcass. Meanwhile, the natives are confined to secondary roles in the background, as bearers of royal personages, hewers of wood and drawers of water; bit-players in their own land.

Thus, as Blaikie observes:

> The myth of the Highlands and, by extension, of Scottish landscape more generally, is one of nature 'as left behind, as lost wholeness'. It is a land of lost content in both senses of the word. The sublime irony is that in 'look[ing] upon a land denuded of cultural reference', we are doing something that is, of course, supremely cultural. (2010: 165–6)

In key respects, the association of land with monarchy is simply the icing on the cake. They are temporary if exotic visitors to their 'estate'; a place to pass their summer holidays. Womack makes an important point about land:

> the land is a double sign. On the one hand, as an object of investment, it is something like a raw material, destined to be valorised by the ingenuity and enterprise of the owner. But the land is also the origin of value; from its natural virtue the landlord derives at once his material wealth, the legitimation of his power, and the standards of propriety by which his artificial works may be judged. (1989: 61)

Land is conventionally seen as a productive asset, from which a return on investment can be had. It is clear, however, that estate economics on Highland estates are weak. The estate, as far as we can tell, costs more money than it generates. Landownership is, as we saw in

Chapter 6, highly concentrated. There must be more to it than economics. And there is. While 'foreign' investment in Highland estates is significant, 'traditional' owners abound (see Callander, 1998; Wightman, 1996). While the orthodoxy is that the loss of economic power among the landed elite is significant, and was a precursor of their loss of political power (see Cannadine, 1990), there is far more to it than that.

First of all, many landowners have high incomes and are sufficiently wealthy so as not to need income from their land. In sociological terms, landowners form a status group rather than a social class. In other words, what matters is social prestige and 'honour', rather than economic returns. In interviews with estate owners in Scotland, we found that the landed elite had responded to socio-economic change by insinuating their own with the nation's 'heritage' which become indivisible. In short, and in the title of our paper, they became 'keepers of the land' (Stewart et al., 2001).

Furthermore, landowners' power relates to their possession of symbolic resources such that their power becomes taken for granted:

> landowners' use of cultural capital binds them to the land in a way which, on the one hand, associates them with Scotland's natural heritage, but, on the other, makes the land their property, and thus allows them a powerful position in the country. In this sense, the relationship conveys a very modern idea of legitimacy – that the laird is the custodian of Scotland's national heritage and consequently the country itself. (Samuel, 2000: 698)

Here is a comment from a residential inheritor we interviewed in our heritage study (Stewart et al., 2001: 397):

> I see great industrial captains [who] just don't have that inherent intelligible, impossible way of expressing attachment to the soil. They don't have the same fusion of spirit and responsibility for the land that I and for that matter my wife's family [who've] been there for a thousand years ... and many of us are wondering what will happen to those great family estates that have been managed in ... a feudalistic way ... [where] you look after your family [and] ... your own and by that I mean the people who look up to you for their very existence. ... We've been here a long time and all things being equal we will be here for a few more generations to come.

He justifies his ownership in terms of family 'breeding' and background: 'It's the breeding and the experience which others coming in don't have and therefore you instinctively know how to treat some of the Highlanders who work here and need careful handling. It's in your blood (Stewart et al., 2001: 397).' Here is an articulation, a defence, of traditional values which is not formulated around swift returns on investment, but on 'historic' values of breeding and blood.

Landowners claim that they are custodians of Scotland's land, and thus the nation, and so insinuate their legitimacy at moments of significant political challenge, namely the setting up of a Scottish parliament at the end of the twentieth century, and central to that is the mobilisation of identity and community. Here is a comment from the Duke of Buccleuch in the context of land reform in 2015: 'I can understand people who have a deep-down visceral dislike of others who own large amounts of land. All I can do is try to make a case for our stewardship of it as being good and responsive to the best interests of the community' (www.express.co.uk/news/uk/556703/Duke-of-Buccleuch-dismay-SNP-land-reform-plans).

Regardless of whether they are incomers, inheritors, foreign or indigenous, there is sufficient ideological cohesion among them to conclude that they have put together a discourse of considerable tactical value. It remains, however, remarkable that who owns land is protected information lest it breaches owners' human right to property and privacy. Comments the journalist David Ross: 'It should be beyond question that there is a public interest in the true identity of who really owns our land being known' (*The Herald*, 2 December 2015).

Our study of Scottish lairds gave us insight into how identities work, interact and mutually reinforce each other. They are able to mobilise a sense of community, both among themselves and the communities they 'serve'. As Akhil Gupta and James Ferguson observed: 'to be part of a community is to be positioned as a particular kind of subject, similar to others within the community in some crucial respects and different from those who are excluded from it' (1997: 17).

The answer to the question (how do landowners justify and defend their positions of power?) is not simply to assert their legal claims to land, but to appeal to their cultural significance as 'keepers of the land', and hence bind their own interests with the nation's. Their space is national property, and their role is to look after it on behalf of the nation, as heritage, what the French call '*patrimoine*', a term which has no easy translation into the English language. What *patrimoine* conveys is a strong sense of national inheritance closely allied with rural imagery and peasant culture which is of continuing political importance in the French Republic. Heritage, land as well as buildings, provides the means for capturing national culture (Hoyau, 1988).

Keepers of the land: knowledge as power

Our second question relates to why this ideological appeal seems to 'work' among the population at large who have no economic interest directly in landownership. This is about insinuating power with 'knowledge'. The French writer Michel Foucault once observed: 'We should admit that power produces knowledge ... that power and knowledge directly imply one another; that there is no power relation without the corrective constitution of a field of knowledge, nor any knowledge that does not presuppose and constitute ... power relations' (1980: 27). The implication of what Foucault was saying is that knowledge influences social practices and has real consequences and effects, so that when it operates effectively according to social interests it becomes a 'regime of truth'. This is not because there is some sort of conspiracy going on to capture and amplify systems of power through knowledge. Rather, there will be different systems or discourses in operation which compete with each other, usually through social agents associated with them.

Discourses of power

Let us apply these ideas to the debate about land in Scotland. Two discourses have domi-nated the debate about land: the 'economic/legal' and 'scientific/environmental'. The first refers to the view that land is an economic commodity grounded in and protected by the legal system which allows land to be traded. The second takes a more 'technical' view of land, and applies the rules of science to its management. By and large, it is the economic/legal discourse which has determined the debate about land: is private ownership a good thing or a bad thing?

Why has the pattern of landownership and land use in Scotland been determined in the way it has? Is absentee ownership harmful, or does it depend on management rather than ownership per se? This is a right and proper debate to have, for we cannot ignore the implications of ownership, but it does constrain the 'discourse' and steer our under-standings of these matters. This discourse has developed its own knowledge dimension in the form of the legal system which carefully documents ownership and handles its disputes (such as the Scottish Land Court).

In the second half of the twentieth century, the 'scientific/environmental' discourse has grown apace. The inverted commas do not imply that it is not 'scientific', or 'objective' in common-sense parlance, but to indicate that it too is a system of knowl-edge, a discourse which sets the agenda for understanding. The scientific discourse about land and the environment needs little explicating. We talk the language of Sites of Special Scientific Interest (SSSIs), of ecological sustainability, of conservation backed up with a vast and growing apparatus of knowledge. Opponents of current practices of land use and tenure have grown increasingly sophisticated and will swap technical jargon with proponents at will in an attempt to knock down key assumptions. Environmental groups have developed their own counter-science to discredit conven-tional wisdoms which they deem to prop up vested interests.

To handle the growing knowledge systems and the disputes about what is best for the land (and sometimes its people), the state has set up its own agencies – Scottish Natural Heritage is one of the most recent of these. Environmental politics has turned into a vast alphabet soup of acronyms: SEPA, CCS, SNH, NHA, SLF, NFUS, SSSI, WWFS, NTS, SOAEFD, APRS, and so on. These agents handle how knowledge is produced, its power and resources. 'Land' is turned into a technical matter, it is 'naturalised'. Indeed, the term 'natural' envi-ronment implies a juxtaposition with the humanly constructed ('unnatural'?), which we know is a false dichotomy. The 'natural' environment has been well and truly shaped by human action. Once more, 'nature' is evidently 'culture'.

Land carries with it a set of cultural, economic/legal and scientific/environmental meanings. These meanings or discourses do not reside somehow 'naturally' in land, but are read into it in its different manifestations by different users and interest groups. Neither are they necessarily discrete from each other. Usually those who own land as a commodity, an ownership sanctioned in law, are able to mobilise scientific/environmental management knowledge in their favour, as well as having preferential access to the sets of cultural significations which attach to it (as 'stewards', keepers of heritage and the nation's history). On the other hand, aligning the economic/legal, scientific/environmental and cultural arguments is an increasingly difficult trick to carry off. Owners of land have grown used to attacks on their 'ecologically unfriendly' practices (such as intensive agriculture, and overgrazing by deer and sheep), while questions like 'whose culture is it anyway?' intrude into the debate more frequently.

To be sure, politics has never been absent. It has long been involved in the land question in Scotland, notably in the crofting lands, and the political dimension has manifestly been growing in the last twenty years. The 'political' also underpins the legal system of landownership, and settles its disputes. It is also largely responsible for the state and quasi-state agencies which provide the scientific expertise and management systems. The state is also a major landowner in its own right through its holding of forestry land and crofting estates, and it is proposed to devolve some responsibilities for the Crown Estates to the Scottish government.[11]

The redrawing of political responsibilities and the resetting of the political discourse have consequences for the economic and scientific interests which have previously had the 'field' to themselves. Traditionally, 'people' were insinuated into the land discourse in a few and well-ordered ways: as they sought to make a living, used it for recreation, and so on. They were deemed to be either legal subjects or technical subjects. However, as 'democratic' subjects, they take on new responsibilities and expectations as these are redrawn by a Scottish parliament. The somewhat restricted technical and legal culture relating to land is inevitably broadened into a more popular culture, one in which people feel they have a right to 'their country' in all its dimensions. They may not 'own' it directly, but undoubtedly they feel that Scot-land 'belongs' to them.

Touring Scotland

Blaikie has made the point: 'Highlandism persists today because it is a reflection of a popular "*mentalité*" in which Scottishness is imagined not just by seeing landscape in particular established ways but through using it symbolically to connect personal, social and national identities' (2010: 137). He also argues that there were two other manifestations of 'land' and identity, from the early twentieth century in particular, but stretching back to the 'invention' of tourism by Walter Scott through his novels. Whereas in the first half of the nineteenth century, the Highlands had at most 100 visitors per year, by the end of the century it could expect a hundred times that number (Durie, 1992).

Scott's own house at Abbotsford near Melrose was attracting over 5000 visitors annually, and by the end of the twentieth century received over 70,000. Ironically, the reinstatement of the 'Borders Railway' in 2015, which is a short walk from Abbotsford, has boosted the numbers significantly. The 'tourist gaze' in Scotland which Scott did so much to invent has come full circle as a result of public investment, and to his descendants' commercial advantage.[12]

Tourism was, in any case, not dependent on actually visiting iconic places, for the invention of postcards and travel literature proved to be essential accessories. Postcards became a cheap and easy way of marking travel and keeping in touch: 'wish you were here' (Morris, 2007). Travel brochures and magazines abounded, notably *Scots Magazine*, which had been founded in 1739, but in 1927 was taken over by DC Thomson to add to their famous portfolio of the *Beano*, the *Dandy* and the *Sunday Post*, and the *People's Friend*. Often accused of being couthy 'kailyard' literature, such publications reinforced the image of Scotland as small town and rural, intimate and parochial. By the inter-war years, bus and car travel had taken off and provided the means to visit the sites/sights. Travel books like H.V. Morton's *In Search of Scotland* (1929) were hugely popular, leading him to a reprise, *In Scotland Again*, in 1933.

All travel, however, was not celebratory. The most baleful was possibly Edwin Muir's *Scottish Journey* (1980 [1935]) in which he contrasted the 'stock enchantment' of the Highlands in their wildest state where they possess 'a thing which is common no doubt to all wild and solitary scenery; that is, the added value which every natural object acquires from one's consciousness that hasn't been touched by the human will' (quoted in Blaikie, 2010: 151).

Here we encounter once more the fable of a land unspoiled by human action, despite its history of clearance and cultural oppression. In contrast there is urban Scotland, damaged by two centuries, according to Muir, by the twin forces of industrialisation and urbanisation which dehumanised people: a process of psycho-social despoliation. Thus, Blaikie points out, 'modernisation begets anti-modernism' (2010: 165), and runs as a theme throughout Scottish literature. The novelist, the late Willie McIlvanney captured it well in his detective novel *Laidlaw* (1977):

Drumchapel engulfed them like a quicksand.

'Some place', Laidlaw said.

'Aye, there must be some terrible people here.'

'No', Laidlaw said, 'That's not what I meant. I find the people terribly impressive. It's the place that's terrible. You think of Glasgow. At each of its four corners, this kind of housing-scheme. There's the Drum and Easterhouse and Pollock and Castlemilk. You've got the biggest housing-scheme in Europe here. And what's there? Hardly anything but houses. Just architectural dumps where they unload people like slurry. Penal architecture. Glasgow people have to be nice people. Otherwise, they would have burned the place to the ground years ago. (McIlvanney, 1977: 32)[13]

So we return to our understanding of landscape. We see that there is an inevitable thesis/antithesis quality to spatial relationships: the urban and rural; the Highlands and Lowlands; the primordial and the post-industrial. Truth to tell, they are mirror images of each other. One reacts to the other. Holloway and Errington in *The Discovery of Scotland* made the point that Scottish art has relied on reaction. Thus, the Glasgow School in the late nineteenth century was antithetical:

> Mountains, and glens, all memorable and historically resonant were rejected, along with sunsets, storms and burns in spate. Out of the purge they rescued and elevated the idea of a picture as an entity in its own right, a structure built out of dabs of paint, tone and colour. (Holloway and Errington, 1978: 141)

They offer a nice juxtaposition of images completed in the same year, 1901, one by McTaggart, *Harvest at Broomieknowe*, and the other by James Pringle, *Muslin Street*, (Bridgeton in Glasgow). Holloway and Errington comment: 'Here are two pictures of mutually exclusive worlds, the one showing the "green places where birds sang and children picnicked", the other "the moving foot of the great city" that the author of Glasgow in 1901 saw laying the green places waste' (1978: 164).

Conclusion: 'Nothing but the land'

So wrote Lewis Grassic Gibbon, which echoes MacDiarmid's 'Nothing but heather'. MacDiarmid, of course, was contrasting this dismissal of Scotland as colonised by heather (*Calluna vulgaris*) to point out the requirement to look far more carefully, to adjust, in other words, our ways of seeing. This is easier said than done, because the dominant modes are so powerful. They get caught up in our language. As Mitchell observed:

> Language and images become enigmas, problems to be explained, prison houses which lock understanding away from the world. The commonplace of modern studies of images, in fact, is that they must be understood as a kind of language; instead of providing a transparent on the world, images are now regarded as the sort of sign that presents a deceptive appearance of naturalness and transparence concealing an opaque, distorting, arbitrary mechanism of representation, a process of ideological mystification. (Quoted in Daniels and Cosgrove, 1988: 7)

The orthodox images of Scotland are so dominant, even hegemonic, that they lend themselves to all sorts of fabrications. One of the best known and amusing is the observation by Forsyth Hardy when he was film critic of *The Scotsman* newspaper in 1953. The Hollywood producer of *Brigadoon* was looking for a suitable site for his movie, a village in the Highlands which would look unchanged after a hundred years. Hardy took the producer all over Scotland, but failed to convince him, and the producer built the set in a Hollywood back-lot, saying: 'I went to Scotland but I could find nothing that looked like Scotland' (in Hardy, 1990: 1).

The quest for the imaginary Scotland has continuing cultural force. One of the latest is the *Outlander* series for television, based on the romantic novels by Diana Gabaldon who by all accounts had never visited Scotland before she wrote her first book.[14] This is a fictional Scotland of the writer's vivid imagination.[15] Notwithstanding, and never willing to pass up a commercial opportunity, the national state-funded tourist organisation VisitScotland has jumped on the passing bandwagon by inviting people to 'Scotland – the land that inspired Outlander':

> If you have found yourself caught in the mystic and spell-binding Outlander saga and wish to be swept away to Claire and Jamie's world, come and experience the land that so inspired the writer Diana Gabaldon and the TV series producers. From ancient and mysterious standing stones to dramatic castles, magnificent stately homes and breathtaking landscapes, visit Scotland and embark on an inspiring journey. (www.visitscotland.com/about/arts-culture/outlander/)

Much as the 'real' Roslin Chapel in Midlothian has not deterred people from visiting the place because they have read Dan Brown's novel *The Da Vinci Code* (2003), Scotland becomes a riddle, wrapped in a mystery, inside an enigma[16] (www.scotland.org/features/the-da-vinci-code-phenomenon/). It raises fundamental questions about who is this 'we', and what is this 'Scotland', and it is to these topics that we now turn.

Chapter summary

So what have we learned in this chapter?

- That people in Scotland invest considerable meaning and significance in landscape; they see it as iconic of Scotland.

- That the association of landscape and national identity is not unique to Scotland, but takes on particularly powerful forms here.

- That we do not experience landscape directly, but through 'ways of seeing', which are culturally and socially charged. Landscapes are terrains of power.

- That, from the eighteenth century, Scotland has been reinvented as a 'land out of time', and the Highlands as a 'peopleless place'.

- That this has come about through its gentrification in the nineteenth century and association with monarchy and aristocracy; and in the twentieth century, with tourism.

Questions for discussion

1. Why does Scotland seem unduly dominated by images of land and 'country'?

2. How would you explain 'landscape' as the most significant symbol of Scotland?

3. How have 'ways of seeing' Scotland altered since the eighteenth century, and why?

4. What has been the role of monarchy and aristocracy in signifying Scotland?

5. Would land reform make a difference to how people see landscape?

Annotated reading

(a) On the meaning of landscape, see D. McCrone and F. Bechhofer. *Understanding National Identity* (2015), chapter 3; R. Williams, *The Country and the City* (1973); S. Schama, *Landscape and Memory* (1996); J. Holloway and L. Errington, *The Discovery of Scotland* (1978).

(b) On Scottish heritage, see P. Womack, *Improvement and Romance: Constructing the myth of the Highlands* (1989); D. McCrone et al., *Scotland – the Brand* (1995); A. Blaikie, *The Scots Imagination and Modern Memory* (2010).

Notes

1 The allusion is to Hugh MacDiarmid's poem 'Scotland small?', which begins: 'Scotland small? Our multiform, our infinite Scotland small? / Only as a patch of hillside may be a cliché corner / To a fool who cries "Nothing but heather!"' (Dunn, 1991: 72).

2 We gave people a card and asked: 'Here are some things which people sometimes say are important to Scottish/English culture. Which one do you feel is the most important? And the second most important?' The lists were as follows: For Scottish culture: Scottish sporting achievements; the Scottish flag (St Andrew's Cross); Scottish music and arts; Scottish sense of equality; Scottish language (i.e. Gaelic or Scots); Scottish landscape. For English culture: English sporting achievements; the English flag (St George's Cross); English music and arts; English sense of fair play; English language; English countryside.

3 For a full account of the findings, see Bechhofer and McCrone (2012a).

4 Non-metropolitan France is often referred to as '*La France profonde*', roughly translated as 'deep France'.

5 The example here is an English landscape, but there is no reason to think that Scotland would be different.

6 The point, of course, is that neither place is in the iconic Highlands.

7 Semiotics is the study of signs and symbols.

8 Presumably, Cosgrove meant Welsh and Gaelic.

9 In 1761, the writer James Macpherson published *Fingal. An Ancient Epic Poem. In Six Books*, together with Several Other Poems composed by Ossian, the Son of Fingal, translated from the Gaelic Language. He was unable to produce the original Gaelic fragments on which they were based, and they were dismissed as a forgery by the likes of Samuel Johnson.

Macpherson fell foul of anti-Scottish feeling in the late eighteenth century aimed at denying the origin-myth of the Scots as a people distinct from the English.

10   Queen Victoria described it in her diary (17 September 1850): 'It is to be thus: I, stepping out of the boat at Loch Muick, Albert, in his Highland dress, assisting me out, & I am looking at a stag which he is supposed to have just killed. Bertie is in the dear pony with McDonald (whom Landseer much admires) standing behind, with rifles and plaids on his shoulder' (https://www.royalcollection.org.uk/collection/403221/queen-victoria-landing-at-loch-muick).

11   At the time of writing (early 2016), this has not been completed. The Scottish Minister for Rural Affairs commented: 'There is a clear and widely supported case for the devolution of the Crown Estate in Scotland in order to promote accountability, transparency and stop the leakage of Scottish revenues to the UK Treasury. Unfortunately, the Scotland Bill goes against the spirit and intention of the Smith Commission proposals and resembles a bit of a dog's breakfast. It is far too complicated, includes restrictions on Scottish Ministers and does not lead to the full the [sic] devolution of the Crown Estate' (http://news.scotland.gov.uk/News/Crown-Estate-devolution-1a26.aspx).

12   The Borders Railway website comments: 'Day visitors can easily reach Abbotsford House, just minutes from Tweedbank Station. A jewel in the crown of Scottish architecture, this luxurious mansion was once home to Sir Walter Scott and guests can explore the elegant rooms where he hosted literary glitterati such as Oscar Wilde and Charlotte Brontë, or discover his life and legacy in the visitor centre' (www.bordersrailway.co.uk/news/2015/september/bordering-on-a-new-golden-age-of-rail.aspx).

13   The writer Alan Taylor chose to use this iconic extract for his obituary of McIlvanney in *The Herald* on 5 December 2015.

14   The provenance is, according to Wikipedia, as follows. In 1988, Gabaldon decided to write a novel for 'practice, just to learn how' and with no intention to show it to anyone. As a research professor, she decided that a historical novel would be easiest to research and write, but she had no background in history and initially no particular time period in mind. Gabaldon happened to see a rerun episode of the *Doctor Who* science fiction TV series titled 'The War Games'. One of the Doctor's companions was a Scot from around 1745, a young man about 17 years old named Jamie McCrimmon, who provided the initial inspiration for her main male character, James Fraser, and for her novel's mid-eighteenth-century Scotland setting.

15   The *Outlander* series is a sequence of multi-genre novels and shorter works written by Diana Gabaldon that feature elements of historical fiction, romance, mystery, adventure and science fiction/fantasy. The franchise has expanded to include the 2014 television drama series *Outlander* on Starz, a 2010 graphic novel and a 2010 musical album called *Outlander: The Musical*. Thus are all commercial possibilities covered.

16   The comment is attributed to Winston Churchill made in a radio broadcast about Russia in 1939.

17

WILFUL FRAGMENTS: CHARACTERISING SCOTTISH CULTURE

In late 2014, the official tourist organisation VisitScotland launched a website encouraging readers to translate famous Scottish icons and landmarks into Mandarin Chinese. These included:

- **Kilt** – 科特短裙 – **Ke-te short skirt** (homophone for 'kilt')

- **The Wallace Monument** – 勇者心碑 – **Monument to brave heart**

- **Royal Mile** – 融蕴美径 – **A beautiful street with long history and profound culture.**

Denise Hill, Head of International Marketing at VisitScotland, said:

> The Great Names campaign has proved a fun and entertaining way for us to engage with Scotland's Chinese market, which is growing year-on-year. These extraordinary new monikers will only serve to lend even more intrigue and romance to places throughout Scotland which in turn will lead to further increases in visits from China. (file:///Volumes/flies/ch%2018%20heritage/ Chinese%20on%20Scotland.webarchive)

In 2014, David Hesse published a book called *Warrior Dreams: Playing Scotsmen in mainland Europe*. He observed:

> In North West Europe, Scottish play-acting is widespread and remarkably organised even if these festivals and associations have received little or no scholarly treatment so far. Only a very small minority among the Scots of Europe claim a family relation to Scotland. They are non-Scots dressing up as Scots. They do so passionately and in impressive numbers. (2014: 2)

This 'play-acting' took four forms: marching pipe-bands; Highland Games; Festivals of Remembrance; and Re-enactments. Said one German re-enactor, Helmut 'McHuck' Huck, who specialised in eighteenth-century Jacobite rebellions: 'I landed in Edinburgh and wondered: why am I the only one wearing a kilt? Have I come to the wrong country?' (2014: 172).

We may shrug our shoulders at these examples of *outré* behaviour, as if they have little relevance to us, and in particular that they have little to do with whom we 'really are'. Surely, we might wonder, other countries (Ireland, for example) are subject to similar cultural fabrications as Scotland, and what harm does it do, anyway, if it brings in tourist dollars? There is more to it than that, and, indeed, such cultural constructions are built upon deeper debates about the nature of Scotland and its cultures, and above all our national identity.

So what lies behind these expressions of Scottish 'culture'? In this chapter, we will explore the cultural origins on which these manifestations are based and examine the arguments that they are distorted expressions of being Scottish which have had a baleful influence on political, social and cultural behaviour.

Chapter aims

- To show why 'heritage' has such a hold in Scotland.
- To examine the strain of cultural pessimism in Scottish intellectual life.
- To analyse the dominant cultural formations which shape how we 'read' Scotland.
- To argue that these debates focus around questions of nationhood.
- To explain how Scotland's dreamscape has become the depository of arguments about modernity.

Scotland – the brand

In 1995, colleagues and I published a book which we called *Scotland – the Brand*. We thought that the title was a neat way of capturing the 'selling' of Scotland by tourism, and the 'heritage' industry. By 'heritage' we did not mean 'history'. Heritage has outgrown its narrow legal definition: that which has been or can be inherited, anything given or received to be a proper possession, an inherited lot or portion.

There is no equivalent in the English language of the French term '*patrimoine*' which captures much better what is involved in heritage; the sense of 'national' inheritance bound up with the sense of a collective *we*, and, in the French case at least, bound up with rural imagery and peasant culture – *cuisine* can be thought of in that way – the meaning of *France profonde*.

What is heritage?

Heritage, to use the rather feeble English-language equivalent, refers to the panoply of material and symbolic inheritances, designed to meet the needs of our modern age to know 'who we are'. As such, heritage is a condition of modernity, reflecting rapid social and cultural change whereby people feel detached from their roots. The search for those roots, real or imagined, is what the heritage industry is about. It is an 'industry' because its roots lie in commerce, in giving – selling – to people who they want to be. Heritage has five aspects:

- Heritage as *commodity*; that it is essentially about selling, thus objectifying, culture.

- Heritage as *consumption*; that it has a product, a set of entrepreneurs, a 'manufacturing' process, a market and, above all, consumers.

- Heritage as *politics* in the widest sense; there is a cultural hinterland which identifies roots, the 'way we were'.

- Heritage as rediscovering the *nation*; the supposed repository of national values – *this* is who we are.

- Heritage as *ideology*; how it is used to justify material and cultural interests, such as those associated with landownership, claiming, for example, that lairds in Scotland are the 'stewards' of the land.

Heritage, however, has far less to do with 'reality' than 'authenticity', how we are represented and constructed. It is the 'exotic' which counts, especially when it comes to selling and marketing, not the everyday. As Dean McCannell pointed out, the aim is to 'knowingly overdose tourists with unwanted pseudo-authenticity' (1992: 31). We are dealing here with pastiche, with what McCannell called 'staged authenticity', performative spectacle.

Is Scotland that much different from anywhere else? The answer comes that Scotland is 'a land out of time', an 'enchanted fortress in a disenchanted world' (Rojek, 1993: 181), a dreamscape. After all, there is a rich vein of filmic cultural constructions such as *Brigadoon* (1954), *Highlander* (1986), *Braveheart* (1995), *Rob Roy* (1995), the cartoon animation *Brave* (2012) and the latest of these, *Outlander* (2014), which we mentioned in the previous chapter.

Inventing Scotland

Scotland represents a rich potpourri of memories, icons, cultural expressions which lends itself to 'authentication'. It is little surprise, then, to find the 'Sinofication' of Scottish places and emblems in the latest tourist campaign, or that sundry Europeans have bought in to the Scottish exotic dreamscape. As David Hesse observes in his book *Warrior Dreams*: 'By playing Scotsmen, the Europeans hope to recover something of their own identity. The Scotland of their imagination serves as a site of memory' (2014: 6).

That allusion to Pierre Nora's concept 'lieu de mémoire' lifts identity out of its association with 'real' place and situates it in *memory* space. This space does not require actors ever to have visited Scotland (remember the woman who 'missed Kintail terribly' even though she had never been there), and if they have, to be disappointed that all is not as it should be. What they might expect is nicely summed up by Peter Womack's comment that: 'All Scots wear tartan, are devoted to bagpipe music, are moved by the spirit of clanship, and supported Bonnie Prince Charlie to a man – all these libels of 1762[1] live on as items in the Scottish tourist package of the twentieth century' (1989: 20).

Two key questions arise: where did all this come from, and what impacts, if any, does it have on 'Scotland' as we experience it today? The Scottish story seems replete with fragmented but powerful narratives, comprising, in William McIlvanney's memorable phrase, 'wilful fragments':

> Not only was our history largely suppressed but those parts of it which were acknowledged were often taught in such a way that they seemed to appear suddenly out of nowhere. A sense of continuity was difficult to grasp. This was the pop-up picture school of history. Oh, look. There's Bonnie Prince Charlie. Where did he come from? And that's Mary Queen of Scots. Somebody cut her head off. Wasn't it the English? Moments of history isolated in this way from the qualifying details of context can be made to mean whatever we want them to mean. Our relationship to them tends to be impulsive and emotional rather than rational, since there is little for rationality to feed on. We see our past as a series of gestures rather than a sequence of actions. It's like looking in a massively cracked mirror. We identify our Scottishness in wilful fragments.
> (*The Herald*, 6 March 1999)

This alerts us to claims about the argument that there is something 'deformed' about Scottish culture, and the ensuing national narrative: the pop-up picture school of history. In Chapter 1, we mentioned the late Marinell Ash's book *The Strange Death of Scottish History* (1980) in which she observed: 'Modern perceptions of Scotland's past are like foggy landscape; small peaks and islands of memory rising out of an occluded background. The name of some of these peaks are Bruce, Wallace, Bannockburn, Mary Queen of Scots, Bonnie Prince Charlie and the Clearances' (1980: 1), perceptions close to those of McIlvanney. Why had this occurred? It was, according to Ash, driven by a form of politics, the failure of national nerve after the Union of 1707 and retreat into the 'emotional trappings of the Scottish past' (1980: 10).

Scottish cultural pessimism

The supposed 'ending' of Scottish history, or at least its caesura[2] caused by the 1707 Union, gave rise to a powerful strain of cultural pessimism among Scottish intellectuals. Scottish culture was seen as split, divided, deformed, characterised by Walter Scott as dividing Scotland between the 'heart' (representing the past, romance, the nation) and the 'head' (the present and future, reason, and, by dint of that, the British state).

The perceived absence of a 'rounded' culture, reflecting the Scottish/British split, mapping as it does onto the culture/politics split, has long had an appeal. Matthew Arnold's Oxford lecture in 1866, 'On the study of Celtic literature', sparked off late nineteenth-century enthusiasm for 'Celticism', and juxtaposed it to 'Saxonism' (Carruthers, 2009). The point about such antinomies was that they were powerful characterisations, not depictions of reality. The classic of the genre was Gregory Smith's notion of the *Caledonian Antisyzygy* (Smith, 1919), the polar turns of realism and fantasy, personified in Robert Louis Stevenson's novella *Dr Jekyll and Mr Hyde* (1886). The 'antisyzygy' was taken up enthusiastically by Hugh MacDiarmid 'to provide the disruptive creative licence and Scottish national difference that his brand of modernism and nationalism required' (Carruthers, 2009: 13). Smith's notion of the 'Caledonian Antisyzygy' would probably have come to nothing were it not that it seemed to appropriate the cultural and political conditions of Scotland at different moments of modernity. The conditions were favourable for adopting it as a dominant trope.[3]

This 'split personality' was a trope which seemed to fit with Scottish social and cultural experiences. Edwin Muir, writing in the 1930s, spoke of a Scotland 'gradually being emptied of its population, its spirit, its wealth, industry, art, intellect, and innate character' (1980 [1935]: 3). George Davie's *The Democratic Intellect* (1961), a powerful indictment of what he saw as the Anglicisation of Scottish culture and education in the nineteenth century, was one of the most influential books of the late twentieth century.

The most trenchant critique of Scottish culture is that by Tom Nairn, writing in his classic *The Break-Up of Britain* (1977). Scotland suffers, he claimed, from 'sub-national deformation', and 'cultural sub-nationalism':

> It was cultural because of course it could not be political; on the other hand, this political action, like, for example, so much Polish literature of the 19th century. It could only be 'sub-nationalist' in the sense of venting its national content in various crooked ways – neurotically, so to speak, rather than directly. (1977: 156)

Heart versus head

Why should we think that Scotland is susceptible to such cultural deformity? By the late eighteenth and early nineteenth centuries, the intelligentsia had been 'deprived of its historic nationalist' role. Said Nairn: 'there was no call for its usual services' (1977: 154) of leading the nation to the threshold of political independence. It had been the historic role of intellectuals, first, to reconstruct the culture, and then spread it more widely such that the whole society became the 'nation' (see Gellner, 1983; Hroch, 1985). After the Union, Scottish intellectuals migrated, in spirit and often in body, to the bigger, more rounded culture of Anglo-Britain, leaving, Nairn thought, a stunted residue of intellectual life in Scotland.

In this context, then, it is easy to explain the Scottish Enlightenment of the late eighteenth century, an otherwise awkward phenomenon to arise in a 'deformed' culture. In essence, Nairn said, it was not really Scottish at all, or rather it represented the belated intellectual fruits of the Union. Operating on a much bigger stage before a larger and more sophisticated audience, it was 'strikingly non-nationalist – so detached from the People, so intellectual and universalising in its assumptions, so Olympian in its attitudes' (Nairn, 1977: 140).

The cultural void in Scotland was aided by the migration of Scottish intellectuals to the richer pastures of England. Macauley, Carlyle, Ruskin, Gladstone and many more were not even thought of as 'Scots' at all. England, says Nairn, was a 'mature, all-round thought-world ... an organic or "rooted" national-romantic culture in which literature – from Coleridge and Carlyle up to FR Leavis and EP Thompson – has consistently played a major role' (1977: 156–7).

This view was supported by the historian Colin Kidd (1993) who argued that Scottish Whig historians looked to England for a progressive and liberating vision of society. Hence, the absence of a nationalist historiography in the nineteenth century was because there was no real – political – demand for one. Liberation and progress were to be achieved through the medium of the Anglo-British state, not via the struggle for national liberation, but in opposition to one for Scotland.

The route to modernity did not involve doubling back to the past. The absence of such a struggle was not, in Kidd's view, because there was insufficient material in Scottish history to construct a myth of national origins, but rather because the 'future' lay with the Anglo-British state; 'Scotland' as such was over. This argument helped to reinforce what became a conventional wisdom about Scottish culture: that it was separated from a nationalist political project, and as a result somehow 'deformed'.

Explaining Scottish cultural formations

So how does this relate to the content of Scottish culture? Here we can apply the concept of 'cultural formations' which the cultural critic Raymond Williams described as 'those effective movements and tendencies, in intellectual and artistic life, which have significant and sometimes decisive influence on the active development of a culture, and which have a variable and often oblique relation to formal institutions' (1977: 117). Such cultural formations help to frame which issues are discussed, and how they are understood.

We have introduced two such 'formations' in previous chapters in discussing Scottish culture, namely kailyard and tartanry, and here we look at them in the context of each other. There is, of course, more to Scottish culture than these sets of images, but the search for a distinctive culture has been so dominated by them that they cannot be avoided. They are important as 'mythic structures' (Craig, 1983) and lie across discussions of Scottish culture, treated as negative, even baleful, influences.

We recognise them as 'habitus', Bourdieu's term for 'a set of everyday social practices and understandings which come to be internalised and hence "objectified"'. Thus, 'objectively regulated and regular without being in any way the product of obedience to rules, they can be collectively orchestrated without being the product of the organizing action of the conductor' (Bourdieu, 1984: 72). They are implicit and 'have no need of words, and ask no more than *complicitous silence*' (quoted in Swartz, 2013: 101, italics in original).

Kailyard

Let us examine in greater detail the lesser of these cultural formations, kailyard, a by-word for parochialism, the other side of 'belonging' which we discussed in Chapter 15. In his collection of essays entitled *Out of History: Narrative paradigms in Scottish and British culture* (1996), Cairns Craig touches a nerve: '*Parochial*: the word has haunted discussion of Scottish culture; it damns up before we start because we must leap in desperation to join 'the world'; condemns us when we finish with having been no more than ourselves' (1996: 11).

Perhaps no other accusation bites so deeply into Scottish consciousness than being 'parochial'; we might think of the English equivalent as 'provincial'. Hence the jibe from the Trump Organization in 2015 when its objection to the offshore wind farm in north-east Scotland was rejected by the Appeal Court: 'parochialism'. Tom Nairn has referred to 'pickle-jar parochialism' (2000: 240), with its own psychic condition of self-colonisation.

It is common to use the synonym 'kailyard' (literally, cabbage-patch) for 'parochial'. However, Kailyardism, properly defined, refers to a popular literary style celebrating Scottish rural quaintness, at its height as a cultural form between 1880 and 1914. Although in formal terms the Kailyard School failed to survive the Great War, its influence on Scottish culture was adjudged long-lasting and malevolent. Much of the Kailyard School's output was produced by Scottish émigrés with rosy, romantic memories of the simple Scotland they had left behind for richer pickings in the south. Their pawky (that is, shrewd) simplicities had a ready market in Scotland, and while kitsch was in no way unique to Scotland, it took on the character of a national–popular tradition.

The implication is that Scottish culture became overwhelmingly *kailyard* and, as a result, a proper 'mature, all-round thought-world' (as in England) could not be Scottish. Revisionist accounts of Kailyardism pointed out, however, that it catered for the émigré market and did not characterise popular fiction in Victorian Scotland. Willie Donaldson argued:

> On the whole, popular fiction in Victorian Scotland is not overwhelmingly backward-looking; it is not obsessed by rural themes; it does not shrink from urbanisation or its problems; it is not idyllic in its approach; it does not treat the common people as comic or quaint. The second half of the 19th century is not a period of creative trauma or linguistic decline; it is one of the richest and most vital episodes in the history of Scottish popular culture. (1986: 149)

If Scotland was 'parochial', it was a view held of the old country by those who had left it, and who required to have their stereotypes confirmed for their own purposes. In this regard, the role of the diaspora in preserving the homeland in aspic is especially important, and we will examine this further in Chapter 20.

That there were differences of *mentalité* between Scots who stayed at home and those who emigrated was asserted by the historian Christopher Harvie, who distinguished between the 'red' Scots – those who leave in search of new opportunities, the outward-bound strain of 'Scot on the make' – and the 'black' Scots – those who stay to nourish the home culture of kailyard and tartanry:

> For the uniqueness of Scotland lies in the power of a 'civil society' divorced from political nationalism, and in an intelligentsia which, lacking a political centre, was divided between two loyalties: the red and the black. The red Scots were cosmopolitan, self-avowedly enlightened and, given a chance authoritarian, expanding into and exploiting bigger and more bountiful fields than their own country could provide. Back home lurked their black brothers, demotic, parochial and reactionary, but keeping the ladder of social promotion open, resisting the encroachments of the English governing class. (1977: 17)

Harvie, whose black/red distinction we introduced in Chapter 15 in the context of 'belonging', does not indicate the origins of, or evidence for, his distinction between 'red' and 'black' Scots. However, the Australian bush poet Henry Lawson published a poem in 1908 called *The Scots*, which used it (www.poetrylibrary.edu.au/poets/lawson-henry/the-scots-0107034).

Lawson's poem (described as a dirge) characterises them as follows:

> The red Scot is angry
>
> Among the sons o' men.
>
> He'll pay you a bawbee,[4]
>
> An' steal it back again.

> The black Scot is friendly
>
> A brither an' a'
>
> He'll pay you a bawbee
>
> An' steal back twa.

Alleged Scottish meanness with money is a key part of the image. It became the stock-in-trade of *Punch* magazine since the nineteenth century,[5] and gave rise to standard jokes such as 'bang went saxpence' (Kington, 1977).

The caption to the accompanying cartoon read:

Peebles body (to Townsman who was supposed to be in London on a visit). *'E-eh, Mac! Ye're sune hame again!'*

Mac: *'E-eh, It's just a ruinous place, that! Mun, a hadna' been there abune twa hoors when – bang – went saxpence!!'*

[The point of the story was that the expenditure of the small sum of sixpence (two and a half pence in decimal currency today) was a large sum to a mean Scot.]

Given the scale of overseas emigration from Scotland which we outlined in Chapter 4, we can understand better that such a typification owed far more to Scots abroad than Scots at home. It was something of a justification for making the move in the first place. How better to retain links with, but also distance from, the 'old country' than by characterising personality types?

Tartanry

It is tartanry, rather than Kailyardism, however, which has been the more significant of the two dominant cultural formations about Scotland. Tartanry is a cultural form which involved the appropriation of Highland symbolism by Lowland Scotland. Nairn called it the 'Tartan Monster' (note the motif of fear, nightmare, neurosis here – sub-Freud: Scotland as a psychiatric condition, a recurring theme in discussions about Scottish culture).

Tartanry was never treated as seriously as kailyard by Scottish intellectuals; perhaps it is too unspeakable to be worthy of their analysis, although they are often linked conceptually together, as in this comment by Christopher Harvie: 'Tartanry attained its fullest extent in the shrewd marketing of the Kailyard authors in the 1890s' (1988: 27).

Tartanry was not a literary movement at all, but a set of garish symbols appropriated by Lowland Scotland at a safe distance from 1745, and turned into a music-hall joke (Harry Lauder (1870–1950) represented the fusion of both tartanry and kailyard – the jokes and mores from the latter, the wrapping from the former; see Figures 17.1 and 17.2, in which history repeats itself).

There are few systematic – and serious – analyses by Scottish intellectuals of tartanry, the set of symbols and images, although there are a number of studies of the history of tartan (Cheape, 1991; Hesketh, 1972; Stewart and Thompson, 1980; Telfer Dunbar, 1962; 1981). The most notorious account is by the English historian Hugh Trevor-Roper (Lord Dacre) in his chapter in the Hobsbawm and Ranger collection *The Invention of Tradition* (1984), in which he attempts a demolition job on tartan itself. The kilt, he claimed, is a purely modern

FIGURE 17.1   Scottish entertainer Sir Harry Lauder on a weighing machine

Source: S&G Barratts/EMPICS Archive

FIGURE 17.2   Scottish First Minister Jack McConnell[6] arrives at the Dressed To Kilt party, held at Sotheby's in New York

Source: ABACA PRESS/ABACA USA/PA Images

costume, first designed and first worn by an English Quaker industrialist, and bestowed by him on the Highlanders in order not to preserve their traditional way of life, but to ease their transformation: to bring them out of the heather and into the factory, presumably because they did not have the wit to do that for themselves (1984: 22).

It is not difficult to demolish Dacre's account of the origins of tartan (see, for example, William Ferguson's *Identity of the Scottish Nation*, 1998), and he certainly had political and cultural axes to grind, as did Hobsbawm. Neal Ascherson (2010) commented:

> Trevor-Roper's Scotophobia, evident even in the letters he wrote as a boy from a Scottish prep school, was not entirely rational. *The Invention of Scotland*, a posthumous selection of some of his essays on the country, is fun to read but spoiled by ignorance of the background, unfamiliarity with recent Scottish research and malicious interpretation. The fact is that he was out of his depth, as he often was when he stepped beyond about 1760. (www.lrb.co.uk/v32/n16/neal-ascherson/liquidator)

We saw in the previous chapter how tartanry's survival and development occurred because a number of factors came together at an opportune moment: the Romantic search for the 'noble savage'; the 'discovery' of the Ossian poems by Macpherson in the 1760s; the raising of Highland regiments after Culloden in 1746. By the nineteenth century, the climate was right for Walter Scott's romantic tales to become bestsellers, the king effectively acting as literary agent by visiting Edinburgh in 1822, accoutred in the way Scott wanted.

The more prosaically named Allen brothers who changed their names to the Sobieski Stuarts had claimed ancestry from Bonnie Prince Charlie and Polish Prince Sobieski. Like Macpherson's Ossian poems, that the manuscript *Vestiarium Scoticum* was a forgery was neither here nor there, for its publication, in 1842, came at a propitious moment to take advantage of the cultural and commercial opportunities which had the royal seal of approval following the royal visit to Edinburgh twenty years before.

The weaving company Wilsons of Bannockburn converted the fantasy into commercial reality by issuing its own '1819 Pattern Book' collating tartans, real and imaginary. The whole enterprise was reinforced, first by George IV in his visit to Edinburgh in 1822, orchestrated by Walter Scott, and then by Queen Victoria's purchase of Balmoral in 1848. This was reflected in the royal iconography which we discussed in the previous chapter. 'Balmorality' even entered dictionaries to define Scottish kitsch, *Collins Dictionary* defining it as 'an idealisation of Scottish traditions and culture'. David Goldie observed:

> Tartanry is, and should be seen as, something of a joke. But we should always remember that jokes are complex things, and remember too that you can do much more interesting things with jokes than simply laugh at them. (2010: 244)

The appropriation of tartan has helped to translate Highland images and identities into Scotland as a whole. Presenting Scotland as 'Celtic' took somewhat longer, for it was not until the second half of the nineteenth century that a discursive separation between 'Saxon' and 'Celt' took place (McArthur, 1994). This distinction became part of an ethno-logical fiction and system of symbolic appropriation whereby Gaelic culture, life and language became the focus of associations required by the external discourse of wider English and European cultures (Chapman, 1992).

Thus did 'Celtic' become a term for non-Anglo-Saxon, an identity constructed around the requirements of modern geo-politics. Chapman argued that Scotland 'has, on the whole, settled for a Celtic and Gaelic definition, in pursuit of difference from England. This accounts for the extraordinary efflorescence of Highland and Gaelic imagery in the self-presentation and assumed genealogy of modern Scotland' (1992: 92). There are also deeper ideological antinomies being employed in this vocabulary:

> the Anglo-Saxon ... appears a brutal soulless figure, disfigured by every wart and sore that industry, cities, pollution, capitalism and greed can cast upon the countenance. The Celt, by contrast, is a magical figure, bard, warrior and enchanter, beyond the reach of this world, and an object of love and yearning for those doomed to wander among material things in the cold light of reason. (Chapman, 1992: 253)

Nor should we think that this characterisation has simply been wished upon a reluctant Scotland from the outside. The social anthropologist Sharon Macdonald (1999) pointed out that within the country itself there is a deep ambivalence between the contrasting tropes of 'improvement/modernity' and 'remaining true to oneself', especially through appropriating Gaelic and Highland culture to convey the essence of a people. She argued that it was only in the second half of the twentieth century that the language of Gaelic came to be seen as central to Scottish identity, and this in the context of continuing decline in the number of Gaelic speakers in Scotland.[7]

The interest in the phenomenon of tartanry as a defining feature of Scottish culture has continued in recent years. Ian Brown's collection of essays, *From Tartan to Tartanry: Scottish culture, history and myth* (2010), distinguished between the dress form 'tartan' and the cultural product which has outgrown its origins 'tartanry'. His book is neither another demolition of 'tartan myths', nor an attempt to rehabilitate them. Rather, it provides useful cultural distance between the iconic 'Scotch Myths' exhibition by Barbara and Murray Grigor in the early 1980s and the analysis of Scottish culture twenty years later in the post-devolution period. The exhibition turned out to be the high-water mark of the critique of tartan kitsch, as well as being highly amusing.

In 1982, the 'Scotch Myths' exhibition designed by film-makers Murray and Barbara Grigor at the Edinburgh International Festival showed the most outré forms of Scottish cultural kitsch. The brochure took the shape of a whisky bottle (see Figure 17.3).

The whole thing was done tongue-in-cheek and was made into a film by Channel 4 (https://www.youtube.com/watch?v=CzZSmVX2M-Q).[8] How, the implication was, could anyone take this stuff seriously?

The Grigors' exhibition had assembled representations of Scotland, from postcards to orange-box labels from California to media representations of Scotland in film and television, and aimed to generate discussion of Scotland's 'deformed' culture. In 1982, the

FIGURE 17.3 'Scotch Myth's' brochure

Source: Author's photograph

Edinburgh Film Festival held a showing of *Scotch Reels*, the film of the exhibition, together with a three-day discussion event around a collection of essays (*Scotch Reels*: *Scotland in cinema and television*, 1982), edited by Colin McArthur.

The remit was clear. In McArthur's words: 'Clearly the traditions of Kailyard and Tartanry have to be exposed and deconstructed, and more politically progressive representations constructed, circulated and discussed' (1981: 25). Much of the evidence was based on graphic representations in film, television and the 'sign media' generally. The semiotics of Scotland, it was argued, are regressive in cultural terms, and in their political manifestations lock us into subordination and dependency.

Tartanry and kailyard were considered to be key to maintaining cultural hegemony over Scotland's sense of itself. McArthur argued that 'a limited number of discourses have been deployed in the cinema to construct Scotland and the Scots, and to give an impression that no other constructions are possible' (1982: 69). These 'pathological discourses', as he called them, could be traced through the ways Scotland is represented, notably in the visual arts.

By the twentieth century, modern cultural media were reproducing the stereotypes, and in film it was the decade and a half after the Second World War which laid down 'the definitive modern statements of Tartanry and Kailyard in the cinema' in Scotland (McArthur, 1982: 45). Films such as *Bonnie Prince Charlie* (1948), *Rob Roy, the Highland Rogue* (1953), *Kidnapped* (1960), *Greyfriars Bobby* (1961), and the doyen of them all, *Brigadoon* (1954),[9] were all Hollywood creations and representations of Scotland. McArthur commented: 'at one level it takes the Romantic representation of Scotland as a given, but at another level ... this representation is revealed as the dream par excellence, as a fiction created to escape from the urban horrors of the twentieth century' (1983: 47).

A decade later, McArthur was still expressing pessimism about a newer genre of films. Movies such as *Local Hero* were still, in his view, being written within dominant Scottish narratives of an 'elegaic discourse', in which 'we tend to be written by the dominant Scottish narratives rather than ourselves writing stories about Scotland' (1993: 102). Such discourses were not inevitable however: 'it has to be understood that the historically dominant narratives about Scotland can impede political advance and must therefore be confronted, deconstructed and replaced with new narratives' (1993: 104). (Note the connection between 'culture' and 'politics'.) The problem, as McArthur saw it, was that the discourses continue, in his words, 'to lurk, iceberg-like, in the Scottish discursive unconscious'. Here we confront a recurring theme of the deformed nature of culture in Scotland – Scotland as a psychiatric condition, which is a powerful discourse in its own right, and one which has dominated discussions about Scottish culture for much of the last fifty years. The discourse does not have to be 'true' to be thought 'real'.

Ian Brown, who edited *From Tartan to Tartanry* in 2010, described the 1983 collection of essays, *Scotch Reels*, by McArthur as the 'locus classicus of anti-tartanry' (2010: 103). Brown quotes Duncan Petrie's analysis of contemporary Scottish fictions: 'both Nairn and McArthur … end up relying heavily on metaphors of psychopathology and an attendant conception of the Scottish national psyche as irredeemably neurotic' (2010: 111). Nairn himself had been pessimistic that this 'psychiatric condition' was treatable. In his classic *The Break-Up of Britain* he had observed that: 'Tartanry will not wither away, if only because it possesses the force of its own vulgarity – immunity from doubt and higher culture' (1977: 165).

Culture and politics

The original Nairn thesis was a key part of a political argument in the 1970s: that the separation of heart from head, culture from politics, had placed a major obstacle in front of the movement for self-government. The failure of the 1979 referendum to deliver a home rule 'assembly' seemed to be proof of that, except a narrow majority had voted in favour, but insufficient to overcome the gerrymander introduced by opponents in the UK parliament (the so-called 40 per cent rule).

The notion that Scots were ambivalent about devolution in 1979 is captured by Ewen Bain's cartoon (see Figure 17.4) published shortly after the result (see Bochel et al., 1981: 198–9 for a selection).[10] The 'don't-knows' won. Furthermore, there was deemed to be no self-governing Scotland because the hegemonic nature of (deformed) Scottish culture prevented it, or so it plausibly seemed, until the recovery of a (devolved) parliament in the late 1990s, and, later, the formation of SNP governments in 2007, 2011 and 2016. By dint of electoral evidence, the 'deformed culture' thesis lost its explanatory political power and with it its lustre.

Nairn's thesis also came under attack from a more conventional 'nationalist' quarter. Craig Beveridge and Ronnie Turnbull, writing in 1989 and again in 1997, promoted as

FIGURE 17.4
The 1979 referendum

Source: Bochel et al. (1981: 198)

the central task of cultural nationalism 'the recovery of Scottish cultural practices', which have to be rescued from the metropolitan-influenced analysis of Scotland. Intellectuals like Nairn were accused of a 'deep aversion to everything native and local' (Beveridge and Turnbull, 1989: 58), which in turn derives from long-standing processes of 'cultural colonisation'. Such processes inflict a Manichean view on Scottish culture: 'In Nairn's description, there are no shades or contours; everything stands condemned' (1989: 58).

Beveridge and Turnbull set themselves the task of identifying and promoting Scottish cultural traditions, untainted by the 'anglicised traditions' of the universities in Scotland (not, of course, in their view, properly *Scottish* universities). For this they relied on the work of George Davie in *The Democratic Intellect* (1961) in which he argued that Scottish higher education underwent an unprecedented and fatal Anglicisation in the late nineteenth century, a thesis described by Lindsay Paterson as persuasive and usually undisputed, but quite wrong in its interpretation of events and processes (1994: 66).

Furthermore, Paterson developed a powerful counter-thesis (in *The Autonomy of Modern Scotland*, 1994) that the lack of self-government in formal terms was a reflection of de facto autonomy for Scottish civil institutions. He observed:

> these institutions are much more subtle and complex than merely a parliament, and this is as true of Scotland as of nations that are formally independent: they are the schools, universities, media, churches and the myriad daily practices that develop informally and slowly. In that sense, nationalists have been successful: they, whether official or oppositionist, have created a world of dense Scottishness which creates a feeling of natural allegiance in nearly everyone who is brought up here, or who has lived here for an appreciable length of time. (1994: 181)

Only when faced with the loss of such autonomy by centralising Westminster governments in the second half of the twentieth century did it take on a more pressing party political form.

Much of the attack on tartanry and kailyard has depended on an uncritical assumption that their impact has been comprehensive and undifferentiated. The essence of Beveridge and Turnbull's thesis was that Scottish culture is deemed to be 'deformed' by intellectuals, and that this arises from 'inferiorism', a form of cultural dependency on the metropolitan, English, power. They presented us with the cultural correlate of the 'dependency' thesis, cultural dependency being the result of employing limited discourses. In crucial respects, however, they made one central assumption: that a single Scottish national culture exists, and remains to be uncovered and rescued from intellectual pessimism.

In their analysis of Scottish culture, Beveridge and Turnbull made the point that those who argue that tartanry and Kailyardism are culturally hegemonic in their effects fail to acknowledge that cultural meanings are never passively consumed, but always subject to selection and adjustment to other discourses. Consumers' responses to tartanry, therefore, are 'not uncritical assimilation, but a complex negotiation dependent on the beliefs and values which are bound up with those of other concerns' (1989: 14). And, in any case, there were alternative cultural models of Scotland.

Clydesidism

From the 1980s, there were attempts to replace tartanry and kailyard with a more 'progressive' cultural formation – *Clydesidism* – which McArthur judged to be 'extremely refreshing in the Scottish context', and not a 'pernicious discourse' (1982: 69). John Caughie argued that the tradition is 'based on working class experiences which, since the twenties, have seemed to offer the only real and consistent basis for *a Scottish national culture*' (1982: 121; my emphasis).

What Clydesidism had in its favour was that it was constructed from 'real' images of working-class life, from the discourse of class, and from naturalism. However, as Cairns Craig (1983) pointed out, it was already becoming a 'historic discourse' by the late twentieth century, even in its heartland of west–central Scotland, and had disappeared in the early years of the twenty-first century.

Its language was redolent of early twentieth-century Clydeside, with its appeal to the 'industrial masses' and to skilled masculine culture. And as Eleanor Gordon and Esther Breitenbach observed, 'skill' is a social construct which is 'saturated with male bias' (1990: 6). It was fine, said Cairns Craig, to break out of the mental traps of the historic myths of tartanry and kailyard, to imagine a future, even a revolutionary future, through which to overcome the static quality of the dominant myths, but we risked embracing a myth based on a fast-disappearing working-class culture.

One might argue that the point was not to find a new, pure, Scottish national culture fit for the twenty-first century, but to recognise that the relationship between cultural forms and political movements is never straightforward. It is tempting to reach back for the classical nationalist formulation of the late eighteenth and nineteenth centuries, described by Gellner, Hobsbawm and Hroch, whereby 'a people', unique in their culture, reach for political self-determination as an expression of that culture.

Rather than there being a single people with a single culture, there seemed to be advantages in diversity and fragmentation, as Cairns Craig has observed:

> The fragmentation and division which made Scotland seem abnormal to an earlier part of the 20th century came to be the norm for much of the world's population. Bilingualism, biculturalism and the inheritance of a diversity of fragmented traditions were to be the source of creativity rather than its inhibition in the second half of the twentieth century, and Scotland ceased to have to measure itself against the false 'norm', psychological as well as cultural, of the unified national tradition. (1987: 7)

If political developments at the end of the twentieth century, notably the recovery of a Scottish parliament, have eroded the view that Scottish culture is peculiar, there is another aspect of the argument to which we now turn: its continuing significance for tourism.

Selling Scotland

VisitScotland's excitement about the Chinese tourist market, with which we began this chapter, is the latest in a long process of 'manufacturing' Scottish heritage (see McCrone et al., 1995: chapter 4). To be sure, tourist boards in most countries are attuned to the commercial possibilities of 'heritage'. In this, Scotland is not unique. It is a lucrative trade but one which manages to hide its pecuniary qualities well. It meets a social and cultural need to provide identity ballast in a rapidly changing world, and it is significant that the more rootless the society, the greater the intensity to search for 'roots'.

Homecoming

Another example of the fusion of culture and commerce was the 'Homecoming', or *The Gathering*, in Edinburgh in 2011, part-funded by the Scottish government to bring 'home' expat Scots. This culminated in a 'clan gathering' in Holyrood Park and a march down the Royal Mile. The event turned out to be a financial embarrassment. Too few people turned up, and the organisers were reduced to appealing to 'affinity Scots' to accommodate those with no known ancestral links to Scotland, but who simply wanted somehow to 'be' Scottish in some way, at least for the moment.

Locals, who are used to this sort of happening in the capital city, let it purposively pass them by. After all, if *anyone* can be Scottish, what sort of club is that? Serious amounts of government money had gone into this event, seeking to cash in (literally) on the diaspora possibilities so well exploited by the Irish government in the past thirty years. Seeking one's ancestors, real or imaginary, is usually good business.

To be sure, there seems to be no shortage of émigré Scots to appeal to. We will explore the 'diaspora' more fully in Chapter 20. However, we encounter claims that diaspora Scots outnumber the resident population by as many as ten to one (see e.g. Basu, 2007: 15). The methodology by which such figures are derived is problematic; how, after all, can one tell, other than by accepting people's claims to family roots? All we can say is that the scale of emigration from Scotland over the last century is such that there is a considerable 'diaspora industry' to which 'roots tourism' such as the 'Homecoming' can appeal (www.visitscotland.com/see-do/homecoming-scotland-2014).

In his 2007 book *Highland Homecomings: Genealogy and heritage tourism in the Scottish diaspora*, Paul Basu observed: 'Scotland is at once a notional and a material reality, an imagined place as much as a geographical territory, a symbol, even a sacred one, that may be yet seen, touched, photographed, driven across, walked upon' (2007: 1). The key point is that this is much more to do with pilgrimage than tourism, for in the words of one of his respondents: 'I am not, and never will be, a tourist in Scotland. I felt Scotland many years before I was there' (2007: 2). It is 'roots' metaphors which are most powerful: 'quest', 'homecoming', pilgrimage'; in the words of another person, 'My soul cannot rest until I reclaim my ancestors' ghosts' (2007: 205). Native Scots, arguably, would be quite taken aback at such sentiments: the belief that there is something 'sacred' about the quest, which simple 'tourism' cannot capture.

Basu's focus is on what he calls 'Highlandism' not 'Tartanry', because the latter he takes to be a genre of 'Highlandist discourse', and in any case tartanry is 'often associated in Scotland with kitsch and bad taste' (2007: 231) and thus to be avoided. He justifies the 'Highland' focus on the grounds that when 'Scotland' is imagined among émigrés, it is *Highland* Scotland which figures, although he does not substantiate this. His fieldwork around the 'Orkney Homecoming' and in the heritage centre at Dunbeath in Caithness does not mention the disputed claims that the Northern Isles and Caithness have a Norse rather than a Gaelic heritage (see e.g. Rosie, 2012).

Basu's is a nice, if unintended, confirmation of the 'Gaelic Vision' of Scottish culture (the title of Chapman's 1978 book), reinforced by the sacral visits of ancestor-seekers. Appeal to 'the blood' ('*we are the blood*', claimed one visitor, alarmingly) is a key part of 'the popular Scottish diasporic imagination, a moral rhetoric of exile [which] comes to dominate a morally ambiguous history of emigration and colonisation' (Basu, 2007: 193). The desire to be a 'child of the Clearances' conveys moral approbation, even if based on dubious historical evidence.[11] Such claims have more to do with societies in which the politics of 'roots' remains live, in settler societies such as Canada, the United States, Australia and New Zealand. People born outwith Scotland and living in Scotland, must wonder about claims that visitors are *more* Scottish because of 'proper' bloodlines; the assumption being that blood trumps residence. In any case, as we shall see in the next chapter, claims to identity through 'blood' in Scotland are treated as problematic.

Imagining Scotland

The cultural capture of Highland imagery has become iconic in the form of Edward Landseer's *The Stag at Bay* (see the previous chapter) and other forms of 'social gaze' in Highland landscapes. Mairi MacArthur's work on Highland tourism from the nineteenth century shows how people were airbrushed out of their history in favour of 'blasted heaths and hills of mist'. Guidebooks and travel memoires focused on three themes: the wild grandeur of the landscape, remoteness and peace, coupled with a dash of romantic history.

Scotland has been subject to an intense 'tourist gaze' for at least 150 years. As we saw in the previous chapter, visitors to the Highlands multiplied by a factor of 100 over the course of the century. The social historian Alister Durie has pointed out that '[Walter] Scott did much to expand and popularise tourism in Scotland. He did not create it, any more than he created Romanticism on which his work fed' (1992: 48).

We can see, then, that key myths and memories of Scotland are sustained by such powerful 'historical' associations, and reinforced by those seeking out their ancestors, however remote or tangential. In any case, even if you cannot claim the blood-links, you can always claim to be an 'affinity Scot'; simply wishing to be one brings it about.

Here, for example, is a description from the 'best-of-Scotland holidays' website of 2015; note the repetition of the word 'home':[12]

> Come to the home of ... Burns; the home of Golf; the home of Whisky; the home of Enlightenment and Innovation; the home of your ancestors.
>
> Has your life been 'touched' in some way by Scotland, whether through family links, having previously visited, lived, worked or studied or are you a member of the many Scottish societies around the globe? If so, the Homecoming Scotland celebrations are the ideal way to rediscover your love of our proud wee nation.
>
> The people of Scotland offer a heartfelt invitation to all 'Affinity Scots' to return to your roots and feature in an inspirational fête of all things Scottish.

Note the care taken to smooth over the distinction between 'affinity Scots' and 'return to your roots'; it is enough that your life has been touched in some way by Scotland. In truth, such a tariff for 'being Scottish' is not difficult to pay.

In his study of *Warrior Dreams*, David Hesse commented: 'By creating "affinity Scots", the marketing people acknowledged that many overseas "Scots" have no ancestral ties to Scotland – and perhaps even that it does not matter much whether they do or not' (2014: 175). This is because 'For Scots only' is not a good marketing label, and somehow you have to make everyone a Scot for the purpose. Hesse's study is of central importance. The 'Scots of Europe' do not have, nor do they claim, proper ancestral roots, but that does not stop them 'playing Scotsmen' for reasons we will explore later in this chapter.

'Scotland' can provide all of this and more, and 'bens and glens tourism' is simply another thing for locals to negotiate their way around as they inhabit an altogether more 'real' Scotland. And yet there lingers a sense that the gap between 'real' and 'fantasy' Scotland is such that so much is expected of us that we become touristic players whether we like it or not.

If tourism is not simply about commercial activities but shapes the production of cultural forms of 'being Scottish', then do these fantastical representations not somehow constrain who we can be, especially in a world where politics and commerce latch on to tourism as they key modern industry? Rojek has pointed out that 'preserving the past in order to escape into it is therefore seen as impossible. For merely to define something as unchangeable alters our relationship to it. Literary landscapes, and for that matter heritage sites, do not preserve the past, they represent it' (1993: 160).

Culture and confidence

So have we left behind arguments that Scottish culture is deeply deformed, ersatz and baleful in its influence on the Scottish 'psyche'? What about the argument that Scotland suffers from a psychiatric–political condition which prevents it from taking its proper place in the world? Is the strain of cultural pessimism which had such a hold on 'imagining Scotland' in the 1970s no longer potent? Does Scotland still suffer from 'pathological discourses'?

On the one hand, the 'political' argument that attaining self-government, at least in the form of a law-making parliament, was limited by this 'inferiorist' condition no longer seems to have the force it once had, given the existence of a devolved parliament, SNP governments in that parliament, and a surge of voting for independence in the referendum of September 2014. We are all (small-n) nationalists now.

Curiously, though, the argument that there is something deformed about the Scottish 'psyche' is an argument that has not gone away. In 2003 Carol Craig published a book with the title *The Scots' Crisis of Confidence* (published by Big Thinking) and set up 'The Centre for Confidence and Well-Being' (www.centreforconfidence.co.uk/information. php?p=cGlkPTY5), supported by the-then Scottish Executive (government). In the words of the author:

> The book attracted considerable press interest and comment. Within a short period of time it was being referred to in speeches and articles from figures in sport, journalism, health, education and from across the political spectrum. It was reprinted several times but from 2009 it was out of print.

In October 2011 Argyll Publishing brought out a new edition of the book. Carol Craig has completely rewritten the introduction and the conclusion and brought her argument up to date. She has also included completely new material on 'mindset' and optimism.

The 2003 edition ended with the comment: 'For Scotland to become a more confident nation and a better place to live we must cease the endless search for Scottishness and renounce our previous obsession with Scottish identity' (2003: 299). She went on: 'In place of the quest for Scottish identity we need a quest for individual identity. We need to encourage individual Scots to go forth and be themselves.' Academic reviewers were critical. The social anthropologist Anthony Cohen observed that Craig 'sees Scottish society as generalizable into a collective psyche to which she applies terms drawn from Jungian analysis, and from which she derives a deterministic culture which explains pretty well everything from economic failure to dreary conformity' (2004: 160).

Undaunted, Carol Craig published another book a few years later called *The Tears That Made the Clyde: Well-being in Glasgow* (2010). Reviewers pointed to similar flaws as in the earlier book. Sean Damer observed: 'By arguing that we need to focus on low self-esteem and unhappiness within the working class, Craig is not only psychologizing a structural problem, but also denying the existence of that unequal structure in the first place' (2011: 152). Cohen and Damer both accuse Craig of failing to comprehend the notion of 'culture' in a social scientific sense.

Both critics were pointing up a perspective with a long critical history, that is assuming that attitudes and values have precedence over social structural conditions, which leads easily into a view that somehow people are responsible for their own (mis)fortunes; it is primarily a matter of will rather than constraining social, economic and political considerations.

There were limits to the extent to which Carol Craig was willing to play the 'confidence' riff, however. She returned to the fray during the Scottish Independence Referendum in

2014 by arguing that, this time, confidence had its limitations, or rather, that simply relying on such a mindset courted 'Pollyanna' tendencies[13] which she aimed at the 'Yes' campaign. In an article 'Why this optimist is voting No' (Carol Craig, 2014), it turned out that confidence was not sufficient, and that serious attention had to be given to the conditions and contexts in which 'confidence' could operate. It was, she said, necessary for people to 'have an accurate knowledge of present realities', so 'grim reality' was required to intrude upon the optimists (https://wakeupscotland.wordpress.com/2014/10/12/carol-craig-on-selfishness-and-the-scottish-independence-referendum/). A sense of confidence, it seems, has its severe limitations, even to those who champion its power.

We might be tempted simply to dismiss such accounts as being of the political moment, but we can also see them as the latest in a long line of thinking of Scotland as a 'psychological condition', employing the use of the language of psychiatry rather than sociology. Here we have a good example of Bourdieu's *habitus* such that everyday understandings have become internalised and hence 'objectified'. The value of such understandings, perhaps, lies far less in their explanatory value for current social conditions in Scotland (or anywhere for that matter),[14] but in triggering an older tradition of invoking psychoanalytic models to account for supposed national neurosis, when social scientific thinking arguably does a far better job.

What is interesting sociologically is not that such accounts explain very much, but that they are deemed to be highly relevant to modern Scotland. Scotland seems not so much a country, more a psychiatric condition, and that is a thesis which is remarkably resilient in the face of social scientific evidence to the contrary. We could be forgiven for thinking that Scots no longer know who they are; that they have been so oppressed by these powerful tropes that they no longer know which way to turn. To reinforce the point: the 'national neurosis' thesis does not stand up to social scientific scrutiny, but it does seem immune to evidence and proof in some quarters.

Scotland as dreamscape

We have seen that much of the debate about Scottish culture takes place within the context of émigré notions of what it means to be Scottish. On the other hand, what if there are people who have no known connection to Scotland as a place, nor are linked to it by blood? Such is the remarkable study by David Hesse, who uncovered what he called the Scottish dreamscape across continental Europe, which involves 'playing Scotsmen', wearing kilts, playing bagpipes, marching up and down, meeting in conventions. What, he asked, is that all about?

It is not all of a piece. Take, for example, *De Scotjes*, literally the wee Scots, in the Dutch town of Tilburg. Set up in the early 1950s by a group of boys who wanted a drum band which was distinctive from others in the area, the father of one of the drummers suggested a Scottish pipe band, because he remembered one marching through the town in 1944 at the time of its liberation from the Germans. Hesse gives the account:

> The British Army's 15th Scottish Division had freed Tilburg from Nazi occupa-
> tion, and acting Major-General Colin Barber declared the city officially liberated.
> To celebrate the victory, the Scots Guards' pipe band paraded through Tilburg
> city centre. The local population lined the streets by the thousands and cheered
> as Major-General Barber led the band. A journalist of the local *Nieuwsblad* was
> pleased with the event but taken aback by the sound of the pipes: 'we do not
> hope that this instrument has now become popular in Tilburg'. If only he had
> known. (2014: 93)

Hesse shows how such events tap into the Scottish dreamscape, and that it is sufficiently
attractive in terms of 'doing', noisily, and with style. Above all, it involves play-acting. The
Scottish dreamscape is familiar; it promises pleasure; and is charged with ideas about heroism and martial valour.

But why Scotland? Hesse explains that there are many presenting reasons, such as pipe
bands liberating Northern European towns, and with such noise and verve, but there is
more to it than that, for the occasions are not mainly commemorative. In his own words:

> The Scots of Europe toss cabers at Highland Games, play soldiers in marching
> pipe and drum bands, commemorate Scottish heroes, and simulate kilted com-
> bat in historical re-enactment clubs. They justify their Scottish performances
> with often elaborate mythologies of kinship: By impersonating Scots they hope
> to recover something of their own lost past. They understand Scotland as a site
> of European memory, a reservoir of shared history. They employ the Scottish
> dreamscape to remember and re-imagine who they were themselves. (2014: 213)

There is an older discovery of 'Scotland' on which much of this rests, namely European
Romanticism, given full expression by Walter Scott. Hesse observes that in the 1820s,
Goethe was attracted to the novels of Scott because he thought German history was dull
compared with Scott's material: 'Scott's magic ... [r]ests on the beauty of the three British
kingdoms and the inexhaustible diversity of their history, while in Germany the novelist
may find no fertile field between the forest of Thuringia and the sand deserts of
Mecklenburg' (quoted in Hesse, 2014: 215). The point is not that twenty-first-century
Europeans are driven to noisy action by reading Scott, but that 'Scotland' is embedded
often implicitly in European Romanticism (see Lukács, 1969).

All of this is reinforced by Hollywood movies such as *Braveheart*, *Highlander* and most
recently *Outlander*: 'The Scots of Europe approach Scotland as a site of memory. They interpret the Scots as survivors from a European pre-modernity and use their musical, athletic
and sartorial traditions to re-imagine their own lost past' (Hesse, 2014: 208).

The appeal of the familiar, the fun and the heroic is a long way from the elegiac searches
in derelict Highland crofts for the bones of one's ancestors, but arguably each compounds the
other, reinforcing ancestor worship with the cultural quest to discover and play out the 'way
we were', whether in Austria, Belgium, Russia or North America. Scotland as a pre-modern
counter-world occupies a central position in European modernity whether we like it or not.

Cue lights, action …

And as if on cue comes the announcement that Steven Spielberg is to direct a movie version of Roald Dahl's *The BFG* (Big Friendly Giant), set in 'Giant Country'. *The Herald* (16 May 2016) commented:

> From The Quiraing on Skye to the Old Man of Hoy on Orkney and the Shiant Isles off Lewis, the acclaimed movie provides another welcome, visual marketing tool for the Scottish tourist industry. It follows on from a series of major block-busters which have led to an influx of tourists in recent years – from James Bond movie Skyfall in Glen Etive to Harry Potter films in Glenfinnan and Glencoe and Michael Fassbender's adaptation of Macbeth in a very atmospheric, not to say wet, Skye.

> Malcolm Roughead, chief executive of VisitScotland, said: 'It's wonderful to hear that the first screenings of The BFG have been a success in Cannes with Scotland playing a starring role once more on the big screen. Set-jetting, where people visit the shooting locations of their favourite movies, is big business.' (www.heraldscotland.com/news/14494446.Steven_Spielberg_s_giant_boost_for_Highland_tourism/)

Conclusion

And so we end up with a conundrum. On the one hand, much of the debate about Scottish history and culture focuses on its fragmented nature, its deformity – that it does not seem to follow the pattern of 'proper' nations which develop coherent narratives of their origins and their identity. We encounter claims that we lack the necessary rounded thought-world, in large part because the Union of 1707 drove a wedge between our culture and politics.

Then we encountered tourism with its ersatz images of who we are, how we dress and how we behave. Furthermore, we have had to live with cultural formations – kailyard, tartanry – which express and reinforce that deformation, and if that were not bad enough, we are told we suffer from a lack of self-confidence. Finding that there are other Europeans who are acting our parts often in an outré form may simply reinforce our sense of unease and even gloom. Living with *wilful fragments* seems part of the Scottish condition.

And yet all is not what it seems. We now know that Kailyardism was a late nine-teenth-century cultural and literary form which had much more to do with people furth of Scotland; strictly speaking, it was not our concern. Tartanry was literally and metaphorically a joke, which did well in the music halls, and sells tat to tourists on the high street, but seems to impinge little on our own behaviour, except when we borrow Highland dress for weddings and graduations, and as uniforms at sporting occasions (see Chapter 21).

If dressing up and doing Scottish in Europe is what some people do, that is their affair, and, in any case, as Hesse points out, play-acting is inclusive; it is some strange kind of compliment, or at least an acknowledgement that we exist. Truth, however, tells a somewhat different tale, as we shall see in the next two chapters when we look at how people do national identity.

Chapter summary

So what have we learned in this chapter?

- That narrative accounts of Scotland, its history, are deemed incomplete, consisting of wilful fragments.

- That there is a strong vein of cultural pessimism running through Scottish intellectual life, partly but not entirely driven by political analysis.

- That two cultural formations, kailyard and tartanry, are thought to be especially powerful, and negative, in their effects.

- That, nevertheless, there are alternative accounts which argue that social and cultural realities are far more subtle and complex in modern Scotland.

- That Scots and Scotland provide a key 'site of memory' for many Europeans.

Questions for discussion

1. What is the significance of 'heritage' in Scotland? How does it relate to 'tourism'?

2. Does Scotland suffer from a form of 'cultural sub-nationalism'?

3. Compare and contrast 'kailyard' and 'tartanry' as key Scottish cultural formations.

4. What connection, if any, is there between cultural and political developments in Scotland over the last fifty years?

5. Are 'Playing Scotsmen' simply playing games, and, if so, to what effect?

Annotated reading

(a) For accounts of Scottish history, see M. Ash, *The Strange Death of Scottish History* (1980); L. Paterson, *The Autonomy of Modern Scotland* (1994).

(b) On political and literary culture in Scotland: T. Nairn, *The Break-Up of Britain* (1977); G. Carruthers, *Scottish Literature* (2009); Cairns Craig, *Out of History:*

Narrative paradigms in Scottish and British Culture (1996); C. Kidd, *Subverting Scotland's Past: Scottish Whig historians and the creation of an Anglo-Scottish Identity, 1689–c.1830* (1993); C. Beveridge and R. Turnbull, *The Eclipse of Scottish Culture* (1989) and *Scotland after Enlightenment* (1997); C. McArthur, *Scotch Reels* (1982).

(c) On filmic representations, see D. Petrie's *Screening Scotland* (2000), *Contemporary Scottish Fictions: Film, television and the novel* (2004) and *The Cinema of Small Nations* (2007).

(d) On kailyard and tartanry: W. Donaldson, *Popular Literature in Victorian Scotland* (1986); I. Brown (ed.), *From Tartan to Tartanry: Scottish culture, history and myth* (2010).

(e) On heritage and tourism: D. McCrone et al., *Scotland – the Brand* (1995); P. Basu, *Highland Homecomings: Genealogy and heritage tourism in the Scottish diaspora* (2007); D. Hesse, *Warrior Dreams: Playing Scotsmen in mainland Europe* (2014).

Notes

1   Womack is referring to post-1745 English demonisation of the Scots, notably in Hogarth's cartoons of 1762, and observes that 'For a brief but rather horrifying period, the Highlander takes on the role of the political devil' (1989: 19).

2   A caesura is a pause or a break, often used in poetry or music, but here referring to a major shift in the narrative of Scottish history.

3   A trope is a figurative use of a word or phrase which provides a motif or cliché for understanding.

4   A bawbee was a ha'penny (half an old penny), usually signifying a trivial amount.

5   *Punch*, also known as the *London Charivari*, was a weekly magazine of humour and satire, founded in 1841, peaking in the late 1940s, closing in 1992, briefly revived in 1996, and closing finally in 2002. It was a staple of doctors' and dentists' waiting rooms.

6   First Minister Jack McConnell was brave enough to model a kilt at a charity fashion show in New York in 2004. He later commented: 'The photograph has come to haunt me' (http://news.bbc.co.uk/1/hi/scotland/7395044.stm).

7   Gaelic ceased to be the language of all of Scotland by the Middle Ages, and was driven back to its north-west heartland by political and cultural pressure from Lowland Scotland and Scots-English (see Durkacs, 1983).

8   The Highlands are memorably described by the Robbie Coltrane character as 'MAMBA country' (Miles And Miles of B***** All).

9   It was *Brigadoon* for which the American producer could find no place that looked like his 'Scotland', so he built it on a back lot in Hollywood (Hardy, 1990).

10   Ewen Bain's cartoons appeared in the *Scots Independent* and *The Daily Record*, notably starring his Highland character, Angus Og.

11   Much like Australians claiming to be descendants of convicts; there are not enough 'convicts' statistically to go round.

12 In 2013–14, Royal Bank of Scotland ran an ad campaign at Edinburgh Airport which proclaimed 'This is Home', cleverly eliding the location of its own HQ with making visitors feel 'at home'.

13 A short version appeared in the *Guardian* newspaper under the title: 'The SNP have become Scotland's Pollyannas' (www.theguardian.com/commentisfree/2014/sep/10/ scotland-yes-campaign-snp-pollyannas).

14 Cohen described them as deriving from 'misconceived theory and the concoction of simplistic generalisations' (2004: 160).

18

NATIONAL IDENTITY: WHO DO WE THINK WE ARE?

To say that Scots have a strong sense of their national identity would seem to be stating the obvious. After all, the national flag, the Saltire (Figure 18.1), is ubiquitous, not only flying on public buildings, but also used as a commercial icon to sell everything from sausages to scaffolding, as well as in people's backyards. It would seem obvious to say that it is a political symbol, highly prominent during the Scottish Independence Referendum in September 2014.

FIGURE 18.1
Flying the flag

Source: Author's photograph

This association of flags with national identity, and in turn with political parties, would seem commonplace. So powerful is the symbol of a flag that, as Emile Durkheim commented, 'we forget that the flag is only a sign, that it has no intrinsic value but serves only to recall the reality it represents; we treat it as if it were that reality' (2008 [1912]: 165).

Chapter aims

- To explore what people in Scotland mean when they say they are 'Scottish', in the context of other social identities they have.

- To examine whether flags are the dominant expressions of being Scottish, or whether other symbols are more significant.

- To analyse the relationship between being Scottish and being British, between 'national' and 'state' identities.

- To ask what people use as 'markers' of national identity, such as place of birth, ancestry, residence.

- To assess how they judge the claims of others to 'being Scottish', whose claims they accept and whose they reject in terms of being 'one of us'.

National identity as banal

The novelist Willie McIlvanney once wrote that

> having a national identity is a bit like having an old insurance policy. You know you've got one somewhere but often you're not entirely sure where it is. And if you're honest, you would have to admit you're pretty vague about what the small print means. (*Glasgow Herald*, 6 March 1999)

McIlvanney followed that up a week later with an essay in the same newspaper in which he said: 'Identity, personal and national, isn't merely something you have like a passport. It is also something you discover daily, like a strange country. Its core isn't something solid, like a mountain. It is something molten, like magma' (*Glasgow Herald*, 13 March 1999).

What McIlvanney was getting at is the implicit nature of national identity, that for most of us most of the time we do not think about it, and for most of us it is 'banal', basic and taken for granted. Only if someone questions our identity credentials, or we visit some place where national identity is disputed, such as on a frontier, do we give it much thought. McIlvanney's insurance policy metaphor nicely captures both its importance (you should not be without one) and yet its everyday insignificance (you are not sure what the small print means).

State and nation

Nor should national identity simply be equated with having a passport, an official piece of paper which validates your citizenship. In any case, you may not think of your national identity in terms of your citizenship anyway. This is especially the case where the state of which you are a citizen is a multinational one, like the United Kingdom of Great Britain and Northern Ireland, to give it its full and official title. The UK is configured as 'multinational', composed of Scotland, England, Wales and Northern Ireland, with 'national' allegiances alongside state citizenship.

This raises a number of questions. While being Scottish, English, Welsh and Northern Irish are officially nested within being British, is that actually how people 'do' their own territorial identity? Do they perhaps forefront their 'national' identity over their 'state' identity, or indeed vice versa? And if so, why?

The whole relationship between people's identification with, and loyalty to, the state vis-à-vis what they see as their 'nation' has a vexatious history. To some people, loyalty to the state, to their citizenship, is the only one which matters. Others identify with the cultural entity, the nation. Indeed, we have grown used to talking about the 'nation-state', which is the fusion of cultural and political elements, only to discover that they derive from different conceptual realms. It turns out that there are few states which are coterminous with nations, and by no means all nations are states; hence the term, 'stateless nations' (see Chapter 3).

Patriotism and nationalism

Writing in 1945, at the end of the Second World War, the author George Orwell made the distinction between 'patriotism' and 'nationalism', the former deriving from loyalty to the state and the latter from loyalty to one's fellow 'nationals' (1945a: para. 2). We can understand why Orwell felt moved to make this distinction, in the aftermath of a world war ostensibly caused by extreme 'nationalism', but the terms he uses are not helpful. Orwell defined patriotism as 'devotion to a particular place and a particular way of life', and 'nationalism' as 'inseparable from the desire for power'.

The distinction is not helpful because 'nationalists' will surely feel a devotion to place and way of life, and may well reject the assumption that they are only interested in 'power'. In other words, it is not a distinction which helps in analytical terms to distinguish different forms of loyalty, and leads too easily to the accusation that '*I* am patriotic, but *you* are nationalistic'.

In territories such as Scotland, we are used to making a distinction between 'nation' and 'state' in formal terms, without assuming that you have to choose between them; that to be Scottish is not to be British. Indeed, supporters of the British Union assert that you can be both, as in the poster issued by the 'Better Together' campaign[1] during the 2014 Scottish Independence Referendum, which proclaimed 'Proud to be Scottish, Delighted to be United'.

The implication for the unionist is that being Scottish and being British are not antithetical; one is nested within the other. For the nationalist, you might be expected to choose one or the other. Nor is this unique to these islands, for in other multinational states like Spain and Canada there is similar debate about being Spanish and/or Catalan and Basque, or being Canadian and/or Quebecois.

Furthermore, this 'political' debate has spawned much academic work about whether, and how, people relate their 'state' to their 'national' identities. It is important to stress that one is not 'better' than the other, that this is a clash between 'reason' and 'emotion', between Orwell's 'patriotism' and 'nationalism'.

After all, many people feel strongly British in emotional terms on the one hand, and 'rationally' Scottish on the other, in the sense that the Scottish level of government and administration is deemed the most appropriate for service delivery. That, after all, is the position of supporters of Scottish devolution within the Union, articulated most coherently by former Prime Minister Gordon Brown in his 2015 book with the telling title *My Scotland, Our Britain*.

Does national identity exist?

There is a view, however, that 'national identity' is unknowable, or even that it is chimerical (Malesevic, 2011). The political philosopher David Miller has said that 'the attitudes and beliefs that constitute nationality[2] [*sic*] are very often hidden away in the deeper recesses of the mind, brought to full consciousness only by some dramatic event' (1995: 18). Here are echoes of McIlvanney's 'insurance policy'; we have one, but we consult it rarely. So Miller is correct when he says that most people, most of the time, do not read the small print, and that only 'some dramatic event' makes them think about national identity.

What is more problematic, however, is Miller's claim that national identity is 'hidden away in the dark recesses of the mind', and hence unknowable. He goes on to say:

> Simple enquiry isn't going to settle the issue, not even empiricism of the kind
> that surveys people's beliefs about their place in the world. You cannot resolve
> the issue of Scottish nationhood by asking a representative sample of Scots, 'Do
> you see yourself as belonging to a distinct Scottish nation?' (Miller, 1995: 18)

The problem with Miller's question is that it conflates two separate issues: 'Do you think there is such a thing as a Scottish nation?' and 'Do you feel you belong to it?' Answering 'no' to his question could be taken as meaning 'yes, there is such a thing as a Scottish nation, and no, I don't belong to it'; as well as 'no, there is no such thing as a Scottish nation, and I cannot belong to something which does not exist'.

This debate may simply be the kind of thing which takes place between philosophers and empirical social scientists, for there is a wealth of relevant material around the subject of national identity, but there is more to it. Among the most intriguing is the work of the social psychologist Michael Billig, who wrote a book called *Banal Nationalism* (1995). Billig used 'banal' not to imply that nationalism is unimportant, but that it is basic, fundamental:

> In so many little ways, the citizenry[3] are reminded of their national place in a world of nations. However, this reminding is so familiar, so continual, that it is not consciously recognized as reminding. The metonymic[4] image of banal nationalism is not a flag which is being consciously waved with fervent passion; it is the flag hanging unnoticed on the public building. National identity embraces all these forgotten reminders. (1995: 8)

Billig was critical of the idea that 'nationalism' refers simply to exotic and passionate exemplars, such that routine and familiar forms, such as the little-noticed flag, have been overlooked. He argued that the daily or 'banal' examples whereby national identity is confirmed and reinforced in everyday life are the key. His point is that people do not passively receive a single ideological message making them conform: 'Each individual is likely to have contrary things to say, as they seek to balance the conflicting themes of common sense' (2009: 348).

What Billig meant by this is that identity, including national identity, is deeply personal. This echoes a famous dictum by the nineteenth-century French writer Ernest Renan (1990 [1882]): that national identity involves a 'daily plebiscite' (*un plébiscite de tous les jours*) such that each person asserts in action their national identity in a matter-of-fact, hence 'daily', way.

Recall Durkheim's comment about flags which we cited earlier: that it is only a sign, and has no intrinsic value but serves to recall the reality it represents even though we treat it as if it were that reality. It is, of course, one symbol among many. In Chapter 16 we pointed out that the most cited cultural icon for Scots was *not* the national flag, the Saltire, but 'landscape'. Furthermore, even those who described themselves as 'strongly Scottish' were only somewhat more likely than other people to see the Saltire as the prime symbol of Scottish culture.[5] The point Billig is making, however, is that 'the flag' is one national symbol among many.

It would seem unequivocal that Scots have a strong sense of being Scottish. This statement should prompt us to ask: compared with whom, and relative to what? And how does being British fit into that, if at all? Are we to assume that you can only have a single 'national' identity and that most people in Scotland say they are Scottish? And if you prefer to say you are 'British', are you making a political statement about the Union? Certainly, one might assume this from the way the 2014 Independence Referendum was portrayed as a binary divide (Figures 18.2 and 18.3): Scots for Independence; Brits for the Union.

Like most such divides, however, that does considerable violence to a complex reality linking 'politics' and national identity. We will discuss the issue more fully in the next chapter.

FIGURE 18.2
Scots for
Independence

Source:
Author's
photograph,
adapted from
Campaign
materials,
2014

FIGURE 18.2
Scots for
Independence

Source:
Author's
photograph,
adapted from
Campaign
materials,
2014

FIGURE 18.3
Brits for the
Union

Source:
Author's
photograph,
adapted from
Campaign
materials,
2014

Who do we say we are?

So let us explore in more detail how people in Scotland do national identity. It is true that if you force people to *choose* between saying they are Scottish and saying they are British, they will opt for the former. The 2014 Social Attitudes Survey (SSA) is the latest in a long line which confirms that. Of people born and currently living in Scotland, fully four-fifths say 'Scottish' and less than one-fifth (18 per cent) say that they are British, so on these figures there are four times more 'Scots' than 'Brits'.

We get that response, of course, because we force people to choose between being Scottish or being British. If, on the other hand, we allow people *multiple* choices, almost everyone in Scotland says they are Scottish (94 per cent), but six people in ten say they are *also* British. So for most people it is clearly *not* a case of being one thing or the other.

Scottish and/or British

This then leads us to ask: how do people relate being Scottish to being British? Since the early 1990s, the preferred measure has been the 'Moreno' question,[6] named after the researcher who introduced it to Scotland from Spain in the late 1980s (Moreno, 2006). It uses a five-point Likert scale[7] ranging from 'Scottish not British' at one end, and 'British not Scottish' at the other, with a mid-point 'Equally Scottish and British', and two further points: 'more Scottish than British' and 'more British than Scottish'.

Moreno borrowed the scale from the political scientist Juan Linz, who designed it for use in Catalonia in Spain in the mid-1970s following the death of Franco and the recovery of democracy. Linz wanted to test out how people in Catalonia balanced up their 'national' and 'state' identities, if indeed they did so at all. It seemed, then, appropriate to apply it to Scotland in the British context too.

Social researchers in Scotland have used the 'Moreno question' since the early 1990s, and have found that roughly a quarter of Scots say they are 'equally Scottish and British'. Nevertheless, Scots seem to be far more inclined than other peoples to emphasise their 'national' (Scottish) over their 'state' (British) identity, by saying they are either Scottish not British ('Only national') or more Scottish than British ('National > state') (see Table 18.1).

These figures make Scotland an outlier in terms of the relationship between 'national' and 'state' identities, but they are a snapshot taken in mid-decade to allow us to compare Scotland with other countries.

The questions were repeated in Scotland in 2014 and suggested a strengthening of the mid-point, 'equally Scottish and British', rising from about a quarter to one-third, making the point that context is important (see Table 18.2). The 2014 survey was carried out during

TABLE 18.1   National identity in comparative context

% by col.	Scotland 2006	England 2006	Wales 2007	N. Ireland 2007	Catalonia 2010	Euskadi 2005	Flanders 2004	Wallonia 2004	Quebec 2007
Only national	35	22	24	19	19	26	7	3	19
National > state	32	17	20	17	28	22	29	11	32
National = state	22	47	32	17	39	35	45	31	28
State > national	4	8	9	24	5	7	8	13	12
Only state	4	6	9	19	7	4	11	42	7
National:state*	8:1	3:1	2.5:1	1:1.2	4:1	4:1	2:1	1:4	3:1
Base	1456	2431	884	1160	2000	1495	517	310	1251

* Ratio of 'mainly national' (rows 1 + 2) to 'mainly state' (rows 4 + 5)

Source: McCrone and Bechhofer (2015: 180)

TABLE 18.2   National identity in Scotland, 2014

National identity	%
Scottish not British	27
More Scottish than British	32
Equally Scottish and British	35
More British than Scottish	3
British not Scottish	2
Other/don't know/refused	1
Base	*1036*

Source: Scottish Social Attitudes Survey, 2014

the Scottish Independence Referendum campaign when 'national identity' was a key part of the political rhetoric. In other words, there is a contextual effect to the question which we need to take into account.

This raises a further question: how *consistent* are the same people in their responses to these identity issues? The normal way of surveying people is by taking a cross-section of the population, which means that different people are surveyed at different time-points. To see whether the *same* people are consistent (or inconsistent), we need to re-survey the same people at different times (this is called a cohort or longitudinal study). This is less common because it is much more expensive to track the same people down and re-interview them.

Nevertheless, we do have such time-series data in Scottish Social Attitudes surveys done at the time of the 2014 referendum, and a year later at the time of the 2015 British general election (see Table 18.3).

The figures (the bold numbers along the diagonal) show nicely that there is a consistent response among those who say they are 'Scottish not British', 'equally Scottish and British'

TABLE 18.3   National identity in 2014 and 2015

	2015				
2014	**Sc not Br**	**More Sc than Br**	**Sc = Br**	**Br > or not Sc**	***N***
Sc not Br	**69%**	17%	8%	6%	169
More Sc than Br	29%	**35%**	30%	6%	199
Sc = Br	5%	15%	**70%**	9%	246
Br > or not Sc	5%	1%	26%	**68%**	78
All	27%	20%	39%	14%	692

Source: Scottish Social Attitudes surveys, 2014 and 2015

and 'British not Scottish, or more British than Scottish'; seven out of ten respond the same way each time, and most of those who do respond differently simply choose the adjacent category. The exceptions are the 'more Scottish than British' where only around one-third give the same answer on both occasions. Roughly equal proportions opted for 'equally Scottish and British' and for 'Scottish not British'.

Why should those who said they were 'more Scottish than British' shift their identities? The plausible answer is that such people found themselves pulled in two directions by a binary 'Yes/No' choice in the referendum. We know from other research that a large number of 'more Scottish than British' preferred as their constitution option 'devolution-max',[8] whereby a Scottish parliament would remain in the Union but have substantially greater powers. It appears that those whose constitutional preferences were not being met by the 'Yes/No' independence options were adjusting their 'national identities' accordingly.

Recalibrating national identity

The five-point 'Moreno' scale is more sophisticated than a simple 'are you Scottish or British?' question. 'Moreno', however, is not without its problems too, for it does not measure how strongly people feel about national identity. Imagine two people giving the same response (say, 'more Scottish than British') but one feeling passionately about it, and one fairly lukewarm. They give the same response; how could we differentiate such people?

One way round this is to measure the strength of being Scottish, and the strength of being British, separately, on respective seven-point scales where 1 is very weak and 7 is very strong. When we use these seven-point scales, we find that people in Scotland are strongly Scottish (almost nine out of ten place themselves at points 5, 6 or 7 on the scale, with a mean score of just over 6; no surprise there).

However, by the same measure, over half (53 per cent) are also British on the seven-point scale (with a mean score of 4.5). More to the point, almost half of all respondents place themselves on points 5, 6 or 7 on *both* scales. In other words, they are strongly Scottish but *also* strongly British; let us call them the 'dualists'. Furthermore, one-quarter of respondents are 'nationalists' such that they are strongly Scottish (5, 6 or 7) but *weakly* British (1, 2 or 3). We can see, then, that people do not simply divide into those who are strongly Scottish and weakly British, and strongly British but weakly Scottish. Plainly, it is not a matter of either/or.

So what kind of people are 'dualists' and 'nationalists'? Apart from party political support such that SNP supporters are disproportionately higher among identity 'nationalists', it is *age* that makes the most difference. Older people (those over 65) are *twice* as likely to be among the 'dualists' and *half* as likely to be 'nationalists'. Indeed, age seems to be a far more powerful factor than, for example, social class, education or sex in accounting for people's national identity choices.

Because this replicates what we found in an earlier 2011 Scottish Social Attitudes Survey, we can be fairly sure that there is a consistent 'age' effect when it comes to relating 'national' and 'state' identities (for more details, see McCrone and Bechhofer, 2015: chapter 8).

Why age should matter is an interesting question. On the one hand, it might be because, as people get older, they may be more inclined to have dual identities; what we might call an 'age effect'. More plausibly, it is likely to be the result of a 'cohort effect'. People born and brought up before and after the Second World War were socialised into thinking of themselves as 'British' far more than subsequent generations, reflecting the war experience, the introduction of the British welfare state, and so on. As they grew older, we can think of many of them *remaining* 'British', unlike their children and grandchildren for whom warfare and welfare were less significant as foundational markers of identity.

Doing national identity talk

Thus far, we have seen that 'national identity' matters to Scots; that, far from being simply an external badge, a certificate confirming our official belonging, it is highly personal, but usually implicit. As the social psychologist Margie Wetherell commented: 'identity needs to be "done" over and over. What "it" is and who "we" are escapes, is ineffable, and needs narrating, re-working, and must be continually brought "to life" again and again' (2009: 4).

Then again, we might wonder whether surveys are the best way of articulating such nuances, given that their forte is standardising responses to allow us to compare results. Can we, however, be so sure of their *validity*: that the measures are getting at the issues we are interested in? Survey responses may produce systematic data but be less good at getting at the *meanings* which lie behind such responses. What, we might ask, do people mean when they opt to say they are 'Scottish not British' or 'more British than Scottish' etc.?

In our research on national identity in Scotland and England, we used a number of methods, from survey-driven quantitative analysis to intensive interviews of a more 'naturalistic' kind. The point was to adopt 'triangulation',[9] looking at a phenomenon like national identity from different points of view, the better to judge how it operated.

Let us start with a simple exercise. If someone is asked to explain their 'Moreno' choice, how do they respond? Here are two examples:

> I would say that I'm a wee bit more Scottish than British but I still feel British.
> ... Because I am Scottish first and foremost, you know.

And another person:

> No. 1 (*Scottish not British*) is out, 'cos I do think myself as British. ... No. 3 (*Equally Scottish and British*) is out. I was looking at that one but I said I was Scottish first, and I stand by that. I live here, if I'd lived in England all my life I would probably have said '*More English than British*'. But if I chose '*Equally Scottish and British*' it would mean I would accept a British football team which I wouldn't, I want a Scottish one.

The first person relies simply on repeating the question, asserting that while they think of themselves as Scottish 'first and foremost', they still 'feel British'. The second person uses a process of elimination: not this, nor that, along with an allusion to sport. In fact, both say they are 'more Scottish than British', but we get a better insight into what lies behind that choice from the second respondent, rather than the first, who does not tell us much about the 'small print' of their national identity.

A third respondent, referring to the letter we sent requesting an interview, bristles at being asked to justify who they think they are:

> But why should I need an envelope through the door to address whether I'm Scottish or not? But then again, it's like breathing, you do it. You don't think about it. It's what you do every day and then somebody says to you 'why are you breathing?' then you've got to stop and think about it. So for me to feel Scottish and then [for] somebody just to come along and say 'why are you Scottish?' I maybe felt like, it's a superficial thought that I've had before. But even the fact that I've been given a week to think about it, I still think that I'm Scottish because I was born here.

It is that taken-for-granted quality of national identity which is most striking ('it's like breathing, you do it'). Here is another Scot talking about national identity:

> It's a sense of identity, isn't it, really? I think that's what things come down to. It's whatever makes you feel comfortable and whatever puts you at ease. If you've got the choice between a scabby, rusty bike and a nice red, shiny bike, you'll choose the red, shiny bike over the other because you can feel proud of it. You can get on it and be the envy of all your friends. Not even the envy, you'll just be the same as all your friends. You have something in which, you have something that reflects, that you're part of, that you're proud to be part of – the country. I'm so proud of my countrymen, not only those who are living but those that have gone before and the contribution that's been made over the centuries. I'm just so proud to be part of that, albeit that I had no input in it whatsoever. I'm proud, by association.

Does *everyone* make this identification? To compare, we are able to draw upon interviews and observations from colleagues in England with whom we worked on the National Identity programme. Susan Condor and Jackie Abell made the important point that 'nationality serves as a vehicle through which to express immediate, authentic, personal experience' (2006: 57). Having carried out interviews in England which formed part of our project, they contrasted how people in Scotland and England talked about national identity. Referring to 'Jenny', the person above who drew the analogy between national identity and 'the red, shiny bike', they commented:

Whereas Jenny, like many respondents in Scotland, presented an image of her sense of self as effectively saturated by, and entirely consonant with, her Scottish national identity, respondents in England almost always represented national identity as something worn lightly, and only partially inhabited. (Condor and Abell, 2006: 69)

Using the distinction adopted by the social anthropologist Clifford Geertz, we might say, then, that Scots tended to adopt a *'thick'* description of their national identity, that is one elaborated and contextualised, whereas people in England tended to adopt a *'thin'* – factual – description.[10] It is not that the English do not care about national identity, nor that they confuse 'England' and 'Britain'.

This 'identity talk' of people in England suggests that they are aware that they are entering difficult territory, and that they have to tread carefully. Condor and her colleagues rejected the commonplace view that the English are simply apathetic, constituting 'a moral or motivational failure, often seen to be the product of arrogance, complacency or lethargy' (Condor, 2010: 527).

Any suggestion that 'national identity' does not matter to the English, at least those who see themselves as 'nationals', seems to be wide of the mark. Both English and Scottish 'nationals' (those born and currently living in either country) choose to prioritise their national over their state identities mainly for cultural and institutional reasons, and not because they are making a 'political' statement about the break-up of the UK. To be sure, most people think that where you are *born* is a key marker of national identity, but that is a matter of fact rather than an affective choice, for plainly it is not within anyone's gift to determine their birthplace.

Contextualising national identity

We saw earlier that feeling 'national' depends on contexts; most of the time it is implicit or 'banal', while at others, it is heightened and more salient. Kobena Mercer has made the point that 'identity only becomes an issue when it is in crisis, when something assumed to be fixed, coherent and stable is displaced by the experience of doubt and uncertainty' (1990: 43). These crises need not be simply 'political' such as might arise during a referendum on independence.

Indeed, it is not simply 'politics' which raises people's awareness of national identity. Scots as well as the English feel more 'national' on sporting occasions, or when encountering landscape or countryside, or experiencing 'national' art or music, or when visiting the 'other' country. All of these contexts make national identity more salient for people. Less important was 'politics', including constitutional devolution, and, if anything, 'politics' seemed to be more important to the English than the Scots in making people feel 'national' (McCrone and Bechhofer, 2015: chapter 3).

It seems that 'culture' matters more than 'politics' in defining national identity, and even somewhat more for the Scots than the English. Given all the constitutional change which has happened since the 1990s, this might seem to be a counter-intuitive finding running against conventional wisdom, but that is what the surveys tell us. There is more to national identity than 'politics'.

Personalising national identity

In any event, national identity is deeply 'personal'. The Norwegian social anthropologist Thomas Eriksen considered that 'nation' is the metaphysical space in which people locate their personal histories, and thus their identities (see Cohen, 2000: 152), so that *personal* identity becomes synonymous with national identity.

People are not told what their national identity ought to be; they actively construct who they are from the materials available to them. This is why national identity is not rigidly fixed but varies systematically according to context and markers such as ancestry, residence and even 'commitment' ('I wasn't born here, but choose to live here') which people can deploy when they migrate to another country.

National identity matters because it is insinuated into people's own sense of themselves. Arguably, when someone says they are Scottish, or American, or whatever, they are making a statement about their own personal identity. Recall our discussion in Chapter 11 when we looked at gender. All forms of social identity involve 'becoming' that person, insinuating the label into 'who we are', and as regards national identity, to the point that 'the person conceives of self as also the nation' (Kapferer, 1988: 161).[11] Condor and Abell used the metaphor of 'lamination' which wraps around personal and collective identity, the one reflecting the other (2006: 58). Cohen has observed that the concept of the nation is something standing outside ourselves but is:

> [s]omething which simply does not require to be well defined, first, because people presume that they know what they are talking about when they refer to it; and second, because the lack of definition allows them scope for interpretive manoeuvre in formulating or inventing or imagining the nation in terms of their selves for the purposes of personal identity. (2000: 166)

Furthermore, people do not simply make identity up for themselves as they go along. The sociologist Stuart Hall commented, for example, that 'we only know what it is to be "English" because of the way "Englishness" has come to be represented, as a set of meanings by English national culture' (1992: 292). Similarly, with being Scottish. We 'learn' to be Scottish, English or whatever in terms of how those identities are portrayed in the media, cultural institutions including education, film, tourism, and so on.

A good starting point for understanding national identity in Scotland and elsewhere is to remember that it takes institutional forms. We are educated, formally and informally, in a 'Scottish' way; we are judged in courts of law in a 'Scottish' manner; and until Scotland became more of a secular society, our relationship to the deity invoked a Scottish way of doing that too. People *become* nationals simply by going about their daily lives, but that process is shaped by what is expected of us.[12] In that sense 'nationalism', as Billig pointed out, is everyday and banal.

There are, then, institutional carriers of 'being Scottish', ways of thinking, of worshipping, of judging, through which we learn 'Scottish' ways. Why such a high proportion of people living in Scotland say they are Scottish has much to do with those cultural carriers of national identity. The creation of the Scottish parliament in 1999 became another such carrier, albeit an important one because it was elected to govern, and to interpret the will of the people in so doing.

The parliament is the result of rising levels of Scottishness in the last few decades and in turn it also 'naturalises' what it means to be Scottish. We might say that it is both cause and effect. There is not a uniform way of doing so, for there are different, even competing, ways of being Scottish. The point is neither that 'the nation' imposes its own identity on 'nationals', nor that they in turn have carte blanche to dream up national identity as they so wish. Richard Jenkins makes the point nicely:

> A group of people without Norwegian passports, with no discoverable historical connections to Norway, and speaking no Norwegian, cannot simply arrive at the Norwegian border and have any expectation of mounting a plausible claim to Norwegian identity or nationality. (2008: 127–8)

Rather, national identity involves a complex and interactive process between institutional conferment and personal involvement. It is a negotiated process.

National and other identities

In Chapter 11, when we discussed gender in Scotland, we saw that women and men ranked 'being Scottish' among their most important social identities. Almost half (45 per cent) of Scots put 'being Scottish' among their top three identities, just below parental status (49 per cent). This contrasted with people in England where only 20 per cent selected 'being English', with one-third of people in Wales 'being Welsh'. So here is confirmation that Scottish national identity is highly salient north of the border relative to other British nations,[13] even though Scots, English and Welsh ranked *other* social identities in a similar way.

In order to be sure of the salience of national identity for Scots, we repeated the exercise in later surveys, each time making it a tougher test. We found that it did not make much difference, for being Scottish was a strongly chosen identity regardless of how we asked the question, whether we included it in the long list of identities, or asked it as an after-thought. True enough, women ranked their gender more highly than men (by 35 to 22 per cent), but both put being Scottish higher still (40 and 41 per cent, respectively). Similarly, working-class people were more likely to choose their class identity than middle-class people (32 to 15 per cent), but, again, both classes rated national identity higher (47 and 40 per cent, respectively). It is true that men in Scotland are somewhat more likely than women to rate their national identity highly, but both sexes see it as an important part of who they are.

There is also a clear age gradient in both Scotland and England, in that young people are more likely than older people to emphasise national identity. Whereas in England, 48 per cent of young men choose national identity, but only 28 per cent of older men, in Scotland the comparable figures were 68 and 40 per cent, respectively. This shows nicely that age makes a difference, but that people in Scotland, whether young or old, rate national identity more highly than south of the border. While there are differences within social categories, it is striking how much higher national identification is in Scotland than it is in England. National identity *does* matter in England, but it matters much more north of the border.

Here is further confirmation that Scots find national identity highly salient. Not only do we find this in systematic survey work, but they seem willing to talk about national identity and to explain it in interviews in a more relaxed and naturalistic setting (see McCrone and Bechhofer, 2015). Relative to other British nations, being Scottish appears to matter disproportionately more to the Scots than it does to the English and the Welsh.

Markers of Scottish national identity

Let us explore in more detail what it is that defines Scottish national identity. What are the social and cultural markers, such as birthplace, ancestry, residence and 'race', which people think are important? And do people use such markers in making judgements about whether or not they consider others to be 'one of us'? We saw, for example, in Chapter 13 that 'race' and ethnicity make a difference as to whether you are accepted as Scottish or not. Can we identify the 'identity rules' which operate behind these markers in such a way that some are deemed more important than others?

By *identity rules* we mean probabilistic rules of thumb whereby, under certain conditions and in particular contexts, identity markers are interpreted, combined or given precedence over others. By 'rules' we do not mean 'laws', which are rules backed up by legal sanctions, but 'rules' as guidelines for social behaviour usually glimpsed only in the transgression. A good example would be social rules about queuing. They are not written down anywhere; we learn by watching and doing, and if we get it wrong, we are usually told one way or another.

So what do you need to be thought of as a Scot? Is it necessary to be born in Scotland, to have Scottish parents, to live in Scotland, to speak with a Scottish accent, and even to be white? Furthermore, if national identity matters so much to Scots, are they much stricter about who counts as a Scot, compared, for example, with the English in England? Put another way, if being a member of the Scottish 'club' really matters to you, do you operate tougher rules about who you would accept as a member?

Scottish 'nationals' tend to conceive of their own Scottish identity, and national identities more generally, as matters of *birth*, and to a much lesser extent, of *belonging*. Migrants find themselves having to make more tentative claims, as in this case:

I: You wouldn't feel able to say 'I'm Scottish'?

R1:   Well, I'm not, because I was born in England. I feel Scottish but I can't introduce myself as Scottish because of the importance of where you're born ... I would feel that if I'm talking to someone that I don't know, they'll say 'Well you haven't got a Scottish accent so you can't be.' It's as if you're claiming something for yourself to make yourself socially acceptable. So I wouldn't tend to do that.

In nice juxtaposition to this comment, here is a Scottish 'national' talking about incomers:

R2:   They can't *become* Scottish; they can be integrated into a Scottish community. I think that's fine but as far as becoming Scottish. To go back to what I said before, not that generation but then the next generation. So if their kids are born in Scotland, if they choose to become, I think that's fine.

Can we go beyond the individual case to work out more systematically what the rules of national identity are? For example, can we find the 'tipping point' at which someone flips over from rejection to acceptance on the basis of someone's credentials? Is it the case, for example, that someone born in England can *never* be treated as 'Scottish', as the second respondent implies?

One of us?

'Real life', of course, may not operate like this, for much will depend on how people behave in particular circumstances or relationships. This is nicely conveyed in the title of an article in an academic journal: 'We hate the English, but not you, because you're our pal' (McIntosh et al., 2004a). There is something deeply personal about the judgements people make about each other, but our interest is in the broad patterns of acceptance or rejection. Nevertheless, as we shall see, the findings are so meaningfully structured that it is highly likely that they reflect actual behaviour and experiences.

Our early findings indicated that someone born in the 'wrong' country, be it England or Scotland, would have their claims to national identity rejected by as many as two-thirds of respondents. In other words, much as articulated by the respondent above, birth outweighs residence, even though none of us have any say in where we were born; as the saying goes, it is an accident of birth.

As we saw in Chapter 13 when we looked at 'race' and ethnicity, a non-white person living in England or Scotland with the requisite 'national' accent and claiming an appropriate identity will, in the absence of other markers, have their claim rejected by around one-third of our respondents (see McCrone and Bechhofer, 2015: chapter 5). Although 'race' (as indicated by skin colour: putatively 'non-white') makes a difference, all things being equal, we found that having a Scottish accent makes a significant contribution to having one's claim to be a Scot accepted, regardless of 'race'.

In other words, a non-white person with a Scottish accent has a better chance of being accepted as Scottish than a white person with an English accent. When we hear a Scottish accent, we read that as indicating that the person has lived in Scotland at least from an early age. All things being equal, non-white people are marginally less likely to be accepted as Scottish than white people with the same characteristics. However, we found that a higher proportion of non-white people in England were *more* likely to be rejected as 'English' than similar people in Scotland. Thus, 17 per cent of English 'natives' would reject a non-white person as 'English' even if they were born and living in England. In Scotland the differential is 12 per cent.

On the whole, people in Scotland and England do not differ greatly in their willingness to accept claims made by someone resident in England or Scotland but born in the 'other' country. People who are older and have fewer educational qualifications are more likely to reject claims. However, someone who thinks of themselves as 'strongly Scottish' is *not* more likely to reject someone else's claim to be Scottish, whereas for the English equivalents, they are.[14]

Important 'political' differences have emerged in the last decade in Scotland and England such that the 'politics of immigration' appears to have a much stronger effect in England than in Scotland in shaping the political agenda, despite the fact that in formal terms immigration is a matter reserved to Westminster. Furthermore, the fact that non-white people in England are far more inclined to say they are 'British' than 'English', while 'hybrid' identities – saying you are a 'Scottish Muslim' – are more common north of the border, might reflect such politics, and in turn reinforce it.

Let us stress the point that we are dealing here with people's attitudes, not how they behave in practice. We do not know the extent to which people will put into practice prior attitudes, or indeed whether they are offset by considerations that, at the end of the day, 'you're our pal', and hence 'one of us'. Take the case of 'English John' as he was referred to by his mates, simply 'one of the boys' when off the football pitch. Originally from Bradford and of Asian origin, 'John' reported that he became 'Scottish John' when he went back to Bradford, because of his accent and 'because he does things Scottish'. It is this complex grammar and syntax of 'national identity' which matters most, rather than rigid markers of who we are.

Here is another example. Shortly before the referendum on Scottish independence, the writer James Meek wrote the following, which makes our point well:

> Were Scotland to vote for independence in September, I'm certain I'd qualify for citizenship of whatever the rump Britain was called. I was born in London, I live there and my mother was born in Essex. Despite my father's Indian birth and early childhood, I'd be pushing my luck to ask for Indian citizenship. My mother's mother was Hungarian, and under that country's sweeping new citizenship law, that would be enough to get me a passport, providing I learned to speak Hungarian.

As for Scotland, it, too, plans generosity for the prodigals. I'd probably qualify for Scottish citizenship on three grounds: my father's mother, Ena, was born there, of impeccable Scottish parentage; I lived there for more than ten years continuously from 1967 to 1984; I have a 'close and continuing relationship' with Scotland. My parents live there. My elder sister lives there. Some of my closest friends are there. The publisher of my novels is there. My bank account is there. I like it there. I have been fostered as a writer there in a way a Yorkshire, Cornish or Mancunian writer would not have been. Scotland has been kind to me. I'd have to apply, though. And perhaps I shall live there again, one day. (2014: 6)

Here we see the richness of the identities available to the author. Rather than a confusion and contradiction, it provides Meek with a full hand of 'identity cards' with which to play his identity game. He can take on different identities according to the circumstances, thus reinforcing the point that national identity (or any other social identity, for that matter) is neither a thing nor an essence, but *a frame of reference*, which social actors manoeuvre around with some skill.

Othering

This brings us to the missing ingredient of identity. It is not simply who you think you are, but who you think you are *not*. All forms of social identity involve *othering*, the issue of the vis-à-vis which provides the alternative. Thus, as Steve Reicher and Nick Hopkins point out: 'For Scottish identity, as indeed for any social identity, who we are depends upon who we compare ourselves to' (Bechhofer and McCroner, 2009: 30). And it is not simply an issue for national identity. It is a feature, too, of gender identities such that being a woman is not being a man, or being middle class is not being working class.

You might well reply that 'woman-ness' and 'middle class-ness' have an essence, and are not simply to be defined in terms of 'the other'. Maybe so, but all social categories have this quality of *othering*, and most of the time it is taken for granted. And in any case, it is rarely reciprocal. We saw previously that women in Scotland are more inclined than men to select gender as one of the most important social identities.

Similarly, working-class people are more likely to choose their social class than middle-class people by a ratio of 2:1. We might draw the conclusion that the less 'advantaged' social group, the greater the internal sense of sharing identities, something found also in studies of ethnicity (Banton, 1997). This vis-à-vis does not imply 'contra' and hostility – but simply *not being* the other for purposes of definition.

How does this apply to national identity? How do people talk about 'notional others'? Here are some examples of how people talked to us:

I: What gives you that sense of being Scottish?

R: I don't know. I think we are … I think we're different. I think the Irish, the Scots, the Welsh and the English, we are different. I think the Scottish people are quite down-to-earth. I think … then again, I don't know whether we're that much different … I don't know, really.

I: But you feel there is some sense of difference between – you mentioned, Welsh, Scots, English and Irish?

R: I can't really put it into words, I think, I'll end up being quite rude, I think the Scottish people are a bit different, or they're different from us, we're different from them. I think there is quite a north–south divide. I think the division of the people is probably ... I think northern English people and Scottish people are quite similar.

Note the caution and hesitancy about the claim to be different, a desire not to give offence ('I'll end up being quite rude'), as well as reference to imputed similarities ('I think northern English people and Scottish people are quite similar').

Justification for a strong claim to being Scottish sometimes comes in being 'taken for' English:

R2: There's certain things that are Scottish. I don't know if it's something to do with the blood system, I don't know, but it niggles a bit when you go abroad and they'll say 'Oh you're English' and you automatically say 'I'm not English, I'm Scottish'. You can just feel your hackles getting up, 'How dare you call me English, I've got a right broad Scots accent.' Then you'd get into, not an argument, it's like a wee heated discussion. The last time we were abroad, they said 'You're British then?' I'd go 'No, we're Scottish.' 'What does your passport say?' I got so fed up I said 'It says Scotland.'

Both of these examples convey the sense of 'other', which does not involve hostility so much as exasperation. Both make it clear that 'the English' constitute 'the other'. Might it not be the case, however, that the commonalities of social class outweigh those of national identity, that working-class Scots feel they have more in common with working-class English people than they have with 'other class' Scots? That certainly is a 'political' claim made during the Scottish independence campaign by the 'No' side. Surely working-class Glaswegians have much more in common with working-class Mancunians and Liverpudlians?

At the time of the first devolution referendum campaign in 1979, when a similar point was being made, surveys asked: 'Whom do you identify with most: an English person of the same class, or a Scottish person of a different class?' In 1979, more Scots put class identity before national identity (by 44 per cent to 38 per cent; see McCrone, 2001: 167). However, when the question was repeated in the 1990s, a considerable majority of Scots opted for 'different class, same nation', and by the mid-2000s (see Table 18.4).

By the middle of the twenty-first century, Scots were clearly identifying with 'nation' over 'class' by more than 2:1, but even a majority of the English now do so, albeit by a smaller ratio (1.3:1). Only the Welsh, marginally, give precedence to class over nation. The fact that only since the 1990s have Scots given precedence to nation over class reflects the extent to which 'national identity' has strengthened recently north of the border.

And what about international comparisons? In 2008–9, we asked: 'Which of these groups do you, as a Scottish/English person, feel you have **most** in common with?'[15] The results are given in Table 18.5.

TABLE 18.4 'Who do you feel you have most in common with?'

% by column	Scots 2006	English 2006	Welsh 2007
Same class, different nation	22	26	34
Same nation, different class	47	35	29
No preferences	17	25	22
Depends on individual	5	5	5
Don't know/no answer	9	9	10
Base	1302	2314	884

Sources: British Social Attitudes Survey, 2006; Scottish Social Attitudes Survey, 2006; Welsh Life and Times Survey, 2007

TABLE 18.5 'National groups with whom you have most in common'

% by column	Scots	English	Scots-English
American people	3	15	−12
Welsh people	8	19	−11
French people	3	2	+1
English/Scottish people*	28	30	−2
Irish people	51	16	+35
None of these	8	16	−8
Base	1156	2080	

* Scots were asked about the English, and the English were asked about the Scots

Sources: Scottish Social Attitudes Surveys, 2008 and 2009

We also asked: 'And which do you have **least** in common with?' The results are shown in Table 18.6.

What conclusions do we draw from these data? On the one hand, as far as Scottish–English relations are concerned, we do find mutuality (28 per cent of Scots and 30 per cent of the English feel they have most common with each other). There is little evidence for mutual hostility; only 1 in 10 Scots say they have least in common with the English, and as few as 1 in 100 English people reciprocate. On the other hand, over half of the Scots say they have most in common with the Irish compared with only one-sixth of the English, whereas the Welsh do not figure much at all for either the Scots or the English.

Does any of this matter? Does people's own sense of nationality make a difference to who they perceive they have most in common with? It seems to matter quite a lot, as we see in Table 18.7.

TABLE 18.6 'National groups with whom you have least in common'

% by column	Scots	English	Scots-English
American people	27	27	0
Welsh people	7	5	+2
French people	50	56	–6
English/Scottish people	10	1	+9
Irish people	5	5	0
None of these	4	6	–2
Base	1149	2110	

Sources: Scottish Social Attitudes Surveys, 2008 and 2009

TABLE 18.7 'Who do you have most in common with, by national identity of respondent?'

% within each national identity category	Most in common with the English	Most in common with the Irish	Base
Scottish not British	18	61	379
Scottish more than British	24	56	414
Equally Scottish and British	40	38	328
British more than Scottish	69	26	35
All	28	51	1156

Source: Scottish Social Attitudes Survey, 2009

The answers are clear cut. The more *Scottish* you feel, the more likely you are to think you have most in common with the Irish (61 per cent). The more *British* you feel, the more likely you are to have most in common with the English (69 per cent). We might read this as a 'political' statement: that who you feel you have most in common with is a proxy for your constitutional politics. It turns out not to be so, for we do not find a strong relationship between feeling you have most in common with the Irish and support for Scottish independence. Similarly, what drives the 'British' Scots to feel they have most in common with English people is not simply support for the Union (McCrone and Bechhofer, 2015: chapter 7).[16]

Conclusion

In this chapter we have seen that Scots do have a strong sense of their national identity; that, relative to their other social identities, being Scottish is one which most people, regardless of gender, age and social class, feel strongly attached to. That, however, is the beginning of the story, not its end, for as Billig commented, 'nationalism' is not some exotic and emotive manifestation so much as it is routine and banal. McIlvanney's point about national identity being something you discover daily, yet 'like a strange country', might seem a contradiction, but it conveys its immediacy and yet its implicit character.

It is, in truth, hard to sustain an argument that national identity is unreal or chimerical, because it figures so much in people's accounts of themselves and others. Nor is it something oddly Scottish, as if few others share our obsessions. Indeed, being Scottish does not require being anti-English, or indeed anti-British, and in that regard it is not a 'political' statement, although it can lend itself to politics as and when required. Nor is it about 'putting out more flags'[17] as if such things incite outrageous behaviour, even violence.

The key point about 'differences', cultural or social, is that they are not inherent, nor necessarily conflictual, but do provide raw materials which might become activated should conditions occur. We need to bear in mind that 'cultural traits are not absolutes or simply intellectual categories, but are invoked to provide identities which legitimise claims to rights. They are strategies or weapons in competition over scarce goods' (Worsley, 1984: 249). The point made by social anthropologists like Michael Banton (1983; 1997) and Thomas Eriksen (1993) is that it is not necessarily 'objective' and long-standing differences, but those which seem salient to actors at a particular time and in a particular context that are the key to the way markers are mobilised.

Furthermore, it is not so much who you *are* as what you *do*. As the writer Philip Pullman points out, 'what we do is morally significant. What we are is not' (2005). Thus, you should not be prosecuted for who you are; rather, for what you do. This does not, however, prevent claims being made that this or that national group, or ethnicity, are a threat to 'our way of life', a point forcefully made by Eriksen in analysing the conflict in the Balkans in the 1990s:

> Ethnic boundaries, dormant for decades, were activated; presumed cultural differences which had been irrelevant for two generations were suddenly 'remembered' and invoked as proof that it was impossible for the two groups [Bosnians and Serbs] to live side by side. (1993: 39)

The relevance of that statement is not to imply that for 'Bosnians' and 'Serbs' read 'Scots' and 'English', simply that activating ethnic or national 'differences' has the potential to be politicised, that they can be 'collectively orchestrated', routinised shorthands which can focus perceptions and ultimately action. It is that important dimension, the relationship between national identity and 'politics', that we now turn to in the next chapter.

Chapter summary

So what have we learned in this chapter?

- That national identity in Scotland is ubiquitous, but usually implicit and taken for granted.

- That people in Scotland give priority to their 'national' (Scottish) identity over their 'state' (British) identity without denying or undervaluing the latter.

- That, while 'politics' is an important context for expressing Scottish national identity, it is not the only one, and is usually of low salience. If anything, 'culture' matters more than 'politics'.

- That judging claims to national identity puts a small premium on matters of 'race' and ethnicity, but issues of birthplace and accent matter more in getting one's claim to being Scottish accepted.

- That national identity involves 'othering', defining oneself vis-à-vis others. Scots judge the Irish to be people most like them, but there is little 'othering' of the English.

Questions for discussion

1. Why do people in Scotland have a strong sense of being Scottish? Is that sense at odds with being British?

2. Is feeling strongly Scottish simply a matter of one's political and constitutional preferences?

3. What are your chances of being accepted as Scottish if you were not born in Scotland?

4. Who do Scots feel they have most and least in common with, and why?

5. Does national identity really matter all that much in terms of accounting for how people behave?

Annotated reading

(a) On national identity: D. McCrone and F. Bechhofer, *Understanding National Identity* (2015); F. Bechhofer and D. McCrone (eds), *National Identity, Nationalism and Constitutional Change* (2009); S. Condor and J. Abell, 'Vernacular constructions of "national identity" in post-devolution Scotland and England', in J. Wilson and K. Stapleton (eds), *Devolution and Identity* (2006).

(b) On social identity: R. Jenkins, *Social Identity*, 3rd edition (2015); T.H. Eriksen, *Ethnicity and Nationalism* (1993); A. Cohen, *Self Consciousness: An alternative anthropology of identity* (1994).

Notes

1   The wording on the poster is a little odd. On the face of it, being 'delighted' sounds more important than being 'proud', and might be read as forefronting being British over being Scottish.

2   'Nationality' is too imprecise a term to be useful here, because it is often simply a synonym for 'citizenship' (think of hotel registers), and cannot be equated with 'national identity' unless one thinks 'state' and 'nation' are the same things.

3   Billig here is using 'citizenry' generically to refer to all people, not simply those who consider themselves 'citizens' of the state.

4   'Metonymy' is a figure of speech where a symbol comes to stand for something else; thus, 'the turf' for horse racing, a 'dish' for a meal, a 'suit' for a man in authority, and so on.

5   Thirty-one per cent of 'strongly Scottish' people thought the flag the main Scottish symbol, compared with 29 per cent of everyone in the sample.

6   I take some responsibility for this. I was one of Luis Moreno's doctoral examiners in 1986 and was editor of *Scottish Government Yearbook*. As a shorthand, I began to refer to the five-point scale as the 'Moreno question', which properly should have been called the 'Linz question' in deference to its original author.

7   A typical five-point Likert scale would take the following format: strongly agree; agree; neither agree nor disagree; disagree; strongly disagree.

8   Scottish Social Attitudes surveys showed that around 30 per cent of people in Scotland had preferred 'devolution-max' as their constitutional preference (http://whatscotlandthinks. org/questions/moreno-national-identity-5#line).

9   Triangulation is a metaphor borrowed from surveying which helps to confirm an object if we look at it from different points of view. In social science, it refers to getting similar results if we adopt different research methods (Bechhofer and Paterson, 2000: 57).

10   The distinction between 'thick' and 'thin' description is usually attributed to the social anthropologist Clifford Geertz (1973). Geertz used examples from the work of philosopher Gilbert Ryle. 'Thick' description refers to contextualised accounts whereby context and circumstances are elaborated. 'Thin' description refers to simple 'factual' accounts.

11   See, for example, Anthony Cohen's book *Self Consciousness* (1994: 156–67).

12   The US daily Pledge of Allegiance is an explicit way of 'making Americans' out of immigrants.

13   'British' was also included in the national lists. Only 11 per cent of Scots, but 27 per cent of the English, and 23 per cent of the Welsh mentioned it as one of their top three identities (McCrone and Bechhofer, 2015: chapter 3, table 3.1).

14   That is, someone who thinks of themselves as 'strongly English' is more likely to reject someone's claim to be English.

15   We asked these questions in Scotland and England of everyone in the sample apart from those who said they were 'British not Scottish/English'. We included 'Americans' as people who shared the common language, and 'French' who did not, but were near-neighbours.

16   As far as the English are concerned, you are more likely to say you have most in common with Scots if you are older and if you think of yourself as 'British'. There is a similar propensity among English people as regards the Welsh – the more British you are, and the more educated you are, the more likely you are to think you have most in common with the Welsh.

17   *Put Out More Flags* was the title of a novel by Evelyn Waugh, published in 1942, and set during the Great War.

19

POLITICS AND NATIONAL IDENTITY

Truisms are often recognised when they no longer apply. British politics has conventionally been seen as the purest expression of 'class politics', because the UK has historically had little of the electoral complexity of other European countries. There is no tradition, at least on the British mainland, of 'confessional politics' where people vote according to their religious affiliation. Neither is there a tradition of 'sectoral politics' in which your vote is based on being a farmer or a city dweller. To be sure, Ireland, north and south, is different, but politics on the 'mainland', in Scotland, England and Wales, at least since the early twentieth century, seemed historically determined by the politics of social class.

That, until the final quarter of the twentieth century, was the conventional wisdom. And then, in the mid-1970s, these assumptions were blown apart. Scotland, seemingly that so 'British' of political nations, which had epitomised 'class' politics for much of its industrial history, appeared to embark on a new politics, a politics of national identity.

In this chapter, we will explore how and why this new politics emerged, and examine more closely the assumptions that national identity is the key dimension of this politics.

Chapter aims

- To set out the transformation of Scottish politics, and in particular the rise of the Scottish National Party.

- To examine the assumption that there has been an identity shift among Scots from British to Scottish.

- To explore how people talk about national identity in political–constitutional terms.

- To argue that, despite appearances, being British still matters to people and, furthermore, that there is complicated relationship between identity and politics.

- To analyse political events in the twenty-first century, notably elections to the Scottish parliament, the British general elections and the Scottish Independence Referendum in 2014.

The divergence of Scottish and British politics

Focusing on recent political events in the twenty-first century, we could be forgiven for assuming that Scottish politics had always been at odds with politics south of the border.

In each of the constituent parts of the kingdom, different political parties dominate: in Scotland, the SNP has 95 per cent of the seats; in England, the Conservatives have 62 per cent; in Wales, Labour also has 62 per cent; and in Northern Ireland, the Unionist parties have 62 per cent. There have been few, if any, occasions in British electoral history when the national territories appear to be so different.

The obvious point to make is that these electoral outcomes show the exaggerated impact of the electoral system, of first past the post, of winner takes all. The respective share of the vote in each nation, balanced against share of seats, shows the lack of correspondence between votes and seats (see Table 19.1).

TABLE 19.1 Share of vote and share of seats for largest party at 2015 British general election by national territory

	Largest party	Share of vote	Share of seats
Scotland	SNP	50%	95%
England	Conservative	41%	62%
Wales	Labour	37%	62%
Northern Ireland	Unionists (DUP + UUP)	42%	62%

Source: www.bbc.co.uk/news/election/2015/results

In Scotland, the SNP got virtually twice the share of seats compared with its share of the vote, based on half of the popular vote, something only ever achieved by the Conservatives and their allies in 1955. The electoral system is supported by the Unionist political parties at Westminster on the grounds that it delivers 'firm government' without requiring coalitions or minority administrations subject to deals and negotiations. Indubitably, then, the 'dis-United Kingdom' is in large part a reflection of the dominant electoral system, which has its own dynamic.

1945–55

What is remarkable is how recent this territorial 'disunity' actually is, especially in Scotland. In the decade after the Second World War, Scotland and England differed very little from each other in terms of the share of the vote for the two main political parties, Labour and Conservative.

TABLE 19.2 Labour and Conservative support in Scotland, 1945–55

Election	Labour advantage in Scotland	Conservative shortfall in Scotland	Combined gap
1945	−0.9	−0.9	−1.8
1950	0.0	−1.0	−1.0
1951	−0.9	0.2	−0.7
1955	−0.1	0.3	0.2

Source: F.W.S. Craig, *British Electoral Facts*, 1981

Indeed, between 1945 and 1955, Labour does marginally *less* well in Scotland than in England, and the Tories somewhat better. We can summarise this as in Table 19.2.

In 1945, Labour had a marginally *lower* share of the vote in Scotland than it got in England (47.6 per cent to 48.5 per cent, a difference of less than 1 percentage point), while the Tories got 41.1 per cent in Scotland and 40.2 per cent in England (once more, and quite coincidentally, a difference of less than 1 percentage point).

We have created a 'combined gap' by adding the percentage point differences together to give a measure of Scottish–English differences. As we can see, these differences in the four elections after the war are negligible, and average out at less than 1 percentage point, indicating that Scottish–English electoral differences hardly existed in the post-war decade.

1955–70

If we do the same calculations for the four elections between 1959 and 1970, we see electoral divergence in terms of vote share for the two dominant parties (see Table 19.3).

There is an important feature to notice: in the 1966 and 1970 elections, the Conservatives do proportionately much worse in Scotland than in England, especially in 1970 when the gap was around 10 percentage points. Indeed, in subsequent years, it is the Conservative shortfall in Scotland which accounts for most of the 'combined gap'.

TABLE 19.3 The beginnings of electoral divergence, 1959–70

Election	Labour advantage in Scotland	Conservative shortfall in Scotland	Combined gap
1959	3.1	2.7	5.8
1964	5.2	3.5	8.7
1966	1.9	5.0	6.9
1970	1.1	10.3	11.4

Source: F.W.S. Craig, British Electoral Facts, 1981

1970–2015

Since 1970, with one exception (February 1974), the combined gap has been in double figures (Table 19.4), and by 2010 it was the largest it has ever been (37 percentage points). Note, too, that the gap does not depend on which party is in power at Westminster. The electoral successes of the Labour Party between 1997 and 2005 did not make an appreciable difference to the gap. Above all, it is the differential Conservative vote in Scotland and England which accounts for most of the gap.

Looking at the period 1945 to 2015 as a whole, we can see just how much Scotland and England have diverged in electoral politics. With the (narrow) exception of 1970, the combined gap in the first twenty-five years is less than 10 per cent. In the second half of the period, it is consistently in double figures, culminating in the 2010 election difference of 37.3 percentage points, and to all intents and purposes continuing on to 2015 when the 'political' divergence rather than the electoral arithmetic became most salient.

The propensity for the Scots and the English to vote differentially for the two main UK parties after 1970 also coincides with the rise of smaller parties, notably the Liberals and the SNP, albeit at different rates of progress. It would, in theory, have been possible for the Scots and the English to continue to vote in similar proportions for Labour and the Tories, as well as for smaller parties to progress, but this has not happened either. We can see this most dramatically if we look at shares of the vote at British general elections in Scotland since 1945 (Figure 19.1).

TABLE 19.4 Labour and Conservative support in Scotland, 1974–2015

Election	Labour advantage in Scotland	Conservative shortfall in Scotland	Combined gap
1974 Oct.	–3.8	14.2	10.4
1979	4.9	15.8	20.7
1983	8.2	17.6	25.8
1987	12.9	22.2	35.1
1992	4.3	21.1	25.4
1997	2.0	16.2	18.2
2001	2.5	19.6	22.1
2005	4.1	19.9	24.0
2010	14.2	23.1	37.3
2015	–7.3	26.1	18.8

Source: British electoral statistics

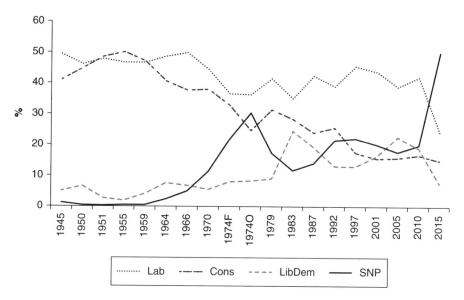

FIGURE 19.1
Share of vote
for parties in
Scotland at
British general
elections,
1945–2015

Source: British
electoral statistics,
1945–2015

Even under the constraining conditions of 'first past the post', we can see that the mid-1970s marked a major transformation in Scottish politics, with the steady decline of the Conservatives and the emergence of the Liberals and the SNP.

Most spectacular of all has been the rise of the SNP, culminating in its electoral success at the 2015 British general election, which followed its electoral success at the 2011 Scottish parliament election, and achieved under a system of proportional representation (AMS) (see Figure 19.2).

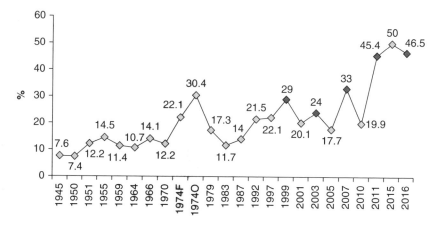

FIGURE 19.2   SNP share of the vote in British and Scottish elections, 1945–2016

Note: Vote share is calculated in terms of seats fought as follows: 1945 (8); 1950 (3); 1951 (2); 1955 (2); 1959 (5); 1964 (15); 1966 (23); 1970 (65); Feb. 1974 (70). Since Oct. 1974, the SNP has contested all the Scottish seats. Scottish parliament elections took place in 1999, 2003, 2007, 2011 and 2016

Source: British electoral statistics, 1945–2016

The SNP vote share was respectable in the seats in which the party stood, although it fought only a handful until the 1960s. By 1970 it was contesting a majority of seats in Scotland, although it was not until October 1974 that the SNP fought all Scottish seats.

Explaining the transformation

The dominance of the two main British class parties, Conservative and Labour, is of a more modern vintage than we might expect. In fact, it is a post-1945 phenomenon, with these two parties regularly taking around 90 per cent of the vote at general elections between 1945 and 1970.

For much of the nineteenth century, Scotland was Liberal territory to an extent that Labour failed to match in the twentieth. Indeed, the Liberal Party won a majority of Scottish seats at every election between 1832 and 1910, except for 1900. Between the 1840s and the 1880s the Liberals notched up huge majorities north of the border, especially in 1847 when 82 per cent of Scots voted Liberal compared with 57 per cent in England, and again in 1865 when the figures were 85 per cent and 59 per cent, respectively.

By the mid-1880s, however, largely reflecting the Liberal crisis over Irish home rule, the differential between Scotland and England in terms of the Liberal vote began to diminish. Between 1918 and the mid-1950s, the Conservative Party was the most popular party in Scotland, winning 37 per cent of all the Scottish seats contested at the eleven elections between 1918 and 1955, compared with the Labour Party and its allies (the Independent Labour Party) who won 35 per cent of seats.

In the period after 1945, the differences between Scotland and England in terms of voting behaviour were small. Only since the 1950s was Labour the dominant party in Scotland, and it has been challenged for the anti-Tory vote by the Liberals who made a modest comeback in this period, and, above all, by the rise of the SNP.

Politics and national identity

Is this transformation of Scottish politics to be explained in terms of the growing importance of national identity? That there is an intimate connection between political behaviour and national identity would seem self-evident, and an opinion poll taken shortly after the referendum on Scottish independence in September 2014 seemed to confirm that relationship (see Table 19.5).

The symmetry of that relationship is obvious: the more Scottish you are, the more likely you were to vote for independence; and the more British, the more likely to vote against.

To what extent has the divergence between Scottish and British electoral behaviour been driven by a strengthening of national identity in Scotland along the lines which the table suggests? Furthermore, is the emergence of the SNP as the major political force in Scotland an expression of that shift?

TABLE 19.5   National identity by vote in referendum

% by row	Yes	No
Scottish not British	84	16
More Scottish than British	61	39
Equally Scottish and British	26	74
British more than/not Scottish	13	87

Source: IPSOS MORI, 18–19 September 2014

It seems tempting to assume that the rise in SNP support reflects an increasing tendency for people to emphasise being Scottish, but as we saw in the previous chapter, the relationship between voting and national identity is not straightforward. Even at the time of the SNP's most successful Scottish election, 2011, the relationship between national identity, identifying with the SNP and constitutional preferences was not clear cut (Figure 19.3).[1]

Most 'exclusive Scots' (Scottish not British) voted SNP, but so also did those who said they thought of themselves as 'more Scottish than British':

- The major shift comes among 'equally Scottish and British' where Labour voting was the most common.

- Those who thought of themselves as 'British' (the final column) were evenly divided between voting Labour and voting Tory (one-third each).

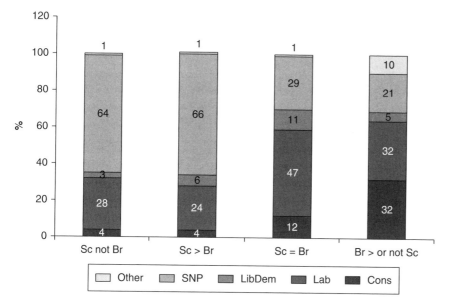

FIGURE 19.3
National identity and vote, Scottish parliament election 2011

Source: Scottish Social Attitudes survey, 2011

SNP vote and national identity

Let us focus on the two 'strongly Scottish' groups. If we compare how they voted in 2007 and in 2011, we can see from Figure 19.4 that the significant voting shift to the SNP came not among 'exclusive Scots', but from the 'more Scottish than British' group, 41 per cent of whom voted SNP in 2007, but 66 per cent in 2011. There was a modest shift to the SNP among 'exclusive Scots' (+4) and even among 'Brits' (+7), but nothing like the increase among those who thought of themselves as 'more Scottish than British' (+15) (see Figure 19.4).

Let us explore in more detail the relationship between national identity, how people vote, along with their constitutional preferences (based on the 2014 Scottish Social Attitudes Survey, with 2011 in brackets). We find that:

- 45 per cent of those who say they are 'Scottish not British' support the SNP (42 per cent);

- 46 per cent of SNP supporters say they are 'Scottish not British' (40 per cent);

- 69 per cent of the 'Scottish not British' support independence (54 per cent);

- 47 per cent in favour of independence say they are 'Scottish not British' (55 per cent).

The key point is that fewer than half of 'exclusive Scots' support the SNP. The inverse is also broadly true: that less than half of SNP supporters are 'exclusive Scots', suggesting that most SNP supporters include some element of 'British' in their national identity.[2]

There is, then, based on the 2014 survey results, a much stronger relationship between national identity and support for independence, namely 69 per cent, in contrast to 54 per cent in 2011. This suggests that the context of the Scottish Independence Referendum (this survey was conducted shortly after the event) had strengthened the

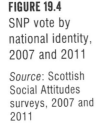

FIGURE 19.4
SNP vote by national identity, 2007 and 2011

Source: Scottish Social Attitudes surveys, 2007 and 2011

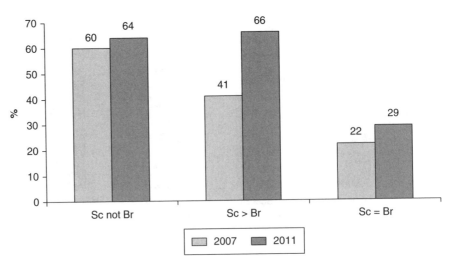

association between national identity and voting 'Yes'. On the other hand, that support for independence was 47 per cent, compared with 55 per cent in 2011, suggests voting 'Yes' was not confined to 'exclusive Scots'.

To complete the picture, we also find the following:

- 59 per cent of people favouring independence supported the SNP (in 2011, also 59 per cent);

- 81 per cent of SNP supporters are pro-independence (in 2011, 55 per cent).

These data show that, while around six in ten pro-independence voters consistently support the SNP, by 2014, at the time of the referendum, a much higher proportion of SNP supporters had swung into line behind the party (up 26 percentage points on 2011). Furthermore, there had been a tightening up since 2011 of the relationship between national identity and independence (+15), and between supporting the SNP and being an 'exclusive Scot' (+6). So that suggests a greater alignment between national identity, supporting the SNP and being pro-independence, possibly because the 2014 referendum campaign reconfigured the association between them.

So to what extent is there a tight overlap between being an 'exclusive Scot', being in favour of independence, and voting SNP? Would we not expect there to be a considerable overlap between all three? In fact, it turns out that only 12 per cent of people do all three, which is marginally up from 10 per cent in 2011, but this still suggests a loose relationship between these three forms of 'nationalism'.

How, if at all, has the relationship between national identity and voting 'Yes' to independence changed over the three years since 2011 when the SNP was elected as a majority government? (See Figure 19.5)

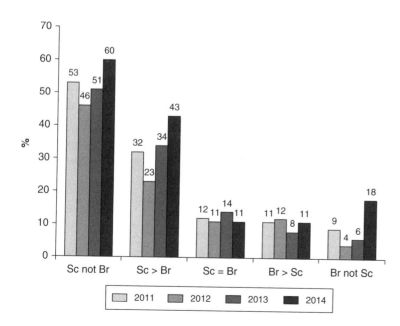

FIGURE 19.5
Percentage in favour of independence by national identity, 2011–14

Source: Scottish Social Attitudes Surveys, 2011–14

Among 'strong Scots' (people who say they are 'Scottish not British' and 'more Scottish than British') we find greater support for independence (up 9 percentage points in each case), but over the four-year period the picture is broadly one of trendless fluctuation. Note too the apparent rise in support for independence among people who say they are 'British not Scottish'. That might seem somewhat contradictory, but only if we think of support for independence in simple identity terms. If, for example, you are not born in Scotland, and, as a result, feel that you cannot claim to be 'Scottish', you might describe yourself as 'British' by default while being in favour of independence.

So, all said and done, does national identity, specifically being an 'exclusive Scot', explain SNP success? Let us focus on the 2011 election where the SNP won a majority. As in all elections, parties are supported differentially by different social groups. So in 2011, men were more inclined to vote SNP than women (57 per cent and 47 per cent, respectively). The same is true of 18–24 year olds, rather than retired people (a differential of 61 to 50 per cent), semi- and unskilled manual workers rather than professional and managerial workers (56 to 43 per cent), those with no educational qualifications rather than those with university degrees (52 to 40 per cent) and people of no religion rather than Catholics (51 to 41 per cent).

We can, then, identify a number of what are called 'marginal' effects – gender, age, social class, education – but we need to use statistical modelling where we put all these variables into the pot to be able to say whether some matter more than others. When we do that, we find that national identity has the major effect; those of age, sex and social class are less important.[3]

There were also modest educational and religious effects which were statistically significant: the more educational qualifications people had, the less likely they were to vote SNP; and Catholics were marginally less likely to vote SNP and more likely to vote Labour (by 41 to 48 per cent). Nevertheless, national identity undoubtedly was the most powerful factor in explaining SNP success.

We can conclude that the nationalist surge in 2011 had little to do with rising support for independence, nor with a rise in people feeling Scottish not British, and more to do with perceptions of competence and leadership, helped by Labour not being perceived as an effective alternative government. This perception of competence helps to explain why there is no simple relationship between electoral success and national identity. The major surge in support was from people who considered themselves 'more Scottish than British', rather than from 'exclusive Scots' who were minded in any case to support the SNP in 2011.

National identity and independence

The decade between 2005 and 2015 has been unprecedented in Scotland: specifically, from 2007 when the SNP became a minority government; 2011 when it won a majority; 2014 when the Scottish Independence Referendum took place; and the British General

Election where the SNP won 50 per cent of the vote, the first party in Scotland to do so for more than half a century.

While the nationalist surge in 2011 was not built upon a surge in support for independence, what effect is there, if any, in the longer term? Might we not also expect that at elections where the SNP was successful, as in 2007 and 2011, there was a strengthening of the relationship compared with ones where the SNP was not?

Let us examine how national identity and support for independence operate over the longer period, and at points where there are British elections or Scottish elections. To what extent, for example, was there a rise in people saying they are 'Scottish not British' at Scottish rather than at British elections? And do we find that there was a higher proportion of 'exclusive Scots' in favour of independence? In any event, we might expect a steady rise over the period (see Table 19.6).

What we see is a degree of 'trendless fluctuation' once more, both with regard to shifts in national identity and support for independence, but also a tightening up of the association between the two in 2014 and 2015. Thus, being an 'exclusive Scot' and supporting independence is over 70 per cent by 2015, in contrast to less than 50 per cent in earlier years, 2014 and 2005 excepted. The more highly charged 'politics of nationalism' since 2011 seems to have had its effect.

TABLE 19.6 Relationship between national identity and support for independence[4]

Elections	Scottish not British	Pro-independence	'Scottish not British' who are pro-independence
1997 (UK election)	24%	28%	48%
1999 (Scottish election)	34%	28%	46%
2001 (UK election)	36%	27%	41%
2003 (Scottish election)	35%	27%	46%
2005 (UK election)	33%	38%	57%
2007 (Scottish election)	28%	25%	48%
2010 (UK election)	29%	25%	46%
2011 (Scottish election)	32%	32%	53%
2014 (Scottish Referendum)	27%	35%	60%
2015 (UK election)	25%	36%*	72%

Note: Based on respondents born and living in Scotland (i.e. 'natives')

* To permit comparison with earlier surveys in the table, we have used the traditional constitutional options

Source: British and Scottish Social Attitudes Surveys, 1997–2015

Talking politics

So far in this chapter we have relied on survey material to explore the relationship between national identity and 'politics'. Why should we assume that people who feel Scottish are making a political statement about the Union? Do we get any inkling from the way people talk about national identity? Let us look at some examples of how people who talk about national identity introduce constitutional politics in their account.

I: Do you think of yourself as being Scottish?

R: *Not in a nationalistic way*, but yes, from an identity point of view, yes.

I: When you say 'from an identity point of view', I just wondered what you meant by that?

R: I relate to Scotland; I think of myself as Scottish, but not to make myself different from anybody else. Just actually to identify who I am.

And this other respondent specifically denies that national identity is 'political':

R: I don't think that I need that [Scottish parliament] to make me Scottish. I feel like Scottish people are very identifiable in their own right anyway. ... and it's not just an accent thing, a temperament thing. It's everything that makes them different so I don't think that you necessarily need to have political autonomy to know that. I think Scots are very confident in themselves and their sense of nationhood, I suppose.

Both accounts are interesting. The first person immediately dissociates national identity from 'politics' by saying '*Not in a nationalistic way*' to underline the fact that they are not making a political statement. The second person makes direct reference to the Scottish parliament, and both stress that being Scottish is not to be taken as 'politics'. Indeed, throughout the interviews, it was rare to find 'being Scottish' used in an overtly political way. Indeed, it seems to be the 'British' who are more likely to stress the politics in their identity statements:

As I've said, I'm quite proud of my Scottish identity, *but I'm not a nationalist.* [This person says they are *equally Scottish and British.*]

And another:

I would tend to think of myself as British. *I'm not a great believer in independence for Scotland, if that means anything* ... I don't think anything in particular comes to mind of being Scottish. You see, this is why I feel that we're all really British because I don't think we're. ... If you asked an Englishman what he thought about that, he probably couldn't tell you either. I feel that although I am Scottish I would rather feel more British. Why? Just because ... *I'm not a separatist.* [*More British than Scottish.*]

'I'm not a separatist' and *'I'm not a nationalist'* are riders far more commonly found among people who include 'being British' in their identity claim than among self-defining 'Scots'. That they choose to interpret the question in that 'political' way without being asked to do so is significant.

National identity: is it political or cultural?

We cannot be sure, of course, how typical or systematic such comments are, and that is why we turn to surveys, which provide us with much more structured material on which to base our judgements. That was why we asked people in Scotland and in England whether they thought that being or Scottish or English was more a matter of 'politics' or of 'culture'. We wanted to test out the commonsensical proposition that in Scotland national identity was likely to be more 'political'. It seemed not an unreasonable assumption that the agitation for, and the setting up of, a parliament in 1999 was fuelled by rising Scottish identity.

On the other hand, we often encounter claims that the English are far less assertive about national identity, that it is more implicit and nuanced, and thus less 'political'. So we asked people a simple question:[5]

> Some people say that being [English/Scottish] is mainly about countryside ['landscape' in Scotland], music, English/Scottish sporting teams, language and literature and so on. Others say that being [English/Scottish] is mainly about, for example, the way England/Scotland is governed, the parliament, and how [England/Scotland] runs its affairs. Whereabouts would you put yourself on a scale between these two positions?

On the seven-point scale, '1' related to cultural matters (countryside/landscape, music, sport, language and literature) and '7' to 'political' matters (government, parliament, etc.), with points in between.[6] This simple distinction has the merit of forcing the issue, and it produced some counter-intuitive results. We found that both Scots and English 'natives' (i.e. people born and currently living in each country) were at the 'cultural' end of the scale, and that Scots were inclined to take a more 'cultural' and less 'political' view of national identity than the English, scoring on average 3.17 on the seven-point scale, compared with 3.79 for the English.

Furthermore, we found no strong relationship between people's national identity and where they placed themselves on the cultural–political scale. We even found that 'exclusive Scots' took a much more 'cultural' view compared with people who were 'more Scottish than British'. Taking these findings as a whole, it seems that there is no systematic and clear-cut relationship between national identity and the cultural–political scale either in Scotland or England.

Nor was this because people did not care very much about the issues. The English and the Scots alike saw *both* culture and politics as important. Around two-thirds of both Scots and English people put 'cultural' *and* 'political' matters in the 'very' or 'quite' important categories, and both Scots and English were remarkably consistent in rating the importance of 'culture' above 'politics' when we repeated the question a couple of years later.

The findings also seemed to confirm what we found elsewhere. We divided people into three categories: the *nationals*, those who said they were primarily Scottish (either Scottish not British, or more Scottish than British); *dualists*, those who said they were *equally* both (Scottish and British); and, finally, *statists*, those who said they were 'mainly British'. We also did the same exercise in England, which gave us useful points of comparison. In accounting for identity choices, it was the 'nationals', whether in Scotland or England, who were much more likely to say that culture, traditions and institutions rather than 'political devolution' lay behind their feelings of being Scottish.

In fact, it was the dualists, those equally national and British, who were most likely to say that 'devolution' was an important determinant of their national identity.[7] In both Scotland and England, however, 'devolution' was a far *less* important factor in accounting for people's identities than cultural and institutional features (history, tradition, cultural concerns). This reinforces the view that 'culture' matters far more than 'politics' when it comes to territorial identities, be they 'national' (Scottish or English) or 'state' (British).

It is interesting that it is not the 'strongly national' identifiers who opt for 'political' statements, but the 'dualists', those who describe themselves as 'equally national and British'. It seems that 'dualists' choose dual identity *because* they are strongly pro-union, presumably thinking that devolution weakens the case for independence. In both England and Scotland, they are asserting that national and state identities are complementary rather than in competition, and they are the most committed to the future of the UK as a multi-national, devolved, state.

What this shows is that there is no simple connection between national identity and constitutional change, and that, if anything, matters of 'culture' rather than 'politics' narrowly defined are embedded in being Scottish. This was captured by Donald Dewar when, as incoming First Minister, he gave his speech at the opening of the Scottish parliament on 1 July 1999. Here is an extract:

This mace is a symbol of the great democratic traditions from which we draw our inspiration and our strength.

At its head are inscribed the opening words of our founding statute: 'There shall be a Scottish Parliament.'

Through long years, those words were first a hope, then a belief, then a promise. Now they are a reality.

This is a moment anchored in our history.

Today, we reach back through the long haul to win this Parliament, through the struggles of those who brought democracy to Scotland, to that other Parliament dissolved in controversy nearly three centuries ago.

Today, we look forward to the time when this moment will be seen as a turning point: the day when democracy was renewed in Scotland, when we revitalised our place in this our United Kingdom.

This is about more than our politics and our laws. This is about who we are, how we carry ourselves. In the quiet moments today, we might hear some echoes from the past:

The shout of the welder in the din of the great Clyde shipyards;

The speak of the Mearns, with its soul in the land;

The discourse of the enlightenment, when Edinburgh and Glasgow were a light held to the intellectual life of Europe;

The wild cry of the Great Pipes;

And back to the distant cries of the battles of Bruce and Wallace.

The past is part of us. But today there is a new voice in the land, the voice of a democratic Parliament. A voice to shape Scotland, a voice for the future.

Walter Scott wrote that only a man with soul so dead could have no sense, no feel of his native land. For me, for any Scot, today is a proud moment; a new stage on a journey begun long ago and which has no end. This is a proud day for all of us.

A Scottish Parliament. Not an end: a means to greater ends. And those too are part of our mace. Woven into its symbolic thistles are these four words: 'Wisdom. Justice. Compassion. Integrity.'

Our survey data seem to show that saying you are *British* is much more of a 'political' statement than saying you are Scottish. This reinforces the point that 'being Scottish', which is the norm in Scotland, is far more 'cultural' than 'political', but nevertheless one which can be mobilised politically as and when required.

Indeed, one of the effects of the long referendum campaign was to channel cultural feelings of 'being Scottish' in a political way and associate it strongly with the 'Yes' vote, reflected in use of the Scottish flag, the Saltire, as a campaigning symbol. One effect has been the strengthening of the association between being an 'exclusive Scot' and supporting independence (see Table 19.6).

It remains to be seen whether this association will remain as strong in the future. It is, however, misplaced to think that the only association which matters is the one between being Scottish and being in favour of greater self-government. Indeed, there is now a good case for claiming that 'being British' is a political statement in Scotland, and it is to this that we now turn.

Does being British matter?

We saw in the previous chapter that around half of native Scots[8] thought of themselves as not only strongly Scottish but also strongly British. These 'Scottish Brits' were more likely to be women, older people rather than the young, more middle class and more highly educated.

What in fact distinguished such people was less their social and demographic character-istics, but more their political–constitutional views, and in particular how they voted at the 2011 election and their constitutional preferences.[9] Thinking of oneself as 'British' was most strongly associated with being anti-independence and not voting SNP in the 2011 election, with age having a modest effect (being older makes you less likely to). Here is evidence once more that saying you are 'British' in Scotland is frequently interpreted as a political–constitutional matter.

The relationship between national identity and constitutional preferences is not a sim-ple one. In the previous chapter, we saw that nine out of ten Scots say they are 'strongly Scottish' but it is a weak guide to constitutional preference. We also saw in Chapter 18 that as many as 53 per cent felt strongly British. It turns out that whether or not you say you are 'British' is a far better guide to constitutional preference. The 'strong Scots' group, who are weakly British, are far more likely to want an independent Scotland and, indeed, to have voted for the SNP at the 2011 Scottish election. For 'identity nationalists', people who link their national identity with nationalist politics, the key features are support for inde-pendence, their age (in this case, being younger) and intending to vote SNP at the next Scottish parliament election.

To sum that up, when we look at the 'Scottish' and 'British' scales, we find a strong political–constitutional effect with regard to these identities. Nevertheless, saying you are *British* seems to have a more powerful effect when it comes to explaining political–constitutional choices than being Scottish.

We can understand better how it was possible for the Better Together campaign during the Scottish Independence Referendum in 2014 to mobilise support for its cause. Calling on people's British identity in Scotland was evidently a powerful mobiliser, given that virtually half of Scots felt British. Furthermore, being British was closely connected to political–constitutional views and, if anything, more powerful than social characteristics such as gender, age, social class and education. Ironically, the same could not be said for

FIGURE 19.6
Yes Scotland campaign badges on display on a campaign stall at Burntisland highland games

Source: Ken Jack/Demotix/ Press Association Images

the pro-independence campaign, precisely because 'being Scottish' was so ubiquitous (and included 'the British'), and hence could not be so easily mobilised to promote 'Yes' (for Scotland) (see Figure 19.6).

There is another aspect of 'being British' which reinforces the point. Even among Scots who do *not* consider themselves personally to be strongly British, there is no deep hostility to symbols of Britishness. Among those people who, in identity terms, deny that they are British, and whom we might expect to be the most hostile, we find fairly positive attitudes towards Britishness. Most Scots feel pride in such things as the 'British past' (56 per cent), the 'British Empire' (57 per cent) and 'British unity' (59 per cent). Even among 'exclusive Scots' the figures do not show a dramatic fall: respectively, 49, 48 and 52 per cent.

As we might expect, there is some variation by political party support. Three-quarters of Conservative supporters react positively to the 'British past' and the 'British Empire'. Yet, even among SNP supporters there is sizeable support for these 'British' options: 44 and 52 per cent, respectively.[10] It is remarkable that just over half of SNP supporters say they are not ashamed of empire, and although they are less enthusiastic about the British past than supporters of other parties, those Scottish nationalists taking a positive view outnumber those taking a negative one.

Furthermore, as many as half of SNP supporters are prepared to accept 'British' as a label that 'unites people living in Britain today', although supporters of other parties are unsurprisingly somewhat more likely to do so.[11] Taking these data together, the dominant impression is that a majority of people in Scotland (and the same is true in England, see McCrone and Bechhofer, 2015: chapter 8) take pride in being British, and although people are more strongly 'Scottish', they do not take a negative view of the British past, its erstwhile Empire or in accepting 'British' as a multicultural and unifying label.

What does 'British' mean, anyway?

Might it be, however, that the Scots and the English have different *conceptions* of what 'British' means; that they use the same term to mean different things? That people have *similar* conceptions of what 'British' means can be gauged from the fact that they chose systematically the same symbols regardless of their own sense of national identity (see Figure 19.7). In the British and Scottish Social Attitudes Surveys of 2006, we asked people to select from a list of symbols they thought most important to British culture, and which the second most important. The point was to ask people what they saw as important symbols of Britain, *not* how they related them to their *own* sense of being British, nor whether they approved of a particular symbol. You may, for example, think of the British monarchy as an important symbol of Britain, while personally holding republican views and disapproving of the institution.

FIGURE 19.7
Vote 'No' pin badges on offer as Jim Murphy MP, former Secretary of State for Scotland, speaks from a soapbox in support of the Union

Source: Jane Barlow/Press Association Images

We found that the English and the Scots broadly agreed on the ranking of the symbols of British culture, and that a constitutional symbol, 'British Democracy', is seen as the most important, and equally so in both countries (see McCrone and Bechhofer, 2015: chapter 8).

'Mainly Scottish' respondents were far more likely to choose 'Fair Play' as a symbol of being British than the 'Mainly English'. The other differences between the 'Mainly English' and the 'Mainly Scottish' groups (a greater tendency for the English to choose the 'Union Flag' and a lesser tendency to choose 'Sport') are smaller.

Across the board, then, it seems that the expected relationship does not hold; a person's sense of their *own* national identity makes little difference to their perceptions of the important symbols of British culture. Furthermore, people do not have to think of themselves as 'British' to rate 'British' symbols in a broadly similar way to other persons living in Britain.

Let us recap the argument:

- First, a substantial proportion of native Scots, those born and living in Scotland, consider themselves strongly British, *as well as* strongly Scottish.

- Second, Scots do not have an aversion to British iconography, that is to the British past, the Empire, or British unity, and if you feel strongly Scottish, this makes little difference.

- Third, Scots, even those who say they are strongly Scottish, are quite able to identify key British symbols, and rank them in much the same way as other Scots as well as the English.

What are the implications of all this? Why, we might wonder, has the politicisation of national identity happened at all? Why do so many politicians and commentators worry about the future of the British state, if a substantial proportion of Scots see themselves as British, take some pride in British icons, and are well able to identify key British symbols, much along the lines of people in England?

How different are the Scots and the English?

Lying beyond such questions are assumptions about the divergence of Scotland and England in terms of political behaviour during the past forty years. The first thing to say is that this divergence does not seem to be driven by differences in social attitudes and values among the Scots and the English (see Table 19.7).

TABLE 19.7   Social attitudes, Scotland and England (2010)[12]

% supporting view that:	Scotland	England	Difference between Scotland and England
Income gap too large	78	74	+4
One law for rich and one law for poor	56	54	+2
Redistribute income and wealth	63	53	+10
Governments should increase tax and spend	40	30	+10
Wrong to be able to buy better health	41	24	+17
Wrong to be able to buy better education	41	28	+13

Source: Scottish and British Social Attitudes Surveys, 2010

Although Scots are more 'left wing' on these measures, only the items on private provision for health and education show large differences. The key to explaining Scottish–English political differences lies far less in assuming that attitudes and values are driving 'politics' than the other way round: that 'politics', and particularly different systems of party competition in Scotland and England, drive social attitudes. Thus, while the main party competition in Scotland is between two centre–left parties, the SNP and Labour, in England it is structured around arguably a neo-liberal agenda between Conservatives and Labour, at least in terms of the vestiges of 'New' Labour deriving from the Blair governments in power from 1997 to 2010.

Defenders of the British Union, notably the former Prime Minister Gordon Brown, are well aware that 'politics' is driving attitudes rather than the other way round. He is highly critical of the sanguine view that there are deep historical associations which will keep the British state together. Brown comments:

> There is a myth that the union can easily survive this new polarisation between Scotland and England because it is held together by longstanding bonds and traditions. But what may have been true in the aftermath of two world wars has given way to a new century where none of our ancient institutions are strong enough or popular enough on their own to bind us together. (*Guardian*, 3 February 2015)

Brown is particularly critical of proposals for 'English Votes for English Laws' (EVEL), which derives from the so-called West Lothian question (WLQ) whereby non-English MPs vote on 'English-only' matters, while such matters are dealt with by, for example, the Scottish parliament and the National Assembly for Wales. Brown has little truck with WLQ, commenting: 'The reality is that having raised the West Lothian question they [the Conservative Party] have not found a workable West Lothian answer, other than by doing what their predecessors refused to do: threatening the very survival of the United Kingdom' (*Guardian*, 3 February 2015).

Because England represents such a disproportionate part of the UK population (84 per cent), Brown comments: 'If anyone's interests are under threat, it is not England's but those of Scotland, Northern Ireland and Wales that are permanently at risk of being outvoted.' In this, Brown is factually correct, for since 1945 Scotland has had a Westminster government it did not vote for 50 per cent of the time, while England has been on the receiving end only 10 per cent of the time, largely in the mid-1970s when neither of the two main UK political parties were able to command a comfortable majority.[13]

It has not been the Scottish tail which has wagged the English dog, but the reverse, which was one of the reasons for creating the Scottish parliament, to redress this 'democratic deficit'. It is the creation of such an institution in 1999 which has provided a powerful political platform for demands for greater self-government, particularly in the hands of the SNP, who have formed the governments since 2007.

The politics of divergence

Let us return to our key question in this chapter, and set our discussion of national identity in context: why has Scottish politics diverged to such a degree from British, or more precisely

English, politics over the last half-century? We can dismiss the simple view that Scottish political behaviour was always 'different'. Scotland and England were remarkably similar in terms of Labour and Conservative voting in the post-war years, and that divergence only became obvious in the 1970s.

There is, however, a more fundamental point to be made: the underlying issues of Scottish politics are as old as the Union itself. The key lies in the nature of that Union and its contradictions. There is little question that the Union of 1707 was, in Tom Nairn's phrase, a patrician compromise between two ruling pre-democratic elites, Scottish and English. To be sure, that Union was not the result of popular will, and if there had been a referendum in its day, it is fair to say that there would have been no Union.

In the event, the Union turned out to be a 'marriage of convenience', a *mariage de raison*, with a single legislature in London, the continuity of the English parliament, but with control over domestic institutions, law, education, religion, parish government, remaining in Scotland. Hence, to use Jim Bulpitt's distinction (1983), 'high' politics – of taxation, warfare and the like – fell under the remit of Westminster, and 'low' politics remained administratively devolved, while under the control of the British government of the day.

Why should that history matter? Because there was a structural contradiction at the heart of the British state; a unitary state, but one where direct responsibility for the governance of Scotland, while notionally under the control of the ruling UK party, remained in Scotland. This not only remained, but was to grow and develop, such that by the 1880s powers were consolidated into the Scottish Office, and rule emanated from St Andrews House in Edinburgh. The following century saw the accretion of further powers, notably under Tom Johnston as Secretary of State during the Second World War, and even as the British welfare state was developed thereafter.

The 'state', then, had different dimensions. Post-1945 welfarism was an integrating and centralising process. Being British had its pay-offs, and the remarkable similarity in voting patterns between Scottish and England in the 1940s and 1950s is testament to that. If, however, we look closely at political trends, we see that electoral divergence began, not in the 1970s, but in the mid-1950s.

Amplifying the Scottish question

Post-war western governments in Europe were 'nationalising' governments, less in the sense of bringing 'the commanding heights of the economy' under state control (notably, coal, steel, power), but more in becoming responsible for 'the national interest'. Post-war politics across Europe involved 'national statism', such that the 'national interest' was interpreted and promulgated by the state, and the British state was no exception (Sørensen, 2016).

The problem as far as Scotland was concerned was that its economic problems, as we saw in Chapter 6 when we analysed elites, happened earlier and to a greater degree than elsewhere.

Tom Johnston's Scottish Office state apparatus in the 1940s was put to work to encourage diversification and inward investment, diversifying the economy away from heavy industry.

This Scottish semi-state, built as it was on separate systems of law, of distinctive institutions of civil society, became the obvious vehicle for bringing about economic and social change. More responsibilities were devolved to Scotland to enable it to undertake economic regeneration, and so the Scottish Office was the key administrative apparatus to transform Scottish economy and society. It helped to generate a Scottish policy community, in Moore and Booth's term, a 'negotiated order' (1989: 150) operating between corporatism and the free market.

In the late 1950s and early 1960s the idea of Scotland as a unit of economic management was translated to the mass electorate via the Labour Party in Scotland, and especially via the Scottish media, and television in particular. Labour's strategy in this period was largely pragmatic: Labour's attitude to the *Scottish question* was based upon the assumptions that the basis of any discontent was economic, and that the electorate were more concerned about the economic goods which they received than with the constitutional mechanism by which they were delivered (Keating and Bleiman, 1979: 151).

The perception of Scotland as a separate unit of political and economic management coincided with the arrival of North Sea oil, which opened up the political possibility of an alternative Scottish future, and which the SNP was to exploit. The post-war belief in 'equal citizenship' was mobilised as equal citizenship for Scots within the UK in such a way that the (British) nationalist assumptions built into the welfare state could be transferred easily in the rhetorical form of Scottish nationalism. Certainly, the ability to shift from one form of nationalism (British) to another (Scottish) occurred at the right moment for the SNP, as well as for many Scots.

By the 1970s, the SNP was in the right place at the right time, making explicit, as well as problematic, the 'national' dimension of the post-war consensus, and providing a political alternative when the British settlement began to fail. Both the Conservative and Labour Parties paid the electoral price, the former more profoundly than the latter. Labour's early success was based on a view of the state as a generator of economic growth.

As Labour was seen to fail to deliver the economic goods in the 1970s, the SNP became increasingly the beneficiary. Ironically, when the next major ideological battle occurred later in the decade – between the radical right with its anti-state project and the defenders of the post-war settlement – Labour in Scotland was in a much better position than the SNP to switch the terms of the struggle onto a left/right dimension, while taking on some of the nationalist mantle.

Nevertheless, the SNP acted as a key electoral catalyst for change, and provided a political home for the socially mobile and the young, in search of a new political identity in a rapidly changing Scotland. It is in the systematic swing away from the Conservatives, however, that we have the most coherent manifestation of the emerging Scottish political system, a system increasingly incompatible with the ideology of the Conservatives' role as the British or English national party.

By the mid-1970s the features of the modern political landscape became clearer. The long, slow decline of the Conservatives was evident, but one which did not culminate in electoral disaster until 1997. The main political struggle was between Labour and the SNP, each swapping political clothing; the Liberals were reduced to walk-on parts, but managed to prosper largely as a useful bolthole for those not attracted to any of the above. Early SNP successes in the mid-1970s lay in its appeal to 'intermediate' workers, and they did particularly well among upwardly socially mobile voters from working-class origins (Davis, 1979).

In this way, the nationalists were beneficiaries of key social changes in Scotland in the 1960s and 1970s – rising affluence, full employment and upward social mobility. Groups who became less reliant on the support of kin as well as more home-centred – Scotland's analogues of the classic 'affluent workers' studied in England (Goldthorpe et al., 1969) – found themselves drawn to the nationalists less for reasons of political ideology than because of their own social detachment from their social class of origin.

This social base paid electoral dividends where Labour was historically weak. For example, Peterhead, a town where the SNP made an early and lasting impact, and which Alex Salmond, who went on to lead the party, won in 1987 as part of the Banff & Buchan constituency, pointed to this important nationalist social base. 'The SNP was most successful in winning affiliations from the upwardly aspirant who were renouncing the class of their homes while not yet entering the middle class' (Bealey and Sewel, 1981: 160).

Perhaps the lack of class connotations in the SNP was the key appeal to this socially mobile group in the 1970s. Such people were susceptible to alternative frameworks of perception, for their traditional forms of social and political identities were weakening. This was also a generation which learned much of their politics via television and the media because their way of life was mobile and privatised.

The Scottish frame of reference

Scotland differed little from the rest of the UK with regard to these social and cultural changes, but from the late 1960s 'Scotland' was a frame of cultural reference through which the political world could increasingly be interpreted. Crucially, the SNP was a political party which could more easily lay claim to this 'Scottish' label, because it was a taken-for-granted reference in much the same way as the Conservative Party in England had implicitly assumed a 'national' identity in England.

In another important respect, the SNP was a 'media' party, well suited to an increasingly volatile electorate. The SNP was in the right place at the right time, making an appeal to the right people. In many ways, we might say that its Scottishness was almost incidental, but, of course, vital. The SNP captured the generation entering political adulthood in the 1960s and 1970s who, in England, tended to vote Conservative or Liberal. Having set the Scottish frame of reference, the collapse of the SNP in the late 1970s left the bulk of its support nowhere to go but to Labour, which, in turn had the effect of turning Labour in Scotland into a proto-nationalist party by the early 1980s. Its opposition to Thatcherism, coupled with its dominance in Scotland (winning forty-one of Scotland's seventy-two seats in 1983, rising to fifty in 1987), gave it little option than to adopt a nationalist mantle.

By the late 1970s, the Scottish stage was set for a new battle over the role of the state, between Labour and the Conservatives, which the latter were singularly ill-equipped to fight. This is the final key element in the process of political divergence between Scotland and England. As we have seen, the slippage in Conservative support began well before 1979 and the election of the first Thatcher government. But the 1980s drove a considerable wedge between the electoral performances of the two nations. Mrs Thatcher may not have created the divergence, but she gave it a flavour all of her own.

And so the main battleground of Scottish politics in the 1990s and 2000s was between Labour and the SNP. Once the Scottish parliament was established in 1999 it was seen as a means to an end, and that end was better government and an expected improvement in social and public welfare. This emphasis on 'instrumental' factors derived from a concern with improving welfare for Scotland as a whole, rather than a highly individualistic perspective of 'voting with your wallet'. We know this because, while most people expected taxes to rise, they were willing to pay the price, in order to raise the standard of social and economic welfare in Scotland generally.

At the time of the 1997 devolution referendum, those voting 'No' were those who also expected taxes to rise, but thought that welfare would not improve on a range of social issues, and these voters tended to be Conservatives (Brown et al., 1999: chapter 7). Indeed, those Tory voters who were minded to support a home rule parliament were caught in a dilemma, and resolved it by voting 'Yes', contrary to party policy.

The Conservatives lost the argument with even their own electorate, and were deemed by the wider one as not having Scotland's interests at heart. The Tories found themselves marginalised not only in the general election of 1997, but also in the referendum four months later, and only the system of proportional representation, which they had strongly opposed, gave them a presence of 18 seats (all list seats) in the 1999 Scottish election for the first parliament, the most they have had in any election since.

Conclusion

By the final quarter of the twentieth century a new kind of 'nationalist' politics had emerged; not simply in the sense of the rise of the SNP, but the intrusion of 'national', that is *Scottish*, politics throughout the Scottish parties and, above all, the electorate. Even when the SNP was not electorally successful, as in the 1980s, the nationalist agenda had been set, and Labour inherited the mantle, culminating in its installation of a devolved Scottish parliament in 1999.

Labour's problem was that it did not know what to do next, trusting that devolution was the 'settled will' of the Scottish people, a phrase credited to the-then Labour leader,

John Smith, or, more aggressively, that it would 'kill nationalism stone dead' in the words of his colleague George Robertson. Neither, history proved, was the case.

Let us return to our question: is Scottish politics primarily 'about' national identity? It depends what we mean. While virtually everyone born and living in Scotland now think of themselves as 'Scottish', a significant number – as many as half – also think they are 'British'. In this sense, Scotland has not developed a simple model of 'identity politics', where knowing how people describe themselves enables us to predict their social and political attitudes and behaviour. In a more fundamental way, however, Scottish politics *is* about 'national identity' in that it suffuses the main social and cultural organisations; it sets the agenda, our framework for understanding.

'The Scottish interest' now dominates our politics, which is why the Scottish parliament came so quickly to be considered the premier institution. Some unionists in the 1970s claimed that devolution would prove to be the slippery slope to full independence. They may feel that their fears have come to pass, but, in truth, there was little they could do to stop the slide, given that the social, political and economic forces had been unleashed much earlier.

The current beneficiaries of those forces are the SNP and their governments. They, above all, are trusted to look after the interests of Scotland, a view held across the supporters of all other political parties. Thus, 60 per cent of Tories, 67 per cent of Labour and 77 per cent of Liberals in Scotland see the SNP as the party most trusted to 'look after the interests of Scottish people in general' (http://whatscotlandthinks.org/questions/how-well-do-the-snp-look-after-interests-of-scottish-people-in-general-6#line).

This, then, is the template of Scottish politics today. The question as to how Scotland's long-term interest should be settled in constitutional terms remains the key one yet to be answered. In the final section of the book, we look at 'representations' of Scotland in the wider canvas, and it is to those these that we now turn, beginning with the 'diaspora'.

Chapter summary

So what have we learned in this chapter?

- That Scottish and English politics have diverged since the 1950s, and particularly since the 1970s in the context of the Scottish frame of reference.

- That 'national identity' is linked to this divergence but not in a straightforward way.

- That 'being Scottish' is significantly more 'cultural' than 'political'.

- That a large proportion of people in Scotland say they are British, and see little conflict with being Scottish.

- That there has been a strengthening of the link between saying you are Scottish and supporting independence.

Questions for discussion

1. Why have Scottish and English electoral politics diverged since 1945, and what, if anything, does national identity have to do with it?

2. How have the connections between people's national identity, their constitutional preferences, and patterns of voting changed since the 1990s?

3. Why has 'being British' remained an important aspect of people's national identity in Scotland?

4. Is being Scottish less 'political' than being British? If so, why is that?

5. To what extent does setting a Scottish political agenda make 'independence' inevitable?

Annotated reading

(a) On identity and politics: see D. McCrone and F. Bechhofer, *Understanding National Identity* (2015), chapter 6; J. Curtice and A. Heath, 'England awakes? Trends in national identity in England', in F. Bechhofer and D. McCrone (eds), *National Identity, Nationalism and Constitutional Change* (2009); A. Brown et al., *The Scottish Electorate: The 1997 General Election and beyond* (1999).

(b) Scottish Social Attitudes: What Scotland Thinks (http://whatscotlandthinks. org/opinion-polls).

Notes

1   These histograms are arranged to allow us to compare how each national identity group voted. Hence, they are of equal size.
2   These data are percentaged in terms of the first-named category, and are not intended to be added together. This means that 45 per cent of 'exclusive Scots' support the SNP, and 55 per cent of them do not.
3   That is, using a binary regression model, we find that age, sex and social class have a diminishing effect when national identity is included.
4   At the time of writing, data were not available for the 2016 Scottish parliament election.
5   In 2006 and again in 2008 (England) and 2009 (Scotland); only people who said they were British *not* English/Scottish were excluded on the grounds that they did not think of themselves in 'national' terms.
6   Any scores less than the mean (3.5) can be taken as 'cultural', and greater than the mean, as 'political'.
7   Around half of the equally national and British group said devolution was important, compared with about a third of the 'mainly Scots' and the 'mainly English' groups.
8   To remind the reader, 'native' Scots are those born and currently living in Scotland.

9 In other words, using binary regression, these 'political' variables were far stronger in explaining who thought of themselves as British.

10 A majority of Labour supporters take pride in the 'British past' (61 per cent) and the 'British Empire' (57 per cent), with comparable figures for Liberal Democrats (respectively, 57 and 62 per cent).

11 Labour supporters (68 per cent) are most inclined to agree, followed by Liberal Democrats (62 per cent) and Conservatives (57 per cent).

12 These are summary data for 2010 when the questions were asked in both Scotland and England. The trends over time for Scotland (2000–13) were discussed in Chapter 7.

13 We calculate these figures by identifying the occasions when Scotland and England got UK governments a majority did not vote for. Because Scotland is only 10 per cent of the UK population, it is much more likely to happen.

20

'MY GRANNY WAS A McTAVISH': CLAIMING DIASPORA IDENTITY

Once, when I gave a lecture on national identity, I was approached at the end by an elderly American who said to me: 'I just wanted you to know that my grandmother was a McTavish'. I found it difficult to respond but murmured non-committally. She was making the point that she considered herself a Scot because, she said, she had 'Scottish blood in her veins'; that her claim was based on her ancestry.

Such has been the power of the 'civic' claim to be Scottish that the ancestral claim, the 'ethnic' one, not one based on birthplace or residence, sits uncomfortably with our conception of ourselves in modern Scotland. 'Blood' is not a marker of being Scottish, which many people living in Scotland give too much credence to, and it is redolent of the darker days of the twentieth century. Recall too our discussion of 'race' and ethnicity which we presented in Chapter 13. Birthplace and residence – you are a Scot if you live and work in Scotland – are criteria we are more comfortable with; Christopher Smout's sense of *place* rather than the sense of *tribe*. But why should that be so, given that many people living furth of Scotland play the ancestral card? We will explore this phenomenon of the *diaspora* which has featured in our discussions of 'belonging', of tourism, and identity.

Chapter aims

- To examine if there are a substantial number of people living furth of Scotland who claim Scottish ancestry and identity.

- To see if such emigrants constitute a 'diaspora' in a sociological sense.

- To ask whether diasporic identity has a meaningful relationship with the 'real' Scotland rather than one of the imagination.

- To discover whether Scots living in England find themselves in an identity dilemma.

In the last decade there has been a plethora of books on the 'Scottish diaspora'. These include: James Hunter's *Scottish Exodus* (2005); Tom Devine's *To the Ends of the Earth* (2011);

Duncan Sim's *American Scots* (2011); Marjorie Harper's *Scotland No More?* (2012); Mario Varricchio's *Back to Caledonia* (2012); Tania Bueltmann and colleagues' *The Scottish Diaspora* (2013); and Murray Leith and Duncan Sim's *The Modern Scottish Diaspora* (2014). Clearly there is a market for such books, reflecting people's interest in where, and who, they have come from.

Spotting the commercial opportunity, VisitScotland (the former Scottish Tourist Board) set up 'Homecoming 2009' designed to attract people of Scottish ancestry to visit Scotland, claiming that 'for every single Scot in their native land, there are thought to be at least five more overseas who can claim Scottish ancestry'. The series of events were as follows:

- On 16 June 2008, Scotland's First Minister, Alex Salmond MSP MP, officially launched Homecoming Scotland 2009 at Edinburgh Castle. The Homecoming started on 25 January 2009 (Burns night) and ran until 30 November 2009 (St Andrews Day).

- On 24 July 2009, a Clan Convention, composed of the chiefs, commanders and leading representatives of Scottish clans, met to discuss the 'Role of the Clan in the 21st century'. The Clan Convention took place within the Scottish parliament.

- The centrepiece event of the year was The Gathering 2009, on 25 and 26 July, centred on Holyrood Park in Edinburgh. The clan gathering included highland games over the two days, a parade up the Royal Mile and a 'clan pageant' on the castle esplanade. Prince Charles, the Duke of Rothesay, was Patron of The Gathering 2009.

As it turned out, Homecoming Scotland 2009 was less than successful in financial terms. We enter the realm of claim and counter-claim as to the events' financial pay-off, that it generated £53 million, or £39 million, depending on assumptions made (www.telegraph. co.uk/news/uknews/scotland/7990211/Homecoming-Scotland-benefits-hugely-exaggerated.html). Lewis Macdonald, MSP, Scottish Labour's tourism spokesman, commented: 'Alex Salmond's claims about the success of *Homecoming* have turned out to be more bogus than Brigadoon.'

Be all that as it may, and quite undeterred, the Scottish government embarked on a less costly Homecoming in 2014, and the tourist industry set about assembling and badging various events, including broadening the appeal to Chinese visitors as we saw in the previous chapter.

The Scottish government meanwhile had commissioned research on the Scottish diaspora, and published three lengthy reports in 2009:

- *Engaging the Scottish Diaspora: Rationale, Benefits and Challenges* (ww.gov.scot/Resource/ Doc/280422/0084484.pdf);

- *Scotland's Diaspora and Overseas-born Population* (www.gov.scot/Resource/Doc/285746/ 0087034.pdf); and

- *The Scottish Diaspora and Diaspora Strategy: Insights and Lessons from Ireland* (www.gov. scot/Publications/2009/05/28141101/0).

The Scottish government made clear its twin aims: 'The Scottish diaspora could assist in spreading a narrative of economic success' and 'diaspora strategy has a role to play in immigration' (from *Achieving Scotland's 2011 Growth Target* (www.gov.scot/Publications/2009/01/15111700/1)).

The exemplar, plainly, was Ireland. The First Minister, Alex Salmond, made a speech at Trinity College Dublin in February 2008, in which he said:

> So I have come to Dublin to set out our aspirations for Scotland's future – how we will create a Celtic Lion economy to match the Celtic Tiger on this side of the Irish Sea. ... The story of Ireland – one of the greatest success stories of the last century, and of this century – is a testament to what the people of Scotland can achieve. (*The Scottish Diaspora and Diaspora Strategy*, para. 2.2, p. 5)

Despite what followed in the 2008 economic crash, and Ireland's economic downturn and banking crisis, the aspirations to learn from the Celtic neighbour as to how to exploit the 'diaspora' remained.

Counting Scots

Just how many 'Scots' there are in the world is a matter of some conjecture. The estimate by VisitScotland that there are fives times as many claiming Scottish ancestry living outwith Scotland compared with people living in Scotland is on the conservative side as such claims go. Thus, the consultants employed by the Scottish government to 'Engage the Scottish Diaspora' were willing to put the ratio at upwards of 12:1. Their breakdown was as follows:

- The 'lived diaspora', which included people born in Scotland as well as those who have lived and worked or studied in Scotland. They estimated that 1.3 million Scottish-born people live outwith Scotland.

- The 'ancestral diaspora': those who can trace their heritage to Scotland. 'They could be second generation migrants, or of ancient historical descent, but they draw a strong link to Scotland as part of their family history' (para. 1.13). These estimates put the number claiming Scottish descent in the United States, Canada, Australia and New Zealand at around 16.9 million.

- The 'affinity diaspora': this is made up of people who 'make a connection to Scotland, without drawing a family link to the country'; they estimate this at between 40 and 50 million worldwide.[1]

The Social Research Unit of Scottish Government was more circumspect (www.gov.scot/Resource/Doc/285746/0087034.pdf). Using available 2001 census data, they calculated that around four-fifths of people born in Scotland currently lived there, with the largest proportion of non-domiciled Scots living in England (just under 800,000, or 18 per cent of people living in Scotland), with 130,000 (or 3 per cent) in Australia, 74,000 (2 per cent) in the United States and 51,000 in Canada (1 per cent).

They concluded: 'Scotland's diaspora is larger than for many of the other countries in this analysis and may even be greater than that for New Zealand and Ireland' (para. 4.1). Furthermore:

> Scotland has the highest percentage of people living outside their country of birth (around 20 per cent) followed by Ireland (19 per cent) and New Zealand (14 per cent). The figures for these three countries are considerably higher than for the other countries considered, which all record figures of 5.6 per cent or less. (para. 3.10)

It is this high proportion of people born in Scotland who live elsewhere which has attracted the attention of researchers and public officials. They provide a base for potential 'reverse migration', or at least they underpin the so-called GlobalScot Network (www. globalscot.com), and public events like the 2009 and 2014 Homecomings. Somewhat more removed are bodies like Global Friends of Scotland which aims 'to promote a contemporary image of Scotland internationally through a network of people who feel an affinity to Scotland; and to showcase Scotland's world-class achievements in culture, sport, education and business'.

The message, then, as regards the Scottish diaspora, is a hard-edged one: it seeks to exploit economic and business links, including inward investment, in a highly competitive global market, and one in which Scotland has been a player since the 1960s.

Migration and the 'diaspora'

The disproportionate scale of emigration from Scotland has a long history. Tom Devine observed in his book *The Scottish Nation* that proportionately more people left Scotland permanently between 1821 and 1915 than from Germany, Spain, Portugal and Italy (2000: 468). During the nineteenth and early twentieth centuries, Ireland, Norway and Scotland consistently topped the league table of Central and Western European countries in terms of emigration per head; and, furthermore, if migration to England is included, 'Scotland ... emerges clearly as the emigration capital of Europe' for much of the period.

The paradox, however, is that Scotland 'was one of the world's most highly successful industrial and agricultural economies after *c*.1860 but was losing people in very large numbers rather than those countries traditionally associated with poverty, clearance, hunger and destitution' (2000: 469). Indeed, by the nineteenth century, the typical emigrant was not the destitute Highlander cleared off the land, but Scots who 'had experience of working within this system of advanced capitalism and had acquired a range of skills that few other emigrants from Europe could match' (2000: 469). Thus, as many as half of Scots who migrated to the United States between 1815 and 1914 were skilled or semi-skilled. In cultural terms, they were mainly Lowland Protestants who spoke English and who had above-average levels of education, and thus escaped both religious prejudice and having to acquire a new language. Some arrived with modest amounts of capital, which represented an 'investment' made by sponsors at their place of origin in the expectation that they would provide added links to the emigration chain for others to follow (Harper, 2012).

Many emigrants sent back money for the fares of relatives so that they too could make the journey. Many were 'returned migrants' who took advantage of seasonal work opportunities in the building trades, returning to Scotland during slack times. As Devine observes: '"Successful" returnees must indeed have been a potent source for spreading knowledge of overseas conditions in local communities, and even a positive influence in encouraging further migration' (Devine, 2000: 478). For those with capital, expatriate Scots notably in Australia and New Zealand were active in land, cattle and sheep companies and thus 'were able to draw on middle-class savings in Scotland through a network of solicitors and chartered accountants who mobilized the capital of the affluent' (2000: 474).

Scottish emigration has a much older pedigree than that occurring in the nineteenth and twentieth centuries. Whether as military mercenaries, commercial traders or small farmers, Scots had been emigrating to mainland Europe, and to Ireland, from at least the sixteenth century, so in Devine's words, 'the custom of going abroad was nothing new' (2000: 480).

The migratory culture, of 'brizing yont' (going forth), even to England, was deeply embedded in Scottish culture such that it helped to define what 'being Scottish' stood for. Thanks to popular writers like John Prebble, we tend to have an image of penurious Highlanders being evicted from their ancestral land, but such emigration belongs mainly to the late eighteenth to mid-nineteenth centuries.

After the 1860s, Highland migration is less significant and overtaken by emigrants from towns, cities and Lowland rural Scotland. 'Expulsion' was the exception, not the rule, and there was always the lure to erstwhile tenant farmers of owning their land. Devine again: 'Much of the movement abroad was therefore aspirational, and ironically, was probably spurred on by the material improvements at home which engendered a new spirit of optimism and desire for even greater opportunities' (2011: 273).

Scottish 'ancestry' was also a useful recruiting tool when it came to raising regiments in the British Empire, such as in Canada where a direct appeal could be made to the 'forefathers' and their military tradition.

A better class of migrant

Those who emigrated encountered a network of Scottish associations such as the St Andrew and Caledonian Societies in the English-speaking world. Unlike Highland Gaelic Societies dedicated to the protection and preservation of culture and, above all, language, St Andrew and Caledonian Societies were self-help organisations, as Kim Sullivan has shown (2014). Their aim was to generate and distribute charitable aid for emigrants who had fallen on hard times, but, she observes, 'underscoring all these societies' benevolent activities was the principle of self-improvement' (2014: 51). Thus the stipulation of the Toronto society in 1879 that 'tramps and vagrants need not apply'. There is also the pertinent example of a grant to enable a newly arrived tradesman to purchase replacement tools for an original set which had been stolen (2014: 55). Sullivan makes the important point that the Scottish societies were expatriate organisations, not indigenous ones.

However, as Devine points out:

> It is more than likely that the Scottish societies, despite their visibility, attracted no more than a minority even of first-generation immigrants. This may help to explain the notable collapse in Scottish associational activity in the USA from the 1920s, in spite of the huge emigration to America from Scotland in that decade totaling more than 160,000. (2011: 275)

While emigration to the United States from Scotland fell away in the second half of the twentieth century, the remarkable revival, or perhaps invention, of the Scottish clan societies in modern times owes its explanation to quite different processes and movements, as we shall see later in this chapter.

The scale of emigration

It is important to underscore the differential importance of emigration from Scotland right up to the present day, and notably overseas.

Using Michael Anderson's data (2012) in his study of Scotland's historical demography (Figure 20.1), we can see just how significant overseas migration was in the years after the Second World War. Nevertheless, as Anderson observes in a forthcoming book on Scotland's historical demography:

> While net emigration overseas continued in almost every year until the 1990s, it never reached the levels even in absolute terms of many of the years before World War One or the early 1920s, though it was especially high in the mid-1960s, peaking at around 29,000 in 1966–67. Meanwhile, net outflow from Scotland to the rest of the UK continued almost unchecked until the early 1990s, again with particularly strong flows in the 1960s, as the Scottish economy was forced to begin its major readjustment to the new competitive environments of the post-war world.

Only in the 1990s does Scotland shift from being a society of emigrants to one of immigrants, as Figure 20.2 shows, charting gross migration to and from Scotland since 1981.

FIGURE 20.1

Net migration from Scotland, by destination/origin, 1947–99/2000

Note: Data for 1947–50 are for calendar years, from 1951 for mid-year starting in the year plotted

Source: Courtesy of Michael Anderson

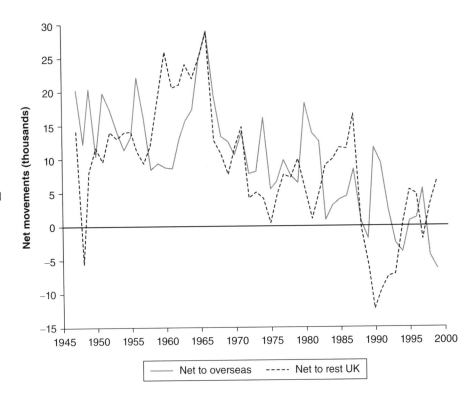

In the modern period, migration to the rest of the UK (mainly England) is more significant than emigration overseas. It is the rise in *immigration*, notably from overseas (including post-1989 Eastern European countries such as Poland), which is the rising trend, currently on a par with immigration from the rest of the UK. It would be easy to think that Scotland's relative

FIGURE 20.2

Gross migration to and from Scotland, by origin/destination, 1981–2 to 2010–11

Source: Courtesy of Michael Anderson

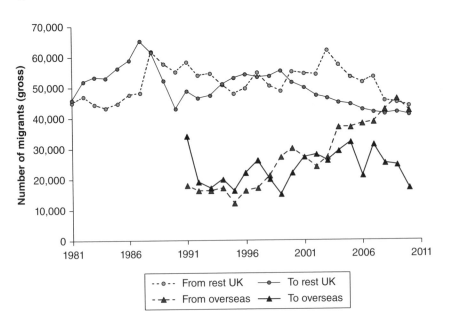

decline in population terms compared with England is the result of low levels of in-migration. However, as Anderson points out, in 2001 Scotland actually had a larger proportion of non-natives than England and Wales, and that this pattern goes back to 1945. What is different is that in-migration to Scotland comes from England, while, south of the border, that in-migration is from overseas.[2]

Understanding the diaspora

So far in this chapter we have treated 'migrants' and 'diaspora' as synonyms for each other. Is it at all meaningful to talk of the 'Scottish diaspora', and, if so, in what senses? Indeed, how applicable is the concept of 'diaspora' to Scotland's emigrants in any case?

'Diasporic studies' came on the academic scene in the 1960s, has had its own journal since 1991 and describes its remit as follows:

> *Diaspora* is dedicated to the multidisciplinary study of the history, culture, social structure, politics and economics of both the traditional diasporas – Armenian, Greek, and Jewish – and those transnational dispersions which in the past three decades have chosen to identify themselves as 'diasporas.' These encompass groups ranging from the African-American to the Ukrainian-Canadian, from the Caribbean-British to the new East and South Asian diasporas. (From journal flyleaf)

In a review of the field, Robin Cohen (2008) identified four phases of writing on diaspora studies. The earliest, in the 1960s and 1970s, focused on the classic examples, Armenian, Greek, Jewish, which still appear in the journal's descriptor above, plus, latterly, Irish and Palestinian. This, described as the 'prototypical' diaspora, is about being a victim. Cohen observes: 'In both established and embryonic victim diasporas the wrench from home must survive so powerfully in the folk memories of these groups that restoring the homeland or even returning there becomes an important focus for social mobilization' (2008: 4).

This conception was stretched in the 1980s by William Safran, who talked of 'metaphoric designation' to include 'expatriates, expellees, political refugees, alien residents, immigrants and ethnic and racial minorities tout court' (Cohen, 2008: 1). This stretching of the concept 'diaspora', however, made it difficult to draw a defining line. The third phase in diasporic studies, from the 1990s, sought to deconstruct the concept of 'homeland' such that diasporas became de-territorialised, home essentially being where the heart is. The final phase, in the twenty-first century, has tried to accommodate the earlier phases by consolidating features of the previous three.

In a critique of the concept and field of study, Rogers Brubaker has written of the *'Diaspora' Diaspora* to make the point that the concept has become so attenuated as to have little analytical leverage. Even where emigrant groups have been largely assimilated into 'host' societies, the concept of 'diaspora' loses its explanatory power. He observes:

The problem with this latitudinarian, 'let-a-thousand-diasporas-bloom' approach is that the category becomes stretched to the point of uselessness. If everyone is diasporic, then no one is distinctively so. The term loses its discriminating power, its ability to pick out phenomena, to make distinctions. The universalization of diaspora, paradoxically, means the disappearance of diaspora. (2005: 3)

Nevertheless, Brubaker tried to reconstitute three key elements of 'diaspora': first, that it is about dispersing people in space; second, that it is oriented to a 'homeland'; and third, that it has to do with 'boundary-maintenance' such that it persists over generations. The problem in his view is that diasporas are treated as bona fide actual entities, and are cast as unitary actors. Brubaker is a critic of what he terms 'groupism', the assumption that if we define people as such they behave accordingly (see Brubaker, 2002). He quotes, with approval, John Armstrong's comment: 'Clearly, a diaspora is something more than, say, a collection of persons distinguished by some secondary characteristic such as, for example, *all persons with Scottish names in Wisconsin* ... [T]he mobilized diaspora ... has often constituted for centuries a separate society or quasi-society in a larger polity' (quoted in Brubaker, 2005: 6; my emphasis).

Brubaker seems to be saying that there is more to a diaspora than sharing a 'secondary characteristic' ('*all persons with Scottish names in Wisconsin*'). They may have little to do with each other, or even know each other. Moreover, Brubaker argues that diasporas are not to be defined from the outside – etically,[3] as it were, from the observers' point of view – but, rather, as a *claim* made by social actors themselves:

We should think of diaspora in the first instance as a category of practice, and only then ask whether, and how, it can fruitfully be used as a category of analysis. As a category of practice, 'diaspora' is used to make claims, to articulate projects, to formulate expectations, to mobilize energies, to appeal to loyalties. It is often a category with a strong normative change. It does not so much describe the world as seek to remake it. (2005: 12)

So the key questions become: Who makes the claim to be a diaspora; and on what grounds, and why? How do they mobilise others they feel should belong? Who is included, and who excluded? Why does the diasporic claim arise at some points and not at others? In short, studying diasporas becomes much more akin to the study of cultural and social movements, set in particular social, cultural and political contexts. It also raises the issue of how successful organisations are at speaking on behalf of the self-defined diaspora. So, in Brubaker's terms, we should treat diasporas as categories of practice, project, claim and stance rather than a bounded group. In that regard, Brubaker is arguing that diasporas are defined in terms of identification and collective action rather than being defined from the outside.

Is there a Scottish diaspora?

We now return to our question: do emigrant Scots constitute a diaspora and, more to the point, do those who make such a claim speak for anyone but themselves? What, if anything, does it have to do with the 'homeland'? And, truth to tell, does that homeland afford recognition to the claimants, and in what sorts of context? These are key sociological questions.

If the Scottish government, speaking ostensibly on the part of 'the Scottish people', is willing to afford special status to 'Scots' of varying ilks – including 'ancestral and affinity Scots' – what should one make of that in sociological terms? If the government is keen to make a success of 'Homecomings', then does it matter that the definition of who is a Scot is a very elastic one? If the Scottish government's consultants number affinity Scots at between 40 and 50 million, vastly outnumbering people who live in Scotland, what are the implications of that, especially when we know that 'civic' rather than 'ethnic' definitions are what matter (see Chapter 13)?

Nevertheless, it is birthplace which is the key marker for being accepted as Scottish. For example, when we asked in 1997 how important or unimportant various markers were in order to be considered Scottish, eight out of ten people in Scotland said place of birth was very or fairly important, and almost half (48 per cent) that it was very important. 'Ancestry', defined as having Scottish parents or grandparents, was thought important by almost three-quarters of people (36 per cent said 'very important'), while living in Scotland – the classic 'civic' marker – by two-thirds (with 30 per cent saying it was 'very important').

So 'ancestry' is not an insignificant marker of being Scottish. Indeed, at the time of the first parliamentary election in 1999, we found that people in Scotland were more willing to give Scottish passports in the event of independence to those born but *not* currently living in Scotland (79 per cent) in contrast to those not born in Scotland but living here (52 per cent). Blood, it seems, matters.

Putative citizens

At the time of the Scottish Independence Referendum in September 2014, the Scottish government declared itself willing to award putative Scottish citizenship to everyone born in Scotland, to those living there and even to those from other backgrounds. Table 20.1 gives us insight into whom Scottish government might consider a 'Scot' in the event of independence.

Thus, everyone born and/or resident in Scotland would be awarded citizenship, including children of 'Scottish citizens' so defined above. Those with a parent or grandparent who qualifies for Scottish citizenship and, finally, migrants to Scotland or those who have spent ten years in Scotland may apply for naturalisation.

This is a broad and inclusive definition, but neither 'ancestral' Scots going back further than grandparents, nor 'affinity' Scots would actually meet the criterion. In any case, as far as diasporic identity is concerned, Brubaker's comment is apposite:

> It appears that what is usually counted, or rather estimated, is ancestry. But if one takes seriously boundary maintenance, lateral ties to fellow diaspora members in other states and vertical ties to the homeland, then ancestry is surely a poor proxy for membership in a diaspora. (2005: 11)

TABLE 20.1   Scottish Government's criteria for citizenship, 2014

Current status	Scottish citizenship?
At the date of independence	
British citizen habitually resident in Scotland on day 1 of independence	Yes, **automatically** a Scottish citizen
British citizens born in Scotland but living outside Scotland on day 1 of independence	Yes, **automatically** a Scottish citizen
After the date of independence	
Child born in Scotland to at least one parent who has Scottish citizenship or indefinite leave to remain at the time of their birth	Yes, **automatically** a Scottish citizen
Child born outside Scotland to at least one parent who has Scottish citizenship	Yes, **automatically** a Scottish citizen (the birth must be registered in Scotland to take effect)
British national living outside Scotland with at least one parent who qualifies for Scottish citizenship	Can **register** as a Scottish citizen (will need to provide evidence to substantiate)
Citizens of any country, who have parent or grandparent who qualifies for Scottish citizenship	Can **register** as a Scottish citizen (will need to provide evidence to substantiate)
Migrants in Scotland legally	May **apply** for naturalisation as a Scottish citizen (subject to meeting good character, residency and any other requirements set out under Scottish immigration law)
Citizens of any country who have spent at least 10 years living in Scotland at any time and have an ongoing connection with Scotland	May **apply** for naturalisation as a Scottish citizen (subject to meeting good character, residency and any other requirements set out under Scottish immigration law)

Source: Scottish Government: *Scotland's Future: Your guide to an Independent Scotland*, 2014: 273

Diasporic claims

So who claims to be part of the Scottish diaspora? Above all, Scottish–American associations predominate. There has been an astonishing growth in expressions of these. Thus, the number of 'Highland Games' in the United States tripled between 1960 and 1980, and then quadrupled between 1985 and 2003 (Devine, 2011: 276). So too has the creation of Scottish clan societies and 'family associations', the popularity of Highland dancing, and Scottish Country Dance groups.

The most prestigious Highland Games is the Grandfather Mountain Highland Games which attracts 30,000 people over four days (see Figure 20.3).

We might assume that this 'ethnic' revival is an expression of Scottish in-migration over the centuries. We find, however, that there has been a decline in such in-migration (by 1970, there were only 170,000 Scots-born people in the United States, fewer than at any time since the 1860s (Devine, 2011: 276)), but there has, in any case, been a falling away of Scottish associational life since the 1920s.

FIGURE 20.3
Grandfather
Mountain
Highland Games
(www.gmhg.org/
events.htm)

Source: Clan
Gathering (I am
grateful to the
Games Committee,
and to James
Shaffer, for
permission to use
this photograph)

This Scottish–American ethnic revival has other roots and causes. As Celeste Ray observes: 'Scottish–American ethnic organizations and celebrations reveal the creative and ongoing process of renegotiating history to produce a heritage that appeals in the present and are an American phenomenon rather than a Scottish one' (2012: 170). In any case, as Devine points out, this is strongly associated with the American South, a region in which few Scots actually settled. Indeed, more than half of what he calls 'neo-clansmen' lived in the South.

At the heart of this is SAMS – the Southern Scottish-American Military Society[4] which takes pride in military prowess; hence, the celebration of warrior culture seen to have infused US militarism. Devine points out that it was in fact the Scotch-Irish (from the North of Ireland) who settled in the South, and who now are enthusiastic participants in 'Highland' paraphernalia. There is a double irony in that these people are celebrating a Highland, Gaelic and Jacobite past which their forebears would have deemed anathema to their Lowland and Protestant values (see Figure 20.4).

FIGURE 20.4
Feeling at home
in the mirk:
Visitors walk
past the tents
and flags of
different Scottish
clans during
the Grandfather
Mountain
Highland Games
in Linville, NC

Source: Chuck
Burton/AP/Press
Association
Images

This exotic efflorescence of ersatz Scottish culture might invoke amusement, even embarrassment, among 'real' Scots, but Devine reminds us that in any case the transatlantic obsession with clans and tartans is simply a few steps away from a nineteenth-century reconstruction of Highlandism and tartanry in the 'old country'. These are differences of degree rather than of kind, reflecting in Devine's words, 'combined Highland dress and Confederate garb, a kind of Bonnie Prince Charlie meets Robert E. Lee lost-cause combo' (Devine, 2011: 285).

So what is it that accounts for this capture of 'Scottish culture' by the American South? Its clearest expression lies in the creation in 1998 of National Tartan Day and its promotion by Republican Senator for Mississippi, Trent Lott, who was Senate Majority leader. Lott's speech was loaded with *Braveheart* allusions, in which Scottish–Americans are constructed as heroic, pioneering and indomitable, and essential to the creation of American values. Euan Hague observed that National Tartan Day is 'simultaneously a celebration of Scotland and Scottish tradition and a commemoration of a romantic and traditional vision of the formation of the United States' (2002: 96). There is not much evidence for the notion that the Declaration of Arbroath in 1320 was the founding document for the 1776 American Declaration of Independence.

Ray points out that 'southerners take to Scottish heritage so well because its present shape draws not only on cultural continuities, but on parallel mythologies which underlie the construction of both Scottish and southern identities' (2001: 133). Ray was criticising a previous article by Edward Sebesta on 'The Confederate Memorial Tartan', who claimed that it was the expression of 'the neo-Confederate movement' with its connection between clan and Klan (Sebesta, 2000).

Ray admits to the plausibility of the connection 'in view of the way southerners often combine the Jacobite and southern "Lost Cause" mythologies' (2001: 135), but rejects the view that the Scottish heritage celebrations are political and racial rather than cultural. She comments:

> What they choose to remember, and celebrate, has little to do with the reality
> of the plantation era. They might be accused of reinventing traditions and history, but they generally embrace a polished vision of 'the past', not one which
> applauds slavery. Heritage is a rhapsody on history. We strike the chords we
> wish to hear. (2001: 137)

Celebrating hybridity

To understand the efflorescence of 'Scottish–Americanism', it is important to appreciate the remarkable turnaround in the notion of 'hyphenated Americans'. In his 1919 address in support of the League of Nations, Woodrow Wilson commented: 'Any man who carries a hyphen about with him carries a dagger that he is ready to plunge into the vitals of this Republic whenever he gets ready.'

In a cartoon from *Puck* magazine (9 August 1899), Uncle Sam sees hyphenated voters and asks, 'Why should I let these freaks cast whole ballots when they are only half

Americans?' (http://communicatingacrossboundariesblog.com/2011/07/27/perspective-of-a-hyphenated-immigrant/).

Ironically, it was black American Alex Haley's TV series *Roots: The saga of an American family* (1976) which breathed new life into the search for hyphenated Americans. Such people were no longer viewed with suspicion as turncoats with divided loyalties, a national identity fifth column, but as celebrants of multiple identities, combining the civic and the ethnic (Waters, 1990). Around 5 to 6 million people in the United States claim Scottish ancestry on the US census form. As Duncan Sim observes, among Americans there is 'a strong desire to be "from somewhere"' (2011: xviii).

In the accompanying notes on the US census form, we find these useful comments about 'ancestry', which are instructive:

The intent of the ancestry question is not to measure the degree of attachment the respondent had to a particular ethnicity. For example, a response of 'Irish' might reflect total involvement in an 'Irish' community or only a memory of ancestors several generations removed from the individual. A person's ancestry is not necessarily the same as his or her place of birth; i.e., not all people of German ancestry were born in Germany (in fact, most were not).

Currently, when someone reports more than two groups for their ancestry in the American Community Survey, only the first two ancestries are tabulated.

Some people identify their ancestry as American. This could be because their ancestors have been in United States for a long time or they have such mixed backgrounds that they do not identify with any particular group. Some foreign born or children of the foreign born may report American to show that they are part of American society. There are many reasons people may report their ancestors as American, and the growth in this response has been substantial.

The ancestry question was added to the census form in 1980, so the earliest information available from this question is from 1980.

About the Ancestry question

The Census Bureau currently collects ancestry data through the American Community Survey (ACS). The ACS question on ancestry is 'What is your ancestry or ethnic origin?' The text after the question provides examples of particular ethnic groups. The response area for the question consists of two write-in lines in which respondents can report ancestry or ancestries with which they identify. We code up to two ancestries per person. If a person reports more than two ancestries, we generally take the first two. For example, if a person reports German, Italian, and Scottish, we would code German and Italian.

What is helpful about these notes from the Census Bureau is that they spell out for us the 'official' rules for 'making Americans', and how to handle hybridity. What we cannot say, however, is how people themselves make use of them in describing who they claim to be.

There is, however, a contrast between Americans who make a claim to Scottish ancestry and recent migrants born in Scotland. Frank Bechhofer observes: 'The claims of the former are often extremely (occasionally laughably) tenuous. The claims of the latter, like Scottish migrants to England, are based on birth or parentage' (2012). The key methodological problem is one of self-selection if we choose to focus on those people who join Scottish–American societies: 'These are American Scots who have chosen to maintain links to their homeland through these various organisations. We learn next to nothing about those Americans of Scottish descent, presumably the majority, who are not involved in Scottish organisations' (2012: 2225–6).

Then there is the question as to what Scots (i.e. the people who inhabit the 'homeland') make of all this. Bechhofer's comment about the claims being 'tenuous' is more polite than most. Devine is similarly restrained: 'American–Scottish identities dramatically diverge from those of the homeland, where celebrations of kinship and supposed blood relationships formed on a clan name at Highland games are, to say the least, uncommon' (2011: 279).

Ray is more forthright. She claims that such activities make Scots feel 'embarrassed, indignant or exasperated about the stereotypical, tartanized notions of Scottish identity that transatlantic Scots embrace' (2012: 170). In truth, we do not know, except to say that the Homecomings of 2009 and 2014 in Edinburgh were not exactly aimed at indigenous Scots. Most probably saw it as an extension of the overseas tourist industry, events to be negotiated around rather than embraced.

This vogue for 'ancestral tourism' gravitates to the Highlands, at least as imagined as the essentialised topos. Ray comments: 'While their actual roots may be in Kelso or Peebles, interviewees often report feeling "more in touch with their Scottish heritage" on the Isle of Skye' (2012: 179). Ray herself recounts the conversation with someone she casually met at the Grandfather Mountain Highland Games in North Carolina and who compared the landscape with that of Kintail in Wester Ross. Her acquaintance said she missed it terribly – but she had never actually been there. 'Place' was vividly imagined through words, songs and film.

There is little intent to deceive. Here is a comment from the president of the Toronto St Andrew Society: 'The thing we [the society] do least well is interpreting present-day Scotland to the membership. We are aware of what is happening in and around Scotland, but the depth of our knowledge is not much more than watching TV news or Braveheart' (quoted in Sullivan, 2014: 63).

There is a nice example of the ambivalence of Scots to this transatlantic translation of Scottishness in the book by the historian James Hunter, who was commissioned by the Clan Macleod Societies worldwide to write up their accounts. He commented: 'To begin with, I was sceptical. Like many Scots, I regard clan societies with suspicion – not least because they purvey, or so it seems to me, a soft-focus and villain-less version of an often brutal and miserable past' (2005: 13). He came to terms with the phenomenon by acknowledging that such societies have their own agenda, and, in contrast, we have our own expectations that, as the homeland, they 'should conform with, or even defer to, our present-day conceptions of what it means to be Scottish' (2005: 25).

The 'diaspora' is perfectly entitled, he says, to its own agenda, for such people are not trying to *be* Scottish. It is about *them*; it is not about us. Nevertheless, there is the issue that, at least in institutional terms, Scots seek to buy into – in tourist terms, quite literally – this diasporic conception of being Scottish, without assuming that it has anything to do with them. Further, if the Scottish government sets out to trade on or with the 'diaspora', is it not buying into a foreign conception owing more to places of destination – the United States, Canada, Australia, New Zealand – not the place of origins?

In any case, as Ray observes:

> Through both physical manipulation and emotional attribution, Scottish–American community members transform spaces into meaningful places mimetic of a Scotland apprehended through folk memories and literature. Topophilia for specific Scottish landscapes is formative of a Scottish–American ethnic identity and serves as an effective hook in marketing 'ancestral tourism'. (2012: 168)

How others see us

We cannot be sure that this has more effect on the 'natives' than we imagine. After all, how others see us is a key support to who we think we are. This is also sustained by literature and film. The 'kailyard' which we discussed in the previous chapter was sustained by an émigré literature. T.D. Knowles (1983) argued that much of the output of writers like MacLaren, Crockett and Barrie was aimed at a wider British and American market, not simply, or not even, a Scottish one (see McCrone, 2001: 137 and 138).

In any case, as Willie Donaldson has shown, the local press was much concerned with social and economic change in Scotland, whereas it was the book trade which essentially catered for London and overseas markets. More recently, we have books with grandiose titles such as: *How Scots Invented the Modern World* (2001), by the American, Arthur Herman, who worked at the Smithsonian Institute in Washington, DC. This has the subtitle *The true story of how Western Europe's poorest nation created our world and everything in it.* That begs so many questions that it is hard to know where to begin. In any case, it is highly unlikely that a Scot would write such a '*here's tae us, wha's like us*'[5] book, and it can only be understood in the context of the émigré genre.

Filmic Scotland

What of film as sustaining a particular set of images of Scotland? Arguably, film (and television) imagery has a particularly powerful impact on how Scotland is imagined, possibly greater than the printed word. There is the now-famous comment by Forsyth Hardy, when he was film correspondent of *The Scotsman*, that the producer of *Brigadoon* could find 'nothing that looked like Scotland' and so constructed the mythical country in a back-lot in Hollywood (McCrone, 2001: 127). Contra those who argue that there is more to Scottish films than *Brigadoon*, Duncan Petrie (2014) has suggested that there are three dominant cinematic representations of Scotland in modern times:

- First, Scotland as a wild and rural periphery, and 'usually an island' if not geographically then culturally speaking. Examples include *Brigadoon* (1953), *Whisky Galore* (1949), *The Maggie* (1954), *The Wicker Man* (1973) and, more recently, *Local Hero* (1983).

- Second, Scotland is filmically represented as 'history', overwhelmingly drawing upon the Jacobites, Walter Scott and Robert Louis Stevenson. This too is 'rural', and draws upon picturesque Highland terrain of bens and glens, and is suffused with 'England' as the (common) enemy: 'This theme has proved particularly popular with Hollywood as it relies more directly on stereotypical "Scottish" signifier, but ideologically it also elides the Jacobites with Washington's forces in the American War of Independence' (2014: 223–4). Without worrying overmuch about historical accuracy, we can see how *Braveheart* ticks the boxes.

- The third tradition is a more modern (or modernist) one, portraying Scotland as urban, industrial and, above all, proletarian. Thus, we get 'gritty' drama with a cross-over between film and television, from *Just Another Saturday* (1975), *Just a Boy's Game* (1979), *A Sense of Freedom* (1980), *Shallow Grave* (1994) and, of course, *Trainspotting* (1996).

These genres, different though they are, help to structure 'Scotland' as filmic place. It is pertinent too that Wikipedia divides 'Films set in Scotland' into seven categories: films set in Glasgow; films set in Edinburgh; Harry Potter; the Jacobite Rising 1745; 'Kidnapped'; the Loch Ness Monster; and films based on 'Macbeth' (http://en.wikipedia.org/wiki/Category:Films_set_in_Scotland).

If you did not know Scotland, you would arrive with a very distorted view of the place. Former First Minister Wendy Alexander was not short of the mark when as Enterprise Minister in the first Scottish government ('Executive') she complained that Scotland is conventionally portrayed by three icons: 'Braveheart, Brigadoonery and bagpipes' (http://wayback.archive-it.org/3011/20130204052926/http://www.scotland.gov.uk/News/Releases/2002/04/1418).

And lest we think such representations are passé, the Pixar/Disney film *Brave* (2012)[6] and the *Outlander* series based on popular novels by the American writer Diana Gabaldon are the latest offerings.[7] Said the vice-president of Amazon Instant Video, which has the film rights: 'Filmed in Scotland and already hugely popular stateside, we can't wait to bring the show and its stellar cast of breakthrough British talent to the UK where we know there is a huge fan following already' (*The Herald*, 26 February 2015).

Does any of this matter? We might take the more sanguine view that these are products of the 'entertainment' industry, but they have a power and capacity to shape what

'Scotland' means. Thus, at the time of its release in 1995 *Braveheart* made good politics, if bad history. Nevertheless, the SNP produced a leaflet for the occasion: 'Today it's not just bravehearts who choose independence – it's wise heads – and they use the ballot box. You've seen the movie – now face reality.'

How Scotland is depicted on screen cannot but have a powerful effect on how others, and ourselves, see us. As Petrie observes, the indigenous film industry compares very badly in terms of financial investment with that of other small nations like Ireland, Denmark and Norway. It seems that we have the images, but not the wherewithal to make them represent Scotland more realistically.

Migrant identities: who do you say you are?

Thus far in this chapter we have dealt in representations, either of how others see us or how we choose to portray ourselves. What is missing from much of this literature is how those who do leave Scotland see themselves and their countries of origins and destinations. As Bechhofer observed, normally we learn nothing about those migrants who do not belong to diasporic associations, and who were born in Scotland. Indeed, most émigré Scots will have gone native, for that is their way, and has been for a century or two (Harper, 2003; 2012). 'Getting on' in the new worlds usually depended upon 'fitting in', working with, rather than against, the host society. Seeing oneself as 'victim' has not been the Scottish way, given that 'getting on' has frequently meant 'getting out'.

Scots in England

And what do we know of Scots who migrate to England, our biggest 'export market' for people? The census tells us that there are three-quarters of a million people born in Scotland living in England, by far the largest number of émigrés furth of Scotland. Are they a 'diaspora' according to Brubaker's criteria? Clearly, they live outwith Scotland, but what sort of orientation do they have to the 'homeland', and do they seek to preserve their national identity vis-à-vis the host society? How do they see themselves? Are they still 'Scots', or do they aspire to being British, or even English?

A key part of our research funded by the Leverhulme Trust involved the study of 'emigrants' – English-born people in Scotland, as well as Scots-born living in England. It is the Scots in England who interest us here (see Bechhofer and McCrone, 2012b). About a hundred were interviewed on three occasions over three years, one group living in Manchester and the other on the south coast of England (www.institute-of-governance. org/major_projects/national_identity_citizenship_and_social_inclusion_1999_2005). For some of these people, migration represented 'escape':

It was a conscious decision to move to England, I was determined that I was going to broaden my horizons, and that I didn't want to stay under the influence of the town, and my family, which I would have if I'd have stayed within a certain radius.

And another:

I knew that if I came to England I could start a new life. I could start to reinvent myself. No-one would know me, I wouldn't have that baggage of everyone knowing my family and telling my parents whatever I did. So it was always my intention to move to England.

Scottish migrants, based on the experiences of Scottish–English relations in Scotland, had mentally prepared themselves for a more difficult reception in England and had been pleasantly surprised. What did they experience when they got there?

I did feel like a typical Scot, off to this foreign land of England, where I probably had a, 'mistrust' isn't the right word, that's the wrong thing to say, more of a preconception about the English than they had of me.

Again:

I was quite surprised how nice everybody was, possibly because when you come from Scotland you are brought up to demonise the English, you know, they're this kind of monster race that keeps coming and killing us and I was quite surprised how civilised and pleasant everybody was.

Almost without exception, the Scottish migrants still claimed to be Scottish, saw such an identity positively, and did not consider themselves in any way to be 'English', nor, indeed, were they taken for such by the English themselves. 'Home' remained Scotland:

Scotland is absolutely definitely home, without any question, but I think it's because I spent most of my life there. And that's why I would think of Scotland as home.

And another:

I think you always go back to the place you're born, if the conditions were better. It's just the way it is in Scotland, at the moment, which is very hard. I'd love to get on a train today, and go back up there and work.

In particular, birth, upbringing, the distinctive Scottish education system, figure strongly in support of Scottish claims. Cultural differences too continued to matter:

The Scottish sense of humour can be very different. When I moved to London, people didn't understand my sense of humour perhaps as well as they did at home. It can be quite sarcastic and quite dry and I think people at times thought I was flippant. And I wasn't at all. If I'd been at home it would have been taken completely differently.

Did they think they had become anglicised willy-nilly? They usually interpreted this as a question about accent. For purposes of being understood, they had modified their accent – for 'English ears' – and find themselves being challenged by friends and relatives in Scotland for 'becoming English':

At work, I am a figure of fun, which I kind of like, 'cos it's very warm humour. I get teased a lot. Never, never in a cruel way, ever ever. But I remember my best friend from home came to visit and a colleague went up to her and said, 'Och aye the noo.' I remember that one time thinking, that's just not even funny, it's so pathetic.

There is no sense, however, that Scottish migrants have moved into a context where they feel under any pressure to become English. Most feel that, as Scots, they have been well received and there is little evidence to suggest that people in England are surprised that they claim their Scottishness rather than falling into a 'we're all British' line. Few Scottish migrants, we discovered, had a more heightened or positive sense of Britishness than Scottish nationals.

Unlike English migrants to Scotland, many Scottish migrants had moved to England to find work or follow a particular career path, and some held onto a 'myth of return' although practicalities relating to careers and family make such a move unlikely. There did seem an interesting contrast with English migrants to Scotland who appreciated the improved quality of life in Scotland, which influenced their unwillingness to return to England.

So what did they make of the host society, England? They spoke of their surprise, even bewilderment that 'English' national identity was underplayed, and that the English seemed in their experience unwilling to celebrate it:

England hasn't got a strongly defined culture. And it's kind of spread it so wide across the world it looks commonplace, so there's nothing definingly English. Whereas, holding onto tartan and kilt wearing is something that really reinforces the fact that we are Scottish, and nobody else does it. So it's a very, very strong icon.

And another:

I don't think the English have got the same sense of identity, which is rather sad. They've lost their identity, it was almost lost with the Empire. Very proud nation been laid low, in a way, laughed at even. I stand quite aloof, really, to some extent, 'cos I'm not English, but I still feel sad. It's dreadfully sad.

English iconography seemed, in their view, to be confined to periodic football tournaments and sporting occasions. These approaches to Englishness were contrasted with Scottish migrants' approach to their Scottishness. Indeed, several made a point of saying that in England they felt *more* Scottish than they had been in Scotland, celebrating their Scottishness by attending Burns' suppers, St Andrew's Day celebrations and wearing a kilt. These celebrations of Scottishness were seen by migrants as positively received by their English hosts, although they are also the context for national banter/jokes in the same way that football/sport is. The one context where Englishness comes to be celebrated by the English is sport, particularly major football competitions, and Scottish migrants not surprisingly saw this as quite natural and acceptable.

England is regarded by Scottish migrants as an identity context where issues of national identity are much less salient with regard to Scottish/English relations. Scots certainly are seen as 'different' by the English, but are judged to be 'acceptable' migrants. A large number of Scots contrasted their easy acceptance into England with what they assumed was a more difficult transition for English people into Scotland:

> I thought, you know, this is nothing like I was taught at all, they're not hooligans, and they're not anti-Scottish, and they don't want to invade our country and rape and pillage and all that sort of thing that's been, you know, drummed into you through the years. And I saw a totally different side of it.

Scottish migrants noted that concerns over migration generally lie elsewhere for the English, around issues of non-British migration, asylum-seeking, illegal entry, ethnic minorities within England, and European issues. The impact of devolution had begun to filter into English accounts, and migrants reported comments about Scottish MPs voting on English issues, the number of Scots in the Cabinet when Labour was in power, the Barnett formula used to calculate Scottish public expenditure, the costs of the Scottish parliament, and issues of public policy divergence notably relating to education (university fees) and health and social care (personal care for the elderly). Few Scottish migrants felt that devolution for Scotland had distanced them from the homeland, and few thought that as émigrés they ought to have had the right to vote back in the old country.

In broad terms, then, the claims to national identity among Scottish migrants to England were similar to those of Scottish 'natives'. They were Scots because of their birthplace and upbringing, and were happy to remain so. The view that national identity is fixed through birth and upbringing, and not open to change, even after lengthy residence in England, was widespread. There was very little evidence, in the eyes of our Scottish migrants at least, that a lack of residence in Scotland undermined their claim to being Scottish:

> I am actually quite proud of being Scottish. I like being Scottish. I just don't particularly want to live there. They are actually two distinct things if you think about it. You are Scottish. But it doesn't actually make a difference to where you live you know.

Another observed:

> I've got a very strong emotional tie with Scotland, but it's <u>not</u> because I live there. It's because all my *origins* are there.

They are, nevertheless, more inclined than Scots who have remained in Scotland to dwell upon 'roots' and ancestry. After all, given that Scottish migrants still wish to claim to be Scottish, because Englishness holds little attraction for them, they try to make the strongest claim they can to Scottishness so certain markers such as birthplace and ancestry figure prominently in national identity claims, to offset the lack of the residential qualification and a perceived marginal loss of accent:

> I think, for me, Scottishness as I was brought up with it, was about being sensibly proud of where you came from, because you, you had a history that was good. And in primary school history, you learnt more about the Scottish inventors, explorers. And I think, at the end of the day, we did believe the education system was very good, and gave you an entry into doing things. So there was a sense of pride in past achievements, the Scots were a nation to be reckoned with. The fact that we actually stood up for things, we seemed to believe and have certain values about things, and weren't afraid to stand up and say so. Honesty. And a sense that part of the Scottish ethic seemed to be you were willing to work hard to achieve things, and take responsibility for things.

And finally:

> I want people to know I'm Scottish. I'm proud of being Scottish, I'm proud of the Scottish Heritage, I'm proud of being part of it. We have lots of traditions, Scottish country dancing, types of music and traditions, the kilts and all that kind of thing, which I think is somehow lacking down here. I feel that's part of my identity. I was brought up with that around, it's part of my identity and the traditions I was brought up with, so in that sense it's important. But it's not the be-all and end-all.

Conclusion

So what conclusions can we draw about a 'Scottish diaspora'? First of all, emigration has been going on for centuries, and hence a large number of people around the world have some basis to claim to have Scottish roots, if they so desire. Some do, but many do not, although we have no way of knowing for certain. Our evidence from Scottish migrants to England is that they retain a strong sense of being Scottish, never think of themselves as 'English', and only rarely, and usually for political purposes, do they claim to be 'British'. 'Home' is Scotland, and seems to remain so even after long sojourns south of the border.

There is talk of 'return', but the constraints of family networks and careers make this unlikely to happen. It is also fair to say that Scots in England do not 'go native', nor do they proclaim national difference publicly. Angela McCarthy's analysis of Scottish voices held in the National Sound Archive at the British Library[8] reinforces our point, and complements what we found in our larger survey of Scots in England. She comments:

> Few Scots who settled in England in the twentieth century ... proclaimed the public nature of their identities. Nor did they reflect much on cultural representations of their identities such as literature, paintings and music. For Scots in England their national identity was less 'institutional' and 'cultural' and more a 'social-mental' conceptualisation. In this sense they were similar to their compatriots interviewed in New Zealand. (2005: 181–2)

Both our evidence and hers affirm the deeply 'personal' nature of national identity which we discussed in the previous two chapters. We are led, then, to conclude that 'diasporic' identity in the Scottish cases does not belong to the world of public and political action, for these are aspirational migrants rather than 'ethnic' players with irredentist longings. And in any case, as we saw in Chapter 13, issues of 'race' and ethnicity play out in different ways in Scotland and in England.

In short, Scotland is the land they have come from, and for which they retain a deep and personal affection, rather than an overtly political project about which they have strong views. In that regard, if Brubaker is correct in saying that 'diaspora' is a category of practice, a way of mobilising loyalties and energies for political action in the homeland, we might conclude that there is no meaningful 'Scottish diaspora' in his sense of the term.

What, however, of the Scottish–American diaspora? It is altogether a stranger, more exotic, phenomenon. It is based on 'ancestral' claims of a rather distant sort, driven very little by matters of what happens in the homeland, and much more by local – American – politics of identity. In short, this 'diaspora' is a creature of that place, that moment, with very little to do with Scotland as such, except as it is usefully imagined for domestic purposes.

For quite different reasons, then, the Scottish–American diaspora is metaphorical, but still worthy of being understood in its own terms. But it too is only a diaspora in a thoroughly attenuated way. There is considerable irony in the Scottish government treating as 'real' what is epiphenomenal, but those are the (post-)modern times in which we live. Lying behind the debates is the question: who is a Scot? Who has the right to make the claim? This leads us to the issue of representing Scotland. In the next chapter, we will tackle the question: who plays for Scotland? How significant is sport?

Chapter summary

So what have we learned in this chapter?

- That there has been a long tradition of emigration from Scotland, since at least the nineteenth century. Scots have been mainly 'economic migrants' with above-average levels of occupational and educational skills.

- That the Scottish diaspora is an imagined, cultural community based loosely on notions of ancestry and aspiration.

- That the Scottish–American diaspora has more to do with the internal politics of hybrid identity in the United States than with direct Scottish ancestry.

- That, in general terms and in that context, how 'Scotland' is represented owes far more to Hollywood than to Holyrood.

- That Scots living in England retain a strong sense of being Scottish while retaining a 'myth of return'. 'Scotland' remains the place they call 'home'.

Questions for discussion

1. Should we treat Scots as 'economic migrants' rather than 'refugees'? How, for example, do the Scots compare with the Irish abroad?

2. Given that so few Americans today have immediate Scottish ancestry, how would you explain the claims to Scottish culture in events like the Grandfather Mountain 'Highland Games'?

3. What are the connections, if any, between how Scotland is portrayed in film and television and the 'realities' of Scotland today?

4. How and why have successive Scottish governments sought to capitalise on the 'Scottish diaspora'? How successful have they been?

5. Are Scots permanently settled in England 'Scottish' in any meaningful sense of the term? Would you consider them to be a 'diaspora'?

Annotated reading

(a) There is a substantial literature on Scottish emigration, including J. Hunter, *Scottish Exodus* (2005); T. Devine, *To the Ends of the Earth* (2011); D. Sim, *American Scots* (2011); M. Harper, *Scotland No More?* (2012); M. Varricchio (ed.), *Back to Caledonia* (2012); T. Bueltmann et al., *The Scottish Diaspora* (2013); M. Leith and D. Sim, *The Modern Scottish Diaspora* (2014).

(b) On the sociological meanings and significance of 'diaspora', see R. Cohen, *Global Diasporas* (2008); R. Brubaker, 'The "Diaspora" diaspora', *Ethnic and Racial Studies*, 28(1), 2005; and the journal *Diasporic Studies*.

(c) On Scots living in England, see F. Bechhofer and D. McCrone, 'Coming home: return migrants in twenty-first-century Scotland', in M. Varricchio (ed.), *Back to Caledonia* (2012b); and A. McCarthy, 'National identities and twentieth century Scottish migrants in England', in W.L. Miller (ed.), *Anglo-Scottish Relations from 1900 to Devolution* (2005).

Notes

1   These estimates are referenced to internal unpublished working papers, so the calculations cannot be checked.

2   Using 1969–70 standardised figures, Michael Anderson calculates that the largest overseas migration came from south-west Scotland, Tayside, Glasgow and the Borders. Glasgow and north-east Scotland had the highest proportions migrating to the rest of the UK at this period.

3   To remind the reader: 'etic' in social anthropology refers to the account generated by the observer; 'emic' refers to that of the social actor.

4   For an example, see www.2jamisons.com/sams.html.

5   'Here's tae us; wha's like us? Gey few, and they're a' deid', is a boasting toast, usually used ironically. See Dictionary of the Scots Language (www.dsl.ac.uk/entry/snd/sndns2008).

6   The first line of the plot sets the tone: 'In Scotland, a child princess named Merida of the clan Dunbroch is given a bow and arrows by her father, King Fergus, for her birthday.'

7   Shot in Scotland and based at studios in Cumbernauld, arguably as culturally distant from the Highland setting as one could get.

8   She analysed six interviews collected as part of the Millennium Memory Bank project. Data are held at the British Library.

REPRESENTING SCOTLAND

21

PLAYING FOR THE NATION

It was a Scot, Bill Shankly, the Liverpool football manager, who growled 'Someone said that football is more important than life and death to you; and I said, "listen, it's more important than that".'[1]

Chapter aims

- To ask if sport matters in Scotland. Do Scots really care?

- To see if sport is 'war minus the shooting', as George Orwell claimed.

- To examine the connection between identity, both national and local, and sport.

- To ask if Scots are 'ninety-minute nationalists'. What, if any, is the connection between sport and politics?

- To examine if the connection between sport and nation/locality has been lost as a result of 'globalisation'.

Sport and politics

The relationship between sport (usually football) and politics is a familiar Scottish trope. Here is the political scientist James Kellas making the point in his book *The Politics of Nationalism and Ethnicity*:

> the most popular form of nationalist behaviour in many countries is in sport, where masses of people become highly emotional in support of their national team. But the same people may display no obvious nationalism in politics, such as supporting a nationalist party, or demanding home rule or national independence. (1998: 28)

This (lack of) connection between politics and sport was famously expressed by the Scottish nationalist Jim Sillars who complained that 'the great problem we have is that we sing

Flower of Scotland at Hampden or Murrayfield and that we have too many ninety minute patriots in this country' (*The Herald*, 24 April 1992). The phrase 'ninety-minute patriots/ nationalists' thereafter entered the political lexicon. The context was important. Sillars' comment was made two weeks after the British general election of 1992 which saw the Conservatives unexpectedly returned to power at Westminster, on an improved share of the vote in Scotland (25.6 per cent and an additional seat (from ten to eleven)). The SNP had only three seats to show for its increasing share of the vote (from 14 to 21.5 per cent).

This statement or its variants – eighty-minute nationalists, in the context of rugby – have served to problematise the fact that people can be fervent supporters of the national football team but fail to transfer that fervour to nationalist politics. Grant Jarvie and Graham Walker, who begin the introduction to their edited book *Scottish Sport in the Making of the Nation* with the Sillars' quote, observed that:

> This is a widely held view among Scots; there are many who share Sillars' exasperation and even more who regard the matter in a resigned way as proof that Scotland lacks the will to control its own destiny. The concept of sport as a 'substitute' in this sense has not been subjected to much critical interrogation; indeed, it has virtually attained the status of another myth. (1994: 1–2)

The focus in this chapter is on Scotland and its iconographic relationship to sport. We might wonder, however, what 'sport' means in this context. It is clear that we are talking about football, possibly rugby, but little else. If we treat football as the dominant Scottish sport (around 1.5 million attended Scottish Premier League games in season 2014–15, despite the absence of Rangers who played in a lower league that season), then it is reasonable to think of it as the premier game, at least in terms of spectators.

Arguably, that is how 'sport' is construed in the context of issues of Scottish culture and identity, although others, notably Grant Jarvie and colleagues, have reminded us that, football apart, there is more to it than that (Jarvie and Burnett, 2000).

We saw in Chapters 18 and 19 that the relationship between national identity and how people do their politics is a complex one, and that in this regard Scotland is not unusual. We may be tempted to dismiss sport as a benign pastime, as something not worth bothering about, but that would be to ignore its economic, social and cultural significance. Huge amounts of money are involved; millions of people are mobilised around the world; for some, it defines who they are. In other words, sport matters.

War by another name?

The writer George Orwell once famously observed that sport is 'war minus the shooting'. In his dyspeptic piece written for the left-wing magazine *Tribune* in 1945,[2] Orwell was commenting on the visit by the Russian football team Moscow Dynamo to the UK where they played Chelsea and Arsenal in London, and Rangers in Glasgow. The Dynamo visit is conventionally taken as signifying the beginning of the end of British hegemony in football, a few years before England were taken apart by Hungary at Wembley in 1953.

Orwell did not think much of the Dynamo visit, possibly reflecting his experiences, a few years before, of the Soviet Union during the Spanish Civil War, but generally he believed that sport is 'an unfailing cause of ill-will'. While playing cricket on the village green can be done for fun and exercise, he went on, 'serious sport has nothing to do with fair play. It is bound up with hatred, jealousy, boastfulness, disregard of all rules and sadistic pleasure in witnessing violence: in other words, it is war minus the shooting'.

While one should make allowances for journalists making a point in order to sell newspapers, Orwell's comments are serious ones. He was clearly having a go at the orthodoxy that if only nations played each other at sport (football and cricket, he thought), then they would have no reason to meet on the battlefield. Plainly, the 'Hitler' Olympic Games in 1936, and England's 'friendly' against Germany in 1938 where the England players were required to give the Hitler salute, reinforced the view that fascism and football went together, and the rest was a well-known history.

Perhaps we do not take sport seriously enough in social science. The 'neglect' in social science reflects the fact that until recently there was no social theorising about sport, merely descriptive accounts of how many people played or watched which sports; what we might call a *sociography* (description) rather than a sociology (explanation).

We might even claim that 'sport' is a modern invention. When our forebears worked twelve hours or more each day, they had little time and opportunity for 'leisure'. That 'sport' is modern might also seem strange, as the ancient Greeks are credited with inventing the Olympic Games, and Romans enjoyed gladiatorial contests. On the other hand, such 'sport' could be seen as an extension of warfare, either as preparation or as celebration of military prowess. '*Morituri te salutamus*' – 'we who are about to die salute you' – was how gladiators saluted the emperor.

Highland Gaming

Scotland has its own examples of the genre. The 'Highland Games' phenomenon, today unrecognisable from its origins, had functional roots. Hill races were opportunities for fleet-of-foot messengers to show their prowess; caber tossing showed proficiency at hoisting roof couples onto houses; and trials of strength which involved throwing weights around were generally useful in the days of heavy agricultural labour (Jarvie, 1999; Jarvie and Burnett, 2000) (see Figure 21.1).

The 'modern' form of such games derives from the nineteenth century and their adoption by lairds and royalty, first, in the early nineteenth century: the Braemar 'Gathering' (1817), St Fillans (1819), The Lonach (1823); and in the second half of the century: Ballater (1866), Aboyne (1867), Oban Argyllshire (1871) and Cowal Dunoon (1871). These subsequently spread to the Lowlands (still called 'Highland Games', however, even in a town like Airdrie) and to North America in the twentieth century. There, as we saw in the previous

FIGURE 21.1
Highland
Gaming: Adam
Patterson,
of Brevard,
NC, prepares
to throw the
hammer during
the 59th annual
Grandfather
Mountain
Highland Games
in Linville, NC

Source: Chuck
Burton/AP/Press
Association
Images

chapter, the most fantastical games took place, dating from the 1950s, the 'Grandfather Mountain Highland Games and Gathering O' Scottish Clans' (mission: *To carry on and promote the annual Grandfather Mountain Highland Games and Gathering of Scottish Clans, to foster and restore interest in traditional dancing, piping, drumming, athletic achievement, music and Gaelic culture* (www.gmhg.org)). 'Highland Games', offering prize money when athletics was strictly amateur, provided a circuit for professionals to make a living.

Does sport really matter?

Those who neither play sport nor follow a team may be properly sceptical. What evidence is there that sport in Scotland matters to people in terms of national identity, and, if it does, to whom? In the 2009 Scottish Social Attitudes Survey (following similar questions in the 2008 British Social Attitudes Survey), we asked respondents:[3]

> Some people feel more Scottish in some situations and less Scottish in others. Where would you put yourself on a scale in the following situations?

• When the national team are playing in a sporting event?

• When you are in Scotland/England (i.e. the 'other' country)?

• When you hear or read about the Scottish parliament (or the National Assembly of Wales)?[4]

- When you see images of or visit the English/Scottish countryside?

- When you hear, read or look at famous English/Scottish music, poetry or paintings?

Our list was attempting to cover a range of contexts: 'politics', iconic images, culture, being 'abroad' and sport. Surely, we might think, 'serious' matters like politics, and culture, would be at the top of that list? Not so; the most important turned out to be 'sport'. Seven out of ten Scots[5] put 'When the national team are playing in a sporting event' at the top of the list. As many as half (51 per cent) said that they felt 'a lot more Scottish' in this context, and 20 per cent 'a little more Scottish', summing to 71 per cent. Sport is ranked more highly than the 'countryside' (66 per cent), 'when in the other country' (i.e. England) (65 per cent) and above 'music, poetry and painting' (61 per cent), with 'devolution' on 30 per cent. So sport matters to people as an icon of national identity, and seems more important than politics in the scheme of things.

Nor is this simply a Scottish obsession, some kind of displacement for not having a 'proper' politics. As far as associating 'sport' with national identity, England is quite similar, with almost two-thirds feeling 'more English' when the national team is playing (44 per cent saying 'a lot more English' and 21 per cent 'a little more') (see Table 21.1).

TABLE 21.1 Contexts in which people feel 'more national'

% saying a lot or a little more national when:	English	Scots	English-Scots
National sports team playing	65	71	–6
Seeing images of/visiting countryside	54	66	–12
In other country (England/Scotland)	52	65	–13
Experiencing music, poetry, paintings	44	61	–17
Scottish parliament/National Assembly for Wales	40	30	+10*
Base	2138	1256	

* That the English feel more 'national' in the context of devolution for Scotland and Wales is an interesting finding, and possibly reflects the sense that growing nationalism in England has been partly triggered by the constitutional process (see McCrone and Bechhofer, 2015: chapter 6)

Sources: Scottish Social Attitudes Survey, 2009; British Social Attitudes Survey, 2008

Nor is it the case that this focus on sport relates to the strong presence of 'Scottish' national (and English national) teams which, unusually for 'stateless nations', play international sport. We find that 'sporting occasions like the Olympics when a British team is competing' figure in making people feel 'more British', even in Scotland. While we might expect English people to say this – and 68 per cent do – Scots are not that far behind (60 per cent), and, importantly, in both cases it far outranks the other items (when abroad, the national anthem, ceremonial occasions) (for full details, see McCrone and Bechhofer, 2015: chapter 3). Fewer Scots feel 'a lot' more British at sporting times compared with 'a little'

(22 to 38 per cent), but nevertheless 'sport' does have the capacity to make Scots feel 'more British' as well, indeed, as 'more Scottish'.

Furthermore, what get Scots annoyed most is when commentators confuse the terms Scottish/English/British in describing sportsmen and women. In the Scottish Social Attitudes Survey of 2011, we included a question asking respondents 'how annoyed' they got when descriptive niceties were not observed, such as calling the monarch the 'Queen of England', or Westminster the 'English' parliament and not the 'British' one, or calling the North of England simply 'the North'.

What riled Scots most? 'When the tennis player Andy Murray is "British" when he wins, and "Scottish" when he loses.' This item, rather than misnaming the monarch or the UK parliament, or getting the geography wrong, turned out to be what annoyed Scots most, with 32 per cent saying it annoyed them 'a great deal' and 17 per cent 'quite a lot'. The more 'Scottish' people said they were, the more annoyed they got (44 per cent of those saying they were 'Scottish not British' were annoyed 'a great deal', compared with only 12 per cent who said they were 'British').[6]

Sport matters – but to whom?

But surely, you might think, this is because the sorts of 'sport' people have in mind is gendered (football, rugby), and that, as a consequence, more men than women are likely to feel 'Scottish' in sporting contexts? Not so, it turns out. While there is a modest gender difference, 76 per cent of men and 68 per cent of women, the remarkable feature is how similar they are in 'feeling Scottish' on sporting occasions.[7]

For comparison, once more the English are not very different: 69 per cent of men and 62 per cent of women feel more English when the national team is playing.[8] When it comes to sporting occasions making people feel 'more British', we find that there is a very small gender difference in Scotland (63 per cent of men and 58 per cent of women) and virtually none in England (respectively, 69 per cent and 68 per cent).

If there was a gender dimension with relation to men and women following different sports, then we might have expected to see an effect generated by the most 'masculine' sports like football and rugby being the ones most 'national' (Scotland playing England, for example). However, we do not find this 'gender' effect, and so conclude that sport *tout court* has a widespread effect on making people, women as well as men, 'nationals'.

But surely there is a social class difference? What of the argument that feeling more 'national' has a social class dimension to it; that working-class people are far more likely than the middle class to be moved by sport? Once more, just as we do not find a major 'gender' gap, we do not find a 'class' one. Around three-quarters of Scots in the top social class (managers and employers) say they feel more Scottish when the national team is playing, compared with 69 per cent of those in manual jobs.

It is safe to conclude, then, that there is very little variation across the social class categories. There is, if anything, greater variation by social class in terms of 'feeling British' on sporting occasions, with those in higher classes tending to feel 'more British' (64 per cent of social class I, but 54 per cent of class V).[9] We get very similar results for English people. Thus, two-thirds across all social classes 'feel more English' when England are playing, and there is a similar differential compared with the Scots as regards 'feeling more British': 72 per cent of social class I and 65 per cent of class V.

So we cannot deny that 'sport' matters to people; it makes them feel more 'national' when 'their' team is playing; and the national character of 'their' may differ according to different sporting contexts – Scottish in football, British in Olympics, and so on. Furthermore, this is as true for women as it is for men, and across the social classes, as well as for the Scots and the English. The stereotype of the working-class Scot (or English, for that matter, the archetypal 'white van man' flying the English flag) being far more moved to national feelings by sport does not seem to stand up. It is as true for the middle class as it is for the working class.

Manly sports and moral fibre

Let us explore why this should be, with the help of some historical material. During the nineteenth century, in Scotland, England, and indeed throughout the British empire, 'athleticism' was a key feature of educational ideology in private schools (see Horne et al., 2011; Mangan, 2010). Athleticism was aimed at developing 'character', frequently underpinned by anti-intellectualism, anti-individuality and conformity (Horne et al., 2011: 863). James Mangan points out that between 1862 and 1890, 'the "games ethic" had spread throughout the middle class schools of Scotland' (2010: 268).

Loretto school near Edinburgh was a particular leader in the field, developing a cult of 'sturdy sporting manliness', under its headmaster, the splendidly named Hely Hutchinson Almond.[10] Principal Almond preferred 'vigorous manhood, full of courage to the languid, lisping babbler about art' (Mangan, 2010: 265). The focus on a 'Sparto-Christian' ideal was supported by a 'regimen of all-weather exercise, cleanliness, comfortably informal dress and fresh air' (Mangan, 2000: 77). An extreme example, Gordonstoun school in Moray, was founded by the German educationist Kurt Hann in 1934, and attracted royal patronage, with both the Duke of Edinburgh and Prince Charles alumni.

The success of 'Lorettonianism', as it was called, went far beyond the Scottish border, as this contemporary comment from the *Public School Magazine* of 1900 makes clear:

> It [inter-varsity rugby match] depicted a unique occasion: two Lorettonians, the respective captains of the Cambridge and Oxford XV's of the year, soberly shaking hands before the annual match and declaring, 'I think we've met before!' This meeting was the high point of a success on Oxford and Cambridge playing fields in the last quarter of the nineteenth century which was quite astounding. Loretto, this small, unpretentious and rather odd school, had five rugby blues

and one cricket blue at Oxford in 1880. The next year, eight out of the nine Lorettonians at Oxford played rugby for the University. In addition, one was captain of the cricket eleven and another president of the boat club. Three years later Loretto had eleven full blues at Oxford and seven played in the University match. Finally between 1884 and 1891 four Lorettonians held the captaincy of the Oxford XV. (Mangan, 2010: 266)

In turn, Oxford and Cambridge played key roles in disseminating this 'athletic culture', and thereafter reinforced the cycle whereby 'public' school appointments were imbued with the Loretto spirit. 'Manly men' had imperial appeal, quickly mimicked by schools abroad. The *Chronicle* reported in 1908:

> One of the nice things about footer [football] in India is that the teams are composed of players from a great number of schools. In our team, Rugby, Haileybury, Marlborough, Sandhurst, Bedford, Kelvinside Academy, Edinburgh Academy and Watson's are among the schools represented … in addition Winchester, Sedbergh, Cheltenham, Loretto and Fettes. (Reported in Mangan, 2010: 275)

We can see that by this time the ethos existed not only in 'public' schools such as Loretto and Fettes, but in merchant company day-schools like Watson's in Edinburgh. Mangan concludes that:

> The middle-class schools of Glasgow were certainly no longer simply Scottish but they were clearly not English. They were British institutions training Scots for the British Empire. As such they furnish fascinating illustrations of ethnic adaptation in the interests of survival, security and prosperity. And sport was central to this adaptation and to the cloning process that followed in its wake. (2010: 275)

Sporting values

In their research in contemporary 'independent' schools in Scotland, Horne and his colleagues show how sport was used to promote educational and social advantage (2011). Sport is judged to be character-forming, teaching creativity, endurance and teamwork, reflecting a considerable investment in sports facilities far in excess of what the state schools can afford. Further, this is as true of girls' schools as it is of boys' and co-educational schools.

To this day, private (and some state) schools in Scotland are involved in a network of inter-school sports, notably rugby, cricket (for boys), and hockey and lacrosse (for girls). The fact that fewer schools in the state sector play these games to any great degree, and rarely have the resources to do so, helps to reinforce the social exclusivity of the 'games ethic', apart, that is, from football (soccer). The rituals of criss-crossing Scotland by bus on a Saturday morning to play inter-school fixtures remains a distinctive feature of this culture, based at least implicitly on *mens sana in corpore sano* (a healthy mind in a healthy body). Out of such activities come key networks of local power and influence; being an 'old boy' (or 'old girl', for that matter) can have a pay-off in later professional life once the hockey pitch is far behind.

The connection between social class and sport is a familiar one. The old saw, attributed to Oscar Wilde, that football is a gentlemen's game played by ruffians, and rugby a ruffian's game played by gentlemen, makes the point. In writing about mountaineering in Scotland, David Brown has argued that mountaineering had two – class – phases. The first, in the 1920s, was dominated by those with sufficient economic and cultural capital, institutionalised in the Scottish Mountaineering Club: 'only the grand bourgeoisie of the SMC had the economic resources to practise the new sport that were way beyond the means of ordinary people' (Brown, 2009: 318).

Working-class mountaineers emerged from the 1920s in Glasgow and Clydebank due to easy geographical access to the mountains. Nevertheless, 'although working-class climbers existed in an almost separate social world from their upper middle-class counterparts, they were influenced by the culture of that world, with the result that there was little in the way of class conflict' (Brown, 2009: 319). The second phase, 'the decades of the proletariat' emerged in the 1950s in the form of 'weekending', which introduced less deferential climbing habits based on a joking culture and climbing ability, rather than on what Brown calls 'bourgeois mysticism'.

So far we have tried to establish that 'sport' is not some optional extra in people's lives and identities, but key to their sense of being Scottish (or indeed, English, and British too), reinforced across genders and social classes. In short, we have to consider seriously the sociology of sport in a wider social, economic and cultural context. Here we encounter the argument that sport has lost its 'local' moorings and become globalised.

Globalising sport

The globalisation thesis can best be summarised by reference to a special issue of the journal *Global Networks* (2007), entitled *Sport and Globalization: Transnational dimensions*. Writing with David Andrews, George Ritzer, possibly best known for his book *The McDonaldization of Society* (1993), focuses on the interaction of the 'global' and the 'local'. Their point is that these are not polarities, but 'complementary and interpenetrative' (2007: 136) and thus mutually constitutive: in particular, 'the *local* has been so effected [*sic*] by the *global*, that it has become, to all intents and purposes, *glocal*' (2007: 137, italics in original).

The interaction generates twin processes: *grobalization*, 'the imperialistic ambitions of nations, corporations, organizations, and the like and their desire, indeed need, to impose themselves on various geographic areas'; and *glocalization*, 'the interpenetration of the global and the local, resulting in unique outcomes in different geographic areas' (2007: 137). Such combinations generate the '*grobal*' and the '*glocal*'. The key organising institution in late capitalist society, they say, is the commercially driven corporation:

The commercial corporation is, effectively, the institutional vehicle through which late capitalism has become grobal; corporatized elements such as sport (education, religion, and health domains being equally applicable in this regard) becoming both a product, and an important process facilitating grobalization of late capitalism. (2007: 141)

The power of commerce

In this way, sport teams/franchises become transnational corporations – as in the English Premier League – which seek to contrive 'local' and indigenous sporting authenticity. Such corporations are adept at 'shaping and using glocal sport practices, symbols, and celebrities as conduits for realizing grobal ambitions' (2007: 141). Thus, Manchester United and David Beckham as exemplars. Further, global corporations such as Adidas, Nike and Reebok, and Coca-Cola, McDonald's and Vodaphone, have global domination of the 'product'. Events such as the Olympic Games, or the World Cup, are suffused with corporate dominance.

In the 2010 World Cup held in South Africa, a Dutch brewery was accused of using women fans to advertise its beer by dressing in identical short orange dresses sold as part of the gift package. 'What seems to have happened is that there was a clear ambush marketing activity by a Dutch brewery company', said the FIFA spokesman, seemingly offended because the official sponsor of the tournament was the competitor, Budweiser beer (www.bbc.co.uk/news/10321668).

Proposing to hold the 2022 World Cup in Qatar at the height of summer in 40°C temperatures, and, following protests, changing it to December just before Christmas, and in a country with no football-playing tradition whatsoever, reflects the power of transnational corporations to call the tune. Relatedly, television rights are the key to 'national' economic success, classically in the English Premier League (marketed internationally by its initials as the EPL), determined by transnational media organisations like News International (Sky Sport), or ESPN ('The World Leader in Sports'), a co-venture between the Disney and Hearst Corporations of America.

As if to make the point, the proportion of 'national' players eligible to play for England in the top four EPL clubs in 2015 (Chelsea, Manchester City, Arsenal and Manchester United, all owned by foreign capitalists) is a mere 22 per cent, down from 28 per cent in the previous season (www.theguardian.com/football/2015/mar/23/greg-dyke-fa-overseas-player-quotas). Put another way, more than three-quarters of the footballers in the top four English teams are 'foreign' nationals. The Chairman of the English Football Association, Greg Dyke, someone with extensive media experience in both commercial and public television, has proposed tough new rules concerning the balance of homegrown and foreign players lest the English national team continue to decline. He is unlikely to get his way with commerce.

Globalisation theorists such as Andrews and Ritzer are not convinced. They observe: 'the rescuing and resuscitating of the sporting local represents a highly questionable form of oppositional intellectual practice' (2007: 148). They say that 'it is impossible to re-assert the global–local distinction, and furthermore, such an assertion is simply to glorify the power of the actor, the local and more recently, the glocal' (2007: 149). Those who would assert the significance of the local, they claim, are simply glamourising the underdog, and showing their localist political sympathies which have no place in the modern, global world; which is quite a claim. Furthermore, this search for local identity and heroism qualifies for the label 'globaloney',[11] 'the elevation of one image – say, the heroic local sport fan and club – to represent globalization in its totality' (2007: 149).

Commodifying sport

The article by Andrews and Ritzer is possibly the most extreme of those in the special issue on *Sport and Globalization* which was edited by Richard Giulianotti and Roland Robertson. Robertson has been credited with creating the concepts of the *glocal* and *glocalization* (Robertson, 1992; 1995), and has combined with Giulianotti whose expertise is in the sociology of sport (Giulianotti, 2005b).

Elsewhere, Giulianotti has commented that 'as a core element of postmodern popular culture, sports dominate greater and greater volumes of media content and are bloated by hyper-commodification' (2005a: 210). Other contributors to the *Global Networks* issue such as Rumford focus on cricket, and argue for its 'post-westernization' with the International Cricket Council (ICC) acting as a 'global entrepreneur'. This is an interesting case, for cricket grew up as a British 'imperial' sport, and is by and large only played to a high standard either in (some of) the white dominions (Australia, New Zealand and South Africa), or in the Indian sub-continent (India, Pakistan, Bangladesh and Sri Lanka) and the West Indies, apart from the 'home' country of England.[12]

One cannot deny that sport has become internationalised; indeed, that is necessary, otherwise national teams would have no one to compete against. Nevertheless, as the social anthropologist Thomas Eriksen observed, Ritzer's approach and theories of globalisation are limited because they rule out the possibility of *anything* being merely local (Eriksen, 2007). Eriksen argued that there are many sports which remain 'local', or at least regional, such as winter sports, and cricket.

Eriksen, a Norwegian, makes the point that most sports are *not* global, but embedded in a selective cultural geography (including winter sports). The best examples are sports played in North America, notably baseball and 'American' football which, with very few exceptions (Cuba and Japan in the case of baseball), are not played professionally anywhere else in the world.[13] That does not prevent them from being thoroughly commercialised, with branding and product accessorising. Thus, teams like the New York Yankees, Boston Red Sox, Dallas Cowboys, LA Lakers and ND Fighting Irish are *global* brands, while playing all their league games in the United States. If we simply focus on sports such as football, which does have (almost) worldwide appeal, then we miss the key point of the relationship with the local fan base.

Global United

What the globalisation thesis tends to do is to treat such a base as 'international' and to ignore the local. After all, one cannot imagine a sports team with no local or national supporters, but simply a global brand. It would, for example, be impossible to think of Manchester United being rebranded as Global United, with its fan base anywhere but Manchester. It is impossible to imagine football teams (and you always require opponents to play against) playing behind closed doors to an Internet audience. That way lies commercial perdition.

Foreign club owners have sought even to change the names of long-standing clubs. Thus, the owner of Hull City, Egyptian-born Assem Allam, wanted to change the name of the club to Hull Tigers to give it greater 'international' appeal, especially in the Far East.[14] Similarly, the owner of Cardiff City, Malaysia-based Vincent Tan, dropped the traditional blue kit and the Bluebird crest 'to appeal to international markets', in favour of red shirts and a dragon motif (conveniently, a Welsh as well as a Far East symbol), later dropping the dragon (www.bbc.co.uk/sport/football/30741073).

Nor can we be sure who supports which teams and why. Eriksen gives the nice example of his 9-year-old son who took against the Swedish footballer Zlatan Ibrahimović. Eriksen assumed that this was for 'national' reasons (historic rivalry between Sweden and Norway), or that the footballer was of Yugoslav origin. It turned out that his son's dislike of the player was because he had played previously for the Italian club Juventus, which clashed with his son's support for the English club Arsenal. Thus had transnational media made viewers familiar with international sport, and, in the nature of it, generated support (and non-support) for quite convoluted reasons.

Defining the local

There are sports, on the other hand, which are closely linked into national dimensions, sometimes for distinctly political reasons. Thus, in Ireland, the Gaelic Athletic Association (GAA) was founded in the 1880s to connect up with nationalist feeling, vis-à-vis 'British' sports such as football, which was known as 'the garrison game', played in towns where British garrisons were located (see Hannigan, 1998). Thus, hurling and Gaelic football were devised as 'indigenous' to Ireland, and not the property of the British coloniser. It is also true, however, that a century later Ireland (the Republic, that is) has a more than passable football team, and in 2015, the all-Ireland rugby team won the Six Nations tournament.

Simply treating the extremes of globalised sport as the norm fails to convey the myriad sports which are based on local and national rivalries. The other aspect which the globalisation of sport thesis underplays is why, in any case, people support a team as 'theirs'.

The most obvious forms of association are usually local (Manchester United, Celtic, Heart of Midlothian, Nottingham Forest), especially where there are historic local rivals (Manchester City, Rangers, Hibernian, Notts County). Without an 'other' vis-à-vis '*our* team', it is hard to generate loyalty, something we can see when the owners of a club move it away from the local area in London. Wimbledon FC became M(ilton) K(eynes) Dons, for example. So infuriated were some supporters that they formed AFC Wimbledon, using the old crest and colours. By 2016, the 'old' club was in League Two and won promotion to League One.[15]

Nevertheless, it is hard to establish new loyalties and associations; for example, Edinburgh Ferranti Thistle, a works team, was renamed Meadowbank Thistle in 1974, and was moved by the owners to Livingston new town in 1995 where it became Livingston FC. (One wonders whether there are any of the original supporters of the works team left who have transferred their allegiances to the West Lothian club 25 miles (40 km) away.)

Nations are us

Such an approach also underplays the 'national', which is the fundamental basis of international sports competitions. We may not wish to argue, with Orwell, that sport is war without the fighting, but supporting 'us' against 'them' is the bedrock of social rivalry and an outlet for national identities (Figure 21.2). The key point about the Olympic Games is that 'our' nation competes, is entered in the league table of medals, and that there is a medals ceremony at which the *national* anthem is played for the winners.

There is sufficient force in 'national' myths that they spill over into politics. Thus, England's victory in the 1966 World Cup was deemed a good omen ('the feel-good factor') for the-then Prime Minister Harold Wilson to call a snap general election – which he won. Again, the hubristic display of the Scotland manager Ally McLeod at the 1978 World Cup,

FIGURE 21.2
Dressed to kill: Scottish fans wait for the kick-off between Scotland and England in their Euro 96 Championship clash at Wembley

Source: BUTLER/ Press Association Images

and notably defeat against Peru, was sufficient to generate a view that it contributed to the outcome of the political referendum of 1979 which resulted in no devolved assembly for Scotland (see the famous cartoon of the 'feart lion' by Turnbull, reproduced in Chapter1; see Figure 1.4).

We do not have to believe in cause and effect to think that the emotive power of sport in symbolising the nation is a powerful one. There is also the presumptions of 'national character' which surround sport, nicely expressed by Winston Churchill who is reputed to have said: 'Italians lose wars as if they were football matches, and football matches as if they were wars' (https://www.theguardian.com/football/2008/apr/01/europeanfootball.sport1).

Globalisation theorists are uncomfortable with locating sport in the 'national' context; 'national society' usually equated with the state. Seemingly, this has been superseded by neo-liberalism and 'international governance' (such as FIFA, IOC, ICC).[16] It is a model which struggles to make sense of national sentiment other than as a residue of outdated social and political forces. Thus, Frank Lechner, in *Global Networks*, analyses the relationship between national identity and football in the Netherlands, notably the Dutch national football team, *Die Oranje*.

Lechner comments:

> In claiming soccer distinction, the Dutch resemble others. This fact suggests that, like many such claims, the Dutch one may in fact embellish a collective memory, idealize a particular view of Dutch soccer, distort its actual record, and turn extraordinary events and people into emblems of perennial Dutch qualities. (2007: 222)

He continues: 'The way the Dutch view themselves as a unique soccer nation fits familiar global patterns. A sociologically informed critique of their romantic soccer self-image displays the myth as myth' (2007: 226). Lechner, we might argue, misses the point: why the 'myth' should be so powerful and persistent, and held to be self-evident among the Dutch *Oranje*, possibly juxtaposed to the German Other, deemed to be 'dour and mechanical' (2007: 216). Globalisation theorists too readily buy into the comment by Ulrich Beck that 'the national [is] a sociological zombie category' (Giulianotti and Robertson, 2009: 172).

Whatever the internationalisation of sport, its association with 'place', whether local or national, is powerful. Otherwise, we have no way of understanding why people in such large numbers pay good money to follow 'their' team, and to identify so strongly with it, unless we simply fall back on arguments about false consciousness on a global scale.

Following the nation

The Scotland vs England fixture is surrounded by media claim and counter-claim. As Moorhouse commented:

the Scots have always crossed the border surrounded by an "ideology" which, probably more than any other travelling support, speaks of battles, raids, armies, troops, invasions, hordes, sacks and the like. This is true of the chants and banners of the fans, but also of media reports in Scotland and England. (1989: 213–14)

Tartan Army

Established in 1980 as the Scotland Travel Club, the Scottish 'Tartan Army' was aimed at improving fan behaviour when 'abroad' (especially England) and received the commendation of Scotland's then-First Minister Jack McConnell for its 'worldwide reputation', in 2002. The deteriorating reputation of England's football fans for hooliganism became the opportunity for Scottish fans to be 'not English', as it were, by behaving contrarily well (see Figure 21.3).

Since the 1980s, the Scots have adopted a holier-than-thou approach: 'The Scots note every "outbreak" of English hooliganism, counterposing them to the "trouble-free" state of Scottish soccer' (Moorhouse, 1989: 218). Indeed, the more following England became associated with the far right and the National Front, the holier, and more progressive, the Scots could be.

Thus, says Giulianotti, 'contrasts were routinely drawn between the gregarious demeanour of Scottish fans and the misdeeds of English supporters at the same [1982] tournament' (2005b: 292). Codes of conduct and forms of 'self-policing' were observed; the kilt became the standard form of dress (a 'Tartan Army tartan' was invented and registered with the Scottish Tartan Authority)[17] and, significantly, all forms of club colours were banned.

FIGURE 21.3
The Tartan Army, Scottish football fans, on the steps in Trafalgar Square

Source: John Stillwell/Press Association Images

Giulianotti commented: 'Football matches provide the Tartan Army with the cultural circumstances in which the sociable interplay of conflict and concord occurs pleasurably and peacefully' (2005b: 293). This is a 'play form of association par excellence', which is playful, expressive, carefree and joking. You are required to 'join in', to take pride in banter and 'crack' (*crac*: fun), and ignore social or economic differences between the supporters. Standing your round of drinks reinforces reciprocity, and cultural conformity is expected in the interests of social solidarity and not 'letting the side down'. Giulianotti concludes: 'the Tartan Army furnishes its individual participants with a common array of identity touchstones, a set of props and audiences, for the creative cultivation of fresh forms of *meaningful* (not egocentric) individuality' (2005b: 301, italics in original).

The 'army' metaphor is well chosen, for it draws upon the military tradition of uniform(ity) and behaviour, evoking a recognisable iconography at home and abroad. As Neil Blain and Raymond Boyle observe:

> No metaphor is so familiar in descriptions of Scottish sport as the military metaphor. It is used frequently by other nations' journalists to describe their teams' performances. But in Scotland it is the core of the nation's perception of itself. (1994: 130)

There are distinct echoes of what David Hesse described as 'warrior dreams' (see Chapter 17), in which Scottish play-acting – non-Scots dressing up as Scots, but without claiming to be such – acted out the parts. The 'real' Tartan Army, as it were, Scots dressing up as 'Scots', simply reinforces the cultural practices. It is also amplified by other 'nationals' dressing up in outré fashions to celebrate their national side, notably *Oranjegekte*, 'Orange craze', during international football tournaments. Revealingly, the comment is made online that '*Oranjegekte* has been compared to the Scottish Tartan Army – both, it is argued, are elements of national identity formation, simultaneously personal and collective, and not rational'[18] (Dejonghe, 2007: 95). So, too, is the *Roligan* movement, a pun on the word *rolig* in Danish, meaning 'calm', and juxtaposed to 'hooligan' (https://en.wikipedia.org/wiki/Roligan). The website refers the reader to 'The Tartan Army, the supporters of the Scotland national team, who are equally renowned for their peaceful nature.' *Plus ça change* …

More than a football team …

It is true, of course, that *Die Oranje* are a far more successful football team than Scotland's, who have not qualified for a major international tournament since 1998, but the performative quality of the fan base belies its dependence on results. That aspect of *Die Oranje* is the key aspect missing from Lechner's analysis of Dutch football. This capacity to be an expression of national identity as 'myth' in the anthropological sense[19] is surely worth noting.

Nor does it not simply relate to national teams. For example, the Catalan football team *Barça* (Barcelona FC) are described as '*més que un club de fútbol*' ('more than a football club'), reflecting their community involvement, but above all, their quasi-national symbolic significance for a 'stateless nation', Catalonia, which does not have institutionalised identity – like Scotland – in international sports.

While it is sensible to focus on the 'international' aspects of global sport, notably football, it is grounded in highly local and national attachments. In any case, being able to identify yourself as a 'nation' or a community is aided considerably by international acceptance. The fact that 'Scotland' has been for more than 100 years part of the 'home nations' in sports such as football and rugby largely created in these islands has helped to reinforce the existence of its nation-ness.

The world's first international football match was played between Scotland and England in 1872 (the score, appropriately, was 0–0), and the British Home Championships were formed in 1884 such that the four British nations (England, Scotland, Wales and (Northern) Ireland) played each other annually until the 'home internationals' were abolished precisely 100 years later.[20]

Who gets to play?

'National' identification with 'the team' is commonplace, and we saw earlier in this chapter that people see in sport a way of feeling 'more national', regardless of gender and social class, and as true of England as it is for Scotland. The criteria for selecting 'nationals' have been stretched in recent years as the pool of indigenous skill and expertise has diminished. The complexity of FIFA's eligibility rules are a wonder to behold (https://en.wikipedia.org/wiki/FIFA_eligibility_rules). The Scottish Football Association (SFA) issued a set of rules as follows:

On the occasion of the meeting of the International Football Association Board on February 27, 1993 the four British associations ratified the following agreement, which came into force on February 1, 1993, on the criteria which should determine the eligibility of the player to be selected for one of the national teams of the British associations:

His country of birth.

The country of birth of his natural mother or father.

The country of birth of his natural grandmother or grandfather.

Where the player, both natural parents, and both natural grandparents are born outside the UK, but the player is the holder of a current British passport, he may play for the country of his choice. (Scottish Football Association)

In 2008, the Spanish-born Nacho Novo, who had played in Scotland for eight years, became the centre of a controversy about who is a Scot for sporting purposes (the 'McNovo' controversy, as it was called).[21] The SFA reinforced its view that the four 'home nations' had a gentlemen's agreement that eligibility would not go beyond having at least one grandparent born in the nation in question.

The Scottish Government Sports Minister at the time, Stewart Maxwell, argued for a far more open criterion based on residence: 'if you pledge your allegiance to Scotland, whether it's because you were born here or whether you are a naturalized citizen,[22] that's entirely reasonable. Everyone should be treated the same way.' Maxwell's 'civic' view did not prevail over the SFA's 'ethnic' criterion, and 'McNovo' never did play for Scotland.

National rivalries

National and international rivalries may be exploited or (mis)interpreted by politicians, but rarely are substitutes for the real thing. There was the instance of *'la guerra del futbol'* between El Salvador and Honduras, lasting for 100 hours, in 1969, triggered by the local qualifying round of the 1970 World Cup, but this was more a catalyst than a cause, an unusual case perhaps of sport being 'war *plus* the shooting' (to paraphrase Orwell). See Ryszard Kapuscinski's book *The Soccer War* (2007) for a good account.

National rivalry, however, runs deep. As befits the oldest 'Internationals' in the world, games between England and Scotland have long been symbols of cultural/political differences. The segregation of fans these days usually means that 'trouble' does not ensue, at least inside the grounds. There are interesting situations in which watching 'the game' in the company of 'the other' may become fraught.

Nor does it require both sets of fans to be present, merely that supporting 'anyone but Scotland/England' may surface, as in the account of one émigré Scottish professor watching – in England – a 2015 World Cup qualifying match between Scotland and Gibraltar, and finding it a most uncomfortable experience (see www.heraldscotland. com/comment/columnists/in-more-than-25-years-of-living-in-england-i-have-never-encountered-such-animosity.122483764).

Scots have long been accused of supporting 'anyone but England' (ABE), especially as Scottish teams rarely qualify for international tournaments these days. This is often seen as an odd, even reprehensible, thing to do, as if supporting your historical rival ('auld enemy') was your next best choice. There are many systematic rivalries such as Australia/New Zealand, France/Italy, even (especially) France/England ('frogs'/les rosbifs) (http://news.bbc.co.uk/1/hi/uk/2913151.stm). And there is nothing quite like a football song sung by English fans, called 'Two World Wars and One World Cup' (to the tune of Camptown Races), which makes the point about sport having a lot to do with war *and* shooting. Presumably sharing the same state makes Scottish/English rivalry less acceptable, at least to some.

Supporting England in lieu of Scotland seems the exception not the rule, sometimes seen as deriving from an 'underdog mentality', or indulging in *Schadenfreude*, taking pleasure in the misfortune of others. Stuart Whigham has pointed out that people's own preferences (what he calls the 'ontological narrative') frequently take second place to the 'public narrative' in which it is expected that ABE will apply to Scots migrants living in England.

In his study, none of his respondent Scots living in England expressed anti-English sentiments but took some satisfaction ('relief', in their words) if and when England were knocked out of a tournament, if only because the (English) media became far less partisan as a result. He also pointed out that having 'English' children made one less vociferous in supporting Scotland. Said one, 'why should I entertain anti-English ideas if my kids are English?' (Whigham, 2014: 169).

For those who live on the border between Scotland and England, there are further challenges if you play sport. Because jurisdictions operate, teams have to register in one country or the other, a pragmatic decision in the main, so as to maximise the number of games. In a study of a women's rugby team, Fiona Gill shows how 'Bordertowners' handle ambiguity in their ascribed identity by embracing and performing it:

> The ambiguity, far from being suppressed or hidden, is expressed through the constant mention of the mixed national character of the town, through the banter between players and throughout Bordertown, which has an explicitly national character. This strategy avoids being confrontational because it is a performance of a local identity expected by outsiders to be ambiguous. (Gill, 2005: 99)

Gill argues that 'performing ambiguity', that is being both Scottish and English, and above all 'local', is their preferred way of behaving and bonding because it minimises conflict.

We have made the point in this chapter that the essence of team sports is that they represent 'us', that they capture who 'we' are, and, crucially, who we are not. Without the vis-à-vis there would effectively be no such sport. Neither would two teams named after their sponsors – let us call them Nike vs Adidas, or Coca-Cola vs Pepsi – be taken seriously as international competitors on the field. Fundamentally, they need us more than we need them. Two teams called Yokohama Rubber (Chelsea FC) and Chevrolet (Manchester United) would draw puzzled looks rather than excite loyalties.[23]

Locality matters

In this next section, we explore local rivalries, and in particular those between Glasgow rivals Celtic and Rangers. This so-called Old Firm rivalry, however, is but one of many rivalries between places, and 'tribes'. In many ways 'place' rivalries are the norm, and not just in Scotland. They are often expressed as 'derbies' between and within cities (Hearts vs Hibs; Aberdeen vs Dundee/Dundee United; St Mirren vs Morton; Inverness CT vs Ross County; and so on). Often they are expressed in ribald caricatures about the opposition and take the form of ritual abuse. They can even reach down to more esoteric local differences (who can explain Ayrshire junior football teams Auchinleck versus Cumnock in anything like rational terms, apart from sheer or mere difference?). When we carried out our ethnographic research on Berwick-upon-Tweed, we encountered complex rivalries with other local towns (Eyemouth, Duns or, indeed, 'anywhere-but-Berwick').

A boys' game?

It is, however, the Celtic/Rangers rivalry which is best known, and elevated into something of a political cause célèbre. Are we dealing here with 'just a boy's game',[24] or are these rivalries deep-seated and reflective of wider social and ethnic divisions? Deciding where you stand on this binary explanation is a dividing line in academic terms. On the one hand are writers who view Old Firm rivalry as the tip of the deeper iceberg of religious bigotry and sectarianism. On the other hand are those like Bruce (see Chapter 14), Rosie and Moorhouse who see it largely as an iceberg with very little depth.

Writing in 1994, Moorhouse commented trenchantly:

> In my view, [the] study of Scottish football and Scottish society would benefit if academics and journalists would put a moratorium on the use of a whole bundle of terms like 'sectarianism', 'sectarian hatred', 'bigotry', 'tribalism' (a lovely example of racism being used to condemn 'prejudice'). (1994b: 192)

He argued that claims of sectarianism ought to be based on hard evidence 'other than the chants at Old Firm games' if we wish to show that a 'religious divide' really does function in modern Scotland. In a later article, Moorhouse (2006) argued that 'football hooliganism' has been dominated by English examples despite being a global phenomenon, and as such is both badly studied as well as over-studied, thus losing much purchase on developments in modern societies, while reflecting a moral panic about violence and sport.

And just to prove that team loyalties are 'leaky' and complicated, even incomprehensible, attaching to the Old Firm is support for adversaries in the Middle East. For reasons no one has properly explained, except in appeals to 'freedom' over 'tyranny' on the one hand, and loyalty, law and order on the other, Celtic fans associate themselves with the Palestinian cause, while Rangers align with Israel.

Given the supposed virulence of Celtic/Rangers rivalries, it is interesting to read the accounts of fans who emigrate to North America, ostensibly taking their loyalties with them (see Giulianotti and Robertson, 2007a). Both clubs have NASCs (North American Supporters Clubs) and use their new culture pragmatically to maintain old identities. While extensive social relationships between club supporters on either side of the Old Firm divide are rare, social and cultural reciprocity is common. Said one of their informants:

> We've got a lot of pals in the Celtic social club, and if we run out of beer … we'll ring them up and they'll send us over a crate, so we've got good friendships … the whole attitude's different. You still get the oddballs, the real bigoted individual, but I don't think it's nearly as bad as it is back home (Rangers social club official, Ontario). (In Giulianotti and Robertson, 2007a: 143)

The point of the comment is not to assume that it is 'as bad as it is back home', but to render the Old Firm attachment appropriate to its new social and cultural context. What exercises both sets of overseas supporters' clubs most of all is the threat that new technology such as 'pay-as-you-go' television will render redundant the desire to meet at the club to share with other people recordings of the latest game, however vicariously, rather than watching it alone on the home sofa.

Only a game?

So does this imply that 'back home' Old Firm rivalry continues unabated, often with violent outcomes? A Scottish-government-funded advisory group on tackling sectarianism in Scotland published in 2015 (http://news.scotland.gov.uk/News/Minister-welcomes-sectarianism-research-1631.aspx) commissioned survey research which showed that 'football' was the most commonly mentioned factor which people *believed* to be contributing to sectarianism (88 per cent, with 55 per cent saying it was 'the main cause'). Loyalists marches came second (79 per cent) and Irish Republican marches third (70 per cent). However, the survey by ScotCen (details at www.gov.scot/Publications/2015/02/5330) showed that a majority (58 per cent) of people in Scotland did not support *any* football team, with 12 per cent each supporting Celtic or Rangers.

The media meanwhile fell back on the equation 'football = sectarianism' as reflected in the covering headline from *The Herald*, 'Official studies: it's football which fuels Scotland's sectarianism, not parades', even though the report pointed to the key role of families, and especially grandparents, as agents for socialising children into sectarian beliefs. Old stereotypes die hard. That figure (58 per cent) that most people in Scotland do not support *any* football team would seem to weaken Shankly's famous statement that football was far more important than life and death.

Conclusion

We have seen in this chapter that sport matters in Scotland. It not only heightens national feeling, across genders and social classes, but might only be accused of mild exaggeration in terms of its life and death possibilities. Plainly, representing the nation on the sports field has a long pedigree in Scotland. Only the Olympic Games in which there is a British presence are the exception, although the authorities reluctantly accepted that, unlike London

2012, there were no 'British' football teams, men or women, at the Rio Games in 2016 because of opposition from Scotland, Wales and Northern Ireland who fear for their institutional independence.[25] That is a measure of how much a cultural carrier national sport is, and why 'playing for the nation' carries such cultural and political power. Its amanuensis has frequently been the 'national' press, and that is the subject of our next chapter.

Chapter summary

So what have we learned from this chapter?

- That sport is a powerful means of expressing identities and rivalries; that it can be regarded as 'war minus the shooting' (Orwell).

- That sport in Scotland catalyses national identity, regardless of gender and social class.

- That despite claims that sport has now been globalised in its appeal and reach, it remains, in the last resort, national and local.

- That local rivalries are at least the equal of national ones, and convey aspects of identity and belonging, as well as attachments to place.

- That sport may not be a matter of life and death in literal terms, but matters for all that.

Questions for discussion

1. Does sport matter in terms of national and local identities, and, if so, why?

2. Why might 'masculine' sports like football and rugby apparently appeal to women as well as men?

3. Are Scots really 'ninety-minute nationalists'?

4. Is there tension between the globalisation of sport at professional levels and people's commitment to nation and locality?

5. How serious is the rivalry between Celtic and Rangers?

Annotated reading

(a) For a history of various sports in Scotland and their cultural significance, see G. Jarvie, *Sport in the Making of Celtic Cultures* (1999); G. Jarvie and J. Burnett, *Sport, Scotland and the Scots* (2000); G. Jarvie and G. Walker, *Scottish Sport in the Making of the Nation* (1994); J.A. Mangan, 'Missionaries to the Scottish middle classes', *International Journal of the History of Sport*, 27(1–2), 2010;

J. Horne et al., 'Capitalizing on sport', *British Journal of Sociology of Education*, 32(6), 2011; D. Brown, 'The Big Drum: the mutability of a sporting habitus: mountaineering in Scotland as a case study', *International Review for the Sociology of Sport*, 44(4), 2009.

(b) On sport and identity, see G. Orwell, 'The sporting spirit', *Tribune*, 14 December 1945; D. McCrone and F. Bechhofer, *Understanding National Identity* (2015), chapter 3; F. Gill, 'National identities in a Scottish border community', *Nations and Nationalism*, 11(1), 2005; S. Whigham, '"Anyone but England"? Exploring anti-English sentiment as part of Scottish national identity in sport', *International Review for the Sociology of Sport*, 49(2), 2014; H.F. Moorhouse, 'Football hooliganism and the modern world', *International Review of Modern Sociology*, 32(2), 2006; I. McIntosh et al., '"It's as if you're some alien …": exploring anti-English attitudes in Scotland', *Sociological Research Online*, 9(2), 2004.

(c) On the 'globalisation' of sport, see R. Giulianotti and R. Robertson, *Globalisation and Football* (2009); R. Giulianotti and R. Robertson, 'Forms of glocalization: globalization and the migration strategies of Scottish football fans in North America', *Sociology*, 41(1), 2007; and the special issue of *Global Networks*, 7(2), 2007, especially the introduction by Giulianotti and Robertson; Rumford (on cricket); Lechner (on Dutch football); Eriksen (on transnational sports); and Andrews and Ritzer (on the *grobal* and *glocal*).

(d) For a comprehensive coverage of a sociology of sport, see R. Giulianotti, *Sport – A critical sociology* (2005); and R. Giulianotti, 'The sociability of sport', *International Review for the Sociology of Sport*, 40(3), 2005.

Notes

1 Attributed to Shankly during a TV chat-show in 1981. This comment has been described as 'fatuous' by Alan Bairner (in Jarvie and Walker, 1994: 9), which fails to appreciate Shankly's mastery of the bon mot put to telling effect.
2 George Orwell, 'The sporting spirit', *Tribune*, 14 December 1945.
3 A similar question was asked of people in England on the 2008 BSA survey. The question was asked of people who described themselves as English/Scottish not British, more English/Scottish than British, equally English/Scottish and British, or more British than English/Scottish. It was not asked of those who said they were British not English/Scottish.
4 We included the National Assembly for Wales because we were trying to convey 'devolution' as a whole and not simply the Scottish parliament. The survey was not carried out in Wales.
5 Defined as people born and currently living in Scotland; elsewhere, we have referred to them as 'native Scots'.
6 The next item in order of 'annoyance' (either a 'great deal' or 'quite a lot') was Westminster as the 'English parliament' (43 per cent). 'The Queen of England' raised the ire of 32 per cent.
7 Fifty-seven per cent of men, and 46 per cent of women, say they feel a lot more Scottish when the national team is playing (a differential of 9 percentage points).
8 The differential (minus nine) saying 'a lot': 49 per cent of men and 40 per cent of women is identical to that for Scottish men and women.

9   Perhaps, on reflection, this should not surprise us. The data exclude those who say they are 'Scottish and not British', and hence are weighted appropriately to those who, at least to a degree, feel British.

10 Having taught at Loretto a few years before, he became proprietor of the school in 1862.

11 The accusation of 'globaloney' is usual the reverse, and more commonly aimed at those who assume that globalisation is a fait accompli. See, for example, Michael Vesteth's book *Globaloney: Unraveling the myths of globalization* (2005).

12 The ICC has over 100 members: 10 full members, 37 associate members (including Scotland) and 59 affiliate members.

13 It has been claimed that the World Series in baseball was named after the newspaper *New York World*, and kept the 'World' title after the paper became defunct in 1931.

14 The-then Hull City manager, Steve Bruce, commented, with some ambivalence: 'For what he has done for the club – and I say this repeatedly – he's put it on the map a little bit and he's put his hard earned money so he's entitled to have his opinion' (www.theguardian.com/football/2015/apr/02/hull-city-tigers-name-change-fa).

15 The *Guardian* writer David Conn commented: 'If they win, it will be Wimbledon's sixth promotion since they began as a newly formed, supporter-owned club in the Combined Counties League following a trial of players on Wimbledon Common. And promotion would put them, after so short a time, in the same division as the Milton Keynes club [MK Dons] they still revile as "the franchise"' (https://www.theguardian.com/football/2016/may/29/afc-wimbledon-league-two-playoff-plymouth).

16 FIFA: Fédération Internationale de Football Association; IOC: International Olympic Committee; ICC: International Cricket Council.

17 See the Scottish Register of Tartans at www.tartanregister.gov.uk/tartanDetails.aspx?ref=4073.

18 It is not clear here why the author describes it as 'not rational', possibly as a synonym for 'emotional'.

19 'Myth' refers to a set of beliefs and social practices held to be self-evident. It does not mean, as in common parlance, something which is untrue.

20 The presenting reason was that fixture congestion placed additional burdens on players and clubs.

21 See www.telegraph.co.uk/sport/football/international/3269766/Nacho-Novo-should-not-wear-dark-blue-of-Scotland-says-SFA-president-George-Peat-Football.html.

22 You can become a naturalised citizen after five years' residence in the UK, but the point is less one of law than of custom and practice when it comes to 'representing the nation'.

23 The Rubbers versus the Chevies does not have much of a ring to it, and sounds like a remake of *West Side Story*.

24 'Just a boy's game' was an iconic TV *Play for Today* (1979) written by Peter McDougall and starring the singer Frankie Miller. It was based in Greenock, not Glasgow, but captured the unspoken but abiding rivalry between Rangers and Celtic in the west of Scotland.

25 This does not rule out badging an 'England-plus' team as 'British'.

22

SEEING OURSELVES: THE MEDIA IN SCOTLAND

Try this as a thought experiment. If there was no 'Scottish press' – no *Herald*, *Scotsman*, *Press and Journal*, *Courier*, no *Daily Record*, no *Sunday Post* – how would we have made sense of Scotland? If we had had to rely on the London-based *The Times*, *Guardian*, *Telegraph* and *Sun*, what would have been the chances of framing an understanding of ourselves?

It is, of course, a '*what if?*' question, because one of the defining features of Scotland is that there has been such a press to reflect and amplify Scottish concerns, to help, indeed, to construct the Scottish frame of reference. And yet, just at the moment when Scotland has never been more politically detached from the British state, the indigenous press has gone into steep decline.

Consider these figures: taking 1973 as our benchmark, the point at which agitation for greater self-government began in earnest, and comparing newspaper sales in 2015, we find that *The Scotsman* has lost 72 per cent of its sales, the *Daily Record* 69 per cent, *The Herald* 62 per cent, *The Courier* 65 per cent, with the *Press and Journal* losing a 'mere' 48 per cent. If the most 'successful' Scottish daily newspaper has barely managed to hold onto about half of its sales, and the rest have lost around two-thirds to three-quarters, then something dramatic is going on. Furthermore, that iconically successful of Scottish newspapers, *The Sunday Post*, which used to sell easily over 1 million copies on the Sabbath, now sells just over 160,000. Neil Blain and David Hutchison set the puzzle: 'It is very strange that the once dominant *Daily Record* – which sold over three-quarters of a million copies in the 1980s – has been so vulnerable to the onslaught of the Scottish edition of *The Sun*, which now outsells it' (Blain and Hutchison, 2016: 20).

Chapter aims

- To explore how and why the 'Scottish' media have declined, especially in the context in which Scottish affairs, political, social and cultural, have never been so salient.

- To examine the role of the media in shaping the Scottish 'growth project' in the second half of the twentieth century.

- To explain why newspapers owned and produced in England have made such incursions into the Scottish market.

- To analyse the relationship between newspaper readership and national identity.

- To focus on three moments of jurisdictional tension which have helped to shape Scottish-British issues, including the Scottish Independence Referendum in 2014.

Imagining the nation

The close relationship between national identity and the media is an obvious frame for understanding Scotland. After all, the media – press and broadcasting – represent one of the key institutional pillars for constructing the nation. As Benedict Anderson observed: 'The convergence of capitalism and print technology on the fatal diversity of human language created the possibility of an imagined community, which in its basic morphology, set the stage for the modern nation' (1996: 46).

How national communities are 'imagined' by means of the print media, and newspapers in particular, is central to Anderson's thesis. This is a highly personal experience. Said Anderson, 'the newspaper reader, observing exact replicas of his own paper being consumed by his subway, barbershop, or residential neighbours, is continually reassured that the imagined world is visibly rooted in everyday life' (1996: 35–6).

Similarly, in the late nineteenth century, the French writer Ernest Renan conjured the metaphor 'daily plebiscite', as a means of imagining the nation; national identity was done on a daily basis. It was typified in the (daily) newspaper, such that readers implicitly communicate with others through their daily consumption.

The press shapes the cultural world, and with it the sense of belonging to the nation. Thus, Eugen Weber in his classic study *Peasants into Frenchmen* (1977) showed how vital the press was in creating French citizens after the revolution. A common language spread 'by newspaper and barracks even more than school' (Weber, 1977: 84) was the means for creating Frenchmen and women. The adoption of the vernacular disseminated a shared identity through communication, not only roads and railways, but above all by newspapers – 'le papier qui parle'.

Likewise, Michael Billig's concept of 'banal nationalism' (1995) represents 'flagging the homeland daily' ('daily' as the everyday as well as 'Daily' newspaper) whereby a national 'we' comes into existence and is sustained by the sharing of a common culture on a daily basis. Continual 'flagging' reinforces a shared sense of 'we': 'Banal nationalism operates with prosaic, routine words, which take nations for granted, and which, in so doing enhabit them. Small words, rather than grand memorable phrases, offer constant, but barely conscious, reminders of the homeland, making "our" national identity unforgettable' (1995: 93).

How, we might ask, does that work in the UK where 'nation' does not equate with 'state'? Scotland would seem to be both a good and a bad fit for Billig's thesis. On the one hand, the press and the media are key institutions which convey, indeed help, to build Scottish national identity, while, on the other, creating (British) citizens by similar means does not easily equate with multiple media representations of 'the nation'. After all, the key question is: *which* nation – Scottish or British? Who is this '*we*', this personal *deixis*,[1] we are being invited to be part of?

The fourth estate

Our first task is to explore the role of media in Scotland. It is the 'fourth estate', reflecting its key role in all modern societies. Philip Schlesinger and Alex Benchimol has noted that since the late eighteenth century,

> there can be no doubt that Scotland's newspaper press has had an important role in articulating national and regional identity in the country and that it has played a part in constituting a distinctive Scottish national sphere within the more encompassing one of the Union – the United Kingdom. (Schlesinger and Benchimol, 2015: 101–2)

We begin the modern account in the post-war period, although a distinctive Scottish press has a much older pedigree. In a review of the Scottish press in the inter-war period, Liam Connell observed that: 'These years witnessed the emergence of a genuine political nationalism in Scotland, as part of a more general process of *écossification* by which Scottishness took on a political significance that had rarely been available to it for some 150 years' (2003: 189).

The modern Scottish National Party was formed by the amalgamation of two smaller parties in 1934, while at the same time there developed a culturalist 'national' movement associated with cultural figures like Hugh MacDiarmid, Lewis Grassic Gibbon, Eric Linklater, Edwin Muir, Violet Jacob and Naomi Mitchison. While not overtly 'political', this cultural movement occurred within the context of the collapse of the English cultural imperium, such that 'English culture' was no longer equated with the culture of England (Cairns Craig, 1996).

The emergence of a 'Scottish' press was both cause and effect of cultural and political change. It was the medium through which a changing Scotland was portrayed, explained and amplified, without being overtly 'political'. Connell quotes the writer James Barke writing in 1936:

> When the race for circulation between the big dailies … was at a crucial stage, they discovered Scotland. … Now the Scottish press had never evinced any interest in Scotland from a nationalist standpoint. The phrase 'Scotland a Nation' would have sounded rank nationalist sedition to editors whose policy was predominantly Unionist … but the English dailies altered all that. (2003: 197)

Claiming to be 'Scottish national' newspapers was a selling point, purporting to provide a unique and comprehensive coverage of Scotland, something which survives today, but with less marketing success.

Modernising Scotland

In the post-war period, a new kind of 'politics' (or 'political economy') emerged in which the state played a much more interventionist role in economic affairs, reflecting in part its directive role in war. Its lodestar was economic growth. Across the western world:

> The state found a new and different response to the legitimacy problems; increasingly it treated industrial growth per se as possessing intrinsic and commanding political significance, as constituting a necessary and sufficient standard of each state's performance, and thus justifying further displacement of the state/society line. (Poggi, 1978: 133)

This was not a peculiarly Scottish phenomenon, for western states took up the challenge of what in France was called *Les Trente Glorieuses*, thirty years of economic growth and prosperity in Europe, including the UK. In the post-war period, Scotland's dependence on declining heavy industry and failure to attract new 'white-goods' industries, for example making domestic appliances, had pushed the Scottish Office, the 'semi-state', to embark on economic planning for diversification. The Scottish Office had put together a powerful administrative apparatus to induce foreign capital to come to Scotland.

This was described (see Chapter 6) by Moore and Booth as a 'negotiated order' such that there was a degree of decision-making and administrative autonomy coalescing around 'the Scottish interest'. This 'negotiated order' operated somewhere between corporatism and free-market pluralism bringing together bodies like CBI Scotland, the STUC, Scottish Council (Development and Industry) and, latterly, the Scottish Development Agency/ Scottish Enterprise. This 'Scottish policy community' mediated through the Scottish Office represented a 'meso-level of the British state' (1989: 150).

An essential part in mediating the policy community was the press in Scotland. Writing in the mid-1970s, James Kellas commented: 'All Scottish papers are part of the economic log-rolling of the Scottish interest groups (among them the trade unions, employers associations, and the Scottish Council (Development and Industry)), who seek further government-aided development in Scotland. The political affiliation of the papers then becomes somewhat irrelevant' (1975: 175–6). All were united in support of the 'Scottish Growth Project', the transformation of the Scottish economy away from heavy industries, irrespective of political affiliation. This included the Conservative Party, which drew upon a tradition of state intervention epitomised in the inter-war years by Walter Elliot MP who, as Secretary of State for Scotland, introduced free school milk for school children[2] and set up the National Housing Company to build prefabricated houses.

Labour was happy to buy into the 'national project' defining the main forms of discontent as 'economic' rather than 'constitutional'. Labour's approach to the 'Scottish question' was to invest in infrastructure such that this discontent could be assuaged by creating jobs (Keating and Bleiman, 1979). In the 1950s and 1960s, unemployment in Scotland was running at twice the UK average, and the mid-1960s saw the highest rates of net overseas emigration (in 1966, a net loss of 30,000 people per annum).

The political consensus focused on economic growth, reflected in the Toothill Report in 1961, commissioned by Scottish Council (Development and Industry) and headed by the Managing Director of Ferranti Edinburgh, John Toothill. Major investments had been made in a steel mill at Ravenscraig in Lanarkshire (1959) and the Rootes car plant at Linwood in Renfrewshire (1961), as well as expansion of the petrochemical refinery at Grangemouth on the Firth of Forth. In 1964, the Forth Road Bridge was opened linking Fife and the Lothians more directly.

The focus on 'regional planning' and state-directed investment had all-party support, and it is significant that all of the investment took place under Conservative governments at Westminster. Labour inherited the Scottish Growth Project when it came to power in 1964, and gave it a twist of its own with Harold Wilson's 1963 speech on the 'white heat of technology', thereby in the words of one trade union leader 'capturing science for the Labour Party'. Labour, which maintained its high share of the vote in Scotland at 45 per cent or more (whereas the Conservatives never won more than 40 per cent after 1964), was both the beneficiary and the driver of public infrastructural investment.

Reporting Scotland

There was no question that all newspapers in the 1950s and 1960s were broadly 'unionist' and supportive of the Scottish growth project. The *Daily Record* supported Labour (but only after 1964; previously it had been Conservative), while other dailies were Conservative or, now and again, Liberal when it suited them. In the early 1970s, the *Record* had a circulation of more than half a million, as had the *Scottish Daily Express* (Kellas, 1975: 172), with the *Glasgow Herald* and *The Scotsman* with more than 80,000, and the Scottish 'regional' papers, the *Dundee Courier* and the *Aberdeen Press and Journal*, on 122,000 and 108,000 respectively. Evening papers flourished, with the circulation of the *(Glasgow) Evening Times* at 181,000 and the *(Edinburgh) Evening News* at 148,000. The iconic *Sunday Post* was bought by over 1 million people and thought to have a readership figure of three times that number.

Into this newspaper culture came television. The TV transmitter at Kirk o' Shotts was built in 1951, and by 1956 one-third of Scots had a TV set. The proportion of TV licences[3] grew from 3 per cent in 1952 to 40 per cent by 1958. Despite the enduring myth that the Queen's Coronation in 1953 was the main catalyst for television sales (in 1954, only 10 per cent of Scots had a licence), it was the late 1950s and early 1960s which saw the growth of television in Scotland; by 1966, for example, 78 per cent had a TV licence. Commercial television – STV – began broadcasting in 1957. At the core of television were 'news and current affairs', with a strong 'industrial' focus – a key part of the Scottish Growth Project.

Scottish 'industrial correspondents' (rarely 'business' or 'economics') were the doyens of such reporting. One such was John Hossack, who moved from the *Scottish Daily Express* to the BBC in 1959, and then to STV in the mid-1960s. His obituary in *The Herald* in 2004 commented:

> He was industrial correspondent at a time when heavy industry was accelerating into decline. Strikes and unrest were rife and competition for news was cut-throat and relentless ... John was a doyen. He already had extensive Labour contacts and at the Express expanded them to include senior CBI figures. Behind the scenes at the Scottish Labour Party he was a tireless activist, writing for senior politicians including Willie Ross. But he never let his political beliefs colour his reporting or his principles of truth and fairness. When he moved to the BBC in 1959, his balanced, unembroidered reports and sound judgment were evident, the timbre of his gravelly tones adding to his growing authority. He interviewed four prime ministers and, as one former colleague noted, probably knew more about Scottish business and industry than all of them put together. His job took him to unusual locations, even reporting from the top of the Forth Road Bridge at its opening. He hated heights. He had impeccable shorthand and a contacts book which was the envy of his peers. So much so, the BBC tried to buy it from him when he left. Without any success. His knowledge was as much in demand behind the scenes as on screen. With George Middleton of the Scottish Trades Union Congress he was instrumental in driving the successful campaign to bring the Rootes car plant to Linwood and he believed passionately in the case for Upper Clyde Shipbuilders. In the mid-1960s he moved to Scottish Television, then forging a path in regional television news coverage. (*The Herald*, 8 September 2004)

Thus we find the intimate connections between industry, politics, newspapers and television in the working career of one person. What lay at the base of such interconnections was the assumption that 'Scotland' was a distinct unit of political and economic management, focused around a 'growth' project which would restructure the economy, reduce unemployment and cut emigration. All the main political parties bought into the project, including the Conservatives. The rise of the New Right and neo-liberalism was rarely to be seen, the preserve of right-wing extremes and think-tanks such as the Institute of Economic Affairs and the Adam Smith Institute.

The media and nationalism

While it was 'unionist', assuming the political and economic coherence of the UK, the media helped to establish Scotland as a geo-political space, built upon a long pedigree of institutional coherence, and one easily adaptable to a project for economic modernisation. This meant that when oil was discovered in the North Sea in 1969 (in the Forties field in 1970 and in the Brent field a year later), it fitted easily into the 'Scottish project', even though there was no (legal) question that it was 'British oil'.

The SNP, however, was in the right place at the right time, making explicit the 'nationalist' assumptions about the Scottish project, shifting it from a British to a Scottish frame of reference. As Labour faltered politically in the 1970s, so the SNP was the beneficiary. Above all, it acted as a catalyst for electoral change, and in particular offered a political home for the socially mobile and the young in search of a new political identity in a rapidly changing Scotland. Kellas' analysis of the SNP's appeal in the 1970s is well put:

> At all times, it seems to have attracted defectors equally from all parties, although this varies from constituency to constituency. Up to 1974 it seems to have appealed to first-time voters or previous abstainers. Its declining support after 1978 was particularly marked among young voters and New Town voters, many of whom had consistently supported the party since the late 1960s. (1989: 141)

The appeal of the party to such social groups was reflected in the volatility and unexpectedness of its successes and failures, as shown by its share of the vote in UK elections: 12 per cent in 1970, rising to 22 per cent in February 1974, and 30 per cent in October of that year, and falling back to 17 per cent in 1979.

The volatile appeal of the SNP to the young, and the socially and geographically mobile, was reinforced by the absence of a significant class base. As we saw in Chapter 19, in the 1970s the SNP did well across all classes, but especially among skilled manual and routine non-manual workers, those groups which were electorally detached from their traditional social bases. The party's appeal was stronger among the 'new' working class – technicians and craftsmen – than it was among 'traditional' manual workers – steelworkers and miners (Davis, 1979).

The SNP attracted the young in high proportions, and did proportionately well among those who had been upwardly socially mobile out of the manual working class. For example, one-third of SNP voters in non-manual jobs had fathers who were manual workers, compared with a quarter of SNP non-manual voters who had non-manual fathers. This suggests that non-manual workers who had been upwardly mobile were especially susceptible to the appeal of the SNP, as were younger workers, and those buying a house with a mortgage.

Home base in a television age

The SNP was the main beneficiary of key social changes in Scotland in the 1960s and 1970s – rising affluence, full employment and upward social mobility. Groups who became less reliant on the support of kin as well as more home-centred – Scotland's analogue of the classic 'affluent workers' studied in England (Goldthorpe et al., 1969) – found themselves drawn to the nationalists less for reasons of political ideology than because of their social detachment from their social class of origin. This social base paid electoral dividends where Labour was historically weak. In Peterhead, for example, which later became the core of Alex Salmond's Banff and Buchan constituency, '[t]he SNP was most successful in winning affiliations from the upwardly aspirant who were renouncing the class of their homes while not yet entering the middle class' (Bealey and Sewel, 1981: 160).

Crucially, the SNP was a political party which easily captured the 'Scottish' label, because it was a taken-for-granted reference in much the same way as the Conservative Party in England had implicitly assumed an 'English' national identity. Furthermore, the SNP was a *media* party, well suited to an increasingly volatile electorate, and one which did not need to make the long march to political power as the Labour Party was required to do at the beginning of the twentieth century. In many ways, the SNP's Scottishness was almost incidental, yet vital. The lack of class connotations in the SNP was the key appeal to this socially mobile group in the 1970s. Such people were susceptible to alternative frameworks of perception, for their traditional forms of social and political identities were weakening.

They were also a generation which learned much of their politics via television and the media. A mobile and privatised way of life provided a more appropriate frame of political and social reference. This generation read their politics off the television. In this regard Scotland was little different from the rest of the UK in terms of economic and social change, with the crucial difference that 'Scotland' was a frame of cultural reference in terms of which the political world could increasingly be interpreted.

Whichever political party was best able to 'speak for' the nation reaped the electoral dividend. Thus, the SNP did well in the late 1970s, and Labour assumed the 'nationalist' mantle in the 1980s. The Conservatives, on the other hand, rapidly fell out of electoral favour, their share of the UK election vote falling almost by half, from 31 per cent in 1979 to 17 per cent in 1997.

The personal and the political

Let us summarise our argument thus far. Scotland's 'fourth estate', the media, while formally unionist in its politics, had, from the 1950s, bought into a Scottish growth project dealing with economic modernisation which was supported across political and civil Scotland. A distinctive Scottish press and, from the 1950s, broadcasting media reinforced the Scottish agenda. As a consequence, the 'frame of reference' was increasingly a Scottish one, without ostensibly threatening the Union.

This state of affairs lasted thirty years from 1945 until the mid-1970s. The 'framing' work had enabled the SNP to take electoral advantage of social and political change thereafter, particularly in its appeal to socially mobile workers, detached from traditional class bases, and who were non- or lightly unionised. This 'politically mobile' electorate, from the

1970s, learned their politics from the media and television in particular, and gravitated to the SNP. The literary critic Raymond Williams (1974) called this process 'mobile privatism', whereby television rapidly expanded in the home and became an important means for acquiring new attitudes, values and perspectives, notably with regard to politics.

The impact of new technologies such as television connected with key social changes in the second half of the twentieth century. Williams observed: 'Socially, this complex is characterised by the two apparently and yet deeply connected tendencies of modern industrial living: on the one hand, mobility, on the other hand the more apparently self-sufficient family home' (1974: 26). Political parties, such as the SNP, which were not defined by a strong social class aura, were much more likely to appeal to this new social cadre whose social and geographical mobility made them more dependent on television for their view of the world and social affairs. Where 'Scotland' was concerned, the attention of the media in general, and television in particular, on the economic project was both personal and political.

The changing press

Let us now return to the conundrum. If the media were especially important midwives in the modernisation of Scotland, economically, socially and politically, then how are we to account for the fact that their role is considerably weakened by declining circulation figures? David Hutchison has commented: 'The political sea change which led to devolution does not appear to have strengthened the loyalty of Scottish readers to Scottish newspapers; in fact, the opposite has happened' (2008: 68).

If a distinctive press and the media are vital to the national deixis, then what has been the effect of declining newspaper readership in Scotland, and in particular readership of the Scottish press? If fewer Scots read newspapers, and especially Scottish ones, then what impact does that have on the national deixis? Might not people feel *less* Scottish in that context?

We could take the view that the decline in newspaper readership in Scotland is simply a reflection of generic decline, at least in the western world.[4] After all, the printed newspaper is a traditional medium, the *carrier* of news, and there may well be other vehicles more appropriate to the age. Nevertheless, the decline of the indigenous press may have particular ramifications in Scotland. Could it be that the less 'Scottish' the media, the less 'national' the frame? If Anderson, Billig and Weber are correct about how the national press implicitly instructs its readers in 'being national' along with carrying news, then it is plausible to expect that people in Scotland might become less 'Scottish' or at least in different ways than previously. In any case, there does seem to be a contradiction in that fewer Scots read Scottish media, and yet political–cultural developments in Scotland seem to reinforce a strong sense of being Scottish. Is it possible to reconcile these?

The short answer to our conundrum is to say that the press was a key catalyst precisely at the moment where the Scottish Growth Project was being created and disseminated, that is in the 1960s and 1970s. While we might have expected the press to benefit in circulation terms from the 'Scotticisation' of public life, it was, to be sure, not inevitable. Thus, newspaper readership has declined in the long term as other media, notably television, have been on the rise. In this respect, the medium is not necessarily the message. In the next part of this chapter we will explore what those 'media' are turning out to be.

Taking Kellas' circulation figures for 1973 as a benchmark, and comparing them with Audit Bureau of Circulation (ABC) sales figures for 2015–16, we find dramatic declines in circulation for 'Scottish' newspapers (Table 22.1).

TABLE 22.1   Sales circulation figures for Scottish-based newspapers (ABC)

	1973	2015	% change
Daily Record	569,137	174,525	−69
The Courier	122,657	43,031	−65
Press and Journal	107,910	56,422	−48
The Herald	85,141	32,141	−62
The Scotsman	80,113	22,740	−72

Sources: For 1973, *Newspaper Press Directory 1974* (J. Kellas, *The Scottish Political System*, 1975: 172); for 2015–16, Audit Bureau of Circulation (ABC) certified figures

All show a massive decline over the forty-year period, ranging from *The Scotsman*, which has lost almost three-quarters of its readers,[5] closely followed by the *Daily Record*, to the 'best', the *Aberdeen Press and Journal*, the only newspaper not to lose more than half its readership.

Declining readership

It is not only sales, but also readership of newspapers which have fallen.[6] Historically, Scotland had a disproportionately large number of newspapers for the size of its population (Dekavalla, 2015), and people were no longer buying multiple titles in Scotland as they did for much of the post-war period.[7] It is a moot point as to whether the ownership of Scottish newspapers has made a significant difference to sales as well as content. *The Scotsman* is currently owned by the Johnson Group, which is based in Scotland, and *The Courier* and *Press and Journal* by DC Thomson of Dundee. *The Herald* is owned by Newsquest, part of the US Gannet media group. There seems to be no obvious relationship between ownership and the decline in newspaper sales in Scotland.

Using Scottish Social Attitudes survey data, we find that whereas 75 per cent of Scots in 1999 said they read a newspaper regularly, by 2014 this was down to 40 per cent. Furthermore, those reading Scottish-produced daily papers (those listed in Table 22.1) had fallen from around half (51 per cent) in 1999 to only 18 per cent in 2014.[8] The proportions saying they read one of the four Scottish broadsheets declined from 20 to 8 per cent, although the decline in the *Daily Record* was proportionately steeper (from 31 to 10 per cent). These declines had occurred during the most politically salient period in recent Scottish history, namely the setting up of the devolved Scottish parliament in 1999, through to the Scottish Independence Referendum in 2014.

Even among self-identifying 'Scots',[9] that is those who considered themselves only or mainly Scottish, the fall in readership of Scottish-based newspapers was steep, from 55 to 19 per cent.[10] Those who described themselves as 'only or mainly British' were even less likely to read one of the Scottish broadsheets in 2014 (a mere 2 per cent, down from 21 per cent in 1999).[11]

This decline in reading newspapers is partly due to changing habits. After all, people may be getting their news from other sources these days, notably from the Internet. Nowadays, as many as half now say they look at a news or newspaper website at least once a week, and one-third do so every day or even more often (Scottish Social Attitudes Survey, 2014). While the survey shows that those who look at websites are more likely than those who read a daily newspaper to get their news online (71 per cent compared with 52 per cent), it is a question of *both* reading a newspaper *and* going online, rather than either/or.

Putting a kilt on it: the 'English' press in Scotland

To what extent do people in Scotland have different patterns of readership compared with the rest of the UK? After all, until quite recently, Scots had a habit of reading more than one newspaper (Dekavalla, 2015). As part of the Leverhulme research programme on nationalism, national identity and constitutional change, researchers carried out a series of quantitative surveys on twelve consecutive days between October 2000 and January 2003. They selected front-page stories, editorial comment and a further selection of randomly selected stories from 'Fleet Street' titles bought in both Scotland and England, and five indigenous Scottish titles (see Table 22.2).

Reflecting technological innovation, most Fleet Street newspapers now print an edition specifically for Scotland, so that while readers in England and Scotland may be buying ostensibly the same titles, the editorial copy may be different. Similarly, while the *Guardian* and *Independent* change very little in Scottish–English copy, the *Sun*, for example, badges itself as *The Scottish Sun* with substantially different stories.

The market share of such 'hybrids' has improved considerably. Indeed, many 'British' newspapers produce specific editions for other markets, notably the Republic of Ireland, a separate and independent state. *The Irish Sun* flourishes in the Republic because it is rebranded and distances itself from its parent title with its little-Englander conservatism, and now sells 56,000[12] copies in the Republic. *The Scottish Sun* sells 218,000 daily copies, over 40,000 more

TABLE 22.2 Daily sales in Scotland and the rest of the UK, August 2005 (% of all sales)

	Scotland	%	Rest of UK	%
Fleet Street 'quality': *Guardian, Independent, Telegraph, The Times*	86,086	6	1,918,885	20
Fleet Street 'mid-market': *Express, Mail*	224,016	15	2,815,551	29
Fleet Street 'popular tabloid': *Mirror, Star, Sun*	511,721	35	4,973,377	51
Scottish-based dailies: *Courier, Herald, Press and Journal, Record, Scotsman*	660,422	45	29,674	<1

Source: Audit Bureau of Circulation (www.abc.org.uk)

than the indigenous *Daily Record* (www.abc.org.uk). *The Scottish Sun* offers its readers a diet of Scottish stories and relates to them in Scottish–national terms, even to the point of supporting independence in 1992 and flirting with a 'Yes' vote in the 2014 referendum, although ultimately declining to do so (www.theguardian.com/media/greenslade/2014/sep/17/sun-rupert-murdoch). In the British general election, it threw its weight behind the SNP, reinforcing the belief that, above all, it likes to be seen to back winners.

The (Scottish) *Daily Mail* also edits out 'English' copy to appeal to readers north of the border, and sells 89,000 copies in Scotland, making it the third most read newspaper in Scotland, after the *Sun* and *Daily Record*. The *Daily Mail* is well ahead of the *Aberdeen Press and Journal* and the *Dundee Courier*, while the *Scottish Daily Express* has a circulation of almost 45,000, comfortably more than *The Herald* and *The Scotsman* (www.abc.org.uk).

Readers in Scotland buy different titles than readers in England, with almost half reading indigenous titles and most of the rest reading heavily Scotticised editions of Fleet Street tabloids. Those titles which do least to tailor their products to Scottish readers (notably, the *Guardian* and *Independent*) do least well north of the border. Thus, in 2014, the bestselling 'English' broadsheets in Scotland were *The Times* (18,000), the *Telegraph* (16,000), followed by the *Guardian* (9000) and the *Independent* (2400) (www.abc.org.uk). Nevertheless, these broadsheets hold their own in Scotland, at 4 per cent in both 1999 and 2014 (Scottish Social Attitudes survey figures).

Reading the papers

These figures, of course, tell us little about the content of these newspapers. Michael Rosie and Pille Petersoo (2009) analysed 2500 articles from three broad categories of newspaper, namely 'Fleet Street England', 'Fleet Street Scotland'[13] and 'Indigenous Scottish', with particular reference to selected 'markers' of national identity. These findings are summarised in Table 22.3.

TABLE 22.3   Summary of selected markers in newspapers in England and Scotland

% by column	Fleet Street England	Fleet Street Scotland	Indigenous Scottish
'British'	36	32	26
'English'	12	11	12
'Scottish'	6	17	47
'Welsh'	4	3	3
'Northern Irish'	2	2	2
'Irish'	2	1	3
'European'	12	12	10
Base	*1026*	*985*	*518*

Source: www.institute-of-governance.org/__data/assets/pdf_file/0008/47375/IoG_Briefing_17.pdf

The largest difference relates to the marker 'Scottish', with 'Scottish Fleet Street' papers three times more likely to use it than their 'English' equivalents. However, 'Indigenous Scottish' papers make use of 'Scottish' in almost half of the articles. Furthermore, the authors observed:

> While newspapers in Scotland are more likely to refer explicitly to 'Scotland' or 'Scots', there is no corresponding finding in newspapers bought in England with regard to 'England' or 'English'. Indeed, we found that a very significant proportion of all articles which used 'English' markers were in fact referring to either the English language, or to England's international sporting teams. One third (34%) of all references to 'England' were found in a sport-related article, far fewer references to 'Scotland' (14%) were sport-related. (www.institute-of-governance. org/__data/assets/pdf_file/0008/47375/IoG_Briefing_17.pdf)

The survey results reinforce the point that there is no 'British national press' despite the historic dominance of 'Fleet Street' (which is no longer the site of the newspaper industry, but continues to be its eponym). Similarly, we can see the differential between the Fleet Street English and Fleet Street Scottish editions, reflecting the care taken to tailor Scottish editions to that market. Simply 'putting a kilt' on a story or item does not make it 'Scottish'. One effect of post-1999 devolution has been that neither 'national' press, English nor Scottish, carried much news from Wales or Northern Ireland, nor did 'English' stories figure prominently in the Scottish newspapers. The researchers commented:

> Newspaper reporting in England and Scotland is characterised by a remarkable degree of concentration on the countries in which the newspapers are sold. Newspaper readers in Scotland receive little information about Welsh, Northern Irish and even English (non-British) current affairs. Their counterparts in England are presented with little news about Scotland, Wales or Northern Ireland. It looks as if constitutional change has reinforced rather than weakened this trend. (www.institute-of-governance.org/__data/assets/ pdf_file/0008/47375/IoG_Briefing_17.pdf)

The conclusion was that readers in England and in Scotland bought newspapers with substantially different referents or 'flags'. While, in England, 'British' flags predominated over 'English' ones (at least in the early 2000s), Scottish newspapers saw themselves as addressing 'Scottish' questions. Thus, while fewer people are in the habit of reading a daily newspaper, the ones they do read cater to their expectations and views.

The research shows that the UK press is a complex mosaic of explicit and implicit 'national' titles. The researchers commented: 'It is doubtful whether readers can be expected to know who *"we"* are, particularly where there may be a wide range of potential *"we's"* to choose from' (www.institute-of-governance.org/__data/assets/pdf_file/0003/47370/IoG_Briefing_12.pdf).

A good example of addressing different *'we's'* can be seen by juxtaposing the front pages of the *Daily Mail* during the 2015 British general election, one designed for England, which carried the banner headline 'Most Dangerous Woman in Britain', and one for Scotland which said, 'Nicola: I want Tories to Win'. Presumably, in Berwick-upon-Tweed on the Scottish–English border, you could choose your paper and your politics.

Who is 'we' anyway?

Newspapers and the media more generally deal in understandings of belonging and identity; that is, deixis, referential words and phrases which require contextual information in order to be understood. Pille Petersoo, who was a member of the team which carried out the analysis of newspapers, observed that 'while "we" helps to draw clear distinction between members and non-members, between *us* and *them*, the deixis "we" can also be used to make this border diffuse' (Petersoo, 2007: 420).

National deixis

This reinforces Anderson's point that readers are encouraged to imagine a community of readers who share key understandings. Petersoo's research was based on analysis of 110 leader articles in *The Herald* and *The Scotsman* during the 1979 and 1997 referendum campaigns. She argued that these newspapers not only mobilise the 'we' in support of their stances, but use it in different contexts to make different references: notably, a newspaper 'we' (we the readers); an inclusive Scottish 'we'; and an all-inclusive British 'we'. She concluded that the Scottish 'we' is the one most commonly used in the Scottish national media. Given below are two examples, one from each newspaper and from each referendum campaign:

> *Why we must vote Yes*
>
> Let **us** take as a premise that it is desirable to sustain the unity of the United Kingdom. Indeed, **our** close and cousinly links with the English, **our** affection for **them** and respect for **their** culture, the degree of domestic, social and economic intercourse between **us** – these facts make separatism ... unthinkable.
> (*The Scotsman*, 23 February 1979, bold italics in original)

Petersoo made the points that: (a) the newspaper is 'addressee-inclusive', imagining the reader as Scottish without explicit mention; (b) it addresses its readers as Scottish, vis-à-vis 'our cousins the English'; and (c) the cousinly metaphor implies an extended family where cousins live happily together.

Here is another extract from a leading article, this time from *The Herald* in the context of the 1997 referendum:

The real decision we face

No one doubts – from the stands at Murrayfield or Hampden to the pages of Trainspotting, from the echoing footfalls of the legal fraternity in Parliament House to the interactions of children and teachers in schools across the land, from fishing boat to computer assembly line – that there is something ***we*** call Scottish about what goes on ***here*** and a place called Scotland which gives meaning to ***our*** lives. ***We*** are now being asked to choose how that sense of identity should be nurtured in a new millennium. (*The Herald*, 20 August 1997, bold italics in original)

The extract is full of national deixes ('the land', 'here', 'a place'). Petersoo commented:

By putting Murrayfield rugby and Hampden football fans, Trainspotting's drug addicts, Edinburgh lawyers, children, teachers, fishermen etc. across Scotland all together into one sentence, the extract suggests that Scotland is one big national family, a thriving imagined community. Scotland is imagined as a unity, and it is assumed that all those different groups of people agree on the single definition of Scottishness. (2007: 427)

The personal deixis 'we' can have different referents; it wanders between the newspaper 'we', the Scottish 'we' and the British 'we'. Petersoo gives an example from *The Scotsman* editorial at the time of the 1997 referendum, to make the point about the 'wandering we':

The rebirth of a nation

A day to seize opportunity

Carpe diem, says the old Latin tag. This morning ***we*** might prefer a sturdier, native injunction. Perhaps it is time now to say that Scots should rise from ***their*** backsides and prove that ***they*** have meant everything ***they*** have said. This day, over all others, brings with it the opportunity to say what sort of nation ***we*** mean to be. The alternative is clear, familiar and failed. It offers few hopes of real progress. It offers nothing for ***our*** self-esteem. Though ***we*** are to choose, it seems to this newspaper that there is no choice if Scotland is to regain belief in itself. (*The Scotsman*, 11 September 1997, bold italics in original)

The Scottish 'we' in the second sentence becomes a Scottish 'they' in the third. The triple Scottish 'they' then becomes a Scottish 'we' again, concluding with mild distancing as Scotland becomes 'it'. What constitutes the national 'we' varies according to context and topic. Petersoo concluded:

Far from just adopting the national 'we' banally and unconsciously, readers may need to work on the different array of 'we's that they confront in the newspaper, and bring in some interpretative knowledge in order to recognise the particular national 'we' invoked in the particular article. And even more so, on many occasions the readers have to cope with a wandering 'we' within the same article. There is no simple and banal national 'we' in the media, but a kaleidoscope of different 'we's' – exclusive newspaper 'we's, inclusive (sub)national 'we's, all-inclusive (supra)national 'we's, and wanderings of all sorts. (2007: 432–3)

Thus, what 'we' means, and who 'we' are meant to be, depend on quite subtle reading and interpretation, nor can we assume it always and simply refers to a national 'we'.

Defining us

Codes of inclusion/exclusion may also require subtleties of language. The most obvious case relates to 'foreign' languages, and as we shall see later in this chapter, the defence and promotion of 'national' languages is an important *raison d'être* for certain newspapers in particular cultures (Schlesinger and Benchimol, 2015). Because Scotland is part of the 'anglosphere', the cultural boundaries are both looser and more porous, providing a threat to indigenous media.

One form of defence is to employ what Fiona Douglas calls Scottish *lexis* (from which derives 'lexicon'), words and phrases subtle enough to appeal to 'we' in the 'know', for example *hame* for home, *bairn* for child, *outwith* for outside/beyond.[14] Douglas observes: 'The use of Scots lexis in the newspapers is as much for symbolic purposes, language display and stylistic considerations as it is for communicative import' (2009: 65). Comparing articles in *The Herald*, *The Scotsman* and the *Daily Record* in 1995 and again 2005, and with *The Times* and the *Sun* as 'controls', she concludes that the newspapers are fairly tokenistic in their use of Scottish lexis ('Scots'), and, in linguistic terms, adopt 'thin' Scottish standard English as the norm.

Scottish *lexis* tends to be found disproportionately in two sections, namely sports pages and in feature articles, the former being a sufficiently bounded 'deixis' to allow and reinforce its content boundaries. Her comparison over time shows that *The Herald* makes significantly less use of 'Scots' in 2005 than in 1995, and the *Daily Record* greater use, possibly because it was under commercial threat from *The Scottish Sun*.[15] Both the *Sun* and *The Times*, which had invested in Scottish editions, also made greater use across the period of Scottish lexis to convey this process of indigenisation.

Newspapers, politics and national identity

There is a long-standing debate about the role and influence of the media in shaping national identity, and even bringing about political change. The most famous, or notorious, example of the claim relates to the *Sun* newspaper at the 1992 British election, an election which Labour was predicted to win. The weekend after the election, the *Sun* carried the headline, 'It's The Sun Wot Won It'.

That headline became 'proof' of the view that newspapers determine the outcome of elections, a point of view reinforced by the defeated Labour leader Neil Kinnock who blamed the *Sun* for his election loss, especially its election day headline: 'If Kinnock wins today will the last person to leave Britain please turn out the lights'. Academic analysis was more circumspect on the grounds that: (a) there is little direct evidence that newspapers change people's minds; (b) people tend to choose newspapers which fit in with attitudes and values; and (c) in any case, many tabloid readers pay little or no attention to editorials as opposed to sport, features and other news items (see Curtice, 1999; https://wiki.leeds.ac.uk/index.php/What_Influence_ did_the_newspapers_have_on_the_outcome_of_the_1997_British_general_election).

The *Sun* has long taken a 'robust' if not entirely consistent view of politics, as reflected in the front page for the Scottish parliament election on 3 May 2007 (Figure 22.1). The desire to be on the winning side helps to explain its later switches of allegiance; above all, it is a matter of selling newspapers.

FIGURE 22.1
The *Sun*'s viewpoint

Source: Institute of Governance, University of Edinburgh, collection

The media and national identity

To what extent are newspaper readership and 'national identity' related? We have seen that people who think of themselves as only or mainly Scottish are more likely to read indigenous Scottish newspapers than those who consider themselves to be only or mainly British. This was as true in 2014 as it was in 1999 (and points in between) although there has been a fall in general newspaper readership as well as in reading 'Scottish' newspapers. The analogue of the 'Sun wot won it' would be that the media have the influence to shape, and even change, people's national identity. To that end, we explored the connection, with regard to Scottish nationals (people both born and currently living in Scotland) and English migrants to Scotland (Kiely et al., 2006).

As far as Scottish nationals were concerned, we found that those who mainly read the Scottish press did so out of habit, in a taken-for-granted and non-contentious way. To take contrasting illustrations, here is an assessment of the media by someone who accounted for their national identity by saying: 'I've never thought about it because I don't consider it. As I say, I consider myself first and foremost Scottish.' Like many Scottish nationals, they took exception when something in the media challenged their sense of national identity. They commented:

> Take the flooding in the south, for instance. Edinburgh's recent flood situation merited about four column inches and half a breath and half a beat on 'Scotland Today' [Scottish current affairs programme]. ... It happens in England for the first time, and it consumes the media. Now that, in itself, that's infuriating. That's probably too strong a word but that is typical of how, because it's us, 'You don't matter because you are who you are and to be honest with you, we don't care. But we want everyone to care about this. We think this is national news and you must care and we don't care if you don't care or not. It will dominate your newspapers and it will dominate your airspace. So you will all listen.'

Contrast that with someone who gave their national identity as strongly British:

> I actually object to getting the Scottish editions because, all these papers now come out with Scottish editions as if Scots now somehow are not interested in what's happening in the whole country as a whole and they give you a bit of it. I object to not reading the same paper in Glasgow as a guy in London, I want to read the same paper. ... When you're watching 'Newsnight' and suddenly it clips over to bloody Scotland and you get some third-rate interviewer and it takes up half the bloody programme and you're watching and you say 'I don't want to see this'. I want to see a national programme, which is dealing with national issues with guys that are, in spite of everything, guys who are right on the ball, pressing national figures.

What we see in these examples is the way people tune into programmes and features according to the ways they define themselves in national identity terms. 'Scots' tend to be critical of instances where Scottish issues are underplayed or ignored, while 'Brits' are critical of Scottish overplay, as they see it. For both, in their different ways, identity and media consumption become contentious when something in the media challenges their sense of identity.

It is, however, among English migrants to Scotland that national identity relates more directly to perceptions and understandings of the media. They come to Scotland and encounter newspapers and television programmes produced entirely in Scotland, as well as Scottish variations on the media with which they are familiar in England. Furthermore, they find themselves in an environment where they have to (re)negotiate who they are, and reassess how their sense of national identity relates to the stance taken by the Scottish media on Scottish, British and English national identity.

Those living in Scotland who described themselves as 'English' often complained about a Scottish national frame of reference in the Scottish media. Other migrants tried to claim a more inclusive sense of being British but, reinforcing the point that the existence of a British national press is an assumption rather than a reality, they struggled to find media compatible with being 'British' in Scotland. Finally, among those who make claims to being Scottish, there is a shift over time in media consumption in favour of a Scottish perspective.

Here are three examples, the first comment from an English migrant who retains her sense of being 'English':

> I think in my heart of hearts I consider my home somewhere in England, not somewhere in Scotland. I can't be specific but it's just certain things like I like the fact that all the papers don't say 'Scottish' version of the Times and stuff. Now which is really bizarre but I think I'm only reacting like that because I've spent so long with people ramming down your throat 'oh this is the Scottish version of this'.

The second example is from someone who says they consider themselves to be 'British':

> I get The Times every day but it does have what it calls the Scottish pages, which are three pages of Scottish news and I keep saying we should buy a Scottish newspaper. My newsagent keeps saying we've been here long enough now to buy a Scottish newspaper because she obviously doesn't consider ... I always assume that the paper is the same everywhere so I sometimes say to my Dad 'oh, did you see that thing in the paper?' He says 'well, it wasn't in my paper'. I say 'it was on page 3'. He says 'well, we don't get all that Scottish rubbish in our newspapers [laughs]'.

Finally, here is someone born in England who has lived in Scotland for many years and considers it 'home':

I'm listening more to Radio Scotland. Most of my news sources come from Radio Scotland and Guardian and Herald. Big issues, I'm conscious that I switch much more and listen to Radio Scotland a lot more and buying The Sunday Herald. Those two are two clear decisions that happened and changes. I'm listening to Radio Scotland because of the Parliament really and it's more likely to carry on.

What the examples suggest is not that it is not a question of 'the media' somehow determining who people are; rather, people interpret and manoeuvre their way around the media in such a way that they fit more congenially into their sense of national identity, especially as this might change over time. Put simply, if you aspire to be a 'national', then you gravitate towards those media which assist you to do so, that you learn how to be 'we', one of us.

The writing on the wall?

The decline of the print media in Scotland is obvious but not unique. As the Scottish Universities Insight Institute observed:

> The scale of this transformation is seen not just in how individuals access and consume news. It is apparent, also, in the rapidly evolving structure of the public sphere itself. The centralised, capital-intensive, top-down, elite-mass media pyramid of the previous century, attached to which the professionalism of the journalist was a guarantee of news' objectivity and democratic value, and the basis for a structural separation of the producer and the consumer of news, is being replaced by a horizontal online network of content-generating users, bloggers, social networkers, citizen journalists, media literate activists and all those who can, because of the communication technology at their disposal, now contribute to the globalised public sphere. They read, but they also write. (Scottish Universities Insight Institute, 2010: ii)

This apparent 'democratisation' of the media masks the domination by media conglomerates such as Google, Amazon and News International. Newspapers in particular are experimenting with mixing hard copy and digital editions, and whether or not to have metered paywalls so as to charge for copy, and/or moving to a subscription-based model for tablets and smartphones (Dekavalla, 2015). There is, moreover, a diverse 'communicative space' (Schlesinger) in modern Scotland.

According to the Scottish Social Attitudes Survey 2014, around half (51 per cent) look at a news or newspaper website at least once a week, and as many as 34 per cent do so at least once a day.[16] Of those who consult a website for news, almost half (49 per cent) use the BBC News website, and no other web source comes close to that figure.[17] Those people who do not read newspapers are more likely to consult a website than those who do read one (71 to 52 per cent respectively).[18]

Print journalism has declined under the twin challenges of digitisation and the Internet, a process of 'creative destruction', according to Philip Schlesinger, and, as a result, 'journalism is condemned to reinvention' (Schlesinger and Doyle, 2015: 306). While 'broadcasting' is a matter reserved to Westminster under the Scotland Act of 1998, cultural and media matters are a concern of the devolved Scottish parliament whether under a Labour/Liberal Democrat administration (1999–2007) or a nationalist one (since 2007). As Schlesinger points out elsewhere: 'The demand for "broadcasting devolution" has become deeply entangled with the exercise of control over the news agenda in Scotland' (Schlesinger, 2008a: 158).

In this section we will explore three points of jurisdictional tension which have helped to frame Scottish–British issues in broadcasting: the television current affairs programme *Panorama* affair (1995); The Scottish Six (1998); and the coverage of the Scottish Independence Referendum in 2014. The point is not to take sides in these disputes, but to forefront them as examples of jurisdictional tensions.

The *Panorama* affair, 1995

The 'affair' refers to a BBC broadcast interview, broadcast throughout the UK, with the-then Prime Minister John Major three days before Scottish local elections on 6 April 1995. This breached the BBC guidelines relating to political 'balance' so close to elections. John MacInnes observed: 'The management of BBC Scotland and the National Broadcasting Council for Scotland made the prospects [of 'interfering' in elections] clear to London and were ignored. Frantic efforts to organise some political balance for the Scottish context were fruitless' (1995: 7). It seemed to MacInnes that Scotland was not important enough to upset a timetable appropriate to England and Wales, and that 'in London, it didn't count' (1995: 8). He concluded:

> The price to the BBC of its own hierarchical centralism was an astonishing inability to understand just how different Scottish civil society in Scotland is from the metropolis where most television is made, and where there is no mechanism for feeding any such understanding into the decision-making process. (1995: 8)

The Scottish Six debacle, 1998

Three years later a more notorious row erupted, one year before the Scottish parliament was established in Edinburgh. Known as the 'Scottish Six', it concerned the proposal to allow BBC Scotland to have an opt-out programme between 6 and 7 p.m. to cover news and current affairs (see Schlesinger, 2004). This proved unacceptable to London. The grounds for rejection proved controversial. The-then Director General of the BBC, John Birt, wrote later in his memoirs: 'I was deeply resistant to the proposal. It could have dire consequences for the BBC and unintended consequences for the United Kingdom. ... The end of a single common experience of UK news', Birt wrote, would 'encourage separatist tendencies' (quoted in Schlesinger, 2004: 20).

On the eve of devolution, this was a major story, and Labour politicians, notably at Westminster, were major opponents of a Scottish Six. The row died away, but left a residue of tension. Writing in 2003, John McTernan, one of Tony Blair's advisors, wrote in the Holyrood magazine: 'Scotland has a Parliament because it is a nation, albeit one within a larger political unit. But because of the strength of nationalism over the last thirty years, there remains a residual fear that doing anything to build national identity is a gift to separatists' (quoted in Schlesinger, 2004: 36, footnote 12). This articulates nicely the dilemma for unionist politicians: that accommodating to self-government in Scotland runs the risk, in their eyes, of ratcheting up the demand for further powers to the point of independence.

Nevertheless, in early 2016, and in the context of renegotiation of the BBC charter, the Corporation announced that it was going to 'trial' a Scottish Six, some eighteen years after the original controversy – a case of better late than never, or perhaps, too little, too late, given the changed political and constitutional context since 1999 (www.bbc.co.uk/news/uk-scotland-35658589).

The Scottish Independence Referendum, 2014

At no point was this more obvious than during the referendum campaign on Scottish independence in 2014. Indeed, the press, in the form of the *Daily Record*, became part of the message rather than the medium. A few days before voting, it published what became known as *The Vow* (see Figure 22.2).

It turned out to be less of an agreement between the three UK party leaders, and more of a creation by a newspaper supporting the 'No' campaign, and, as we have seen, suffering something of a sales crisis. (For an analysis, see Roy Greenslade in the *Guardian*: www.theguardian.com/media/greenslade/2014/oct/31/daily-record-scottish-independence.)

Accusations were made that the BBC and STV were favouring the 'No' campaign in their news outputs. Writing in a pamphlet for The Saltire Society, the journalist Iain Macwhirter absolved the media of conscious political bias at work. Rather, he said, it reflected 'the groupthink of the UK and the Scottish press' (2014: 82). He continued:

> The agenda of most BBC news and current affairs programmes, even in the internet age, still comes from the press. They don't simply lift stories from the papers, of course, but they look at the press for their themes – especially *the Guardian, the Daily Mail, the Times, the Telegraph* and in *Scotland, the Herald, the Scotsman*, and *the Daily Record*. As editors and presenters scan the headlines of these papers, and cross-reference them with the news events of the day ... a view emerges of the 'feel' of the day. When they brief their presenters on what issues to question politicians on breakfast news programmes, editors will advise them to cover the questions being raised in the press. (2014: 83)

FIGURE 22.2
The Vow

Source: Institute of Governance, University of Edinburgh, newspaper collection

Macwhirter's analysis is plausible, in that he worked as a BBC political correspondent at Westminster, as well as presenting Scottish current affairs programmes and being a columnist for *The Herald* and *Sunday Herald*.

The point about 'groupthink' was also made by Andrew Tolson in a book edited by Neil Blain and David Hutchison (2016) called *Scotland's Referendum and the Media: National and international perspectives*:

> The determining factor in all of this is not simply bias, or even geography – it is to do with the institutional organisation of British broadcasting. In particular, Scotland (and Wales, and Northern Ireland) are traditionally defined as regions, and in British broadcasting regional news follows, and is secondary to, national news. This means that even when Scottish politics is critical, as it was in May 2015, to the UK's political formation, in the news agenda, it is usually a secondary matter. (Email comment to Neil Blain, 2016: 234)

There is, of course, irony in the view that, as newspapers decline in circulation, their influence is maintained in the broadcasting media which are reliant on them to help to set the agenda. As Dekavalla observed:

> issues which are constructed as Scottish and those constructed as UK-wide have different protagonists. This means that the political debate on the two types of issues is exclusive to sources in the respective nations and is presented as not being of concern to sources in the other nation. There is an isolation of the mediated debate around 'Scottish' issues, which seems related to a deficit in the coverage of Scottish affairs in the rest of the UK after devolution, also noted by other researchers (e.g. Rosie et al., 2006; Schlesinger, 1998). (2012: 336)

One of the major effects of the 2014 referendum has been to embed many of the arguments for and against independence, and to reinforce a common conclusion that, in terms of setting the agenda, the winners (No) lost and the losers (Yes) won. Schlesinger wrote, perceptively a decade before the referendum, that 'it is increasingly clear (though still not openly acknowledged) that the spectre of independence has haunted the calculations of devolutionist politicians' (2004: 36). The inherent complexities of the devolved Scottish condition mean that 'the levers of statehood may still afford decisive policy advantages that those of mere autonomy within a state do not' (Schlesinger, 2008b: 48).

As part of the 'anglosphere', Scotland is particularly vulnerable to incursions by non-indigenous newspapers, in a way in which they are less so in other small countries where there are distinct languages and cultures to defend and promote (Schlesinger and Benchimol, 2015). The role of the media, broadcasting and press is an important dimension in the pursuit of distinctiveness in small nations, whether independent or not. Where 'culture' is permeated through a distinctive language, the issue is clearer. In Denmark, Norway, Catalonia and Quebec, there is a perceived need to find appropriate business models for sustainable media in globalised conditions. Despite historical and cultural differences, in small nations in particular, political and cultural matters are closely aligned.

Conclusion

In looking at the media in Scotland, let us adopt MacInnes' stricture that 'it is important to avoid reducing analysis of the national character of the mass media to an assertion that the mass media ought to be national' (1993: 97). Such reductionism would convey a misleading sense of the complex way the media operate in Scotland, and, in any case, we have seen that the relationship between the media, national identity and politics is not straightforward.

Besides, there is no necessary contradiction between declining newspaper circulations and the greater 'politicisation' of Scotland in the last two decades. We have seen that the press and media played an important role in the 1960s and 1970s in setting a new 'frame' for Scotland, but once established, other institutions, notably a devolved parliament and, more broadly, civil society, reinforced the Scottish frame of reference. We might say that the Scottish media helped to channel and shape Scottish national identity, but did not determine it.

The emergence of Scottish editions of Fleet Street newspapers is a reflection of this need to address Scottish issues. Those newspapers which decline to do so do not sell well north of the border, and, in turn, the Fleet Street press, both broadsheet and tabloid, know that they cannot simply reprint copy which appeals to 'little England'. In any case, newspapers are sensitive to the possibilities of boycott, as Merseyside's popular ban on the *Sun* for mis-reporting the death of ninety-six Liverpool football fans at Hillsborough makes plain (see, for example, www.theguardian.com/football/2016/apr/26/how-the-suns-truth-about-hills-borough-unravelled).

At a time when newspapers are losing readers and are dependent on quite fickle changes in the market, 'loyal readers' are in short supply. In any case, the future is all to play for, given the serious upheaval in broadcasting and media. These are times when a variety of business models are being played out, and none seem the obvious way to go. The press and media generally may seem all-powerful, but the skill lies in coming to terms with people's expectations and aspirations. In a Scotland whose constitutional future is as yet quite uncertain, this is quite a skill.

If the 'national' press have lost their position as agenda-setters in Scotland, it alerts us to the impact of global forces, and this is the subject of the next chapter.

Chapter summary

So what have we learned in this chapter?

- That the press and the media were critical in helping to assemble the 'Scottish frame of reference' in the 1960s and 1970s, especially in the context of the 'Scottish Growth Project'.

- That there has been long-term and significant decline in newspaper sales in particular, especially those produced in Scotland.

- That nevertheless the media as a whole, and especially television, have helped to refocus the cultural and political agendas on Scottish issues.

- That, especially in a declining market, how people choose to vote and their constitutional preferences are not determined by the newspapers they read.

- That the issue of how Scottish questions are 'framed' remains a vibrant question as in the case of the Scottish Independence Referendum of 2014.

Questions for discussion

1. How distinctive are the Scottish press and media, and why?

2. How would you explain the decline in newspaper readership in the context of political and constitutional developments since the 1990s?

3. What is the relationship, if any, between national identity and the newspapers people read in Scotland?

4. Does it matter that fewer Scottish newspapers are owned and controlled in Scotland? Why have 'English' newspapers in Scotland seen less of a decline than 'Scottish' ones?

5. To what extent did the media shape and determine the outcome of the Scottish Independence Referendum in 2014?

Annotated reading

(a) For the history of the press and media in Scotland, see N. Blain and D. Hutchison (eds), *The Media in Scotland* (2008); L. Connell, 'The Scottishness of the Scottish press, 1918–39', *Media, Culture and Society*, 25(2), 2003; and F. Douglas, *Scottish Newspapers, Language and Identity* (2009).

(b) On Scottish politics and the media, especially around the 2014 referendum, see I. Macwhirter, *Democracy in the Dark: The decline of the Scottish press and how to keep the lights on* (2014); N. Blain and D. Hutchison (eds), *Scotland's Referendum and the Media: National and international perspectives* (2016).

(c) On the media in the twenty-first century, see P. Schlesinger, 'Broadcasting policy and the Scottish question', in T. Gardam and D. Levy (eds), *The Price of Plurality: Choice, diversity and broadcasting institutions in the digital age* (2008); and P. Schlesinger and G. Doyle 'From organizational crisis to multi-platform salvation? Creative destruction and the recomposition of news media', *Journalism*, 16(3), 2015; P. Schlesinger and A. Benchimol, 'Small nations, the press and digital challenge', *Media, Culture and Society*, 37(1), 2015. See also M. Dekavalla, 'Evaluating newspaper performance in the public sphere: press accounts of Westminster elections in Scotland and in England in the early post-devolution period', *Journalism*, 13(3), 2012.

Notes

1 *Deixis* refers to words or phrases such as pronouns like 'me' and 'here' which can only be understood according to the context in which they are used.
2 There is political irony that as (English) Secretary of State for Education in the Conservative government, Mrs Thatcher achieved notoriety for abolishing free school milk in 1971.

3 All households with television sets in the UK are required by law to hold a licence. The income from licence fees funds the BBC.

4 See, for example, as regards the United States, the Pew Research Center's Report (www.journalism. org/2015/04/29/newspapers-fact-sheet/).

5 *The Scotsman* sells only 14,000 at full price, the rest (over one-third of its 'sales') being discounted or given away. *The Herald*, on the other hand, does not do give-aways.

6 ABC (Audit Bureau of Circulation) is the industry body for media measurement, and provides certificated sales figures (www.abc.org.uk). 'Readership' refers to the number of people who claim to read a newspaper, and who may not necessarily buy it.

7 The evidence for this claim appears in House of Commons, Scottish Affairs Committee, 2009, 1 July, 'Crisis in the Scottish Press Industry: Report, Minutes, Oral and Written Evidence'.

8 Extrapolating from sales figures, the 2015–16 readership is likely to be closer to 15 per cent.

9 These data are based on Scottish Social Attitudes surveys in 1999 and 2014 which asked people about their newspaper reading habits, and, in the later period, which websites, if any, they used for news. The survey also asks about respondents' national identity.

10 The rate of decline in newspaper readership among 'Scots' was roughly the same for readers of the *Daily Record* (36 to 12 per cent) as it was for readers of the Scottish broadsheets (from 19 to 7 per cent), ratios of approximately 3:1.

11 Readership of the *Daily Record* among 'Brits' fell from 11 to 6 per cent, a less steep decline.

12 All ABC circulation figures have been rounded to the nearest thousand in order to show orders of magnitude.

13 'Fleet Street England' refers to those sold in England, and 'Fleet Street Scotland' to those sold in Scotland.

14 Douglas' dataset generated 6204 discrete newspaper articles for the 1995 corpus, and 8510 for 2005, which were examined for the use of Scots lexis, words and phrases of Scottish provenance.

15 The *Daily Record* also mounted a long-running poster campaign headlined 'Real Scots Read the Record', implying that its 'English' rival did not appeal to 'real Scots'. Sales patterns suggest that it did not work.

16 Thirty-seven per cent never do so, some of whom do not have Internet access.

17 The *Guardian* is the closest at 7 per cent.

18 Of people who do not consult a news website, 54 per cent read a newspaper regularly compared with 46 per cent who do not, suggesting a small compensation difference, but we cannot be sure that this amounts to substitution.

23

SCOTLAND AND STUFF: THE SOCIOLOGY OF CONSUMPTION AND LIFESTYLE

> To study stuff, we need ourselves to be where stuff is. Right there, in the living room, the bathroom, the bedroom and the kitchen. This is where most of modern life is lived. Families are created in bedrooms and sometimes divorced there. Memories and aspirations are laid out in photographs and furniture.
> (Miller, 2010: 109)

We start with this comment by Daniel Miller, not because there is anything unusual about Scotland in relation to 'stuff', but because there is not. Like any other advanced capitalist society, our relationship to consumption is defined by economy and culture. What is produced and consumed is not so different from other comparable societies.

Chapter aims

- To ask why consumerism is a central feature of modern capitalism.
- To argue that 'taste' is culturally and socially produced such that production and consumption are part of the same process.
- To examine the argument that what we buy is the brand rather than the object itself.
- To explore the view that 'stuff' is in fact culture rather than simply its expression.
- To locate 'stuff' in the wider global economy in examining 'fast' and 'slow' fashions.

Scotland and consumption

Let us start with a few statistics to make the point that Scotland is not so different when it comes to consumption. In terms of gross disposable income per head – what people have to spend – Scotland is close to the middle of the distribution for the 'economic regions' of the UK with just over £15,000 (2011 figures), ranging from £13,500 in Glasgow to £18,000 in Shetland (UK Statistics Authority, 'Official Statistics in the Context of the Referendum on Scottish Independence', MR 6-2013). Put another way, the average weekly expenditure per person in Scotland for 2011 was £200, compared with the UK figure of £201 – virtually identical.

The major items of weekly expenditure were (UK figures in brackets):[1] recreation and culture, £55 (£60); housing net of mortgage payments, £53 (£60); and food and non-alcoholic drinks, £52 (£53). As regards clothing and footwear, Scots spend £22 per week, the same figure as the UK as a whole. Scots spent 5.1 per cent, compared with a UK figure of 4.7 per cent, in terms of their household expenditure on clothing and footwear as a percentage of total expenditure in the period 2009–11 (http://webarchive.nationalarchives.gov.uk/20160105160709/; http://www.ons.gov.uk/ons/rel/family-spending/family-spending/2012-chapter-5/art-chapter-5—weekly-household-expenditure—an-analysis-of-the-regions-of-england-and-countries-of-the-united-kingdom.html).

In this chapter we will make sense of Scotland's relationship to consumption without implying that it is unusual. Where there are particular 'Scottish' aspects, most obviously in treating 'Scotland' itself as a consumable object (Scotland itself as *the brand*), we will analyse these, but our aim is to provide a framework within which Scotland's relationship to 'stuff', to use Danny Miller's useful term (Miller, 2010), can be analysed. Miller observes:

> Stuff is ubiquitous and problematic. … The idea that stuff somehow drains away our humanity, as we dissolve into a sticky mess of plastic and other commodities, is really an attempt to retain a rather simplistic and false view of pure and prior unsullied humanity. (2010: 5)

Understanding consumption

As Jan Webb (2006) has observed, there are two conventional views about contemporary consumerism: on the one hand, that it is about the sovereign and individual consumer making rational choices in the marketplace (the neo-liberal view); and, on the other hand, that people are 'cultural dopes' (Lasch, 1979) who are manipulated into acquiring false needs, and subsequent entrapment in a web of debt and excess, leaving little scope for human agency.

While such a view is conventionally associated with Marxist-informed economics, it has a wider appeal, such as in the popular analysis in the 1950s by Vance Packard of advertisers as *The Hidden Persuaders* (1957), inducing consumers to buy products according to 'compelling needs'.[2] Packard's account built upon the work of Thorsten Veblen at the turn of the twentieth century, in his *The Theory of the Leisure Class* (1899), in which he attacked the wasteful aspects of 'conspicuous consumption' for status-seeking among the rich.

Seeing people as rational consumers on the one hand and 'cultural dopes' on the other is too stark and lacking in nuance to be satisfactory. In any case, Webb observes:

> Through organisational marketing, modernity's ideal of an individualised self-identity is connected to choices between branded and symbolically loaded artefacts and services – clothes, cars, furniture, travel, entertainment and so on – in multiple and differentiated markets. (2006: 54)

In other words, the notion of the sovereign and individual consumer making free and easy choices is itself a cultural construction which is designed to serve the neo-liberal zeitgeist.

Governments in the post-1945 economy made consumerism a key instrument of economic policy such that the vices of self-indulgence and hedonism became virtues, even a moral imperative, in order to sustain employment and taxes. 'Debt' became a duty whether applied to houses or consumer durables in order to sustain the economy. Only by spending more could we make the economy grow: 'The expansion of markets was not simply a matter of selling more goods, but of associating consumerist values and attitudes with self-esteem and a sense of citizenship' (Webb, 2006: 57).

The sustained economic boom ended in the mid-1970s, by which time buying on hire purchase (HP), the 'never-never', was the norm, having displaced the pre-war distaste for buying on 'tick'.

Following the financial crisis and bank crash of 2008–9, there was another volte-face which blamed high levels of household debt for damaging consumer confidence. With almost half of households in debt in 2008–10, politicians began to claim that people's debt was a substantial burden, and that they were required to rein in household spending. 'Debt' was no longer seen as a necessary good (or evil). Further, governments sought to draw direct parallels between households and government in terms of the virtues of 'balanced budgets' (see www.ft.com/cms/s/0/71d48fce-74a1-11e4-8321-00144feabdc0. html#axzz3dyHZPVQS).

Thus did the consumer wheel come full circle, although what economic impact this might have had on both households and governments is unclear. In any case, British governments soon changed their tune and encouraged spending on houses and cars with cheap money in order to stimulate the economy. Certainly, it would require a major change in how each person relates to consumption to effect a major rebalancing of the economy. Old habits, in any case, die very hard, and governments have come to depend on people spending more than they have.

The sociology of consumption

So why is consumption sociologically interesting? The most obvious point to make is that consumption is in essence a *social* activity, even when carried out ostensibly by solitary individuals. Drawing upon the work of Max Weber, Erin McDonnell (2013) has argued that we cannot understand how goods, services and experiences affect social interaction and human well-being without understanding how people organise *socially* to select, acquire, possess and use such things. Even a focus on subjective disposition and constructions ('meanings') misses how individuals structure and organise the economic activities of consumption.

McDonnell argues that what Max Weber called 'budgetary units' are relatively durable social groups and not to be reduced to atomised individuals. Thus, 'budgetary units are composed of members with some intersubjective orientation to each other, possessing a minimal collective identity and norms for enforcing group behaviour' (2013: 309). In any case, Weber's classical distinction of classes, status groups and 'parties' was designed to separate, and articulate, the three dimensions of power, respectively: economic, social and political.

Of these dimensions, status group, or lifestyle, is closest to matters of 'consumption', reflecting how people choose to portray their social identities. Weber's point was that 'status' (social power) and 'class' (economic power) are analytically distinct but connected in practice, for in the real world one informs the other. As Bryan Turner pointed out:

> Social status involves practices which emphasize and exhibit cultural distinctions and differences which are a crucial feature of all social stratification. ... Status may be conceptualized therefore as lifestyle; that is, as the totality of cultural practices such as dress, speech, outlook and bodily dispositions ... while status is about political entitlement and legal location within civil society, status also involves, to a certain extent *is*, style. (Quoted in Jenkins, 1992: 130, italics in original)

A strictly 'materialist' account would explain what people consumed in terms of 'class'; that is, in the sphere of production. In such a perspective, where people stand in relation to the means of production determines what they are able to consume, because you can only buy what you can afford. Furthermore, Veblen's theory of the 'leisure class' was based on the view that idleness, and not 'work', was the mark of social status, and that 'conspicuous consumption' was the external measure of one's wealth. In that regard, Veblen followed Marx in arguing that one's place in the system of 'production' largely determined what was affordable, and hence people's place in the system of consumption. For Marx, *Homo faber*, the worker, took precedence.

The cultural production of taste

The writings of Pierre Bourdieu in the 1970s and 1980s, notably his 1984 book *Distinction: A social critique of the judgement of taste*, focused on the link between social class and lifestyle. Bourdieu was interested in the sociology of cultural consumption, and in particular the uses to which culture was put, and the manner in which cultural categories are defined and defended.

To take an example, class determines and constructs what we are allowed to photograph; that is, what we think of as acceptable objects. The point is that it is the social rules which frame what is permissible: rules of composition, which occasions can and should be photographed, and which are off-limits. Thus we can photograph weddings, christenings, but not funerals, at least not the private bits. Public displays of eminent cortèges are encouraged, and the public scenes of mourning during and after Princess Diana's funeral in 1997 were widely reported by the media. Holiday photos are within-limits, what used to be called 'holiday snaps', but intimacies are off-limits. Nevertheless, the ubiquity of smartphones has generated phenomena such as 'revenge porn', the circulation of sexually explicit media without the consent of the subject, and the law struggles to keep up with legal redress.[3]

Manufacturing 'good taste'

Bourdieu's point was that there is a hierarchy of legitimacies with regard to cultural goods and tastes, with 'aesthetics' at the pinnacle, which have to be learned and internalised (as 'good taste'). Theoretically, no one is excluded from having such taste but the effect is that only those with education and 'breeding' are deemed able to appreciate such cultural goods (think of art in museums and galleries). Bourdieu identified the intellectual field within which creations of this sort occur: first, in the medieval and early modern period when art was dominated by Church and Court, and subsequently, modernity, with a shift to a 'market' situation wherein a new bourgeoisie could learn taste and have it expressed on their walls.

Bourdieu was critical of the notion that 'cultural taste' is pure or innate, for cultural classification is rooted in the class system and socially acquired. Thus, 'people learn to consume culture and this education is differentiated by social class' (Jenkins, 1992: 138). 'Taste' becomes one of the key signifiers and elements of social identity, operating as much within social classes as between them. Bourdieu argued that individuals meet and marry *within* rather than between lifestyles, giving expression to 'cultural capital' – education, speech, dress, physical appearance. In most cases, economic capital and cultural capital are closely related but not intimately so. Thus, the rich can have 'poor taste' ('more money than sense', as the saying goes) and the highly educated, 'high taste' but without the economic capital to match.

So 'lifestyle' becomes a system of classified and classifying practices with distinctive signs such that there is an 'elective affinity' between classes of products and classes of consumers (Jenkins, 1992: 142). This produces a 'system of differences' which is diverse, changing and contestable. Bourdieu was interested in the disjuncture between subjective expectations and their objective probabilities such that 'displaced intellectuals' gravitate towards certain employment spheres which he calls 'social' work.[4] He does not omit class interests from the schema. Jenkins pointed out that 'Bourdieu's central argument in *Distinction* is that struggles about the meaning of things, and specifically the meaning of the social world, are an aspect of the class struggle' (1992: 147).

'Habitus' and taste

The notion of 'habitus', a set of social practices and understandings which are internalised and hence 'objectified', comes into play in such a way that 'the working class habitus is both an adaptation to the realities of working class life and a defence against them' (Jenkins, 1992: 146). Bourdieu's point was that 'habitus' does not require explicit guidance but is 'objectively regulated and regular without being in any way the production of obe-dience to rules [such that] they can be collectively orchestrated without being the product of the organizing action of the conductor' (Bourdieu, 1984: 72).

Jenkins argues that much of Bourdieu's thesis is, nevertheless, deterministic, and ignores processes of *cultural* production. While class fractions are defined in terms of employment status, lifestyles are not immediately self-evident, and thus 'the reader is left uncertain about the social meaning of the bundles of practices and attributes identified as "lifestyles", and relationships they have with each other' (Jenkins, 1992: 148). In any case, working-class people seem no less concerned to make social and cultural distinctions than anyone else, and Jenkins believes that Bourdieu (who died in 2002) should have dusted off his anthropologist's hat and spent more time among the people about whom he wrote, the better able to report their patterns of consumption.

Production or consumption?

The theoretical division into 'production' and 'consumption' has been criticised by George Ritzer on the grounds that 'there is no such thing as either pure production (without at least some consumption) or pure consumption (without at least some production), the two processes always interpenetrate' (2015: 2). To circumvent this, Ritzer proposes a new con-cept of *prosumption* which he derives from Alvin Toffler's book *The Third Wave* (1980).

The rise of *prosumption*

At one level, the new concept, *prosumption*, seems unnecessary, because production has always required consumers, and, furthermore, that which is consumed has to be produced. Nevertheless, Ritzer is arguing that a new world of *prosumption* has emerged. He claims that the most abundant and revolutionary examples are digital, notably associated with the Internet, which, Ritzer argues, is the 'home' of this new world. The examples he gives include:

- lining up in a fast-food restaurant to collect food, and, later, disposing of the leftovers (Ritzer was the author of the bestselling book *The McDonaldization of Society* (1993));

- self-checkout systems at supermarkets;

- IKEA furniture DIY assembly;

- self-provisioning one's travel and hotel arrangements online or at kiosks;

- using an ATM rather than a bank teller;

- using three-dimensional (3D) printers;

- and tele-teaching and Internet-based online learning (MOOCs – Massive Open Online Courses).

Ritzer argues that such *prosumption* has knock-on consequences such that newspapers dispense with journalists in favour of online bloggers; that *prosumers* do all sorts of free work once done by paid staff. We might think of 'zero-hours contracts' for those who are kept on the books without working any hours at all, and obviously getting no pay.

While there is much that is thought-provoking about Ritzer's notion of *prosumption*, we might doubt if it is quite as new as he implies. Thus, door-to-door deliveries of shopping, or buying at the door, were features of nineteenth-century shopping across the social class divide. 'Home delivery' may not be the modern invention some think it is. Bloggers have not replaced journalists, so much as trying to get a foot in the paid journalistic door. In any case, the dilution of labour, as Marx documented, is not a new phenomenon, but one dependent on relative control (or the lack of it) of one's scarcity value. Nor are 'new' ways of production so revolutionary, but dependent upon capital/labour relations. In a period in which labour has lost much of its bargaining power, it is easy to assume that this is a new process rather than a very old one.

Ritzer's argument that 'to the contemporary capitalist, the uncommodified labor time of the prosumer is preferable to the commodified labor of the proletariat' (2015: 10) only makes sense if one discounts the 'freedom' of the prosumers to take their business elsewhere. 'No contract, no pay' means that the employer has no hold over the prosumer, who, like unpaid interns, can trade their experience for a 'proper job' should one arise elsewhere. Ritzer also finds it odd that in 2014 Facebook paid $19 million for the messaging company WhatsApp, which at the time was making very little money. The point is, surely, that Facebook saw WhatsApp's potential as a money-maker dovetailing with other parts of its business; just as it has long been a feature of capitalism to acquire a 'loss-making' business with a view to taking its market share or its capacity to extend the core business.

What is paid for such a business is not a reflection of its current profitability, still less its value. Further, while it may be the case that for the likes of Amazon 'the greatest value of an online company lay in the consumer data it collected' (Ritzer, 2015: 11), 'big data' or information of this sort only works if there is a market for the product (to say nothing of the advantage of selling books and 'stuff' at monopoly prices). Indeed, there is the notion of the 'attention economy' where the point is for companies to cash in, literally, on consumer attention as they search for the 'product'. We are waylaid by adverts which may cause us to deviate, and for which advertisers are paid handsomely. While 'attention economics' is deemed to be new and a creature of the digital age, in the early 1970s Herbert Simon observed that information consumes the attention of its recipients (1971).

Doing-it-yourself

While the 'do-it-yourself' economy dovetails with aspects of neo-liberalism, it is not all one-way traffic. After all, assembling IKEA furniture can be traded out to carpenters or those with the time and skills to fit it all together. To take a Scottish example of getting someone literally to do the dirty work, people living in tenement flats can hire out the social (and legal) obligation to take their turn at cleaning the communal stair rather than doing it themselves. 'Your turn to clean the stair' no longer requires hanging a notice on your neighbour's doorknob, but paying your share of professional stair-cleaning to a third party.

Ritzer's claim that 'the arrival of the new prosumer not only makes the market less necessary; we witness, in fact, demarketization' (2015: 15) may indeed be the reverse: its 're-marketisation' particularly for those who are money-rich and time-poor. 'Walking the dog' is no longer your responsibility. Some even claim that professional dog-walkers can earn £64,000pa (www.dailymail.co.uk/news/article-3105155/Professional-dog-walkers-earn-64-000-year-trust-look-pooch.html). One does not have to buy into those claims to reflect that what were once household responsibilities such as cat-minding and dog-walking, to say nothing of stair-cleaning, can be 'farmed out' if the price is right. 'Taking care when you're not there' eases the conscience. Everything has its price if someone is willing to pay the money for the service.

Perhaps we might think that there is something slightly distasteful about farming out 'personal' responsibilities to those who would take them on at a price. Some argue that almost everything has its price. In the 1960s, the economist Gary Becker claimed that even that most intimate and personal 'good' – having children – had its price. Children, in Becker's words, should be seen as a 'consumption good'. He commented: 'It may seem strained, artificial, and perhaps even immoral to classify children with cars, houses, and machinery' (1960: 210). He continued:

> Children are viewed as a durable good, primarily a consumer's durable, which yields income, primarily psychic income, to parents. Fertility is determined by income, child costs, knowledge, uncertainty, and tastes. An increase in income and a decline in price would increase the demand for children, although it is necessary to distinguish between the quantity and quality of children demanded. The quality of children is directly related to the amount spent on them. (1960: 231)

It may seem shocking to consider children in this way, but our concerns are with the sociology (rather than the economics) of Becker's position. We might argue that putting a 'price' on children is far *less* common than it used to be when peasants had large families to provide the necessary labour on the land; after all, you could hire out your children's labour. And what better way to guarantee a labour force of your own? It has been argued that in north-east Scotland the high rate of illegitimacy in the nineteenth century was a deliberate checking of fertility potential to provide future necessary labour (see Ian Carter's study *Farm Life in Northeast Scotland, 1840–1914: The poor man's country*, 1979). There was no point in taking on marginal farming if you could not generate your own family labour to help support it.

It is true, historically, that boys were valued more highly than girls (*male* primogeniture was the norm, after all), and, in any case, Becker's reference to 'psychic income' in the quotation above somewhat gives the game away. Enjoying children is not like enjoying a cup of coffee. We might go 'upmarket' for better coffee, but children are not to be bought off the peg once we have compared quality against price. And 'psychic income' is a metaphor rather than something an economist can easily price.

In addition, price and value should not be confused, as reflected in the accusation that someone knows the price of everything and the value of nothing. The late Neil MacCormick, an eminent theorist of law, observed that: 'The truth about human individuals is that they are social products, not independent atoms capable of constituting society through a voluntary coming together. We are as much constituted by our society as it is by us' (1999: 163).

The point is that society does not come about because individuals decide after the event to come together. Rather, society *makes* individuals in the first place. In other words, we are *contextual* individuals whose identities are manufactured and maintained by the societies we inhabit. The failing of a strictly economistic view is to locate the individual outwith the social order. On the contrary, 'consumption' is a social act rather than an individual one, and what we 'want' is socially manufactured. Does that imply that we are, then, 'cultural dopes', manipulated to consume whatever the 'hidden persuaders' want from us? That is a beguiling viewpoint, but too simple.

Buying into the brand

Products need to have symbolic meanings and qualities injected into them by means of advertising, marketing and branding (Webb, 2006: 58). Thus, the 'substance' of a product matters far less, if at all, than what it *signifies*, and what sort of lifestyle is conveyed. We may think that 'a washing machine is a washing machine is a washing machine', that is material functionality is all, but such a strategy does not sell many washing machines in the marketplace.

Instead, people must be persuaded to upgrade their washing machine/car/computer/wardrobe for something more stylish and up to date, more in keeping with self-identity. That is the purpose of advertising. As Webb observes: 'How else can people be persuaded to replace last year's clothing, car, mobile phone or kitchen, when "last year's model" is perfectly functional?' (2006: 58).

There need not be an immediate revenue pay-off from advertising a 'new' product, but 'branding' is all. Brand identity by Microsoft, Coca-Cola, Nike and Apple relies on lifestyle identification ('the new range', 'cool', 'this season's'), an assumed sharing of values, a sense of community – being, for example, an 'Apple person' or belonging to the 'MacTribe' (rather than someone simply using a run-of-the-mill PC).

To say that Apple is an American technology company does not begin to convey its appeal. One of its founders, Steve Jobs, chose the name 'Apple' because it resonated 'fun, spirited and [was] not at all intimidating', and thus Apple became iconic.[5] There is more to the product than a piece of technological kit. Said one BBC correspondent at the 2011 launch of a product in London: 'The scenes I witnessed at the opening of the new Apple store in London's Covent Garden were more like an evangelical prayer meeting than a chance to buy a phone or a laptop' (Alex Riley, writing for the BBC, www.bbc.co.uk/news/business-13416598).

By 2015, Apple was posting quarterly revenue of $58 billion and a quarterly net profit of $13.6 billion (www.apple.com/pr/library/2015/04/27Apple-Reports-Record-Second-Quarter-Results.html?sr=hotnews.rss). Its managing director's catchphrase – 'no-one wants to buy sour milk' – is challenged by criticisms of its labour practices, notably in China (the so-called Foxconn suicides in 2010, and the Shenzhen factory making circuit boards for the iPhone and iPad; see www.globallabourrights.org/reports/exhaustion-has-no-limit-at-apple-supplier-in-china). We will see later in this chapter, in relation to the 'fast fashion' industry, how extended and complex supply chains make public accountability much more problematic. The challenge too is to keep coming up with a new product, a fresh example of the brand.

Apple is but one major corporate global player which has a host of interconnected products: desktop computers, laptops, iPod (2001), iPhone (2007), iPad (2010) and the Apple Watch (2014).[6] The focus is far less on the individual product and much more on lifestyle – being an Apple person, buying into the range – where the technology can seem less important than the marketing.

Apple designer Jonathan Ive commented: 'What people are responding to is much bigger than the object. They are responding to something rare – a group of people who do more than simply make something work, they make the very best products they possibly can. It's a demonstration against thoughtlessness and carelessness' (John Arlidge (2014) 'Jonathan Ive designs tomorrow', *Time*, 17 March (Time Inc.)). Whether having a lengthy supply chain over which it is hard to practise vigilance constitutes thoughtlessness and carelessness is a moot point.

Buying the lifestyle

Such corporate brands are not simply selling a useful piece of kit, but a lifestyle, even membership of a community, a set of values which are tied up with the product. Webb points out that Nike presents itself as 'enhancing people's lives through sport and fitness', while Polaroid is no longer a camera but a 'social lubricant' (2006: 60). The trouble is that this does not guarantee survival, for the Polaroid Corporation (founded in 1937) was bankrupted in 2001 and again in 2008, and has reinvented itself as a brand licensor to companies that distribute consumer electronics and eyewear. In 2010 it appointed Lady Gaga as the 'creative director' for the company, a talent many of her fans were unaware that she possessed.

Polaroid Eyewear, actually owned by Italian company Safilo, announced the closure of its Vale of Leven factory in Dunbartonshire in 2016, on the grounds that 'the current supply chain could not support the global brand expansion in a sustainable way' (BBC, 'Polaroid plant closure at Vale of Leven', 9 February 2016). The factory had begun as a film plant in 1965, made cameras in 1969, and ended production of both in 1996. Eyewear production (sunglasses, to you and me) began in 1972, ending in 2016.

Worshipping consumption

Setting is all. Without it, we cannot believe. That is the essence of Jean Baudrillard's comment (1983) that the 'real' is no longer real, and Umberto Eco's observation that 'absolute unreality is offered as real presence' (1987). We have discussed in Chapter 17 how 'staged authenticity' relates to tourism in Scotland, but McCannell's concept (1992) conveys the importance of providing a meaningful forum for activities. It is inappropriate to set up a shop in a funeral parlour, but you can actually buy cheese in the foyer of Edinburgh Royal Infirmary. The setting has to be right to make it believable.

The fuzziness of the distinction between shopping, advertising and entertainment present challenges and opportunities. The Disney Corporation's theme parks are monuments to their own contrived reality of cartoon characters 'made real'. The first Disney World arrived in California in 1955; Florida in 1971; Tokyo in 1983; and EuroDisney in 1992, possibly the least successful in terms of custom, and requiring refinancing of debt by the parent corporation. Why that should be so may have something to do with its locale, its setting, 20 miles (32 km) from Paris in northern France, which lacks the Florida weather.

Cathedrals of consumption

Ritzer (1999) describes such settings as 'cathedrals of consumption' because they are 'quasi-religious' and enchanted places which 'have become locales to which we make "pilgrimages" in order to practice our consumer religion' (1999: x). His descriptor 'cathedral' is eye-catching, but begs the question as to its metaphorical usefulness. Cathedrals are centres of religious faith requiring high priests, a faithful, and the belief in a transcendental being. Metaphors have their limitations as well as their uses.

Other types of settings rush to emulate cathedrals of consumption, places like universities, hospitals, 'accessory shops' at sports venues where you can buy the accoutrements to support your team even if you cannot afford a ticket to see them play. The problem, though, says Ritzer, is that the 'cathedrals' become evermore disenchanting to the jaded customers they have been designed to attract.

So added fixes of 'enchantment' are required: new products, new performances, new practices. Thus, the largest shopping venue in the United States[7] is the self-styled Mall of America, built in Minnesota in 1992, which is dedicated to selling *'nu stuff'* on top of a children's theme park in the basement (Nickelodeon Universe, and Sea Life Minnesota), and which makes no effort to disguise its shed-like quality (see Figure 23.1).

Added fixes of spectacle are needed, such as building an ice castle 12 metres tall made of icicles using 4 million gallons (15 million litres) of water in the winter of 2012–13.

FIGURE 23.1
nuStuff: Mall of America, Bloomington, Minnesota

Source: Author's photograph

'Spectacles' of this sort are deemed necessary to attract customers and increase footfall. Despite the fact that the Mall of America is dominated by the usual brand shopping (an Apple Store, LEGO, Hard Rock Café, for example) it has struggled to fill its stores: in 2015 it was 4 per cent empty, but as high as 40 per cent ten years previously, especially its fourth floor where footfall has proven hard to come by.

The Mall of America is a good example of the constant need to 're-enchant', in order to attract customers, especially as, according to Ritzer, the average length of visit to shopping malls has dropped to seventy minutes (down ten minutes in thirty years). The fact that most of the shops are familiar 'high street' names (but no longer selling on the high street as such) reflects Ritzer's view that superstores are 'category killers' which drive out the variety and low prices offered by specialty shops.

The search for the extravaganza conforms to Baudrillard's 'real unreal'. Ritzer gives the example of Las Vegas:

Where else can you find New York City, Monte Carlo, Bellagio, Venice and Paris within a few minutes walk of one another? Even if you went to one of those 'real' cities, you would be able to experience only it and not the others. In any case, the tourist areas of those cities have themselves become simulations. (1999: 118)

Then there is the real Death Valley, a few hundred drivable miles away, but few visiting Las Vegas actually travel there. Ritzer's view: 'For a society raised on the movies, television, video games, and computer imagery, Death Valley can seem dull and uninteresting' (1999: 118). Much better, he thinks, if some Vegas entrepreneur were to erect a themed casino called 'Death Valley'. Punters could 'die' there every night, and go back the next day to repeat the exercise.

Scotland has its own struggles with realities. While the Pictavia Visitor Centre (http://pictavia.activclient.com/About/About.aspx) in north-east Scotland attracted a good crowd with youth appeal, the more 'academic' Archeolink Visitor Centre, which opened in 1997, finally closed its doors in 2011 (www.e-architect.co.uk/aberdeen/archaeo-link-visitor-centre). Pictavia announced in late 2014 that it too would close (www.thecourier.co.uk/news/local/angus-mearns/137229/pictavia-founding-team-member-surprised-it-has-lasted-so-long/).

The message? That 'consumer enchantment' requires the sanitisation of history such that history becomes 'heritage', a pastiche of itself, and we enter a process of 'Disneyfication'. In short, 'the market relies on the generation of unlimited needs and desires for goods, which by definition must not satisfy wants, making people susceptible to unstable assessments of self-worth and stimulating dissatisfaction' (Webb, 2006: 73).

The sociology of stuff

The weight of argument thus far might incline us to think that consumers are open to manipulation; that they are indeed 'cultural dopes'. The social anthropologist Daniel Miller takes a different view: that 'stuff' actually *creates* us in the first place, and is not some add-on extra; indeed, people are much more in control of culture than is usually implied. It is customary, Miller says, to see clothing as *semiotic*, as objects which signify or represent us. In other words, we aspire to belong, to identify, and we adopt the appropriate uniform. Rather, he says, 'the whole system of things, with their internal order, make us the people we are' (Miller, 2010: 53).

Culture comes, above all, from *stuff*. His own fieldwork in Trinidad convinced him that clothes, for example, are not some *reflection* of who we are, but the *essence* of who we are. Thus, in Trinidad, it is style, not fashion, which matters, being able to strut your stuff, or 'gallerying', as it is called. Poor people in Trinidad have many pairs of shoes because strutting your stuff, quite literally, is the essence of identity. Trinidadians define themselves and each other in terms of consumption, not production; not in terms of what you work at, but what car you drive or the houses you furnish; and cross-overs between the two: cars are heavily upholstered rooms on wheels, and decorated accordingly.

People, says Miller, do not succumb to what is on offer; they know what they want, and use it to good effect. We do feel alienated by consumer culture, but we keep our anonymity and distance through picking and choosing, and protecting our persons through the use of money, the purest expression of stuff. In that regard, consumption is less oppressive than production, 'so Baudrillard could not have been more wrong' (Miller, 2012: 57).

Miller argues that 'consumer culture should be regarded as authentic, but it has also rejected the assumption that it is necessarily individualistic, materialistic, competitive, or, indeed, capitalist' (2012: 63). In any case, he says, so-called tribal societies are often *more* materialistic than ours (cargo cults, for example in Melanesia, are based on the belief that performing ritual acts will lead to the bestowing of wealth). The extent and significance of material cultures are far more complex and nuanced, and when aboriginal people drift to towns and cities, they lose much of their cultural wealth.

It is not enough simply to consume stuff; it is necessary to exchange it, as much social anthropology makes us aware. Thus, 'through exchange, people learn to "get a life"' (2010: 66). Miller is making the point that 'we do not start from what societies do with things, it is the circulation of things that creates society ... society and stuff are actually artificial separations out of the same process' (2010: 67).

Stuff is us

We too have our own versions of that. When it comes to gift exchange, it is a bit insulting to send someone a present of money (unless the recipient is an impecunious teenager with complicated and baffling tastes).[8] Even the act of sending a Christmas card implies that some thought and effort has gone into the object; rather more, perhaps, than the less time-consuming act of sending people e-cards – possibly the same one (to say nothing of sending someone an e-goat, or donating to charity on their behalf; noble, perhaps, but somehow less intimate, saying more about the donor than the recipient). The 'object' somehow matters more, even if the card sits for a couple of weeks on a mantelpiece along with many others, and is then 'recycled'.

Clothes in particular are not to be viewed as objects which signify or represent us 'from the outside in'; that are principally signs or symbols which stand for the person. Stuff of this sort, says Miller, actually *is* 'us' in the first place; clothing in that sense is not superficial. Thus, 'clothing plays a considerable and active part in constituting the particular experience of the self, in determining what the self is' (2010: 38).

His own research on London streets makes an important point about territorial differences. He observes: 'in London clothing was found to be a source of anxiety, precisely because of the increasing pressure on individuals to express themselves, combined with the growing difficulty in determining one's own individual taste' (2010: 40). London, he avers, has a 'spectacular sense of drabness' (2010: 38). There is 'a suspicion in London of genres such as designer brands which for adults may be seen as vulgar or stupid. Entirely different from the situation in Madrid' (2010: 37) where classic, smart and expressive clothing is the norm; the *Madrileños* equivalent of strutting your stuff. 'Style' matters, but then in London it does too, even if it is of a different order.

Selling places

There is a Scottish version of this. In 2004, Glasgow adopted the branding slogan: 'Glasgow: Scotland with style'. (At its launch Glasgow declared itself as 'the new black' (http://news.bbc.co.uk/1/hi/scotland/3547313.stm).) It was picking up on a self-belief that Glaswegians are wedded to 'style', that its 'Style Mile' has popular appeal. It reproduced with approval the *Lonely Planet Guide*: 'Boasting the UK's largest retail phalanx outside London, Glasgow is a shopaholic's paradise. The "Style Mile" around Buchanan St, Argyle St and Merchant City is a fashion hub, while the West End has quirkier, more bohemian shopping options' (https://peoplemakeglasgow.com/things-to-do/shopping).

It is a key part of city branding, and it has clever implications. Thus, Glasgow as 'Scotland with style' might imply that *only* in the city do you find 'style' (that the rest of Scotland is a style desert), or that you can have both Scotland *and* style if you visit the city. Its 2004 strap-line was the successor to the one adopted in 1982, 'Glasgow's Miles Better', using the Mr Happy icon (from *Mr Men*). That itself was cleverly nuanced: Better than what? Than it used to be? Than you think it is? Than Edinburgh, its historic rival?

At a time when the tendency is to stress the homogenisation of culture under the impact of globalisation, here are interesting examples of the vibrancy of local cultures and styles – finding the niche – even if they are in large part the product of ad agencies, which, in any case, do not 'lick it off the floor', as the saying goes in Scotland.[9] There has to be resonance in the locality for it to 'work'; contrast Glasgow's with Edinburgh's feeble 'Inspiring Capital' (2005) or, worse still, 'Incredinburgh' (2012) which inspired incredulity and ridicule in the local media. Local rivalries were nicely captured by the cartoonist Steven Camley (see Figure 23.2).

The most unfortunate slogan was (past tense, because it was quickly dropped) 'Curious Suffolk', the English county, which, unwittingly, implied unfortunate mental capacities in its residents. Dundee has stuck steadfastly, if somewhat boringly, for two decades to 'City of Discovery' (after the sailing ship moored at its docks), and timidly venturing to 'One City: Many Discoveries' in 2009.[10] Aberdeen, as Scotland's third city, and per capita its wealthiest, has no strap-line, but did 'win' the award in 2015 for Scotland's most dismal place: 'The Plook on the Plinth'.[11] Perhaps only places in need of cultural and economic bootstrapping go in for advertising strap-lines.

Uniform blue jeans

While clothing and footwear only represent around 5 per cent of household expenditure in Scotland (much on a par with the rest of the UK), in cultural terms it seems far more significant to people's everyday lives. Let us then return to Miller's arguments about such

FIGURE 23.2
Selling cities

Source: I am grateful to Steven Camley for permission to use his cartoon which appeared in *The Herald* (29 April 2016)

consumption, and in particular the ubiquitous blue denim jeans. He observes: 'to understand jeans we have to push ourselves out of the frame where we take them for granted, and instead stare at them as something incomprehensible' (2012: 91).

What is it, he asks, which makes them so common that 50 per cent of people in the world wear them? Miller rejects the argument that global capitalism – 'the market' – is responsible and has forced us into standard uniform. Jeans are not only ubiquitous, but highly intimate and personal, even to the extent that they are 'weathered' for us (distressed, for example, by stone-washing, or being slashed at the knees) in advance of purchase. Wearing blue jeans is not about 'being American', although that is where they originated (in truth, the fabric originated as hard-wearing indigo-dyed cotton, '*serge de Nîmes*', and there is a modest museum in that French town).

Nor is it about 'designer jeans' of an aspirational sort. Miller observes that in a metropolis like London (to which he attributes a grunge culture in any case, 'a kind of particular nowhere'), jeans are 'garments of transition': 'Migrants now use jeans to become and be seen as ordinary in much the same way as do non-migrants' (2012: 104). They are described by wearers as 'comfortable', culturally and socially, if not corporeally. It is not that people are conformist, but that jeans allow people to 'fit in', 'be themselves', be 'comfortable' in that sense.

Miller's point is that objects should be taken at face value and not reduced to their 'symbolic' relationship to persons. He broadens his argument: 'The single main problem with conventional writing about consumption is that it seems to consist largely of authors who wish to claim that they are deep by trying to show how everyone else is shallow' (2012: 107).

Miller's general disposition to consumption is at odds with what has become the conventional wisdom. What we consume, above all what we wear, is not wished upon us by global capitalism. Our jeans may be stone-washed, but their wearers are not brain-washed. Rather than 'the economy' being rational, scientific and intelligent, Miller thinks that it is remarkably stupid, usually having to chase the fashion after it has been adopted, and slow on the uptake. Where it is successful (and he uses his Trinidad examples to make the point), the role of advertising is to translate the product into the locality, such as Coca-Cola, the classic global product, which can only 'work' if it is translated and indigenised. In key regards, it is the consumers who are 'in charge'.

Doing the shopping

Miller's own detailed ethnography involved following people around as they did their shopping, which is nuanced and complex. Shoppers are 'different people' as they shop in different situations; subdued and respectful in John Lewis (as befits its class aura), and more boisterous and joshing in the local markets. They are more than capable of this 'code-switching' depending on socio-economic contexts, and know how to 'behave' appropriately.

Miller found little evidence of advertising guiding people's shopping choices, whether in London or Trinidad. He did find, however, that people distinguished between 'bog standard' shopping for food and other necessities which people – usually women (shopping is 'gender-saturated') – did almost on a daily basis (the 'housewife' role) versus 'Shopping' as high ritual – what we might call Saturday afternoon shopping, which involves 'treats'.

Thus, says Miller, 'the action which acts to make thrift work effectively turned out to be the "treat"' (2012: 81). 'Treats' are seen as rewards for buying 'necessities' – 'an act of labour on behalf of the household' – as a reward to self. If you practise 'thrift' on behalf of the family, then you allow yourself a 'reward', often in the form of chocolate. Miller comments: 'shopping as sacrifice is not experienced as a religious rite, but it is saturated with the devotion we associate with love' (2012: 85), a means of expressing devotion to those we care about, including pets.

Miller, then, is arguing that shopping is not a programmed activity carried out by automatons at the behest of consumer capitalism, but that it confers choice and empowerment for people, in Trinidad and on Camden High Street alike. Such consumer behaviour is often contradictory. People express the value of having local shops, but continue to shop at the supermarket; or to approve of ethical shopping, while recognising that being 'organic' comes at a price, at the expense of ubiquitous 'thrift': thus, 'moral concerns for one's own family are experienced as a kind of natural and warm attitude. Concerns for the planet and exploitation are focused on more distant and abstract goals, which don't carry the same sense of immediacy and warmth' (2012: 89).

The home as temple to stuff

Above all, Miller claims, houses are 'the elephants of stuff' (2010: 81). Not only are they containers for smaller stuff, but are themselves the most expensive stuff that most of us are likely to buy. Housing as stuff is complex, and has been a big disappointment to many architects. Le Corbusier liked to say that a house was a machine for living in – and, hence, functionality was all – but, as Miller says, 'he had no defence against "nice" and "pretty"' (2010: 83).

It is a well-known practice for home owners to change their kitchens (and/or bathrooms), not because the previous are inadequate, but because they wish to put their personal signature, their stamp, on the dwelling. Nor is this the result of brainwashing by the kitchen- or bathroom-fitting industries, but the desire of the consumers to make it their 'own'. A good example of that is what is known in Scotland as the 'bought house', purchased by long-standing tenants of their former council houses. Their first act is to change the front door for one which signals the change of ownership: this is me.

Regardless, people have ingenuity and individuality when it comes to their gardens, as any casual survey shows.[12] The growth of the DIY industry emerged out of house moves in the last thirty years and the desire to put one's stamp on property. Miller comments that DIY usually involved gender alliances: women as the drivers; men doing the physical work:

> The rise of DIY in effect saved men's sense of their own masculinity and gave them an appropriate role within the house … but without the aesthetic direction of women, men felt they could do nothing. Without the manual labour of men, women felt they could do nothing. (2010: 88)

IKEA-building was an activity in which both were required, if only because self-assembly is usually impossible with only one pair of hands.

It has become a truism in sociology that 'home-centredness' is a central life value for people, regardless of whether they own or rent. We began this chapter with the quotation from Miller, in which he said: 'right there, in the living room, the bathroom, the bedroom and the kitchen. This is where most of modern life is lived' (2010: 109). Not only are they major stuff containers, but houses are stuff in their own right – big stuff. We fill them with personal items, decorate their mantels and sideboards with mementos and photographs, usually of kith and kin, with the message: this is who we are; this is who we have come from.

Other people's stuff

The trauma of clearing out 'stuff', especially that of a relative who has died, presents us with challenges and traumas because stuff resonates with biography; it tells us who we are. The 'house clearance' industry offers another personal service which makes it somewhat less painful if it is left to strangers to sort through family stuff and dispose of it. In any case, our attitude to 'stuff' has changed across the generations.

The superfluity of 'charity shops' in the UK does not signify the emiseration of the population so much as the desire to rummage among other people's stuff to find the quixotic and fashionable. For my parents' generation, the equivalent would have been a mark of penury and stigma (arguably still associated with the US Thrift shops, but not the 'garage' sale). One of the earliest charity shops in the UK was opened by the Edinburgh University Settlement in 1937 as 'Everybody's Thrift Shop'. *The Scotsman* newspaper of the day noted that: 'One woman went off triumphant with a handsome suit worn, it was whispered, by a professor'; and the ubiquitous Oxfam began in Oxford in 1947.

The rise and rise of the student generation from the 1960s gave new value to second-hand clothing, opportunities for new 'style' to emerge, before spreading throughout the population for whom browsing in charity shops has become a national pastime. The challenge for such shops is how to maintain the flow of goods, as they jostle with each other on the high street.

Miller's perspective on consumption is a healthy antidote to the more conventional sociology which views 'capitalism' as determining our consumption of stuff, with advertising its helpful assistant. Rather, he takes the view that 'material culture appears as society made tangible, the hard, strong material presence that displays itself forthrightly such that we cannot escape its presence' (2010: 155). This is set against the capacity of stuff to fade from view, to become naturalised, the background frame for our behaviour; 'stuff achieves its mastery of us precisely because we constantly fail to notice what it does' (2010: 155).

The strength of Miller's approach is in giving us a detailed understanding of how and what we consume, almost on a day-to-day basis. There is, though, another aspect to be considered: where stuff comes from, the 'political economy' of stuff, and it is that to which we now turn.

Fast and slow fashions

In a remarkable display, the Museum für Kunst und Gewerbe (MK&G)[13] hosted an exhibition on Fast Fashion in Hamburg in 2015. Its accompanying book comments:

> In no other area of the consumer goods industry does the principle of creating new needs function as well as in fashion. Fast Fashion, a success story which has been surging upwards since the 1990s, has increased this 'must have' motivation exponentially: within a fortnight the big fashion names, thanks to verticalization, manage to launch their new collections on the market. The price of clothing is dropping, and with it the quality.

Whereas haute couture has catered for the premium market in women's fashions since 1886 (when *Chambre Syndicale de la Haute Couture* was founded), the ready-to-wear (prêt-à-porter) market focused on clothing tailored according to standardised size tables and industrially manufactured products, usually designed by a named designer, using quality materials and with small production runs at locations in relatively high-wage countries such as Italy.

Many haute couture designers (like Yves Saint Laurent; Chanel) got into prêt-à-porter, recognising the added value in terms of sales, and drip-feeding the mass market. However, as Angelika Riley observed:

> Copying is in the DNA of fashion, we might even go as far as to say: no fashion without imitation. Fashions in clothing came about through the fact that a large group of people emulate someone seen as a model and copy their style of dressing. (MK&G, 2015: 65)

Fast and cheap fashion

'Product piracy' is not easy to police. There was a shift to developing countries in the 'new international division of labour', especially in clothing production where supply chains are highly complex and characterised by a high degree of intermediary trade and subcontracting. This made it virtually impossible to trace the lineage. Large manufacturing companies receive orders from buying companies, and they assume responsibility for samples production, fabric procurement, garment styles, product quality control and even design itself.

Work stages such as sewing, printing, packaging and so on are outsourced to smaller sub-manufacturers who may be in other regions, or even countries. A pair of jeans may be designed in the Netherlands, the cotton grown in Uzbekistan, the spinning and weaving done in India, dyeing in China or Indonesia, sewing in Bangladesh, finishing (notably sand-blasting) in Turkey, retailing in Germany, and disposed of as used clothing, ending up in Zambia (MK&G, 2015: 38–9).

The 'liberalisation' of the Multi-Fibre Agreement (MFA) – the global textile agreement[14] – opened up markets in developed societies to developing countries which often created 'free export zones' to attract foreign investors through low wages and tax exemptions, with few questions asked.

Textile processing in these countries consumes large quantities of non-renewable resources (such as water) and frequently offers few protective measures against toxic chemicals. Global comparisons of fibre consumption showed a three-fold increase in chemical fibres between 1992 and 2012, a modest one in cotton (+1.3) and a decline in the use of wool (a decline in this period of 40 per cent) (2015: 53).

The Fast Fashion study asked: 'why is it possible that today a T-shirt costs less than an XL coffee, a dress the same as a big ice-cream sundae or a pair of trousers the same as a cinema ticket?' (2015: 15). The answer is that 90 per cent of clothes are now produced in low-wage countries, mainly in Asia.

The worldwide production of fast fashion goods

Because parts of the production process are passed on to sub-manufacturers, inspection cannot be carried out. Indeed, premier buyers turn a blind eye, or claim to be unaware of the intricacies of the production process as long as it produces at the price and volume required.

FIGURE 23.3
No irony
intended

Source: Fast
Fashion exhibition;
author's
photograph

Transparency only arises when disaster strikes, as in the Rana Plaza disaster in Bangladesh in 2013, when the building collapsed, killing over 1000 workers (www.theguardian.com/world/rana-plaza). The factories in the building included high street names such as Benetton, Monsoon, Matalan, Primark and Walmart, many of whom claimed not to know their goods were being manufactured there (the irony is nicely captured in Figure 23.3).

Slow fashion

The contrasts with other forms of the fashion business are instructive. 'Slow Fashion' seeks to focus on sustainable, aware and ethical fashion (analogous to the 'slow food' concept), where as far as possible products are mostly locally sourced from existing, sustainable and innovative materials, with a short production chain, and where the steps from fibre to processing remain visible.

FIGURE 23.4
Cheap at the price

Source: Author's photograph

"We work for about 12-14 hours a day. We work on Sundays and holidays. Yet, we don't get a wage that could fulfill our basic needs."
Krishanthi, garment worker in Bangladesh

Shirt
€ 0,10

Nevertheless, the authors of the Fast Fashion report calculated that the price of a T-shirt made by 'slow fashion' at €19.90 contains 3 per cent in wages, compared with the 'fast fashion' T-shirt which cost €4.99 (and only marginally less wage component at 2.6 per cent). The middle-price version cost €29 with less than 1 per cent in wage costs (2015: 48–9) (see Figure 23.4).

Throw-away fashion

Where does such clothing end up? The authors of the Fast Fashion report calculated that Germans spent around 4.6 per cent of household consumption on clothing and footwear[15] (virtually identical to what the British spent, at 4.7 per cent; Scots spent 5.1 per cent). As much as 40 per cent of clothing in German wardrobes was unworn, and the ratio of new clothes consumption compared with what was disposed of is just under 2:1 (the EU ratio is 2.5:1), as befits the most affluent country in the EU.

Around two-thirds of used clothing which is discarded either by owners or charity shops is exported to developing markets for resale locally, where it undergoes a complex sorting process, with high-value brands going to Eastern Europe and Russia, good-quality summer wear to Africa, and low-quality items to South Asia (see Lucy Norris, MK&G, 2015: 142–7). India imports more than 100,000 tons pa of used clothing for industrial recycling.

The material is sorted into piles by colour, and then shredded with a view to being carded and spun as regenerated yarn. Panipat in northern India has more than 300 mills recycling old clothes into yarn, turning it into 'shoddy',[16] a technology invented in nineteenth-century Yorkshire, and a term which took on wider significance thereafter in the English language to refer to anything sub-standard. Thus, the simple product of the T-shirt has a complex, and often dangerous, geography and a history.

Conclusion

As elsewhere in the western world, people in Scotland have an obsession with stuff. In that regard they are no different from anyone else, and if Daniel Miller is correct, no one on the planet escapes this obsession. That is not to say that everyone has the same relationship to stuff. In a system of global production, people in Scotland consume far more stuff than they ought to, both in terms of their per capita share of the world's resources and in buying into the stuff chain such that we occupy a much more elevated position in that chain.

A century or more ago, our forebears were much more likely to consume stuff which was produced locally. Those who could afford stuff went to local producers, had their clothes made by local tailors, or, more likely for most of the population, relied on hand-me-downs, wearing other people's trousers (recall the person who was proud to purchase 'a professor's suit' from Edinburgh's first charity shop in 1937). The rise in affluence in the post-war period, coupled with the cheaper cost of stuff, meant that cheap labour elsewhere produced the stuff we bought, and as a consequence drove manufacturers out of business.

There is irony in the fact that the early Industrial Revolution in Scotland was based on textiles, on linen and flax, on cotton and jute produced elsewhere but processed in Scotland. Nowadays, we wear clothes made anywhere but Scotland, and, if we do, we pay much more for them. Think of the Harris Tweed industry (www.harristweed.org).

At the same time, the perceived value lies far less in the objects themselves, their utility, their use value, and far more in what they represent to others, their brand image. Stuff gives off the message: we are *these* kinds of people; we value *these* sorts of things; *we* have taste. So much consumption has to do with differentiating ourselves from *those* people; of wearing our values on our sleeves. In the next chapter, we will look at the phenomenon of 'globalisation' and Scotland's place within it. Stopping the world and getting off is not much of an option.

Chapter summary

So what have we learned in this chapter?

- That consumerism is the central feature of contemporary capitalism and, more to the point, it is a belief system, an 'ism'.

- That the production and consumption of stuff are inextricably linked; that almost everything has its price.

- That erecting warehouses of stuff locks into lifestyle choices; that shopping becomes an end in itself rather than simply a means to keeping ourselves provisioned.

- That stuff is 'us' in the first place, rather than being an externalisation of our needs and desires.

- That our consumption of stuff has direct implications for people around the world; that our consumption practices have deep implications for people's ways of life.

Questions for discussion

1. Why is consumerism a central feature of contemporary capitalism? How has this come about, and over what period?

2. Is people's consumer taste simply determined by their social class?

3. To what extent do we buy the 'brand' rather than the object itself? How influenced are we by marketing and branding in deciding what to buy?

4. Have 'cathedrals to consumption', the shopping malls, been inextricably damaged by online shopping? If so, why?

5. Is the exploitation of producers in the Third World inevitable in our pursuit of cheaper and faster fashion?

Annotated reading

(a) On the sociology and anthropology of consumption, see J. Webb, *Organisations, Identities and the Self* (2006); D. Miller, *Stuff* (2010) and *Consumption and its Consequences* (2012); E. McDonnell, 'Budgetary units: a Weberian approach to consumption', *American Journal of Sociology*, 119(2), 2013; P. Bourdieu, *Distinction: A social critique of the judgment of taste* (1984); and R. Jenkins, *Pierre Bourdieu* (1992).

(b) On the fusion of production and consumption, see G. Ritzer, 'The "new" world of prosumption: evolution, "the return of the same", or revolution?', *Sociological*

Forum, 30(1), 2015; G. Ritzer, *The McDonaldization of Society* (1993); and G. Ritzer, *Enchanting a Disenchanted World* (1999).

(c) On the global fashion industry, see Museum für Kunst und Gewerbe (MK&G), *Fast Fashion: The dark sides of fashion* (2015).

Notes

1 Variations are largely the result of the high figures for London and south-east England, notably on housing expenditure.

2 Packard's subsequent books, *The Status Seekers* (1959) and *The Waste Makers* (1960), also became bestsellers.

3 A law outlawing revenge porn was passed by the Scottish parliament in March 2016.

4 Bourdieu is not referring to the (British) profession of social work, but to forms of employment which require high levels of social capital and interpersonal skills but are relatively poorly paid.

5 The story goes that the bite out of the apple was to avoid people confusing it with a cherry.

6 One review of the Apple Watch commented: 'Apple Watch is good, but better suited on the wrists of early adopters and boutique shop regulars. It's convenient but there's a learning curve you have to overcome and a high price that some people won't be able to get around' (www.techradar.com/reviews/wearables/apple-watch-1264567/review). It sells for around £250.

7 The largest mall in North America is actually in West Edmonton, Alberta, Canada.

8 A friend puzzled over what to give 14-year-old girls for Christmas. She 'googled' the question, and found that bobble hats were the current in-thing. Thereafter she was thought to have very cool taste.

9 That is, picking up the local vibes.

10 Perhaps there might be a plan to have 'One Discovery: Many Cities'.

11 A 'plook' in Scots is a disfiguring pimple, that is a 'carbuncle'.

12 And the garden has the merit of being able to be surveyed unobtrusively, unlike the house interior. Take a stroll down any street and note the variations in exterior décor.

13 Roughly translated as the Museum for Arts and Crafts.

14 The Multi-Fibre Agreement imposed quotas on Third World production of clothing, and lasted from 1974 until 2004. From 2005, there was a massive expansion of cheap products into western markets from countries like China and Bangladesh.

15 Women's annual expenditure on clothes in Germany was twice that of men's (€4400 to €2200).

16 Shoddy was an inferior quality yarn or fabric made from the shredded fibre of waste woollen cloth or clippings.

24

SCOTLAND AND THE WORLD

Consider this. Just at the point at which the political movement for Scottish independence has never been stronger, indigenous control of Scottish industry has never been weaker. The Scottish economy has been hollowed out by 'globalisation'; it is hard to deny the 'branch-plant' status of Scotland (see Chapter 8). This applies to heavy industry and manufacturing, such as is left. The banking crash of 2008 removed the Scottish banks from their historic hub status at the centre of the Scottish economy. What appears to be left is the semblance of Scottishness, not its substance. The puzzle we confront in this chapter is how to reconcile the political demands for greater self-government with the hollowing-out of the Scottish economy.

FIGURE 24.1
'Scotland ... obviously!'

Source: Courtesy of the National Map Library in Edinburgh to whom I am grateful for permission to use this billboard image

Chapter aims

- To define 'globalisation' as conventionally understood.
- To ask whether the concept helps analytically to make sense of the modern world.

- To apply it to Scotland, with a view to understanding the wider political and cultural implications.

- To re-examine the nexus between politics, economics and society so as to rebalance our understanding of Scotland in the modern world (cf. Figure 24.1).

In the previous chapter we saw that 'globalisation' has transformed consumption in Scotland, and in Chapter 21 that it was an influential framework for understanding sport. It has been argued by some that the 'global' has reshaped the local and the national so as to reduce their value and meaning significantly (Held et al., 2010). In this chapter we will look at the argument that 'globalisation' has altered the social world so significantly that 'the world has become a single place'.

There is, however, another view of these things, to which we will return at the end of this chapter, which argues that the 'globalised' economy of pre-1913 Scotland evolved in the subsequent century into a much more self-reliant entity (Tomlinson, 2014). Far from Scotland being 'hollowed out' as an economic nation, it has become, arguably, much more of a 'community of fate'.

This has implications for how we interpret the transformation of Scottish politics and society. If there is precious little 'economy' left to control, how are we to explain the rise of nationalism in Scotland and the creation of a home rule parliament? Do we simply adduce that this amounts to closing the door after the economic horse has bolted? Is the rise of 'nationalism' simply the ideological after-effect of economic and industrial transformation?

There is a view that latter-day nationalism simply evokes the desire to 'stop the world – I want to get off'; that it is an emotional reaction to the loss of real political, economic and cultural control (Ignatieff, 1994). David Held has argued that 'democracy and most govern-ance concepts that assume the integrity of the nation-state must live with the fact that this assumption becomes increasingly challenged as we shift from a world of national commu-nities to "overlapping communities of fate"' (2014: 494–5). He concludes: 'The state is no longer a silo; it cannot be treated as a self-contained unit' (2014: 494–5). One might, of course, argue that it never was such a thing; that much of the globalisation thesis depends upon contrasting the globalised present with a presumed non-globalised past. To claim that 'the state' was ever as self-contained as this is contentious, but that is to anticipate a later argument.

What is globalisation?

Let us begin with the definition by Held and McGrew:

> Globalization denotes the intensification of worldwide social relations and interactions such that distant events acquire very localized impacts and vice versa. It involves a rescaling of social relations, from the economic sphere to the security sphere, beyond the national to the transnational, transcontinental and transworld. (2007: 2)

The authors argue that globalisation is a historical process characterised by:

- a stretching of social, political and economic activities across political frontiers;

- the intensification of interconnectedness in almost every sphere of social existence;

- the accelerating pace of transborder interactions and processes;

- the growing extensity, intensity and velocity of global interactions and, in particular, the enmeshing of the local and the global.

Held and McGrew conclude:

> Rather than growing interdependence between discrete bounded national state, or internationalization, the concept of globalization describes a structural shift underway in the organization of human affairs: from a world of discrete but interdependent national states to the world as a shared space. (2007: 3)

This definition has a number of features which are worth drawing out. First, the focus is on *social* relations, which is used as a generic term encompassing economic and political dimensions. Held and McGrew's focus is much more on the latter two dimensions than the 'social' more narrowly defined.

Second, the implication is that the four key elements of globalisation – extensity, intensity, velocity and impact – are premised on the assumption that these are qualitatively and quantitatively different than previously, and so transformative in their effect.

Third, the impact is primarily on 'states', sometimes described as 'national states' (Tilly, 1990). Because they are 'understated',[1] nations such as Scotland are presumed to be subject to similar processes, but even less in control of key institutions, and hence, if anything, *more* vulnerable to globalisation. The counter-argument is that understated nations are reflecting the *decline* of current state autonomy. As the possibility of state break-up becomes more likely, so we can think of such understated nations as a symptom rather than a cause.

Tracking globalisation

Although the term was first used in the 1960s, 'globalisation' came into fashion in the late 1980s in order to reflect the growth of transnational corporations, which grew in number from 7000 in 1970 to 80,000 in 2013 (Eriksen, 2014: 2). The transformation of markets, and in particular the hugely enhanced speed of financial transactions, revolutionised ways of doing business. In the UK and the United States in particular, from the 1980s policies of deregulation and privatisation were promoted by key international players such as the International Monetary Fund and the World Bank, aided and abetted by the respective Treasury departments (known as the 'Washington Consensus').

Neo-liberal economics found a new lease of life after monetarism,[2] and in the UK was thought to be both inevitable and desirable by Labour and Conservative governments alike. Tony Blair's 'New Labour' regime from 1997 bought enthusiastically into the project, as reflected in the HM Treasury report 'Long-Term Global Economic Challenges and Opportunities for the UK', 2004 (http://news.bbc.co.uk/nol/shared/bsp/hi/pdfs/02_12_04_pbr04global_421.pdf). Held observed:

> The Blair–Brown governments simply took globalization as a given, and argued that in a world of free financial and economic flows, the options of the nation-state had been radically reduced. So all that could be done was to adapt to global markets. (Held, 2014: 494)

By the time former Chancellor Gordon Brown became Prime Minister in 2007, the implications were working their way through the economic and political systems (see Crouch, *The Strange Non-Death of Neo-Liberalism*, 2011). The banking crash of 2008 provided a momentary respite, before the financial merry-go-round cranked up again. Globalised trade, complex supply chains and outsourcing reflected new ways of doing business, and states played catch-up.

Globalisation was championed in the early 1990s by journalists like Martin Wolf of the *Financial Times*. His book, *Why Globalization Works* (1994), was a celebration of the virtues as well as the inevitability of the process, and received encomiums in the financial press including the *Wall Street Journal* and *The Economist*. A decade later, Wolf was expressing misgivings that society was in danger of being hollowed out by globalisation, and that the social inequality which resulted threatened to destabilise the social, and ultimately the economic, order.[3]

The hegemony of globalisation?

Globalisation, is, in any case, not simply an 'economic' process, but a political, social and cultural one. Roland Robertson, whose writing on sport we encountered in Chapter 21, defined globalisation in the early 1990s as the compression of the world, and the intensification of the consciousness of the world as a whole (1992). Here was an altogether more ambitious and transformative process beyond simply describing new ways of doing business.

The social anthropologist Thomas Eriksen has described globalisation as a process of 'disembedding' (Eriksen, 2014) such that anything can be accessed anywhere, but above all it is de-territorialised such that things, people, ideas are lifted out of their original context. This is 'global modernity', which involves a disembedding process with transnational and global reach.

What George Ritzer famously called 'McDonaldization' brought together both economic and cultural processes:

> McDonaldization is the process by which the rational principles of the fast-food restaurant are coming to dominate more and more sectors of society and more societies throughout the world. It leads to the creation of rational systems – like fast-food restaurants – that are characterised by the most direct and efficient means to their ends. (Ritzer and Guppy, 2014: 12)

Such systems have four characteristics, namely a focus on:

efficiency, with an emphasis on using the quickest and least costly means;

calculability, with emphasis on 'quantities', not the quality, of food (thus, *big* Macs);

predictability, producing a standardised product and service globally, whether you were in Bangkok or Baltimore; and

control, using precisely the same processes in frying hamburgers, for example. There is little prospect of asking to have your hamburger well done or rare; you get what the company at its Oak Brook, Illinois HQ decides.

Ritzer's study of McDonaldization caught the eye because it combined an account of the economic, organisational and cultural aspects of modern capitalism. McDonaldization stood as an exemplar of globalisation. The fast-food restaurant not only was an ubiquitous way of consuming food, but became iconic of society itself, with the focus on efficiency, calculability, predictability and control, set, of course, within the parameters defined by the process. To its critics its food was fast, homogeneous and tasteless, designed to leave people wanting more.

Accounting for globalisation

What are we to make of globalisation, and its contention that the world has become a single place? The concept of 'globalisation' seems to explain too much as well as too little. While there is a case for saying that 'economic' processes have been transformed by the easing of capital flows, by the impact of the Internet, by the ability of high-frequency trading to shape markets (Mackenzie, 2014), it is quite another to claim that this is inevitable, driven simply by the dictates of markets and technologies.

Embracing such processes by the Blair–Brown Labour governments in the early 2000s was a *political* choice, not an economic given. Politicians are often accused of ignoring the 'laws of economics' (Stephanie Flanders, *Financial Times*, 29 December 2015),[4] but the reverse is at least as true: that economics fails to give due credence to 'politics'. The old term 'political economy' has much to commend it.

Other states (by all accounts, Canada) held to traditional and tighter ways of doing financial business leading up to the financial crash, adopting a more 'conservative' strategy in terms of financial deregulation, with fewer destructive effects on the 'real' economy. That British choice to hitch its wagon to financial deregulation left subsequent Labour governments in considerable difficulty after the bank crash of 2008, and arguably undermined the Labour Party election strategy in 2015. It was difficult to turn around an alternative political programme if one had to apologise for adopting enthusiastically a 'neo-liberal' policy set a decade earlier.

Our task in this chapter is to assess 'globalisation' in sociological rather than economic terms. One of the problems with the globalisation thesis is that it seeks to make arguments well beyond its 'economic' remit. Hence Robertson's early claim above that globalisation was about 'the compression of the world and the intensification of the consciousness of the world as a whole', and Giddens' view that 'the world has become a single place'. The riposte is to ask (a) how can we tell that this is now the case; and (b) what is the historic benchmark which permits us to come to that conclusion?

Writing as Editor of *Globalisation: Studies in anthropology*, Eriksen commented:

> The scope as well as the substance of globalisation seems to represent every-thing that a good social anthropologist should be wary of: grand comparisons often underpinned by flimsy evidence, whimsical and eclectic methodologies, a fondness for sweeping generalisations and, hovering in the background, the spectre of evolutionism. (2003: 3)

Eriksen proposed that we should get rid of the term itself, because 'it is a promiscuous and unfaithful word engaging in a bewildering variety of relationships, most of which would be better off using more accurate concepts' (2003: 4).

In a later book published in 2014, Eriksen seems to have done something of a volte-face, even allowing for the intensification of global processes. He talks about a 'compressed world', and argues that 'global modernity' involves a series of disembed-ded processes with transnational and potentially global reach. 'Disembedding' implies that anything can be accessed anywhere, that 'de-territorialisation' has taken place, and, further, that a shift from the 'concrete' and the tangible to the 'abstract' and intangible has occurred.

Included in this is religion. 'Concrete' society is based on intimate, personal relation-ships, memory, local religion and orally transmitted myths, whereas 'abstract' society is one based on formal legislation, archives, a book religion and written history. Perhaps, as we shall see later in this chapter, globalisation should be treated as the latest in a long line of social theories which are determined to explain the radical transformation of 'national societies' into one (world) Society (capital S).

Eriksen does argue that nationalism, 'often seen as an obstacle to globalization is a prod-uct of the same social forces that are shaping the latter'. This is because

> nationalism as a mode of social organization represents a qualitative leap from earlier forms of integration. Within a nation-state, all men and women are citi-zens, and they participate in a system of relationships where they depend upon, and contribute to, the existence of a vast number of individuals whom they will never know personally. (2014: 30)

At one level this may seem unexceptional, as a statement about the modernity of nation-alism and nation-states, much as described and analysed by Ernest Gellner (1983), but it is quite removed from assumptions that such states – and societies – have been replaced by a global system.

Questioning globalisation

The most sustained critique of the globalisation thesis is that of Paul Hirst et al.[5] (2009). The authors take issue with the claim that 'we live in an era in which the greater part of social life is determined by global processes, in which national cultures, national economies, national borders and national territories are dissolving' (2009: 2). They are critical of the ways in which the term 'globalisation' has the capacity to inflate its meaning, and, further, that the myth exaggerates the degree of helplessness in the face of wider economic forces. They argue for an alternative case:

- that the current highly internationalised economy is *not* unprecedented in history;

- that genuinely transnational companies are relatively rare;

- that the shift of investment and employment from advanced to developing countries driven by capital mobility is far less than is thought;

- that the world economy is far from being genuinely 'global';

- that major economic powers, notably in Europe, East Asia and North America, are able to exert powerful governance pressures over financial markets.

In short, the authors take the view that there is an *'inter*-national' economy rather than a globalised one, and that there is danger in exaggerating the degree of political helplessness in the face of contemporary economic forces. They conclude: 'the opposite of a globalized economy is not ... a nationally inward-looking one, but an open world market based on trading nations and regulated to a greater or lesser degree by both the public policies of nation-states and supranational agencies' (2009: 21). Far from the nation-state being undermined by the processes of globalisation, 'the state's national and international role continues to play an essential part in making and regulating cross-border activity' (2009: 23).

Bearing in mind that the ultimate task of this chapter is to locate Scotland in this globalisation debate, what are the implications of this view? The first point to make is that this is an argument about the role of *states* in the modern world. Nevertheless, a similar argument applies to would-be states. The assumption that from the 1990s neo-liberal capitalism had swept the board was alleged to reduce nation-states to 'the local authorities of the global system' (2009: 225). Their task was simply to provide the infrastructure and public goods required by business at the lowest cost. In short, the view was that national politics came more and more to resemble municipal politics in terms of providing services to business.

In the first place, however, most businesses continued to be local and/or national, and did *not* operate on the necessary global scale. As such, they required governing frameworks more suited to their scale of operations. Furthermore, controlling economic activity was less a matter for 'government' and more for systems of *'governance'*, that is purposive action undertaken by a range of public and semi-public bodies, and not strictly political systems narrowly defined.

In any case, most firms are embedded in national cultures and institutional arrangements which operate *within* the national state. Hirst et al. argued: 'Nation-states are now simply one class of power and political agency in a complex system of power from world to local level but they have a centrality because of their relationship to territory and population' (2009: 239). The role of the state as law-maker reinforces its institutional power, even where it is involved in translating supranational law locally (as in the cases of EU law, or the Human Rights Act).

The basis of legitimating the modern state is democracy. Thus, 'democratic elections and the rule of law legitimated the sovereign powers of state institutions and provided a better foundation for the state viewed as the organ of a self-governing territorial community than did the will of a prince' (2009: 223). By extension, where the legitimacy of the (British) state is questioned, as in Scotland, an alternative nationalism (re-)emerges, seeking to redraw state boundaries.

None of this implies that the crisis of state legitimacy forces people to look simply to the global level. Hollowing out the state helps to undermine its authority when alternative state forms – notably from below – become more legitimate. Further, it is to the state, current or future, that people look for redress, not to 'no state' at all.

One of the key arguments of those supporting 'Brexit' in the 2016 referendum, the proposal that the UK leaves the EU, was to reassert the power of the British state to control immigration, employment law, health and safety, not to *diminish* its power. After all, what neo-liberals seem to want is 'Free Market, Strong State', as Andrew Gamble (1994) pointed out. Thus, populations remain bound to a state, even if they seek to transfer allegiances to another. We should be careful too in assuming that migration between states in the early twenty-first century is greater than it was in the previous two centuries, whether in the form of forced or economic migration. Simply assuming that this is the case, in order to support a globalisation thesis, does not make it so.

Further, the emergence of transnational systems like the EU, or the North American Free Trade Agreement (NAFTA), indicates that supra-state bodies take on some of the political and governance tasks of individual states, especially where these are deemed too difficult for each state to deal with by itself.

The European Community/Union has developed as a way for member-states to 'export' their difficult problems of economic and social transformation – agriculture, industrial development – on to the supra-national level. Writing in 1992, the economic historian Alan Milward was critical of the view that there is a zero-sum competition between European integration and the sovereignty of the national state: that is, 'it implies that the economies, societies and administrations of these national entities become gradually merged into a larger identity' (1992: 2). There is, said Milward, no antithesis because the evolution of the European Community (EC, as it then was) had been an integral part of the reassertion of the nation-state as an organisational concept, and that without this process of integration, the Western European nation-states would have been struggling to retain the support and allegiance of their citizens. Far from there being even a trade-off of power to the detriment of the national level, 'the EC has been its buttress, an indispensable part of the nation-state's post-war construction. Without it, the nation-state could not have offered to its citizens the same measure of security and prosperity which it has provided and which has justified its survival' (1992: 3).

On the other hand, the controversy about the Transatlantic Trade and Investment Partnership (TTIP), a proposed trade agreement between the EU and the United States which would liberalise trade and reduce regulation with regard to environmental legislation, banking regulations and food safety law, and reduce as a consequence the powers of individual states, has mobilised a European Citizens' Initiative aiming to increase direct democracy in line with the Treaty of Lisbon in 2007 (http://waronwant.org/what-ttip).

Reasserting the state

One of the problems with the concept of globalisation is that it implies that states no longer matter and, as a consequence, nationalism, which is the pursuit of statehood in the interests of the nation, is thereby redundant. This is to confuse the 'global' with the 'international'. There is a considerable difference between a global economy and an international one, which provides an essential base from which national companies can trade. In short, there are many multinational companies, but very few genuinely transnational ones.

The national level, then, remains a political–economic base for most companies to operate from. If companies remain, by and large, national, then populations remain firmly bound to a territory. The people remain 'nationalised' insofar as the state regulates their migration, labour activities and social security. While the capacity of the state to control its territory has been reduced by the extension of international markets and communications media, it still retains considerable capacity to regulate its population. The result of this is that:

> States remain 'sovereign', not in the sense that they are all powerful or omnipotent within their territories, but because they police the borders of a territory and, to a degree that they are credibly democratic, they are representative of the citizens within these borders. (Hirst and Thompson, 1996: 190)

We might conclude, then, that the 'nation-state' is not dying, merely that it is undergoing radical transformation (Beetham, 1984; Mann, 1997). No longer could the state solve its key problems by itself; increasingly it looked to an association with its neighbours to solve common difficulties. This was a political–economic strategy of 'regionalisation', which reflected the impact of new global forces, driven by a new international division of labour (Keating, 1996).

The state was not ending but transforming, as it sought to come to terms with the new world economy. In the process, it found itself under challenge from above, the supra-state level, as well as below, from nationalist and regionalist movements who were asserting rights of greater self-determination in the new world order, made easier by the collapse of communism and greater liberalisation.[6]

We might say that globalisation has *engendered* nationalism, not *endangered* it. In part, this is because localism is the other side of the coin from globalism. It is also because 'globalisation' is a bundle of different but interconnected processes which impact at different speeds in different ways on different territories. The shifting geo-politics of the modern world alters the balance of forces between territorial levels.

Scotland today retains both the marks of its origin as well as later transformations designed to enable adjustment to modern international markets. The Scottish economist Neil Hood once observed:

> Scotland may be a small economy, but it speaks to the world. Its Gross Domestic Product may account for less that 9% of that of the UK. But it is, as it has historically long been, one of the most open economies in the world. Scotland has needed no lectures from a McKinsey manual on globalisation. Openness to trade and investment has, for more than a century, been one of its defining characteristics. (1999: 38)

In a prescient 1997 paper called 'Has globalization ended the rise and rise of the nation-state?', the sociologist Michael Mann pointed out that national and international networks proceeded alongside the expansion of transnational power relations: 'Thus the past saw the rise of transnational capitalism, and cultural identities alongside the rise of the nation-state and its international system. They have always possessed a complex combination of relative autonomy and symbiotic interdependence' (1997: 477). The error was to assume that *trans*-nationalism equates with 'globalisation'. Mann concluded:

> We must beware the more enthusiastic of the globalists and transnationalists. With little sense of history, they exaggerate the former strength of nation-states; with little sense of global variety, they exaggerate their current decline; with little sense of their plurality, they downplay inter-national relations. (1977: 494)

Mann was making a valid sociological observation that human societies are never to be equated simply with the political form of the state, but that they involved multiple, overlapping and intersecting networks of social interaction within and across them, and, reflected in the title of an earlier paper by Mann, that nation-states are diversifying, developing, not dying (1993).

Let us underline the point made earlier in this book that assuming that the political world is inhabited by 'national states' fitting together like a jigsaw puzzle is misguided. The demise of 'bloc politics' following the collapse of communism has made it easier for non- or understated nations – like Scotland – to assert their right to self-government. Tom Nairn has commented:

the old question used to be: 'Are you big enough to survive and develop in an industrializing world?' The advent of globalization is replacing this with another, something close to: 'are you small and smart enough to survive, and claim a positive place in the common global culture?' (2008)

The case of Denmark

Let us take another example, this time of a small state, Denmark, which has a population comparable with Scotland's. John Campbell and John Hall pointed to the economic success of small advanced capitalist countries like Denmark. What is it, they ask, which has given Denmark its competitive advantage? They argue that small countries tend to be culturally homogeneous and thus better able to develop institutional capacities to cope with vulnerabilities deriving from the global political economy. Such states develop strong and cohesive national identities, and in turn 'an ideology of social partnership which augments the possibilities for cooperation, sacrifice, flexibility and concerted state action in the national interest' (2009: 548).

Not only is size not everything, being small has the potential for market advantage. Note 'potential', for these are tendencies, not actualities. In the case of Denmark, which had been a 'big little country' in the sense that for much of its history it punched far above its demographic weight in political and economic matters, the loss of territory (notably Schleswig-Holstein south of Jutland in the 1864 war with Prussia) required a radical reconfiguration of *Danskhed* (Danishness). Influenced by the cultural nationalist Nikolaj Grundvig, Danish identity drew upon three characterisations of Danish culture: *Hygge* (cosiness/intimacy), *Tryghed* (security) and *Trivsel* (well-being), described by Schwarz as the 'three graces of Danish culture and socialisation' (in Østergård, 1992: 25).

Out of these (re)constructions came the modern notion of Danishness, stressing moderation and the democratic spirit as basic virtues. By the twentieth century, communitarian peasant traditions of solidarity and cooperation were transmitted from pre-modern village society to social democracy. This attracted an emerging working class, social democracy as a political ideology lasting well into the late twentieth century and beyond.

Campbell and Hall make this key point: 'common culture and persistent vulnerability unified the people as a nation and fostered an ideology of social partnership in which all the important social actors agreed to work together for the common good' (2009: 557). This is especially important because Denmark was an 'open' economy. The state encouraged economic diversification notably in agriculture, and in particular the switch, for geo-political reasons, from German to British markets in the late nineteenth century.

More recent challenges to cultural homogeneity reflecting migration patterns in the twenty-first century have presented the Danish cultural and political systems with further issues, especially to its underlying cultural values, reflected in the rise of right-wing social movements (Meret and Siim, 2013). Campbell and Hall conclude:

if threats to survival – nationalist as well as international – are extreme enough, then they can create incentives powerful enough for people to overcome deep-seated cultural differences and forge a national identity and an ideology of social partnership that facilitates cooperation, self-sacrifice, flexibility, and concerted state action that seem central to the socioeconomic success of small countries in today's world. (2009: 566)

The cosmopolitan view

Debates about globalisation, however, derive less from a careful assessment of the empirical evidence and more from the assumptions and perspectives through which analysts view such matters. Craig Calhoun has commented that discussion about global civil society is framed by two competing perspectives: 'On the one side was the utopia of cosmopolitan liberalism. On the other was the specter of reactionary nationalism or fundamentalism' (2003: 531).

Or rather, that is how 'globalists' might perceive the divide, for it is unlikely that dissenters from the globalisation thesis would describe themselves as reactionary nationalists, still less fundamentalists. Nevertheless, Calhoun's point about the rhetorical juxtaposition between 'liberal cosmopolitanism' and 'illiberal localism' is worth exploring further.

Writing in the journal *Global Policy* in 2010, Held et al. claimed that we are seeing 'the unraveling of the state-building process under the impact of globalisation'. The central paradox of our time, they believe, is that: 'the collective issues we must grapple with are increasingly of global scope and reach and yet the means for addressing them are national, weak and incomplete'. What is required, in their view, is a 'global strategy' because national governments are too weak, and self-interested, to act. There is a paradox in their analysis. On the one hand, governments are too weak to act collectively, and yet they are preoccupied by 'short-term national considerations' so as to prevent global action. The answer, in their view, is to create 'global governance'.

Calhoun, however, observes that such a 'cosmopolitan' outlook, based as it is on liberal theory, 'has not focused on the sources or nature of solidarity, but rather the relationship of individuals to states mediated by citizenship' (2003: 533). Thus, Campbell and Hall's study of the basis of Danish social solidarity would have little meaning for such an outlook. Not only, in Calhoun's view, do the 'new cosmopolitans' have no strong sense of social solidarity, but they theorise about a world inhabited by autonomous, discrete and culture-less individuals, and as such make common cause with economic liberals in dismissing the 'social' as restrictive and potentially authoritarian:

> At least in their extreme forms, cosmopolitanism and individualism participate in this pervasive tendency to deny the reality of the social. Their combination represents an attempt to get rid of 'society' as a feature of political theory. It is part of the odd coincidence since the 1960s of left-wing and right-wing attacks on the state. (2003: 536)

Calhoun makes the telling point that all identities and solidarities are neither fixed nor simply fluid, but may become more or less fixed under different circumstances and contexts. Neither do economic liberals offer a strong account of social solidarity or of the role of culture in social life, giving little weight to belonging, or at least viewing it as 'resistance', thus preventing global action.

What we perceive here is a classically 'liberal' view of the world in that social actors or freestanding individuals operate without the constraints of social ties. In this regard, it is an *a*-sociological account of human action, one which juxtaposes 'state' and 'individual', usually, but not always, driven by enlightened self-interest. The American political philosopher Michael Sandel put it well:

> If we understand ourselves as free and independent selves, unbound by moral ties we haven't chosen, we can't make sense of a range of moral and political obligations that we commonly recognize, even prize. These include obligations of solidarity and loyalty, historic memory and religious faith – moral claims that arise from the communities and traditions that shape our identity. Unless we think of ourselves as encumbered selves, open to moral claims we have not willed, it is difficult to make sense of these aspects of our moral and political experience. (2009: 220)

This is, in essence, a sociological point. We cannot account for people's actions and thoughts except insofar as they take account of other people's. They are not *individually* determined. Calhoun's point about cosmopolitans is that they too readily buy into an individualised Benthamite philosophy where 'the community is a fictitious body composed of the individual persons who are considered as constituting, as it were, its members. The interest of the community then is what? – the sum of the interests of the several members who compose it' (quoted in Calhoun, 2003: 536). It is but a short step to claim, as Mrs Thatcher once did, that 'there is no such thing as society. There are individual men and women, and their families' (Margaret Thatcher, talking to *Woman's Own* magazine, 31 October 1987).

'Cosmopolitans' such as Held and Kaldor would dissent from being Thatcherite, perhaps even from being Benthamite liberals, but their *Weltanschauung* predisposes them to underplay, even deny, the relevance of social solidarity, or, if they do, perceive it as a barrier to progress. Here is Calhoun's characterisation of 'extreme cosmopolitanism':

> It is ... constructed out of the concrete conditions of cosmopolitan mobility, education, and participation in certain versions of news and other media flows. It is the culture of those who attend Harvard and the LSE, who read *The Economist* and *The New Yorker*, who recognize Mozart's music as universal, and who can discuss the relative merits of Australian, French, and Chilean wines. It is also a culture in which secularism seems natural and religion odd, and in which respect for human rights is assumed, but the notion of fundamental economic redistribution is radical and controversial. This culture has many good qualities, as well as blindspots, but nonetheless it is culture and not its absence. (2003: 544)

His final point in that quotation is the key one. Claiming 'individualism' is itself a cultural statement, even though it is premised on not being 'cultural' at all. Says Calhoun, 'solidarity is not the "bad other" to individual choice', and 'buying into some neoliberal discourses about freedom actually means celebrating the tyranny of the market' (2003: 549).

Rarely is the argument about juxtaposing 'cosmopolitanism' and 'nationalism', for the former is usually implicit and the latter explicit (just like juxtaposing 'patriotism' and 'nationalism'). Tom Nairn observed: 'A nationalist ... by definition speaks from somewhere; the internationalist speaks (or claims to speak) from nowhere in particular' (1993: 156). Nairn refers to 'the new "*intelló*" fad of cosmopolitanism – the aloofness deemed ethically appropriate for the globalizing times' (2008).

The road to 'globalisation'

Theorising about globalisation does not spring out of the air. In sociological terms, we need to ground the thesis in the context of post-war social thought, because it is the latest in a long line of theories which assert the homogenisation of social life. Social science, it seems, has a liking for theories which judge that the world has become a single place, and that 'society' (lower case) has become 'Society' (upper case). Each theory runs into the other.

The convergence thesis

The first was the 'convergence thesis' associated with the American writer Clark Kerr whose book *Industrialism and Industrial Man* was published in 1960. Kerr and his associates took the view that economic and technological requirements of industrial development produced marked uniformities in the occupational structures of advanced societies; hence, 'convergence' occurred as societies industrialised. This derived from the need of 'industrialism' to require a core set of social structures.

Critics of the convergence thesis identified a number of problems:

- That what constituted 'industrial society' as a general category was ambiguous, and, relatedly, that the thesis assumed what it set out to explain, namely that similarities in occupational composition resulted from industrial development, rather than being its cause.

- Second, it gave primacy to technology as the key driver of social change, treating it as the key independent variable.

- Third, there was an assumption, usually implicit, that the United States was the exemplar of 'industrialism', and hence a model for others to follow. Only later did arguments for 'American exceptionalism' come to prominence (Lipset, 1997).

Subsequent empirical work on occupational structures undermined the convergence thesis. There seemed little evidence that such structures and, as a consequence, systems of social stratification, were becoming the same (see e.g. Erikson et al., 1983; Garnsey, 1975). Erikson and his colleagues concluded that 'the course of change in national occupational and class structures may make for divergence as well as convergence in mobility patterns' (1983: 328).

Post-industrialism

In the 1970s, a new but related thesis emerged: that of 'post-industrial society'. Associated with Daniel Bell in *The Coming of Post-Industrial Society* (1974), the argument was that the 'post-industrial' economy shifts from the production of goods to services, driven by the emergence of the 'knowledge economy', and with it the transformation from blue-collar to white-collar employment. Critics pointed out that it was dubious that 'knowledge' was *not* a feature of 'industrial' or even 'pre-industrial' societies, and that the descriptor 'post' simply said what it was *not*, rather than describing the new society.

The cultural theorist Cairns Craig has made the wider point, that '"Post-isms" have proliferated everywhere at a speed that has led only to banalisation and confusion' (1996: 211). He comments that this post-world has three key ideas: it is a world in which relativity rules, with no absolutes because language, image, style and media are part of a discourse which can neither be proved or disproved; information, the domain of signs, dominates over what were once thought of as 'realities'; and the post-world is one without centres, with no fixed authority or absolutes. While this is a perspective grounded in studies of literature and culture, social science became interested in the 'post-modern' – in 'post-modernity' (see Giddens, 1990) – and its link with globalisation (1990: 52).

World-system theory

Also emerging in the 1970s was the more radical 'world-system theory', created by Immanuel Wallerstein (1974, 1979), which we introduced in Chapter 8 in the context of industrial and occupational change in Scotland. Wallerstein departed from convergence or modernisation theories to argue that capitalism should be seen as a 'world system' rather than as a mode of production operating within autonomous states.

The key in his thinking lay in spatial relationships between core, periphery and semi-periphery such that there was a global division of labour with some territories performing key and subordinate services for the 'core'. In this regard, world-system theory shared many of the perspectives of theories of under-development (associated with Andre Gunder Frank, notably in his book *The Development of Underdevelopment*, 1966, and applied mainly to South America) which took the view that certain territories were systematically and structurally under-developed by the core rather than failing to 'develop' and 'modernise' by dint of inadequate cultural habits and practices.

The notion of 'under-development' turned out to be a fruitful one, and was applied in the 1970s by the Aberdeen sociologist Ian Carter to the economic history of the Highlands (Carter, 1971; 1974). Carter was using 'under-development' to escape from the conventional wisdom that the Highlands were 'backward' because they were '*un*developed'. Systematically oppressed militarily, culturally and economically, the region was a paradigm case of conservative modernisation, in which the landed classes used a variety of levels to hold down the labour force in making the transition to commercial sheep farming (Carter, 1974: 301).

When the first edition of my book *Understanding Scotland* was published in 1992, the debate about Scotland's economic and social development was vibrant, and Wallerstein sought to explain Scotland's development in terms of his approach. Economic development in Scotland, he argued, proceeded 'by invitation'; that is, as allowed by the Anglo-British state in the context of a growing empire.

We saw in Chapter 8 how the historian Christopher Smout took issue with Wallerstein's explanation. Smout argued that 'dependency' per se did not block economic development in Scotland, but rather was beneficial and benign: 'Dependency in Scotland's case was far from being a crippling handicap. Trade was not an engine of exploitation, but a cause of growth' (1980a: 628). Scotland, it seems, had been able to move (in Wallerstein's terms) from peripheral to semi-peripheral to core status because of its early 'dependency'. Here was my own assessment in 1992 which is worth repeating:

> The value of Wallerstein's world-system theory lies in its insistence – not always adhered to – that economic structure be viewed as a dynamic process of ebb and flow, in its startlingly simple but useful assumption that since the sixteenth century there has been but one capitalist world economy and a multiplicity of political and cultural systems, and in its characterisation of this economy in terms of a single division of labour with core, semi-periphery and periphery, allowing surplus value to be extracted (sometimes literally) and retained by the core. World-systems theory is concerned with explaining broad changes at the level of the 'world-economy', and is less satisfactory when handling individual societies, which it tends to treat in a 'black box' manner, as if only external factors are important. (McCrone, 1992: 47)

In the 1960s and the early 1970s, debates in Scotland about its 'colonial' status within the British state were popular, given social and political change. As we discussed in Chapter 6, there were concerns about the 'branch-plant' status of Scotland's economy; the emergence of the SNP as a political force gave credence to the view that economic and political 'liberation' went together. However, as we saw in Chapter 8, attempts by the American sociologist Michael Hechter to describe a process of 'internal colonialism' and characterising Scotland as an 'ethno-nation' did violence to historical evidence which, to use Tom Nairn's more apposite descriptor, was much more of a 'junior partner' in British imperialism than one of its victims (for the full account, see McCrone, 1992: chapter 3).

It is possible to see, then, a legacy of ideas in the post-war period which draws a common thread through convergence thesis, post-industrialism, post-modernity, world-system theory and globalisation in the sense that each asserts, rather than proves, the de-centring of society, under the impact of global trends and influences. The shift of focus from the local and national to the global, however, carries risks that all is not what the theories might tell us. In the final section, we will bring the story firmly back to Scotland.

Scotland's global development

Scotland, nevertheless, remains something of a puzzle. Its nationalism does not appear to conform to the conventional wisdom that processes of globalisation and uneven development are responsible. When Scotland was swept by forces of economic, social and cultural change of this type, it did not generate the kind of nationalism so common in other parts of Europe in the eighteenth and nineteenth centuries. A political movement recognisable as nationalism only emerged in Scotland in the final quarter of the twentieth century, and not when other European nations were being forged.[7] We would be mistaken in thinking, however, that globalisation has had nothing to do with nationalism in Scotland. On the contrary; it has everything to do with what emerged in the late twentieth century, as forces of global change transformed the constitutional arrangements of the UK.

Conventional theories of nationalism do not apply easily to Scotland (McCrone, 1998). In the first place, it made the transition to modernity as early as the middle of the eighteenth century, and by the mid-nineteenth century it was, after England, the most intensively industrialised country in the world. Its social, economic and cultural institutions had been revolutionised, and yet it did not evolve a political nationalism worthy of the name. That was to come over a century later.

Nationalism comes later

Why was there no recognisable Scottish nationalism in the high period of the early nineteenth century when so many other European societies were liberating themselves from imperial and colonial yokes? The short answer is that the classes which elsewhere used nationalism as a political vehicle – the bourgeoisie – had little need of it in Scotland. They had sufficient power already (Paterson, 1994). The Union of Parliaments in 1707 brought Scotland and England (Wales and Ireland effectively did what England required of them) together in a curious state (Nairn, 1977).

Great Britain – later renamed the United Kingdom when Ireland was formally annexed in 1801 – was a 'marriage of convenience' for both Scotland and England. For Scotland, the Union gave merchants access to English markets at home and abroad at a time when

England had been practising restrictive mercantilism against foreign trade. The burgeoning American colonies were especially important following the failure of Scottish commerce to establish continental trading posts in the Americas. For England, the Union solved the political–military problem of the Scottish–French alliance dating back to the late thirteenth century, and which frequently squeezed England between its two neighbours. Furthermore, the United Kingdom was a unitary rather than a federal state, for it had a single parliament although it was manifestly a multinational state. That contradiction has never been properly resolved in these islands.

In truth, it was a strange Union: a Union of unequals, a Union made by the ruling class of aristocrats and patricians rather than on behalf of the 'people' who would figure iconically in later nationalisms and forms of state-building. The contrast with Ireland was striking. While Irish 'Unionists', both the Ascendancy in the south and the Orangemen in the north, were incorporated into the British state, that left substantial proportions of native Irish, marked by Catholicism, alienated and disaffected. A relatively simple spark in the form of the Easter Rising of 1916 set the island ablaze.

Scotland was different. It had its own legal system, its own national – Presbyterian – church, its own education and social systems; in short, its own civil society (Devine, 2000). In that regard, it had a large measure of self-government in a pre-modern Union which created a single UK parliament at a time, 1707, when legislatures were pre-democratic and fairly unimportant.

The Union was, like so much else in Great Britain, an antiquated compromise between the old aristocratic order and a newer democratic one, a social and political transformation effected without radical upheaval, or, at least, outright social conflict. Scotland, then, was self-governing, but a society without its own domestic legislature. Instead, the British parliament passed Scottish legislation as and when it had to, and largely left the Scots to their own devices.

Scots on the make

Such devices were often to be found within the growing British Empire, notably the Dominions. English commentators complained of 'Scots on the make', that their northern neighbours were seeking, and getting, undue influence in matters of economy and governance at home and abroad. There is little doubt about the role of Scots in the empire: they saw it as their oyster (see Figure 24.2).

Here was an expression of the connection between God and mammon, David Livingstone's missionary zeal and colonial adventure in southern Africa. Roughly at the same time as his 'discovery' and naming of the 'Victoria Falls' in honour of the imperial monarch, the imperial army in India invented a new drink.

Camp coffee was the first 'instant coffee' mix, of coffee essence, sugar and chicory, created by The Paterson Company of Glasgow in 1876 at the request of the Gordon Highlanders on field campaigns in India. The BBC/British Museum's History of the World comments:

FIGURE 24.2
Converting
the world:
Mary Slessor
and David
Livingstone

Note: Mary Slessor
(1848–1915) was
a missionary in
Calabar, Nigeria,
who followed
David Livingstone
(1813–1873).
Slessor also
followed
Livingstone on
the Clydesdale
banknotes in 1997

Source: I am
grateful to The
Clydesdale Bank
for permission to
print these

'Originally the picture depicted the Sikh as carrying a tray of coffee – an intermediate version, with the Sikh standing but the tray missing; it is widely believed that this was changed to avoid the imperialist connotations of the Sikh as a servant' (for the image,[8] see www.bbc.co.uk/ahistoryoftheworld/objects/XG1CiGSCTzqb05nDwIhhjg).

Meanwhile, Scotland remained that constitutional curiosity: a nation without a state, or, rather, without the formal trappings of statehood, but with considerable institutional autonomy. The UK, meanwhile, was a state without a nation in the sense that Scotland and England ran their own social affairs, as to a lesser extent did Wales and Ireland.

Much of this did not matter as much as running an empire, and so 'Britain' was largely under-developed at home in terms of systems of governance, and over-developed abroad in the sense that its resources and energies went into running the largest empire the world had ever seen. The historian Eric Hobsbawm (1969) described Britain as a 'world island', as an 'automatic switchboard' which ran so much of the world's trade and commerce. It was the home of laissez-faire, and Scotland bequeathed to it the greatest economist of them all, Adam Smith, whose *Wealth of Nations* has never been out of print since it was published in 1776, the year, ironically, of the American Declaration of Independence in Britain's largest colony.

Scotland and the Union

The Scots learned to live in two different worlds: that of imperial prospects and opportunities; and that of the home base, cultivating the former by shaping the institutions of the latter to their advantage. They learned to be both British and Scottish, and for much of the subsequent 200 years were content to do so. They were 'unionist–nationalists' in the sense that their own sense of being Scottish was amplified by being British, for as long as Scottish civil life was protected, then they saw no contradiction between national (Scottish) and state (British) identities (Morton, 1999). This was, at the time, the best of both worlds, and certainly gave to Scotland unimaginable economic and political leverage which it could not possibly have hoped to have as a small, relatively poor and peripheral northern European country.

That Scotland was transformed by this political–economic Union cannot be doubted. Such a transformation depended on global markets, as these were developed and protected by the British Empire, which used its military muscle to dominate world trade. It was not a question of Scotland being 'allowed' to develop its economy in a complementary way to that of England (McCrone, 1992). After all, in the home of laissez-faire, the state was neither inclined nor able to make such decisions, for it was the market which had to decide.

We saw in Chapter 8 that Scotland was not some over-specialised corner of the economic empire, but a full and competitive player in the second half of the nineteenth century – the imperial century. Scotland's industrial structure mirrored that of the UK as a whole, while Wales – depending as it did on coal, iron and steel – was undoubtedly a specialised producer with a niche role in British imperial markets (McCrone, 1992: 66). If anything, Scotland mirrored the UK's industrial structure, and was more 'British' than the other economic regions of the kingdom (Lee, 1995).

Scotland remained a country within the British state with a high degree of civil autonomy within the structure of that state, and was not reduced to a region of England. Scotland was especially well adapted to take advantage of the UK's highly advantageous structural position within a world economy itself shaped around the UK's interests. Scotland's long-term problems derived from over-adaptation to imperial opportunities, not under-adaptation.

Scotland and globalisation

We recognise that globalisation made modern Scotland precisely because it was incorporated into the capitalist world. Adam Smith in *The Wealth of Nations* observed that capitalism had the capacity 'to unite, in some measure, the most distant parts of the world, by enabling them to relieve one another's wants, to increase one another's enjoyments, and to encourage one another's industry' (quoted in Nairn, 1997: 148). The internationalisation of the modern economy is at least 200 years old, and in that crucible, modern Scotland was formed.

This was not, however, a 'global' economy, for while there are continuities with earlier forms of globalisation, there are distinct processes in the modern form.

The conventional wisdom about Scotland and its economy is that it has been hollowed out by globalisation. Indigenous control of its historic staple industries – heavy engineering, shipbuilding, textiles – once owned by Scottish capitalists has come to an end (see Chapter 6). There is, however, a counter-view, expressed by the economic historian Jim Tomlinson, that 'the idea of a national economy, in the sense of the nation as an economic "community of fate", is far from outdated, even in an era of globalisation' (2014: 171).

The first great age of globalisation occurred in the second half of the nineteenth century, under the aegis of the British Empire. Thus, up to 1914, the UK was the most globalised economy in the world, and, within the Union, Scotland was even more globalised than the UK as a whole. All Scotland's major industries were heavily dependent, directly or indirectly, on international markets, notably shipbuilding, heavy engineering and locomotives. Cotton thread (in Paisley) and jute (in Dundee) depended upon raw materials and world markets.

Tomlinson argues that high levels of economic instability and insecurity were offset by cheap food grown in the empire, notably Australasia and Canada. At the same time, its major industries, its financial institutions and banks were owned and controlled within Scotland. Overall, comments Tomlinson, 'we can argue that by 1913 Scotland probably had the most globalised economy in the world' (2014: 172). There was, however, little economic 'community of fate':

> The economic livelihoods of Dundonians rested largely on the monsoon in Asia, the intensity of Calcutta competition in jute and the state of the American market; that of Glaswegians rested on global levels of trade feeding through to demand for ships, and fluctuations in the world market for capital goods. (2014: 172)

The twist in the argument is that the inter-war period brought about a process of *de*-globalisation. In the first place, the political response to industrial decline in Scotland was to push for Union-wide solutions, first through the Conservative (Unionist) Party which had a strong Scottish presence until well into the 1960s, and the post-war Labour Party, reinforcing unionist politics.

A shared community of fate

As we saw in Chapter 8, a second phase of de-industrialisation occurred in Scotland from the 1950s, and the state, in the form of the Scottish Office, was inexorably drawn into a process of restructuring. Public ownership was one side of the equation, and state direction and inducement to locate in Scotland (steel-making at Ravenscraig, automobiles at Linwood) was the other.

Later, inward investment by US multinationals to have access to European markets, and encouraged by substantial regional policy subsidies, came in the form of 'Silicon Glen' and, a couple of decades later, went, for easier and cheaper pickings elsewhere in Asia and Eastern Europe. What Tomlinson describes as the 'adventurist' policies of the post-1979 Thatcher government put an end to such corporatist thinking as there was, and as a result industrial employment in Scotland fell as a share of total employment from 42 per cent to 11 per cent over 60 years.

Ironically, a key feature of the last thirty years has been the growth of public sector employment such that the historic differential in unemployment rates in Scotland vis-à-vis the UK has diminished significantly. In that regard, says Tomlinson, the growth of public sector employment has been a significant component of de-globalisation. De-industrialisation also undermined the influence of 'unionist' solutions achieved through the organised labour movement, especially with neo-liberal Conservative governments in power from 1979 to 1997. Labour unionism had lost its clout and capacity to deliver. Tomlinson concludes:

> from a globalised industrial economy, reaching its peak in the years before 1914, Scotland has become a significantly post-industrial economy with strong de-globalising elements. A much greater amount of the forces acting upon the Scottish economy than ever before is now internal; above all, political decisions made about public spending in Edinburgh, within some constraints imposed from London, matter a great deal. (2014: 176)

Thus, he argues, 'there is now more of a "national economy", imagined as a "community of fate" than ever before in Scotland's history' (2014: 176).

The 'national' economy

Here we have a nice twist to the arguments about globalisation. Tomlinson's work has the merit of using empirical data (for an analysis of the Dundee jute industry, see also Tomlinson, 2014; Tomlinson et al., 2011), and is not driven by 'flimsy evidence and a fondness for sweeping generalisations' identified by Eriksen as one of the failings of the academic literature on globalisation.

While it is true that industrial restructuring in Scotland has removed swathes of the Scottish economy from indigenous control, in its heyday there was little approximating to a 'community of fate' in the nineteenth century in comparison with the early twenty-first century. Even the idea of a 'national economy' was lacking in the nineteenth century, and arguably the concept of an 'economic nation' with national systems of accounting only emerged in the post-war period (Sørensen, 2016).

Producing 'national statistics' on the assumption that the economy was coterminous with the polity is a modern idea, reflected in the notion of 'the national interest'.

The twist is that this 'national interest' has migrated since 1945 from the British to the Scottish level, reinforcing political and institutional autonomy north of the border. Thus, economic nationhood has attached to Scotland, whether or not this results in eventual political 'independence'; paradoxically, globalisation and de-industrialisation can have unexpected consequences.

Conclusion

Is 'globalisation' the answer? We might reply: it depends what the question is. The strength of the globalisation thesis is that it attempts to link up the key structural changes in our modern world: economic, cultural, social, political, technological. Its weakness is that it asserts rather than proves the interconnections between them. In his book *Globalization* (2014), Eriksen seems to have succumbed to its appeal. One might say that, since 2003, Eriksen has become a believer, possibly because since 2012 he has been leading a comparative project on 'the crises of globalization' (2014: xi).

A flavour of this conversion can be had from the strap-lines which he uses in key chapters:

'Nowadays we are all on the move' (chapter 5, p. 99, from Bauman).

'The battleground of the twenty-first century will pit fundamentalism against cosmopolitan tolerance' (chapter 6, p. 117, from Giddens).

'Neo-tribal and fundamentalist tendencies, which reflect and articulate the experience of people on the receiving end of globalization, are as much legitimate offspring of globalization as the widely acclaimed "hybridization" of top culture – the culture at the globalized top' (chapter 8, p. 153, from Bauman).

There is, of course, the possibility that Eriksen was being ironic, and presenting these assertions as truths held to be self-evident to their authors, rather than borne out of careful consideration of evidence. The trouble with such statements is that they beg far too many questions. Indeed, the globalisation thesis has a peculiar relationship to data and evidence. For example, Eriksen observes that: 'There can be no effects of say, global capitalism, the Internet, or politicized Islam, that are not mediated by human understandings and experiences, and they vary. Most empirical generalizations about globalization are therefore false' (2014: 8).

What Eriksen means by this is that we cannot generalise about the impacts of globalisation because human beings have the capacity to interpret social change in quite complex ways. Still, apart from the assertion that 'one typical consequence of globalization has been the rise or rekindling of various forms of identity politics' (2014: 189), we are left none the wiser about how these are connected up. Indeed, if we take at face value the claim that empirical generalisations about globalisation are 'false', what is the nature of evidence that it has the impact it has, or might it simply mean that globalisation is something you either believe in, or you do not?

There is a wider point to be made. In an excoriating book entitled *Learn to Write Badly: How to succeed in the social sciences* (2013), Michael Billig takes issue with Ulrich Beck's concept 'cosmopolitanisation' (2013: 157–8). Billig observes that Beck does not put forward 'cosmopolitanisation' as an interesting hypothesis to be tested. Beck and his colleague 'use the phrase "really-existing cosmopolitanization" a number of times ... writing about the need to "understand the really-existing process of cosmopolitanization of the world", which they contrast with the "unreal science of the national"' (2013: 157–8).

How we are to decide that one sphere is 'real' and the other 'unreal' is not clear, except from within the theory itself. This, to borrow from Bourdieu, is substituting the reality of the model for the model of reality. You either believe in the model, or you do not. Truly, says Billig, this is no way to do social science, and, further, people are written out of the account: actors are 'not persons but types of sociology' (2013: 158). Billig argues that this writing people out of social science accounts is systemic:

> the big concepts which many social scientists are using – the *ifications* and the *izations* – are poorly equipped for describing what people do. By rolling out the big nouns, social scientists can avoid describing people and their actions. They can then write in highly unpopulated ways, creating fictional worlds in which their theoretical things, rather than actual people, appear as the major actors. (2013: 7)

In choosing to write about Scotland, we can be accused of 'methodological nationalism', when, to quote Eriksen, 'it is plainly impossible to understand a single nation-state, even a huge one, if the analysis is not based on an understanding of transnational processes. Transnationalism must be a premise, not an afterthought' (2014: 78).

No one can dissent reasonably from that, but the same stricture applies to what we might call 'methodological globalism', especially where even 'empirical generalisations' are not required. Rather, we might rely better on mark 1 Eriksen and his comment about 'flimsy evidence, whimsical and eclectic methodologies, a fondness for sweeping generalisations' to understand both Scotland and the world we inhabit.

Chapter summary

So what have we learned in this chapter?

- That globalisation is seen by its proponents as the intensification of worldwide social, political and economic relations, such that these are disembedded from their territorial surroundings.

- That critics argue that globalisation explains too much as well as too little, and makes arguments about society, culture and politics well beyond its economic remit.

- That 'globalisation' is the latest in a long line of social theories presuming the homogenisation of the world.

- That the links between globalisation and neo-nationalism are complex, the state remaining an important platform for social change.

- That the concept of the 'national economy' is not outdated in an era of globalisation, and is a catalyst of neo-nationalism as in Scotland.

Questions for discussion

1. How does 'globalisation' connect up economic, social, political and cultural change in the modern world?

2. To what extent can it be said that globalisation explains too much as well as too little?

3. Has globalisation ended the rise of the 'nation-state'?

4. Are globalisation and nationalism opposites rather than complements?

5. How well does globalisation explain economic and social development in Scotland over the last century?

Annotated reading

(a) The globalisation thesis: D. Held and A. McGrew, *Globalization/Anti-Globalization: Beyond the great divide*, 2nd edition (2007); R. Robertson, *Globalization: Social theory and global culture* (1992); D. Held et al., 'The Hydra-headed crisis', *Global Policy*, February, 2010; T.H. Eriksen, *Globalization* (2014).

(b) Critics of the globalisation thesis: P. Hirst et al., *Globalization in Question*, 3rd edition (2009); T.H. Eriksen (ed.), *Globalisation: Studies in anthropology* (2003); M. Mann, 'Has globalization ended the rise and rise of the nation-state?', *Review of International Political Economy*, 4(3), 1997; C. Calhoun, '"Belonging" in the cosmopolitan imagery', *Ethnicities*, 3(4), 2003.

(c) Scotland and globalisation: T. Nairn, 'Globalization and nationalism: the new deal?', *OpenDemocracy*, 11(4), 2008; J. Tomlinson, 'Imaging the economic nation: the Scottish case', *Political Quarterly*, 85(2), 2014; J. Tomlinson et al., *The Decline of Jute: Managing industrial decline?* (2011).

Notes

1 'Understated' is a more appropriate descriptor than 'stateless', given the institutional apparatus short of formal statehood.

2 Monetarism, associated particularly with the work of Milton Friedman in the 1970s and 1980s, focused on the role of governments in controlling the amount of money in circulation.

3   In 2015, Wolf published another book, *The Shifts and the Shocks: What we have learned – and have still to learn – from the financial crisis.* Despite his belief in the higher priority of economic forces, Wolf is highly political, hence his support for the British state during the 2015 British general election campaign. 'The SNP has no interest in my country's success. It cares only about what it can extract from us' (*Financial Times*, 16 April 2015) is a statement of his political values ('*my country*', '*us*', is manifestly not a reference to Scotland but to England/the UK).

4   Flanders asserted: 'Politicians like to behave as if the laws of economics do not exist.' It is a moot point as to whether there are 'laws' of economics comparable with the 'laws' of physics, and, if so, whether there are 'laws' of politics too.

5   Paul Hirst died in 2003, and his name appears as first author as a mark of respect by his colleagues.

6   The terms 'liberal' and 'liberalisation' are used here in an 'economic' (as in 'neo-liberal') rather than a 'social' sense. In essence, these are European rather than American expressions, and not to be taken as equivalent to 'liberal/conservative' divisions as they usually are in the United States.

7   It has been asserted (Pittock, 2009) that the Jacobite risings in the eighteenth century were a form of Scottish nationalism. While such risings undoubtedly sought to mobilise Scottish sentiment against the Union, they had much more to do with reinstating a Stuart to the *British* throne.

8   I am unable to reproduce the images on the printed page because of the restrictive practices of copyright holders. The reader might like to 'google' them for themselves.

EPILOGUE

I didn't think it would end like this ...

At the start of this book, I commented that there is no conclusion to the sociology of Scotland; hence this epilogue, a theatrical device to allow the author to address the audience directly. Its point is to stand back and ponder how far we have come, as a society as well as a sociology. Tom Burns, the first professor of sociology at a Scottish university, was fond of saying that 'society' was much more interesting than 'sociology'. By that he meant that trying to make sense of the world around us was much richer and more rewarding than contemplating our disciplinary navels. Sociology, he would say, is only useful if it turns handles to help us make sense of society. Perhaps sociology has become too self-reflexive and concerned with internal debates, and insufficiently interested in the world 'out there'. That is for others to judge, and beyond the scope of this book. The task here has been to make sense of Scotland in sociological terms. There is little point in being precious about it, for the boundaries between history, politics, social anthropology and cultural studies are properly fluid such that influences flow from one to the other. Trying to make sense of Scotland in the round requires that. A Scottish way of doing sociology deals in the language of universals while doing so in the grammar of the particular.

The emergence of sociology at Scottish universities has coincided with the rising salience of 'Scotland' as an object of social, political and cultural study. Manifestly, this is in large part due to 'political' events. The period between 1975 and 2015 has seen unprecedented change in Scotland and the wider UK of which it is currently part. That forty-year period crystallised and made overt deeper and long-standing developments, notably between Scotland and England. The most obvious changes have been political, in the sense that the recovery of a parliament and the growing divergence in electoral behaviour north and south of the border have been its obvious manifestation.

Emerging Scotland

So how are we to account, in sociological terms, for these changes? How do we set them in a sociological context? It matters that for most of the history of the past millennium Scotland was an independent state. To say that does not imply that becoming independent once more is inevitable, nor that the state of independence in the twenty-first century will revert back to its eighteenth-century condition. However, thinking of Scotland as an independent state does not require a great leap of the imagination. Arguably, the historical precedent of an independent Scotland in these islands distinguishes it from Wales. This helps to make the point that 'understanding Scotland' can only be done in comparative terms, and specifically in the context of neighbourly relations around the Union of 1707. That Union, a significant development of the Regal Union of 1603, yoked Scotland and England (and by default Wales and Ireland) into a marriage of convenience.

In his book *Independence or Union*, Tom Devine commented: 'In general, the birth of Great Britain was greeted with muted indifference north of the border. It was not a happy portent for the future' (2016: 4). That was then, and this is now, but history matters. We might argue that bribery and corruption brought the Union about, but it had a major pay-off for Scotland. Devine again: 'there is broad historiographical agreement today that union was a necessary precondition for Scottish economic growth but not in itself sufficient to guarantee that it would happen' (2016: 50). The savagely racist caricatures in the 1760s in which Scots were portrayed as 'greedy mendicants growing rich on England's rich pastures' (2016: 54) were a sign of Scottish success, not failure. Scots took to the opportunities of union with enthusiasm, for transatlantic trade was unthinkable without the Union. And not simply transatlantic trade: 'In the decades after the Union streams of eager Caledonians from genteel but impoverished backgrounds poured into the British empire at every point from the Arctic wastes of Canada to the teeming cities and plains of Bengal' (2016: 70).

Severing sinews

The Union 'worked', but it remained a marriage of convenience, a *mariage de raison*, as the French would say, given that indigenous institutions of governance – law, religion, local state functions, what are called 'low' politics – remained autonomous; having your cake and eating it, as it were. That lack of enthusiasm for union which Devine spoke of, seeing it as a device for economic and political aggrandisement, was bound to wane as the British fiscal–military state began to decay. It may have seemed to many English people profound ingratitude, but Scots saw in union a means to an end, and by the twentieth century, as the bargain seemed less so, the sinews of state began to weaken.

Two further institutions bound Scots to that union: religion and war. To be sure, Scots did not embrace the English church, but securing Presbyterianism within the Treaty of Union removed a potent source of constitutional opposition. The British union state held because Scots had considerable autonomy over things which mattered to them, including their ways of worship. War was also significant because it bound the Scots into the imperial war machine, and granted them pride of place in many military campaigns. General Wolfe's alleged comment in the eighteenth century, that it was 'no great mischief' if the Scottish regiments suffered untoward casualties, did not breed resentment but pride.[1] The iconography of the Scottish soldier became a key element of national(ist) identity. The National Theatre's play *Black Watch* in 2006 was testament to that. Almost by stealth, The Royal Regiment of Scotland (2004) created a Scottish army, and one of the institutions of union, the military, was 'nationalised'.

Religion, warfare, welfare. The creation of the post-war welfare state in 1945 was the third sinew which bound Scotland into the Union. It generated a politics of economics and of class, and Scottish and English electoral behaviour were virtually identical for the next decade. Reflecting that, the Labour Party dropped its commitment to home rule in 1950, and the Scottish Conference of the Labour Party withdrew support at the end of that decade. The Scots were British, or so it seemed.

But all was not what it seemed. The transformation of the Scottish economy, the desperate attempts to stem the tide of emigration, to restructure the Scottish economy, had created a political–economic infrastructure with the Scottish Office at its heart. A Scottish frame of reference, which in any case had never gone away, was reinforced, this time in economic rather than cultural terms. Or rather, periodic cultural revivals such as that in the 1920s and 1930s, and again in the post-war period, helped to underpin and give expression to Scottish difference.

This was not overtly 'political', but the focus on Scottish matters insinuated into electoral politics slowly but surely. Above all, it was the weakening of the sinews which held Scotland in the Union which made the difference. The Union simply could not hold if it were based on sentiment alone. Presbyterianism, made safe for and by the Union, lost its cultural force in a secular age. Warfare was not required in the long period of economic prosperity and rising living standards – what the French called *les Trente Glorieuses*.

Imperceptibly, the Union, which in any case had been a 'convenience', came to matter less. The British state never quite 'got' the Union; its *mentalité* was always centralist if usually benign. Institutions like the BBC did not know quite what to make of Scotland: it came up with an oxymoron, that Scotland was a 'national region'. Perhaps because the UK had never been transformed into a federal state, which would have married federalism and multinationalism, it lost its opportunities to restructure. The defeat of 'Home Rule all round' in the 1880s and again before the Great War, the departure of most of Ireland in 1921, the reinforcing of democratic centralism in 1945, failed to notice Scotland's glacial slide away from the union state.

Political voice came with the sudden rise of the Scottish National Party in the 1970s, and Labour in particular scrambled to recover its commitment to home rule. Too little, too late. The discovery of oil in the North Sea helped to change the political psychology of Scotland, allowing an alternative economic future to be imagined. All the while, the Scottish Office sought to reassert its legitimacy, but from as early as the mid-1950s it had become obvious that Scotland and England danced to different political tunes. A Scottish Assembly might just have held in 1979, but it was swept away by an incoming Conservative government intent on holding the union line. Its leader Mrs Thatcher told one of her Scottish acolytes, Michael Ancrum, 'Michael, I am an English nationalist and never you forget it'.[2]

Margaret Thatcher turned out, unwittingly, to be the recruiting sergeant, or, to change the metaphor, the midwife of Scottish Home Rule. Her long reign was swept away in 1990 by her own party, fearing defeat, and then left without a single Scottish MP in 1997. A devolved Scottish parliament, stronger than the Assembly offered in 1979, was created ('reconvened' if you were Winnie Ewing) in 1997. It was more than a 'political' institution, because it had been the creature of civil society in Scotland designed in the long, dark days of opposition in the 1980s and 1990s. It quickly established itself as the premier focus for Scottish domestic politics, elected by proportional representation. Labour saw it as a way of seeing off the SNP; the Conservatives first considered it the beginning of the end of civilisation, only for it to be their means of survival. The SNP saw it, with a few traditional dissenters, as a means to a longer term end, a stepping stone to ultimate independence. Some politicians warned that it was the thin end of the wedge, the slippery slope to independence, but there was little they could do about that. Labour was in power for the parliament's first two terms, but in truth it did not know what to do with power: 'doing less better', was one of its less edifying slogans.

And so, less than two decades after the parliament was set up, Devine's words ring true, 'the SNP has virtually turned Scotland into a nationalist polity' (2016: 270).[3] The unionist parties (Labour, in some desperation, had taken to wearing the mantle which it had long avoided because of its association with Conservatism and Protestantism) agreed to a referendum on independence in 2014, but only on condition it allowed for a 'Yes/No' answer. The ostensible aim was to see off the independence vote 'for a lifetime', despite (or because of) the fact that as many as 30 per cent of people in Scotland wanted a more powerful parliament within the UK (so-called devolution-max). When the polls narrowed the gap, the unionists issued The Vow that in the event of a 'No' vote they would consider extending the powers of the parliament. Making up policy on the hoof is never a good idea, and the Smith Commission convened after the result, and delivering within six weeks, was never able to hold the line. Labour in particular was taken aback by David Cameron's interpretation of the result as requiring a solution to the 'English' question (EVEL, English Votes for English Laws). Labour felt it had been treated, in Lenin's phrase, as useful idiots in order to save the Union.

The British general election of 2015 turned out to be a continuation of the referendum campaign, and under first-past-the-post, the SNP swept up almost all (95 per cent) of the Scottish seats, on 50 per cent of the popular vote, last achieved, ironically, by the Conservatives in 1955. One year later, at the Scottish parliament elections, the SNP held onto power, but without the overall majority it achieved in 2011. This was a function of the Additional Member System which militated against any single party getting a majority of seats. That the SNP did so in 2011, winning 53 per cent of the seats, was the unusual effect of getting virtually the same proportion of the votes in both constituency and list votes (respectively, 45 and 44 per cent). In 2016, 46 and 42 per cent of the votes gave the SNP 49 per cent of the seats.

Scotland's futures

And so to another referendum, this time on British membership of the EU in 2016. If there is such a thing as a sociological law, it is that of unintended consequences – which means of course that one can never predict precisely what will happen. Social and political life seldom follow a predictable path, although we are rather better at explaining how things come about *after* the event.

When the UK government announced its intention of having a referendum on the UK's membership of the EU, it was a device for a prime minister to get himself off a political hook: that a substantial proportion of his own party were profoundly Eurosceptic, even Europhobic. It was not difficult to see that this had much wider implications: that if England voted Eurosceptically, Scotland might not. There was no guarantee of this, for public opinion north of the border had long been 'healthily' Eurosceptic, but rarely Europhobic. This was in part because nationalist opinion in Scotland promoted the European Union as an alternative to the British one: 'Independence in Europe', after all, had been the SNP's slogan, as much for tactical advantage than anything else.

A proto-English nationalism defined itself vis-à-vis 'Europe', a proverbial black box into which almost anything could be read. It did not take a crystal ball to predict that 'Brexit' would provide a convenient slogan for a myriad, inchoate set of discontents. Quite apart from the 'vis-à-vis' question, nationalism in Scotland had long taken a different path, one which recognised that 'independence' in the modern world was always going to be partial and complex. Alongside the ideological framing that did not see 'Europe' as the 'other' (unlike England), successive Scottish governments had cultivated the material resources which the European dimension brought to the table.

To a small, sparsely populated country on the north-west fringes of Europe, with substantial natural resources, Europe offered more credits than debits. It also provided a narrative which defined Scotland once more as a European country. That the Scottish result on 23 June 2016 was so much in contrast with that in England (and Wales, for that matter, which makes the term 'England and Wales' trip more readily off the tongue)[4] provided the means of propulsion from the British Union. Given the events of the previous few years, and with hindsight, we can see below how the trajectory worked.

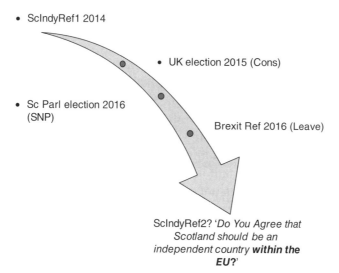

- ScIndyRef1 2014

- UK election 2015 (Cons)

- Sc Parl election 2016 (SNP)

Brexit Ref 2016 (Leave)

ScIndyRef2? '*Do You Agree that Scotland should be an independent country **within the EU**?*'

None of the points on the trajectory were, or are, inevitable: that a majority 'No' vote in 2014 would mean that the winners lost, and the losers won, the ideological battle; that the Conservatives would win the 2015 UK election; and that the prime minister would be held to his promise made in 2013 to hold a Brexit referendum; that the SNP would be re-elected in an electoral system which made an overall majority hard to achieve; or that the UK (more precisely, England and Wales) would vote 'Leave'.

If none of these were predictable, neither is Scottish independence, either in the sense that a majority would vote 'Yes' in a future referendum, in contrast to 2014 (and, if so, in what proportion to confer legitimacy), or in the sense that the political conditions for such 'independence' would be achieved, at least within the EU. Social scientists, in any case, are not very proficient at prediction, given the sheer complexities of social, political and economic life. What we can say is that the scenario which occurred, an English 'Leave' vote and a Scottish 'Remain', presents the conditions for propelling Scotland out of the British Union, while making it not at all certain that this will happen, nor the form it would take.

But what, you might point out, of my claim that it is the sociology, not the politics, of Scotland which matters? The short answer is that in the modern age we cannot make a hard and fast distinction between 'sociology' and 'politics', between society and state. The two run into each other. In the post-war period, the state in all modern societies plays a central role in the quest for economic growth, even while governments adopted a neo-liberal, hands-off, view of these matters. The line between 'state' and 'society' is virtually impossible to discern.

Translating that to a Scottish context, the parliament is not simply a 'political' instrument, but the means of social transformation and change (hence the term 'social politics'). We might say that Scotland has not changed because of its politics; rather, its politics have changed because Scotland has.

Different policy communities in Scotland, namely education, health, housing, the economy, the arts, and so on, look to the Scottish parliament/government to act as the transmission system of policies. In this way, the parliament/government itself becomes the most important 'policy community' of all. The new politics of Scotland since 1999, which quickly established itself as the premier terrain in the minds of voters, has reinforced and given expression to social aspirations and demands.

The parliament and government have become the key bricks in the wall of Scottish civil society. Where this will go in constitutional terms is impossible to say. Much hinges on that useful sociological expression given to us by Max Weber, the unintended consequences of human action.[5] Nothing is set in stone, nor planned out exactly in advance. Events and processes unfold; there is no blueprint in a rapidly changing world. Just how society/state relations develop in Scotland will depend as much on events and processes elsewhere.

And so this book is written in that context. This is how we have got here. This epilogue acknowledges that the tale is not ended, nor that it will have a predictable end. Others will have a different tale to tell, or tell it in a different way. Tom Burns' stricture that the business of sociology is to conduct a critical debate with society about its social institutions, whatever the outcome, continues to ring true. Let us end with words from Jackie Kay, the Scots makar (national poet), written to celebrate the 2016 opening of the fifth session of the Scottish parliament:[6]

> Find here what you are looking for:
>
> Democracy in its infancy: guard her
>
> Like you would a small daughter
>
> And keep the door wide open, not just ajar,
>
> And say, in any language you please, welcome, welcome
>
> To the world's refugees.

Notes

1   Wolfe is alleged to have said of Highland soldiers during the Seven Years' War with France (1754–63): 'They are hardy, intrepid, accustomed to a rough country, and make no great mischief if they fall.'
2   Quoted in Tom Devine's *Independence or Union* (2016), but attributed to James Naughtie's *The Rivals* (2001: 21).
3   Note the small 'n' in 'nationalist' to make the point that 'Scotland' is the prime focus for people living in Scotland. Capital-N Nationalism implies voting for and identifying with the Scottish National Party.
4   By dint of a majority voting for Brexit, Wales appears to have bound itself more closely to England.
5   Weber used it in the context of the relationship between the Protestant ethic and the spirit of capitalism.
6   The poem is available on the Scottish Poetry Library's website (www.scottishpoetrylibrary.org.uk/poetry/poems/threshold).

APPENDIX: TIMELINE, 1900–2016

1900	United Free Church of Scotland formed by union of United Presbyterian Church of Scotland and Free Church of Scotland.
1901	Irn-Bru is first produced as Iron Brew by A.G. Barr in Falkirk.
	RRS *Discovery* is launched in Dundee.
	The Glasgow International Exhibition opens in Kelvingrove Park.
1902	Edinburgh's North British (now the Balmoral) Hotel opens.
	A stand at Ibrox stadium in Glasgow collapses during an England versus Scotland football match: twenty-five are killed.
1903	The North British Locomotive Company of Springburn in Glasgow is formed.
	Aberdeen Football Club is founded.
	Hampden Park stadium opens in Glasgow as the home of Queen's Park Football Club.
	Opening of Willow Tearooms in Sauchiehall Street, Glasgow, designed by Charles Rennie Mackintosh for Catherine Cranston.
1904	*The Scotsman* newspaper moves to new offices at North Bridge in Edinburgh, remaining there until 1999.
1905	First rugby match between New Zealand and Scotland played at Murrayfield.
	Scottish Motor Traction (SMT) is set up in Edinburgh as a motor bus operator.
	Thirty-nine men die in a fire at a model lodging house in Watson Street, Glasgow.
1906	New Argyll Motor Works is opened for production of the Argyll car at Alexandria, West Dunbartonshire.
	Yarrow Shipbuilders moves from London to Scotstoun, Glasgow.
1907	The British Aluminium Company begins producing aluminium at Kinlochleven.
1908	First ship launched from Yarrow Shipbuilders' new yard.
1909	Construction of Rosyth Dockyard for the Royal Navy.
	Riot by fans after replay of Scottish Cup Final between Rangers and Celtic at Hampden Park.
	The Scotch whisky brand name Johnnie Walker is introduced.
	The Harris Tweed trademark is registered.
1910	The whisky-based liqueur Drambuie is first marketed commercially in Leith.
1911	At the Singer Manufacturing Co. sewing machine factory in Clydebank, 11,000 workers go on strike in solidarity with 12 female colleagues protesting against work process reorganisation; 400 alleged ringleaders are dismissed.
	New building for the Mitchell Library opens in Glasgow.
1912	Unionist Party created in Scotland following merger of the Liberal Unionist Party with the Conservative & Unionist Party in England.

1913	Edinburgh Zoo opens.
	Coal mining production in Scotland peaks at 43.2 million tonnes, employing over 140,000 men and women, who, with their families, make up 10% of the Scottish population.
1914	A royal visit to Scotland is interrupted by suffragettes: one attempts to reach the King and Queen's carriage at Dundee.
	First World War begins. The Royal Navy cruiser HMS *Hawke* is sunk by a German U-boat off Aberdeen with the loss of 524 crew members.
	Sixteen Heart of Midlothian FC players enlist en masse – seven die in action before the war ends.
	Glasgow becomes the first UK city to employ women conductors on public transport for the duration of the war.
1915	Great Britain's worst train disaster occurs at Quintinshill (near Gretna Green) in which three trains collide, with the loss of 227 lives.
	Glasgow revolutionary socialist anti-war protester John Maclean is arrested for the first time under the Defence of the Realm Act and dismissed from his job as a teacher.
	Naval bases are established at Scapa Flow in Orkney and Invergordon.
1916	Conscription to the armed forces begins.
	British Grand Fleet leaves Scapa Flow for the Battle of Jutland.
	Edinburgh-born Black Watch private John Docherty is shot at dawn for desertion, the first Kitchener's Army volunteer to be executed.
1917	UK Parliament votes to give votes to women over 30 for the first time.
1918	John Maclean tried in the High Court for sedition.
	Armistice Day – the First World War ends on the eleventh hour of the eleventh day of the eleventh month.
	German battle fleet surrenders to the allies in the Firth of Forth prior to being interned at Scapa Flow.
	English industrialist William Lever, Baron Leverhulme (known as 'the Soap man'), buys the Isle of Lewis.
1919	'Bloody Friday' riot – mass rally of strikers in Glasgow's George Square repeatedly charged by police. Tanks and army patrol the streets.
	The naval yacht *Iolaire* struck a reef on approaching Stornoway Harbour at 2 a.m. Despite being only 20 yards (18 m) from shore, 205 out of 260 Lewis men and 24 crew died as the overloaded boat sank.
	German fleet scuttled in Scapa Flow.
1920	Scottish Protestant League founded by Alexander Ratcliffe.
1921	First women jurors in Glasgow Sheriff Court.
	Church of Scotland Act 1921 given Royal Assent, recognising the Church's Articles Declaratory and thus its status as the national church in Scotland but independent from the state in spiritual matters.
	Helen Fraser is the first woman to stand in Scotland (for the Liberal Party) as an official party candidate for parliament in UK general election.
	The *Aberdeen Press & Journal* is first published under this title following a merger between the *Aberdeen Journal* and the *Aberdeen Free Press*.

(Continued)

(Continued)

1922	Hunger March sets out from Glasgow to London.
	British Broadcasting Company (BBC) is formed.
	UK general election. Conservatives win election; Labour is biggest party in Scotland with twenty-nine MPs out of seventy-one. Winston Churchill loses his seat in Dundee.
1923	BBC Scotland begins broadcasting from Glasgow.
	The steam train 'Flying Scotsman' goes into service with the London and North Eastern Railway (LNER), on the London (King's Cross) to Edinburgh route.
	The Caledonian Railway, Highland and Glasgow and South Western Railways are merged into the London, Midland and Scottish Railway; and the North British and Great North of Scotland Railways into the London and North Eastern Railway.
	The Duchess of Atholl is elected Unionist Party MP for Kinross and Western Perthshire.
1924	Westminster debates a Home Rule Bill for Scotland, but it is not voted on.
	Ramsay MacDonald becomes the first Labour Prime Minister of the United Kingdom, leading a minority Labour government.
1925	First moving image on a television screen when John Logie Baird transmits the image of a 15-year-old office boy in his London workshop.
	National Library of Scotland established by Act of Parliament.
1926	General Strike, the first in British history, 3–12 May.
	Launch, under the auspices of the Scots National League, of a new monthly Nationalist newspaper entitled *The Scots Independent*.
	Sacramento River stern-wheel paddle steamers *Delta King* and *Delta Queen* are shipped from William Denny and Brothers' yard at Dumbarton to California.
1927	The Scottish National War Memorial is opened at Edinburgh Castle.
	Glasgow University Scottish Nationalist Association formed.
1928	The National Party for Scotland is founded.
	People over the age of 65 receive a state pension for the first time, of 10 shillings (50 pence) a week.
	Voting age for women reduced from 30 to 21, the same as for men.
	John Logie Baird transmits first colour television.
	Scotland defeat England 5–1 at Wembley stadium.
1929	The Church of Scotland and the United Free Church of Scotland unite.
	Local Government (Scotland) Act 1929 enacted. Aberdeen, Dundee, Edinburgh and Glasgow are confirmed as having city status.
	Legislation requires both parties to a marriage in Scotland to be at least 16 years old (although no parental consent is needed).
	Aluminium smelter at Fort William opened in conjunction with Lochaber hydroelectric scheme.

1930	Island of St Kilda evacuated.
	First section of the 132 kV AC National Grid, the Central Scotland Electricity Scheme, is switched on in Edinburgh.
	Formation of the Scottish Party by members of the Unionist Party favouring establishment of a Dominion Scottish Parliament.
1931	Ramsay MacDonald forms a UK 'National Government'.
	Invergordon Mutiny by 1000 sailors against pay cuts.
	National Trust for Scotland established.
	The Unionist Party wins a majority of Scottish seats as the National Government retains power with a landslide victory throughout the UK.
1932	First contingent of the National Hunger March leaves Glasgow.
	Wendy Wood leads a group of nationalists into Stirling Castle, at this time an army barracks as well as a heritage attraction, to tear down the Union flag and replace it with a Scottish standard.
1933	First alleged sighting of the Loch Ness Monster.
	The first regular air service in Scotland is established, from Inverness to Wick and Orkney.
	Scottish Democratic Fascist Party founded by William Weir Gilmour and Major Hume Sleigh to oppose Irish Catholic migration to Scotland.
1934	Scottish National Party founded with the amalgamation of the National Party of Scotland and the Scottish Party.
1935	Glasgow Subway electrified service opens.
	The Communist Party of Great Britain candidate, Willie Gallacher, wins the constituency of West Fife in the general election.
1936	The 'Oor Wullie' and 'Broons' cartoon strips first appear in the *Sunday Post*.
	First radio outside broadcast in Gaelic, a religious service from Iona Abbey, transmitted by the BBC.
	Kincardine Bridge opens across the Firth of Forth.
1937	A British record attendance at a football match is set when 149,547 watch Scotland play England at Hampden Park, Glasgow; Scotland won 3–1.
	The first issue of children's comic *The Dandy*, including the character Desperate Dan, is published.
	The National Trust for Scotland acquires its first part of the site of the Battle of Culloden.
1938	First edition of the long-running *Beano* comic is published.
	Rugby first appears on British television: England versus Scotland at Twickenham in London.
	Queen Elizabeth is launched at Clydebank.
	Iona Community established by Rev. George MacLeod in Glasgow.
	The Empire Exhibition, Scotland 1938, is held at Bellahouston Park, Glasgow.

(Continued)

(Continued)

1939	UK attendance record for a club football match created when 118,567 attended the Rangers versus Celtic match at Ibrox stadium.
	Outbreak of war: German submarine sinks HMS *Royal Oak* in Scapa Flow, Orkney, with the loss of 810 lives.
	Civil servants of the Scottish Office begin to occupy its first office in Scotland, St Andrew's House on Calton Hill in Edinburgh.
	A dust explosion at the Valleyfield colliery in Fife kills thirty-five miners.
1940	Rationing of sugar, bacon and butter introduced.
	RMS *Queen Elizabeth* makes her maiden voyage on delivery from Clydebank to New York.
	The Marriage (Scotland) Act 1939 prohibits 'irregular' marriages ('marriage by declaration' or 'handfasting') from this date, ending the practice of 'anvil marriage' at Gretna Green.
1941	SS *Politician* runs aground on Eriskay in the Outer Hebrides, creating the basis for Sir Compton MacKenzie's novel *Whisky Galore*.
	Tom Johnston is appointed Secretary of State for Scotland.
	The Clydebank Blitz (13–15 March): over 500 killed and 48,000 made homeless.
1942	Military scientists begin testing of anthrax as a biological warfare agent on Gruinard Island.
1943	Creation of the North of Scotland Hydro-Electric Board to bring electricity to all parts of the Highlands and Islands.
	Ferranti opens a plant at Crewe Toll in Edinburgh, originally to manufacture gyro gunsights for aircraft.
1944	'Pay As You Earn' (PAYE) Income Tax introduced for the first time.
	In the Kirkcaldy Burghs by-election, the Scottish National Party candidate Douglas Young comes close to winning the seat, which is held for Labour by Thomas Hubbard.
1945	First Scottish Nationalist MP is elected. The Scottish National Party gained its first electoral victory when it won the by-election in Motherwell and Wishaw by a majority of 617 votes.
	Victory-in-Europe Day, end of the Second World War in Europe.
	First general election after the Second World War – a sweeping victory for the Labour Party.
1946	Scottish edition of the *Daily Mail* begins publication in Edinburgh.
	The last election for a university constituency in the UK takes place when the Combined Scottish Universities by-election is held. Walter Elliot (Unionist) wins decisively.
1947	Coal mines nationalised and brought into public ownership.
	East Kilbride designated as the first New Town in Scotland under powers of the New Towns Act 1946.
	First Edinburgh International Festival opens.
	The Broadway musical *Brigadoon* opens in New York.
1948	A Scottish Region of British Railways begins to operate as a result of nationalisation of rail transport in Great Britain under the Transport Act 1947.
	Glenrothes is designated as a New Town under the New Towns Act 1946.
	The National Health Service begins operating as a result of the National Health Service (Scotland) Act 1947.
	Bread rationing ends in Great Britain.

1949	The National Covenant for Home Rule is launched by John MacCormick.
	Scottish Gas Board established.
1950	Petrol rationing, introduced during the Second World War, is ended.
	First official Edinburgh Military Tattoo staged at Edinburgh Castle as part of the Edinburgh Festival.
	The Stone of Destiny is removed from Westminster Abbey in London.
1951	The cartoon character 'Dennis the Menace' appears for the first time in the *Beano* comic.
	Festival of Britain: Exhibition of Industrial Power in Glasgow.
1952	Identity cards, introduced as a wartime security measure, are abolished in Great Britain.
	First television programmes broadcast from Kirk o' Shotts, Central Scotland.
	'Pillar Box War': First GPO pillar box of the present reign to be erected in Scotland is attacked because it carries the Royal Cipher of Elizabeth II, the regnal number being considered historically incorrect in Scotland.
1953	Rationing of chocolate and sweets finally ends.
	Coronation of Queen Elizabeth II. Objectors who said that Scotland had never had a 'Queen Elizabeth I' were told that in future the 'highest number will be used' where there is such a conflict.
	Royal yacht *Britannia* launched at John Brown's shipyard, Clydebank.
1954	Food rationing officially ends.
	Work on construction of Ravenscraig steelworks is authorised.
1955	The South of Scotland Electricity Board (SSEB) is formed by merger.
	UK general election: in Scotland, as throughout the UK as a whole, the Conservatives have a majority of seats.
	Cumbernauld is designated a New Town.
1956	The first telephone cable connecting the UK and North America goes live: 2240 miles (3600 kilometres) long, the cable runs from Gallanach Bay, near Oban in Argyll and Bute, to Clarenville, Canada.
	The National Library of Scotland's first purpose-built premises are opened on George IV Bridge in Edinburgh.
	Edinburgh and Dundee Tramways cease to operate.
1957	Scottish Television starts broadcasting.
	Construction of a missile testing range on South Uist begins.
	Scotland's first nuclear power station at Dounreay is commissioned.
1958	Aberdeen Corporation Tramways last operate, leaving Glasgow as the only system in Scotland.
	St Ninian's Isle Treasure discovered in Shetland.
	Christmas Day is a public holiday in Scotland for the first time.
1959	UK general election results in a record third successive Conservative victory. The Unionist Party in Scotland loses four seats.

(Continued)

(Continued)

1960	Glasgow Cheapside docks fire: nineteen firemen killed.
	Real Madrid beat Eintracht-Frankfurt 7–3 at Hampden Park to win the European Cup for the fifth year in succession.
	'National Service', which required all fit young men to train in the armed forces, ends.
	Glasgow area suburban train services electrified.
1961	Scotland defeated 9–3 by England at Wembley, a record score for a football match between the two countries.
	Holy Loch US nuclear submarine base opens.
	The British Motor Corporation's Bathgate Lorry Plant begins production.
1962	Scottish Opera founded.
	Livingston is officially designated as a New Town.
	The North British Locomotive Company of Springburn goes into liquidation.
	The last steam locomotive built in Scotland.
	Last tramcar runs in Glasgow (to Auchenshuggle).
1963	Rootes car factory opens at Linwood, making the Hillman Imp.
	Kinross and West Perthshire by-election: Conservatives retain the seat allowing Prime Minister Alec Douglas-Home to enter the House of Commons.
1964	Forth Road Bridge opens. At 6156 feet (1876 m) long and with a centre span of 3300 feet (1006 m), it is the longest in Europe at the time.
	Aberdeen typhoid outbreak.
	University of Strathclyde chartered.
	Hunterston, a nuclear power station, opens.
	Labour defeats Sir Alec Douglas-Home's Conservatives, and the Unionist Party in Scotland loses eight seats.
	First stretch of the M8 motorway between Glasgow and Edinburgh opens.
1965	Cruachan hydroelectric scheme opens.
	Highlands and Islands Development Board is formed.
	Corpach pulp and paper mills open.
	Union Canal officially closes to navigation.
1966	Tay Road Bridge opens.
	Heriot-Watt College in Edinburgh is designated Heriot-Watt University.
	Construction of a prototype fast breeder nuclear reactor at Dounreay on the north coast of Scotland is announced.
	First Red Road Flats in Glasgow officially open.
	Irvine is designated as a New Town.
1967	Celtic FC win European Cup, beating Inter Milan 2–1 in Lisbon.
	University of Dundee, which was incorporated into the University of St Andrews in 1890, is constituted as a separate university.

	The liner *Queen Elizabeth II* is launched at John Brown's shipyard at Clydebank.
	University of Stirling instituted by Royal Charter.
	Hamilton by-election: Winnie Ewing wins for the Scottish National Party, taking the seat from Labour.
1968	The General Assembly of the Church of Scotland permits the ordination of women as ministers.
	Upper Clyde Shipbuilders formed.
	Declaration of Perth: the UK Conservative Party leader, Edward Heath, proposes a directly elected Scottish Assembly.
1969	Closure of the Waverley Line (the Edinburgh–Galashiels–Hawick–Carlisle Railway).
	The Longhope lifeboat sinks in the Pentland Firth with the loss of eight men on board, all from the small island of Hoy.
	Everyone in the UK over the age of 18 is allowed to vote in parliamentary elections. The minimum age of 21 had been set in 1928.
	First announcement of the discovery of high-grade crude oil in the North Sea.
	Debut of Scottish Ballet at the King's Theatre, Glasgow.
	Death penalty for murder is formally abolished in the UK.
1970	Kingston Bridge over the River Clyde in Glasgow officially opens. At the time, it was the longest bridge in any British city.
	The 13th Commonwealth Games open in Edinburgh.
	UK general election: Labour wins in Scotland with forty-eight MPs out of the seventy-one available, but the Conservatives win a majority across the UK. The SNP wins its first MP elected at a general election.
	BP announces the discovery of the massive Forties Oil Field in Scottish waters.
1971	Ibrox Park disaster: sixty-six supporters killed on stairway 13.
	Decimal currency is introduced, abandoning 12 pennies to a shilling and 20 shillings to a pound.
	Invergordon aluminium works starts production.
	Erskine Bridge over the River Clyde opens.
	UCS work-in begins at John Brown's Clydebank shipyard led by activist Jimmy Reid.
1972	UK joins the European Common Market (now called the European Union).
	The uninhabited island of Rockall, 290 miles (467 kilometres) out in the Atlantic from the Western Isles, is formally incorporated as part of Scotland.
	Last ship launched at the former John Brown & Company Clydebank yard.
	Rangers win the European Cup Winners Cup in Barcelona, beating Dynamo Moscow, 3-2
1973	The Kilbrandon Report is published and recommends the establishment of a directly elected Scottish Assembly.
	Glasgow Govan by-election results in Margo MacDonald of the SNP winning the seat from Labour on a 26.7% swing.

(Continued)

(Continued)

1974	The general election results in the first hung parliament since 1929, though Labour wins a majority of seats in Scotland. The SNP wins seven seats.
	Professional football is played on a Sunday for the first time.
	The second general election of the year results in a narrow victory for Harold Wilson, giving Labour a majority of three seats. Labour also wins a majority of seats within Scotland, while the SNP secures its highest ever Westminster representation up to this date with eleven seats.
1975	The *Scottish Daily News*, the first workers' cooperative national newspaper, is published (closed after six months).
	Local Government (Scotland) Act (1974) comes into force and the thirty-three counties and four city councils are replaced by nine regional, fifty-three district and three island councils.
	Referendum held on British membership of the European Community.
	In Scotland 1,332,286 vote 'Yes' and 948,039 vote 'No'. Turnout is 61%. Only Shetland and Western Isles have majorities against.
	First oil pumped ashore from British oilfields in the North Sea.
	Local government reorganisation (replacing counties and burghs for administrative purposes with regions and districts).
1976	The Scottish Labour Party is formed.
	Scottish MP David Steel is elected as new leader of the Liberal Party.
1977	Scottish District Council elections held, with Labour suffering significant losses.
	Scotland's 2–1 victory over England at Wembley is followed by a pitch invasion during which sections of pitch and crossbars are removed by fans.
	Tam Dalyell MP asks 'the West Lothian question'.
1978	Launch of BBC Radio Scotland.
	Glasgow Garscadden by-election: Donald Dewar retains the seat for Labour with only a 3.6% swing to the SNP.
	Hamilton by-election: George Robertson retains the seat for Labour, thwarting a strong challenge from the SNP.
	The Scotland Act 1978, to establish a Scottish Assembly, receives Royal Assent.
	First North Sea oil comes ashore at the Sullom Voe Terminal in Shetland via the Brent System pipeline.
1979	Referendum to create a Scottish Assembly wins a majority but fails to win 40% of electorate. Act is repealed without being put into effect.
	UK general election: the Labour Party wins the majority of seats in Scotland but the Conservatives win by a majority of forty-three seats across the UK as a whole.
1980	Scottish District local elections result in big gains for the Labour Party.
	Criminal Justice (Scotland) Act 1980 decriminalises private homosexual acts between two consenting persons aged over 21 in Scotland.
1981	Peugeot closes the Talbot car plant at Linwood, Renfrewshire, which was opened by the Rootes Group eighteen years earlier as Scotland's only car factory.
	George Wood (Aberdeen) Ltd ceases trawler operations.

1982	Roy Jenkins wins the Glasgow Hillhead by-election for the Social Democratic Party.
	Kessock Bridge opens over the Beauly Firth.
	The Carron Company ironworks of 1759 at Falkirk goes into receivership.
1983	Aberdeen FC beat Real Madrid 2–1 to win European Cup Winners Cup.
	Glasgow Central Mosque built.
1984	Miners' strike began in March, and lasted twelve months.
	Scotland win the rugby 'Grand Slam' at Murrayfield for the first time in fifty-nine years.
1985	Scottish Bus Group is reorganised into new regional companies.
	Freuchie in Fife win the Village Cricket Cup at Lord's Cricket Ground, the first for a Scottish club side.
1986	Commonwealth Games are held in Edinburgh.
	The millionth council house in the UK is sold to its tenants in Scotland, seven years after the right-to-buy scheme was launched.
	Bus deregulation takes place in Great Britain.
1987	General election: the Conservatives win just ten of the seventy-two constituencies in Scotland, but are re-elected to power at Westminster due to the scale of their election victory in England.
1988	Explosion aboard North Sea oil rig 'Piper Alpha': 167 lives are lost.
	'Sermon on the Mound': Margaret Thatcher, the Prime Minister of the UK, addresses the General Assembly of the Church of Scotland.
	The SNP wins the Glasgow Govan by-election from Labour with a swing of 33%.
	Scotland on Sunday newspaper, a sister paper of *The Scotsman*, is published for the first time.
	Pan Am Flight 103 blows up and crashes at Lockerbie, Dumfries, killing 243 passengers, 16 crew and 11 Lockerbie residents.
1989	The Claim of Right is signed at the General Assembly Hall, on the Mound in Edinburgh, by fifty-eight of Scotland's seventy-two MPs.
1990	Strathclyde Region Council applies for 250,000 summary warrants against rate-payers refusing to pay the 'Poll Tax' (introduced in Scotland in April 1989).
	Glasgow's year as Cultural Capital of Europe.
	Privatisation of the Scottish Bus Group begins.
	Scotland beat England 13–7 at Murrayfield to win the rugby 'Grand Slam'.
	British Steel announces the closure of the hot strip mill at Ravenscraig with the loss of 770 jobs.
	Alex Salmond wins the SNP leadership election, succeeding Gordon Wilson.
	Labour wins by-elections in Paisley South and Paisley North, retaining both seats despite swings to the SNP of 11.7% and 14%, respectively.
1991	Inauguration of full electric service on British Rail's East Coast Main Line from London King's Cross railway station through to Edinburgh Waverley.

(Continued)

(Continued)

1992	The general election results in Labour winning a clear majority of MPs in Scotland, with forty-nine out of seventy-two elected. However, the Conservative Party, with only eleven MPs in Scotland, becomes the UK government.
	Ravenscraig steelworks, the largest hot strip steel mill in Western Europe, closes.
	University of the Highlands and Islands is established as a Millennium Institute.
1993	Oil tanker MV *Braer* runs aground on Shetland, spilling 84,700 tonnes of crude oil into the sea.
	The Council Tax replaces the Community Charge as a means of raising revenue for local government.
	Glasgow Caledonian University is created by the merger of Glasgow Polytechnic and The Queen's College, Glasgow.
1994	Local government reorganisation, replacing the regions and districts with single-tier councils.
	John Smith, leader of the Labour Party, dies.
1995	Bridge to the Isle of Skye opens.
	The film *Braveheart*, directed by and starring Mel Gibson as William Wallace, is released.
	Perth by-election: Roseanna Cunningham wins for the SNP with a swing of 11.6%.
	Scottish Constitutional Convention publishes its blueprint for devolution, *Scotland's Parliament, Scotland's Right*.
1996	The Stone of Destiny is returned to Scotland, to be housed in Edinburgh Castle.
	Sixteen children killed in Dunblane school massacre.
	Reorganisation of local government in Scotland, with thirty-two unitary councils introduced.
	Stone of Scone (Destiny) is installed in Edinburgh Castle after it was removed from Scotland by King Edward I of England in 1296.
1997	Newly elected Labour UK government under the leadership of Tony Blair legislates for a referendum on a devolved Scottish parliament, which is passed by a large majority.
	The bill to establish the Scottish parliament is unveiled by Secretary of State for Scotland Donald Dewar.
1998	Torness Nuclear Power Station is commissioned.
	Scottish Socialist Party is established.
	New Museum of Scotland opens in Edinburgh.
1999	A Scottish parliament sits for the first time in 272 years: the start of a 'new sang'. Donald Dewar of the Scottish Labour Party is elected as First Minister and forms Scottish Executive in coalition with the Scottish Liberal Democrats. Election for the new Scottish Parliament results in 56 Labour MSPs, SNP 35, Conservatives 18, Liberal Democrats 16, Greens 1, Scottish Socialists 1, Independent 1.
	Sunday Herald newspaper is launched.
2000	Scotland's first Minister Donald Dewar dies suddenly.
	The Royal Bank of Scotland succeeds in a hostile takeover battle for its larger English rival, NatWest Bank, successfully defeating a rival offer by the Bank of Scotland.
	The Abolition of Feudal Tenure etc. (Scotland) Act 2000 receives Royal Assent.
	Repeal of controversial Section 2B of the Local Government Act 1988 which prevented local authorities from 'promoting homosexuality'.

2001	Motorola factory in Bathgate closes with the loss of 3100 jobs.
	Jack McConnell elected First Minister of Scotland, succeeding Henry McLeish.
	The UK general election results in Labour winning 56 of Scotland's 72 MPs, with the Liberal Democrats winning 10, the SNP 5 and the Conservatives 1.
	The Bank of Scotland and the Halifax merge to form HBOS plc.
2002	Longannet, the last deep coal mine in Scotland, closes, after being flooded along a 5-mile (8 km) mineshaft.
	Falkirk Wheel boat lift opens in Scotland, also marking reopening of the Union Canal for leisure traffic.
2003	The Land Reform (Scotland) Act 2003 receives Royal Assent.
	Scottish parliamentary election: the Labour and Liberal Democrat coalition led by Jack McConnell win a majority of the seats and remain in power. The Scottish Green Party and the Scottish Socialist Party significantly increase their representation.
	The High Court in Glasgow imposes a minimum sentence of twenty-seven years for Al Ali Mohmed Al Megrahi, the Libyan convicted of bombing Pan Am Flight 103 over Lockerbie.
2004	Opening of the new Scottish Parliament Building.
	Edwin Morgan becomes Scotland's first ever official national poet, The Scots Makar, appointed by the Scottish parliament.
2005	Gaelic Language (Scotland) Act is passed by the Scottish parliament, the first piece of legislation in the UK to give formal recognition to the Scottish Gaelic language.
	The UK general election results in Labour winning 41 of Scotland's 59 MPs, with the Liberal Democrats winning 11, the SNP 6 and the Conservatives 1.
	The Smoking, Health and Social Care (Scotland) Act 2005, banning smoking in enclosed public spaces, gets Royal Assent.
2006	Dunfermline and West Fife by-election: Willie Rennie of the Liberal Democrats wins, the first time the Labour Party has ever lost a seat it was defending to the Liberal Democrats, the SDP or the Liberal Party at a Scottish by-election.
	Moray by-election: Richard Lochhead holds the seat in the Scottish parliament for the SNP.
2007	The SNP becomes the largest party in the Scottish parliament and forms a minority government.
	Gordon Brown succeeds Tony Blair as Prime Minister of the UK.
	St Andrew's Day is for the first time a designated bank holiday in Scotland, under the St Andrew's Day Bank Holiday (Scotland) Act 2007.
2008	The Labour Party wins the Glenrothes by-election.
	Health Secretary Nicola Sturgeon is named Scottish Politician of the Year.
2009	The Scottish parliament rejects the budget tabled by the SNP administration. The Presiding Officer casts the deciding vote after the result is originally tied at sixty-four in favour and sixty-four against. The Scottish parliament approves the minority SNP administration's budget at the second time of asking.
	The SNP tops the poll in the European election in Scotland, winning two of Scotland's six MEPs.
	The Calman Commission recommends that the Scottish parliament be given greater control over tax and legislation such as setting speed limits.

(Continued)

(Continued)

2010	UK general election: with no Scottish seats changing hands, Labour maintains a stronghold in Scotland with 41 out of 59 Scottish Westminster seats. The Liberal Democrats have 11 seats, the SNP 6 and the Conservative Party hold its single Scottish seat.
2011	The SNP under Alex Salmond gains an overall majority of the Scottish parliament.
	The SNP urges British Prime Minister David Cameron to amend the Scotland Bill to give the Scottish parliament greater legislative powers.
	Scottish First Minister Alex Salmond unveils a legislative programme for the coming year which includes plans to create a single police force and a single fire service for Scotland.
	Newly elected MSP Ruth Davidson is elected as leader of the Scottish Conservatives.
2012	The Scottish government announces that it plans to hold an independence referendum in the autumn of 2014.
	Local elections result in the SNP making sixty-one gains and winning the largest number of councillors in Scotland, as well as gaining control of Dundee and Angus. Labour makes forty-eight gains and wins control of West Dunbartonshire and Renfrewshire. The Liberal Democrats lost over half of their councillors allowing the Conservatives, who also lost councillors, to end the day as the third largest party in local government.
2013	The Church of Scotland's ruling General Assembly votes to allow actively gay men and women to become ministers.
	Cockenzie coal-fired power plant closes.
	Prime Minister David Cameron rejects an invitation for a head-to-head TV debate on Scottish independence with First Minister Alex Salmond.
2014	European Parliament election held: the SNP wins the popular vote and retains two MEPs, Labour retains two, the Conservatives retain their single MEP and UKIP wins the final seat from the Liberal Democrats.
	Scotland has a referendum on national independence. Result is to remain part of the UK, by 55% to 45%.
	Nicola Sturgeon succeeds Alex Salmond as Leader of the Scottish National Party and First Minister of Scotland after she was the only candidate to put their name forward in the party's leadership election.
	Johann Lamont resigns as leader of the Scottish Labour Party with immediate effect, triggering a leadership election.
	The Smith Commission, established by David Cameron to look at enhanced devolution for Scotland following the referendum, publishes its report, recommending that the Scottish parliament should be given the power to set income tax rates and bands.
	Leader of the House of Commons William Hague sets out Conservative plans for English votes for English laws, which could see Scottish MPs prevented from voting on legislation that does not affect Scotland.
2015	The SNP wins 50% of the popular vote in the UK general election, securing 56 of the 59 seats in Scotland.
	Scotland's population grew by 19,900 to reach 5,347,600 in 2014 according to the Office for National Statistics.

Rail transport returns to the Scottish Borders after forty-six years with the reopening of the Waverley Route between Edinburgh and Tweedbank, under the name of the Borders Railway.

The voting rights of Scottish MPs are to be restricted after the Conservative government wins a vote on its controversial 'English votes for English laws' (EVEL) plans.

2016   The SNP is returned to power at Holyrood with 63 MSPs; the Conservatives have 31, Labour 24, the Greens 6 and the Liberal Democrats 5.

One month later, the referendum on UK membership of the European Union is held. Scotland votes 62% to remain; England, 53% to leave. The UK votes to leave the EU by 52% to 48%. A new chapter in Scottish and British politics opens.

BIBLIOGRAPHY

Aebi, M.F. (2004) 'Crime trends in Western Europe from 1900 to 2000', *European Journal on Criminal Policy and Research*, 10(2–3), 136–86.

Aebi, M.F. and A. Linde (2010) 'Is there a crime drop in Western Europe?', *European Journal on Criminal Policy and Research*, 16(4), 251–77.

Aebi, M.F. and A. Linde (2012) 'Crime trends in Western Europe according to official statistics from 1990 to 2007', in J. van Dijk, A. Tseloni and G. Farrell (eds), *The International Crime Drop: New directions in research*, Basingstoke: Palgrave Macmillan.

Allan, C. (1965) 'The genesis of British urban redevelopment: the Glasgow case', *Economic History Review*, 18, 598–613.

Amir, S., N. Blain and D. Forbes (1999) 'New ethnic and national questions in Scotland: post-British identities among Glasgow Pakistani teenagers', *Ethnic and Racial Studies*, 22(5), 821–44.

Anderson, B. (1996) *Imagined Communities: Reflections on the origin and spread of nationalism*, revised edition, London: Verso.

Anderson, M. (2012) 'The demographic factor', in T.M. Devine and J. Wormald (eds), *The Oxford Handbook of Modern Scottish History*, Oxford: Oxford University Press.

Anderson, M., F. Bechhofer and J. Gershuny (eds) (1994) *The Social and Political Economy of the Household*, Oxford: Oxford University Press.

Anderson, R.D. (1983) *Education and Opportunity in Victorian Scotland*, Edinburgh: Edinburgh University Press.

Anderson, R.D., M. Freeman and L. Paterson (eds) (2015) *The Edinburgh History of Education in Scotland*, Edinburgh: Edinburgh University Press.

Anderson, R.D. and S. Wallace (2015) 'The universities and national identity, c1830–1914', in R.D. Anderson et al. (eds), *The Edinburgh History of Education in Scotland*, Edinburgh: Edinburgh University Press.

Anderson, S. (1999) 'Statistics and the "problem of crime" in Scotland', in P. Duff and N. Hutton (eds), *Criminal Justice in Scotland*, Aldershot: Dartmouth Publishing.

Andrews, D. and G. Ritzer (2007) 'Sport and globalization: transnational dimensions', *Global Networks*, 7(2), 135–53.

Ascherson, N. (2010) 'Liquidator', *London Review of Books*, 32(16), 10–12.

Ash, M. (1980) *The Strange Death of Scottish History*, Edinburgh: The Ramsay Head Press.

Ashworth, A. (2005) *Sentencing and Criminal Justice*, Cambridge: Cambridge University Press.

Atkinson, A. (2015) *Inequality: What can be done?*, Cambridge, MA: Harvard University Press.

Audit Scotland (2012) *Reducing Reoffending in Scotland*, November (www.audit-scotland. gov.uk/uploads/docs/report/2012/nr_121107_reducing_reoffending.pdf).

Baines, D. (1991) *Emigration from Europe, 1815–1930*, Basingstoke: Macmillan.

Baird, S., J. Foster and R. Leonard (2004) 'Ownership of companies in Scotland', *Quarterly Economic Commentary*, 49, November, 45–53.

Baird, S., J. Foster and R. Leonard (2007) 'Scottish capital: still in control in the 21st century?', *Scottish Affairs*, 58, Winter, 1–35.

Baird, S., J. Foster and R. Leonard (2011) 'Who owns Scotland's jobs?', *Scottish Left Review*, 64, 1–5.

Bannister, J., J. Pickering, S. Batchelor, M. Burman, K. Kintrea and S. McVie (2010) *Troublesome Youth Groups, Gangs and Knife Carrying in Scotland*, Edinburgh: Scottish Government Social Research.

Banton, M. (1983) *Racial and Ethnic Competition*, Cambridge: Cambridge University Press.

Banton, M. (1997) *Ethnic and Racial Consciousness*, 2nd edition, London: Longman.

Banton, M. (2015) 'Ethnic boundaries: a critical rationalist perspective', in J. Jackson and L. Molokotos-Liederman (eds), *Nationalism, Ethnicity and Boundaries: Conceptualising and understanding national and ethnic identity through boundary approaches*, London: Routledge.

Basu, P. (2007) *Highland Homecomings: Genealogy and heritage tourism in the Scottish diaspora*, London: Routledge.

Baudrillard, J. (1983) *Simulations*, Paris: Semiotext(e).

Bauman, Z. (1990) *Thinking Sociologically*, Oxford: Basil Blackwell.

Bealey, F. and J. Sewel (1981) *The Politics of Independence: A study of a Scottish town*, Aberdeen: Aberdeen University Press.

Beaune, C. (1985) *Naissance de la Nation France*, Paris: Gallimard.

Bechhofer, F. (2012) 'Review of *American Scots: The Scottish diaspora and the USA*', *Ethnic and Racial Studies*, 35(12), 2225–6 (http://dx.doi.org/10.1080/01419870.2012.708427).

Bechhofer, F., B. Elliott and D. McCrone (1978) 'Structure, consciousness and action: a sociological profile of the British middle class', *British Journal of Sociology*, 29(4), 410–36.

Bechhofer, F. and D. McCrone (2008) 'Talking the talk: national identity in Scotland and England', in A. Park et al. (eds), *British Social Attitudes, 24th Report*, London: Sage.

Bechhofer, F. and D. McCrone (eds) (2009) *National Identity, Nationalism and Constitutional Change*, Basingstoke: Palgrave Macmillan.

Bechhofer, F. and D. McCrone (2012a) 'Imagining the nation: symbols of national culture in England and Scotland', *Ethnicities*, 13(5), 544–64.

Bechhofer, F. and D. McCrone (2012b) 'Coming home: return migrants in twenty-first-century Scotland', in M. Varricchio (ed.), *Back to Caledonia*, Edinburgh: Edinburgh University Press.

Bechhofer, F. and L. Paterson (2000) *Principles of Research Design in the Social Sciences*, London: Routledge.

Becker, G. (1960) 'An economic analysis of fertility', in *Demographic and Economic Change in Developing Countries*, New York: Columbia University Press (www.nber.org/chapters/c2387).

Beetham, D. (1984) 'The future of the nation state?', in G. McLennan, D. Held and S. Hall (eds), *The Idea of the Modern State*, Milton Keynes: Open University Press.

Bell, D. (1974) *The Coming of Post-Industrial Society*, New York: Basic Books.

Bell, D. (2003) 'Mythscapes: memory, mythology and national identity', *British Journal of Sociology*, 54(1), 63–81.

Berger, J. (1972) *Ways of Seeing*, London: BBC and Harmondsworth: Penguin Books.

Berger, P. (1963) *Invitation to Sociology: A humanistic perspective*, Harmondsworth: Penguin Books.

Beveridge, C. and R. Turnbull (1989) *The Eclipse of Scottish Culture: Inferiorism and the intellectuals*, Edinburgh: Polygon.

Beveridge, C. and R. Turnbull (1997) *Scotland after Enlightenment: Image and tradition in modern Scottish culture*, Edinburgh: Polygon.

Billig, M. (1995) *Banal Nationalism*, London: Sage.

Billig, M. (2005) *Laughter and Ridicule: Towards a social critique of humour*, London: Sage.

Billig, M. (2009) 'Reflecting on a critical engagement with banal nationalism – reply to Skey', *The Sociological Review*, 57(2), 347–52.

Billig, M. (2013) *Learn to Write Badly: How to succeed in the social sciences*, Cambridge: Cambridge University Press.

Bishops' Conference of Scotland (2006) *Religion in Scotland's Schools*, European Council of Episcopal Conferences (www.chiesacattolica.it/cci_new/PagineCCI/AllegatiArt/30/Scozia_ingl.doc).

Blaikie, A. (2010) *The Scots Imagination and Modern Memory*, Edinburgh: Edinburgh University Press.

Blain, N. and R. Boyle (1994) 'The marking of Scottish identity in sports journalism', in G. Jarvie and G. Walker, *Scottish Sport in the Making of the Nation*, Leicester: Leicester University Press.

Blain, N. and D. Hutchison (eds) (2008) *The Media in Scotland*, Edinburgh: Edinburgh University Press.

Blain, N. and D. Hutchison (eds) (2016) *Scotland's Referendum and the Media: National and international perspectives*, Edinburgh: Edinburgh University Press.

Bloor, M., M. Gannon, G. Hay, G. Jackson, A.H. Leyland and N. McKeganey (2008) 'Contribution of problem drug users' deaths to excess mortality in Scotland', *British Medical Journal*, 337, a478.

Blumstein, A. and R. Rosenfeld (2008) 'Factors contributing to US crime trends', in A.S. Goldberger and R. Rosenfeld (eds), *Understanding Crime Trends: Workshop Report*, Washington, DC: National Academies Press.

Bochel, H. and C. Bochel (2016) 'Women candidates and councillors in Scottish local government, 1974–2012', *Scottish Affairs*, 25(2), 161–85.

Bochel, J., D. Denver and A. Macartney (eds) (1981) *The Referendum Experience*, Aberdeen: Aberdeen University Press.

Bond, R. (2011) 'The national identities of minorities in Scotland: anticipating the 2011 Census', *Scottish Affairs*, 75, 1–24.

Bond, R. (2016) 'Sub-state national identities among minority groups in Britain: a comparative analysis of 2011 Census data', Mimeo.

Bonino, S. (2015) 'Scottish Muslims through a decade of change: wounded by stigma, healed by Islam, rescued by Scotland', *Scottish Affairs*, 24(1), 78–105.

Botterill, K. (2014) 'Family and mobility in second modernity: Polish migrant narratives of individualization and family life', *Sociology*, 48(2), 233–50.

Bourdieu, P. (1984) *Distinction: A social critique of the judgement of taste*, London: Routledge & Kegan Paul.

Bourdieu, P. (1986) 'The forms of capital', in J. Richardson (ed.), *Handbook of Theory and Research for the Sociology of Education*, New York, Greenwood.

Boyd, S. (2014) 'Labour market changes and implications for policy and labour market information (LMI) in Scotland', *Fraser of Allander Institute Economic Commentary*, 38(2), 63–80.

Brand, J. (1978) *The National Movement in Scotland*, London: Routledge & Kegan Paul.

Breitenbach, E., A. Brown and F. Myers (1998) 'Understanding women in Scotland', *Feminist Review*, 58, Spring, 44–65.

Breitenbach, E. and F. Mackay (eds) (2001) *Women and Contemporary Scottish Politics: An anthology*, Edinburgh: Polygon.

Breitenbach, E. and F. Wasoff (2007) 'A gender audit of statistics: comparing the position of women and men in Scotland', Scottish Executive Social Research (www.gov.scot/Resource/Doc/172901/0048232.pdf).

Brierley, P. (1999) *UK Religious Trends*, Volume 1, London: Christian Research Association.

Brierley, P. and F. Macdonald (1995) *Prospects for Scotland 2000*, London: Christian Research Association.

Broun, D. (1994) 'The origin of Scottish identity', in C. Bjørn, A. Grant and K.J. Stringer (eds), *Nations, Nationalism and Patriotism in the European Past*, Copenhagen: Academic Press.

Broun, D. (1998) 'Defining Scotland and the Scots before the Wars of Independence', in D. Broun, R.J. Finlay and M. Lynch (eds), *Image and Identity: The making and remaking of Scotland through the ages*, Edinburgh: John Donald.

Broun, D. (2013) *Scottish Independence and the Idea of Britain*, Edinburgh: Edinburgh University Press.

Broun, D. (2015) 'Rethinking Scottish origins', in S. Boardman and S. Foran (eds), *Barbour's Bruce and its Cultural Contexts*, Martlesham: Boydell & Brewer.

Brown, A. (1996) 'Women and politics in Scotland', *Parliamentary Affairs*, 49, 26–40.

Brown, A., D. McCrone and L. Paterson (1999) *The Scottish Electorate: The 1997 General Election and beyond*, Basingstoke: Palgrave Macmillan.

Brown, D. (2009) 'The Big Drum: the mutability of a sporting habitus: mountaineering in Scotland as a case study', *International Review for the Sociology of Sport*, 44(4), 315–30.

Brown, G. (2015) *My Scotland, Our Britain*, London: Simon & Schuster.

Brown, I. (ed.) (2010) *From Tartan to Tartanry: Scottish culture, history and myth*, Edinburgh: Edinburgh University Press.

Brown, R. (2015) 'Explaining the property crime drop: the offender perspective', *Trends and Issues in Crime and Criminal Justice*, No. 495, Canberra: Australian Institute of Criminology.

Brubaker, R. (2002) 'Ethnicity without groups', *Archives Européennes de Sociologie*, XLIII(2), 531–48.

Brubaker, R. (2005) 'The "Diaspora" diaspora', *Ethnic and Racial Studies*, 28(1), 1–19.

Bruce, S. (1992) *The Red Hand: Protestant paramilitaries in Northern Ireland*, Oxford: Oxford University Press.

Bruce, S. (2011) *Secularization*, Oxford: Oxford University Press.

Bruce, S. (2014) *Scottish Gods: Religion in modern Scotland 1900–2012*, Edinburgh: Edinburgh University Press.

Bruce, S. (2016) 'The sociology of late secularisation', *British Journal of Sociology*, 67(4), 613–31.

Bruce, S. and A. Glendinning (2003) 'Religious beliefs and differences', in C. Bromley, J. Curtice, K. Hinds and A. Park (eds), *Devolution – Scottish answers to Scottish questions*, Edinburgh: Edinburgh University Press.

Bruce, S., T., Glendinning, I. Paterson, and M. Rosie, (2004) *Sectarianism in Scotland*, Edinburgh: Edinburgh University Press.

Bruce, S. and A. Glendinning (2016) 'Sectarianism in the Scottish labour market: the 2011 census', *Scottish Affairs* (forthcoming).

Bruce, S. and S. Yearley (1989) 'The social construction of tradition: the restoration portraits and the Kings of Scotland', in D. McCrone, S. Kendrick and P. Straw (eds), *The Making of Scotland: Nation, culture and social change*, Edinburgh: Edinburgh University Press.

Bueltmann, T., G. Morton and A. Hinson (2013) *The Scottish Diaspora*, Edinburgh: Edinburgh University Press.

Bukodi, E., J.H. Goldthorpe, L. Waller and J. Kuha (2015) 'The mobility problem in Britain: new findings from the analysis of birth cohort data', *British Journal of Sociology*, 66(1), 93–117.

Bulpitt, J. (1983) *Territory and Power*, Manchester: Manchester University Press.

Burman, M. and F. Cartmel (2005) *Young People's Attitudes Towards Gendered Violence*, Edinburgh: NHS Scotland.

Burns, L.A., D.J. Williams and P.D. Donnelly (2011) 'A public health approach to the evaluation of the Glasgow community initiative to reduce violence', *Scottish Institute for Policing Research*, Summary No. 7.

Burns, T. (1970) 'Sociological Explanation', Inaugural Lecture, Edinburgh University, 8 February. Reprinted in D. Emmet and A. MacIntyre (eds), *Sociological Theory and Philosophical Analysis*, London: Macmillan (www.sociology.ed.ac.uk/tomburns/burns_inaugural196_sociologicalexplanation.pdf).

Burns, T. and G.M. Stalker (1961) *The Management of Innovation*, London: Tavistock.

Cairney, P. (2014) 'The territorialisation of interest representation in Scotland', *Territory, Politics and Governance*, 2(3), 303–21.

Cairney, P., M. Keating and A. Wilson (2015) 'Solving the problem of social background in the UK "political class": do parties do things differently in Westminster, devolved and European elections?', *British Politics*, DOI: 10.1057/bp.2015.39.

Calhoun, C. (1993) *Habermas and the Public Sphere*, Cambridge, MA: MIT Press.

Calhoun, C. (2003) '"Belonging" in the cosmopolitan imagery', *Ethnicities*, 3(4), 531–53.

Callander, R.F. (1998) *How Scotland is Owned*, Edinburgh: Canongate.

Cameron, J. (1983) *Prisons and Punishment in Scotland: from the middle ages to the present*, Edinburgh: Canongate.

Campbell, J.L. and J. Hall (2009) 'National identity and the political economy of small states', *Review of International Political Economy*, 16(4), 547–72.

Cannadine, D. (1990) *The Decline and Fall of the British Aristocracy*, New Haven, CT: Yale University Press.

Carruthers, G. (2009) *Scottish Literature*, Edinburgh: Edinburgh University Press.

Carstairs, V. and R. Morris (1989) 'Deprivation: explaining differences in mortality between Scotland and England and Wales', *British Medical Journal*, 299, 886–9.

Carstairs, V. and R. Morris (1991) *Deprivation and Health in Scotland*, Aberdeen: Aberdeen University Press.

Carter, I. (1971) 'Economic models and the history of the Highlands', *Scottish Studies*, 15, 99–120.

Carter, I. (1974) 'The Highlands of Scotland as an underdeveloped region', in E. DeKadt and G. Williams (eds), *Sociology and Underdevelopment*, London: Tavistock.

Carter, I. (1979) *Farm Life in Northeast Scotland, 1840–1914: The poor man's country*, Edinburgh: John Donald.

Caughie, J. (1982) 'Scottish television: what would it look like?', in C. McArthur (ed.), *Scotch Reels: Scotland in cinema and television*, London: BFI Publishing.

Cavadino, M. and J. Dignan (2006) *Penal Systems: A comparative approach*, London: Sage.

Centre on Dynamics of Ethnicity (2013) 'Who feels British? The relationship between ethnicity, religion and national identity in England', *Dynamics of Diversity: Evidence from the 2011 Census* (www.ethnicity.ac.uk/census/CoDE-National-Identity-Census-Briefing.pdf).

Chapman, M. (1978) *The Gaelic Vision of Scottish Culture*, London: Croom Helm.

Chapman, M. (1992) *The Celts: The construction of a myth*, London: Macmillan.

Charsley, S. (1986) '"Glasgow's Miles Better": the symbolism of community and identity in the city', in A. Cohen (ed.), *Symbolising Boundaries: Identity and diversity in British cultures*, Manchester: Manchester University Press.

Cheape, H. (1991) *Tartan: The Highland habit*, Edinburgh: National Museums of Scotland.

Checkland, S. and O. Checkland (1984) *Industry & Ethos: Scotland 1832–1914*, London: Edward Arnold.

Clarke, S. (2013) 'Crime trends in detail: trends in crime and criminal justice, 2010', Eurostat Statistics Explained web-resource: Statistics in Focus 18/2013 (http://ec.europa.eu/eurostat/statistics-explained/index.php/Crime_trends_in_detail).

Claval, P. (1980) 'Centre–periphery and space: models of political geography', in W. Gottman (ed.), *Centre and Periphery: Spatial variations in politics*, London: Sage.

Cohen, A. (ed.) (1982) *Belonging: Identity and social organisation in British rural cultures*, Manchester: Manchester University Press.

Cohen, A. (1985) *The Symbolic Construction of Community*, London: Tavistock.

Cohen, A. (1986) *Symbolising Boundaries: Identity and diversity in British cultures*, Manchester: Manchester University Press.

Cohen, A. (1994) *Self Consciousness: An alternative anthropology of identity*, London: Routledge.

Cohen, A. (2000) 'Peripheral vision: nationalism, national identity and the objective correlative in Scotland', in A. Cohen (ed.), *Signifying Identities: Anthropological perspectives on boundaries and contested values*, London: Routledge.

Cohen, A. (2004) 'Review of *The Scots' Crisis of Confidence*', *Scottish Affairs*, 49, Autumn, 160–2.

Cohen, R. (2008) *Global Diasporas*, 2nd edition, London: Routledge.

Colley, L. (1992) *Britons: Forging the nation, 1707–1837*, New Haven, CT: Yale University Press.

Commission on Women Offenders (2012) Final Report, Edinburgh: Scottish Government (www.gov.scot/Resource/0039/00391828.pdf).

Condor, S. (2010) 'Devolution and national identity: the rules of English (dis)engagement', *Nations and Nationalism*, 16(3), 525–43.

Condor, S. and J. Abell (2006) 'Vernacular constructions of "national identity" in post-devolution Scotland and England', in J. Wilson and K. Stapleton (eds), *Devolution and Identity*, London: Palgrave Macmillan.

Condor, S., S. Gibson and J. Abell (2006) 'English identity and ethnic diversity in the context of UK constitutional change', *Ethnicities*, 6, 123–58.

Connell, L. (2003) 'The Scottishness of the Scottish press, 1918–39', *Media, Culture and Society*, 25(2), 187–207.

Cosgrove, D. (1994) 'Terrains of power', *Times Higher Education Supplement*, 11 March, p. 24.

Cowley, P. (2012) 'Arise, novice leader! The continuing rise of the career politician in Britain', *Politics*, 32(1), 31–8.

Craig, Cairns (1983) 'Visitors from the stars: Scottish film culture', *Cencrastus*, 11, 6–11.

Craig, Cairns (1987) 'Twentieth century Scottish literature: an introduction', in C. Cairns (ed.), *The History of Scottish Literature, Volume 4, The Twentieth Century*, Aberdeen: Aberdeen University Press.

Craig, Cairns (1996) *Out of History: Narrative paradigms in Scottish and British culture*, Edinburgh: Polygon.

Craig, Cairns (1999) *The Scottish Modern Novel*, Edinburgh: Edinburgh University Press.

Craig, Cairns (2001) 'Constituting Scotland', *The Irish Review*, No. 28, *Ireland and Scotland: Colonial Legacies and National Identities* (Winter), 1–27.

Craig, Cairns (2012) 'The literary tradition', in T.M. Devine and J. Wormald (eds), *The Oxford Handbook of Modern Scottish History*, Oxford: Oxford University Press.

Craig, Cairns (2015) 'The case for culture', *Scottish Review of Books*, 10(3).

Craig, Carol (2003) *The Scots' Crisis of Confidence*, Glasgow: Big Thinking.

Craig, Carol (2010) *The Tears That Made the Clyde: Well-being in Glasgow*, Glendaruel: Argyll Publishing.

Craig, Carol (2014) 'Why this optimist is voting No', *Scottish Review*, 9 September.

Craig, D. (1961) *Scottish Literature and the Scottish People, 1680–1830*, London: Chatto & Windus.

Craig, D. (2014) *London Review of Books*, 36(17), 13–15.

Craig, F.W.S. (1981) *British Electoral Facts, 1832–1980,* Chichester: Parliamentary Research Services.

Crick, B. (1992) *In Defence of Politics*, London: Weidenfeld & Nicolson.

Croall, H. (2006) 'Criminal justice in post-devolutionary Scotland', *Critical Social Policy*, 26(3), 587–607.

Croall, H., G. Mooney and M. Munro (eds) (2010) *Criminal Justice in Scotland*, Abingdon: Routledge.

Croall, H., G. Mooney and M. Munro (eds) (2015) *Crime, Justice and Society in Scotland*, Abingdon: Routledge.

Crompton, R., M. Brockmann and C. Lyonette (2005) 'Attitudes, women's employment and the domestic division of labour: a cross-national analysis in two waves', *Work, Employment and Society*, 19(2), 213–33.

Crouch, C. (2011) *The Strange Non-Death of Neo-Liberalism*, Cambridge: Polity Press.

Crouch, C. (2013) *Making Capitalism Fit for Society*, Cambridge: Polity Press.

Crow, G. and C. Maclean (2013) 'Community', in G. Payne (ed.), *Social Divisions*, 3rd edition, Basingstoke: Palgrave Macmillan.

Croxford, L. (1994) 'Equal opportunities in the secondary school curriculum in Scotland', *British Educational Research Journal*, 20, 371–91.

Croxford, L. (2015) 'Inequalities', in D. Murphy, L. Croxford, C. Howieson and D. Raffe (eds), *Everyone's Future: Lessons from fifty years of Scottish comprehensive schooling*, London: Institute of Education Press.

Croxford, L. and L. Paterson (2006) 'Trends in social class segregation between schools in England, Wales and Scotland since 1984', *Research Papers in Education*, 21, 381–406.

Cumbers, A. (2000) 'Globalization, local economic development and the branch plant region: the case of the Aberdeen oil complex', *Regional Studies*, 34(4), 371–82.

Currie, R., A. Gilbert and L. Horsley (1977) *Churches and Churchgoers: Patterns of church growth in the British Isles since 1700*, Oxford: Oxford University Press.

Curtice, J. (1999) 'Was it the Sun wot won it again? The influence of newspapers in the 1997 election campaign', CREST Working Paper 75, September.

Curtice, J. and A. Health (2009) '"England awakes." Trends in national identity in England', in F. Bechhofer and D. McCrone (eds), *National Identity, Nationalism and Constitutional Change*, Basingstoke: Palgrave Macmillan.

Daiches, D. (1997) *Two Worlds: An Edinburgh Jewish childhood*, Edinburgh: Canongate.

Damer, S. (1974) 'Wine Alley: the sociology of a dreadful enclosure', *Sociological Review*, 22, 221–48.

Damer, S. (1989) *From Moorpark to 'Wine Alley'*, Edinburgh: Edinburgh University Press.

Damer, S. (2011) 'Review Essay: The peculiarities of the Clydesiders', *Scottish Affairs*, 74, Winter, 147–54.

Daniels, S. and D. Cosgrove (1988) 'Introduction: iconography and landscape', in *The Iconography of Landscape*, Cambridge: Cambridge University Press.

Davie, G.E. (1961) *The Democratic Intellect: Scotland and her universities in the nineteenth century*, Edinburgh: Edinburgh University Press.

Davie, G.E. (1986) *The Crisis of the Democratic Intellect*, Edinburgh: Polygon.

Davie, G.R.C. (1994) *Religion in Britain Since 1945*, Oxford: Blackwell.

Davies, C. (2011) *Jokes and Targets*, Bloomington: Indiana University Press.

Davies, N. (2011) *Vanished Kingdoms: The history of half-forgotten Europe*, London: Allen Lane.

Davis, H. (1979) *Beyond Class Images: Exploration on the structure of social consciousness*, London: Croom Helm.

Dawson, A. (2009) *So Foul and Fair a Day: A history of Scotland's weather and climate*, Edinburgh: Birlinn.

Dejonghe, T. (2007) *Sport in de wereld*, Ghent: Academia Press.

Dekavalla, M. (2012) 'Evaluating newspaper performance in the public sphere: press accounts of Westminster elections in Scotland and in England in the early post-devolution period', *Journalism*, 13(3), 320–39.

Dekavalla, M. (2015) 'The Scottish newspaper industry in the digital era', *Media, Culture & Society*, 37(1), 107–14.

Devine, T. (2000) *The Scottish Nation, 1700–2000*, London: Penguin Books.

Devine, T. (2011) *To the Ends of the Earth: Scotland's global diaspora*, London: Allen Lane.

Devine, T. (2012) 'A global diaspora', in T. Devine and J. Wormald (eds), *The Oxford Handbook of Modern Scottish History*, Oxford: Oxford University Press.

Devine, T. (2016) *Independence or Union: Scotland's Past and Scotland's Present*, London: Allen Lane.

Devine, T. and J. Wormald (eds) (2012) *The Oxford Handbook of Modern Scottish History*, Oxford: Oxford University Press.

Dickson, N. (1990) 'Brethren and Baptists in Scotland', *The Baptist Quarterly*, 33, 372–87.

Dickson, T. (ed.) (1980) *Scottish Capitalism: Class, state and nation from before the Union to the present*, London: Lawrence & Wishart.

Donaldson, W. (1986) *Popular Literature in Victorian Scotland*, Aberdeen: Aberdeen University Press.

Douglas, F. (2009) *Scottish Newspapers, Language and Identity*, Edinburgh: Edinburgh University Press.

Dubois-Nayt, A. (2015) 'The "Unscottishness" of female rule: an early modern theory', *Women's History Review*, 24(1), 7–22.

Duff, P. and N. Hutton (eds) (1999) *Criminal Justice in Scotland*, Aldershot: Ashgate.

Dunn, D. (1992) *Scotland: An anthology*, London: Fontana.

Durie, A. (1992) 'Tourism in Victorian Scotland: the case of Abbotsford', *Scottish Economic and Social History*, 12, 42–54.

Durkacs, V. (1983) *The Decline of the Celtic Languages: A study of linguistic and cultural conflict in Scotland, Wales and Ireland from the Reformation to the twentieth century*, Edinburgh: John Donald.

Durkheim, E. (1952 [1897]) *Suicide*, London: Routledge.

Durkheim, E. (2008 [1912]) *Elementary Forms of the Religious Life*, Oxford: Oxford University Press.

Eco, U. (1987) *Travels in Hyper-Reality: Essays*, London: Pan.

Elias, N. (1978) *The Civilising Process*, Oxford: Basil Blackwell.

El-Nakla, N., G. Macbeth and F. Thomas (2007) *Muslim Women's Voices: Report presenting the findings of a Scotland-wide listening exercise conducted with Muslims*, Glasgow: Amina.

Emejulu, A. (2013) 'Being and belonging in Scotland: exploring the intersection of ethnicity, gender and national identity among Scottish Pakistani groups', *Scottish Affairs*, 84, Summer, 41–64.

Engender (2014) 'Gender inequality and Scotland's constitutional futures' (www.engender.org.uk/content/publications/Gender-equality-and--Scotlands-constitutional-futures.pdf).

Eriksen, T. (1993) *Ethnicity and Nationalism*, London: Pluto Press.

Eriksen, T. (ed.) (2003) *Globalisation: Studies in anthropology*, London: Pluto Press.

Eriksen, T. (2007) 'Steps to an ecology of transnational sports', *Global Networks*, 7(2), 154–67.

Eriksen, T. (2014) *Globalization*, London: Berg.

Erikson, R., J. Goldthorpe and L. Portocarero (1983) 'International class mobility and the convergence thesis: England, France and Sweden', *British Journal of Sociology*, 34(3), 303–43.

Eriksson, B. (1993) 'The first formulation of sociology: a discursive innovation of the 18th century', *European Journal of Sociology*, 34(2), 251–76.

Eski, Y., P. McGuinness and M. Burman (2011) *Changes to Scotland's Criminal Justice System Post-Devolution: Main legislative developments, major reviews of policy and procedure, and the introduction of 'new' bodies*, Edinburgh: Audit Scotland.

Farrell, G. (2013) 'Five tests for a theory of the crime drop', *Crime Science Journal*, 2(5). DOI: 10.1186/2193-7680-2-5.

Farrell, G., N. Tilley, A. Tseloni and J. Mailley (2010) 'Explaining and sustaining the crime drop: clarifying the role of opportunity-related theories', *Crime Prevention and Community Safety*, 12(1), 24–41.

Farrell, G., A. Tseloni, J. Mailley and N. Tilley (2011) 'The crime drop and the security hypothesis', *Journal of Research in Crime and Delinquency*, 48(2), 147–75.

Fenton, S. and R. Mann (2013) '"Our own people": ethnic orientations to nation and country', in T. Modood and J. Salt (eds), *Global Migration, Ethnicity and Britishness*, Basingstoke: Palgrave Macmillan.

Ferguson, A. (1966 [1767]) *An Essay on the History of Civil Society*, Edinburgh: Edinburgh University Press.

Ferguson, W. (1998) *The Identity of the Scottish Nation: An historic quest*, Edinburgh: Edinburgh University Press.

Field, C. (2001) '"The haemorrhage of faith?": Opinion polls as sources for religious practices, beliefs and attitudes in Scotland since the 1970s', *Journal of Contemporary Religion*, 16, 157–75.

Field, C. (2013) 'Scottish Social Attitudes Survey 2011', *British Religion in Numbers*, May (www.brin.ac.uk/news/2013/05/).

Finlay, R. (1994) 'Controlling the past: Scottish historiography and Scottish identity in the 19th and 20th centuries', *Scottish Affairs*, 9, 127–42.

Firn, J. (1975) 'External control and regional policy', in G. Brown (ed.), *The Red Paper on Scotland*, Edinburgh: EUSPB.

Flanagan, A. (2016) *Review of Governance in Policing: To the Cabinet Secretary for Justice*, Scottish Police Authority Report (www.spa.police.uk/assets/128635/337350/337362).

Flinn, M. (1977) *Scottish Population History from the 17th Century to the 1930s*, Cambridge: Cambridge University Press.

Ford, M. and R. Goodwin (2014) *Revolt on the Right: Explaining support for the radical right in Britain*, London: Routledge.

Foucault, M. (1980) *Power/Knowledge*, Brighton: Harvester.

Fournier, M. (2013) *Émile Durkheim: A biography*, Cambridge: Polity Press.

Frank, A. Gunder (1966) *The Development of Underdevelopment*, New York: Monthly Review Press.

Frank, A. Gunder (1967) *Capitalism and Underdevelopment in Latin America*, New York: Monthly Review Press.

Fry, M. (1987) *Patronage & Principle: A political history of modern Scotland*, Aberdeen: Aberdeen University Press.

Fujita, S. and M. Maxfield (2012) 'Security and the drop in car theft in the United States', in J. van Dijk, A. Tseloni and G. Farrell (eds), *The International Crime Drop: New directions in research*, Basingstoke: Palgrave Macmillan.

Fyfe, N. and A. Henry (2015) 'Reform, research and re-invention', *Scottish Justice Matters*, 3(2), 21–2.

Fyfe, N.R. (2010) 'Policing Scotland', in H. Croall, G. Mooney and M. Munro (eds), *Criminal Justice in Scotland: Critical perspective*, Cullompton: Willan Publishing.

Gallagher, T. (1991) 'The Catholic Irish in Scotland: in search of identity', in T. Devine (ed.), *Irish Immigrants and Scottish Society in the Nineteenth and Twentieth Centuries*, Edinburgh: John Donald.

Gamble, A. (1994) *The Free Economy and the Strong State*, London: Macmillan.

Gamoran, A. (1995) 'Curriculum standardisation and equality of opportunity in Scottish secondary education, 1984–1990', *Sociology of Education*, 69, 1–21.

Garland, D. (1999) 'Preface', in P. Duff and N. Hutton (eds), *Criminal Justice in Scotland*, Aldershot: Dartmouth Publishing.

Garnsey, E. (1975) 'Occupational structures in industrial societies: some notes on the convergence thesis in the light of Soviet experience', *Sociology*, 9(3), 437–58.

Geertz, C. (1973) *The Interpretation of Cultures: Selected essays*, New York: Basic Books.

Gellner, E. (1964) 'Nationalism', in *Thought and Change*, London: Weidenfeld & Nicolson.

Gellner, E. (1983) *Nations and Nationalism*, Oxford: Basil Blackwell.

Gellner, E. (1994) *Encounters with Nationalism*, Oxford: Basil Blackwell.

Gellner, E. (1996) 'Do nations have navels?', *Nations and Nationalism*, 2(3), 366–70.

Gibbon, L. Grassic (1934) *Scottish Scene, or the Intelligent Man's Guide to Albyn*, London: Hutchinson.

Gibbon, L. Grassic (1946) *A Scots Quair: Sunset Song*, London: Hutchinson.

Gibbon, L. Grassic (1967) *A Scots Hairst: Essays and short stories*, London: Hutchinson.

Gibbon, L. Grassic (1994) 'The Land', reprinted in *The Speak of the Mearns*, Edinburgh: Polygon.

Giddens, A. (1985) *The Nation-State and Violence*, Berkeley, CA: University of California Press.

Giddens, A. (1990) *The Consequences of Modernity*, Stanford, CA: Stanford University Press.

Gifford, D. (ed.) (1988) *The History of Scottish Literature, Volume 3, The 19th Century*, Aberdeen: Aberdeen University Press.

Gill, F. (2005) 'National identities in a Scottish border community', *Nations and Nationalism*, 11(1), 83–102.

Giulianotti, R. (2005a) *Sport – A critical sociology*, Cambridge: Polity Press.

Giulianotti, R. (2005b) 'The sociability of sport', *International Review for the Sociology of Sport*, 40(3), 289–306.

Giulianotti, R. and R. Robertson (2007a) 'Forms of glocalization: globalization and the migration strategies of Scottish football fans in North America', *Sociology*, 41(1), 133–52.

Giulianotti, R. and R. Robertson (eds) (2007b) 'Sport and globalization: transnational dimensions', *Global Networks*, 7(2), 107–12.

Giulianotti, R. and R. Robertson (2009) *Globalisation and Football*, London: Sage.

Glasgow Centre for Population Health (2014) *Ten Years of GCPH: The evidence and implications* (www.gcph.co.uk).

Glasgow Centre for Population Health (2016) *History, Politics and Vulnerability: Explaining excess mortality in Scotland and Glasgow* (www.gcph.co.uk).

Glasser, R. (1986) *Growing Up in the Gorbals*, London: Chatto & Windus.

Goldie, D. (2010) 'Don't take the high road: tartanry and its critics', in I. Brown (ed.), *From Tartan to Tartanry: Scottish culture, history and myth*, Edinburgh: Edinburgh University Press.

Goldthorpe, J. (1980) *Social Mobility and Class Structure in Modern Britain*, 1st edition, Oxford: Oxford University Press.

Goldthorpe, J. (1987) *Social Mobility and Class Structure in Modern Britain*, 2nd edition, Oxford: Oxford University Press.

Goldthorpe, J., D. Lockwood, F. Bechhofer and J. Platt (1969) *The Affluent Worker in the Class Structure*, Cambridge: Cambridge University Press.

Gordon, E. and E. Breitenbach (1990) *The World is Ill-Divided: Women's work in Scotland in the nineteenth and early twentieth centuries*, Edinburgh: Edinburgh University Press.

Grant, A. (1994) 'Aspects of national consciousness in medieval Scotland', in C. Bjørn, A. Grant and K. Stringer (eds), *Social and Political Identities in Western History*, Copenhagen: Academic Press.

Gray, A. (1981) *Lanark*, Edinburgh: Canongate.

Gray, J., A. McPherson and D. Raffe (1983) *Reconstructions of Secondary Education: Theory, myth and practice since the war*, London: Routledge & Kegan Paul.

Greenfeld, L. (1993) *Nationalism: Five roads to modernity*, Cambridge, MA: Harvard University Press.

Gupta, A. and J. Ferguson (eds) (1997) *Culture, Power, Place: Explorations in critical anthropology*, London: Duke University Press.

Hague, E. (2002) 'National Tartan Day: Rewriting history in the United States', *Scottish Affairs*, 38, 94–124.

Hall, S. (1992) 'The question of cultural identity', in S. Hall, D. Held and T. McGrew (eds), *Modernity and Its Futures*, Cambridge: Polity Press.

Halsey, C.H. (2004) *A History of Sociology in Britain: Science, literature, and society*, Oxford: Oxford University Press.

Halsey, A.H. and W.G. Runciman (eds) (2005) *British Sociology: Seen from without and within*, British Academy Publishing Online (http://britishacademy.universitypressscholarship. com/view/10.5871/bacad/9780197263426.001.0001/upso-9780197263426).

Handley, J.E. (1964) *The Irish in Scotland*, Glasgow: Burns.

Hannigan, D. (1998) *The Garrison Game: The state of Irish football*, Edinburgh: Mainstream.

Hardy, F. (1990) *Scotland in Film*, Edinburgh: Edinburgh University Press.

Harper, M. (2003) *Adventurers and Exiles: The great Scottish exodus*, London: Profile Books.

Harper, M. (2012) *Scotland No More? The Scots who left Scotland in the twentieth century*, Edinburgh: Luath Press.

Hart, F. (1987) 'Neil Gunn's Drama of the Light', in Cairns Craig (ed.), *The History of Scottish Literature, Volume 4, The Twentieth Century*, Aberdeen: Aberdeen University Press.

Hartley, L.P. (2004 [1953] *The Go-Between*, Harmondsworth: Penguin.

Harvie, C. (1977) *Scotland and Nationalism*, London: Allen & Unwin.

Harvie, C. (1988) 'Industry, religion and the state of Scotland', in D. Gifford (ed.), *The History of Scottish Literature, Volume 3, The Nineteenth Century*, Aberdeen: Aberdeen University Press.

Harvie, C. (1995) *Fool's Gold: The story of North Sea oil*, London: Penguin Books.

Hastings, A. (1997) *The Construction of Nationhood: Ethnicity, religion and nationalism*, Cambridge: Cambridge University Press.

Hearn, J. (2000) *Claiming Scotland: National identity and liberal culture*, Edinburgh: Polygon.

Hearn, J. (2001) 'Taking liberties: contesting visions of the civil society project', *Critique of Anthropology*, 21(4), 339–60.

Hearn, J. (2012) *Theorizing Power*, Basingstoke: Palgrave Macmillan.

Hearn, J. (2015) 'Demos before democracy: ideas of nation and society in Adam Smith', *Journal of Classical Sociology*, 15(4), 396–414.

Heath, A. and N. Demireva (2014) 'Has multiculturalism failed in Britain?', *Ethnic and Racial Studies*, 37(1), 161–80.

Hechter, M. (1975) *Internal Colonialism: The Celtic fringe in British national development, 1536–1966*, London: Routledge & Kegan Paul.

Hechter, M. (1982) 'Internal colonialism revisited', *Cencrastus*, 10, 8–11.

Held, D. (2014) 'Interview', *Globalizations*, 11(4), 491–502.

Held, D., M. Kaldor and D. Quah (2010) 'The Hydra-headed crisis', *Global Policy*, February (www.globalpolicyjournal.com/articles/global-governance/hydra-headed-crisis).

Held, D. and A. McGrew (2007) *Globalization/Anti-Globalization: Beyond the great divide*, 2nd edition, Cambridge: Polity Press.

Henderson, I. (1969) *Scotland: Kirk and people*, London: Lutterworth Press.

Herman, A. (2001) *How Scots Invented the Modern World: The true story of how Western Europe's poorest nation created our world and everything in it*, New York: Three Rivers Press.

Herzfeld, M. (1997) *Cultural Intimacy: Social poetics in the nation-state*, London: Routledge.

Hesketh, C. (1972) *Tartans*, London: Octopus Books.

Hesse, D. (2014) *Warrior Dreams: Playing Scotsmen in mainland Europe*, Manchester: Manchester University Press.

HEUNI (2014) *European Sourcebook of Crime and Criminal Justice Statistics*, 5th edition, European Institute for Crime Prevention and Control, affiliated with the United Nations, Publication Series No. 80.

Hills, L. (1994) 'Why engender?', *Chapman*, 76, Spring, 45–50.

Hirst, P. and G. Thompson (1996) *Globalization in Question: The international economy and the possibilities of governance*, Cambridge: Polity Press.

Hirst, P., G. Thompson and S. Bromley (2009) *Globalization in Question*, 3rd edition, Oxford: Blackwell.

Hobsbawm, E.J. (1969) *Industry and Empire*, Harmondsworth: Penguin Books.

Holloway, J. and L. Errington (1978) *The Discovery of Scotland*, Edinburgh: National Gallery of Scotland.

Hood, N. (1999) 'Scotland in the world', in J. Peat and S. Boyle (eds), *An Illustrated Guide to the Scottish Economy*, London: Duckworth.

Hopkins, P. (2004) 'Everyday racism in Scotland: a case study of east Pollockshields', *Scottish Affairs*, 49, Autumn, 88–103.

Hopkins, P. (2007) '"Blue Squares", "Proper" Muslims and transnational networks: narratives of national and religious identities amongst young Muslim men living in Scotland', *Ethnicities*, 7(1), 61–78.

Horne, D. (1969) *God is an Englishman*, Sydney: Angus & Robertson.

Horne, J., B. Lingard, G. Weiner and J. Forbes (2011) 'Capitalizing on sport', *British Journal of Sociology of Education*, 32(6), 861–79.

Houchin, R. (2005) *Social Exclusion and Imprisonment in Scotland: A report*, January (www.scotpho.org.uk/downloads/SocialExclusionandImprisonmentinScotland.pdf).

Hoyau, P. (1988) 'Heritage and "the Conserver Society": the French case', in R. Lumley (ed.), *The Museum Time Machine*, London: Routledge.

Hroch, M. (1985) *Social Preconditions of National Revival in Europe*, Cambridge: Cambridge University Press.

Humphreys, L., B. Francis and S. McVie (2014) 'Understanding the crime drop in Scotland', *AQMeN Research Briefing* No. 1 (www.aqmen.ac.uk/node/1907).

Humphreys, L., B. Francis and S. McVie (forthcoming) 'Temporal dependence of covariates on aggregate measures of crime in Scotland: comparing and contrasting crime and offence types', *European Journal of Criminology*.

Hunter, J. (1999) *Last of the Free: A millennial history of the Highlands and Islands*, Edinburgh: Mainstream.

Hunter, J. (2005) *Scottish Exodus: Travels among a worldwide clan*, Edinburgh: Mainstream.

Hussain, A. and W. Miller (2006) *Multicultural Nationalism: Islamophobia, Anglophobia and devolution*, Oxford: Oxford University Press.

Hutchison, D. (2008) 'The history of the press', in N. Blain and D. Hutchison (eds), *The Media in Scotland*, Edinburgh: Edinburgh University Press.

Hutton, N. (1999) 'Sentencing in Scotland', in P. Duff and N. Hutton (eds), *Criminal Justice in Scotland*, Aldershot: Dartmouth Publishing.

Iannelli, C., A. Gamoran and L. Paterson (2011) 'Expansion through diversion in Scottish higher education, 1987–2001', *Oxford Review of Education*, 37, 717–41.

Iannelli, C. and L. Paterson (2006) 'Social mobility in Scotland since the middle of the twentieth century', *The Sociological Review*, 54(3), 520–45.

Iannelli, C. and L. Paterson (2007a) 'Education and social mobility in Scotland', *Research in Social Stratification and Mobility*, 25, 219–32.

Iannelli, C. and L. Paterson (2007b) 'Social class and educational attainment: a comparative study of England, Wales, and Scotland', *Sociology of Education*, 80(4), 330–58.

Idle, J. (1993) 'McIlvanney, masculinity and Scottish literature', *Scottish Affairs*, 2, Winter, 50–7.

Ignatieff, M. (1994) *Blood and Belonging: Journeys into the new nationalism*, New York: Farrar, Straus & Giroux.

Institute for Economics and Peace (2013) *UK Peace Index: Exploring the fabric of peace in the UK from 2003 to 2012* (http://economicsandpeace.org/wp-content/uploads/2015/06/UK_Peace_Index_report_2013_0.pdf).

Jackson, L., N. Davidson and D. Smale (2015) 'Scottish Police Force amalgamations and mergers: a historical perspective', *Scottish Justice Matters*, 3(2), 3–4.

Jarvie, G. (1999) *Sport in the Making of Celtic Cultures*, London: Bloomsbury T&T Clark.

Jarvie, G. and J. Burnett (2000) *Sport, Scotland and the Scots*, East Lothian: Tuckwell Press.

Jarvie, G. and G. Walker (eds) (1994) *Scottish Sport in the Making of the Nation*, Leicester: Leicester University Press.

Jenkins, R. (1992) *Pierre Bourdieu*, London: Routledge.

Jenkins, R. (2008) *Rethinking Ethnicity*, London: Sage.

Jenkins, R. (2015) *Social Identity*, 3rd edition, London: Routledge.

Johns, R., L. Bennie and J. Mitchell (2012) 'Gendered nationalism: the gender gap in support for the Scottish National Party', *Party Politics*, 18(4), 581–601.

Jones, T. (1977) 'Occupational transition in advanced industrial societies – a reply', *Sociological Review*, 25(2), 387–407.

Justice Analytical Service (2014) *User Guide to Recorded Crime Statistics in Scotland*, November (www.gov.scot/Resource/0046/00464153.pdf).

Kapferer, B. (1988) *Legends of People, Myths of State*, Washington, DC: Smithsonian Institute Press.

Kapuscinski, R. (2007) *The Soccer War*, London: Granta Books.

Karlsen, S. and J. Nazroo (2015) 'Ethnic and religious differences in the attitudes of people towards being "British"', *Sociological Review*, 63, 759–81.

Kaviraj, S. (2001) 'In search of civil society', in S. Kaviraj and S. Khilnani (eds), *Civil Society: History and possibilities*, Cambridge: Cambridge University Press.

Kaviraj, S. and S. Khilnani (eds) (2001) *Civil Society: History and possibilities*, Cambridge: Cambridge University Press.

Kay, B. (2006) *Scots: The mither tongue*, Edinburgh: Mainstream.

Keating, M. (1996) *Nations against the State: The new politics of nationalism in Quebec, Catalonia and Scotland*, London: Macmillan.

Keating, M. (2010) *The Government of Scotland: Public policy making after devolution*, 2nd edition, Edinburgh: Edinburgh University Press.

Keating, M. and D. Bleiman (1979) *Labour and Scottish Nationalism*, London: Macmillan.

Keating, M. and P. Cairney (2006) 'A new elite? Politicians and civil servants in Scotland after devolution', *Parliamentary Affairs*, 59(1), 43–59.

Keating, M. and D. McCrone (eds) (2013) *The Crisis of Social Democracy in Europe*, Edinburgh: Edinburgh University Press.

Kellas, J. (1975) *The Scottish Political System*, Cambridge: Cambridge University Press.

Kellas, J. (1989) *The Scottish Political System*, Cambridge: Cambridge University Press.

Kellas, J. (1998) *The Politics of Nationalism and Ethnicity*, New York: St. Martin's Press.

Kelly, E. (2004) 'Review: Ethnic diversity in Wales', *Scottish Affairs*, 48, Summer, 81–4.

Kelly, E. (2005) 'Review essay: sectarianism, bigotry and ethnicity – the gulf in understanding', *Scottish Affairs*, 48, Summer, 106–17.

Kemp, A. (2011, 2012) *The Official History of North Sea Oil and Gas*, 2 volumes, London: Routledge.

Kenny, M. (2013) 'The Scottish Parliament's record on women's representation is in the balance', Democratic Audit UK (www.democraticaudit.com/?p=1392).

Kenny, M. (2014) *The Politics of Nationhood in England*, Oxford: Oxford University Press.

Kenny, M. (2015) 'Women and the 2015 general election: shattering the political glass ceiling?', *Scottish Affairs*, 24(4), 389–408.

Kenny, M. and F. Mackay (2014) 'When is contagion not very contagious? Dynamics of women's political representation in Scotland', *Parliamentary Affairs*, 67(4), 866–86.

Kerr, C. (1960) *Industrialism and Industrial Man*, London: Pelican Books.

Khilnani, S. (2001) 'The development of civil society', in S. Kaviraj and S. Khilnani (eds), *Civil Society: History and possibilities*, Cambridge: Cambridge University Press.

Kidd, C. (1993) *Subverting Scotland's Past: Scottish Whig historians and the creation of an Anglo-British identity, 1689–c.1830*, Cambridge: Cambridge University Press.

Kidd, C. (2008) *Union and Unionisms: Political thought in Scotland, 1500–2000*, Cambridge: Cambridge University Press.

Kidd, S. and L. Jamieson (2011) *Experiences of Muslims Living in Scotland*, Edinburgh: Scottish Government.

Kiely, R., D. McCrone and F. Bechhofer (2006) 'Reading between the lines: national identity and attitudes to the media in Scotland', *Nations and Nationalism*, 12(3), 473–92.

Kington, M. (1977) *Punch on Scotland*, London: Robson Books.

Kirby, M.W. (1981) *The Decline of British Economic Power since 1870*, London: Allen & Unwin.

Kitsuse, J. and A. Cicourel (1963) 'A note on the uses of official statistics', *Social Problems*, 11, 131–9.

Knowles, T.D. (1983) *Ideology, Art, and Commerce: Aspects of literary sociology in the late Victorian Scottish Kailyard*, Gothenburg: Acta Universitatis Gothoburgensis.

Kumar, K. (1993) 'Civil society: an inquiry into the usefulness of a historical term', *British Journal of Sociology*, 44(3), 375–95.

Lasch, C. (1979) *The Culture of Narcissism*, New York: W.W. Norton.

Lea, J. and J. Young (1984) *What is to be Done About Law and Order?*, 2nd edition, London: Pluto Press.

Lechner, F. (2007) 'Imagined communities in the global game: soccer and the development of Dutch national identity', *Global Networks*, 7(2), 215–29.

Leddy-Owen, C. (2014) '"It's true, I'm English … I'm not lying": essentialized and precarious English identities', *Ethnic and Racial Studies*, 37(8), 1448–66.

Lee, C. (1979) *British Regional Employment Statistics, 1841–1971*, Cambridge: Cambridge University Press.

Lee, C. (1995) *Scotland and the United Kingdom: The economy and the Union in the twentieth century*, Manchester: Manchester University Press.

Leith, M. and D. Sim (2014) *The Modern Scottish Diaspora*, Edinburgh: Edinburgh University Press.

Lenman, B. (1977) *An Economic History of Modern Scotland*, London: Batsford.

Leonard, T. (1984) 'Unrelated incidents', in *Intimate Voices: Selected work, 1965–83*, Glasgow: Galloping Dog Press.

Levitt, I. (ed.) (2014) *Treasury Control and Public Expenditure in Scotland, 1885–1979*, Oxford: Oxford University Press.

Levitt, S.D. (2004) 'Understanding why crime fell in the 1990s: four factors that explain the decline and six that do not', *Journal of Economic Perspectives*, 18(1), 163–90.

Leyland, A., R. Dundas, P. McLoone and F.A. Boddy (2007) *Inequalities in Mortality in Scotland, 1981–2001*, MRC Social and Public Health Sciences Unit (www.inequalities inhealth.com).

Lipset, S.M. (1997) *American Exceptionalism: A double-edged sword*, New York: W.W. Norton.

Lockwood, D. (1958) *The Blackcoated Worker: A study on class consciousness*, London: Allen & Unwin.

Lucas, S.R. (2001) 'Effectively maintained inequality: education transitions, track mobility, and social background effects', *American Journal of Sociology*, 106, 1642–90.

Lukács, G. (1969) *The Historical Novel*, Harmondsworth: Penguin Books.

Lukes, S. (2004) *Power: A radical view*, 2nd edition, Basingstoke: Palgrave Macmillan.

MacArthur, M. (1993) 'Blasted heaths and hills of mist', *Scottish Affairs*, 3, 23–31.

MacCormick, N. (1999) *Questioning Sovereignty*, Oxford: Oxford University Press.

MacDiarmid, H. (1978) *The Complete Poems*, London: Martin Brian and O'Keefe.

Macdonald, S. (1999) 'The Gaelic renaissance and Scotland's identities', *Scottish Affairs*, 26, 100–18.

MacDonald-Lewis, L. (2009) *Warriors and Wordsmiths of Freedom: The birth and growth of democracy*, New York: Tower Books.

MacGregor, N. (2014) *Germany: Memories of a nation*, London: Allen Lane.

MacInnes, J. (1993) 'The broadcasting media in Scotland', *Scottish Affairs*, 2, Winter, 82–98.

MacInnes, J. (1995) 'Astonishingly stupid: the Panorama affair', *Scottish Affairs*, 12, Summer, 1–8.

MacIntyre, A. (2007) *After Virtue: A study in moral theory*, London: Duckworth.

MacIntyre, S. (1980) *Little Moscows: Communism and working-class militancy in inter-war Britain*, London: Croom Helm.

Mackay, F. and M. Kenny (2009) 'Women's political representation and the SNP: gendered paradoxes and puzzles', in G. Hassan (ed.), *The Modern SNP: From protest to power*, Edinburgh: Edinburgh University Press.

Mackenzie, D. (2006) *An Engine, Not a Camera: How financial models shape markets*, Cambridge, MA: MIT Press.

Mackenzie, D. (2014) 'A sociology of algorithms: high-frequency trading and the shaping of markets', June (www.sps.ed.ac.uk/__data/assets/pdf_file/0004/156298/Algorithms25.pdf).

Mackie, A. (1973) *The Scotch Comedians*, Edinburgh: Ramsay Head Press.

Mackie, J.D. (1964) *A History of Scotland*, London: Penguin Books.

MacLaren, A. (ed.) (1976) *Social Class in Scotland*, Edinburgh: John Donald.

Macwhirter, I. (2014) *Democracy in the Dark: The decline of the Scottish press and how to keep the lights on*, Saltire Series No. 5, Edinburgh.

Maguire, M. (2012) 'Crime statistics and the construction of crime', in M. Maguire, R. Morgan and R. Reiner (eds), *The Oxford Handbook of Criminology*, Oxford: Oxford University Press.

Malesevic, S. (2011) 'The chimera of national identity', *Nations and Nationalism*, 17(2), 272–90.

Mangan, J.A. (2000) *Athleticism in the Victorian and Edwardian Public School*, London: Frank Cass.

Mangan, J.A. (2010) 'Missionaries to the Scottish middle classes', *International Journal of the History of Sport*, 27(1–2), 262–78.

Mann, M. (1986) *The Sources of Social Power, Volume 1, A history of power from the beginning to AD 1760*, Cambridge: Cambridge University Press.

Mann, M. (1993) 'Nation-states are diversifying, developing, not dying', *Daedalus*, 122(3), 115–40.

Mann, M. (1997) 'Has globalization ended the rise and rise of the nation-state?', *Review of International Political Economy*, 4(3), 472–96.

Marsh, C. (1986) 'Social class and occupation', in R. Burgess (ed.), *Key Variables in Sociological Investigation*, London: Routledge & Kegan Paul.

Marx, K. (1959 [1869]) *The Eighteenth Brumaire of Louis Bonaparte*, extract in L.S. Fever (ed.) *Marx and Engels: Basic writings on politics and philosophy*, New York: Doubleday Anchor.

Maxwell, S. (1976) 'Can Scotland's political myths be broken?', *Q*, 19 November, 5.

Maxwell, S. (2013 [1991]) 'The Scottish middle class and the national debate', reprinted in S. Maxwell, *The Case for Left Wing Nationalism*, Edinburgh: Luath Press, pp. 138–61.

Mayhew, P. (2000) 'Researching the state of crime', in R. King and E. Wincup (eds), *Doing Research on Crime and Justice*, Oxford: Oxford University Press.

Mayhew, P. (2012) 'Researching the state of crime: local, national and international victim surveys', in R. King and E. Wincup (eds), *Doing Research on Crime and Justice*, Oxford: Oxford University Press.

McAra, L. (2005) 'Modelling penal transformation', *Punishment and Society*, 7(3), 277–302.

McAra, L. (2006) 'Welfare in crisis: key developments in Scotland', in B. Goldson and J. Muncie (eds) *Comparative Youth Justice*, London: Sage.

McAra, L. (2008) 'Crime, criminology and criminal justice in Scotland', *European Journal of Criminology*, 5(4), 481–504.

McAra, L. (2010) 'Models of youth justice', in D.J. Smith (ed.), *A New Response to Youth Crime*, Cullompton: Willan Publishing.

McAra, L. and S. McVie (2010) 'Youth crime and justice in Scotland', in H. Croall, G. Mooney and M. Munro (eds), *Criminal Justice in Contemporary Scotland*, Cullompton: Willan Publishing, pp. 67–89.

McAra, L. and S. McVie (2012) 'Critical debates in developmental and life-course criminology', in M. Maguire, R. Morgan and R. Reiner (eds), *Oxford Handbook of Criminology*, 5th edition, Oxford: Oxford University Press.

McAra, L. and S. McVie (2015) 'The reproduction of poverty', *Scottish Justice Matters*, 3(3), 4–5.

McArthur, C. (1981) 'Breaking the signs: "Scotch myths as cultural struggle"', *Cencrastus*, 7, 21–5.

McArthur, C. (ed.) (1982) *Scotch Reels: Scotland in cinema and television*, London: BFI Publishing.

McArthur, C. (1983) 'Scotch reels and after', *Cencrastus*, 11, 2–3.

McArthur, C. (1993) 'Scottish culture: a reply to David McCrone', *Scottish Affairs*, 4, 95–106.

McArthur, C. (1994) 'Culloden: a pre-emptive strike', *Scottish Affairs*, 9, 97–126.

McCaig, E. (ed.) (2005) *The Poems of Norman MacCaig*, Edinburgh: Polygon.

McCannell, D. (1992) *Empty Meeting Grounds*, London: Routledge.

McCarthy, A. (2005) 'National identities and twentieth century Scottish migrants in England', in W.L. Miller (ed.), *Anglo-Scottish Relations from 1900 to Devolution*, London: British Academy.

McCartney G., C. Collins, D. Walsh and G.D. Batty (2011) 'Accounting for Scotland's excess mortality: towards a synthesis', April, Glasgow Centre for Population Health.

McCollum, D., B. Nowok and S. Tindall (2014) 'Public attitudes towards migration in Scotland: exceptionality and possible policy implications', *Scottish Affairs*, 23(1), 79–102.

McCrone, D. (1992) *Understanding Scotland: The sociology of a stateless nation*, London: Routledge.

McCrone, D. (1994) 'Getting by and making out in Kirkcaldy', in M. Anderson et al. (eds), *The Social and Political Economy of the Household*, Oxford: Oxford University Press.

McCrone, D. (1998) *Sociology of Nationalism: Tomorrow's ancestors*, London: Routledge.

McCrone, D. (2001) *Understanding Scotland: The sociology of a nation*, 2nd edition, London: Routledge.

McCrone, D. (2010) 'Recovering civil society: does sociology need it?', in P. Baert et al. (eds), *Conflict, Citizenship and Civil Society*, London: Routledge.

McCrone, D. and F. Bechhofer (2015) *Understanding National Identity*, Cambridge: Cambridge University Press.

McCrone, D., A. Morris and R. Kiely (1995) *Scotland – the Brand*, Edinburgh: Edinburgh University Press.

McDonnell, E. (2013) 'Budgetary units: a Weberian approach to consumption', *American Journal of Sociology*, 119(2), 307–50.

McEwen, J. (1977) *Who Owns Scotland? Study in Landownership*, Edinburgh: EUSPB.

McGuiness, D., L.M. McGlynn, P.C. Johnson, A. MacIntyre, D.G. Batty, H. Burns et al. (2012) 'Socio-economic status is associated with epigenetic differences in the pSoBid cohort', *International Journal of Epidemiology*, 41, 151–60.

McIlvanney, W. (1975) *Docherty*, London: Allen & Unwin.

McIlvanney, W. (1977) *Laidlaw*, London: Coronet Books, Hodder & Stoughton.

McIlvanney, W. (1985) *Strange Loyalties*, London: Sceptre.

McIlvanney, W. (1991) *Surviving the Shipwreck*, Edinburgh: Mainstream.

McInnes, J. (2004) *The Summary Justice Review Committee Report to Ministers*, Edinburgh: Scottish Executive.

McIntosh, I., D. Sim and D. Robertson (2004a) 'We hate the English, but not you, because you're our pal', *Sociology*, 38(1), 43–59.

McIntosh, I., D. Sim and D. Robertson (2004b) '"It's as if you're some alien …": exploring anti-English attitudes in Scotland', *Sociological Research Online*, 9(2) (www.socresonline.org.uk/9/2/mcintosh.html).

McKay, A. (2013) 'The debate over Scotland's future: do women care?', OpenDemocracyUK (https://www.opendemocracy.net/ourkingdom/ailsa-mckay/debate-over-scotland's-future-do-women-care).

McKendrick, D. and M. Hannan (2014) 'Oppositional identities and resource partitioning: distillery ownership in Scotch whisky, 1826–2009', *Organization Science*, 25(4), 1272–86.

McKinlay, A. and C. McVittie (2011) '"This is jist my life noo": marriage, children and choice in a Scottish fishing community', *Discourse and Society*, 22(2), 175–89.

McManus, J. (1999) 'Imprisonment and other custodial sentences', in P. Duff and N. Hutton (eds), *Criminal Justice in Scotland*, Aldershot: Dartmouth Publishing.

McNeill, F. and S. Batchelor (2004) *Persistent Offending by Young People: Developing practice*, Issues in Community and Criminal Justice Series, London: National Association of Probation Officers.

McPherson, A.F. (1983) 'An angle on the Geist: persistence and change in Scottish educational tradition', in W.M. Humes and H.M. Paterson (eds) *Scottish Culture and Scottish Education, 1800–1980*, Edinburgh: John Donald.

McPherson, A. (1992) 'Schooling', in A. Dickson and J.H. Treble (eds), *People and Society in Scotland, 1914–1990*, Edinburgh: John Donald.

McPherson, A. and J.D. Willms (1986) 'Certification, class conflict, religion, and community: a socio-historical explanation of the effectiveness of contemporary schools', in A.C. Kerckhoff (ed.), *Research in Sociology of Education and Socialization* (Volume 6), Greenwich, CT: JAI Press.

McPherson, A. and J.D. Willms (1987) 'Equalisation and improvement: some effects of comprehensive reorganisation in Scotland', *Sociology*, 21, 509–39.

McVie, S., S. MacQueen, B. Bradford and S. Fohring (2011) *The Scottish Crime and Justice Survey 2008/09: User guide*, Glasgow: Scottish Centre for Crime and Justice Research.

McVie, S., P. Norris and R. Pillinger (2015) 'Is poverty reflected in changing patterns of victimisation in Scotland?', *Scottish Justice Matters*, 3(3), 6–7.

Meek, J. (2014) 'The leopard', *London Review of Books*, 36(12), 19 June, 3–10.

Meek, J. (2016) 'Trains in space', *London Review of Books*, 38(9), 5 May, 23.

Meer, N. (2015) *Citizenship, Identity and the Politics of Multiculturalism: The rise of Muslim consciousness*, Basingstoke: Palgrave Macmillan.

Mercer, K. (1990) 'Welcome to the jungle', in J. Rutherford (ed.), *Identity: Community, culture, difference*, London: Lawrence & Wishart.

Meret, S. and B. Siim (2013) 'Multiculturalism, right-wing populism and the crisis of social democracy', in M. Keating and D. McCrone (eds), *The Crisis of Social Democracy in Europe*, Edinburgh: Edinburgh University Press.

Miles, R. (1994) *Racism after 'Race Relations'*, London: Routledge.

Miller, D. (1995) *On Nationality*, Oxford: Oxford University Press.

Miller, D. (2010) *Stuff*, Cambridge: Polity Press.

Miller, D. (2012) *Consumption and its Consequences*, Cambridge: Polity Press.

Mills, C. (2014) 'The Great British class fiasco: a comment on Savage et al.', *Sociology*, 48(3), 437–44.

Mills, C. Wright (1959) *The Sociological Imagination*, Oxford: Oxford University Press.

Milward, A. (1992) *The European Rescue of the Nation-State*, London: Routledge.

Mitchell, J. (2014) *The Scottish Question*, Oxford: Oxford University Press.

Mitchison, R. (1977) *British Population Change since 1860*, London: Macmillan.

MK&G (2015) *Fast Fashion: The dark sides of fashion*, Hamburg: Museum für Kunst und Gewerbe (fastfashion-dieausstellung.de).

Modood, T. and J. Salt (2011) *Global Migration, Ethnicity and Britishness*, Basingstoke: Palgrave Macmillan.

Mooney, G. and L. Poole (2004) 'A land of milk and honey? Social policy in Scotland after devolution', *Critical Social Policy*, 24(4), 458–83.

Mooney, G. and G. Scott (2005) 'Introduction: themes and questions', in G. Mooney and G. Scott (eds), *Exploring Social Policy in the 'New' Scotland*, Bristol: Policy Press.

Mooney, G. and G. Scott (2015) 'The 2014 Scottish independence debate: questions of social welfare and social justice', *Journal of Poverty and Social Justice*, 23(1), 5–16.

Moore, C. and S. Booth (1989) *Managing Competition: Meso-corporatism, pluralism and the negotiated order in Scotland*, Oxford: Clarendon Press.